YANKEES
AND
GOD

By Chard Powers Smith

NOVELS
Artillery of Time
Ladies Day
Turn of the Dial

POETRY
Along the Wind
Lost Address
The Quest of Pan
Hamilton
Prelude to Man

BELLES LETTRES
Pattern and Variation in Poetry
Annals of the Poets

HISTORY
The Housatonic

YANKEES
AND
GOD

CHARD POWERS SMITH

HERMITAGE HOUSE   NEW YORK

To

Nannette, Cepe, Dusty and Kendall

Preface

A N ORTHODOX PREFACE is not a preface but a kind of subjective appendix. The writer makes his proclamation, his boast, of what he has done or thinks he has done; and he makes his fruitless apologies for some of his mistakes and oversights. Thus he may be of some service to the gentle reader, the gentle prospective reader, the gentle critic, and the ungentle critic.

As to any proclamation of what this book is about, that is written plain in the early part of the text and needs no separate announcement. What the text does not contain is a statement of its own method, the approach to the material and the treatment of it. In this respect this work differs from history with which I am familiar. It is written neither from the political slant, the military slant, the economic slant, the sociological slant, nor—though this is closer—the psychological slant. It is history written from the religious, including the theological, slant. It is not a history of American religion or theology, but of one of our two dominant cultures whose central thread began as a religion well garnished with a theology, and has ended as a subconscious psychological system which, with the godly root removed, yet flourishes in the patterns of the religion and the theology.

It is not in the present intention to announce a general Theological Interpretation of History—though the subject has been so long and so disgracefully neglected in lay writing that a little overemphasis might be briefly salutary. It simply happens that the culture discussed here, one of America's two great and surviving cultures, has a Religious Frame and can not be remotely understood without a close examination of that frame. It is my belief that our other great culture, that of the Old South, should also be taught primarily in terms of its central framework, which is not religious but Aristocratic. Each culture should be perpetuated in terms of its strength, and no effort should be made to synthesize them until such point in history as the synthesis actually began, and that was, historically speaking, just this morning, just this New Industrial morning, this new morning of the School Decision. During the three centuries when Yankee culture flourished and built its own nation, it had nothing in common with the South except a few political and military events and a few political doctrines which each interpreted differently. If in trying to delineate the central reality of the Puritan and the Yankee I had for a moment let my eyes wander sympathetically south of the Line, my perception would have blurred, and for too much of such wandering I think most of our history is blurred. Yankees are first, foremost, today and always a religious people, and to associate them at their psychological center with any other motivation is to disregard them entirely.

In this book I have not attempted anything so impossible as to *prove* my thesis, to write Scientific History based on an accumulation of factual evidence. I have never seen an attempt at this kind of "honest" Germanic writing that did not end by foisting the writer's furtive prejudices on the innocent reader. In the first part of this book I proclaim at length what my prejudices, my hypotheses, my guesses, are as to the qualities of these Yankees. None of this could I *prove* as they prove things about mice. I hope only to caution the reader as to what my slant is. After that I proceed upon the unquestioned assumption that it is correct. In all candor I can not conceive of any other way of writing history.

The people I would be especially pleased to reach with this book are those Americans who are still under the various materialistic prejudices which were popularized by debunking historians between 1900 and day before yesterday. Much good recent history has spoken to them, but it has spoken too gently and not widely enough. Everywhere I find Americans still using that absurd word "Puritanism" to describe traits which to the Puritans evinced the most dangerous Heresey or Error. It is still true that most of America is ignorant of the history of America, and carries along these trivial predispositions which conceal our powerful past with all it has to give us in the present and the future. This widespread and bland ignorance on the part of persons who have heard of education is matter of fury to any who are troubled with flashes of honest patriotism. Wherefore, this book is in stretches an angry book, and my only regret is that I have not the great voice of the prophets to stand on the Mountain and declare the Day of the Lord. The world needs our prophecy, and the world-wide pity is that we have it to give. Several times we have been in sight of a very great light. And afterwards in our depraved, false humility we have turned away from it and denied it three times.

As to apologies, confessions of inadequacy, I have two to make. The first is that I have here written about Yankees and God and have dealt fully with only one sect, the Congregational. Early there were Presbyterians, Quakers, Baptists, Episcopalians. In the late eighteenth century came the Methodists, in the nineteenth the Catholics and numerous Evangelical sects. Each of these has had its influence on Greater New England, but I am not persuaded that any of them has appreciably altered the culture. The Baptists and Presbyterians were, of course, of the same Calvinist stamp as the original Puritans. Of the others, the Episcopalians have been the nearest to the history of this people; but through the eighteenth century their influence was an alien one, the stuff not of Yankees but of Tories. Today Catholicism also is of very great import, but its power is young, and in few places has it actually fused with the culture under the needful mutual concessions. To treat fairly and fully the contributions of these other sects would have enlarged and confused the book. And in fine not any of them, or all together, has been more than a minor theme in the Puritan symphony.

More humbly I must make my apologies to the Commonwealth of New Hampshire, and especially to Maine. I have travelled the reaches of that great Northern Empire with its fierce and independent race, and I have known that, while they had much in common with the inlanders of Massachusetts and Connecticut, there was something alien too and that it was beyond my grasp. I conceived that to write of them as part of the rest of New England would be like writing of Scotland as part of Old England. The clans might descend and burn my books and destroy the type. It is true also that their contribution of migrants to the Greater New England that stretches to the Pacific has been far less than that of their "sister republics" to the southwest.

These are all the apologies I have to make, though there are plentiful matters in the text to make me anxious. The archaic Capitalization is a trial balloon. When I was working in seventeenth century texts I found myself imitating their haphazard method of emphasis, and since the entire American language, like our cultures, is today in revolutionary flux, I thought to toss this into the current. The true method of using it of course is to have No Method, to use it whimsically whenever your mind singles out a word and says it to you with special Emphasis. It is subtler than italics and separate from phonetic emphasis, being all of the eye. It may be that a sophisticated use of it could be synchronized with phonetic emphasis. I did systematize the capitalization with respect to the more prominent theological-psychological terms which are of frequent and usually emphatic occurrence. Otherwise, I have capitalized whimsically, as I might indulge any other mannerism, when the subconscious spirit moved. Sometimes I have gone through many pages with no compulsion to capitalize other than conventionally. Surely here is material for the ungentle and hurried critic.

There is a basic thesis or prejudice in this book which to the best of my recollection is nowhere expressly stated and which is more essential than verbal mannerisms, or matters calling for apology, or even theories of historiography. It is assumed, as others are assuming these days, that a dash of religion might be a good thing for many of us individually and for the country generally. It is assumed that the ways of materialism do not invite any very full expression of the human potential, that they therefore occasion repressions and the familiar current neuroses and psychoses, and that these neuroses and psychoses, acting collectively through the two great materialistic World Powers, are likely to produce contentions of the greatest ugliness. At the end of the book I even suggest that the only hope of preserving the species and the planet is in some religious departure which will fuse Christianity and Buddhism.

Starting with this unoriginal assumption, a basic thesis or prejudice implied here is that a certain particular approach to religion is especially desirable for this country. It is an approach which would be broadly in the Puritan tradition, though only broadly, for no religion can continue to speak its unchanging truth in unchanging language century after century. We have today the Authoritarian religions in which the communicants are sustained by identification with a great Institution, and presume that the perceptions of its leaders are more certainly of Divine Inspiration than those of other men. Also we have the Emotional religions which are at the opposite extreme, presuming that intense Individual Experience is sufficient evidence of union with Truth. The implied thesis of this book is that a third category of religion is also called for if we are to remain an individualistic and self-governing people.

This is the category of religion represented by Puritanism and the other Calvinist sects at their best. It is religion from the Intellectual approach, and the recommendation of it is an unwelcome one to a generation unaccustomed to engage the mind beyond the requirements of mathematical and physical formulae, and most of whose people do not think beyond the common sense rationalities of materialist economics, materialistic sociology and materialistic internationalism. The implied thesis here is that many of us, certainly the forty million or so of New England tradition, can not be integral without a religion in which we do our own thinking. Accordingly, I have ventured, from a layman's point of view, to examine some of the theological principles that first characterized Puritan religion and still, under different names and in terms of different symbols, characterize Yankee psychology. I hope it will be found that they are nothing other than universal expressions of familiar experiences which we have for a good while been pinching within the immediate and confining patterns of our sciences.

Acknowledgments

M Y PRIMARY OBLIGATION on account of this book is to those other
works, mentioned in the "Bibliographical Comment" at the
back, which have inspired it or contributed notably to it, each in
its fashion.

For personal assistance verging on collaboration, I am indebted
to Barbara Damon Simison of the Yale Library. She supplied me
with anecdotage and statistical material, especially for the seventeenth and nineteenth centuries, so voluminous that I have been
compelled, under the limitations of space, to omit much more than
I have used. With respect to the Westward Movement alone, I have
in hand sufficient material to compose a volume of anecdotes on its
pioneer phase. Without Miss Simison's help, the book would doubtless have been written, but in human terms it would have been a
more meager offering.

My other very great debt for personal cooperation is to Robert
Ronsheim of the Harvard Graduate School. Coming into the picture when the work was well advanced, he poured in source material at weak points in the structure, rechecked many factual statements and citations, assembled the notes, did most of the index,
and saw the book through its final typing on the part of a heroic
battalion selected from among his neighbors. During a critical period
I was able to rely on his scholarship, industry and loyalty.

For prolonged hospitality of a luxuriousness such as no writer
is entitled to enjoy, I am indebted sucessively to Daniel Merriman,
Master of Davenport College, Yale, and Basil Duke Henning, Master of Saybrook.

At various road blocks in the progress of composition, conversa-
tions with Mark Van Doren, Richard R. Niebuhr, and Leonard
Labaree were stimulating. I am grateful to Professor Labaree for
putting me on the trail of the Cole *mss.* in the Connecticut Histori-

cal Society. Professor Norvin J. Hein of Yale Divinity School provided important criticism of my sally upon the surfaces of Buddhism at the end of the book.

My wife Marion Chester Smith, Margaret Cheney Dawson, Eleanor Sureda, Professor Van Doren and Mr. Niebuhr all read large sections of the manuscript in progress and made valuable suggestions.

The bulk of my research was under the courteous auspices of the New York Public Library, the Connecticut Historical Society, the Harvard Libraries, and, more than any of the others, the Yale Library. Once more I wish to offer special praise to the Reference Librarians at Yale, where Dorothy Bridgwater and Jean Smith especially never failed to step in as required to help out Miss Simison who carried the major load.

C. P. S.

Contents

PART ONE:

Greater New England

will work out for the best—Millennialism—The Ridgepole: Believe something—The Covenant of Grace—The Chimney: The Truth seen in Grace is Aesthetic Perception, a balance between reason and emotion.

PART TWO:

Yankees and God

1. First Puritanism (1630-1660)

Rounding out The Bay—The Holy Commonwealth—Winthrop —The saintly suffrage—The College—Roger Williams the bad boy—Rhode Island—Mrs. Hutchinson the good and emotional girl—John Wilson the moral and rational man—The two great heresies, Antinomianism or Emotion, and Arminianism or Reason—Trial, banishment and excommunication of Mrs. Hutchinson—Note on tolerance—Rounding out The River—Hooker and the secularization of Equality—Plymouth and Mediocrity —Rhode Island and Individualism—The Cambridge Platform— Fall of the three great pillars, Hooker, Winthrop and Cotton— Wilson, Endicott and persecution—Harmless Baptists and offensive Quakers—The Halfway Covenant—Connecticut in flames—Two kinds of Arminianism or Rationalism: 1) Legal Arminianism or Moralism, becoming Old Calvinism or Conservatism—2) Intellectual Arminianism or Liberalism—End of First Puritanism—Note on orthodoxy.

2. First Decline (1660-1700)

Wealth and complacency—The Restoration—Undesirable immigration—Decline in education—Licentiousness—Greed—Free Enterprise emerging out of mercantilist socialism—Calamities —King Philip's War—Post-war debauch—God's Controversy with New England—Increase Mather—Synod of 1679—Effort to legislate virtue—Legal Arminianism and hell fire—Intellectual Arminianism or Liberalism and Solomon Stoddard—Newtonian science, American Puritans and the Royal Academy—Confusion of Science and Religion—Cotton Mather cures bewitched and bewitching girls—The Devil loose at The Bay— Samuel Sewall favors the living lady—Boston displaces Heaven —Humor—Yankees emerging out of Puritans.

1. Second Puritanism (1700-1760)

An independent little nation—Note on Conservatism—Anglican triumph—Quaker triumph—Baptist triumph—Civil war at The Bay—Thomas Brattle, Benjamin Colman and John Wise

PART ONE

Greater New England

I. Geography

IT IS THE PURPOSE of this book to examine the essentials of one of the two ancient cultures of the United States, that of New England and the northern tier of states settled dominantly from New England. Although the religious sun at the center of Puritan character is now burning on irreligious fuel, it is nevertheless still burning. Also, the psychic planets which circle around it have solidified into distinct traits in their own right. In whole or in part, the system descends into the private cosmos of every contemporary Yankee. The primary purpose of this book is to trace that descent.

A secondary and inferential aim is to raise the question whether, in the present devitalized state of our two basic cultures, we may look for a revival of them in some state of fusion applicable to the entire nation, or of either of them singly, or whether both are mortally stricken beyond recovery.

Our other basic culture, besides that of New England, is that of the Old South, and we shall notice it only for contrast. It is chiefly in their respective virtues that these three-century-old rivals differ from each other, and the virtues of each are most apparent when seen against the opposite virtues of the other. At the outset, if we would envisage them in terms of their real and distinctive qualities rather than indulge the sentimental tendency to conceal mutual contempt and mutually given scars, we should call them what their people called them at the time of their epic collision when they both were strong.

The word "Yankee" is etymologically uncertain and probably of trivial origin, perhaps a mistranscription of the Algonquin way of pronouncing "English," or perhaps "Anglais," more likely a Dutch term of contempt meaning "Little John" and applied by the New Amsterdamers to their eastern neighbors. But whatever its derivation, it is synonymous with "New England," and is the name of the culture that emerged out of Puritan culture about two centuries ago. More precisely, it is the name of those New Englanders in whom, increasingly after 1760, the solemn belief in the God of the Old Testament faded out in favor of that sense of cosmic irony called Yankee humor. The word "Rebel," on the other hand, has a definite meaning, and any true Southerner is proud to bear it. It signifies that romantic individualism which, while it has sponsored much evil, yet when monitored by aristocratic idealism, has provided a great part of what is noble in our history.

So far, the Rebel and Yankee cultures are between them the allegedly "United" States. Although we have enjoyed important contributions by Indians, Spanish, Germans, French, Irish, Scandinavians, Dutch, Poles, New York gamblers, Pennsylvania Quakers, and many others, yet the New English and the Old Southern cultures are the only ones without both of which America today would be unrecognizably different from what it is. In 1860 the line between them was called the Mason-Dixon line. It included in Yankee territory the people of Pennsylvania, Delaware, New Jersey and New York City, an honor which few of them coveted or deserved. In drawing the line today we must relegate these, along with the people of a few Middle Western states, to their separate cultures which belong in neither of the great categories. The southern limit of greater New England begins on the beach of Long Island Sound in Greenwich at the southwest corner of Connecticut; runs westward and northwestward across northern New Jersey and along the northern boundary of Pennsylvania; down the Allegheny and Ohio Rivers to the Mississippi; up the Mississippi to the southern boundary of Iowa; west on this boundary to the Missouri River; down the Missouri and the eastern boundary of Kansas to Oklahoma; westward along the southern boundaries of Kansas, Colorado and Utah; northward, westward and southward around Nevada to the elbow in its western boundary; thence southwestward across northern California to the fiords of the Pacific in the vicinity of Point Carmel. The country north of this is Greater New England, from Portland pronounced "Putland" to Portland pronounced "Porrtland," from Greenwich pronounced "Grenich" to Greenwich pronounced "Greenwitch." It is about half the nation geographically and a little more than two-fifths of it in population. But for the big cities and a few unassimilated foreign islands, the dominant culture is that of the Yankees whose generations pulsated westward after the Revolution to claim "God's Waste" for His Kingdom. Partly south of this dominion and partly within it, the smaller cultures we mentioned total a little less than a fifth of the nation. And south of them, lying across the Continent mostly in contact with the boundary of Greater New England, is the Greater

South, comprising the remaining two-fifths of the country. But for foreign islands analogous to those in Yankeedom, its dominant culture is that of the Old South, essentially that of the original Tidewater Aristocracy of Virginia and Carolina.

The Greater South and Greater New England are nearly equal in total population, about 60,000,000 as against about 65,000,000. For purity of culture each can claim perhaps two-thirds of its people, 40,-000,000 and 42,000,000 respectively.[1] The remaining third contains the individualists who violate the respective cultures, in the North and increasingly in the South the industrial or economic individualists who run the nation today, more exclusively in the South the social individualists who are a by-product of aristocracy. Both north and south the individualists imitate the traditional local culture. But in each region they have lost the spiritual or imaginative center. Their ways of life neglect the more profound human hungers. They are, therefore, not cultures but pseudo-cultures. Their respective countries are a Pseudo-South and a Pseudo-New England. A current historical question is whether the individualism is now passing, so that the true cultures may revive, or whether it is to continue leading us toward anarchy and tyranny.

It is a common mistake of current historians to present our two ancient cultures together, as if the political nation that includes them were unified, as if the material defeat of one destroyed its imaginative or actual reality. In spite of their common English origins and the modern efforts of both materialists and sentimentalists, they remain to this day as different as the cultures of any adjoining European states, as uncongenial as those of France and Germany. They do share certain over-emphasized American faults and vulgarities, but in their virtues, for which they ought to be remembered, they are as different as people of the common Western European heritage could well be.

Under the recent fashion of the economic interpretation of everything, the causes of the differences are said to have been topographical and climatic. The view taken here is otherwise. While economic factors were powerful, the controlling distinctions between the cultures were psychological from the beginning, derived from the contrasting standards of their founders and their cultural descendants. The leaders of the seventeenth-century South patterned their lives upon a social system, that of the English country gentry. The leaders of seventeenth-century New England patterned theirs upon a religious system, that of moderate English Puritanism. There ensued, as in England, a civil war's worth of differences of which the important ones survive today. In the South conduct is directed by an idealized Code, in New England by uncodified Idealism. The South is Individualistic, New England is Equalitarian. The South is Aristocratic and Anarchistic, New England is Democratic. The South is Emotional, New England is Rational. The South is Extrovert, New England Introvert. The South is Gay, New England is Humorous. The South has a Military tradition, New England an Intellectual tradition. People bred from infancy to such different social environments have never understood each other and they do not today.

One major historical development New England and the Old South shared, not only with each other but with every nation of Western Christendom. At some time in the nineteenth century—two or three generations later than England—they were both attacked by economic individualism or greed which gutted their respective Idealisms, left them as pseudo-idealisms within pseudo-cultures, and gave America over to Materialism. As Rebel culture had borne fruit earlier, namely in the leadership of the Revolution and the Federalization, so it showed dangerous symptoms of the infection earlier, namely in the 1810's when political and economic power was passing from the aristocracy to the new rich of the new Cotton Kingdom, whose cupidity was one of the two chief causes of the Civil War. By the '30's and '40's the South was drugging itself with ignorance behind a cotton curtain, and living on its emotions. The war cured the disease of cupidity by destroying the economy. The South lapsed from economic individualism into the social individualism or self-assertiveness which is its persisting blight.

Because New England had always been a carrier of the virus of Greed in the Calvinist Economic Virtues of Diligence and Frugality, it seems to have developed a partial immunity and did not show dangerous signs of the infection until the South was already prostrate. The attack was strong by the 1830's in the industrial and urban form already familiar in England, at the very time when Yankee culture was active both in its literary "flowering" and in its Humanitarian crusade which later conspired with the economic motive of the South to cause the War. The disease entered the Yankee bloodstream at the height of the struggle, when the profiteers, who had opposed the war but had made a patriotic adjustment enabling them to slaughter the army with putrid food, shoddy clothing and defective ordnance, captured the Republican Party and achieved the high tariff of 1863. In 1896, when the people of the North knowingly voted in the new industrial wealth over traditional agrarianism, Yankee culture succumbed to the rule of Yankee pseudo-culture. There is dubious comfort in the chronological coincidence that the years 1696 and 1796 marked comparable crises when Puritan-Yankee culture was comparably ill of some kind of individualism, though not yet economic individualism. But in 1697 and 1797 respectively there were in process upward turns which continued into revivals of the true culture and involved most of the population. So far we have seen no intimation of reawakening except that of the religion of self-expression of the 1920's. But in view of the vast changes in population and in physical and psychological factors since 1796, we need not yet conclude that the tradition is hopelessly poisoned, that another of the world's great cultures has had its day.

Before attempting any account of Yankee culture, it may be well to call attention to the two schools of domestic history which, each in its way, have disguised America for about a century and a half. There was before 1800 a respectable list of historians who might be grouped as a Godly School because most of them found the motive of history in God's will. But this classification would exclude some of the best of the eighteenth-century historians, and there was no community of method or style among them anyway. The first true school of historiography found its integration in the self-important nationalism which followed the War of 1812 and vitalized the ensuing expansion under Manifest Destiny. This was the sentimental or "Filio-pietistic" School—beginning with Bancroft and reaching its reduction to absurdity in Palfrey—which taught most students until 1917, and teaches many of college age today, that all Americans in the past were peerless heroes, and that all foreigners, especially British, were barbarians who massacred innocents on the bloody cobblestones of State Street, Boston.

It was necessary that this inflated image of America, so appropriate to its "Victorian" period, be punctured, and Brooks Adams threw the first, mostly just and accurate, darts at his own New England, beginning in the 1880's.[2] Adams deflated better than he knew, and so stands at the head of our second major school of historiography, the Debunking School which by the 1920's was distorting truth farther in materialistic and libidinous directions than the Filio-pietistic school had done in tender and saccharine directions. Because there are survivors of this school still active, and because many of its textbooks are still perverting the young, it is necessary to issue a warning against it.

The Debunking School had two Wings, a respectable one and a disreputable one. The respectable or Economic Wing simply adopted the Marxian, economic interpretation of history, and so created a mechanical America, a body without a soul. It is perhaps difficult to understand that scholars could have seriously accredited as ever having existed anywhere a thus subhuman humanity, a mankind without imagination, without any but the stark animal impulses and

the even more stark experimental reason. But we must remember that
American culture, and especially Puritan culture, was putridly decadent in the "Victorianism" of the end of the nineteenth century,
and there was something almost affirmative in the fun of breaking
all the colored glass and the fancy china, stripping down all the velvet and bead curtains, stripping off all the plumes and corsets and
revealing the economic machinery which perhaps did represent all
the health that remained. Charles A. Beard was the distinguished
leader of this Respectable Wing of the Debunking School. To him
the Reformation was a rationalization, a derivative of its contemporary Mercantile Revolution. The English Revolution of the seventeenth century was mercantile in motivation, and was called "Puritan" only because of the "intellectual climate" of the age, because
"the thought of the times was still deeply tinged with Theology."
The settlement of New England was impelled exclusively by economics:

> [In 1629] Charles I began to rule his subjects without Parlia-
> ment; and for eleven years he laid taxes, imprisoned objectors,
> and collected forced loans on his own authority. . . . Deprived
> of their voice in the House of Commons, the landed gentry of
> the middle rank, the yeomen, the merchants, and the artisans
> on whom the burden of the royal exactions fell, were now
> roused to revolutionary fervor. Those who belonged to the
> fighting school of the Cromwells and the Hampdens raised the
> standard of revolt. . . . Others despairing of freedom and vic-
> tory at home, decided to emigrate in search of liberty to the
> New World.[3]

Beard's error is not in his indication of economic motives, but in
his denial of religious motivation as primary in what was in fact one
of the largest and most consequential religious migrations in human
history. It is not the purpose here to make an equal and opposite
error. The causes that Beard names, or others as physical, were doubtless compelling with the indentured servants, most of whom were
penniless, and with a few of the yeomen who were the bulk of the
migration. But they were not dominant with most of the yeomen or
most of the artisans, and their influence on the leadership was negligible. We shall see economic motivation at work ubiquitously in
Greater New England in the form of Necessity, the need to wrest
adequate nourishment, clothing and shelter from a stubborn soil;
but we shall see remarkably few periods, regions or individuals in
whom we can say with assurance that even this least degrading of
economic motives was stronger than idealism. Rarer, but of more
historical significance than Necessity has been the economic motive
of cupidity, Greed, the desire for wealth beyond necessity. In the

seventeenth century, as we shall see, this motive was present but far secondary in strength to the Idealism. In the twentieth century it may be triumphant. The interpretation of New England history offered here sees it as the dramatic struggle between these forces. Generally, while there is no disposition in this book to deny importance to material forces or to claim that ideational ones are always supreme, yet it is believed that the preponderance of the long record shows that for more than two-thirds of the life of New England culture—that is, through the Civil War—the religious or other idealistic motives were stronger. The apparent victory of Greed is recent, and we need hardly accept it as final.

The disreputable or Nasty Wing of the Debunking School differed from the Economic Wing in the completeness of its vision of human depravity. Accepting the Economic Interpretation as a matter of course, it went psychotically farther to roll in that infantile, Victorian prurience against which its pseudo-Freudianism pretended to be in revolt. There is scarcely a great man in our history who, during the '20's, was not celebrated for some kind of sexual irregularity.

Among historians of New England, James T. Adams was probably the most vicious because at his best he was so sound as to throw the reader off guard against his sordid preoccupations. He was probably at his worst in his arraignment of Massachusetts in *The Founding of New England*. Since he ignores religion he is able to avoid giving any hint of the true and affirmative qualities of the culture. He neglects most—all but two—of the healthy leaders, and diminishes one of them with faint praise. By revelling in the half dozen disgraceful episodes in the history of Massachusetts, exaggerating their melodramatic features, and giving disproportionate attention to the three brutal and possibly pathological leaders who engineered them, he succeeds in laying upon Boston something of the fetid sultriness of an abattoir. In the midst of this portrayal he slips in by way of a footnote a revealing piece of nasty-nice Victorian demureness, touching the procedure, then universal in the world of English law, of having a committee of matrons appointed by the court examine for witch signs the genitals of accused women. Passing judgment upon a society of typically robust, healthy and often bawdy seventeenth-century Englishmen, Adams blushes and confides to us that "one of the curious elements in the psychology of the Puritans was their morbid interest in the most indecent sexual matters." This Victorian preoccupation with sex as at once indecent, secret and nice was the heart of the Nasty Wing of the Debunking School of American history and biography.

Neither the Nasty nor the Economic Wing contributed anything of value except a comment on themselves and the period that produced them. Their object was not to create but to destroy. The primary impulse was hatred of religion, because the addicts of the school, having grown up in a decadent remnant of Puritanism and being justly in revolt against it, were unable to conceive a new expression of its reality, and so sought self-justification in denying it altogether. This central motive they expanded into denial of all affirmation, all principle, all "glittering generality," all meaning. Truth was only in the negative, the immediate and the brainless. Beard did not believe that the major motives of the Puritans were economic, nor James T. Adams that they were carnal. They both knew that their dominant motives were religious. And, since they could not present these motives, the object of their books was to seduce others to the state of imaginative vacuity in which they found themselves. Already their work is fading out of serious history. It will take its place alongside other forms of publicity which preyed for power or profit upon the more depraved instincts of humanity.

During the past fifty years many peculiar attributes have been fixed upon the Puritans and identified with "Puritanism." They are qualities which, like their opposites, can be ascribed to any ancient culture by emphasizing special periods, sections and individuals. We are here dealing with a culture covering three centuries and a quarter and including incalculable millions. While the falsity or limited truth of most of the generalizations that have been attempted upon these millions will be implied in the main text, a cursory notice of them would seem appropriate in this introductory survey:

The Puritans were moralistic—Puritanism is synonymous with moralism. Generally untrue. Puritanism was in the front of the Reformation, one of whose principal complaints against the Church of Rome was moralism, the offer of Salvation by Works. The Puritans believed in Salvation by Faith, and Faith came through the unpredictable Grace of God. Good Works—that is, obedience to the Law— were usually recognized as a *sign* of Grace, though not a conclusive sign. Moralism was a heresy with the Puritans, known as Arminianism. It was prevalent between 1677 and 1697, and these are the twenty years the Puritan-baiters delight to expand into three centuries. It was espoused by many sects and leaders between 1800 and 1860, and was probably dominant between 1860 and 1900 when Puritanism was in its greatest and possibly final decline. The qualities now popularly identified with "Puritanism" are the Victorian qualities that characterized these forty rococo years.

The Puritans lived under a code of exceptional restrictions called

"Blue Laws." Ridiculous. The "Blue Laws" were the fabrication of one Samuel Peters, an Anglican minister and Tory of Hebron, Connecticut, who was visited by the Liberty Boys and claimed that his gown was torn, fled to England and published his libellous and often amusing satire, the *General History of Connecticut.*

The Puritans were fundamentalists. Untrue. They believed the Bible to be the Word of God, but knew it had to be interpreted by Right Reason.

The Puritans were prudish. Ridiculous. They were Elizabethans and extremely realistic. It is reported that in one case a female church member complained to the minister that her husband was neglecting her, not charging adultery or desertion but simply neglect of normal, healthy sexual routine. The minister expostulated with the husband to no effect. Then the wife complained to the whole congregation, and the culprit was excommunicated. John Dunton, the Boston bookseller of the last quarter of the seventeenth and the first quarter of the eighteenth centuries, recorded the following fragment of a conversation with a "Boston maiden" who rode with him to Ipswich. The subject was "Platonick love." The lady is speaking:

> For my part . . . whene'er I love, I will propose some End in doing it; for that which has no End, appears to me but the Chimera of a Distempered Brain: And what end can there be in love of Different Sexes, but Enjoyment? And yet Enjoyment quite spoils the Notion of Platonick Love: You must excuse me therefore . . . if I . . . declare myself against it, and oppose real Fruition, in your Platonick Notion.[4]

The Puritans were prohibitionists and generally denied all pleasure. Absurd. The greatest Moralist or Arminian in the history of Puritanism called wine a "good creature of God." The consumption of rum in 1700 is said to have been two bottles a week per man, woman and child. "I will tell you," declared Samuel Nowell in a public address,

> how we breed up Souldiers, both in old England and New, every Farmers Son, when he goes to the Market-Town, must have money in his purse; and when he meets with his Companions, they goe to the Tavern or Ale-house, and seldome away before Drunk, or well tipled. It is rare to find men that we can call Drunkards, but there are abundance of Tiplers in *New-England.*[5]

Dancing was ubiquitous, though as bona fide dancing, not as public exercise in unconsummated concupiscence. The robust act of fornication was usually condoned, but furtive and unconsummated sexual preoccupation, such as characterized Victorianism, was unknown.

The Puritans were intolerant and persecuting bigots. False as of their time; true as of ours. In the seventeenth century, when God and the puzzle of Being were generally considered of more importance than financial gain or political rights, all religious parties in all countries persecuted their opponents as a matter of course as soon as they came into power. Time out of mind, heretics everywhere had been treated with the branding iron, the shears, the noose, the stake, the decree of banishment on pain of death. The law of banishment on pain of death which Massachusetts adopted against the Quakers, as did Virginia—though not Connecticut or Rhode Island— was milder than the statute against all non-conformists that Bishop Laud had at hand for use against the Puritans. In the year 1630, when the Reverend Thomas Hooker, M.A., Emmanuel College, Cambridge, recognized even by the bishops as one of the chief theologians of England, in the year that Hooker, with the help of the Earl of Warwick who took custody of his family, escaped into Holland from the summons of Laud's Court of High Commission, in the same year another non-conformist minister of comparable standing was pilloried, whipped, branded, slit in the nostrils and clipped of his ears.[6]

Until 1660, Massachusetts was about equally intolerant with Virginia, being more tolerant than England or New York. Connecticut was more tolerant than any of these, but less so than Maryland. Rhode Island was the most tolerant commonwealth in Christendom. Between 1660 and 1700 old England emerged out of intolerance faster than New England, and Pennsylvania appeared as a new seat of tolerance in America. Both Massachusetts and Connecticut reached a high degree of tolerance between 1700 and 1730. Massachusetts continued to advance. Connecticut suffered a lapse into intolerance in the 1740's, but resumed progress in the '50's. Although comparison is difficult, it is perhaps true that New England as a whole throughout the colonial period was less tolerant than Maryland and Pennsylvania, but more so than Virginia, New York or England.

In all of these communities intolerance was simply one of those expressions of gusto and aggressive perfectionism which marked the inhabitants as Elizabethans, Renaissance men, typical Englishmen of the day, men who lived to extremity in terms of all their faculties all the time, neither repressing their physical impulses, as did some of their descendants, nor repressing their imaginations as do their later descendants. Everyone lived by the maxim that John Cotton expressed in commenting on the controversy with Roger Williams: Either I am right or I am wrong; if I am right, my opponent must be wrong. The Puritans who settled New England neither expected

toleration nor professed it. They did not found a remote commonwealth at mortal danger and great cost in order to provide a refuge
for the persecuted of Christendom, but in order that they by themselves might worship without persecution or other interference. They
did not question the right of the king and his bishops to "harry them
out of the land," and they insisted upon the same right to harry out
of their new land whomever they found offensively guilty of that
word of heavy omen, "Errour."

In the main, intolerance is not worth special notice among the
Puritans. Of more importance in their history are those cases where
the tenor of the intolerance was not that of godly service of the
objective Christian idea, but of egocentricity, self-service and self-
aggrandizement. Such was the case with the notorious John Endicott
who upon landing as *pro tem* governor of the advance party at
Naumkeag (Salem) in 1629, immediately began qualifying himself as
the darling of the debunkers by dispossessing of their houses the "Old
Planters," his seniors in residence, hewing down at Merrymount—
successively thereafter Mt. Dagon, Mt. Wollaston and Braintree—the
maypole of the scamp Thomas Morton, and banishing two of his
best people, the Browne brothers, because they were mild Puritans
and used the Common Prayer in their private devotions. The most
charitable account of the long and brutal career of "strong, valiant
John" is that he had a social inferiority complex in the company of
the gentlemen who were the rest of the magistracy of Massachusetts
Bay, and that his ecstasies of zeal were calculated to impress his betters, his inferiors, and himself. In contrast to Endicott's antics was
the banishment by Plymouth Colony of the Reverend Thomas Ly-
ford, an Anglican minister sent out in 1624 as an affront by the "adventurers" or investors at home, and who, after professing great love
for the settlers and being honored by their choice of him to be the
teacher of their church, at once organized a plot to destroy the hegemony in religion for which the Pilgrims had risked their lives and
lost half of them, and to set up the Anglican service. His banishment,
with every consideration for his comfort, would seem for the age and
in view of the religious foundation of Plymouth, a just and mild proceeding consistent with selfless Christian profession.

*The Puritans were given to censoriousness, mutual spying, tale
bearing and pathological witch hunting.* Generally untrue. They did
have church trials, but were forbearing in the use of them, tolerant
of all vices but lying, and chary of the serious penalty of excommunication. Generally, the periods of malicious tale bearing conform with
those of Moralism. Purveyors of false reports were usually ostracized
and sometimes publicly reprimanded. The only "witch-hunt" they
indulged in was the famous one of 1692, and this was the result of the

moralistic preaching which the ministers had agreed in 1679 to try as a possible correction for the licentiousness that followed King Philip's War. Massachusetts' convictions for witchcraft were probably the most numerous in the colonies—some records of the Virginia trials have been lost. But they were per capita greatly below those of Great Britain and Europe during the same and the preceding century.

The Puritans were ignorant fanatics of the lower orders of society. Absurd. The intellectual level of the citizenry of early New England was probably higher than that of any commonwealth in Western Christendom in the seventeenth century, and possibly higher than that of any whole considerable population in human history. In 1640 there were 113 university men[7] in a population of perhaps 24,000, a much larger proportion than in Old England. Their clergy were the leading Puritan ministers who because of their prominence had been silenced by Bishop Laud, and the Puritan clergy in general was of a higher intellectual mean than the Anglican clergy. The yeomanry, who were perhaps three-quarters of the people, were theologically literate. Though few of them had the liberal learning of the universities, their knowledge of the Bible was comprehensive, as was their knowledge of Calvin, Preston, Perkins and Ames, the formulators of Puritan doctrine, and of the Anglican liturgy against which they were in revolt. They were those farmers, socially the next cut below the squires, who are often celebrated as the backbone of England. Being Calvinists, their approach to religion was intellectual, and they not only tolerated but insisted upon "painful"—that is, finely reasoned—sermons that turned the hourglass twice.

The social level of the Puritans was only a little lower than the intellectual level. Their backing was in a strong minority of the peerage, of whom Lord Rich (the Earl of Warwick), Lord Brook (the Earl of Lincoln) and Lord Saye and Seal were particularly interested in Massachusetts Bay, and the last two of whom would have emigrated but for the hardly expected success in the Civil War. Among the actual settlers, Sir Harry Vane, bart., and the two daughters of the Earl of Lincoln, Lady Arbella Fiennes, wife of Isaac Johnson, and Lady Sarah Fiennes, wife of John Humfry, were the only scions of high nobility. Of the squirearchy were John Winthrop, lord of the manor of Groton, Essex, and William Pynchon, lord of the manor of Springfield, also Essex. Among representatives of great county families were Thomas Dudley, Simon Bradstreet, Isaac Johnson and John Humfry, while of the new gentry only recently accredited as such out of the merchant class, were Sir Richard Saltonstall, William Coddington, John Haynes, Richard Bellingham, Appleton Hough, Theophilus Eaton, founder of New Haven, and many others less prominent. The

Puritan movement both in its religious and mercantilist aspect, was the liberal movement of the seventeenth century and its personnel was that combination of aristocracy and intellectuality which generally characterizes liberal movements.

The Puritans were especially superstitious. Untrue. They were no more or less superstitious than other people of the seventeenth century. What we mean by superstition is that they believed things we do not believe, as did everybody else in their time. They believed that the cosmos was in tension between a positive, centrifugal, loving force called God and a negative, centripetal, selfish force called the Devil. No smallest event happened anywhere in the universe without the instigation of one of them. John Winthrop, Sr., observed with gravity that certain mice in the granary of John Winthrop, Jr., coming on a Greek Testament, a Psalm Book, and a Book of Common Prayer, all bound together, showed themselves good Puritans under God's direction by eating every page of the last and not touching a corner of the others.[8] Identical with Winthrop's superstition in this matter was the uproar in Anglican Cambridge University in 1626 over the discovery of a religious tract in the mouth of a codfish. High academic and clerical authorities pontificated upon this Providence of God, and even Archbishop Ussher wrote, "The incident is not lightly to be passed over."[9] So of the works of the Devil, generally contained within the field of witchcraft, New England exercised itself over a few of them, but Old England scouted out and punished incomparably more.

The Puritans were ruled by their ministers in a "theocracy." Untrue. The ministers were the most influential citizens till the Revolution, after which they were gradually supplanted by the lawyers, and then the "business men"; but none of these had any official authority.

The Puritans were cruel in criminal procedure. Diametrically false. There was hardly a point at which seventeenth-century New England was farther advanced in liberality out of the practices of Old England than in criminal procedure. During the reign of James I, there were in England 31 capital crimes, and the list increased to 223 in 1819. In their first criminal codes in the early 1640's, Massachusetts and Connecticut had twelve capital crimes each, New Haven had fourteen. In each commonwealth the number decreased thereafter,[10] and, incidentally, most of the capital laws were rarely, if ever, applied. In the matter of cruel punishments—including those of witches—New England was far ahead of all of Europe. No witch or other felon was ever "burned" in New England, though this punishment was common enough in Britain. Of the savageries that continued the Middle Ages, the minimal "corrections" of the whipping post, the pillory, the branding iron and the ducking stool were general in New England as everywhere. The ear clippers were sometimes appealed to, though very rarely. For incorrigibility in petty misfeasance a placard, sometimes with scarlet lettering, was often used. But the bloody abattoir that was British and continental justice—the rack, the gibbet, the boot, the forceps, the drawing and quartering—none of this had any counterpart in English America. That the Puritans were conscious of leniency in these respects appears in Law 46 of the Massachusetts Body of Liberties of 1641: "For bodilie punishments we allow amongst us none that are inhumane, Barbarous or Cruel." Torture as a means of extracting evidence was early abandoned, except of one convicted of a capital crime, to compel him to name his accomplices.[11]

The Puritans and Yankees were generally economically motivated, avaricious, and given to sharp dealing. Untrue. The late effort of the debunking historians to belittle the Holy Commonwealth by ascribing to it dominantly economic motivation seems trivial today beyond the need of serious attention. To be sure, there was plenty of economic motivation for leaving an England that was breaking up under incompetent wars, predatory kings, corruption, irresponsible new wealth, the enclosures which were ousting peasants by the scores of thousands and making them criminals on the highways, and a current depression in the wool market that affected the yeomanry. There was economic motivation enough for emigration, and political motive enough, too, what with Parliament closed after '28 and Charles ruling as a tyrant. But the destination for the economic-minded was not New England, where the land was poor and dear, but Virginia and the West Indies; and many Puritans did go to both. "If any come hither to plant for worldly ends," wrote Thomas Dudley to the Countess of Lincoln, "he commits an error, of which he will soon repent him; but if for spiritual . . . he may find here what may well content him."[12]

All of the leadership and the overwhelming majority of the following that went to New England did so in the consciousness that they were to be responsible members of the Holy Commonwealth where the wrongs of Old England would be righted, and where a Second Advent might in due course occur. Of the early settlers, perhaps half of the adults were church members, and another quarter pious Puritans who, for personal or doctrinal reasons, would not or could not pass the theological inquisition before the elders and the congregation which was the condition of admission. These were motivated primarily by religion. With their children, they accounted for about three quarters of the population, including the dominant, land-owning part of it. The remaining quarter were artisans, indentured servants and their families, and miscellaneous adventurers. Some of these were good Puritans, but more were probably godless and disturbers of the peace.[13] They provided most of the court records, and it is among this class, and this class alone, that we may presume that economic motivation was dominant.

As absurd as the charge of economic motivation in the settling of New England is the charge of avariciousness and sharp dealing against the Puritans and Yankees generally. They were thrifty, frugal and shrewd, both because the Bible according to Calvin taught them to be and because these qualities were necessary to survive in a land where extravagance or a bad swap of an animal might mean privation in the coming winter. But they were not primarily concerned with the amassing of money and power. Avariciousness in the form of abnormal profit-taking, the setting of prices above the market, or misrepresentation was punished legally by the Puritans, was looked upon with contempt by the eighteenth-century Yankees, and was not general and admired as a mark of intelligence until after the Civil War.

The Puritans never laughed. Generally true. They were gay and inebriate, but every detail in God's creation was too important to be a butt of humor or "levity." Humor appears with the disillusionment that increased through the First Decline (1660-1700), and it was common by 1750. The possession of it by the Yankees is taken in this book as the quality chiefly distinguishing them from the Puritans.

The Puritans discouraged art. True in so far as they looked with suspicion on art for art's sake, as on anything which distracted the imagination from God and the cosmos. Untrue in that their aesthetic perception was perpetually active in ordering their ideas, in trying to see the cosmos and its details as a unit, in music and dancing, and in performing beautifully all works of craft and construction.

So much for the trivial and mischievous charges that are brought against the Puritans and their culture. More fundamental and dangerous, though even less founded, are the charges that the culture was and is of small scope in time, in space, or in both. It is the pleasure of both domestic and foreign snobs to observe that America is young, its culture not yet developed. Or, if there may at one time have been something like a culture along the Atlantic coast, it was confined to that declining region, and bears no relation to the vast area now occupied or to the still amorphous proto-culture of the people found therein.

It is chiefly by these last people and for their consolation that the charge of youthfulness has been promulgated. In their spacious view the real America is the America of wide landscape and great material power, and all the activities of Americans for about three centuries before 1900 were not those of a mature culture but of a kind of gigantic social foetus exercising in preparation for the recent birth and the present greatness. It is, of course, impossible to combine this theory of immaturity with the smallest fund of historical knowledge. It may be doubted whether any group of people can live in settled proximity even two generations without evolving that common intellectual and moral machinery for coping with social life which we call culture. It is obvious from the record that many Americans have so lived together for more than three centuries. Wherefore, in order to maintain the illusion of childishness, it is necessary to foreshorten the vista of time so as to emphasize the foreground and bedwarf the two ancient cultures upon both of which our material greatness represents no advance but a decline. The device of our infantilist historians is to emphasize recent over past history. Textbooks assign about half their space to events since the Civil War, three-quarters or more of it to the period since the outbreak of the Revolution, and a quarter or less to the colonial period. If we desired to educate our children in the meaning of their society instead of in its surfaces, the proportions should be reversed. Half of textbook space and teaching time should be allotted to the pre-Revolutionary period, and three-quarters up to the Civil War. By that time our two cultures had matured and made their contributions to mankind, and since that time little or nothing has been added to either of them. As history is taught today, virtually all students emerge from the primary and secondary schools with only a generalized knowledge of the colonial age, and that usually falsified with a sentimental or Filio-pietistic slant which drives them presently to the opposite extreme of the Debunking view. In the colleges they are liable to get the latter directly, or at best to be exposed to a broad-minded effort to find some good in the Puritans in spite of their "witch-burnings." It is small exaggeration to say that if a student wants to find out the significance of his country today, he must do work on the graduate level.

The powerful people in whose flattery the politicians maintain our system of education in contemporaneity are themselves the best evidence of our youthfulness. They are our galloping hordes of new rich, with their rattles and horns, their conventions and tours, their public universities increasingly innocent of academic atmosphere, their mediocrity of taste, their sordid magazines and their mass media, their deep sense of intellectual inferiority and compensating will to persecute ideas, their deep sense of social inferiority and compensating isolationism and will to persecute foreigners, their brutal rapacity on the one hand and their childish generosity on the other. They are man for man probably more humane and hardly more offensive than their H-less brothers of Britain, their crew-cut comrades of Germany, their little and porky-eyed partners of France. The unique crime of the American new rich is that they are more numerous than all of these together. The evidence of our youthfulness is daily renewed in the fact that our Texans and Oklahomans are still gushing, while those of Europe have dried into jealousy these two or three generations. The French particularly are concerned with the myth of our infantilism, finding it difficult to choose between our vulgarities and those of the Russians. Long matured out of emotion, they have never understood the barbarian cultures northeast, north, northwest, and west of them, even when they have heard of them. Lacking humor, they must subsist upon their superiority, and can therefore be trusted to the last Frenchman to reassure themselves upon our infancy and to give us crumbs of approval for those of our writers who are outside our tradition. It is going to be almost inconceivably difficult for the French to learn a few things which can be learned only from some barbarians, and which they must learn if they are to survive in the not inconceivably distant first general culture of the world.

As for our American new rich sixth-graders, whose sixth-gradism is so helpful to the self-esteem of our Allies, they are in fact the most apparent hope of the planet. Only too evidently, they are the renewing body, the living, material strength, of the generic Western superculture. And so long as they bully and brag, we may be sure that the soul also goes marching on. For their ostentation is the acknowledgment of their inferiority before the ancient American idealism which invites them and which they despair to fulfill. Their truculent aggressiveness and burning of the books provide a guarantee that their children will have "the best education that money can buy," that their grandchildren will slip unobtrusively into the great tradition and, like all responsible Americans, will lose the favor of the attention of the French. The loud new rich are our babies, our trouble, our strength and our hope. When they are Yankees, they are at once the extreme decadence of New England culture and the evidence of its survival. Their America, as Wilde said, is not in its childhood but in its second childhood. The danger of real newness, of the triumph of callowness, is not in them but in the quiet new rich, in the powerful and the great who are so ignorant, so stripped of idealism and responsibility, that in their subconsciousness they suffer no intimation of their vacuity. Show me a Texan or a Labor Leader who is modest, well-behaved according to the book, and really lacks an inferiority complex, and I will show you something truly young and terrible, something before which we would all do well to prostrate ourselves and close our eyes and tremble.

The possibility of the ascendance of these good people finds support in the now ominous length of the current decline of New England culture. It began in the 1860's, and under the increasing weight of materialism in philosophy, politics, economics and manners the culture may have been crushed out of being into memory. Any age of transition in a culture is a kind of death of one social body, whether physical or psychic, and the birth of a new one, and it is impossible to know, except with hindsight, whether the cultural soul in decline is merely in process of transmigration or whether it has completed its cycle and returned into annihilation in God. The English transition of the sixteenth and seventeenth centuries was part of the actual death of the Feudal Superculture which God had directed through established Authority, and part of the birth of the Bourgeois Superculture which God would direct by speaking, in one way or another, to individuals. But the transition of the industrial revolution in the eighteenth century was the mere substitution of one mechanical body for another. So the apparent shrivelings of the religious soul of New England between 1660 and 1700, and again between 1760 and 1800, we know at this distance to have been mere declines, and each in turn was followed by an awakening. But who can say as much with certainty of a decline that has lasted almost a century, with no revival yet that has involved most of the people? It may be that Materialism spells not a decline but the death of the culture wherein God spoke to individuals, and the beginning of the one wherein He does not speak at all. In that case our two old American cultures are indeed dead after what will have been about three centuries and a half of life, a span about a century shorter than that of the feudal culture which preceded them. If they are dead, then America and the rest of Western Christendom are indeed young, and in the keeping of the well-mannered new rich who doubtless have their mysterious wisdom. In their hands we are on the threshold of a new and frankly materialistic culture in which only Russia has preceded us. It is impossible in our near view to know whether or not this is so. This book will proceed in the hope that it is not, that there is still a chance that the complete human being—call him Puritan, Yankee, Rebel, or some combination of them—will stir out of his long servitude.

To rebut the popular notion that America is young, it is necessary to fix approximately the dates of its two cultures, and particularly, for present purposes, of New England culture. To do this, it is first necessary to know what we mean by "culture."

In the present text we shall not use the word in its individual

sense, in which it is synonymous with "cultivated," and means that
a person or a group is the product of the cultivating or educative
forces of society. Here we shall use the word Culture in its original
bio-social sense, referring to a collection of many individuals and
meaning the quality or qualities common to them and in terms of
which they are a unit. Beyond that it is difficult to find a generally
accepted meaning. T. S. Eliot in his *Notes Toward a Definition of
Culture*,[14] seeming to speak as a somewhat over-professionalized,
over-supercilious Englishman, identifies culture with the medieval-
isms of catholicism and hereditary classes; thus he is of no help to
candid inquiry into existing bourgeois and post-bourgeois culture,
except as we are willing to retire before his implied over-simplifica-
tion to the effect that such cultures do not and can not exist. H. Richard Neibuhr in *Christ and Culture*[15] gives a clear and impressive
definition of culture as what man imposes upon nature, what is social in distinction from what is private; but at the shallow extreme
this would include within culture much gadgetry which often dis-
guises and disrupts it, and at the deeper extreme it would require
difficult distinctions in the area where native impulses, particularly
social and religious ones, merge into their artificial rituals.

Taking our definition of culture as the integrating quality or
qualities of a collection, it becomes desirable often to differentiate between this essence of the collection and its outward activities which
sometimes express it but may also sometimes belie it. This suggests
the classic distinction between Culture as the soul, the life, the
meaning of a society, and Civilization as its body, its mechanics, its
economy, its surfaces. The distinction does invite quibbling where
the elements of civilization are the close expressions of the culture
within. In a square-dance, the fiddle is civilization, but the music is
culture; the boots of the men and the ribbons of the girls are civilization, but the dancing is culture. The standard New England
farmhouse after the middle of the seventeenth century had a graceful roof line which thereafter was retained, in the common substyles,
at some loss of useful space within. The house was part of civilization,
but the impulse which devised and retained the style was of the
stuff of culture. Like Dr. Niebuhr's distinction between Culture and
Nature that between Culture and Civilization is sometimes difficult
to draw. But in the latter case the difficulty is all at the upper or
shallow end of the scale; at least we can take it that all essential elements, in the individual and in society, are of the stuff of Culture.
Also, this distinction suggests a principle, applicable in the present
inquiry, that a man can change his civilization, but probably can
not change his culture.

Cultures exist in family trees, and it is not in the present purpose

to suggest any modification of the nomenclatures that leading scholars have proposed for them and their ramifications. In Western
Christendom there have been successively the great trees of the
Roman, Feudal and Bourgeois supercultures, and each, however
named, has its main limbs, as French bourgeois culture, English
bourgeois culture, or Scotch bourgeois culture. Each of these in
turn has its smaller subdivisions or subcultures which differ variously in their physical features of topography and economy, in their
civilizations, and in their deeper cultural elements. Because of the
complexity of inter-reactions, it becomes always a question of great
and perhaps unprofitable semantic nicety to determine whether
the relation of two kindred cultures is one of parallel development
out of the main trunk, as would be the case with Scotch and English
bourgeois cultures, or whether one is a subculture sprung from the
other, as would be the case with New Zealand and English bourgeois
cultures.

With regard to New England, we might assume that English
bourgeois culture dates from about 1500 and that New England
culture, therefore, is a subculture of this larger limb. Or we might
postulate that English bourgeois culture was fluid and immature
until the Revolution of 1688, and in that case New England bourgeois culture would be a parallel and independent rather than a
derivative growth. Either approach can be supported, and for
purposes of simplicity the view taken here will be the latter one,
that New England culture is not a subdivision of English bourgeois
culture but a close parallel to it and taking many influences from it.
Our real question is, when can we say that there was *a* mature culture
in New England, whatever its affinities, derivations or classification?
Taking such a critical year as 1660, when the second and native-born
generation was in control, and was effecting great changes in ecclesiastical and civil polity, and when the hostile Stuarts were restored in Old England, taking such a year, our question is whether
New England was then still a group of expatriate Englishmen not
yet independently integrated, or whether it was already a mature cultural unit, seeded from the same medieval tradition and sprouting
from the same evolving Puritan roots as bourgeois England, and
therefore closely resembling it, but having also its own special and
local qualities that marked it as independent and self-sufficient.

As already implied, there are usually two elements of a culture.
First, and most important, there is an element of human or internal
nature; and second, and usually related, there is an element of locale
or external nature. The internal element is something of the heart.
It is a community of assumptions and psychic processes which may
once have been theories of original or revolutionary minds but are

now realized by experience, habitual, colored by emotion, shared by all, rarely any longer examined except by intellectuals, and implemented by a civilizationful of practices. Ultimately they are stronger in individuals than the desires for the common gratifications, and are often in conflict with individualism in the common forms of physical, economic or social self-assertion. The assumptions of a mature culture include the deep instinct of religion, irrespective of the outer rituals, the deep instinct for right conduct, irrespective of codes or even customs, the deep sense of the soul's relation to authority, irrespective of social and political institutions. They are the furniture and the vestments in which each member of the culture must be cradled from birth, for they cannot be acquired in maturity at a level deeper than the conscious mind.

The external or local aspect of a culture is pertinent to it but does not define it. The notion, current on high authority now for fifty years, that physical matters, notably topography and the economy that fits it, are definitive in culture, can find only partial support. In many contiguous countries of Europe and Asia we have profoundly contrasted cultures subsisting on identical terrains with almost identical economies. To be sure, the assumptions and attitudes of the culture must suit the uses of the land, and indeed often involve the uses of the land, and there is interplay between them. But in many advanced cultures the deep human elements of religion and morals are not only independent of practical uses but violate them, and it is the deep human elements that are definitive. More essential to the real matters of the culture is the actual landscape itself, the look of it and its appropriateness, either functional or simply associative, to the deeper assumptions. To be part of a local culture a man must either have been born in its landscape, or in a landscape so like it as to be immediately recognizable. People of the same culture are or might have been natives of the same terrain.

In a Culture, then, we have the deep human assumptions, and we have the locale. And expressing or implementing both, we have the surface tools and mechanisms of the Civilization. Although the first settlers of New England came from what were probably three subcultures with their subcivilizations, namely those of the West Counties, London and East Anglia, they nevertheless accomplished on the new ground a very rapid unification and adjustment in civilization, if not in culture. Under the pressures of common religion, common government, common hardships and problems, the people of Lincoln and Dorset, of London and Devon, being now the people of Boston, Charlestown, Roxbury, Watertown, Newtown (Cambridge) and Dorchester, were by the middle 1630's losing their differences of manners and speech, and were becoming identical in the ways of dress, agriculture and the crafts. Their civilization had already a New English distinctiveness in local improvisations and the adoption from the Indians of features of dress, domestic economy and the cultivation of the soil. Within ten years after landing the fundamental subsistence farming was established in these and four dozen other townships, in all of which the forests were burned down into common pastures and privately owned strips that were under cultivation.

At the beginning, as in the succeeding centuries, the "frontier" phase of Puritan settlement was always brief. Each new plantation carried its civilization and indeed its culture with it in the form of an ecclesiastical and a political unit organized before departure, set them down in the wilderness on a spot already staked out in all its subdivisions, and within a year had them rooted and flourishing as a church, a school, a militia, a village of substantial houses within a fortified enclosure, and a supporting agriculture outside taller than the charred and berry-buried stumps of the original forest. In 1640 there was still a newness of structure upon some of fifty villages with their treeless and muddy commons, their thatch, shingles, clapboards, and exposed frames not yet weathered out of the natural yellow. But there was no newness in the social and economic mechanics that used the structures. It could be argued that New England was a going Civilization by 1632. It is conservative to say that it was one by 1640.

As for the Culture underlying the civilization, the basic assumptions and attitudes which were to found and qualify it were all brought in some form by the Puritans from England, beginning in 1620 and especially after 1629. Roughly, they were of three varieties. First, there were the basic Idealism and Mythology which they shared with Christendom. Second, there were the principles of the Calvinist wing of the Reformation which they shared with the body of English Puritans and in terms of which their forbears for four or five generations had been in determined, passionate and dangerous revolt in England, from the yeoman's farmhouse to the baron's hall; it was largely upon these principles that the immigrants proposed to found a *new* England to take the place of the Old England which they believed was going to dissolve in bankruptcy and rapine. These two sets of elements, the generic Christian ones and the generic Calvinist-Puritan ones, were already of the emotional and psychic profundity of culture. Besides them, there was a third set of common assumptions and attitudes not yet so deeply founded: these were certain theories and doctrines that were more or less controversial among the Puritans themselves, were special to these emigrés, and were still not quite out of their cocoons of theory. Subsequently we shall look with some care at all of these elements that went to found New England culture. For the moment we shall notice only the few that seem specially pertinent to its maturing. Some of them are those that came to America in relatively theoretical and little tried form, and some are special New English adaptations of basic English Puritan or of generic Christian principles. As long as any of these fundamentals remained amorphous, it could hardly be said that there was any such thing as New England culture.

Perhaps the unique development among the American Puritans, and their unique legacy to their country, was Equalitarianism. It drew from the Reformation's doctrine of the Equality of all before God, Luther's principle that every man should be his own priest; but in the Anglican Church, and indeed among most of the English Puritans, it was lost in practice beneath inviolable aristocratic assumptions. It survived in the doctrine of Congregationalism, that of independent, early Christian congregations ruled by their own members or "saints." This doctrine was espoused by a few Puritan academicians, and practiced in England at great peril by the Brownists, among whom were the American Pilgrims. Possibly in part through the influence of the Pilgrims, but surely through the fact that the leading divines of the great migration to Massachusetts in 1630 were of Congregational disposition, the system was from the start and permanently established in New England. It was not merely in theory that every man went before God alone. In immediate fact every church member stood up before the other members of his congregation and spoke his mind and had his vote. More important than the beginnings of political democracy, which were indeed involved, was the religious assumption which became channeled in the tradition at this early time before democracy amounted to much. This was the assumption that one man in his soul was as good as another, the deep persuasion, not only that I am as good as you are but that you are as good as I am. The superficial conditions of the frontier village helped the underlying assumption. And the aristocratic tradition, also present, may have militated somewhat against it. Before the culture could be called mature, these differences had to be refined away in the fires of controversy.

The fires burned at first in Boston which, while it was rich in equalitarian warmth, was nevertheless dominated by the oligarchy of the magistrates and very early showed a tendency toward dynastic aristocracy. Roger Williams interpreted the doctrine of equality as meaning something like individualism, both ecclesiastically and civilly, espoused the principle of minimal government, and so set spinning a pinwheel of angry debate which in 1635 spun him out of The Bay to found Rhode Island. In 1637 Anne Hutchinson was preaching wholly private religion—the Antinomian Heresy—and so spun after Williams. Meanwhile in 1636, Thomas Hooker, complaining of the centralization of government at The Bay, spun off to The River to father the Fundamental Articles of Connecticut which broadened the central government and increased the weight of each man in his town. By 1640 there had been achieved a separate integration in each of the three principal colonies, and a kind of mutuality of disagreement between them. At The Bay there was Aristocracy becoming hereditary—though under special equalitarian limitations which would make it unique among aristocracies. At The Island there was individualism, anarchy, almost no political integration. In the culture as a whole it was a valuable safety-valve, a catch-all for Quakers, Groaners, Familists and other originals who translated equalitarianism into emphasis upon their private consequence. At The River Equalitarianism was least confused by conflicting tendencies, an aristocratic surface being accepted, but not taken so dynastically, or otherwise so seriously as to jeopardize the underlying humanity. Beneath a slightly democratized polity, The River preserved and developed the deep equalitarian impulse which, even when its religious base was gone, was going to distinguish the culture of Greater New England and America. While this larger development was yet far off, by 1640 the relation of each colony to the principle of equalitarianism was settled, and with respect to this key quality the culture was mature.

From the doctrine of Equalitarianism there ramified early corollaries which were essential to the culture. Since all men were equal before God, all men were, with respect to their fellows, Independent in matters pertaining to God, that is in matters of private opinion. From this there followed two reciprocal features of New England culture. First, this inner independence, at a time when the most profound human qualities were still considered the most important, gave every man an inner assurance and dignity which made him socially responsible and, like any aristocrat, willing to defer to better qualified authority in all outward matters. Second, it gave every man, subject to the externals of social responsibility, a tolerance of the private views of every other man, for the other fellow was as good before God as he was. Wherefore, we find generally that the early enactments against Quakers and other heretics who threatened the several Commonwealths yet exempted them from punishment if they kept their heresies to themselves and did not "broach" them in public. Mrs. Hutchinson was not banished for her opinions but for publicizing them and causing "disorders." By the time of the persecution of the Quakers and the Baptists in the 1650's, we find the towns neglecting to inform on members of the hated sects who obviously were holding secret meetings within their bounds. By that time, and presumably much earlier, there was established the quality thereafter and to date so characteristic of communities in Greater New England, that anybody may hold any wild opinions he wants to so long as he conforms to the outward civilities and intrudes on no one else's right likewise to hold his wild opinions.

Corollary to Equalitarianism, also, and to the principle of inner Independence within outer conformity, was an early enhancement, within the New England populace, of that Idealism which, as we shall see, is a basic assumption of Christianity. Far more fully than the English, who generally took not only their social code but their ideas from the aristocracy, the American Puritans must work out each his own complete Central Idea by which he would live. The best outward evidence of this inward ferment of ideas among the early settlers comes from Rhode Island where there was little external restraint upon their expression, and by the 1640's we find Coddington, Gorton, Harris and others boiling with comprehensive notions that are to save both God and mankind. So, under their greater restraint, boiled the Idealism of all the New England Puritans.

Still another effect of the doctrines of Equalitarianism and of Internal Independence was the stimulus they gave to the application of the Covenant of Grace which, as we shall see, being matter of controversy among the English Puritans generally, was the central and distinguishing doctrine of the New English. It held in brief that Belief in the Atonement was a sure sign of Regeneration and Election. The central aim of the New Englander from the very beginning was to find out whether he believed or not. And this proclivity, like that for Equality and for a controlling Central Idea, was something that by 1640 was ready to be woven into the fabric of an inclusive culture.

Peculiarly American, also, was the enlargement given to the generic Puritan doctrine of finding all Revelation in the Bible. The rule became at once and remained standard in New England, and out of it grew the special and secular American trait of requiring and depending on written constitutions. Contributory also was the dependence from the beginning upon royal Charters. By 1634 we find the people of Watertown rising to a constitutional point of their rights under the Charter. In 1639 we have the Fundamental Articles in Connecticut, together with similarly organic legislation in Plymouth, and in 1641 the Bodie of Liberties in Massachusetts. By that time the distinct American trait of Constitution-consciousness was established and channeled.

Then there was Millennialism. This came over from England with those leaders who suspected that the New England they were founding might well become the Kingdom where the New Jerusalem would descend. Once in the new country, the idea spread widely among the farmers, being the first form of that Optimism which was from this time typically American.

All these new elements, together with the fundamental Calvinist doctrines and practices which the Puritans brought over with them, and their body of English culture to fill in the chinks, all of these elements were synthesized and in mature shape in the solidly founded towns by ten years after landing. By 1640 the deep religious and social assumptions of Greater New England were founded, and a state of culture existed. But it could hardly yet be called a state of local New England culture. Indigenous refinements of importance had been matured, major differences had been ironed out, and the period of adjustment was over. Yet the bulk of the basic assumptions had been brought by these Englishmen from Old England, and their roots and their external symbols and associations were still there. New England was not the place where they and their culture had been bred together. Their social and religious doctrines might have matured in this scene, but they had not grown through childhood and youth here. They and their details, together with the rest of the minutiae of their inner landscapes—the mountains and cliffs and hidden springs, the swift and the sluggish rivers, the patterns of walls and hedges, the dwellings with lighted windows and those with darkened windows, the nights when monsters roamed, the dawns when the light of Grace drove them away—these inner, psychic features were not reflected and strengthened in the particular outward hills and ponds and seas that surrounded these immigrants now. Their inner landscape had been formed in the frame of a different outer one, and when they came to die they would identify their resurgent youthful hopes with other hills and other trees. They were Englishmen who had carried their culture, together with great and revolutionary ideas, into the wilderness, and had planted them well. But for them it remained, nevertheless, a transplanted and modified English culture. In 1640 the culture of New England was delineated. It was past the stages of random trial and adjustment. Physically, its civilization was past the disruptions and confusions of settlement. But the culture itself was not yet mature on this ground.

What the first generation Puritans accomplished with their homogeneity and their rapid adjustment was to make possible the completion in two generations of major social changes which usually take three. The babies brought in by the original immigrants or born in New England in the 1630's grew up in the complete outer stuff of the new civilization and the complete inner stuff of the new culture, and both were identified with the actual Bear Mountain and Long Pond and Witch Swamp which at the same time were the first places their senses were printing on their memories. When these babies should become the dominant personnel of New England, its culture would be mature. Their influence becomes noticeable after the more or less concurrent deaths of the three first great leaders, that of Hooker in '47, that of Winthrop in '48, that of Cotton in '51. Throughout the '50's, while the second-rate survivors of the first generation were debasing piety with frightened violence, the youngsters were diluting it with liberal attacks upon established church polity. In 1657 they accomplished in the Halfway Covenant such a revolution as would have changed the course of New England during the Antinomian controversy only twenty years earlier. But in them New England culture was now founded, more deeply than church polity, more deeply even than doctrine. The sense of human Equality and of the sources of truth, and other essential assumptions and patterns of thought, while they were still expressed in terms of religion, were already more deeply channeled even than religion.

By the end of the 1650's New England was settled in its combination of peasant economy, half-bourgeois half-aristocratic morality, and aristocratic independence and standards of excellence. In the century that lay ahead the new culture was going to be attacked from within and without, it was going to swing now into the great Heresy of Reason called Arminianism, now into the great Heresy of Emotion called Antinomianism. But in all these changes, and others that were to follow, the basic assumptions and mental patterns of the people would not be disturbed. After about a century and a half of transition out of the culture of the English Middle Ages, New England was by 1660 rooted and mature on its own ground.[16]

But those who must insist upon the cultural insignificance of America will hardly be impressed by ascription of an age of about three centuries to one or both of our two cultures—for the maturity of the Old South is of at least equal antiquity. Even if it be true that seventy-five to a hundred thousand remodelled Englishmen did represent a kind of crude integration in the last half of the seventeenth century, how, it is asked, can that be compared to two thousand years of the recorded cultures of Europe? The reply, of course, is that there are no cultures in Europe of anything approaching two thousand years' antiquity, and only one that approximates our own three hundred.

Glancing back at that mid-seventeenth century, how much of it can we recognize in the Europe of today? Where now are the cultures of France of the ascendant and absolute Bourbons, Spain of the descending and absolute Hapsburgs, Germany of the Peace of Westphalia and the Empire dissolving into little duchies? They are in the records and the monuments which are as available to us as to their national heirs. If France has a mature bourgeois culture today, it was

born into transition in 1789 and matured in 1870. If Italy has a similar bourgeois culture, it was born in 1848 and as late as the 1930's
was so immature as to lapse into tyranny. And who today can identify
a state of culture in Germany or Spain? On the other hand, where is
the bourgeois culture of Britain which, after a century and a half of
transition out of medievalism, matured with the Revolution of 1688?
Precisely and without fundamental change it is in most of the people
of the present British Commonwealth. And where is the bourgeois
culture of New England which, after a transition out of medievalism
partly identical and partly parallel with that of England, matured
with the Halfway Covenant in 1657? Precisely and without fundamental change it is in most of the people of present New England,
Upstate New York, Ohio, Michigan, Indiana, Illinois, Wisconsin,
Minnesota, Iowa, Kansas, Colorado, Utah, Montana, Wyoming,
Idaho, Washington, Oregon, and Northern California, and in many
of the people of New Jersey, Pennsylvania, the Dakotas, Nebraska,
Oklahoma, Texas, Arizona, New Mexico, Nevada and the rest of
California. In these, seventeenth-century New England survives in
their social, political, moral and religio-psychological assumptions,
as well as in a civilizationful of legends, songs, dances, gestures, pos-
tures, accents, quirks and crotchets that have come down little
altered from parent-and-community to child through changing social
surfaces, doctrines and locations on the earth. Their culture is now
almost wholly ruled, and in some part drugged and perverted, by
Industrial Plutocracy, more so than the equally old, parallel, bourgeois culture of England. But if there is saving virtue in tried and
ancient wisdom, these two cultures between them are the best hope
of the West. The critical problem is whether Greater New England
can be awakened in time to rise through its decadent Economic Individualism to face the modern world. The fate of mankind for a
forthcoming millennium may hang on the question of whether in its
fat and lurid autumn it retains the vitality to stage another spring.

Besides the common inference that New England culture is young,
another assumption of the debunkers and the snobs is that it is
geographically small. Even though it may have had a measure of
antiquity, this was limited to a quaint little section whose significance
disappeared at the latest with the horse and buggy. Puritan culture
was always contained behind the electric fence of the New York
line. The moment a Yankee crosses the Hudson he is no longer a
Yankee.

The question of the current significance, or the lack of it, of the six states of original New England is not one that immediately concerns us—their current decline in economic leadership may or may not be a sign, along with others, of returning health. What is of first importance in our consideration of the scope of Yankee culture is the notion that it never went west anyway, that our Greater New England, consisting of the northern half of the country, is a fiction, that the frontier was always a separate culture and took nothing of consequence from the older cultures whose people settled it.

The notion had respectable support in the Frontier Hypothesis of Frederick Jackson Turner. The theory has been pretty well discredited as far as academic America is concerned,[17] but it is getting a new life in the current attempt to apply it to the whole, expansive, post-Renaissance West, to show that the farmers of Argentina and Montana have more in common than the first have with the Spanish or the second with the English.[18] Its effect is to identify humanity with its primitive, infantile and evanescent behaviors which are appropriate on the frontier, and correspondingly to renounce the channeled instinct for excellence and the other expressions of accumulated wisdom which are marks of cultural maturity. Reinforcing the Respectable Wing of the Debunking School of American History in general, and particularly in denying both the virtues and the scope of Greater New England, the Turner Hypothesis has done great harm to the self-understanding and self-respect of the nation. Because a consideration of it offers a convenient means of presenting the expansion of New England culture across the continent, I am going to give it relatively more notice than it any longer merits.

Among the inconsistencies spread large through the papers collected to make Professor Turner's book,[19] the one notable consistency is assumed rather than stated. It is an extreme form of the Economic Interpretation of History, dismissing not only inheritance but even the cultural environment as an influence upon psychic and social growth, attributing everything to the physical environment. The Hypothesis holds that America has developed as a series of successive frontiers, upon each of which, beginning with those of Jamestown and Plymouth, substantially the same conditions have been encountered. In meeting them, the people have developed substantially the same traits, prominent among them individualism, self-reliance, hospitality, optimism, physical resourcefulness and inventiveness. These supposedly frontier traits, among the people of the now ancient as well as of the recent frontiers, are, in the Turner view, the typical American qualities. The elements of American culture have not moved horizontally from east to west with the people, like their animals. They have risen vertically and de novo, like local plants, upon each new strip of western wilderness, and having so grown, have remained the cultural qualities there. Pin all of these strips together, and you get the United States. The uniform formative influence upon America has been the availability, until the 1880's, of a body of free land.

The Turner Hypothesis contained several truths, most of them minor. While the Frontier did not produce the primary traits usually associated with it, such as the virtues of self-reliance, hospitality and optimism and the vices of narrowness, anarchy and lynch law, it did provide a setting that encouraged their development among those already disposed toward them by their original culture. In a state of sparse settlement, the individualism or self-assertiveness which underlies all these traits could expand and flourish, whereas within the more populous regions it would have been compressed toward either social responsibility or criminality. Likewise, the secondary virtues of physical resourcefulness and inventiveness, while they were and still are the normal conditions of both of the two great agrarian cultures from which the bulk of the pioneers came, yet they did receive a special fillip in the equipmental void which was always part of the initial dilemma of the pioneer.

The Frontier did exert original influence upon the regions behind it through the reports of strange and colorful peoples and of gargantuan and heroic deeds. These reached the home cultures by either of two routes, of which the most effective until recently was that of personal account or current journalism, getting its immediate effect in histrionic imitation by little boys and similarly minded elder morons. Here the influence came back immediately from existing or very recent pioneers, not from any section's own forgotten frontier of generations gone. New York State and Ohio, for example, having been settled rapidly between 1790 and 1810, remembered their own frontiers and their hardships through their third generation which was approximately the Civil War generation. But any frontier influence on them since that time has come back from farther west. It has not involved the Iroquois, the Algonquins, Hiawatha, Sir William Johnson, the Brants, Rufus Putnam, Moses Cleaveland, the Coonskin Library and Tippecanoe, but the Sioux, the Cheyennes and the Apaches, Rain-in-the-Face, Crazy Horse, Sitting Bull and Geronimo, Custer, the James gang, Deadeye Dick and Buffalo Bill. In this case the cultural influence does not rise vertically from the past, in the Turnerian fashion, but moves horizontally among living people as asserted here.

The other reportorial or literary effect of the frontier is in the accumulating folklore, which does rise vertically from the more or less local past as Turner would have it. As long as there were surviving islands of actual frontier life, the direct reports of them carried more weight than the ancient tales. Until 1900 Sitting Bull outshone Powhatan or Massasoit, and Custer was esteemed above John Smith or Miles Standish. But now the living frontier is gone, the folklore, duly adorned by its bards, begins to take its place in our culture comparable to that of the Trojan War in the culture of Greece, the adventures of Aeneas in that of Rome, the glorious deeds of Arthur and Lancelot and Percival. And in so far as each corner of America retains its own special folklore, its presence is an exhibit, and the only persuasive exhibit, in support of the Frontier or vertical Hypothesis.

A point in which Turner implies an important truth indirectly and unintentionally is in his emphasis upon the availability of an area of free land as a formative influence upon American character. With him, this is merely a restatement of his general doctrine. Actually, during long periods and over large regions, the availability of free land has undoubtedly had a serious, degenerating effect on the culture adjoining it, holding ajar a door of escape from immediate problems, thus encouraging intellectual mediocrity and moral anemia, both at home and on the Frontier. In that invitation to the glorious freedom of the wide open spaces we have the origin of much that is just in the modern arraignment of America. Fortunately, this vacuous influence of the frontier was not operative upon New England culture during its formative time.

A fundamental error of the frontier theory, and one which has suppressed much significant American history, was its assumption that the Frontier was a unit, its failure to recognize the two sharply contrasted frontiers, each reflecting one of the two contrasted basic cultures. At the time Turner wrote his definitive papers—in the 1890's—he seems to have been ignorant of New England and under a compulsion to detract it. Consequently he applied to all the frontiers from the earliest Atlantic beginnings the qualities of the Southern or Rebel frontier, which is to say, the qualities of Rebel culture. He suppressed knowledge of the Yankee pioneers who moved out of New England, keeping north of Pennsylvania, the Ohio River, and the cultural boundary running westward to the Pacific, and emphasized those who moved out of the South and westward below this line. Thus he concealed the more numerous body of pioneers and emphasized the less numerous.[20] More significantly, he suppressed the qualities of his own region, the Old Northwest of Ohio, Indiana, Michigan, Illinois and Wisconsin, for no perceptible reason except that they were New England qualities. And he suppressed the great contributions its people had made to America, and the still greater contributions they were beginning to make in his time, for no perceptible reason except that they were such contributions as might be expected of Yankees, and the people who made them were mostly New Englanders or their cultural descendants. In place of the tremendous and enlightened idealism that had actually motivated them he must needs attribute to them the infantile qualities which distinguished their neighbors to the south.*

Although Turner nowhere presents together all the traits of his typical frontiersman, who is a Rebel frontiersman, he somewhere admits them all, though diffidently. Besides the virtues of politeness and hospitality—sometimes ostentatious, sometimes courteous, there is always the central individualism, and there are its major subdivisions and analogues of truculence, boastfulness, physical recklessness, romantic optimism, ignorance, contempt for learning and reliance upon emotion, revivalist religion, contempt for government and reliance upon summary justice. These qualities distinguish

* Whatever Turner's personal motives may have been, there can be little doubt of the general social motive represented by his celebration of the Middle West for supposed qualities which, if they had been real, would have equated it with the South upon a mutually low scale. At the time when he was organizing his theory, around 1890, the old Middle West, whose capital was Chicago, being two to four generations from its frontier, was finally losing its just and sustaining pride in the performances of its pioneers. With the idealism of its proper culture, it was awakening to realize that its passage of privation had greatly drained it of the methods and paraphernalia of civilization which were necessary to the full expression of the culture. The Middle West was passing into an awkward age of inferiority complication vis-a-vis the supposedly "cultured," effete, and therefore greatly hated East of its origins. Persons of imagination set about to meet the challenge and supply the defect, and they succeeded in less than half a century, leading the second literary "flowering" of New England culture, leading the nation for a time in liberal thought, developing what is perhaps still our best system of public education. But meanwhile the great and unimaginative body of the citizenry must have a prescription for their inferiority complex in the face of their cousins back East, a mythology to celebrate their special virtues which New England did not possess. This Turner kindly provided, supplying a palliative to jealous little egos and giving no help to the great men who were already struggling to restore the Middle West to a parity with or superiority to New England in terms of the real virtues of the common culture. It is comforting to know they have so far succcceeded that the Old Middle West today has lost its sensitiveness, needing nobody's reassurance as to the importance of its major contributions to mankind.

Turner's disservice to America is little vitiated by the fact that he was a great and beloved teacher, nor by the fact that he was a great scholar who chose to doff his scholarship for the purpose of his unfounded generalizations. He is the more reprehensible in that his later and less celebrated papers show that in the intervening years he had learned much of New England and its complete community with the Old Northwest, yet refused to repudiate the early papers that had reputed him. Indeed it is necessary to acknowledge that the phrase "Greater New England," which is used here to include together the Yankee East and West, was used by Turner to the same purpose in his later papers when he had lived many years in New England. (See, "The First Official Frontier of the Massachusetts Bay" in *Publ.*, XVII [1914], 250-71, reprinted as Chapter II in *The Frontier in American History* [1920] using the phrase in question in page 66 of the book; also, on the same page, the editor's citation of "Greater New England in the Middle of the Nineteenth Century," in Proceedings of the American Antiquarian Society, XXIX [1919].)

equally the backwoodsman in his coonskin cap and his cabin with the smoke going up in the frosty morning, and the cowboy with his easy horsemanship, his solitary soul, his kindness grown inward and explosive. These types—neither of which any Yankee ever became unless he had to leave home suddenly—are now generally accredited as the stock frontiersmen of the whole nation, doubtless because, as compared to the qualities of the Yankee pioneers, they are the more primitive and colorful in an age that abhors maturity and intelligence, and ignores drama in favor of melodrama.

These qualities of the Rebel pioneers—generally expressions of Individualism—do suggest the crudities of the Frontier better than do those of the Yankee pioneers, and they were surely extended and aggravated by frontier life. Yet their origins were in quite unfrontier-like conditions of Southern culture, and, it may be observed, they tend to survive in Southerners generations after the Frontier has been loaded with skyscrapers. Their beginnings were in everything opposed to them, namely in the aristocratic virtues which the planters had developed in their children before the end of the seventeenth century. The second and third generation from the first settlers, frequently educated in England, were already of Christian feudal quality,[21] which meant that the best of them had a genuine courtesy, including a large humanity or sense of basic human equality. Of the Southern Aristocracy after 1700 the boast can be made that is usually reserved for military heroes, that seldom have so few people affected so profoundly the lives of so many. The gentry itself was never over two hundred families,[22] perhaps on the average 1,500 individuals, most of them concentrated in the East. Yet they not only provided the leadership of the Revolution and the Federal period; for three centuries they have indoctrinated directly or indirectly millions of Rebels with their stereotyped ideas of the Knight and Gentleman, and at least a pretense of his courtesy, hospitality, responsibility and serviceability. And in an unreckonable number among the millions there is still a measure of substance beneath the pretense.

Besides the virtues of the code, individualism was implicit in it from the beginning, both for better and, rather more noticeably, for worse. The virtues prescribed ran to the service of persons not principles, of your neighbor not God. Also it was the rare Galahad—the rare Washington, Jefferson or Lee—who did not have a fundamental sense of his own importance as the primary condition of his service to the people of the parish, the county, the state and the nation. And the people of the parish and the county, while they put on the graces of the quality, were at the same time, each in his degree, aware of their humble place, resentful of it, and proud to belligerency of what they could claim. By the end of the seventeenth century the more enterprising of these were going up-country into the Piedmont, some under the economic necessity of exhausted tobacco lands, all in search of a freer arena for their self-respect, their self-concern, their self-expression, their Individualism. Besides the encouragement to their subjectivity provided by the dangers of the wilderness, there also developed, in contrast with the hospitality they brought with them, a suspicion of strangers who might be either royal tax collectors or rent agents of the gentry upon whose patents they often were squatting. So the generosities of aristocracy and the truculences of individualism were found mixed in those who before the Revolution were already a majority of Southerners; and it would be a guess of temerity that would venture to say generally where the one quality prevailed, and where the other. In the Tidewater Aristocracy itself, and in those Virginians who moved out to become border people along the Ohio, we may suspect that the generous virtues, the culture of the Old South, remained dominant. Among the people of the Virginia and Carolina Piedmont, probably the most populous part, it would be idle to try to apportion the two sets of qualities. As for the run of frontiersmen before 1800, the people of the mountains, most of those westward in Tennessee, and perhaps in Kentucky, it can be inferred from the record that the individualism they brought with them had been aggravated and fixed by the Frontier, that they were already mostly of the Pseudo-South, of the angry breed in whom ignorance and violence were stronger than the gentle inheritance.

After 1800 both the individualism and the aristocracy got reinforcement, partly in the older parts but mostly on the new frontiers of Western Georgia, Alabama, Mississippi, Arkansas and Texas. Across this Deep South, just then opening, charged armies of Scotch-Irish and Scotch Highlanders, dragging the new cotton gin and their newly acquired slaves behind them. Natively they were cut to a duality almost identical with that of the Southern pattern. Their traditions were of gallantry, courage, and Bonnie Prince Charlie, and equally they were of clans, feuds, intrigue, brutality and generally ornamental violence. At the outset the violence predominated, but in course it was softened in some degree. Those who succeeded in the battle royal for cotton land set about transforming themselves and their children into gentry by marrying as fast as they could into the old aristocracy. At their best they succeeded by the time of the Civil War. At their near best they produced two other valuable classes, one a pseudo-aristocracy which imitated the graces of the gentry but missed its learning and its responsibility, the other a body of substantial, middling farmers who made out with three to five slaves and no pretentious nonsense. At worst, the immigration, because of the ruthlessness of its battle royal, accelerated the growth of the Poor White class, with its illiteracy, superstition, dreams of grandeur,[23] green alcohol, boastfulness, bowie knives, gouging, lynching and all kinds of murder. All four of these classes were the frontier of the Deep South, and they spread north and west to reinforce the old frontier of the mountains and the western rivers. Among them altogether the Individualism was surely predominant. It flourished on the Frontier, but it was not instigated there. As at first it came as a by-product of the aristocracy of the Tidewater, so now it came as a primary product of the clans of Scotland.

Erecting a composite Rebel who combined the less extreme of both the vices and the virtues, Turner made him the generic Frontiersman from the northern source to the southern mouth of the Father of Waters. He accomplished the absorption into this character of the more numerous Yankee frontiersmen partly by a misuse of words usually familiar to historians. He attributed to his stock frontiersman the "Individualism" of the Rebel which was exceptional among Yankees before the industrial revolution; but he equated it with "Equalitarianism," a fundamental Yankee quality which no true Rebel ever understood, desiring to be not equal to his neighbors but superior to them, desiring his neighbors to be his equals as a matter of Christian principle but his inferiors as a matter of social and physical fact. Still more remarkably, Turner attributed to his type frontiersmen "Democracy," using it as a vague synonym for his already inconsistent individualism-equalitarianism and not at all in its proper meaning of a form of government, a form which the Yankees had developed naturally out of their equalitarianism, but of which no "Southern Democrat" ever heard, least of all the "Jacksonian Democrats" of the frontier. To them government was a matter of the challenge, the trigger, the knife and the feud. To them even more than to their better enlightened cousins east of the mountains, "democracy" meant local independence and individualism, not a form of government but a synonym for anarchy. At best it was a truce between fighting men. Each planter, whether in Georgia or Missouri, held himself lord of his domain. His political relations were with his adjoining neighbors whom he met from time to time at their boundaries or in their houses or in the county towns, each complete with retainers and panoply, wanting only armor and pennants to reproduce similar parlays between similar illiterate lords of similar manors in the dark ages. As for democracy!—If any mollycoddle Yankee tried to tell these bravos to defer to a majority of his neighbors, they must know what they were asking for! Equality?—what did they want to do, free the Niggers? Real gentlemen, real Jacksonian Democrats, real Individualists didn't discuss such things.

Most deceptive among Turner's misuses of words is that of "Idealism." His generic frontiersman is an "Idealist." By this he means—in a triumph of paradox—a materialistic idealist. The brave frontiersmen bore their hard lot in the high "American Dream" that their children would have a "more abundant"—that is, a monetarily richer—life tomorrow. That most of them, north and south, did have some such dream is likely, and the maintenance of it in the face of seemingly insuperable hardship and often impending death was a proof of great courage. But that any such dream, before the Civil War, was the dominating "ideal" of any representative body of Americans, north or south, that it contained, as James T. Adams would have it, the "Epic of America," is ridiculous.

The most profligate Rebel planter and the most criminal Rebel backwoodsman had each the same controlling idea of himself as a gracious gentleman one of whose gentlemanly qualities was that he would not stoop to work for money—a proclivity which he attributed to his enemy the mean and grubbing Yankee; and the maintenance of that hospitable ideal, often in obvious squalor, was a far nobler course than the persistence of any dream of wealth could be. Correspondingly, the typical pre-Civil War or pre-Materialist Yankee, whether in Old New England or the Old Northwest, had an ideal of social amelioration, especially an ideal of the Union as the haven for a better—not a richer—humanity, which was the strongest thing in his life and comprised the Yankee cause—to match the Rebels' economic cause—of the Civil War. This passionate Idealism—which Turner and the other economic interpreters prefer to neglect—was very possibly stronger among the pioneers of the Old Frontier, the Old Northwest, than it was in the East, for along the Ohio they were in close and often violent contact with the Rebels who had no time for their nonsense, and in the War their humanitarian dream overcame their economic interest which was rather with the South than with New England. Without that powerful Idealism—not at all peculiar to Lincoln—the war would probably never have been fought, and it surely would not have been won. The War showed, as nothing else had shown, the gulf between the two great cultures. It showed the gulf as deepest on the Frontier where the geographical gulf was narrowest. By emphasizing the irreconcilable standards of the two frontiers, it showed the triviality of Turner's composite pioneer with his piddling financial "ideal," and at the same time it revealed the whole fallacy of the doctrine of the Frontier's uniform and dominating influence.

The contrast between the cultures was nowhere more evident than in the typical Rebel and Yankee methods of pioneering. The aristocratic-individualistic-anarchistic Rebels migrated with a scout in the smallest groups consonant with minimal safety. When they reached a likely region, they scattered as widely as possible, and concerned themselves with their individual subsistence farming, and with the erection of a manor shack where at the earliest possible moment they would have in the neighbors for such show of hospitality as the flesh and the pulps and the juices of the forest afforded. They made no provision for schools, except in so far as those of wealth among them hired Yankee tutors as was the custom back east. They were slow in the erection of churches, but most of them were susceptible to revivals and camp meetings where the Spirit was not averse to the use of a little green spirits, and heavenly love might find expression in chasing the girls into the bushes.

In all respects the pioneering methods of the equalitarian, communitarian and democratic Yankees were different, and were even more expressive of their basic culture. They migrated typically in large companies, organized before departure into a congregation and a township, complete with minister, schoolteacher, selectmen, surveyor, justice of the peace and constable. Their first echelon was not, as Turner says, the trapper and the scout, but a committee who went out to inspect an area in the howling wilderness advertized by some private or public company, put off their city clothes as late as possible, prospected and selected a site where they had had no predecessors, surveyed and staked out among the great trees the common, the church, the school, the home lots and the farm lots. Their second echelon was their complete civilization and culture—in one case, according to a not wholly trustworthy report, a congregation carried the frame of its church all the way from Connecticut to Ohio. On the way out they never missed a church service, and rarely a school session; and before the stockade was complete around the village— if they made a stockade—before any houses were finished, they would have both church and the school settled and functioning. As soon as the Indian peace was secure they would subscribe with other settlements to found one of those little colleges that are still the milestones of the path of New England across the Continent.

As Perry Miller says of the first Puritans, so their descendants "conceded nothing to the forest." Their effect on the frontier was immediate and clear. The effect of the frontier on them was negligible. In the popular or Turnerian sense, it was not a frontier at all. It was just the edge of expanding New England that, continuing as it had started from the eastern beaches in the 1620's, unrolled slowly toward the Pacific and along its advancing line grew immediately the outer paraphernalia of civilization and the inner assumptions and tried ways of a culture.

In 1630 the line was within the sound of the Atlantic. In 1660 it was on the Connecticut River and the northern boundary of Massachusetts. In 1760 it was at New York and a third of the way up New Hampshire. After the Revolution the great march began. By 1800 the line included all of Vermont and most of Upstate New York, with a long salient down across Ohio to Cincinnati. By 1820 it included all of Ohio, with a salient running down along the River across southern Indiana and out to Collinsville in Illinois. By 1840 it had swelled to take in half of Michigan, a third of Wisconsin, all of Illinois—though still under plenty of Rebel competition, had crossed the Mississippi to include a strip of Iowa and send a Mormon salient out to Independence, Missouri, while two new lines had bulged in from the Pacific, one to enclose some of the Spanish in California, the other to set up the missionary post at Walla Walla in what was going to be Washington. By 1860 all of Iowa and Wisconsin and half of Minnesota were in Greater New England, with a great salient sweeping south and westward to include most of Kansas and Colorado, and all there was of Utah, while the California frontier had moved in to the Sierras, and the northern one had enclosed Portland, Salem, Seattle and Olympia and had sent a salient up the Columbia valley and across Idaho to Missoula in Montana. After the War the old line swept westward across the Dakotas, Nebraska, Wyoming and Montana, and by 1880 it had met the Pacific advance at Helena. Greater New England was complete in outline, and it remained only to fill in the spaces where the bison still ran.

The effect on New England culture of the successive frontiers it enclosed was slight. Hardly greater was the demoralizing effect upon the general morale of the availability of an "area of free land" whither it was possible to disappear in escape from responsibility and trouble. Until 1675 there was plenty of free land in New England, but so strong was the religious cohesiveness of the culture that it was taken up only under religious schism or actual economic necessity. From 1675 until 1760 the New England frontier was shut tight on the Massachusetts line by the hostile French and Algonquins and on the New York line by the officially friendly Iroquois. Within this closed region New England was populously compressed and its culture refined to the point of caricature. One of the refinements was an adjustment, not to the hope of free land, but to the fact of pinched, costly, irregular, eroded, stony and worn-out land. After the elimination of the French and the Algonquins in 1763, the Yankees exploded northward to fill Vermont, New Hampshire and Maine, not in any dream of liberty but for the preservation of life. After the elimination of the Iroquois in 1777 they exploded westward from their still overpopulated and further devitalized soil, and by 1800 the houses on the hilltops were beginning to fall unheard into their cellar-holes, and the roses and apples to run wild in the returning forests. But even in that migration the motives were still chiefly schism and need. It was not until materialism was already boring within the culture in the time of the golden mirages of the 1840's that cupidity became a common cause of pioneering. It was not until after the Civil War that any Yankee would have understood, let alone heeded, any talk of freedom and a "more abundant life" in the "wide open spaces."

Instead of a hypothesis holding the frontier to be a recurrent source of culture, it would seem that a doctrine of the Continuity of Culture would more closely fit the facts of the history of the United States. People of a given culture tend to retain it and to transmit it to their cultural descendants, regardless of race, migration and changing physical environment, unless and until they are overwhelmed by a different culture. Most obviously, the continuity and present scope of Yankee culture is evinced in the still inhabited footprints from ocean to ocean: Hartford, Conn., New Hartford, Conn., Hartfords, N. J., Vt., Me., and N. Y., New Hartford, N. Y., Hartford, O., Hartford City, Ind., Hartfords, Mich., Ill., Wisc., Io. and Kan., New Hartfords, Io., Minn. and Mo., Hartfords, S. D. and Wash. So fifteen Salems or New Salems, twelve Fairfields, Springfields or New Springfields, Plymouths or New Plymouths, eleven Burlingtons and Warrens, ten Cantons, nine Cambridges, Farmingtons, Kents and Manchesters, seven Portlands, six Amhersts, Hillsdales, Litchfields, Morrises, New Havens and Watertowns, five Bostons and Greenfields, four Goshens or New Goshens, Lawrences, Norwalks, Norwiches and New Londons, and hundreds of other repeated names, besides the further hundreds of classically and otherwise Europeanly named towns—the Atticas, Athenses, Homers, Syracuses, Uticas, Romes, Carthages, Elyrias, Palmyras, Ciceros, Cincinnatis, and Ravennas, the Napleses, Venices, Havres, Lisbons and Oxfords whose highfalutin titles showed the traditional hope of emigrating Yankees not to let "learning be buried in the graves of our fathers."

From the first settlers of these villages came back the thousands of letters we still can read, bringing much great news to their friends and relatives at home; how now in the first month we have organized our school which is holding in so-and-so's sod hut; how now at the end of six months we have completed our church; how the case of rain-soaked books we almost jettisoned on the way out has become a set of shelves and once more we have for company Plato and Calvin, Pope and Franklin, Scott, Irving, Cooper, the Word of

God and the sermons of Edwards, Hopkins, Dwight, and our own dear Grandpapa; how there are "unprincipalled" people hereabouts who drink too much whiskey and cheat the Indians and make them dangerous, but we are getting our village in order, and now we have dances in our log tavern to which we take our daughters; how we have all had our dark hours when we have dreamed of giving up and returning, but we have not forgotten how to joke temptation away; how we know in our hearts that an omniscient Providence has led us here and is using us toward the building of a greater and better Union and bringing nearer the Kingdom of God.

One can not but wonder whether those who espouse the frontier hypothesis have well enlightened themselves upon these expressions of a passionately idealistic people, or, if they have read them, how they can suppose that a culture so powerfully evinced can be lost, any more than the uses of the hand or the tongue can be lost, in a few generations of changed surroundings. It is difficult to conceive that a company of Yankees who left the Township of Hartford, Connecticut, early in the nineteenth century and founded Hartford, Ohio, were any the less Yankees for their trek and at the outset a little greater hardship than they were accustomed to at home, or that they brought up their children any differently on the good topsoil than they would have brought them up among the native rocks. And the same of a company who a little later set out and founded Hartford, Iowa, probably under greater hardship than had come with the founding of Hartford, Ohio. And the same of a company who still later set out and founded Hartford, Washington. And the same of the founders of all the fourteen other Hartfords between. Is there any reason to suppose that in their basic cultural assumptions and habits of mind the descendants of the settlers of these younger Hartfords are any farther from the New England culture of 1860, 1760 and 1660 than are the descendants of those who stayed back in Connecticut? Indeed, may it not be that the inhabitants of Hartford, Iowa, and Hartford, Washington, are today nearer to the eighteenth-century culture of Hartford, Connecticut, than are the inhabitants of Hartford, Connecticut?—just as the maligned Western "R" may be nearer to Elizabethan English and New English than is either the flat adenoidal of modern Boston or the mellow tonsillar of modern Oxford. And is it conceivable that the people of the younger Hartfords today are psychologically as far removed from the people of the older Hartfords as they are from the unassimilated descendants of immigrants from say, South Carolina or Bohemia, who settled in their area at about the same time their ancestors did. Of course, if the people of different cultures have fused in a single community, then one culture may absorb the other, or a hybrid may result. In numerous rural areas, particularly in Wisconsin, Minnesota, the Dakotas and Nebraska, as well as in most of the big cities, Yankee culture has either never existed or in one way or another it has succumbed. But that has nothing to do with the frontier. Those are cases of the conflict of cultures.

It is not to be supposed, of course, that all or most of the inhabitants of all these New England towns are descendants of the people of New England. The people of the Yankee towns today are from every racial background on earth. Where the culture is strong it takes but one native generation to make a Yankee. Once a youngster of no matter what derivation has grown through adolescence in that atmosphere, no emigration will change him. Similarly, if anyone after adolescence immigrates into Greater New England from a big city or other alien environment, he will never be a Yankee. But his children will be as pure as they come.

Any attempt to estimate the number of people of reasonably pure New England culture can proceed only by a kind of balancing of probabilities. The entire population of the area of Greater New England is 67,000,000.[24] But this area includes five states containing considerable rural islands of unassimilated foreigners, in two of which, Wisconsin and Minnesota, Yankee assumptions and habits of mind are probably dominant over those of Germans, Scandinavians, Swiss, Bohemians and Poles,[25] and in three of which, namely the Dakotas and Nebraska, they are probably weaker. Wherefore the latter three states must be excepted from Greater New England, leaving a population of 65,000,000. Within this number, the rural population of municipalities of 2,500 or less, totalling 21,000,000, and the population of cities ranging between 2,500 and 50,000 numbering also 21,000,000, are mostly of Yankee Culture; while the people of cities over 50,000, totalling 23,000,000, are mostly of the Yankee pseudo-culture in which materialism and economic individualism or Greed have replaced the original idealism. Thus out of a gross population of 65,000,000 in Greater New England, we can presume that 42,000,000, or about two-thirds, are of reasonably pure Yankee culture.

Of the 85,000,000 and more who are the balance of the country, 25,000,000 are in the borderland of New York City, New Jersey, Pennsylvania and Delaware, together with the Dakotas and Nebraska. The remaining population of 60,000,000 is that of the Greater South. Any attempt to estimate the ratio there between those of the true or aristocratically flavored Rebel Culture and those of the socially individualistic Pseudo-culture would not have for guidance even the rough probabilities we used in Greater New England. Until recently we might have presumed that in the South the true culture was a little stronger in the cities, and the truculent pseudo-culture a little stronger in the rural areas. But today the Southern cities seem to be succumbing to the same industrialization and economic individualism which a century ago began capturing the Yankee cities and undermining Yankee culture. On the other hand, we suspect that this is a new kind of industrialism that has progressed beyond the predatoriness of the nineteenth century toward responsibility within some new culture or some revival of old culture which is still nebulous. And this new industrial responsibility is as evident in the North as in the South. Any new and mutual cultural integration that may be involved will represent the first real move in all our history toward an obliteration of the old cultural barrier between the regions.

There is no basis for even a guess of cultural distribution in the South. We can only presume, doubtless optimistically, that its ratio between those of the culture and those of the pseudo-culture is similar to that in the North. Under such a presumption, two-thirds of the population of 60,000,000 would retain the genuine courtesy, perhaps also something of the public responsibility, which comes down from the old aristocracy, while a third would be given over to the individualistic pseudo-culture in which formal politeness is all that remains of the courtesy. Thus we would have a working guess that a total of 80,000,000 people, north and south, about half of the population of the nation, still retain some cultural center, some assumptions and habits of mind which are more valuable to them than the various insatiabilities of hedonism and individualistic self-assertion.

It may be that these bearers of the remnants of the old cultures will continue to shrink in numbers and decay in quality as they have been doing now for a century more or less. In that case the cultural integration we may be approaching, while it will retain filaments of the old, as bourgeois culture retained threads of feudalism, will be so different at the center that it will be the third, and perhaps the first composite, culture of the United States. It will be our first unqualifiedly materialistic culture, in which the individual is entirely reduced to a mechanism, and in which all curiosity and intimations touching the cosmos and the human predicament will be pronounced unreal and placed under taboo. The new industrialism might help advance this trend, which the old industrialism started and has carried a good way. Its leaders would be the newest and least idealistic flight of new rich who are already in authority in a great pyramid based in the Deep South and pointing up through the New or trans-Mississippi Middle West to Minnesota and Dakota. Some likelihood of the emergence of such a more perfect materialism might be inferred from the fact that we have yet a little way to go before reaching the state of pure degredation in which Russia precedes us. It may be that a course once started must complete its devolution into absurdity before it can be reversed. Against the emergence of such an absolutely materialistic culture is the fact that the subhumanities of it, developed through the eighteenth and nineteenth centuries, are now old tales that all of Christendom is weary of, and the more important fact that today the priests of reason and mathematics are confessing their mysteries inadequate, and are offering mankind back to the mysteries of the priests of God.

The new industrialism, and perhaps the naïve and innocent newest-new rich, might conceivably move in the direction of a revival of the two old Cultures in some state of fusion of their respective immaterialistic standards. Both pseudo-cultures do seem to be emerging from their respective economic individualisms. Even the Pseudo-Yankees of the cities are rarely any longer concerned with bigger and better things. While they continue strong for gadgets and comforts, tend to adjust submissively to the various administrative systems in which they find themselves, and rarely work out any comprehensive Idea around which to center existence, yet they no longer put their own financial success at the top of the aims of life. More significantly, the South is educating itself for the first time since it began celebrating its Peculiar Institution a century and a quarter ago, and so is facing its race problem frankly and removing the more vicious and hopeless elements of its individualism. Also, since the actual aristocracy has now finally vanished, its tendency perennially to renew the individualism of imitation and jealousy is also gone. But its great legacy of Christian courtesy in some part remains, and in smaller part its political responsibility which, as in the North, the individualism has denied. The New South, for the first time since it surrendered to Cotton, is coming into a phase of honesty and realism wherein it is not inconceivable that it might face the fact of essential human Equality which its greatest gentry faced while they were still in control, and the denial of which, since they lost control, has been one of the chief incompatabilities between it and New England.

Both Rebel and Yankee culture have lost their original nucleii, the Rebels an integrated aristocracy with its code, the Yankees an integrated religion with its theology. The people of each culture, however, retain in their minds a channel worn by the ancient process, the one a disposition toward some code of "honor," the other a disposition toward idealism, an assumption that some set of ideas comprises the reality of life, and a habit of trying to acquire and to live by such a set of ideas. When Yankee Religion was failing in the eighteenth century, the necessary idealism filled its place with a genuine and selfless Political Ideal. When the Political Ideal was giving way to Greed in the nineteenth century, the idealism took the form of one of the world's great Humanitarian movements. When Greed captured the culture, then the Yankees must make of it, must make even of evil and selfishness, a lofty ideal, that of Success, of Making Good, to be served at no matter what personal inconvenience. When, in the 1910's and '20's, the intellectuals revolted against the standard of Success, they must needs set up the high idea of Self-expression or Self-indulgence in its place, and must sin with a devotion no less consecrated than that of Thomas Hooker to the God of the Cosmos. The Yankees have lost their great ideals, but they have never lost their idealism. In any future fusion comprising in some part a revival of both old cultures, Yankee culture is likely to provide the central element of Faith, and Rebel culture the central element of Law or Works, the tension between these being essential to any culture. In their fusion will lie the stuff of the First Great Commandment, the Love of God, while in the fusion of Rebel courtesy and Yankee equality will lie the stuff of the Second Great Commandment, the Love of the Neighbor. Once these major qualities were fused, the other differences between the two ancient cultures would soon evaporate.

It would seem, then, that if the United States is to turn aside from final, materialistic dehumanization, and is to move into a new cultural incarnation, then the culture of Greater New England will have important contributions to make. We have touched superficially upon two of these possible contributions, namely, idealism and equalitarianism. Both need more profound examination. Moreover, they, and many other qualities as unique to the culture, are contained within a wonderfully integrated, a tightly wrapped and everywhere interdependent, system which was at first a system of Religion in which the central idea was the Drama of Redemption. Today it is merely a Psychological System, a pattern of thought and a habit of relating thought to action, which characterizes some forty million Yankees. We have asserted the fact of the psychological system; we have founded it geographically across the continent from Putland to Porrtland; and we have surmised its importance to the future of the nation. It remains to examine it more fully, to try to describe the actual structure of the system, the typical houses inhabited by the people of that considerable region which is its country.

II. Architecture

ULTIMATELY PURITANISM was and is an aesthetic, a way of perceiving, ordering and expressing reality. But as primarily stated in the language of its heyday, it was a Religion, a Cosmic Drama, specifically the Christian Cosmic Drama, a method of adjusting human life to forces that both transcend and include the observed forces of Nature. In application the religion was a Psychological System, and this survives today as the habitation of each of 40,000,000 Yankees, even though most of them have forgotten its religious origin and nomenclature. The religion and the psychological system are identical in structure, each including a philosophy, a cosmology, an ethics, a morality, a mythology, a deology, an eschatology, an ecclesiasticology, a jurisprudence, an economy, a sociology, a literary standard, a logic, and many lesser systems that are appropriate to complete living.

All these are interdependent, being closely fitted and pegged together in a single structure, the Puritan House. There are the great structural members, the more or less hidden masonry and frame, which were originally the conscious doctrines of the religion, and are now the equally essential but more or less subconscious elements of the psychology. There is all the secondary structure of joists, studs, partitions, doors and inner finishings, which are the conscious beliefs of the individual occupant. These may or may not have been set up by him, and always include one room, normally the ancient kitchen with its big fireplace, which is his private shrine and secret retreat. And there is the external finishing of clapboards, shingles, windows and doors which are the stuff of civilization and usually conform to the same in the houses of the neighbors. Generally, the heavy inward members are permanent, and if, through the failure of the clapboards to cover it, one of them rots into weakness, it must be replaced at peril. The external covering, being subject to the vicissitudes of the weather, is always in process of renewal, and since it is also subject to the

47

vicissitudes of fashion, these renewals gradually accumulate into a complete change of civilization and aspect, a change which every Puritan House has sustained at least twice. Between the inner structure and the outward appearance, the secondary structure of floors and partitions is influenced by both. But it is also the individual part where the householder is most likely to impress his own personality, as against the powerful conservatism of the frame and the social conformity of the exterior.

The once universal practice of self-examination in the private diary has declined among Yankees as agnosticism and superficiality have replaced Puritanism and profundity. But it is not entirely lost. Let us imagine an average Yankee, a literate and thoughtful, though not a highly educated farmer, who has suffered the normal agonies and joys, the frustrations and rewards, that overtake humanity. From time to time, he has set down his observations about living, and in maturity he puts them together in a Credo representing what he has learned so far. He does not order his findings according to their importance, but divides them into two groups, of which he calls the first "General Notions" and the second, which is full of practical precepts about business and people, he calls "Special Notions." His "General Notions" are our concern. In them, he has set down in all innocence the main headings of the Puritan Psychological System, and with a changed nomenclature they are also the main headings of the Puritan Religious System, the Christian Cosmic Drama. We shall present them in his language and order, but with our numbering and comments pointing them out to be the masonry and the frame, the main structural members of the Puritan House.

I. *The Bed Rock*
Keep your eyes and ears open, but look for the truth in your own mind.

This is the *Idealism* which in Puritanism, as in most religions, is less an item of express doctrine than an assumption. Few of even the more distinguished Puritans were philosophers, for their theology forestalled their inquiry into the nature of ultimate Reality. For them it was not in comprehensible Concepts and Archtypes of Idealism any more than it was in comprehensible Material Forms. It was in an axiomatically incomprehensible God who was before all archtypes and material forms and created them. The archtypes, to be sure, are the thoughts or emanations of God, but they are not God. It was basic to Puritan, as to most Christian doctrine, that God must be separate from His creatures, including His thoughts. Else the current of his Love, which can run only to things outside itself, could not run to them.* If pressed to attribute to God either Matter or Idea for His clothing—and the difference between them was real to the Puritan—he would choose in favor of Idea. But he would prefer not to be pressed.†

Puritan Idealism was not so much in the philosophical as in the colloquial sense, meaning the governance of life by some "idea" or more or less unified set of "ideas" in the mind. Like our average Yankee who inherits the Puritan House, every Puritan must pursue Truth in the form of some such "idea" till he found it. "O Truth, Truth!" cried Augustine, who after Paul is set as second in this "idealistic" or subjective line of Christianity, "how inwardly . . . did the marrow of my soul pant after Thee . . . I hungered and thirsted not even after those first works of Thine, but after Thee Thyself, the Truth. . . ." And here is Thomas Hooker, preaching in tiny Hartford, thirteen hundred years later: ". . . Look at the soul in respect to the end for which it was created, and that impression which is estamped and left upon it unto this day, whereby it's restlessly carried in the search, and for the procurement of that food for which it was made. . . ."[1]

And so when our Yankee writes down, "Look for the truth in your own mind," he is recording the long agonies of self-searching and failure and more questing and finally success which every Puritan and every Yankee has endured. The great chimney at the center of the House has many significances which we shall notice later, but among its meanings, rising as it does out of the bed rock of idealism, is Aspiration to that Central Idea or Truth which the Puritan and Yankee must find to survive. The function of the chimney's fire, among other things, is to keep that Central Idea lighted and warmed.

In the heyday of Puritanism the householder's specific Central Idea, resting on the general Bed Rock, was consciously as big as the whole house and included all the members of the religious frame

* Among American Puritans of record, only Jonathan Edwards dared go all the way into philosophical idealism. To him the archtypes or basic ideas, while they were indeed the thoughts or "suppositions" of God, were not mere creations or emanations of Him. They were themselves "God's acting" or *God acting*, immediately parts or aspects of Him. Thus Edwards laid himself open to the charge of the heresy of pantheism, the identification of God with his creation. (Paul Russell Anderson and Max Harold Fisch, *Philosophy in America*, [New York, 1939], 76. Edwards' *Works*, Sereno E. Dwight, ed., 10 vols. [New York 1829-30] I, 671 and 674.)

† Most Puritans, and apparently all of the leading American Puritans, were followers of Petrus Ramus, the "French Plato" who, being a Calvinist, was murdered during the massacre of St. Bartholomew's Eve. But the Puritans' concern was with his "logick," his intuitive or imaginative method of presenting and examining aspects of reality, rather than with his more or less Platonic account of reality. For a discussion of Ramian "Platonism," see Perry Miller, *The New England Mind, The Seventeenth Century*, Chap. V.

which we are going to examine. The kitchen fireplace was augmented by other fireplaces, four or five of them, likewise giving into the central chimney and heating the rest of the house. But those other fireplaces are bricked up now, and most of the house is heated by an impersonal furnace that squats mechanically on the idealism of the cellar floor. The ancient frame is as necessary as ever to the survival of the house, and it, with its "General Notions," are still subconsciously part of the present occupant's Central Idea. But his active interest is rather in the "Special Notions" which are more or less peculiar to him, and which comprise the walls, the doors, the decorations and the furniture of the one room, once the kitchen, now his "den" or "library," that is still heated by the fire in the great chimney and is his private domain. His ancestors' Central Ideas were as large as a theology, as large as human capacity. Now for all practical purposes his have shrunk to the dimensions of the one room whose contents are nobody else's business, being a series of simple aphorisms, such as "Four sprays for apples, two for peaches"—"Go to bed"—"Don't tell on a neighbor but let him know you know and maybe he'll quit"—"Talk to an ornery bull but keep your mouth shut with an ornery woman"—"Democrats are sometimes human"—etc., etc.

But for all its triviality, that central shrine is still a holy and a passionate thing, an "idea" lighted and heated by the fire of Faith in the chimney of Aspiration, and the Yankee must at all costs maintain it intact. If a dimension of it or an item of furniture or a color in it is changed otherwise than after long contemplation, the Yankee will grow apprehensive. If the secret room is destroyed, either because he removes a partition to make a sensible enlargement into another room, or because one of the great members of the house falls and lets the whole collapse, then either the fire will flare and burn down the ruins, which means the Yankee will go alcoholic, or it will sink to coals under ashes, which means he will continue to live in his house, being coldly and quietly mad.

II. *The Foundations*

Here our Yankee is still among underlying assumptions, rather than the particular doctrines, of Puritanism. The four walls standing on the bed rock of idealism and supporting the house are the elements of those monotheistic religions which by the nineteenth century dominated most of the world.

1) *There is probably something hereabouts besides me.*

This has been and is the primary assumption of all religions, namely that this apparent cosmos, this roundabout, this seeming

earth and stars and distances and durations beyond human understanding, is something which actually exists. Like the Jews, like the
Buddhists and the Mohammedans, the Puritans started their theology in a state of wonder at the fact of "incomprehensible, first and
absolute Being,"[2] before which human "reason is too finite to com-
prehend the infinite, 'too shallow to contain the deep, the bottomless; too narrow to grasp the boundless; too little comprehensive to
include this incomprehensible Object.' "[3] This belief of every Yankee
in external reality keeps him, for all his practicality, out of the modern tradition of experimental reason which is based on Descartes'
solipsism, "Cogito, ergo sum," and today leaves the individual alone
with his self-contained id, ego and superego.

   2) *There must be some point to it.*

   This is the second basic assumption of the four world-wide monotheisms and many of the paganisms, namely that the cosmos has
some Meaning or Purpose or Order, some integrating factor which
they call *God*, some kind of cosmic drama of which He or It is the
author and producer. Even more than the principle of the existence
of objective Being, this religious assumption, still subconsciously
made by every Yankee, is heretical to the great modern superstitions.
It implies in the cosmos mental qualities like orderliness and purpose, even free will, so admitting doubt of the sacred foundations of
materialism and its "unalterable law"—a doubt, by the way, which
the mathematicians are coming by, so we may look for a present stam-
pede of the scientific sheep into a corner, not of religion of course,
but of a kind of cosmic psychology. Furthermore, the assumption of
the existence of a Meaning or God goes beyond the permitted recognition of man's body as part of the material universe, and implies
in man's mind also a possible relation to reality, belief in which
becomes for materialists the dangerous sin of Anthropomorphism.
Perhaps most serious of all, this surviving suspicion by Puritans and
Yankees of an integrated Meaning of all things throws doubt on the
great twin dogmas of Deweyesque Pluralism and Relativity in which
modern "philosophers" delight to rest from the tedious quest for
reality. In this doubt all monotheists commit the Unforgivable Sin
of Absolutism.

   3) *Pull with the Stream.*

   This is the basic ethic of the great religions, namely to find out the
direction of external truth and then try to conform to it. For the
Puritan-Yankee this truth is the same as that definitive Central Idea
to which we saw his basic Idealism aspiring. The Puritans called its
dynamic aspect the *Will of God*. Here is Roger Williams writing to
his wife:

> [An] . . . argument of the spiritual health and temper is when
> the affections work strongly and lively after God; . . . after
> God as a portion and inheritance; after God as a husband. It
> is . . . when we can say as the Lord Jesus said, it is our meat
> and drink to do our Heavenly Father's will; when we are active
> and ready at the commands of God and can say (when the Lord
> asketh, "Whom shall we send?"), "Send me," as the prophet
> Isaiah said (Isa. 6:8). . . .[4]

This compulsion to adjust to actual, external truth is especially
the mark of the monotheisms. It distinguishes them from the pure
paganisms where the concern is not to lose oneself in some external
reality not rationally confirmed, and therefore unreliable and precarious, but to develop this known and central self vis-à-vis the immediate environment of people and things which is convincingly
perceptible. In the ancient paganisms the impulses of this central
self were identified with divinities who must be propitiated, which
partial objectification gave the old cults some color of religion. The
modern paganism of psychiatry makes no such irrational compromise. In attributes the Id is a modified Ishtar or Aphrodite, the ego
just another Zeus, the superego a little bundle of Athenes and
Apollos. But where these old gods were worshipped on external altars
and even sometimes observed among the affairs of surrounding nature, the rituals of their modern counterparts are entirely subjective.
The current priests of course recognize the need of objectivity for
health, and they duly direct their communicants into such diverting
activities as sport and art. Some of them even recognize value in the
self-dedication of religion. But it is not likely that religion approached at their suggestion or with their encouragement will do
their patients much good. For their purposes are by profession utilitarian and subjective, and their advised objectivity is no objectivity.
They seek the expression and mental health of the individual, and
there is no surer way of forestalling the expression and mental health
of the individual. Who serves Iaveh or Civa or Allah or Christ in order
to gain his own soul will not gain it. But who serves them in entire
concern for their glory and power and in the entire sacrifice of his
self, his ego, his superego and his soul, he will find that new self and
that new soul which he never asked for. Psychiatry and other cults of
rationalism perform secondary services for religion. But religion can
not serve psychiatry or any other irreligious objective and remain religion. Religion, the identification of the soul with the Fact of Being
can not occur in relation to any calculated quest.

4) *You Can't Pull Against It Anyway.*
This is the remnant of the grand principle of *Predestination* which

characterizes the four great monotheisms and without which any religion is suspect of the smaller or irreligious concern. The doctrine follows necessarily from the predication of an omnipotent Control or Meaning or God of the Cosmos whose dimensions transcend human observation. Within Its or His inclusive Will, it is inevitable that spontaneous, original or free human will be either non-existent or permissive and limited. Also, His principles of order and justice may well be outside the understanding of a group of His creatures on one of the planets of one of the star systems of one of His galaxies.

This deference to supernal reality is intellectually inescapable, and it characterizes every major theology, not only of Judaism, Buddhism and Mohammedanism, but also of each of the four great subdivisions of Western Christianity, the Roman, the Anglican, the Lutheran and the Calvinist. Yet the doctrine of Predestination has never rested easily upon occidental individualism. Ethically, the European resists the impugnment of his individuality, his liberty, his free will. Theologically he resents the injustice, by human standards, that permits pain in the world, and seems sometimes to reward the irresponsibly wicked and to punish the responsibly good. Especially since the Reformation, every sect has hedged against it in order to hold its communicants. And as we approach our own time, wherein physical standards are tending to supplant mental ones, we find an increasing number of supposed Christians who deny the doctrine with impatient scorn. Thus, while it is a basic principle which Christianity shares with the other monotheisms, we must from the outset recognize that it is different, and generally weaker, in Christianity than in the other systems. Even in noticing it within Puritanism, where it was relatively strong, we shall find little that would be equally acceptable to the Mohammedans or the Buddhists.

Calvin himself hedged no jot against Predestination, and the Puritans and their English and American sects which were most lastingly influenced by him—notably the intellectual sects, the Congregationalists and the Presbyterians—hedged less and later than the Romans, the Anglicans and the Lutherans. Although the Puritans attributed both Justice and Mercy to God, they knew that in human terms the two were incompatible, and they meant merely that the Cosmos had Its own Justice and Mercy which, like everything else about it, were beyond the grasp of human or "Natural" reason. Puritanism, being an aesthetic, had only a secondary interest in moral values anyway. Its primary interest was in the Greatness, the Wonder, not the Goodness or Badness, of God. To the Puritan there was less satisfaction in the notion that God might have human virtue than in the mere percept of His superhuman Glory.

In the seventeenth century men would rather be damned by an inscrutable and omnipotent Lord than saved by an anthropomorphic and legalistic One. "All from him and all for him," preached Thomas Hooker, "he is the absolute first being, the absolute last end, and herein is the crown of his Glory."[5] William Adams, the minister of Dedham, Massachusetts, showed the typical Puritan combination of mystical awe before God's Creation and eager curiosity about the rising Galilean astronomy:

> His hand has made and framed the whole Fabrick of Heaven and Earth. He hath hung out the Globe of this world; hung the Earth upon nothing; drawn over the Canopy of the Heavens . . . ; Created that Fountain and Center of Light, Heat and Influence in this lower World, the Sun . . . the Seas, the vast Mountains also, and the Wind so indiscernable in its motions . . . they are His Work. . . . Those notable changes in the World in the . . . exalting or bringing down of Kingdoms, Nations, Provinces, or Persons, they all are wrought by him. . . .[6]

Jonathan Edwards dated his mystical awakening, long before his acceptance of Predestination, from a sudden perception while in solitude in the fields of the inclusive meaning of a passage in First Timothy—"Now unto the King eternal, immortal, invisible, the only wise God, be honour and glory for ever and ever." By and large the seventeenth-century Puritans, and decreasingly the eighteenth-century Yankees, shared emotionally Edwards' unified concept of the universe, though generally lacking his power to analyze it. The Cosmos, including Man, was a single work of art executed by God, its dimensions outside of time, and the apparent sequences of its details not so much causal as aesthetic. What seemed to be events and "causes" were simply objects or concentrations of waves that in the Beauty or "Excellency" of the universe must needs lie alongside each other just as they did, having been inscribed that way by the creative Meaning or God. Predestination did not mean succession in time but the whole spectacle of Creation as it actually has been, is, and will be, now and forever. Among its infinite details are the impulses of choice, of the seeming free will, of every individual. They lie longside his actions in the panorama of the Cosmos, because it was just so and not otherwise that the Painter put them there.

To the Puritan it was enough that he had a place somewhere in the great mosaic. Typically, he lacked Edwards' penetration, and conceived it all under the common human illusion of time as duration, breaking up the mosaic into sequent fragments composed into a moving picture. He lived every moment, like the Hebrew prophets and the Mohammedans, in the aggressive humility that comes with the sense of pulling with the current of truth. The certainty that the destiny of his soul had been decided once and for all by the authority that runs the stars, leaving no problem for him but that of discovering whether or not he was among the "Elect," this certainty was a more energizing motive than the dubious promise of a dubious reward for piling up a little store of voluntary good deeds the required quantity of which was nowhere stated. Whatever the end, the Puritan had his assigned part, his prescribed entrance and his line to speak in the Drama of Redemption which had been written before the beginning of the world. It would not occur to him to ask, or even to desire in his minute interest, any change in the script. Win or lose, he was fighting in God's cause, and the harder he fought, the more he worked for God's glory, the greater the likelihood that he was in fact predestined to the grand list, that he was already among the Elect! And even if it turned out that he was not redeemed, that he was to be cast into the bottomless pit of psychotic fire, still what greater privilege could there be than for this brief moment to be striving on the side of the universe, the privilege—perhaps a more Christian privilege than that of being saved—of being "damned for the glory of God"? ". . . As often happens," say Miller and Johnson, ". . . the believers in a supreme determining power were the most energetic of soldiers and crusaders. The charge of Cromwell's Ironsides was, on that particular score, proof positive of the superiority of the Puritan over the Anglican, and the Indians of New England learned to their very great sorrow how vehement could be the onset of troops who fought for a predestined victory."[7]

Within this general sense of cooperation with the whole current of Being, the Puritans' Occidental hedges in the direction of the individual's importance and control of his destiny were slighter than those of the non-Calvinist sects. A basic reservation which they shared with other Christians held that man had not always been helpless of independent choice, and would not always be. But for unpredictable and seemingly spontaneous sports which were the presages of free will, Nature in its evolution before man's emergence was entirely predestined—in our scientific language, predetermined—under the Will or Meaning or God of the Cosmos working through what we call Natural Laws. Among these laws, dominating all living things, were those imposing the hungers of self-preservation and self-propagation, and the "higher animals," whether or not they enjoyed intimations of consciousness and deliberative reason, were absolutely driven by these. Out of this Nature and in response to the Will or God that controlled it, Man emerged, whether as a relatively sudden sport or as the product of slow evolution. He emerged out of predetermined Nature into the "Image of God," which included that spontaneous and objective or Imaginative Perception* which impels equally spontaneous or undirected action, and which we call Free Will.† In this state of "Innocence" the old hungers of self-perpetuation remained active, but, whether through some psychic mutation or a concurrence of the forces controlling climate, they no longer preempted his attention, but were subservient to his free perception and consequent free action. In a world of Reality, Spirit or Imagination, it was his unique activity to perceive the essence of outer things, which was to "name" them, which was to create or have "dominion" over them.

In this condition of Free Will "in the image of God" man lived a long time—in our timetable, perhaps some millions of years of the warm Pliocene, perhaps some hundreds of thousands of years in one of the warm interglacial periods of the Pleistocene. At the end of this period, whether under the inducements of changing weather or in pursuance of his own curiosity, in the exercise of his still uncoerced imaginative perception he chose gradually to turn it inward upon himself, to change his selfless objectivity for a self-centered subjectivity. Thus he voluntarily resubmitted himself to the domination or determination of Nature's hungers of self-perpetuation. Only they were reinforced now, and extended immeasurably beyond their strength and scope in other creatures, by the previously free imagination which, by this choice, was "enslaved" to the self and so "ruined," but it was not destroyed. What in the state of nature had been an unconscious impulsion became, through self-consciousness, self-knowledge, or simply "knowledge," a rapacious self-concern, intent not upon self-preservation and continuance, but upon self-ascendance, both absolutely and relatively to other beings.

Furthermore, the "fallen" imagination, though now enslaved to the now dominant law of self, preserved some inverted remnants of freedom or spontaneity, by which it could perceive originally and devise external means of advancement far beyond the compulsions of natural law. As part of "knowledge," the mind became complicated and adroit in the processes we call Reason and that the Puritans called Natural Reason. Man became a creature distinguished not for spiritual understanding but for Material accomplishment. God's primordial laws of self-perpetuation had been ruthless and brutal, but Man's self with its implement of perverted imagination made them more ingeniously and destructively brutal.

---

* "Nothing can induce or invite the mind to will or act anything, any further than it is perceived. . . ." (*The Freedom of the Will,* in Clarence H. Faust and Thomas H. Johnson, eds., *Jonathan Edwards,* 268.)

† In this book "imagination" is used, as I have used it elsewhere, to mean the poetic faculty which perceives the reality within the appearance of things, an antonym rather than a synonym of "fancy" which conjures unreal figments.

Still further, he was not left in the integrated and happy state of a single-minded fiend. The psychic pattern of free imagination was not able to concentrate exclusively upon its new business of self-expression, but must needs suffer, as it continues to suffer, occasional flashes of "conscience" or pure objective or innocent perception, disquieting reminders of the original purpose for which the God or Meaning of the Cosmos evolved or created it. While churning continually and consciously in the interest of its master, the self, it all the time knows subconsciously that this labor is a violation of its godlike mission and capabilities. So its "knowledge" is not only practical but moral. It is the "knowledge of good and evil." Into this state of psychic conflict between a compulsive inward and a remembered outward intent of the imagination, into this state of "Degeneracy" or "Reprobation," every individual is born or early conditioned by his social environment. But his state is not hopeless. If and when he is able to escape from this conflict, to turn his eyes completely and permanently outward from the self, then in this state of "Regeneration," this restored objectivity or Image of God, he will recover permanently his capacity for original perception and correspondingly original action, his Free Will.*

Within the frame of this basic idea of a period of "Reprobation," with the possibility of escape from it into "Regeneracy" and freedom, the Puritan's concern, like that of all Christians and, in their different vocabularies, like that of Jews, Buddhists, and Mohammedans, was to understand how this restoration and reintegration might be attained. And here, rather than in matters of daily conduct, was where the question of Predestination, here specifically called "Election," was of greatest personal import. Was each individual's return or failure to return into a state of imagination and freedom as absolutely predetermined as was his tenor of self-preoccupation which blocked that return? Or does everyone retain from his long inheritance sufficient free imagination and power of free action to reverse his self-concern and the predatory course of action it impels, to lift himself by his bootstraps out of the dilemma in which he finds himself along with his billions of equally confused cousins? Upon this point no two theologians of any religion or sect have ever fully agreed. Among the Puritans, we can distinguish three general views.

First, there were the pure Calvinists who were absolutely consistent intellectually. The race of Man, by its choice of self-concern, plunged all of its members into a state of moral helplessness from

---

* "Rectifie therefore the apprehension, and heale the disease; labour to have judgment informed, and you shall see things as they are." (John Davenport, *The Saints Anchor-Hold*, [London, 1661], 67-68.) This "rectified" perception, as experienced today, may be taken as generally aesthetic or specifically religious. It is noticed more fully in the Discussion of Grace.

which no return to Innocence is possible except through entirely unpredictable Election by the inscrutable Will or God of the Cosmos. Chief among these true mystics and predestinators were, in the seventeenth century, John Cotton of Boston* and in the eighteenth century Jonathan Edwards of Northampton.† One of the objections to their position was and is, of course, that it relaxes the sense of moral responsibility. Election comes to each man unpredictably from God as an emotional intuition and without any relation to his acts or will, and similarly after his Regeneration equivalent emotional intuitions and the actions they impel are likewise of divine sanction.

Theoretically, and usually in practice, these religious "experiences" were subject to confirmation out of the Bible, as interpreted by the subject's minister, his congregation, or both. But sometimes in individuals and localities and over considerable periods they were interpreted privately by those who enjoyed them, without submission to any human censorship. This reliance upon subjective emotional conviction we today call Revivalism. The Puritans called it the Heresy of Antinomianism—Against-the-Law-ism—and they associated it with Libertinism. Within the memory of the older men among the first immigrants, there had occurred bloody examples of its application in Europe, and they passed down into the New England tradition a great fear of it, with a corresponding distaste for excessive emotion generally.

The danger of Antinomian excesses as a result of their absolute predestinationism was a matter of concern to both Cotton and Edwards. It is worth observation that of the two distinguished Puritans who were banished for religious reasons in the century and a half of the colonial period, one was Anne Hutchinson, the exuberant disciple of Cotton, and the other was Edwards himself. They were not banished for their predestinationism, but for the embarrassing and embarrassingly proclaimed views it drove them to, in the guileless Mistress Hutchinson the assertion that God spoke personally to her, in the fastidious and equally guileless Edwards the published recognition of "surprising works of God" in the peculiar antics of some of his converts, and the insistence that some such emotional sign of Regeneration was a condition precedent to admissibility to the church. Predestination is an inescapable intellectual inference from

* "A man is as passive in his regeneration as in his first generation." (*The New Covenant* [London, 1654] 55.)

† ". . . it is . . . as repugnant to reason, to suppose that an act of the Will should come into existence without a Cause, as to suppose that a human soul, or an angel, or the globe of the earth, or the whole universe should come into existence without a Cause." "Every event, which is the consequence of anything whatsoever . . . must be ordered by God. . . ." (*The Freedom of the Will*, in Faust and Johnson, *Edwards* 292, 305).

the monotheistic concept of an omnipotent God. But to little minds it becomes on the one hand an impugnment of their little importance, and on the other a warrant of licentiousness. In restraining them as libertarians it confirms them as libertines. It is essential to the grandeur of the mystic's perception of the spectacle of all Being, but for general application it presupposes a world wherein everyone, like Mistress Hutchinson and Edwards, is already Regenerate—born again—and restored to Innocence.

At the opposite extreme from the utter Predestinators and their sometime heresy of Antinomianism were the Rationalists and their more prevalent Heresy of Arminianism—named after a Dutch Anti-Calvinist Jacobus Arminius—which hedged so far against Predestination as to destroy it. The Reason in Arminianism was not the "Right Reason" we shall notice as characterizing Imaginative Perception, but the reason of fallen and Reprobate man, the reason of either logic or common sense which the Puritans called "Natural Reason." It took either of two forms, of which one, Intellectual Arminianism, associated with Science and Liberalism, makes no appreciable appearance until the eighteenth century. Throughout the seventeenth the common form of the heresy is Legal Arminianism, that Moralism which the Puritan-baiters are pleased to identify with "Puritanism" generally, the naive notion that the God of the nebulae will reward boy scouts for conforming to certain admirable social regulations. From the earliest days, in the person of the Reverend John Wilson of the First Church of Boston, to the final collapse of the decayed Calvinist one-hoss shay in the nineteenth century, this heresy was usually lurking somewhere in the churches, too often in the pulpit. It had its periods of ascendancy, notably under its most distinguished adherent, Increase Mather,* during the First Decline between 1677 and 1697, and again in the Third Decline after the Civil War when God was retiring behind a veil of scientific scepticism. Although its addicts usually professed orthodox Predestination, they did it for rhetorical rather than serious purposes, to frighten rather than to inspire their listeners. Actually, they denied it by making the disposition of each individual's soul dependent upon his own supposedly free moral choices and conduct. Thus, as their opponents pointed out, they made the Will of God, the Will of the Cosmos, wait upon the wills of His or Its creatures. This of course was to take the life out of Puritanism, which is a cult not of morals but of God.

Between the extreme Predestinators and the extreme Free Willists or Arminians, most Puritans occupied a middle ground in which,

* Men "should do such things as have a tendency to cause them to Believe." (*Soul-Saving Gospel Truths* [2nd. ed., Boston 1703, Boston 1712], 22-23.)

while they maintained an undiminished percept of the glory, omnipotence and omniscience of the God of the Universe, they yet saved a limited area wherein a man's imagination and will, however fragmentary and "ruined," could yet make a contribution to his Regeneration. These middle-of-the-road Puritans, of whom Thomas Hooker of Hartford was the leader and well-spring, had a vision to which our contemporary psychology seems at last to be agreeing, namely, that most of our actions are subject to determinism, but that there is yet within the larger frame an area of spontaneity or free will. Hooker carefully eschewed Arminianism, always asserting that Election, the offer of Regeneration, came to an individual in God's good pleasure, without any derivation from his previous acts or choices. But once the offer was made, it was possible for a man to *reject* it.* In that rejection or acceptance there was a free choice.

Moreover, before the actual offer and the completion of Regeneracy, there was frequently a preliminary intimation, a half-dawn followed by a kind of probation, a period within which the individual was allowed a scintilla of free will, still feeble and unregenerate but sufficient to enable him to prepare himself,† by study and contemplation rather than external good works, to recognize and accept divine Election when it should finally offer. Hooker was here, as he was always, psychologically the earthiest of the great Puritans. He was describing the human experience of Imaginative Perception, of which Regeneration was merely the extreme and definitive case. No man can force such a perception. It may come as a sudden and complete flash. Or, and more frequently, it may come slowly and by steps, each step strengthening the subject a little more to make the next. At the first intimation a man should put himself in a posture of contemplation and humble waiting, together with study or other preparation. This will not compel predestined revelation, but it will facilitate the recognition of it when it comes. It will reduce the danger of missing the magic moment.

A very common Puritan hedge against the awesome concept of implacable predestination made a distinction between it and a predetermination that was not necessarily final. The distinction was implicit for those who chose to find it in the phrase "Free Grace." This intended merely to state the fact of the general doctrine, that God would bestow Regeneration on whom He would and withhold it from whom He would, irrespective of their previous actions. But in the phrase "Free Grace" it was possible to imply that the decision had not been made final for every individual, the play written

---

* "Thou canst resist a Saviour, but not entertaine him, doe what thou canst." (*The Soules Vocation* [London, 1638], 230-1.)

† "The soule of a poore sinner must be prepared for the Lord Jesus Christ, before it can receive him." (*The Unbeleevers Preparing for Christ*, 2.)

and the script closed before the beginning of time. There was always a chance that God might "change His mind." In His infinite mercy even at the last minute He might have pity on poor little me. Thus God's omnipotence was saved, but His stature and the grandeur of His timeless universe were qualified by intimate and pathetic association with the pettiness of time and man. The doctrine of unpredestined and yet Free Grace was not Arminian, since it did not require God to reward sinners who tried their little best. But it carried a hope that people's actions might matter, and so it tended in the Arminian direction. Incidentally, it was congenial to modern cosmic mathematics which are at last coming to the common monotheistic insight that the universe behaves like nothing so much as a Mind, a Mind which, while proceeding in the main according to consistent laws—that is, conservatively—yet Itself exhibits a measure of spontaneity, capriciousness, or free will.

Besides the several hedges against Predestination, which on the whole subtracted little from the glory and omnipotence of God, there were corollaries to the general doctrine which tended to brighten the shadows of uncertainty and terror that might fall across timid souls who caught no gleam from Eternity but were genuinely motivated by impulses of goodness, the love of their neighbors, in Time. It was generally accredited that Good Works, though they did not induce Election, might yet be a "sign" of it. Sound enough in itself, the doctrine often produced such a scramble to display "signs" of Regeneracy as was hardly distinguishable from the Arminian anxiety to *earn* salvation by means of them. Another important corollary was the doctrine of the "Covenant of Grace" which gave assurance that mere "Belief" in Christ was a sure sign of Redemption, and which we shall consider at length later. Finally, the emergence out of Reprobation into Regeneracy was usually marked by a definitive emotional Experience or Conversion, and whoever had known that experience, especially if the Church had confirmed it by receiving him, though he might afterwards be guilty of misconduct in his degree, yet rarely doubted that all would come well with him in the end.

The Puritans on the whole did well with their doctrine of Predestination. Most of them maintained the larger view of God and the Universe of which it was a part, while preserving to individuals enough moral responsibility to avoid the Antinomian excesses that it seemed to excuse to a small and self-indulgent logic. But even in their own day it was already unpopular with the Anglicans and the Lutherans of Europe. And for three centuries it has declined as Christianity and humility have declined and secular Individualism has risen to replace them. In America today, where the Glory of the Self has perhaps been most successfully substituted for the Glory of God, it is rare any longer to find anyone who so far lives to his imaginative capacity that he espouses even the diluted doctrine of Free Grace. In their bombardment of Puritan culture, the debunkers were able to make popular ammunition of its underlying assumption that the individual is of less significance than the Cosmos. The large view is generally suspect by psychiatrists, who curiously deplore the full expansion of the mind although their whole profession is directed toward the expression of the self! In their view, apparently, to tolerate any notion of a Meaning or God of things generally is to be guilty of either a father or a mother complex! As if there were anything abnormal in seeking inclusive Reality outside myself! They speak for the age, in which everything must be cut down to the scale of the many and the small. Imagination is taboo except in art, and the subjects of art are less regarded than composition and design. The best art is abstract art in which the subject may be eliminated.

Our average Yankee, who knows the adventure of Being is bigger than he is, is nevertheless affected by the modern tendency to small Individualism which tells him that he's a pretty big shot himself. If you ask him straight out about Predestination, he will probably deny it in conscious self-importance that will brook no restraint, thanking you kindly, upon its freedom of action. Yet in his honest solitude every Yankee retains the larger view. Typically he still lives, if not on a farm, yet in sight of the dimensions of nature, and the consciousness of irresistible cycles tends to keep his self humble and his imagination alive to the larger and mysterious cycle that contains them. His sense of being part of some enormous spectacle within which he is negligible is evident in his deliberate rhythm, in his awareness that the Universe is not dependent on his doing, that the Control of it is not going to be greatly embarrassed whether he lives or dies, in his intellectual caution that is chary of absolute predictions and qualifies its statements with "It would seem" or "It may be that," in his idiom of understatement and therein his characteristic humor. And withal he still goes about his work with that dedication which was once the ennobling belief that it was a calling assigned to him by Destiny. Knowing that he is helpless in the hand of the God who made him as he is and who runs the weather, he yet takes pride in working to his capacity for the furtherance of that same God's plans. Like Thomas Hooker, he knows that somewhere in the premises his own will and self-determination matter. Like all the Puritans, he remains in the hands of predestining Power the most indefatigable of voluntary workers.

III. *The Sills*

We have seen that the foundation walls of the Puritan House were four principles common to the great monotheisms of Judaism, Buddhism, Mohammedanism and Christianity, namely that the universe Exists, that it has a Meaning or Control, that it is desirable to adjust to the Control, and that the Control is Irresistible anyway. Upon this foundation the four sills are the elements of the peculiarly Christian cosmic drama, and they are entirely shared only with the other subdivisions of Christianity.

1) *Most men to begin with are not much different from hogs.*

This is the Christian doctrine of *Original Sin*. In discussing Predestination, we saw that man, under the controlling Force or God of the Cosmos, evolved into the state called the Image of God, a condition which included, as a basis for Free Will, an objective Imagination. Actually this objectivity, this selfless perception of essences, is what in the Christian vocabulary is called Love. Man's authorization to "name" the things of the world and to have "dominion over them" was only this power to perceive them as they actually were, to move into them and identify himself with them, not a power to coerce them in their action and evolution. Indeed, it was the condition of this perception or Love that, as far as man was concerned, the object should have free will. The beloved should be qualified by an independence, a rational unpredictability which invited the equally free imagination of the lover.

In the Christian view, such Love or perceptiveness was the central quality of the Meaning or God of the Cosmos. Although possessed of absolute dominion over all Being, yet it was the nature of God that he should dissipate His power in this motion, this projection of Himself from here to there. As distinguished from the ultimate reality of the Buddhists, which is repose, the beginning and the end of the Christian universe is primal, uncreated movement. He must go out perceptively and responsively into every electron of His creation, wherefore to each electron and concentration of electrons He was a "personal God." Being is dynamic. Basic and final status is not different from force. As our scientists with their rational method finally identify their matter with motion, they come in some triumph upon a paradox which is revealed to every person whose self has been broken, so that he has stood out of time in that absolute receptivity which our dull vocabulary calls "understanding," and which the Puritans called the Grace of God and Regeneration. Shortly now our hierophants of Natural Reason will be admitting with professional modesty their discovery of a paradox which was intimated by Isaiah and Plato, and was taken as axiomatic by Christianity a long time ago.

The Christian myth begins with this loving God, this "Word." In the midst of a universe He utterly controlled He required something He could not control, something toward which He could exercise

this devoted uncertainty, this outgoing current, this anxiety to see
the object perfect without His domination. Wherefore, at a laborious
length of some billion years He evolved man in His own independent
and loving "Image"—together, no doubt, with analogous free and
imaginative creatures on other fragmentary rafts among the stars.
And responsive to his "Creation," man's chief love or perception
during the entire period of his unself-conscious "Innocence," was
that of God Himself, the Meaning of the Cosmos Whom he then
understood and with Whom it was his pleasure to walk and talk
in the cool of the evening.

The authors of the Christian classics had no way of estimating
how long the race of man lived in Love and Imaginative Understanding, whether some million years of the warm Pliocene or a
shorter age in the tropical regions or warm interludes of the Pleistocene. At any rate, something eventually happened—perhaps the
coming of the Ice Ages or of one particularly severe glaciation—to
tempt them to turn their free perception into self-consideration and
self-concern. Whether through external necessity or internal vanity
and curiosity, man presently chose to break the current of imagination between himself and God and turn back into himself, to love
himself instead of God and His external roundabout, to take charge
of his own destiny and "justle the Almighty out of the Throne of
his Glorious Soveraignty," and so to *"be above God, and be happy
without Him."*[8] Thus, as we have seen, he "fell" back into Nature
which is determined or predestined under the laws of self-perpetuation without love or imagination. Only he did retain in "ruined"
form his imagination which was henceforth "enslaved" to his Self.
It turned inward from a God-centered Cosmos—sometimes called
Heaven—to a self-centered Cosmos—sometimes called Hell. Only in
this inward Hell it still tends to see troublesome sparks of summer
lightning which are remnants of the original current of outward
Love. In some individuals, the light flickers down and out into complacency and ceases to trouble them. In these the Fall is at last
complete. They are those whom Christ called "hypocrites," the responsible rulers of society of whom He said, "They have their
reward."

This major turn in man's evolution, this break in the psychic circuit or Love that connected him with God,* this setting himself
above God, is what is called *Original Sin,* and any subsequent acts
which widen the gap by further expressing or encouraging self-
concern are called "Sins." The state of Original Sin is called Reprobation or Unregeneracy and it involves, as we have seen, the loss of

---

* Sin "makes a separation between God and the soul." (Thomas Hooker, *The
Application of Redemption* [London, 1659], 59.)

Free Will to perceive truth and act accordingly. Furthermore, as we have seen, it is held by Christian doctrine to be a state into which all of mankind is born or conditioned in infancy. The chances of emerging from it are identically those of recovering a Will free of the domination of self, and among the Puritans we saw bearing on the question the three general views on Predestination. The view of Absolute Predestination, usually called Total Depravity, holding that each man is helpless to emerge except under God's immutable decree;* the Arminian view that allows man a large remnant of Free Perception or Will to influence his emergence;† and the intermediate view that allows man a modicum of choice and a limited period in which he may voluntarily prepare himself to recognize and accept Election when it is proffered.‡

The doctrine of Predestination, even in its milder, Arminian forms, has been the darling of the Puritan-burners, especially its corollary professed by some, though not the more enlightened, Puritan divines, that unbaptized and therefore ipso facto unregenerate babies were destined to "the easiest room in hell." It drove all Puritans, both in youth, and periodically throughout their lives, into dreadful periods of soul-searching for evidence of whether their Original Sin had been atoned and "forgiven," and that they were therefore Elected. There was Thomas Hooker's own protracted and only generally recorded struggle while a lecturing fellow at Cambridge,[9] or the comparable experience of his son-in-law and successor in the church at Cambridge, Massachusetts, Thomas Shepard, who wrote in his autobiography about "the spirit of god wrestling with me" when he was in Emmanuel College, and how "a godly Scholler walking with me, fell into discourse about the misery of every man out of Christ viz: that what ever they did was sin . . ."[10]

These were the profitable periods of powerful minds, which indeed most Puritan minds were. It was through them that both the idealistic and the intellectual traditions of the culture were maintained. Better thunder for the debunkers is provided by the cases of possible neurosis in children induced by the terrors of hell fire, especially as in due course we shall see it preached to them in the decadent period of the 1680's and 1690's.

* ". . . The redeemed are in everything directly, immediately, and entirely dependent on God . . ." (Jonathan Edwards, *God Glorified in the Work of Redemption* [Cambridge, 1731], quoted in Perry Miller's *Jonathan Edwards*, 30.)

† ". . . The gospel promises . . . not only tell us what it is that God requires of Sinners . . . but they do also give us to understand after what manner God will by his Grace convey a pardon to Sinners." (Samuel Willard, *A Remedy Against Despair* [Boston, 1700], 42-3.)

‡ "It is the Lord's Almighty power that hath possest us with this libertie and freedom from iniquitie, but yet not withstanding before we can come to injoy a full libertie from all iniquitie, we must fight for it, and wage the battle of the Lord." (Thomas Hooker, *The Saints Dignitie, and Dutie* [London, 1651], 38.)

The doctrine of Original Sin has of course suffered much prurient perversion on the part of eager and repressed Fundamentalists who have enjoyed associating it—and sin generally—with particular usually deliciously sensual acts for their own sake. More reasonably, the modern psychologists associate it with the sense of guilt and its sometime complications. Curiously, however, the psychological method of resolving the complications is rarely to encourage the full expansion of that imagination whose frustration in our world of self-emphasizing materialism is a main cause of the sense of sin or separation from Truth. Rather, modern psychology tries to break the complex by denying the existence of the reality the imagination seeks, and offering it some partial diversion, such as an aesthetic exercise which must be less than satisfactory precisely because it is deliberately assumed out of self-concern as a piece of self-therapy instead of being involuntarily compelled or predestined as is the case with true art. It is perhaps the soundest feature of generally psychologically sound Christian doctrine that it knows what the "guilty" imagination wants, knows precisely what the egocentric blocks are, and offers in the Forgiveness of Sin what comprises—along with the Buddhist discipline—one of the two possible remedies that man has yet found. Also, as psychiatry doubts that the complacent and comfortable need treatment, Christianity doubts that they *can* be treated, even by God—"they have their reward."

The Puritans and the Yankees after them made generally healthy use of the doctrine and sense of Original Sin, finding in them much of the motive power of that search for truth which was central in their culture. No true Yankee has ever settled into that self-centered universe of complacency which is a confession of the surrender of the quest for truth. On the other hand, our average Yankee has no time for those almost self-centered people who worry about elevating themselves in the world, or who simply worry about themselves on any score. He knows the Puritan paradox that, while the good life depends upon thinking through to some kind of explanation of the world and your place in it, yet there is nothing so sure to block the discovery as self-concern and self-attention in the quest. He understands the common experience of Christians, who, because of the extraordinary purity of their vision of selflessness, believe themselves in the very possession of that vision to be the most self-vaunting and extraordinary of sinners. He would understand Jonathan Edwards' record of his feelings in the year 1739, only a few months before the beginning of the Great Awakening which he launched quite unintentionally through the unconscious power of his selfless soul:

> Often, since I lived in this town, . . . I have had a vastly greater sense of my own wickedness, and the badness of my

heart, than ever I had before my conversion. It has often appeared to me, that if God should mark iniquity against me, I should appear the very worst of all mankind; . . . and that I should have by far the lowest place in hell. When others, that have come to talk to me about their soul concerns, have expressed the sense they have had of their own wickedness, by saying that it seemed to them, that they were as bad as the devil himself; I thought their expressions seemed exceedingly faint and feeble, to represent my wickedness.[11]

Our Yankee would know Edwards' feeling of the depth and power of the volcano of self. But, like Edwards, he knows also that there are opposite forces on the planet which can draw off and eliminate the greatest and deepest of magmas.

2) *Some kind of readjustment must have been made to get us out of the mess we've got ourselves into.*

Here our Yankee is stating the basic Christian principle which is the second sill of the Puritan House, namely, the doctrine of the Atonement. Man's choice, in the exercise of his free will, to turn his imagination and love inward upon himself broke the circuit of Love with God, and thereby was created, on however minuscule a scale, a cosmic dislocation or irritation which, like some disquieting image obscurely disturbing the mind, invited the attention of the general Control. As in all derangements of the processes of Being, the general laws of repair set to work, as in the healing of a wound of a tree or an animal, as in the adjustment of a species to a changed environment, as in the wearing down of mountains after a geologic upthrust that has broken the organic and inorganic routines, as in the gathering of electrons into new systems after a cosmic explosion. Under God's interrupted will to love a creature he had created free and therefore capable of love, the forces of variation and adaptation set out to mend the circuit.

At the human pole there was also an impulse to re-establish the current in the form of the residual objective impulses of the "ruined" imagination. But the force of this impulse was rarely strong enough, poetic or prophetic enough, to send a spark of imaginative perception all the way back to God, and so revive the circuit. Generally each man, through the influence of inheritance or environment, made again for himself the definitive or Original choice to be dominantly self-concerned.

But from God's pole the force of repair was much stronger, for the power of Love was unmixed. In due course, just as the whole vitality of a mind can concentrate upon some small thought or image, so the entire universal flow of God's Love or Cosmic Imagination poured into this planet and one individual of its recalcitrant species who, besides thus becoming for practical purposes God, was also fully man and early conditioned to Self-Concern or Original Sin. Thus the cosmic force of Love, absolutely selfless and fearless, took on a particular form of self-centered subjectivity which, if it had dominated God's omnipotence, would have occasioned permanent and at least local derangement in the whole state of Being. But being selfless, the Godliness overcame the self-aggrandizing manliness and accomplished the total immolation of the latter as no simple individual's remnant of Love could succeed in doing.

Thus, in simplest terms—to interpret a cosmic event with earthly or Natural Reason—there was set up an example that might encourage and strengthen men in their struggle to escape from their dichotomy. More profoundly, this act of self-sacrifice on the part of the Control of the Cosmos had an actual and powerful effect on the psychic inheritance of the species—and any other species in whose interest it was performed—just as any consummated concept or idea in the mind accomplishes an alteration in each of the numberless smaller concepts and images which it contains. Henceforth the members of the human species were at least strengthened in their impulse to return to the state of selfless innocence which they could not alone regain. It was as if a great river all of whose drops at first ran to the ocean nibbled its way through its containing dikes and turned aside into a desert where it gradually thinned and vanished in the sand. Then the ocean, being beyond another range of dikes, tore a channel through with a tidal wave, so that thereafter at least a part of the river turned before desiccation and found the sea.

In Christian theology this process of cosmic disturbance and repair is often presented in legalistic symbols. The Original divorce from God or Sin is presented as a kind of juridical misfeasance—technically, the breaking of a Covenant or contract of Works—for which a penalty or price must be paid. Man's ensuing discomfort, the sense of conflict or guilt in which he finds himself, is said to be the more or less automatic, early working of this penalty. The attitude of God toward this state of affairs is, to human understanding, dual and paradoxical. On the one hand the theology attributes to him a Justice which imposes the penalty as a kind of interim measure while working out a larger intention. This attribute of divine Justice might be called the force of masculine love in the cosmos, the deterministic tendency to complete the evolution of this free and loving species, according to the divine Idea of it, correcting its current errors and perfecting it in its own capacity to love and enjoy free will. In apparent conflict with this impulse of creativeness or order, theology also gives God an attribute of Mercy, which might be called the force of female love in the cosmos. This is the impulse, not to prolong this creature's state of uncomfortable maladjustment by compelling it toward some perfect form, but, in spite of its defiant and prodigal self-concern, to hasten unconditionally the work of the forces of repair and adaptation, to the end that the discomfort may be ended forthwith.

All agree that the Atonement was a divine or cosmic act of combined Justice and Mercy. Through the God-man's immolation of manly self-concern, the penalty imposed by divine Justice was paid. But as to the general applicability of this act there is disagreement. Is God's act—in the legalistic vocabulary—"Imputed" to all men at once, whereby all have met the requirements of Justice and are so "Justified"—a term signifying Regeneracy in this its legal aspect? Or is some remaining step of Imputation to each individual still necessary?

Almost all Christians and almost all Puritans held that such a remaining step was required, which is to say that no mutation could be so abrupt that the genes and the social environment of all persons born after a certain date would alike be purged of all self-centering tendency or influence. The effect of the cosmic visitation would at first be scattering, which is to say that in the early stages God would touch some individuals and miss others. This second act of God, which is generally conceived as an act of Mercy rather than Justice, and which heals the dislocation, disturbance or conflict in the individual mind, is the one called "Grace." And the individual's ensuing condition of Justification and Regeneration is called the "State of Grace." As the Atonement was an act of combined Justice and Mercy, the bestowal of Grace upon individuals is one of Mercy exclusively, as no one can ever be perfectly certain that he has received it, or, having received it, whether he has not rejected it and "fallen from Grace"; the final bestowal is generally conceived as postponed to immortality. In 1647 Thomas Hooker lay on his deathbed, a victim of the current 'flu epidemic in Hartford. One of his parishioners stood by him weeping and said, "Sir, you are going to receive the reward of your labours." Said Hooker, theologian and anti-Arminian to the last, "Brother, I am going to receive mercy." And in a few moments he was dead.[12]

The three Puritan schools we have noticed with respect to the general matter of Predestination and Free Will had each its appropriate interpretation of Grace or the Imputation of the Atonement to individuals. By the school of Hooker it was imputed to those who were able, by a faint act of Free Will, to Prepare themselves to recognize the offer of Election when it came. By the Arminians it was imputed to all who morally deserved it. By the School of Total Depravity it was imputed to whom it would be imputed, and the individual will was helpless. Besides these views, in each of which Justice was stronger than Mercy, there appeared in the eighteenth century a fourth view, that of Universalism, in which Mercy was stronger than Justice. Christ died for everybody, wherefore everybody, with or without a future period of purgation, will be Justified, Elected, Regenerated and Saved willy-nilly. If anyone interposes a stubborn, individualistic, reprobate Free Will, it must be overcome for his own good. There is here no more freedom than in the school of Total Depravity, but there is a high anthropomorphism, a greater concern for man's glory than for God's, an attribution to God of a Humanitarianism that must needs resolve everybody's tensions and make them comfortable in universal understanding.

Our typical Yankee probably does not belong to any of these schools of nice distinction. He is simply sure that somehow, somewhere, there is a way of getting out of this mess of misunderstanding and seeing things straight. With his disposition toward Predestination, he may not be sure that all men have brains enough to know the answer when they hear it. The best that he or any man can do is to keep his ears open to catch it when it comes by.

3) *When you see it, it's quick like the sun breaking through a gray sky, and at first you don't know where you are.*

Here our Yankee is describing the flash of any real idea, and specifically his memory of the integration of his central bundle of Ideas by which he lives. This experience is the one we have noticed already as a completion of the Atonement, the Imputation of it to individuals which the Puritans called *Grace*. It is another aspect of that generic *Regeneration* which, being for individuals the climactic event of the Christian drama, is set in a landscape of near synonyms reflecting it from different angles. In its relation to Predestination, Regeneration is God's *Election* of some individuals while neglecting others. We have seen it also in its legal aspect as the *Justification* of criminal man by the Atonement's satisfaction of his sentence for Original Sin. We have seen the further legalisms of the *Imputation* of the Atonement to individuals, which accomplishes their *Redemption* from the state of *Reprobation,* and so inaugurates the state of Regeneration or Regeneracy. Psychologically, we have seen it as the restoration of clear *Imagination* or *Perception,* and, as identical with Perception, we have seen it as the revival both of *Free Will* and of the current of *Love* with God and his cosmic cast of Creatures. Finally, if this state of Regeneration is not vitiated by a second "Fall" of the individual, we shall see it leading him to emerge from the temporal Drama into a timeless state called *Salvation,* while those never Elected, along with those caught in the nadir of a second Fall, emerge into a different timeless state called *Damnation.*

Meanwhile, the dramatic development from the Atonement on is all motivated by the *Grace*—that is, the Mercy, the Graciousness—of God. However, in all Christian theology, as we have seen, Grace tends to be identified especially with its individual application, the Imputation of the Atonement to those Elected. In the ritualistic and Arminian sects, where Grace and Redemption are identified with external maneuvers, the meaning of the word is contracted no farther than this. But in all the true Protestant sects, where Grace is an exclusively internal event, and specifically among the Puritans, its original meaning tends to be further violated. It is reversed and applied, not so much to the gift of God to the individual, as to the experience of the individual in receiving the gift. The experience of Grace becomes a synonym for *Conversion,* thus acquiring a more intimate and poignant meaning than the solution of a legal tangle, or even than the application of the Mercy and kindness of the Meaning of the Cosmos. At the same time it remains a larger word than Conversion, retaining something of the sweep of the Cosmic Drama and of the boundless Compassion and tenderness of God in concerning Himself to untangle one of His creatures from the web of self where it is snared.

As the Atonement and its Imputation are the center of Christian theology, so Grace is the center of Christian experience. It is the same, whether its bestowal follows one or another of the courses we have noticed, that is the Universal course, the Predestined course, the Arminian, or the Preparative. It differs with times and persons, not in quality but in degree of intensity, varying from the highest voltage down to a feebleness where its authenticity may be doubted. Thus, it is professed by many gentle church-goers as a slow and easy awakening, and as such is commonly admitted by their ministers. But in indubitable cases of its reception, it is a single and powerful event, possibly spread over a brief period. Once that event has made its imprint on a personality, the individual comes into the *State of Grace* which, as Grace is the personal analogue of Regeneration, is the personal analogue of the State of Regeneration or Regeneracy. When a person, once having enjoyed Redemption and its benefits, chooses, with his restored Free Will to "fall" back into the State of Self or Reprobation, we do not say that he has fallen from Regeneracy, which is correct, but that he has "Fallen from Grace," a larger phrase meaning that he has moved out of the state of God's Attention and Love.

The State of Grace is precisely the *State of Love,* a continuing level condition punctuated by ecstasies which renew its instance. It is also precisely the *State of Imagination* which is a continuing condition of sensitive objectivity punctuated by ecstatic moments of specific perception. In discussing Grace it will be easier to notice these specific visitations of it, while remembering that they are the peaks in one continuous Christian uplift or mountain range. The experience of Grace usually has its intimations and its bordering twilights, but it is unmistakable in its fullness as a single and unshadowed event. It usually shows some or all of certain psychic phenomena which we shall notice separately, remembering that they actually comprise one experience. As our Yankee describes the sudden and staggering breaking in of a clear idea, so there is always about the authentic experiences of Grace a sense of inevitability, of urgency and speed, which leads to the doctrine, common though not universal among the Puritans, of *Compulsive Grace.* Like the artist, or any kind of fanatic, when the beneficiary of Grace is touched on the shoulder, he can hardly escape. Edwards tells how "towards the latter part of my time in college; . . . it pleased God to seize me with a pleurisy; in which he brought me nigh to the grave, and shook me over the pit of hell." And a little later, "God would not suffer me to go on with any quietness; I had great and violent inward struggles. . . ."[13]

This violence of God accomplished only a partial conversion of Edwards. More effective was the quiet compulsion that marked his awakening to his central perception of Predestination:

> From my childhood up, my mind had been full of objections against the doctrine of God's sovereignty, in choosing whom he would to eternal life, and rejecting whom he pleased; leaving them . . . to . . . be everlastingly tormented in hell. It used to appear like a horrible doctrine to me. But I remember the time very well, when I seemed to be convinced, and fully satisfied, as to this sovereignty of God, and his justice in thus eternally disposing of men, according to his sovereign pleasure. But never could give an account, how, or by what means, I was thus convinced, not in the least imagining at the time, nor a long while after, that there was any extraordinary influence of God's Spirit in it; but only that I now saw further. . . .[14]

A large-scale and dramatic example of the compulsiveness of Grace is provided by the Great Awakening of the 1730's and 40's, of which Edwards was the instigator and the English revivalist George Whitefield the eventual dynamo. There was a kind of breathless urgency that seemed to sweep in enormous gusts through communities and regions, what Edwards' biographer calls "a spiritual hurricane,"[15] and concerning which the figure of wind was used by others. Speaking of his own Northampton in '34-35, Edwards says that ". . . the noise among the dry bones waxed louder and louder."[16]

In 1740, under Whitefield, the Awakening reached its peak velocity. We have the account of the farmer Nathan Cole of Middletown, Connecticut, who having followed Whitefield's approach in the news with increasing excitement, responded to a "messinger" who came "all on a suding" one morning with the news that he was to preach at the Center at noon, ran "with all my might" for his wife and his "hors," then by alternately riding and running covered the twelve miles in an hour; as he neared the village he saw a fog and heard steady thunder, but as he approached the highway along the river the fog became a dust cloud and the thunder the rumble of horses, and he could see men and horses "sliping along in the cloud like shadows" while "every hors seemed to go with all his might," and the river bank was black with people and horses, and the "fery boats running swift forward & backward the oars roed nimble & quick every thing men, horses & boats all seamed to be Struglin for life."[17]

In such accounts of urgency, we may, if we wish, find "mob psychology," but that is only to confess that here is some kind of phenomenon that we can not really name, and it is at least as descriptive to speak of "the spirit of God moving over the face of the waters," or to remember at Pentecost "a sound from heaven as of a rushing mighty wind." What is certain is that Grace is a definite experience, and that it is usually preceded, whether in individuals or in masses, with a sense of compulsion and necessity and speed.

We have already mentioned the central quality of the experience of Grace, that of Imaginative Perceptiveness. In the attempts to describe this quality it is distinguished from other and natural perception as a kind of *Clairvoyance,* a sense of supernal clarity which is usually associated with *Light,* and which our Yankee likens to the sun breaking through a cloud. Speaking probably to his congregation in Cambridge, Thomas Shepard introduces Light less as a metaphor than as a fact. He said there is a knowledge which some men have

> from the book of creation, some by the power of education, . . . some by the letter of the gospel, and so men may know much and speak well. . . .

But beyond this is a further knowledge that comes only with Grace, whereby they

> see things in another manner; to tell how they can not; it is the beginning of the light of heaven.[18]

Shepard's father-in-law, Thomas Hooker of Hartford, uses, as is his practice, a more homely and a more striking figure, but the sense of light breaks over it. "Sound contrition and brokenness of heart," preached Hooker, brings a strange and sudden alteration into the world, varies the price and valew of things and persons beyond imagination . . . , makes things appear as they be. . . .*

When young Edwards lay sick for three months in a stranger's house, he waited eagerly each morning for the dawn in his window, for

> it seemed to be some image of the light of God's glory.[19]

Edwards, as we shall see again, is probably our best expositor of Grace as "an entirely new kind of perception."[20] To Edwards sin was simply the inability to perceive the reality of things, actually a deficiency in the imaginative or poetic faculty. His descriptions of his early experiences of Grace are usually in terms of light:

> . . . I walked abroad alone, in a solitary place in my father's pasture, for contemplation. And as I was walking there, and looking up on the sky and clouds, there came into my mind so sweet a sense of the glorious *majesty* and *grace* of God, that I knew not how to express. I seemed to see them both in a sweet conjunction; majesty and meekness joined together. . . . After this . . . the appearance of every thing was altered; there seemed to be, as it were, a calm, sweet cast, or appearance of divine glory, in almost every thing. God's excellency, his wisdom, his purity and love, seemed to appear in every thing; in the sun, moon, and stars; in the clouds, and blue sky; in the grass, flowers, trees; in the water, and all nature; which used greatly to fix my mind.[21]

In expository vein also Edwards uses visual imagery and light less as metaphor than as actual experience. It is precisely the perceptiveness of the artist when he is objectively identified with his material. Under the light of Grace, Edwards says,

> the ideas themselves that are otherwise dim and obscure, are by this means impressed with the greater strength, and have a light cast upon them; so that the mind can better judge of them. As he that beholds the objects on the face of the earth, when the light of the sun is cast upon them, is under greater advantage to discern them in their true forms and mutual relations, than he that sees them in a dim starlight or twilight.[22]

Both the Compulsiveness and the Clairvoyance of Grace are functions of a third quality which is at the heart of Christianity, the quality of Humility or Selflessness, in active terms *Self-Loss*, the receipt by Imputation or Cosmic Compulsion—or in some part the

---

* Hooker here uses "imagination" as synonymous with fancy. (*The Application of Redemption,* 55.)

vicarious experience—of the Atonement which was Man's self-immolation on the Cross. It is only through this "Brokenness of Heart" or "Poverty of Spirit"—supposed never to have been absolute in any man but Christ—that the individual is reduced to that nothingness, that "blank sheet of paper," upon which perceptions are clear, unblurred by the imposition of the desires and opinions of the self. In the breathless haste of the farmer Nathan Cole to hear Whitefield, though he was not in Grace but only on the fringes of Grace, there was an impersonality, a complete objectivity within a spectacle in which he was nothing. If a man would be a Christian, said John Cotton in "Purchasing Christ,"

> he must first be a foole, and be content to bee counted a foole, and heare every carnall man to count him a foole.[23]

So Roger Williams, who was seldom deficient in self-appreciation, yet proclaimed humility with the assurance of personal experience:

> I speak peace and joy to the weakest lamb and child in Christianity that is so low, so weak, so little, so poor in its own eyes, that it sometimes saith it hath no Christ, no spirit, no faith, no love, no, nor true desire in itself. To this poor weak one I speak peace and joy, and say that this spiritual poverty is blessed and is the first step or round of that spiritual ladder.[24]

And here is John Winthrop, the founding Governor of Massachusetts, interrupting one of his supreme love letters to his wife to rejoice in humility before God:

> . . . Let us entertaine and love him with our whole heartes: let us trust in him and cleave to him, with denyall of our selves, and all thinges besides, and account our portion the best in the world.[25]

And here is Edwards remembering his youth and the early phases of his conversion:

> There was no part of creature holiness, that I had so great a sense of its loveliness, as humility, brokenness of heart and poverty of spirit: My heart panted after this, to lie before God, as in the dust; that I might be nothing, and that God might be ALL, that I might become as a little child.[26]

But the anxiety for selflessness does not always rest at this tender and lamb-like station. Our record of Edwards in this respect is the only full one among the great Puritans, but we may suspect that he speaks for the known rest, and for the thousands unrecorded. Here is his report of his feelings some years after those just noticed, and there is in it a seeming incongruity in so great a Christian, an air of fatuousness, of an unhealthy, even a hypocritical, posture of self-immolation:

> I have greatly longed of late, for a broken heart, and to lie low before God; and, when I ask for humility, I cannot bear the thoughts of being no more humble than other Christians. It seems to me, that though their degrees of humility may be suitable for them, yet it would be a vile self exaltation in me, not to be the lowest in humility of all mankind.[27]

And in another passage, reporting on the same period as the above, he shows with seeming sincerity a sense of his own sinfulness commensurate with his anxiety for self-abasement:

> My wickedness . . . has long appeared to me perfectly ineffable, and swallowing up all thought and imagination; like an infinite deluge, or mountain over my head. I know not how to express better what my sins appear to me to be, than by heaping infinite upon infinite, and multiplying infinite by infinite.[28]

Finally, in a third passage reporting on the same period—which was that of his high maturity—Edwards gives us an inkling of the reason for all this extravagance, this superlative strain to humble himself beneath all other men and to confess his sinfulness, his self-centered separation from God, the greatest in the world. Edwards had no humor, but he did have clarity of introspection and awful sincerity. We may presume that what he saw in himself was really there:

> The very thought of any joy arising in me, on any consideration of my own amiableness, performances, or experiences, or any goodness of heart or life, is nauseous and detestable to me. And yet I am greatly afflicted with a proud and self-righteous spirit, much more sensibly than I used to be formerly. I see that serpent rising and putting forth its head continually, every where, all around me.[29]

In other words, one of the world's great saints, one who was in fact about to display a remarkable selflessness in the ordeal of his persecution and dismissal from Northampton, one of the world's great Christians, looking into himself, saw, not the meek simplicity of his Christ-like vision, but "joy" in his popularity, accomplishments and kindness, and "everywhere," "all around" in those depths of self, a "proud and self-righteous spirit." It would seem that in proportion that his capacity for self-loss and Grace exceeded that of most men, the magmas of self boiling in him were deeper and stronger than in most men. One recalls the adage that only the greatest sinners can become saints. One remembers Augustine's long struggle against vanity and lust. Pertinent is Hooker's ordeal in the period of his conversion, when he was already a teaching fellow at Cambridge. The report is Cotton Mather's, no match in any respect for either Hooker or Edwards, yet a curious and personable mind, undoubtedly qualified by his own experience to understand the nature of this inner conflict. Mather reports of Hooker that

> in the time of his agonies, he could reason himself to the rule, and conclude that there was no way but submission to God, and lying at the foot of his mercy in Christ Jesus, and waiting humbly there till he should please to persuade the soul of his favour; nevertheless when he came to apply this rule unto himself in his own condition, his reasoning would fail him, he was able to do nothing.[30]

There are available no private papers of Hooker in which he confesses in maturity, as Edwards did, the depth of his sense of his own wickedness. But in one of his greatest sermons, probably preached during his last years, he describes the consciousness of sin with a passion that seems to be fueled by experience:

> . . . [The sinner] hath seen what sin is, and what it hath done, how it hath made havock of his peace and comfort, . . . made him a terror to himself, when he hath looked over the loathsom abominations that lie in his bosom, that he is afraid to approach the presence of the Lord to bewail his sins, and to crave pardon, . . . afraid and ashamed lest any man living should know but the least part of that which he knows himself, and could count it happy that himself was not, that the remembrance of those hideous evils of his might be no more. . . .[31]

It would seem that the explanation of this conflict in men of great intellectual and moral power was not quite the simple, "idealistic" and relativist one that in proportion that one's vision is lofty one sees oneself failing to realize it in action. Nor, if we are human beings, can we rest in the materialistic view, that all mental activity other than that of intelligent animals is neurotic or psychotic. It would seem more probable that in this particular matter the confessions of the saints are true. All elements are in pairs that are equal and opposite. Greatness in Godliness is also greatness in Selfliness or Sin. The great Imagination is born, or early conditioned in the Reprobate or "ruined" state, wherein it is directed and empowered by the Self in its Self-centered Cosmos, and in which phase it were better called for some purposes Fancy, and for other purposes Reason. In these forms it directs the individual life intelligently, arriving at many perceptions and inductions of value and gratification on the plane of Self or Nature.

Subsequently, when at the compelling touch of Grace from without it becomes truly Imagination and moves out from the self to perceive God and His God-centered Cosmos, it does not become a new process, a new fact, a wholly new life, but a new and wider and unbounded exercise of the old one, "not a new faculty of understanding, but . . . a new kind of exercises of the same faculty of understanding."[32] Indeed the Regenerate Imagination could hardly have responded to Grace if it had not enjoyed much Preparative activity in the Unregenerate state, and the larger or "greater" its final and selfless perceptions, the larger or "greater" must have been the Natural landscape in which it first explored and discovered. The leaf at the top of the tree is at last drawn out by the Sun of Grace and disports unselfed in His Glory; yet it was the sap of self coming up through Reason and Fancy from the dark roots of Nature that lifted him there above Nature. The flame in the lamp is there by the match of Grace, but oil crawled in the wick before there was Light, and both wick and oil must continue to work if the flame is to continue to be seen. And in degree that the leaf and the flame are high and pure in their selfless perception, so sensitive will they be, looking down, to the tough trunk of Nature, the red seething crater of Self, from which they can not detach themselves while they flutter and flicker in time. In proportion that Hooker or Edwards or any other Christian knows the experience of Grace with its "calm, sweet . . . appearance of divine glory" on "everything," making "things appear as they be," in that same proportion each is "a terror to himself" as he perceives "the loathsom abominations that lie in his bosom," and sees "every where" the "serpent" of "a proud and self-righteous spirit . . . rising and putting forth its head continually." In that passage where Edwards demands to be the lowest of mankind, he is indeed expressing the greatest and most fatuous egoism of mankind. But he is also perceiving, from a proportionately elevated, selfless clairvoyance of Grace, the magnitude of that egoism and his helplessness to overcome it. No man can become Edwards or Hooker or Lincoln, or whoever has seen farthest and deepest and most humbly, who has not been first, and remained in the lower depths always, the greatest of egoists, the farthest from God, the greatest of sinners America has known.

And in this paradox Christianity is not mocked but is confirmed. For it is just at this point of the utter helplessness of the greatest saints that the need and meaning of the Atonement and of Grace are most richly apparent. It is only now that the Prodigal Son comes home in full brokenness of heart and can be forgiven. It was not for a theological quip but rather for joy in Belief in the Atonement that Hooker in his dying sentence corrected his friend who had said, "You

are going to receive your reward," and substituted, "I am going to
receive mercy." As his knowledge of the hopeless enormity of his self-
concern was great, so great was his exultation in Belief in the vastness of the Compassion that would "forgive" and heal and eliminate
that self-concern.

There is a fourth quality of the experience of Grace which often
balances the sense of personal nothingness in a healthy way that
eliminates the excruciating sense of self-centeredness which occasionally—and indeed only occasionally—tortured the Greatest Christians.
Without this compensation one may doubt whether any considerable
imagination could for long remain a Christian. This quality, which
we noticed as essential to a grasp of Predestination, is the perpetually
overwhelming sense of the Glory and Grandeur of God. We saw
Nathan Cole, in his race to hear Whitefield, entirely forgetful of
himself and lost in the spectacle of all Creation around him "strug-
glin for life." We saw Edwards combining his sense of his own
smallness with that of God's greatness:

> . . . My heart panted after this, to lie before God, as in the
> dust; that I might be nothing, and that God might be
> ALL. . . .[33]

Of his early period of conversion, Edwards wrote of his frequent
sensations of being

> alone in the mountains, or some solitary wilderness, far from all
> mankind, sweetly conversing with Christ, and wrapped and
> swallowed up in God.[34]

And in the passage we noticed for its sense of Light in connection
with Grace, he mentioned in conjunction "majesty and grace," and
again "majesty and meekness."

It is as if the loving self, going out to be lost in the Cosmos, draws
after it the great and fatuous hulk of the natural self from which it
emerges, and sends it ahead to indulge its megalomania in vicarious
glory, identifying itself with the grandeur and vastness of the beloved. Thus there is no division in the person. The self is both lost
and glorified, "swallowed up in God." Hooker, who usually exceeded
Edwards and everybody else in metaphorical power, gives us, in one
of the finest passages in Puritan literature, the whole feeling of
Grace; the compulsion, the luminosity, the selflessness and the glory:

> So I would have you do, loose your selves, and all ordinances,
> and creatures, and all that you have, and do, in the Lord Christ.
> . . . Let all bee swallowed up, and let nothing be seene but a
> Christ. . . . As it is with the Moone and Starres, when the
> Sunne comes, they loose all their light, though they are there

in the heavens still; and as it is with rivers, they all goe into the Sea, and are all swallowed up of the Sea. . . . So let it bee with thy Soule, when thou wouldest finde mercy and grace.[35]

If all of the Puritans and Yankees could at all times have lived in the inclusiveness of that passage, most of the sense of sin would have been purged from the Elect, Puritanism might not have weakened before Materialism, and we might never have had any "Puritanism" at all. It was when the imaginations of Hooker and Edwards were drowsing that they experienced and perceived the horror of their residual egoism. It was in the periods when the imagination of the culture as a whole was similarly lapsing that smaller men than Hooker and Edwards, experiencing their egoism without perceiving it or struggling to abate it, released it instead to resounding moral and political purposes, and strengthened the body of the nation and weakened the soul.

The theory and experience of Grace is general in Christian doctrine. But in the Protestant sects it is a more decisive experience as it is adjusted particularly to each individual. Among the Protestants, the true Calvinists, including the moderate or middle-of-the-road Puritans, as distinguished from the Arminians insisted on the Emotional Experience of Grace, and as distinguished from the various Antinomians gave the experience the closest discipline and so ultimately the greatest significance. As a definitive psychological experience it comes down to our Yankee long after he and his culture have lost awareness of its religious frame. He knows the Compulsion and the sense of Light in waking up to any persuasive notion. And as he begins to put his ideas together into a system, he knows the universal senses of Nothingness and of Grandeur that are really the same and the secret of the business.

4) *Heaven and Hell are here and now.*

This was probably the enlightened Puritan view of the generic Christian doctrine of *Salvation,* the doctrine that, following a *Last Judgment,* the Redeemed will be received into eternal bliss in a locale called Heaven and the Damned into eternal damnation in a locale called Hell. There is no doubt that most Puritans, and most Yankees until well along in the nineteenth century, had at least a strong suspicion of the material existence of these post-mortal institutions of joy and misery. Yet it was not until the Arminian decadence after 1679 that the ministers preached post-mortal "hell fire."[36] Cotton, Shepard, Hooker and Davenport never did. Both Regeneracy and Reprobation were present states, and while the ministers made plentiful references to their continuance in future time, the references were rhetorical rather than critical. The object of living was to attain a state of beatitude or self-loss, to set up

with God the circuit of Grace and Faith—that is, Love—right
here and now. Puritanism was a psychological system for attaining
a happy adjustment of all the human impulses in the existing present. The Puritans, like other Christians, lacked positive information
about post-mortal states, and found them useful for purposes of
metaphor rather than of promise or threat. So long, preached
Hooker,

> as these rebellious distempers continue, Grace and Peace, and
> the Kingdom of Christ can never be established in thy heart.
> For this obstinate resistance differs nothing from the plagues
> of the state of the damned. . . . Know, that by thy dayly con-
> tinuance in sin, thou dost to the utmost of thy power execute
> that Sentence upon thy soul: It's thy life, thy labor, the desire
> of thy heart, and thy dayly practice to depart away from the
> God of all Grace and Peace, and turn the Tomb-stone of ever-
> lasting destruction upon thine own soul.[37]

It is difficult, perhaps in this case impossible, for us to elicit literal,
prosaic lineaments in the poetic structures of the seventeenth century. Still surrounded by the riches of medieval superstition, notably
the colorfully pictured Roman Catholic Arminianism of rewards
and punishments, accustomed to think and speak in metaphor, it was
inevitable and proper that the Puritans should have recourse to the
vast armories of psychological symbolism provided in the images
of post-mortal Heaven and Hell. Yet it is impossible to find an expression by any of these educated minds that shows convincingly
that they were really interested in these dubious matters of which
they knew nothing by experience or dependable authority. After the
Synod of 1679 many of them did set out deliberately to frighten their
people into being good by promising lurid punishments if they did
not. But even then, and even on into the eighteenth century, we can
only guess how much was prediction and how much was just ornamental fire and smoke. Certainly the famous hell fire of Edwards'
Enfield sermon aimed merely to portray and to incite present psychic
torture in the hope of introducing present psychic integration or
Grace. The premise of all of Edwards' theology was timelessness, and
he saw things not as they were becoming but as they were already,
decreed, executed and settled in the Order of the Cosmos. Hell fire
was in the present blindness that could not perceive the Meaning or
God of things today, tonight, right here in the Enfield Meetinghouse.
Only God's hand, His Love, was holding helpless souls from dropping into that fire hopelessly and forever. Heaven was just as clearly
the present objective perception which is not only Grace but present
and actual Salvation. For Edwards, "the parting between heaven
and hell is located not in the regions of the sky or under the earth,

not even in the Last Judgment, but in the human perception; the function of art is to make the distinction unmistakable."[38]

All Puritans and Yankees were at all times more or less busy laying up treasures in Heaven, and many, perhaps most of them, doubtless did believe that Heaven was the name of a city which had the Best Bank in the Cosmos. But many others looked for their reward in the present fun of the "laying up," and they were content with the present combination of the outward bank of New Haven or Hartford and the inward bank of their own clear understanding. It is out of this second tradition which grew stronger as religion declined, that our typical contemporary Yankee gets his worldly notions of Salvation and Damnation. As to eternal time after death, he finds that to be matter upon which his information is insufficient, and he thinks that people who bother about such things are fools. Generally, in his observation people get what is coming to them here. If they've thought mostly about money, or about their own righteousness, they usually end up in a nervous state that makes them a trouble to themselves and to everybody else. But if they've taken things easy and tried to understand people and the world as it is, they generally end up in a fairly comfortable condition.

IV. *The Cornerposts*

In the four common Christian doctrines of Original Sin, Atonement, Grace, and Salvation, our Yankee has described in his Credo the four sills of his Puritan House. Next he sets up four further principles which are special to Protestantism or its Calvinist branch, and particularly to Puritanism, whether English or American. These are the great cornerposts of the house.

1) *Go it alone.*

This is the remnant of the primary doctrine of the Reformation, and the first cornerpost of the Puritan House, the inner or *Religious Independence* that was an aspect of the generic *Philosophical* Individualism of the Renaissance, the principle embodied in Luther's phrase, "Every man his own priest," that more than another founded the modern world. Falling on a population of Europe that had always depended upon its "betters" for all standards, major decisions and leadership, the new emphasis on the individual did not in the sixteenth and seventeenth centuries effect any great change in the aristocratic surface of society. Most noticeably the class of the "betters" was reinforced from among the once despised merchants; but in their third and second, even their first generations, they hastened to recostume themselves as traditional gentry. Even in religion, the

Church of England did no more than substitute the King and his hierarchy for the Pope and his. It was only on the lunatic fringes of society that any outward and leveling expression of this inward and novel theory was proposed.

And yet this theory of every individual's spiritual independence, the inviolable importance of his soul before God, was in the English air, at least strongly enough to nourish a lunatic fringe of Quakers, Ranters, Seekers, etc., and to frighten the bishops into violence. As we shall see presently in considering Congregationalism, it was very consciously in the air among those slightly left-of-center Puritans who came to New England. It was the honest hope of their ministry, or most of it, that all of the people should be raised to a point where they might indeed become each "his own priest," and to this end they labored endlessly to clarify the finest points of the Drama of Redemption, and to prepare every simpleton for the intelligent receipt of Grace. In their theory the minister was not the direct mouthpiece of God, but a specialist trained to advise and assist laymen in their own interpretations and experiences. To be sure, many violated the theory in their instinctive identification of the Divinely and the Socially Elect. Yet they must not fail to give the theory lip service. In 1708 the Saybrook Platform was promulgated by an exceptionally reactionary group of Connecticut ministers for the purpose of holding their own power and blocking innovation; yet in the Confession of Faith they must needs repeat hypocritically the letter of Religious Individualism from the English Savoy Platform:

> . . . Those things which are necessary to be known, believed and observed for Salvation . . . are so clearly propounded and opened in some place of Scripture or other, that not only the learned, but the unlearned, in a due use of the original means, may attain unto a sufficient understanding of them.[39]

Meanwhile, this inner Independence, which must be sharply distinguished from the modern American individualism of self-assertion, was widening in application beyond the original fringe of Antinomian libertines in Germany and the more ignorant sects in England among which the exhibitionists who came to New England as Quaker missionaries were the most offensive. The highly respectable Mistress Anne Hutchinson declared that God not only assured her of her state of Grace but continued to instruct and to direct her; and she had many followers, both respectable and disreputable, and enjoyed for a time the support of Master John Cotton, late Dean of Emmanuel College, Cambridge, Teacher of the First Church of Christ in Boston. The trend first found numerous expression in the Great Awakening and its aftermath in the 1740's and '50's when, in a reckless extension of the carefully limited Religious Individualism of Jonathan Edwards, itinerant ignoramuses went ranting about New England, proclaiming that the trained ministry was not regenerate, and encouraging everyone who had been wrought up enough to believe himself "saved" to do whatever God told him to. This religious individualism of the eighteenth century was virtually coextensive with the social and political individualism which at the time was leveling the Yankee landscape. But the social and political leveling proved to be more permanent. After this first hurricane, revivalism did not again widely sweep territorial New England. It moved west into Greater New England, but even there, and even during the lapse in education on the early Middle Western frontier, it did not commonly march up and down the camp meetings as it had first done in the Connecticut Valley, and as it continued to do south of the Ohio.

From the beginning, Religious Individualism in New England was jacketed in certain restraints, and it is jacketed in them in our typical Yankee today. In the deep doctrinal matters which were the foundations and frame of the Puritan House, the original yeomen tended to defer to the opinions of their educated betters, and in the outward clapboards and shingles which the world saw daily they generally conformed comfortably to local public opinion. It was in all that intermediate construction which I called the flooring, the partitions and the inward finishing that each citizen from very early lived in an independent world where his ideas were his own, and among these independent ideas was the idea that his neighbors' ideas were also their own. It was in this living part of the house that they tolerated and hid the Baptists and the Quakers, so long as they kept outward decorum, when the government was persecuting them in the 1650's. It was in this part of the house that they developed and set up the economic and political ideas that resented taxation and legislation for them on the part of an alien power, and it was from the mantel in this part of the house that they took down their muskets. Somewhere between an outward decorum and an inward metaphysical frame that no common man can build easily, the Puritan knew that he lived as a free and inviolable individual in God's sight. In that living interior of his house he was independent, absolute and alone. And in the same part his cultural descendant knows himself still to be independent, absolute and alone. Where Yankee culture has degenerated into Industrial Pseudo-culture, the original, circumscribed Individualism has broken out socially to join similar currents from the Pseudo-South to produce that contemporary American Individualism which now holds the blown and cracked eggshell of the planet in its exuberant hands. But where the culture has remained strong the individual has also remained strong and has been content to stay in his house which is still his impregnable castle.

2) *Education is the thing.*

In this affirmation of the value of Book-Learnin', our Yankee states a principle which, though religiously based, became one of the greatest secular forces of cohesion in the culture. In the beginning the "Book" involved, the authoritative repository of truth, was the Bible, but in due course it took the special form, at first concomitantly and afterwards dominantly, of the *Written Constitution,* the instrument of government. In the interpretation, the *Learnin',* we find one of those paradoxes by which Puritanism was able to embrace apparently conflicting principles where each was in its fashion right. As we shall notice presently in Congregationalism or Politics, so in Education, the Puritans, and the Yankees after them, were able to maintain Equality in principle, while applying Aristocracy as a matter of course in practice.

Yankee Book Learnin', in its original form of reliance upon and familiarity with the *Word of God,* was the second great cornerpost of the Puritan House. Concomitant with the principle of *Religious Individualism* in the Reformation was the doctrine that God's Will is revealed, not through the pronouncements of the Church, but through the Bible. Since God dictated it to his prophets and evangelists there has been no later Revelation. And as it was clear to all Protestants what the Book was, so it would seem also that the proper Learnin', the true method of using the Book, was self-evident. By the basic doctrine that every man should be his own priest under God, it would seem that every man should interpret the Bible as God would tell him. But here the doctrine ran into an infrangible wall of long practice and prejudice everywhere mortared with idealism and buttressed by common sense. On the question of the interpretation and application of the Bible churches, sects and nations proceeded to split in schism and in blood. And specifically it was one answer to this question that launched those thousands of ships westward to found a new England.

For it was here, probably more than in matters of vesture, ritual and sacramentation, that a large minority of the communicants of the Church of England in the sixteenth and seventeenth centuries desired to "purify" it of the methods of Rome farther than their archbishops had done. The Puritans agreed that much of the Bible needs adjusting for modern application, but in their notions of the proper method of adjustment they found themselves in individualistic advance of their orthodox brethren. The Anglican divines agreed that it was all God's Word, but it seemed to them evident that He intended much of it exclusively for an ancient pastoral tribe, and not at all for enlightened Englishmen of the days of Elizabeth and James. Which parts were applicable specially to the old Jews, and which were of contemporary application was a question which, under the ancient and never questioned doctrine of intellectual aristocracy, fell naturally within the province of the trained reason of the bishops.

To which the Puritans cried "Popery," the presumptuous interposition of man's will to interpret God's will. To them the "reason" which the Anglicans used to sift what of the Bible was applicable from what was not was "Carnal" or "Natural" Reason, "ruined" by man's Original Sin and his continuing reprobate or self-centered condition. "Though arguments be never so plaine," wrote Thomas Hooker, "and Scriptures never so pregnant; yet a carnall wretch will carry himselfe against all, and say, it is not my judgment, I am not of that Mind."[40] Natural Reason, said John Norton, successor of Cotton as Teacher of the First Church of Boston, is no better than "Star-light" which

> cannot make it, otherwise than night. The light of nature since the fall, compared with the light of the image of God, before the fall, hath not the proportion of Star-light, to the bright Sun-light at noon-day. This indeed is but darkness. But, if compared with the light of the Gospell, it is worse than gross darkness.[41]

According to the Puritans, the Anglican method of selecting what of the Bible was currently applicable was an impious use of Natural Reason. To them every word of the Bible applied to all men at all times, and the adjustment should be not by selection, but by interpretation. This also was beyond the Carnal or Natural Reason of the Unregenerate. But it was within the power of *Right Reason* which is a function of that Imagination, that power of objective perception, which man lost at the fall and which is restored by Grace, the return to innocence that removes the film of self from things and makes them "appear as they be." The Puritans, to be sure, delighted in Natural Reason and its uses in the unfolding universe of Galileo, Bacon and presently Newton, and they supplied the Royal Academy with a disproportionate number of distinguished scientists. Yet it would not have occurred to them that the materials, processes and findings of Natural Reason or "Natural Philosophy" were anything but superficial embellishments upon the generic glory of Creation. The Puritan's distinction between Natural Reason and Right Reason is one of those nice points which the Puritan-burners delight to point out as scholastic quibbles. But, like most of the Puritan's quibbles, it contains a distinction of aesthetic importance. What it really means is that you can't read any creative literature, including the Bible, unless you are yourself in a creative mood, which is to say an imaginatively sensitive or gracious mood. Rational or New Criticism can sit down scholastically and tear into interesting pieces the Bible or the *Symposium* or *Hamlet* or *Moby Dick,* and thereby it will proportionately destroy their meaning. But to read them with imagination, trusting the perceptions of Grace which in these things come to all men, that is to read them with Right Reason and to read them truly.

In the pursuit of this critical principle of the superiority of Imagination or Right Reason over Natural or Analytical Reason, some eighty thousand people, most of them from substantial homes, moved westward in the first fifty years to risk their lives on a cold and unmastered ocean and in a colder and unknown wilderness. And yet the individualistic principle that was implicit in the critical one, though they professed it with passionate hypocrisy in major pronouncements, yet in practice was honored mostly in the breach until the great or Jacksonian collapse of standards in the nineteenth century. In the seventeenth century scarcely anybody, whether educated or ignorant, had yet questioned "the conception of religion as a difficult art in which the authority of the skilled dialectician should prevail over the inclinations of the merely devout." . . . Very few Englishmen had yet broached the notion that "any Tom, Dick or Harry, simply because he was a good, honest man, could understand the Sermon on the Mount as well as a Master of Arts from Oxford, Cambridge, or Harvard."[42] Grace might come to anyone, but all would have agreed that the Elect can recognize and apply it "all the better if they know Latin, Greek and Hebrew."[43] With the consent of all to this general proposition, the same class of men assisted the American Puritans to interpret the Bible as issued its interpretation by fiat to the Anglicans. The former were ready to die for the principle that every man was his own priest. But in administering his priestly duties each must turn for advice as a matter of course to those trained by the universities to give it.

Thus the great Puritan cornerpost of the Word of God or Book-Learnin' was in its original, oaken heart an aristocratic cornerpost, albeit in terms of a special kind of aristocracy which distinguished it from that of the Old Country. The American Puritans deferred to their educated ministers, not because they were gentry, not even because they were anointed priests, but simply because they were educated. Except in Boston and a few other purlieus of The Bay where Europe was never outgrown, New England aristocracy was not dynastic but intellectual. For two centuries it was presumed that those specially trained to interpret God's Word were the ones best qualified to interpret it. Which meant that it was presumed that the educated were the best leaders for society. During the first century and more, when God's Word was almost exclusively the Bible, the leadership was by and large of the ministers. In the eighteenth century, as God's Word tended to get identified with Man's Word in matters of Rights and Government, the aristocracy became increasingly that of the lawyers. After the Civil War, when God's Word and Man's Word alike submitted to material Power, the aristocratic tradition lapsed entirely. Or it remained in faint diffusion among all college graduates in whom, as they increased in numbers, education proportionately thinned away until it was on the average shallower than that of the seventeenth-century farmers. So Learnin' passed, and the individualistic inference of the Reformation at last won a literal triumph. The great tradition, however, has not yet passed among those Yankees who have not gone to college and who, therefore, have not been disabused of the ancient belief that they are institutions of learning that teach the things that people ought to know.

But the intellectual tradition of the Puritans was not aristocratic in the narrow sense. In the seventeenth and eighteenth centuries when means were found for educating the deserving, whether they had money or not, the learned ruling class was open to all. Furthermore, it was supposed that everyone might receive enough education to prepare himself for the receipt and exercise of Grace. In a Holy Commonwealth, there was no need for anyone to be in the dilemma of Hooker's "ignorant sinner" who was like

> a sick man remaining in a Apothecaries shop, ful of choycest Medicines in the darkest night: though be the choycest of all receipts at hand, and he may take what he needs, yet because he cannot see what he takes, and how to use them, he may kill himself or encrease his distempers, but never cure any disease.[44]

Out of this recognized need for learning, there arose and flourished from the beginning the first, eventually the largest, and until recently the finest free, compulsory, Universal Educational System in the world. Every colony except Rhode Island, and most of the individual plantations or towns, adopted and applied school ordinances within their first dozen years. The earliest orders of the General Courts are directed to the education of particular children who were not getting it at home. Then, beginning with Massachusetts in 1642, that colony and New Haven and Connecticut passed general acts requiring parents and masters of apprentices to see to the education of their charges to the point of being able to read the Scriptures and understand "the principles of religion," under penalty of having them taken away and farmed out with more solicitous foster parents. In 1645 New Haven established the first public school, and in 1647 the famous "Old Deluder" statute of Massachusetts,* adopted soon after by Connecticut, compelled towns of fifty houses to set up public elementary schools by means of which parents and masters could fulfill their legal duties to educate the young, and towns of a hundred houses to establish also grammar—our high—schools to prepare for "the college at the Bay"—Harvard, 1636. And after 1644 Massachusetts, Connecticut and New Haven were all sending grain for the maintenance of poor scholars in Harvard, that the quality of the ministry might not decline. From that time New England education flourished as long as intellectual standards did. In the western reaches of Greater New England it is at least vigorous and original today.

Conformable to the spirit that was creating this system, New England in the 1640's and '50's probably enjoyed the loftiest level of General Education—as distinguished from that of a ruling class—of any whole community in human history. Out of a population of 24,000 it had over a hundred English university graduates—a higher ratio of higher education than was found in England—together with its two or three score graduates from Harvard's early classes. Most distinguishing of all, it had a yeomanry well grounded in theology if not much in the humanities, its very servants able to hold their own in the refined discussions of Grace and Works, Free Will, "Means" and "Providences" before the blazing chimneys on winter nights. Unlike the Anglican ministers, who cajoled their congregations with mellifluous rhetoric and easy content, the Puritan preachers gave their people the toughest, most "painful," intellectual analysis of cosmic forces of which they were capable, and the people listened for two, three, and four hours in unheated meeting houses and not only took it but demanded it. It is reported that in 1637, when the detachment of Massachusetts men under Captain Underhill was doing a forced night march through the woods to join Captain Mason of Connecticut for the attack on the Pequots, they fell into a debate whether in this service they were acting under the Covenant of Grace or a Covenant of Works—theological concepts of the distinction between impulsion by Faith or Imagination and Law or Duty. The argument grew so heated that the disputants mutually demanded

* "It being one chief project of that old deluder Satan, to keep men from the knowledge of the Scriptures, as in former times by keeping them in an unknown tongue, so in these latter times by persuading them from the use of tongues, . . . and that learning may not be buried in the graves of our fathers, . . . it is therefore ordered . . ." etc.

that they be halted until the matter should be settled. "The greatness of the Puritans," says Perry Miller, [45] "is not so much that they conquered a wilderness, or that they carried a religion into it, but that they carried a religion which, . . . narrow though it may have been in some respects . . . , was nevertheless indissolubly bound up with an ideal of culture and learning. In contrast to all other pioneers, they made no concession to the forest, but in the midst of frontier conditions, in the very throes of clearing the land and erecting shelters, they maintained schools and a college, a standard of scholarship and of competent writing, a class of men devoted entirely to the life of the mind and of the soul." It might be added to their greatness that even their half-educated took their half-education seriously as a gift of God, a "talent" putting on them a responsibility to use it for the Glory of God and the betterment of his Holy Community.

Fundamental to the doctrine of God's Word, with its corollaries of Intellectual Aristocracy and Education, was of course the assumption that there is such a thing as God's Word. *Truth Exists* and can be discovered by Prayer—that is, concentration—and the application of Right Reason or Imagination. Truth in the beginning was truly from God; it was assumed to be cosmic, since it was then assumed that a cosmos existed. In the eighteenth century it contracted to the realm of certain assumed Rights of Man. In the nineteenth century it contracted further to the Right, a standard which was not uniform, but it was at least assumed to exist and proclaimed by lawyers and statesmen. It was not until the end of the century, when the last absolutes were falling, pragmatism was in, and relativism and pluralism were around the corner, that the Right gave way to the merely Legal, and the traditional search for Truth to an exercise in expediency and chicanery in the interest of gain.

Coincident with the assumption that Truth Exists and that it can be conjured forth by the application of educated Right Reason, we still have deep in Yankee character a fond belief in the *Invincibility of Reason*. It is perhaps our greatest asset in and contribution to the councils of nations today. Confronted by a tired, old-world diplomacy within which the council table is just another bazaar, we still believe not only that Truth Exists but that it can be dug out by a group of suspicious enemies through concerted, rational effort, and being so reasoned out will forthwith and happily persuade them all. That we are sometimes cheated is neither astonishing nor disgraceful. It would seem more disturbing when we regret that our Puritan idealism, using Right Reason, is cheated by materialism, using Natural Reason, wherefore we propose to surrender and to learn to practice the principles of bargaining.

Probably the most spectacular, and the most continuously successful derivative of the tradition of God's Word is *Government by Written Constitution*. In the early years the Bible and the several covenants or contracts found in it, together with the royal Charters, provided the organic civil as well as the moral law of the colonies, and throughout the seventeenth century the magistrates were instructed by the General Courts to enforce biblical law where no secular law had been provided.* The Bible and the Charters were the first American constitutions which, when they were applicable, supplanted English Common Law until the Bible in turn was replaced by more appropriate "Fundamentals." Through the habit of biblical interpretation the Puritans were from the beginning not only education-minded men, not only legal-minded men, but also constitution-minded men, men accustomed to govern themselves under a body of organic statutes which were taken to embody the Truth and could be changed only with difficulty.† Thus they prepared themselves for self-government under the Constitution of the United States.

All of these elements or derivatives of the cornerpost of the Word of God, the tradition of Book-Learnin', are on the aristocratic side, the side of the Learnin'. Gradually the individualistic side, the implicit principle that every Tom, Dick and Harry, if he thinks he is in Grace, can interpret the Book, has worked its way out of theory into practice. Being nothing other than a school of illiterate criticism, it is an aspect of that ignorant Individualism which has progressively taken over most aspects of American life. For all their espousal of emotional inspiration as the command of God, Mistress Hutchinson and her friends looked to the ministers she accredited for the interpretation of God's Word. During the more extensive Antinomian performances of the Great Awakening, many illiterates itinerated about as ministers of the Word and did not hesitate to

---

* In 1636 John Cotton wrote to Lord Saye and Sele, one of the patrons of Massachusetts Bay:

"I am very apt to believe what Mr. Perkins"—William Perkins, the great Cambridge Puritan scholar—"hath, in one of his prefatory pages to the golden chaine, that the word, and Scriptures of God doe contayne a short *upoluposis*, or platforme, not onely of theology, but also of . . . ethicks, economicks, politicks, church-government, prophecy, academy. It is very suitable to Gods all-sufficient wisdome, and to the fulnes and perfection of Holy Scriptures . . . to prescribe perfect rules for the right ordering of the commonwealth. . . ." (Miller and Johnson, 209).

It is significant that at the time of this writing Cotton was on a committee to draw up a body of "fundamentalls" for Massachusetts. For a discussion of New England's "Covenant-constitutions" from God, see Alice M. Baldwin, *The New England Clergy and the American Revolution*, 13-14.

† The Bible of course could not be amended, and the Charters only through what were virtually diplomatic channels. The "Fundamental Orders" of Connecticut (1639) and the "Body of Liberties" of Massachusetts (1641) could be amended by ordinary legislative process, but in their truly organic features they were treated with special respect and were in fact amended but rarely.

pronounce upon it; but not many of their converts took upon themselves to do the same. In the nineteenth century the real decline started, and it accelerated. On the frontier of the Old Middle West, when education was hard to come by for a generation, the notion that an ignorant minister is dearer to God than an educated one spread rapidly, and led to the common assumption that anybody who was sufficiently excited was inspired by God to interpret His Book. Parallel to this view there appeared for application by sane illiterates the phenomenon of Fundamentalism, the practice of the supposedly literal interpretation of the Bible by people unqualified to make either a literal or a critical interpretation. From a glance at the statistics of the size and distribution of the revivalist sects, it would seem that a majority of the Protestants in the country today, perhaps even in Greater New England, are of the persuasion that a little prayerful analysis of, say, the Book of *Revelation,* will fetch an ignoramus closer to God's meaning than an exposition by some jackanapes from a college. One wonders whether, for purposes of biblical interpretation, the more desiccated parts of Greater New England—notably Kansas—should not be excluded from the domain of our typical Yankee who still honors education.

So long as all of this remains in the category of more or less honest pseudo-religion it is cause for apprehension, but not for despair. But when intellectual individualism eschews even the safeguards of pretended religion, to the end that any dolt who was miseducated in a current college becomes an authority on matters of diplomacy, art, letters, government, and religion, with the power of life and death over those who have devoted their lives to getting educated in these matters, then indeed the Reformation is mocked. One begins to doubt that mankind can ever govern itself, and regrets that Luther ever nailed his theses on the church door. In this crisis our Yankee with his instinctive respect for learning is perhaps the last hope of the nation. He is conservative and not critically literate, and he can be disturbed by the lurid press. But he knows ignorance when he sees it face to face. Being ignorant himself, he knows that it is not qualified to run the country. And when he sees it pretending to more education than it has, he turns away. He has a sure nose for any kind of fake, and this one he likes less than most.

3) *Keep plugging.*

Here our Yankee refers to the third Puritan cornerpost, that of the *Calling,* including as corollaries the *Economic Virtues* which have instigated much of the expansive energy of modern empires, and latterly, when the sanction of religion has been removed, the irresponsible rapacity which has undermined them, together with the aimless momentum, the neurosis and the carditis of Americans. The identification of cupidity with Calvinism, which the debunkers have found easy to make by selected references to Calvin's *Institutes,* is unjust to Calvin himself, is in some degree just to the English Puritans, and is in the main unjust to the American Puritans until well along in the nineteenth century when Puritanism was almost dead.

Calvin aimed to integrate spiritual and secular living, to make no radical distinction between the battles of the soul and those of current politics, business and warfare. He did differentiate this world from the next, but made them equally part of God's drama, conceiving life in time as a kind of curtain-raiser for life in eternity. A man's behavior here was an exercise under godly control, seen by Calvin's Arminian followers as a period of trial and probation, and by the truer Calvinists, including the Puritans, as an arena in which to exhibit "signs" that one was among the predestined Elect. In either case it was desirable to do the Lord's work; and high among the categories of the Lord's Works was the injunction to tend to your earthly business.

The divine injunction to the Economic Virtues was found more explicitly in the Old than in the New Testament. Here is a list of common texts from *Proverbs* that were popular with the Puritans:[46]

> . . . Go to the ant, thou sluggard; consider her ways, and be wise; Which having no guide, overseer, or ruler, Provideth her meat in the summer, and gathereth her food in the harvest. . . . He becometh poor that dealeth with a slack hand: but the hand of the diligent maketh rich. . . . Wealth gotten by vanity shall be diminished: but he that gathereth by labor shall increase. . . . A good man leaveth an inheritance to his children's children: . . . The rich ruleth over the poor, and the borrower is servant to the lender. . . . He that tilleth his land shall have plenty of bread: but he that followeth after vain persons shall have poverty enough. [*Proverbs,* it may be recalled, abounds equally in texts for the principle that piety and moral goodness are superior to wealth.]

The homely virtues here advised for their practical results Calvin emphasizes as the commands of God:

> . . . All these things are given to us by the Divine goodness. . . . They are, as it were, deposits intrusted to our care, of which we must one day give an account. We ought, therefore, to manage them in such a manner that this alarm may be incessantly sounding in our ears, "Give an account of thy stewardship." (Luke xvi, 2) Let it also be remembered . . . that this

account is demanded . . . by him who has so highly recommended abstinence, sobriety, frugality, and modesty; who abhors profusion, pride, ostentation, and vanity; who approves of no other management of his blessings, than such as is connected with charity. . . .

And Calvin integrates the several economic virtues within his famous doctrine of the *Calling*, which is the earthly application of the doctrine of Predestination:

. . . The Lord commands every one of us, in all the actions of life, to regard his vocation . . . he has appointed to all their particular duties in different spheres of life. . . . Every individual's line of life, therefore, is, as it were, a post assigned him by the Lord, that he may not wander about in uncertainty all his days. . . . Hence . . . will arise peculiar consolation, since there will be no employment so mean and sordid [provided we follow our vocation] as not to appear truly respectable, and be deemed highly important in the sight of God.[47]

From this central statement of Calvin's doctrine of business, it is evident that he himself does not deserve the charge of advocating cupidity, or of espousing the economic interests of mercantile capitalism which was rising rapidly in his day. While the qualities he enumerates—"abstinence, sobriety, frugality, modesty," the abhorrence of "profusion, pride, and vanity"—are indeed among those that in an expanding economy will accelerate accumulation of wealth, yet it is notable that Calvin does not include among them that epoch-making command to "diligence" which, as pronounced by his followers, became the goad that drove great nations and their millions upon world-encircling adventures of conquest and greed. The Reformation's expression of the religious aspect of the individualism of the Renaissance was, of course, congenial to the political or democratic and the economic or capitalistic expressions of it, and they undoubtedly supported one another in the mutual epic advance that hardly faltered till the twentieth century. But there is no evidence that Calvin had any interest in the political and economic expressions except as they bore on the religious expression.

In reminding his followers that a man's calling was "a post assigned him by the Lord," and that he must one day "give an account of his stewardship," the inference that he be industrious in his business is only as a healthy alternative to pitying himself because his Calling might be "mean and sordid" in comparison to those of others. Calvin was only saying that all Callings are of equal importance in the eyes of God, that if you do a good job at your particular stewardship, which was assigned to you by God and is part of His business, you will be happier than in giving yourself to worldly intrigue to get a more desirable stewardship and so "wandering about in uncertainty all your days." In the sixteenth century the profitable Calling of trade was still generally considered "mean and sordid," and Calvin may well have had in mind to comfort the merchants, along with the obscure poor, with the assurance that they were doing God's business. But this was not to encourage, or even to condone, the rapacity of some of them.

It was the English Puritans who, accepting Calvin's list of modest virtues that aimed at contentment in one's lot, amended them with the injunction to that zealous industriousness of which gain was the obvious and intended result. "Zeal and diligence," declared the Puritan teacher Richard Baxter, "are the victorious enemies of sin and satan."[48] A shameless little manuscript volume, *The Tradesman's Calling*, attributed to Daniel Defoe, and probably though not certainly intended as Satire[49] goes far beyond the norm of English Puritanism in justifying avarice as commended by God. "Prudence and Piety were always very good friends. . . . You may gain enough of both worlds if you would mind each in its place." Even "a preposterous zeal" in religion, by which is meant "neglecting a man's necessary affairs upon pretense of religious worship," is deplored as pursuing the less rather than the more godly end; and profiteering is advocated in the suggestion that a man should not fail to "take the advantage which the Providence of God puts into his hands."[50]

It is not probable that many English Puritans would have followed the doctrine of the Economic Virtues to such frivolous extremity, and, so far as appears, no Americans did. The Puritans of early Massachusetts Bay and Connecticut were watchful to punish cases of sharp dealing, or even such profiteering above a fair gain as would today be admired as simply good business.* Such diaries as are available show a concern for the results of the writers' mercantile adventures, but they show a greater anxiety lest his interest be more in his profit than in doing God's work.[51] Two sermons of John Cotton, both bespeaking the spirit of their Calvinist source, are fair statements of the ascendance in New England of piety over the cupidity which the Economic Virtues invite. The first, entitled "Christian Calling," was probably preached in Cotton's church in Boston, England, shortly before his emigration:

> . . . Faith drawes the heart of a Christian to live in some warrantable calling . . .: An instance you have in the Prodigall

---

* Massachusetts disciplined its rich Captain Keayne, and Connecticut Springfield's also rich and leading citizen William Pynchon, each for some kind of commercial overreaching.

son, that . . . comming home to his Father, the very next thing after confession and repentance of sin, the very next petition he makes, is, *Make mee one of thy hired servants.* . . .

. . . when faith hath made choyce of a warrantable calling, then he *depends* upon God for the quickning, and sharpning of his gifts in that calling . . . Though he have never so much skill and strength, he looks at it as a dead work, unlesse God breathe in him . . .

. . . Faith about a man's vocation . . . *encourageth* a man in his calling to the most homeliest, and difficultest, and most dangerous things his calling can lead and expose himself to . . . Take you a carnall proud heart, and if his calling lead him to some homely businesse, he can by no meanes embrace it . . . ; but now faith having put us into a calling, if it require some homely employment, it encourageth us to it. . . .

. . . Faith hath another act about a mans vocation, and that is, it takes *all successes* that befall him in his calling with *moderation,* hee equally beares good and evill successes as God shall dispense them to him. . . .[52]

Another and more penetrating sermon of Cotton's states the paradox—one of the most profound of the several Puritan paradoxes—which was at the bottom of the combination of genuine zeal in business with genuine and dominant piety. This economic paradox goes back to Paul and his advice to "use this world, as not abusing it: for the fashion of this world passeth away."[53] Calvin, after quoting the passage in its obvious meaning as an injunction to moderation, amends it so as to give it a more profound significance, "to use this world as though we used it not. . . ."[54] And Cotton, with that aptness of metaphor which so often characterizes the Puritan "Plain Style," plants one of the seeds of the American Puritan and Yankee soul:

There is another combination of vertues strangely mixed in every lively holy Christian, And that is, Diligence in worldly businesses, and yet deadnesse to the world; such a mystery as none can read, but they that know it. . . . [Again a Christian may] bestir himselfe for profit, [and yet] bee a man dead-hearted to the world . . . his heart is not set upon these things, he can tell what to doe with his estate when he hath got it.[55]

And to the same purport is the injunction to love the world with "weaned affections."[56]

Here is stated what is indeed a "mystery as none can read but they that know it," and we could almost add that only they can "know it" who are of either American or English Dissenting Calvinist tradition. It is incomprehensible to the contemporary materialist mind which can not conceive that what it actually admires as "hard-headed realism" should be indifferent to its "realistic" results, that the apparent "realist" should find his true realism in an imaginative or idealistic realm which to the materialist can not be other than a figment of hypocrisy. And yet this paradox of living in the world as if one were in it not, dominated the organization and administration of increasing areas of the planet for three centuries, and it provides such idealism as may yet be found in our politics and commerce. It has made both Britain and America powerful and hated, enabling them to perpetrate on the surface acts as shameless as those of French, German or Italian imperialism, while all the time maintaining toward their victims a genuine, generous, active and often self-sacrificing kindliness. The worldly paradox that came down from Calvin has retained the wisdom to remain a paradox, recognizing both of its horns at once, not attempting the literal logic and fierce consistency of the Lutherans who have held that the individual must be either in the world or out of it, that rational necessity knows no irrational tenderness. The German mind, and to a degree the French mind, sees truth in black or white and must resolve paradoxes. The Puritan mind sees truth precisely in paradox. The true Calvinist has continued to live in the world at once with energy and with indifference.

There is, to be sure, an hypocrisy here, but it is of a special kind, an inversion of the usual kind. It is what we might call *The Grand Hypocrisy* in which the pretense is of self-concern and the secret reality is of selfless idealism. The Puritan, in Tawney's phrase, was "the practical ascetic, whose victories are won, not in the cloister, but on the battlefield, in the counting house, and in the market."[57] The dedicated chastity of the Puritans, which has made them the by-word of the literal-minded and literal-passioned, perhaps found its ridiculous extremity in the unhealthy behavior of their latest daughters the famous demi-virgins of the 1920's, together with their latest sons the youthful male virgins, who disported themselves in all the abandonments of licentiousness except only the final commitment of normal consummation. They exercised notoriously and shamelessly in a world of self-indulgence; yet they did it with "weaned affections." Reality was still in idealism, although by the 1920's it was a pathetically contracted idealism. It is of course highly unfair to the robustly carnal Puritans to compare them with these bloodless and brainless decadents upon that Victorianism which was itself a major decadence. Yet these wraiths did illustrate in caricature that paradox of their ancestors by which they worked with great and shameless energy in the world of self-aggrandizement, at the same time doing it with "deadnesse" and indifference to the results, for it was not their true world.

But by the time of its sensual attenuation in the 1920's, the Grand Hypocrisy in its original and economic form was long reversed, negated and forgotten. The great materialist change, though traceable from the first settlement, hardly provided the general character of Greater New England until after the Civil War. In the seventeenth century, especially in Boston, we find individuals and fashions assuming that as Works were a sign of Grace, and wealth a sign of the Economic Virtues which figured among Works, therefore wealth was a sign of Grace and the plutocracy was also the Elect. But even under this sordid tradition—and it had many addicts as long as the Grand Hypocrisy lasted—these financially Elect took small pleasure in the evidence of their Election. Their wealth was chiefly a source of unquiet and a worm in their consciences gnawing with the fear that their concern for it was more than the sense of a stewardship for which they must give an account. It is not until the strong rise of both materialist philosophy and industrialism in the 1840's and '50's that we begin to see the Grand Hypocrisy generally reversing into Common or Petty Hypocrisy in which the pretense is of selfless objectivity and the concealed fact is of self-indulgence and Greed. As the great factories multiplied, there grew also the blight of Victorianism under which the owners professed that they were running them for the moral good of the employed, while increasingly they were pinching the latter into industrial slavery. After the Civil War even the pretense of virtue was gradually thrown away. By 1900 even Petty Hypocrisy, which at least recognized the standard of selflessness, had succumbed to that bestial frankness which survives, in which we proclaim without shame that the possession of wealth is not a sign of divine Grace, but is itself the experience of reality.

Generally, the Grand Hypocrisy, superimposing materialistic actions upon idealistic motives, lasted as long as the original idea of God lasted. Under the belief that the Economic Virtues were enjoined by God, and that their rewards were incidental, the Puritan and his family could live in humility and assurance. But once the larger sanction was removed, the Yankee moved into today's state of mere industrious momentum in which he must needs "die in the saddle," a treadmill on which he does in fact die young, meanwhile himself deserving the disagreeable charges that ignorant and jealous foreigners have long thrown at his social ancestors. Having lost the understanding of the ancient paradox that was the Puritan's secret, he exercises Diligence and Frugality for the professed purpose of accumulating wealth without even a pettily hypocritical pretense of piety. He has fallen into a naïve form of the logical consistency which characterizes the Germans, the Russians and the Latins. In the world forum he plays with them at their game instead of his. And he does not play well.

This is the degraded state of the contemporary American that the world sees, and he represents not New England culture but New England Pseudo-culture. The case of the typical Yankee who "keeps plugging" on the farm or in the small town is not so hopelessly sad. By and large his plugging is practical, it is nearer to the reality of necessity, and so does not have the aspect of a beltless pulley spinning in a vacuum. Also, his sense of the Economic Virtues is still an absolute moral sense, not relative to gain, nor is it quite reduced to an empty habit. The impulsion is not a meaningless, nervous momentum; it is more a sense that he "ought" to do what he is doing. And behind that "ought" there is the assumption that there is a source of all value, a Meaning of life, a God. This intimation of reality, this ghost of the Grand Hypocrisy, is evident in the Yankee common sense that restrains its possessor from the slightest exultation or change in his tenor or any concession to vanity in case he does get rich. The cornerpost of the Calling, with its Economic Virtues and its Grand Hypocrisy, is a member of the Puritan House that is still part of the average Yankee's conscious Central Idea that is still heated by the living fire in the ancient chimney.

4) *It is what you think that matters, not what you do.*

This cornerpost is the great doctrine of *Salvation by Faith Not Works,* which was one of the fighting slogans of the Reformation and embodied the chief complaint against the Roman Church, that against indulgences and the whole mechanism of Salvation administered by men. To the Puritans, and in Yankee instinct today, Faith means the established relation of the individual to cosmic Truth. In the Puritan it was the continuing state of loving God, which was the continuing state of that Imaginative Perception which is Grace. In the Yankee it is the continuing state of Imaginative Perception or Grace which is his Central Idea and what he means by "what you think."

Faith is realized as part of the gift of Grace. It is the response to Grace, as Puritan John Ball said, "the gift of God, and the act of man; a wonderful and supernaturall gift of God, and a lively motion of the heart renewed by grace. . ." [58] The continuing State of Grace and Faith describes a single established relationship between God and the Individual, the same circuit of Love, differing only in the direction of the current. Grace is God's accolade and continuing assurance to man, and Faith is man's acceptance and continuing fealty to God. Grace is God's affirmation, and Faith is that of man.

From the beginning of Puritan history, we find the occasional confusion of *Faith,* an imaginative and emotional state, with *Belief* in some specific event past, such as the Crucifixion, or forthcoming, such as immortality in time, or the Second Advent; and both the Fundamentalists and the debunkers have substituted belief in divers absurdities for the true Faith of the Puritans which was Communion with God. Presently we shall notice how, under the Covenant of Grace, the Puritans emphasized Belief as a sign of Grace, and how the religionless Yankees sometimes make it the center of Faith and even a substitute for Faith. But first we should distinguish the imaginative and emotional inclusiveness of Faith from the simple factuality of Belief which may or may not comprise part of it.

There is probably no line along which the Puritans quarrelled so bitterly and ceaselessly among themselves as that between conduct and faith, between what they called the "Covenant"—or Contract—of Works and the Covenant—or Contract—of Grace. All agreed that Adam in Innocence had been under a Covenant of Works, being God's agreement that He would keep him in a state of timelessness if he did not violate God's command not to take an interest in himself. But he did voluntarily take on self-knowledge and self-concern, thereby vitiating the Contract and lapsing out of timelessness into time. Thereupon God substituted for the broken Covenant of Works the Covenant of Grace which we shall notice in a later section. Substantially it was God's promise that, while he would extend Grace to some and withhold it from some in his own good pleasure, yet anyone's Belief in the Atonement was a sure sign that he was in Grace, that he was Elected. For the individual Puritan, therefore, the primary aim of life became, not the performance of "Works," but the attainment of sincere Belief, identified in some way with an emotional experience of Grace. And for most the secondary aim became the persuasion of the local congregation of the validity of the Experience and the Belief, to the end that the congregation might accept him into Sainthood and the Church Visible, thereby strengthening the probability that he was indeed on the Great List of the Elect.

All agreed that the object of active life was to glorify God and to hope for Grace and Faith, and that Works had nothing essential to do with it. Said John Preston, Master of Emmanuel College, Cambridge, England, and the author of much doctrine that came to America,

> You might meddle with all the things in this world, and not be defiled by them, if you had pure affections, but when you have an inordinate lust after anything, [that is, when it diverts your real attention from God or Man to yourself] then it defiles your spirit.[59]

And, said Samuel Willard of the Old South Church of Boston: "I tell you this, the Saints of God shall commit greater sinnes and goe to Heaven, when thou lesser goe to Hell."

Nothing was farther from the Puritan moral concept than the value of any kind of conduct for its own sake, let alone peccadillos to which later Fundamentalists attached importance. "Drink," said Increase Mather, minister of the Second Church of Boston, "is in itself a good creature of God and to be received with thankfulness, but the abuse of drink is from Satan." Here is Roger Williams beginning a letter to Governor John Winthrop, Jr., of Connecticut, in February, 1660:

> Sir,—Loving respects to yourself and Mrs. Winthrop, &c. Your loving lines in this cold, dead season, were as a cup of your Connecticut cider, which we are glad to hear abounds with you, or of that western metheglin, which you and I have drunk at Bristol together, &c. Indeed it is the wonderful power and goodness of God, that we are preserved in our dispersions among these wild, barbarous wretches. . . .[60]

Although the Puritans limited the consumption of spirits by law, the limitation was to a quantity which, by one estimate, was two quarts of rum a week for every man, woman, and child in New England, not counting cider, beer, cordial, applejack, and metheglin.

Because there has been broadcast, now for two or three generations, so much nonsense about "Puritanism" and the Calvinism from which it derives, it may be valuable here to quote the Genevan himself on the use of the Things of the world:

> . . . the Scripture . . . fully instructs us in the right use of terrestrial blessings. . . . If we must live, we must also use the necessary supports of life; nor can we avoid even those things which appear to subserve our pleasures rather than our necessities. It behooves us, therefore, to observe moderation. . . . There have been some, in other respects good and holy men who . . . [have permitted] men to use corporal blessings no further than their necessity should absolutely require. This advice . . . committed the very dangerous error of imposing on the conscience stricter rules than those which are prescribed to it by the word of the Lord . . . according to them, it would be scarcely lawful to drink anything but bread and water. . . . On the contrary, many . . . who see a pretext to excuse intemperance in the use of external things . . . assume . . ., what I by no means concede . . ., that this liberty is not to be restricted by any limitation; but that it ought to be left to the conscience of every individual. . . . I grant, indeed, that it is neither right nor possible to bind the conscience with the fixed

and precise rules of law in this case; but since the Scripture de-
livers general rules for the lawful use of earthly things, our practice ought certainly to be regulated by them.

. . . the use of the gifts of God is not erroneous, when it is
directed to the same end for which the Creator himself has
created and appointed them for us. . . . Now if we consider
for what end he has created the various kinds of aliment, we
shall find that he intended to provide not only for our necessity,
but likewise for our pleasure and delight. . . . Shall the Lord
have endued flowers with such beauty, to present itself to our
eyes, with such sweetness of smell, to impress our sense of smell-
ing; and shall it be unlawful for our eyes to be affected with
the beautiful sight, or our olfactory nerves with the agreeable
odour? . . . In a word, has he not made many things worthy
of our estimation, independently of any necessary use?

Let us discard, therefore, the inhuman philosophy which . . .
not only malignantly deprives us of the lawful enjoyment of
the Divine beneficence, but which cannot be embraced till it
has despoiled man of all his senses, and reduced him to a senseless block. But, on the other hand, we must with equal diligence
oppose licentiousness of the flesh; which, unless it be rigidly
restrained, transgresses every bound . . . it will be one check
to it, if it be concluded, that all things are made for us, in order
that we may know and acknowledge their Author, and celebrate
his goodness to us by giving him thanks. What will become of
thanksgiving if you overcharge yourself with dainties or wine,
so as to be stupefied and rendered unfit for the duties of piety
and the business of your station? Where is any acknowledgement
of God, if your body, in consequence of excessive abundance,
being inflamed with the vilest passions, infects the mind with
its impurity, so that you cannot discern what is right or virtuous? Where is gratitude towards God for clothing, if on account of our sumptuous apparel, we admire ourselves and de-
spise others? if with the elegance and beauty of it, we prepare
ourselves for unchastity? . . .

. . . We should learn . . . to enjoy abundance with moderation. . . .[61]

Calvin's twin rule—first, to make use of all the things of this world,
and second, to use them moderately—was at the center of the Puritan
concept of morality. Nothing in itself, but anything in excess, was
forbidden. Moderate drinking and moderate profit in business were
both favored, but excess in either was condemned. Beauty was celebrated as the principle of order or harmony, in all human works, but
the Puritans looked dubiously on sensual material in art as tending

to the diversion of the imagination from the things of God. In the seventeenth century, England had, as we have seen, some thirty capital crimes; Massachusetts and Connecticut reduced them to twelve and rarely enforced the laws against any but murder, burglary, arson, and rape. Diligent research finds in two centuries no execution for fornication, and only three for adultery,[62] these exceptional cases arguing some kind of special unseemliness or hardship upon third parties. In the public records, it is sometimes pathetic to see the magistrates of Massachusetts and Connecticut trying to put an end to some illicit liaison in the interest of the general tone of the Holy Commonwealth, but without ever considering prosecution under the capital laws. Pre-martial fornication and pregnancy were condoned by confession and marriage, and in most places and periods they left no social stain. The authorities were always ready to "correct" or punish excessive sensuality, but they were equally opposed to excessive or unhealthy chastity. We noticed the report of a husband who was excommunicated from a congregation on his wife's complaint against him for continence, and of the Boston maiden who complained of "Platonick" love that it denied the normal "use" of love which was "Enjoyment."

Although most Puritans theoretically concerned themselves first with Faith, second with the rule of Moderation in conduct, and ignored the Covenant of Works, yet there were considerations that kept them precariously near the abyss of the latter. Orthodox from Calvin down was the doctrine that good works might be a "sign" of Grace, not a guarantee but an intimation, a condition on which the local Congregation should look favorably in making their guess whether an applicant was one of the Elected "saints." It was true that God by his inscrutable standard might damn the righteous and save the licentious, yet on the whole it was presumed that if you were in Grace you would be more disposed to serving Him than indulging in such "wastes of time" as, say, alcoholic or sexual excesses. And it is probable that this doctrine of Works as a Sign provided a stronger impulsion toward pious carriage than could any Fundamentalist promise of Heaven as a reward for a sufficient score in legal acts and abstentions. To keep on piling good deed on good deed, with no assurance that the column would ever be high enough, was a tedious business tending toward self-righteousness, neurosis or despair. But to know that even now you were once and for all either on or off the Great List of the Elect, that the problem was simply to find out which, and that every good work done in Faith was a "sign," that was to make good deeds a joy and morality a joyful standard. When you did a kindly work with your eye honestly on God or your neighbor, it was hard not to suspect in all humility that you were already one of the saints chosen to glorify the God of the Cosmos for ever and ever. This was a long way from moralism or "Puritanism"; but if Faith and true Puritanism should fail, perversion would be easy.

Equally precarious with the doctrine of Works as a Sign was that of works as a Preparation for Grace. Most of the preachers of early New England, following Thomas Hooker, recognized the value of works not as inducing Grace, but as Preparing the soul to recognize and receive Grace when it should come. It was chiefly on this ground that Anne Hutchinson condemned the Boston ministers for preaching in effect a Covenant of Works, and that she declared of Hooker that she "liked not his spirit." "An inn," preached Hooker, "must be prepared to receive the guest, else he will pass by to another lodging." And again, God "watcheth the time till your hearts be ready to receive and entertaine him."[63] Thomas Shepard, Hooker's son-in-law and successor in Cambridge, taught how the soul must learn to "lie like wax beneath the seal" as it waited for God.[64] "Doe what you are able to doe," said Hooker. "Put all your strength, and diligence unto it."[65] And Peter Bulkeley of Concord told his people frankly that if they came to God with confession, penitence and contrition, He would receive them into the Covenant of Grace—"Thus you see the way to enter into the Covenant with God."[66] One step beyond was the practical moralism of Solomon Stoddard of Northampton, grandfather of Jonathan Edwards, who preached that Works—among which for this purpose he included the sacrament of Communion—might be a *Means* to Grace. And one step beyond that was the straight doctrine of Arminianism and Works that the ministers, beginning in 1679, preached for twenty years in order to encourage the many indifferent and dissolute of that time to behave themselves and restore respectability to New England. "You may make a *Tryal*," said Cotton Mather, for, "Never, I am perswaded, never any Soul miscarried, that made such Applications."[67] This was almost the language of the original Jacobus Arminius, who had declared that God will not refuse any one who does what he can.

But in spite of the always prevalent doctrine of Preparation, and the easy slip from it into a straight doctrine of Works, the slip was not made by many, except in the brief period just referred to and in the double debacle of Victorianism and Fundamentalism after the Civil War when it was no longer meaningful to address a spiritless age in any terms but those of concrete rewards and punishments. The Puritans, and today the Yankees, have always felt contempt for a minister who scolded them and told them to stop drinking and gambling lest they go to hell. They have always had, and they have today, a suspicion that the real values of life lie in what a man thinks, not in what he does. If he thinks straight, and keeps his eye on the things he concludes, nobody needs to worry about what he will do.

V. *The End Rafters*

The Bedrock of Idealism underlying the Puritan House is of the general stuff of humanity. The Foundations were imported from all the great monotheisms. The Sills were cut and planed by the Christian fathers, with the final fitting done in New England. The Corner-posts were cut and planed by Calvin and the English Puritans, with a recutting and all the fitting done in New England.

There remain to be described the End Rafters and the Ridgepole. These also were planned in England, but they were not widely adopted there. Which is to say that they were cut in the rough there, but the final cutting, the planing and the fitting were done on the ground in New England after the rest of the frame was up. The first of them we shall notice became one of the peculiar features of American Puritan culture.

1) *Every man is as good as I am.*

This is the End Rafter of *Congregationalism,* which in due course became New England and American *Equalitarianism.* Of the Yankee's major qualities it is probably the one that is most nearly unique in the world. There are large elements of Equalitarianism in other great cultures, notably those of England and of France, but even today they are probably less deeply founded and more adulterated by self-assertive Individualism than is the case in the Puritan-Yankee-American tradition.

The theory of Congregational polity is extreme Separation from any established church order. Each congregation is entirely self-governing, free of the control of bishops or presbyters. The notion was current in sixteenth- and seventeenth-century English Puritan circles, but it was espoused by few, among them the Brownists from whom emerged the American Pilgrims. At the beginning of the principal settlement on Massachusetts Bay in 1630, the main body of the Puritans, possibly influenced by the Pilgrims, adopted this form of organization, and it became the seed of America. Subsequently, in 1633, Cotton and Hooker each brought in the doctrine on his own hook and made it authoritative.

The integration of each congregation was around a Church Covenant, a brief and dignified paragraph typified by that of the First Church of Boston wherein the signers agreed to "walke in all our wayes according to the Rule of the Gospell, & in all sincere Con-

formity to his holy Ordinances, & in mutuall love, & respect each
to other, so neere as God shall give us grace." It was a simple document, but it laid great responsibility on the signers. For each of
these "Saints," as they were called, in revival of the practice of the
early Christians, acknowledged himself and all the other subscribers
to be in the State of Grace, the state of selflessness in which their
Imaginations were the channels of the Will of God. It was the assumption of God's business, at least with respect to each other, a
tremendous assumption which imposed an equivalent humility.

Thus Equality was established on the deepest level that human
consciousness can reach, that level on which man was first evolved
in the Image of God and which, though it is deeply overlaid, still
sends up its currents and its tremors to trouble the surfaces. The
"Image of God" meant the possession of pure perception that could
see the essentials of all things and people. Thus the Puritan church-
members saw or "named" the world around them as Adam had done,
and each saw in the other this same clean, God-like perceptiveness
which was here and now of the stuff of timelessness or eternal life.
Within that community, that Communion of heavenly perception,
the state of sensed equality was virtually absolute. It was so profound that on its surfaces the usual differences between men—of
position, opportunity, even talent—were no more than matters of
administration. There was no paradox but simply a recognition of
God's division of labor in the Puritans' aristocratic assumption that
every job should be done by the one best qualified to do it. A similar
equalitarianism was in fact essential in the old codes of chivalry,
including that of the American Old South, though the living sense
of it under the codes was probably never as widely diffused among
all classes as it was in New England. America's earliest statement of
Equalitarianism was written by a Puritan who at the time of writing
was still an English aristocrat, on shipboard on his way to New
England, passionately anti-democratic, one whom our individualists
today would call a supreme "snob":

> . . . Noe man is made more honourable than another or more
> wealthy etc., out of any particular and singuler respect for him-
> selfe but for the glory of his Creator and the Common good of
> the Creature, Man. . . .[68]

And again, a more elaborate statement which our current persecutors
of intellectual and unintellectual minorities might read with interest:

> . . . Wee must be knitt together in this worke as one man, wee
> must entertaine each other in brotherly Affeccion, wee must
> be willing to abridge our selves of our superfluities, for the

supply of others necessities, we must uphold a familiar Commerce together in all meeknes, gentlenes, patience and liberality, wee must delight in eache other, make others Condicions our own rejoyce together, . . . allwayes haveing before our eyes our Commission and Community in the worke, our Community as members of the same body, soe shall we keepe the unitie of the spirit in the bond of peace. . . .[69]

Although the Puritans knew that no man in the flesh could be wholly in Grace, they yet proceeded as if all of the church members were, as if they were all qualified to expound the Bible and other evidences of God's will, in both ecclesiastical and secular matters. If the assumption were correct, God's will being always single, they should have had a unanimous vote on every question, and the wonder is not that they sometimes failed to get it but that they missed it so rarely and usually by such small margins. After sometimes acrimonious debate, they would proceed to a vote, normally "by erection of hands," in the belief that if the proposition was God's will and not that of unregenerate men, unanimity would be obtained. The theory was that as long as there was a single dissenting vote, something must be amiss. They had two ways of coping with disagreement. One was internal and preventive. The other was external and therapeutic.

The internal method depended on the aristocratic tradition. Proposals were first discussed and agreed upon among the leaders of the church, that is the minister and elders, who were usually men of learning and so of social standing to whom the less qualified tended to defer. In the meeting one of them propounded the carefully prepared proposal, which few if any of the lesser brethren had heard, and he and others of the elders explained it. Opposition was rare, and an act of social courage. Normally, when the "erection of hands" was called for, the unanimous vote was obtained. If the opposition was one or two, the matter was usually considered carried, but if it was large, though still a minority, determination was usually postponed to another day and further discussion and prayer.

Recourse was had to the "external" way of resolving controversy only when the split seemed irreconcilable, as when the leadership was itself divided. Then, after months of wrangling, either the minority or the majority would secede and move out to found a new church in the wilderness. Thus unanimity, the equality of all in the perception of God's will, would be restored to both parties. The expansion of New England in the seventeenth century was chiefly impelled by such schisms. As the Faith declined, in the eighteenth and nineteenth centuries, and the deep sense of equality was blurred by competitive individualism, rule by unanimity gave way to ma-

jority rule, power replaced perception. It is interesting that while
the Yankees have gradually abandoned what was in intention the
direct rule of God speaking through His Saints, their ancient Antinomian enemies the Quakers have maintained it with success to
the present time.

Congregational Equalitarianism has had its different developments in different sections. In Boston it was early qualified by the rule
of a powerful, dynastic aristocracy whose members, under the theory
of the Economic Virtues that wealth was a sign of Grace, became
approximately coextensive with the leadership of the churches. So
confirmed, and enjoying equality among themselves in the fashion
of the citizens of Athens, they proceeded, as the enfranchised
Athenians had done, to rule over a large and subject population.
Christian equalitarianism did not expand beyond the churches into
social equalitarianism in Boston, and in consequence the suffrage was
not extended beyond the Saints until a Royal order compelled it.
Yet the tendency toward general equality has tugged at Boston consciences down the generations. They were an aristocracy, but perhaps
the plainest aristocracy the world has known since Sparta, the one
most desperately driven by the necessity of lifting the lot of mankind,
and depressing their own lot a little—though not too inconveniently
much—to meet it. High intellectual standards combined with gray
styles and English diet to distinguish some of the world's richest
and most strongly entrenched families. Not a suffering human, beast,
fish or insect on the planet but must have an association founded
for its amelioration. And if anybody wanted an audience and publication for his dangerously radical ideas, let him look to the reactionaries of Beacon Hill.

All this in Boston was the work not of good equalitarianism but
of bad conscience for the denial of equality, not of tolerance but
of the theory that one ought to be tolerant. Just a little outside
Boston, however, in its own suburbs, and so down, out and up across
New England, the equalitarianism from an early date expanded
beyond the fellowship of the churches to include the community.
Not only did the Puritans tend to tolerate their neighbors in those
intermediate parts of the Puritan House where was the life of every
day, but they tended to protect, in terms of the fundamentals of the
foundation and the frame, heretics like Baptists and Quakers with
whom they agreed no more than did the central government that
was persecuting them. And as widely as the sense of human equality
expanded, so widely political equality tended to follow it. Wherefore, in the backwoods towns of Massachusetts, outside the arc of
The Bay, we find an actual local suffrage larger than that of the Saints,
irrespective of what the organic law of the Colony might prescribe.

It was at The River that equality from the beginning transcended the churches to include virtually everybody, becoming a generic feeling toward all men, a sense of universal Equality eventually independent of its religious origin; and as such it spread westward to characterize the nation. It is important always to distinguish it, being a function of selflessness or objectivity, from that self-exalting Individualism with which it is commonly confused. Philosophically, Individualism and Equality are equivalents, but in practice in our competitive society they become opposites. The common business man and common snob does not want his neighbor to be his equal but his inferior.

Similarly, Equalitarianism provides the best basis for Democracy, but the two concepts are not coextensive. The tendency of some of the leaders of early Connecticut to recognize wide limits of human equality was probably responsible for the extension of the suffrage beyond the church membership; but our modern democracy, which provides the rules for a battle royal for power between individualists, denies equality. In the eighteenth century the general equalitarian frame of society provided a check on both the religious individualism of the Great Awakening and the political individualism that was developing from Locke and Wise. The deadly competition which we have come to associate with democracy was not prevalent till well along in the nineteenth century when rapacity at the top and jealousy at the bottom were squeezing out the equalitarian instinct, and science was eliminating that religion from which equality must from time to time be renewed. Our interest here is not in democratic institutions for their own sake, and our concern with individualism is only as a force inimical to the culture we are describing. Our interest here is with that Yankee Equality which derives from Puritanism, which retains a kind of social mysticism even after it is divorced from religion, and without which it is unlikely that democracy and the nation can survive.

The sense of equality in a society probably depends upon the entertainment by its members of a common idea so inclusive as to engulf the competitive instincts, so lofty as to keep all persons in the same state of humility in contemplation of it, while enjoying at the same time a satisfying self-expansion in identification with it. Such equalitarianism as the British enjoy is based in their idea of Royalty, enriched by the artifices of pageantry and enlarged by the fictions of royal sovereignty and imperial power. The French retain traces of equalitarianism that originally derived from the high principles of their Revolution.

New England Equalitarianism was founded in an idea deeper, stronger and more inclusive than either of these, the idea of God before whom each individual lies in "brokenness of heart," nothingness, and around this nothingness a sense of light and Glory. In the first half of the nineteenth century, as this idea failed, it was replaced by the millennial concept of the Union as the hope of mankind, and this flourished in Greater New England for two generations before the Civil War and has its remnants today, especially among freedom-struck immigrants. But at the very time when this idea was containing the Yankees in equality and perceptiveness during their great creative period, it was already being undermined by the competitive idea that was reconceiving freedom and the American utopia in the image of blind and unperceptive power. By the end of the century this materialistic and idea-less idea had replaced both that of God and that of Utopia, and any surviving equalitarianism would seem to have been without living roots.

But in such detachment Yankee Equalitarianism does survive in every little town across the continent and in every Yankee who went to the city from the little town. When it was already beginning to be a quality in itself, without any surviving ideational envelope, both Emerson and Theodore Parker described it in the same un-Christian and un-Utopian terms, each independently and apparently without knowledge of the other's expression. Both said in effect that it is less important for a young man to know that he is as good as every man than it is for him to know that every man is as good as he is. This is the subconscious assumption of every Yankee today. Upon that base, his own security, his own equal standing with all men, is so profound that nothing can greatly disturb it. If a braggart goes about confessing his lack of self-reliance by asserting it, the Yankee is faintly troubled for him, but consciously he is amused, and a touch of salty sarcasm is called for. When a person is deferring overly, is abasing himself or fawning, the social violation is more extreme. Confronted by such behavior, whether false or sincere, the Yankee is simply embarrassed and wants to get away. He is contemptuous of swagger but he understands it, for he used to swagger himself when he was a boy. But self-effacement below the dignified level of absolute equality seems unhealthy and is beyond his comprehension. Perhaps he feels as a Puritan would have felt if someone, professing Christian belief, yet held himself so low that even with Christ's help he could not be lifted into Grace.

Materialistic historians can of course supply an economic base for Yankee equalitarianism. To be sure, it was buttressed by the economy of small farming, by approximate equality in wealth, and by the ingrowing, neighborly society of township and village. But it was not inaugurated by these economic and social factors, was never chiefly dependent on them, and today survives them. However, we may well doubt whether this major characteristic can last forever without either its religious foundation or these practical props. Perhaps more strongly than any other feature of the Puritan House, it has survived the materialist change, not only within the proper Yankee culture but even within the pseudo-culture of the cities and the banks and the corporations. The wealthy industrialist of Yankee background, equally with the Yankee farmer, knows deeply and inarticulately that every man is as good as he is. Alike they are amused at the fool who tries to patronize them. Alike they are embarrassed by the simpleton who defers to them. Together they have something precious in common that might yet contribute to the rebuilding of the world.

2) *The less said the better.*

This is the end rafter of forensic and literary theory called the *Plain Style* which adjoins the end rafter of Equality and with its help eventually becomes Yankee taciturnity and *Humor*. Though the substance of the writing and sermonizing of the Puritan was typically intricate and "painful," they yet aimed to present it with a direct simplicity in distinction from the colorful method of the Anglican divines. "God's Altar needs none of our polishing" was a fair statement of literary theory by Richard Mather in his *Preface* to the *Bay Psalm Book*. To be sure, the Plain Style of the New England ministers incorporated plenty of figures of speech, but they were of a homely rather than an ornamental nature, and tended rather toward prosaic illustration than the incisiveness of poetry. Here John Cotton is distinguishing a hypocrite from a saint:

> —When two men walk together, a dog follows them, you know not whose it is, but let them part, then the dog will follow his Master.[70]

And here is Hooker on the body that will rise at the last trump:

> Take a great Onyon, and hang it up in the house, and it will grow bigger and bigger: what is the cause of it? not because any thing is added, but because it spreads itself further; so then there shall be no new body, but the substance enlarged and increased.[71]

It may be that out of this clerical theory and practice of plain, homely, prosaic and incredibly humorless expression a similar habit of literal, direct and concise expression developed in the habit of common speech. It was this habit of simple and humorless statement, whatever its source, that in the eighteenth century emerged as that packed understatement which paradoxically we know as Yankee humor. At its best it is unintentional, being a simple, factual statement that is funny because, being true, it is incongruous with other facts upon which it is a comment. As the political candidate ranted his principles before a village meeting, a Yankee farmer who was deaf leaned to his neighbor and whispered, "What's that feller talkin' about?" And his neighbor leaned back and whispered the plain truth, "He don't say."

Yankee Humor was the child of the *Plain Style,* and its other parent was that Equalitarianism which consisted in a mutual nothingness before God. Not only had the Individual overcome the Original Sin that wanted to assert itself, but he was surrounded by other individuals who likewise had lost their selves and were likewise committed to a life without any self-assertion. The tacit understanding among them was, in the vernacular, that none of them would "show off." Each, in return for his not showing off, would be protected from the distress of hearing anyone else do the same. Hence Puritan, and presently Yankee, society was characterized by a great chariness of speech, a terror of loquacity, a general personal reticence wrapped around an inward observatory minutely and passionately watching the truth and falsehood in the outer sky. Wherefore, when comment did emerge it was as driven by irresistible necessity to name the truth in contrast to the current appearance. And under such impulsion out of such restriction, it must be consummately succinct, packed and apt. Indeed, until he is overwhelmed by such necessity the Yankee, today as always, does not speak at all. The taciturnity, to be sure, is characteristic of many country people. But the explosive and accurate statement of truth, the unintended irony and humor, characterizes no numerous people of Western culture except the Yankees.

3) *Look at any question from both sides.*

This is the end rafter of *Ramist Logic,* a balanced system which the Puritans, especially the American Puritans, took over from the "French Plato," Petrus Ramus, who was killed on St. Bartholomew's Eve. It lacks the flavor of Puritanism on several scores, and represents the strong classical disposition of the Puritans which had them in several contradictions, though no essential ones. From the central Puritan point of view, the Ramian system was false, or at least shallow, because it did not depend on the possession of that Right Reason which came only with Grace. The Ramian Logic, subject to certain cautions, could be applied by the mere Natural Reason of an unregenerate mind, because even in Reprobation and ruin the mind of man closely corresponds to the entirely logical structure of the world. Petrus Ramus understood this structure in full detail, and set it out in a kind of blueprint of the universe from which any intelligent sinner, if he would read the instructions, could figure out the answer to any problem whatsoever.[72]

What of Ramus is of surviving interest is not his chart of the universe, but his and the Puritans' way of using one part of it. He arranged many of his "principles of art" in dichotomies or pairs of opposites by means of which any proposition at all could be tested by simple common sense. The facts always fitted one of the pairs of opposites and not the other. This method was *Ramian Logic*, though there was in it nothing of the systematic discipline that we associate either with the syllogism of Aristotle or with scientific or inductive reason. It was no more than a harnessing of aesthetic, imaginative or idealistic perception within convenient limits. By dividing a problem into successive pairs of opposites, it was possible to "prove" anything at all. In his *The First Principles*,[73] the Reverend James Fitch of Norwich, Connecticut, took up the eternal question of whether the world was created or eternal, a question which Aristotelian logic had never entirely resolved. But for Mr. Fitch and Ramian logic, the solution was easy. Either the world was created or it was not. If it was not created, then there is neither cause of its existence, nor any design or purpose in it. But these conditions are palpably absurd to common sense. Wherefore, the world was created. Furthermore, it was either made by God or it made itself. But the second condition is absurd. Wherefore, it is "proven" that God made the world.

Such was the convenient "logick" commonly used by the Puritan ministers throughout the seventeenth century. It is perhaps worth observing also that such became the rhetoric—the convenient alternative rhetorical question—of nineteenth-century oratory. Is the Federal Government, demanded Webster in his reply to Hayne, "the creature of the state legislatures or the creature of the people?" If it is the creature of the states it is "the servant of four-and-twenty masters," which is an absurdity. Wherefore, it is the creature and servant of the people. In the "house divided" speech, Lincoln declared that the country must presently be "all slave" or "all free," and to his listeners the dichotomy was just and its solution plain.

And so the intuitive and *a priori* "logick" of the "French Plato" of the sixteenth century comes down as an instinctive method of thought of the modern Yankee. The matter is black or white. The universe exists or it does not. Common sense, the mind of unregenerate man, still corresponds to the mind of God and so provides the answer. The method, as we observed earlier, is un-Puritanical in that it uses Natural or Carnal Reason, rather than the Right Reason which is true Imaginative Perception; and it does this because it is of humanist rather than Calvinist derivation. We may observe further that it does not conform to the habit of paradox that typifies the Puritan system, and this for the same humanist or classical reason. Consequently, though Ramian logic is common in Puritan sermons, it is probably not characteristic of the great and penetrating passages. Similarly with our contemporary Yankee, he will use the balanced method in ordinary thinking, as a kind of formula of broad-mindedness, yet we may suspect that in the greater problems of his central idealism he will wait, as his forebears did, for the unsystematized light.

4) *America will come through.*

This optimistic fourth end rafter is that of Millennialism. With the Puritans it was of two varieties, mutually congenial, the one realistic and qualified, the other unrealistic and unqualified. The realistic Millennialism was that of some of the English Puritan peers—especially Lord Saye and Sele and Lord Brooke the Earl of Lincoln—who proposed to prepare a new England, a place to which a saving remnant, including themselves, might retire if they were defeated in the increasingly hot war with the King for power and with the Archbishop of Canterbury for a "purer" church. To this end they supported the Massachusetts Bay Company, and to this end they sent over John Winthrop the younger to prepare a plantation specifically for them, which he duly did at the mouth of the Connecticut River, naming it Saybrook after them.

The unrealistic New England Millennialism was that of the bulk of those who actually took up their roots and emigrated westward into the cold and the dark. With them the interest was not in some line to fall back upon in the future. It was in a retreat now to a new England, in company with others like-minded, an opportunity to be one of a selected group—very possibly a group elected to this consummation from all eternity—who in appreciable numbers were to carry a mutually agreed definition of perfection to an unblemished country and there to consecrate every energy to the possibility—if ever there were such a possibility—of realizing that perfection on earth. New England was to become *the* Holy Commonwealth, the Kingdom of God,[74] "the place where the Lord will create a new Heaven, and a new Earth,"[75] where the New Jerusalem would descend presently, as prophesied in *Revelations.* Said Jonathan Mitchell in 1662, "The Latter Erecting of Christs *Kingdom* in whole *Societies* . . . was our Design, and our Interest in This Country. . . ."[76] American Puritans, or many of them, identified themselves with the Children of Israel who were driven into the wilderness to find the Promised Land where Christ would set up his Kingly Office and the Cosmic Drama would merge into eternity. It was part of this prospect that all the inhabitants would become saints and the state would wither away into "Holy Anarchy" that would need no government. When we find the magistrates and ministers impatient with the licentiousness of their lower classes, it is well to remember that they had their eye on the holy prospect with which godlessness and self-indulgence comported badly.

This Millennialism which was general in early New England and did not lose its original zest until the decadence after 1676, revived again in the eighteenth century, and grew particularly strong in the nineteenth, both in sects of which the Millerites were the most numerous, and in the utopianism that had no doubt that the Federal Union was going to be the first perfect government on earth and the haven of mankind. Remnants of it lurk in the Yankee mind today, in the form of uncompromising confidence in America, and probably in the characteristic American Optimism which knows no obstacle too great to be overcome.

VI. *The Ridgepole*
Believe Something.

This last important member of the frame of the Puritan House was, in Puritan language, the *Federal Theology,* the theology of the Confederation, Contract or *Covenant of Grace.* Like the rafters which it binds together, it was conceived, planned and cut in England, but was in all respects finished and fitted in America. All five of these members supporting the roof were controversial and not generally adopted among English Puritans. But, so far as appears, the divines of New England were to a man Congregationalists, Plain Stylers, Ramists, Millenarians and—professing the Federal theology of the Covenant of Grace—Federalists.

The whole concept of the Covenant or Contract is to us ridiculous and amusing, with its application to religion of the vocabulary of mercantilism, its frequent mention of the receipt of Grace as "closing with Christ," its notion of getting God's enforceable signature and seal—supplied by the Bible—on His bond to save those who do as he requires. But to at least the great cornerposts of Protestantism, the Word of God, and Salvation by Faith not Works, it added strengthening amendments, and, binding together the rafters and so the roof, it provided for the more fundamental members of the frame a practical protection against the outer world and weather. It provided a systematic method for individualistic religion. It specified what of the Bible should be studied and grasped. It suited and integrated in application the Puritan intellectual approach, the identification of Grace with Imagination, and of Salvation with the maintenance of a mental posture. Especially, it provided at least partial answers to the main complaints against Puritanism by both of the major heresies: the complaint of the Antinomians that the Orthodoxy gave no assurance of Election, leaving everyone to toss in anxiety all his days; the complaint of the Arminians that it guaranteed no human justice to one who might struggle to gain moral perfection, for even if he succeeded he still might fail to attain Grace and so would be damned.

In the Covenant of Grace God very nearly met both of these objections by committing Himself of His own free will—thus saving His omnipotence and omniscience—to redeem individuals upon certain stated and comprehensible conditions. It appeared that He had made the commitment by His Covenant with Abraham, duly engrossed in the Seventeenth Chapter of *Genesis,* and variously in *Deuteronomy.* There God promised to give the land of Canaan to Abraham and his children forever upon condition that they "be perfect" with Him, and the "perfection" required was that they *believe* that God would do as He promised. The *Covenant of Grace* translated the promise to Abraham forward into the conditions of the Christian Atonement. By the Fall men had disqualified themselves to fulfil the Covenant of Works under which God had planned that they should enjoy eternal life. By the Atonement God "paid the debt" and gave them another chance whose condition was psychological rather than moral. As Abraham had been required, as the condition of the Covenant, to believe in a *future* act of God, all that was required after the Atonement was that one believe in a *past* act of God. Whoever merely understood and believed in the Divinity of Christ, the Crucifixion, the Resurrection and thereby the Atonement of every man's Original Sin of self-concern, that person was thereby psychologically identified with Christ's sacrifice, which was thereupon Imputed to him, so that he was forthwith the recipient of Justification, Grace and Faith. The condition was clear, and the promise was certain. Belief became in effect a Work, of all Works the most unmistakable sign of Grace.

The Covenant of Grace was a fair answer to the Antinomians. They had never asked human justice of God, but they had asked some means by which a person who was Justified could be assured of it. In the pursuit of their heresy they accepted as assurance anybody's private emotional assurance, though these experiences were always unique, usually extraordinary beyond intelligent analysis, and sometimes socially dangerous. The requirement of mere Belief very nearly solved their problem. It was as private and authentic as an emotional Experience; indeed it usually was an emotional experience. Although Belief was an orderly, intellectual standard, it was a standard which any minister and his congregation could administer without questioning or tampering with private experience or invoking special standards of their own. No complicated theology was called for. A simple condition for assurance of Grace and admission to the company of the Saints was provided for any sincere Christian. It is perhaps worth observing that Jonathan Edwards eschewed the Covenant of Grace and returned to stark Predestination, and that the Great Awakening of the eighteenth century, occurring in large part under his preaching up and down the Connecticut Valley, was the first numerous outbreak of Antinomianism in New England.

The Arminian Heresy was less certainly satisfied by the Covenant of Grace. To be sure, Belief as a condition of Salvation was to any Calvinist mind a fair requirement. Also, the doctrine made it eloquently clear that by Belief you had God firmly caught by His own bond from which He could by no subterfuge escape! Furthermore, many of the ministers reduced the profession of Belief to a form with which any hypocrite could comply. By the end of the seventeenth century some were proclaiming that merely to be in a community where it was possible to hear the Word of God preached every Sunday was an offer of Grace which left everything else up to the individual's wishes. The second-rate ministers did their little best to blow away the last filmy mists of Predestination from the will to be saved. Yet the awful truth remained that God could bestow Belief on whom he would, and withhold it from whom he would. However a man might "try," he might still fail of the rewards due him by human Justice. It is perhaps significant that there was always a strong Arminian minority in New England, whereas the only impressive Antinomianism was that of the Great Awakening when the Covenant of Grace was for the moment laid by.

It is possible, though far from certain, that the search for honest Belief caused more anguish of soul than the mere search for a convincing and unspecified Religious Experience. But a greater danger of the Covenant of Grace was probably in its intellectuality, its tendency to identify casual and facile Belief with the great and overwhelming event of Faith. This cool possibility may have eased the drift into the Age of Graceless Natural Reason, the Enlightenment, of the eighteenth century. On the other hand the Covenant provided a door to Grace and Faith for many who might otherwise not have found one.

In our typical Yankee's irreligious system there is an equivalent danger of over-intellectuality. Instinctively he knows the difference between the Perception of Grace—what he calls the sun breaking through a cloud—and mere Opinions on a number of things. Yet his religious training does not emphasize the necessity of Imaginative rather than Rational Perception, and his Central Idea or bundle of notions may rest precariously in the latter. We can only conjecture that such a Yankee is rare, that in our typical farmer the criterion of a "Belief" is, like that of his Puritan forebears, that it be not simply known with his mind but *felt* like a secret glow.

VII. *The Chimney*

Enjoy yourself, but not too much. Think, but not all the time.

The great stone chimney with its capacious kitchen fireplace is the center of the house, and without it the householder would have neither heat, cooking nor light. It is in fact the reason for the house, the living fire around which the rest is a shelter against the weather, the Christian life around which the frame we have been examining is for the most part doctrine, rationalization, reduction of the living principle to comprehensible application and rule. In the chimney we see graphically enacted the crux of the Puritan's Cosmic Drama, of the drama of his Culture, and of himself individually. We said earlier that this central structure itself, rising out of the Bedrock of Idealism, is the Puritan Aspiration toward Truth. Now we see also the fire in it as the Faith or Love that rises through the self to vanish upward and outward into God's selfless and placeless firmament. The light that the fire throws on the utensils and furniture in the room is Right Reason or Imagination. The draft of the fire depends on a mystery, a secret ratio between the size of the flue and the amount of fuel, which only the mason knows. Wherefore, the mason is God, and His building of the central core of the chimney through Love and without pay was the Atonement. In the beginning, also, He was the only man in town who had a reliable flint and steel. As He was very busy and His appearance unpredictable and usually inconvenient to the householder, His lighting of the fire was the touch of Grace, both Free on His part and Compulsive upon the recipient. Before His coming, the care of the latter to keep the fire laid and ready for him was the practice of Preparative Works.

Once the fire is lighted by Grace, the significant thing about the ensuing flame of Faith is, as we have seen, its power of the imagination, in the Image or likeness of God, to perceive or name the essence of things. And this power to perceive the reality of separate things is also the power to perceive the generic Order, the Beauty or "Excellence," which is necessary to the integration and existence of them together. Here is Miller's paraphrase of Edwards' aesthetic, combined from the *Religious Affections* and the unpublished "Notes":

Scatter a few dots or lines on a paper: there is no 'good' to be
found in them; then group them into symmetrical patterns or
designs, and immediately the mind recognizes a pleasure . . .,
a disinterested joy in the 'equality' of the arrangement. The dots
or lines, like stones in an arch or sounds in a melody, remain
what they were, but the mind is so constructed that . . . it perceives things in systems of order, in time and space, in proportion and law. The mind perceives and is pleased with beauty no
less because it has itself bestowed that beauty upon things
which in themselves are neither beautiful nor ugly.[77]

Here there is a new observation, namely that the "equality," the
excellence or beauty, of the arrangement is not in the "dots and
lines" themselves, but is "bestowed" upon them by the perception
of the Imagination* in the State of Grace. The objects perceived
do, according to Edwards, have an extraneous existence which is reported into the mind by the senses. But it is the Gracious Imagination which, with an emotion or "joy" which Edwards generally called
"the sense of the heart," sends back Beauty upon them—"Beauty
properly denotes the Perception of some Mind."[78] And as this
Beauty, this Order, is the reality of things—Hooker's "things as
they be"—it follows that the Regenerate Imagination, being freed of
Sin or Self, creates by perception, gives form, "a local habitation
and a name," to the things, the concentrations of waves, that the
senses intimate in the world around it.

And as man creates what he sees, so God's perception is the faculty
or Attribute of Him by means of which He Creates everything in
the Cosmos. Separate waves or particles—some mathematicians today call them "wavicles"—may give what Edwards called "consent"
to being such as they are. But for their concentrations into things
they require the act of an extraneous mind to perceive them:

> Particles can consent to being this or that individual particle,
> . . . [but they] call upon God as the ultimate beholder to give
> them significance by perceiving them.[79]

And this significance, cast upon things by God's perception, and
recast upon them by the human Imagination with its accompanying
"sense of the heart," is the ultimate and single beauty or reality of
all Being.

* It is perhaps desirable to point out again what was noted earlier, that "Imagination" is used in this book to signify the faculty that perceives the reality
behind appearances. Edwards habitually uses it in the other accredited sense to
mean the faculty that conjures unreal fragments. With the authority of Shakespeare, Coleridge and others, and because I used it so in my treatise on poetry, I
am holding to the first meaning, while deploring any confusion that might arise
from a comparison of this text with Edwards'.

. . . Unless this is seen, nothing is seen that is worth the seeing; for there is no other true excellency or beauty. . . . This is the beauty of the Godhead, and the divinity of divinity . . ., the good of the infinite fountain of good; without which, God himself (if that were possible) would be an infinite evil; without which we ourselves had better never have been; without which there had better have been no being.[80]

Thus religious people from the beginning of history have attributed creative Imagination to the Control of the Cosmos, and have asserted that Attribute of God to be *the* one He assigned to man in making him in His Image. Thus they lay themselves open to the light charge of anthropomorphism, the comfortable charge by means of which materialists excuse themselves from the tiresome exercise of considering God, dismissing him with the proposition that if He exists He must be grand beyond condescending to share any qualities with His little creatures. They do not consider that it might seem more likely, even to materialistic or Natural Reason, that all things or concentrations of waves within Being share something, or everything, with the central Meaning of Being. It is of course unlikely that man created that Meaning, that God. But that Meaning surely created or evolved man and gave him all his qualities, all presumably drawn from the qualities or characters of the Meaning Itself. God is not anthropomorphic, but it is hard to conceive man or any other creature as other than deimorphic. Among the qualities that the Cosmos evolved in us, it happens that the Imagination—however widely it may be shared by other creatures, organic or inorganic—is the quality we specialize in. Although neither we nor any other creatures possess any quality which is not an image in God's mind, yet we think of this one as special, as *the* Image of God. This faculty, even more than consciousness, even more than life, we associate with the mystery of motion that seems to be general in Being. What this whole motion of God is we do not know. But we think it contains this small stir of ours, this immaterial flashing from here to there, from me to you, this blown flame from the most inward subjectivity sweeping out into the most outward love and objectivity, this wind of light pouring into creative identification with all particulars, this volcanic self curving up and away into selflessness, this fire of Faith rising in the chimney of Aspiration, this shine on all things, this warmth, this convincing semblance of existence, this "Excellency," this "sense of the heart." We do not say it is God, but we do presume that He contains it, and that we have it from Him.

This Imaginative Perception which is Grace and Faith, this fire in the chimney of the Puritan House, is in all respects precisely the "creative imagination" of the artist. Just as the original lighting of the fire by Grace came from an external force, unpredictable, arbitrary, compulsive, subject perhaps to Predestination or concurrence of cosmic forces, so it is the common experience of artists that the final and illuminating "inspiration" to a composition comes unforeseeably, often at inconvenient moments, as a seemingly intrusive and irresistible force from without themselves, traditionally associated with the whisper of their alter ego, their "genius."

Again, as most Puritans believed that "Works," the laying of the fire for lighting, while they could in no sense induce Grace, yet were a valuable "Preparation" for the receipt of the spirit when it came, so artists suppose that their general training, and their specific "spade work" such as preliminary studies and sketches, while they will in no case accomplish the real work, may yet be indispensable to its final perception and transcription.

Again, that Right Reason which with the Puritan is the shining of the general illumination of Faith upon particular objects in the room, is the artist's application of his general sense of Form to particular details, integrating them as they have to be into the whole. Generally, as a condition of Grace and the lighting of the fire of Faith is "brokenness of heart," the humbling of the spirit, the loss of the soul to find it, so the artist, in proportion that his perception is effective, is objectified in his material, is outside himself and has no self. And it may be added that just as a work of art may be uneven, showing true perception in some parts or aspects and mere rationalized "works" or undisciplined emotion in others, so Grace also may be partial, transitory, momentarily had and lost, the fire of Faith burning but imperfectly or only for the clairvoyant moment.

Finally, the identity between Puritanism and art, and perhaps the central quality of both, is contained within the mystery we noticed in the construction of the chimney, the secret relation of the size of the flue to the amount of Fuel to be burned in the fireplace, a relation which only the mason God knows and on which the draft of the fire depends. It was never reduced to a doctrine, for it could not be. But it was implicit in all doctrine and in all living. It is what the Yankee meant in the last entry in his Credo, unconsciously describing the chimney of the house: *Enjoy yourself, but not too much. Think, but not all the time.*

This is an expression of that Puritan *Moderation* which we observed in connection with Calvin's doctrine of the proper "use" of the things of the world. It can be taken as a principle of unilateral denial of excess in any particular "use" or category of experience, a kind of Holy Mean. But more subtly, and especially in fundamental matters, the Mean was less like a medial point, a kind of normal in the thermometer of any given kind of experience, than it was a balance between two contrasting kinds of experience, both positive, not so much a Holy Mean as a *Holy Ratio*. Our Yankee is not so much concerned about being moderate in his fun, and also moderate in his submission to the discipline of thought or reason, as he is in striking a balance between them, a mixture of freedom and discipline in precisely the right ratio. And this Ratio at bottom is between the Self-indulgence of Emotion, what in theological terms we saw as the heresy of Antinomianism, and the Self-indulgence of Reason, what in theological terms we saw as the heresy of Arminianism.

In the great chimney the flue is Reason, Natural Reason, and the fuel of the fire is Emotion. If God in His construction had made the flue and its throat too large, or if the householder had not piled in enough fuel, then the flames and the heat would all go up the chimney; there would not be enough fire to warm, feed and light the family who would be put to continuous tense, self-concerned calculation just to maintain life. On the other hand, if He had made the flue or the throat too small, or if the householder piled in too much fuel, then the fire wouldn't draw but would smoke and flame out into the kitchen and blind everybody; again the family would creep around in an anxious, self-centered existence, and they would be lucky if the house didn't burn down around them. But since God adjusted the flue to the fuel by the mysterious rule of moderation, the Holy Ratio, the householder needs only to keep a normal fire and it will warm the kitchen and send heat to spare into any other rooms that may be in use, will cook for the family and light the kitchen with a glow on beams and benches and table, on copper and pewter and iron utensils, throwing them into proper relief and clarifying the use and meaning of each. The fire as it rises in the chimney is contained by the discipline of the flue, and it originates in the heat from the fuel, but it is not either. It is a wholly separate experience, a special kind of perception and application of the perception in experience.

The effort to strike the Holy Ratio, Moderation, the way of the Cosmos, the Will of God, in every aspect of living was the whole concern of the Puritans. They frowned on excessive sensuality, whether in or out of marriage, but they frowned equally upon celibacy or unnatural continence. They encouraged the normal use of wine, but held drunkenness to be "of the devil"—defining drunkenness, incidentally, as the inability to walk. They frowned upon a monastic abstinence from self-interest in the affairs of the world, but they punished acts of cupidity that exceeded conscience or the current norm of profit-taking. They encouraged creative art and exemplified the principle of beauty in everything they made, but they discouraged salacious art that invited attention to the self and away from the principle of beauty or "Excellency" as embodied by the perceptive Will of God in all aspects of Being.[81] Taking into account that their over-celebrated bigotry and persecution were not in themselves excessive for their time, it is noticeable that their intolerance of religion was precisely of what seemed to them extreme. They excluded the early Quakers and Baptists because they were obviously guilty of the Error of excessive Emotion or Antinomianism. They excluded the Anglicans and Roman Catholics because they were just as obviously guilty of the Error of excessive Reason or Arminianism. They tolerated the Quakers and the Baptists as soon as they had soothed their rages down to a normal tenor. They continued to exclude the Romans and—if they had not been compelled otherwise—would have continued to exclude the Anglicans, because they failed to make an equal and opposite move out of rationality toward Moderation.

In the seventeenth century of violent religious controversy, the Puritans were the Liberals. The Anglicans, tending more and more into Reason or Arminianism, more and more back toward an authoritarianism like that of Rome, were the Conservatives. At the other limit, professing their Emotional or Antinomian-like doctrine of direct communication by God with each individual, the Quakers, Ranters, Levellers and the like were the Radicals. Between these walked the Puritans, trying to extract and to reconcile what was true in each of the others, and to avoid what in each was extreme, immoderate, self-asserting and evil. In America they hoped to be free of harassment from either the Right or the Left. If ever the Protestant ideal of giving every man the learning and discipline to be "his own priest" could be realized, it would have a chance in this Holy Commonwealth, established by a qualified and homogeneous group, in a new and clean country.

As the guide of each Puritan's life was the hope of Grace and Faith, so the central and sustaining expression of the Holy Ratio between Reason and Emotion was not in doctrine but in personal religious experience. In a mysterious mixture of these irreconcilable elements, the true fire of Puritan Faith burned. Ministers were warned not to "raise the affections without informing the mind," lest they perform "a fruitlesse unprofitable labour" which "serves but to make zeal without knowledge."[82] A "sudden Blaze of thought, tho' never so bright, will not lay open the hidden Mysteries of divine Things to our View, unless the Mind be brought by Meditation to an holy Pause upon them."[83] Cotton said that while "knowledge is no knowledge without zeal," yet "zeale is but a wilde-fire without knowledge."[84] And conversely, Edwards had it that, while heat without light is not "heavenly," yet "where there is . . . light without heat . . . there can be nothing divine in that light."[85] The memorable part of Edwards' life was as a "theologian of mediation," devoted to fighting some of his Antinomian followers with one hand and the Arminians with the other. "More deeply passionate than Davenport and more finely intelligent than Chauncey, he was accused by the one of being too intellectual and by the other with being too emotional."[86]

Like every true artist, every true Puritan was engaged throughout his life in both resisting and inviting both Reason and Emotion, in seeking the quiet sense of perfection, the Holy Ratio, Edwards' Sense of the Heart, which all recognize when it comes but which is dissipated by the effort to capture it and hold it in formula. As Coleridge said that poetry depends upon unusually strong emotion held within unusually strong discipline, so in the near background of the experience of Grace there must be both an irresistible demand of passion and an orderly and immovable frame of thought. The contents of the perceptions of Poetry and of Religion may differ, but in each case the manner of perception is, so far as man can know, the creative method of Being and is single and uniform. In both religion and art it is the feeling of looking afresh upon renewed and uncomplicated Creation, a wide and quiet country of understanding that is beyond any stir of doubt or question, and beyond any emotion but the still memory of it, a country of light wherein "the appearance of every thing" is "altered" under a "calm, sweet cast, or appearance of divine glory," a light that is "the beginning of the light of heaven." This is the country of the Holy Ratio wherein the Puritans, out of the close Reason of the Schools and the free Emotion of Anne Hutchinson, were able to distil the Sense of the Heart, the ability to perceive, and so to create, the quiet relation of things that is as close as men have approached to understanding of the intention of God. This Holy Ratio was the condition of the fire in the central chimney of the Puritan House, the fire of Faith that for two centuries warmed and lighted a culture until in the nineteenth century, under the impulse of too much Reason, too much Intellectual Arminianism, the chimney was rebuilt and enlarged without consulting God. No one has yet built a fire large enough to throw heat into the room. The house begins to have the chill of a tomb.

But still today the sense of balance between the extremities of reason and emotion is the mentor of every Yankee from Vermont to Oregon. In perfecting his Central Idea, or bundle of ideas, that he must have to live, he follows the principle of neither cogitating himself into blankness nor running off after the latest hot notion that comes along. He knows that there is a quiet kind of electricity that holds the stars and the seasons in balance, and it is neither too violent nor too calm. A man who lives by his whims is a fool, but a man who has a system for licking the chances of life and the weather is a worse one. The Yankee has compassion alike for the drunk and the prohibitionist, for he knows they are both damned.

With the consideration of the Chimney and its Holy Ratio of Moderation, we end our description of the main parts of the Puritan House which are still the foundation and sustaining framework of our average Yankee's Central Idea. In the beginning this frame that today supports and protects some forty million Yankees was both a Religious System and a Psychological System for daily living. In fact, for men who lived primarily in the Cosmos and the Imaginative Predicament, instead of on the planet and in the physical predicament, there was no difference between the religious and the psychological system. Today only the psychological system survives, and it is not as strong as when it was consciously identical with the secret working of the Cosmos. We cannot be certain that without the full understanding of the Imagination, without the support of all the mental faculties that man once exercised, the psychological system will be able to stand indefinitely against increasing, self-centering individualism which, of course, can lead nowhere but back into tyranny and the end of this cycle of history. Meanwhile, there are those optimists who claim to see signs of weakening both of Individualism and of the Materialism on which it depends, with a trend back toward Equalitarianism and that interest in things and people outside the self which is essential to Religion and a fully living humanity.

If America does enjoy a revival of human potentials, the new way will of course change the names of all the main members of the Puritan House, as it will build new outside and inside finishings. It is neither possible nor desirable that the nation should move back into the whole House of Winthrop and Hooker, Edwards and Hopkins, Channing and Finney. Yet the substance of the old foundation and of the frame were for all mankind and for all foreseeable time. The names will change, but the actual stones, the sills and the cornerposts, will be the same. It should be helpful to us in approaching the matter of their new nomenclature, the vocabulary of a new theology, to familiarize ourselves with the old nomenclature and vocabulary, which are the only ones the nation has known. Surely

there can be no harm in reminding ourselves that there was a time
in this country when men put the large things before the small,
when the mystery of existence and the things of the universe were
taken more seriously than the perquisites, comforts and span of the
life of the individual's body, when cosmic truth was put above every
other truth, the Rights of God above even Civil Rights, even the
Rights of Man. There can be no harm in reminding ourselves of
that, if only to help us descend from our debunked exoticism and
for a starting point to set foot on the rocks of our tradition. It is not
helpful to presume sentimentally that our ancestors were paragons
and all other persons scoundrels. But it is important to know that
they did have a complex, precise and well integrated system of living
which gave very many of them—as human affairs go—wisdom, con-
secration, assurance and secret satisfaction to stand against greater
hardships than we latterly have so far known. There can be little
harm in inquiring into the reality, the secret strength of their large
and inclusive Central Idea, "to try"—in the always Elizabethan
language of Thomas Hooker—"to get an interest in Jesus Christ."

In our inquiry thus far we have considered Puritan culture as
static, a House with its foundations and its principal members which
are among the permanent things of humanity. From now on we shall
consider it historically, as existing in time. For this purpose we
must change our image from that of something standing to that of
something moving, from a House to a River, the River of Puritan
history. The three central elements which we saw in the fire in the
Chimney will take the form of three different currents of the River,
variously impinging upon each other. The Central Current will be
that of Imaginative Perception or the clear, deep, smooth, limpid
flow of the Holy Ratio which is a mysterious compound of Reason
and Emotion and yet is neither Reason nor Emotion, and whose
course and vicissitudes are those of the central thread of New England history. On the right of the central current flows the wide and
muddy one of Arminianism, sometimes moral in aspect and called
Legal Arminianism, sometimes intellectual and scientific and called
Intellectual Arminianism. On the left is the uneven flow of Antinomianism, alternating between rocky pools and sudden cascades.
The Central Current of Imagination, being smooth and selfless or
objective, reflects the Sky of outer reality that arches over the River.
But the Arminian current, being muddy with self-righteousness and
small calculation, sees no sky; and the Antinomian current, while momentarily reflecting the sky in its pools, soon loses the reflection in the
cascades of emotional self-indulgence. The drama of the history of
New England is in the widening of the flanking currents to cover
and efface the central one with their respective kinds of Original Sin

or self-concern. As they succeed and the central current is narrowed, the outer sky it reflects, the world through which its love flows, and the God who is the meaning of that world, are also narrowed and contracted. Sometimes when the sky seems to contract or lower, it has not really contracted, the flanking heresies have not really intruded upon it. Rather the general light, the intensity of Faith, has failed for its own reasons and the great River, while as wide as ever, flows for a time in twilight. This happens when Puritanism, losing its Faith, becomes Yankeeism, as it began to do at the end of the seventeenth century, as it did fully at the end of both the eighteenth and nineteenth centuries.

Generally, in the three completed centuries of Puritan history the central current of Imagination has flowed clearly, reflecting its world, through the first six decades of each century, but after 1660, 1760 and 1860 respectively the light has dimmed for various reasons and the Perceptiveness of Faith has declined, only to revive again at the beginning of the next century. But in each case, when the revival lightens the world again, its sky, and the God who is the Meaning of the Sky, are found to be contracted from their scope of the preceding century. In the seventeenth century, it was a sky as large as human perception could reach; the scene was the World of the Cosmos. In the eighteenth century it was contracted to the size of an abstraction called Man; it was the World of Man. In the nineteenth century it was further contracted to the scope of particular Men and their interests; it was the World of Men. And in the futile effort to revive Puritanism in the twentieth century the sky addressed was no larger than the private Self trying to express or realize itself alone; it was the World of Me. We shall follow this contraction chiefly as we see it in terms of the scope, the outlook, of the people of Greater New England. It represents also a philosophical contraction from Idealism into Materialism, Pragmatism, Relativism and Pluralism. And it represents a moral contraction from the God-centered Christian Cosmos into the self-centered and self-emphasizing cosmos of Paganism that in Renaissance Christendom was identified with witchcraft, the forces of self or Original Sin personified as the Devil, and is identified today with the cult of psychiatry which, with the philosophy of pluralism, is at war with the Meaning of Creation.

To return for a moment to our original figure of the Puritan House, this contraction of the sky over the River represents the contraction we noticed first from the Puritan's occupancy of his whole house to the Yankee's occupancy of one room of it, the old kitchen where the big fireplace is, though the rest of the house yet stands unoccupied and unheated around him. This shrinkage of the river of his culture and of the scope of his own Central Idea, with the presently bruited possibility of re-expanding them in some new vocabulary comprehensible to our times, are matters to give our average Yankee pause. They are matters which, in the normal care and maintenance of his House, his own shrunken Central Idea, he might well take into consideration, retiring for the purpose to his secret room, as is his custom, stirring up the emotional fire of his demand for Truth, and sitting there in silence a long time, perhaps a generation or two, or perhaps a century, of time.

PART TWO

Yankees and God

I. The World of the Cosmos (1630-1700)

1. FIRST PURITANISM (1630-1660)

BY THE YEAR 1634 God's empires of New Plymouth and Massachusetts Bay were well morticed into their rocks, and the Control of the Cosmos was directing them in trends some of which were going to be American. The ordeals by cold and starvation of the first winterings were long past. Caves, tents and conical huts were no longer the habitations of gentry who had left great houses in Cornwall, Devon, Dorset and Gloucester, in London, Sussex, Essex and Lincoln, and of yeomen from the same shires whose homes had been as sturdy and often as large. Even the first shacks of palings and mud—"wattel and daub"—were becoming the mark of the shiftless or the newly arrived. Since the accession of Puritan-hating William Laud as Archbishop two years before, the Great Migration had increased in volume, and some of the villages of Massachusetts Bay were taking on metropolitan pretense.

The empire of Plymouth had shared little in the growth. Its five plank-and-thatch hamlets had together a population of scarcely 400.[1] Four years ago it had made its valuable contribution of Congregationalism to Massachusetts and America—though not an indispensable contribution, for just last fall John Cotton and Thomas Hooker, both distinguished Anglican divines now immigrating as Puritans on the ship *Griffin,* declined to baptize the former's brand new baby "Seaborn" on the ground that, being for the moment without congregations, they were therefore not properly ministers. Plymouth had probably influenced somewhat the decision of the immigrants of 1630 to adopt Congregationalism. Whereafter, in pursuance of its uncalvinistic Calvinism of ignorance and submissive endurance in this vale of tears, Plymouth had settled into that equalitarianism of mediocrity which was to be part of the remote future of America but no part of the New England tradition.

In contrast was the empire of Massachusetts Bay, commonly called

"The Bay." Upon its fourteen hamlets, with a total growing population of more than 4,000,[2] the Control or Meaning of the cosmos had laid the aggressive duty, not of enduring this vale of tears but of transforming it into the triumphant Kingdom of God. Its capital of Boston, while it was never to become properly of New England, was about to begin its long role of originating and disgorging westward in revolt against itself the ideas that became New England and America. The town was a peninsula in the form of a starfish with lopped arms—now long since buried far back in the mostly man-made city. Alone of the early villages, it knew itself impregnable from the beginning and was not palisaded, its only connection with the mainland being the fifty-yard-wide, surf-swept, sentry-guarded Roxbury Neck with its one-track road that is Washington Street today.

The village, with a population in 1634 of perhaps 750[3], was centered around modern State Street, beginning at the shore of Town Cove—today a good quarter mile inland at Merchants Row—and running a scant hundred yards up to Market—presently High and now Washington—Street. Along this forum, shortly to be called King Street, and especially around the upper end where it attained a good hundred feet of width, were ranged the great central institutions and the temples of the gods. On the shore a little north of the street was Samuel Cole's Tavern, conveniently available whether by land or by sea. Halfway up, on the south side at about present Congress Street, was the Meetinghouse, foursquare, with its pyramidal roof of thatch, its belfry and bell, devoid of ornament and more barn-crude than the houses, not through parsimony but through Puritan avoidance of Anglican "popish" trappings. Appropriately alongside it was the house of Governor John Winthrop,[4] saintly guardian of the Holy Commonwealth and purest Puritan of the early Massachusetts laymen of record. At the upper or west end of the Street, squarely on the site of the modern Old State House, was the Town House which was also the capitol of the empire, and had for suitable flankers—along modern Devonshire Street—on the north side the clergy, being the house of the Reverend Master John Wilson, Pastor of the Church, and on the south side the merchantry, being the house of Captain Robert Keayne, presently convicted of sharp dealing, but withal a philanthropist and founder of the Ancient and Honourable Artillery. Around this Center, and along Market Street (Washington), Prison Lane with the Jail (now Courthouse Square), and Sentry Lane with the School (now School Street) continuing across the Highway to the Common (Tremont Street) and (as modern Beacon Street) up Sentry (Beacon) Hill, along these and a lacing of narrower and more crooked lanes clustered the fifteen or twenty houses of the gentry, and of the wealthier yeomanry whose children would be of the gentry.[5] Continuing along the Common and modern

Tremont Street and northward along the shore were scattered the cottages of the poor, of similar frame-and-rubble construction as the mansions of the great and variously approaching them in pretense. The eleven names of property holders along the central forum included, besides those already given, those of William Aspinwall, John Leveritt and James Oliver, but they may or may not have had their houses there. Approximately on modern Adams Square was the mansion of Magistrate and Colony Treasurer William Coddington, and on modern Tremont Street that of Magistrate Bellingham, these perhaps the only structures of brick at this early date.[6] Somewhat farther removed, on Cotton Hill (modern Pemberton Square) was the new house of Reverend Master John Cotton, arrived last fall with Reverend Master Thomas Hooker, now settled in Newtown (Cambridge) and destined to share with Cotton the theological leadership of Puritan New England, as they had shared it for their generation in Puritan Old England.

The style was universally Jacobean, the heavy and sometimes red-painted frames showing, filled in most cases with miscellaneous rubble, plaster and mortar, those of Bellingham, Coddington, and possible others of the gentry, filled with brick. The windows were generally casements with diamond panes, some of the smaller "cottages" doubtless retaining the original oiled paper. The roofs were high pitched, most of them thatched with marsh or "salt" hay, the eaves usually down to the first story. Doubtless the more pretentious mansions copied the English manor plan, with two peaks perpendicular to the street. Many houses were no more than one long room, usually parallel to the street, the interior having the colossal fireplace of mud, with suitable hardware, at one end, and a long loft above, with or without shallow dormers. Some may have already exemplified the plan that became that of the typical New England house,* basically two equal rooms—a "keeping-room" and a "parlor"—on

---

* Just how the standard, one-chimney New England house, with or without the secondary lean-to that made it a "saltbox," was inaugurated at this time is still debated. One account is of a nuclear long room, at one end the great chimney; to which increasing wealth or another generation added another room on the other side of the chimney; and the third advance was a lean-to spanning the back of both front rooms and becoming presently the kitchen, with terminal pantry and buttery and the biggest fireplace of all (J. Frederick Kelly, *Early Domestic Architecture in Connecticut*, 12-17), and see the account of the accretion of the Hull House in Boston in Morison, 137. See also the Whipple house in Ipswich and the Hempstead House in New London.

The other account holds that the plan of two rooms and lean-to with central chimney was brought fully developed from England by the seventeenth-century yeomen. (Anthony N. B. Garven, *Architecture and Town Planning in Colonial Connecticut*, 116-20.)

A theory I have not seen advanced is that in houses where the central chimney is eccentric, giving a keeping-room on one side of the entrance larger than the parlor on the other, in such houses the one-room nuclear method was either used or imitated; but where the rooms are symmetrical round the chimney, the imported plan was used or imitated.

either side of the chimney, with one long room or kitchen behind, for second story two corresponding bedrooms and a long, low and narrow back attic behind them, and for third story a narrow and lofty loft. Because lime was scarce in early New England, and mortar therefore unstable in the weather,[7] some of the houses were probably clapboarded from the beginning. Also, by 1634 big shingles may have begun to replace thatch,[8] permitting the pitch of the roofs to be flatter, the walls and eaves higher, the second-story rooms more spacious and the whole house deeper.

Such was the aspect of Boston on its slope from Town Cove part way up Sentry (Beacon) Hill, a cluster of high-peaked roofs, most of them thatched, some shingled, resting on big-timbered walls filled with miscellaneous masonry, a few clapboarded over, with lower imitations of them straggling north and south along the shore. And such, in their varying topography and surrounded by their high palisades of sharpened logs, were the aspects of the other surrounding hamlets, notably Charlestown, Roxbury, Dorchester, Mt. Wollaston (Braintree), Newtown (Cambridge), Watertown, Agawam (this year to be rechristened Ipswich), Sagus (Lynn) and Naumkeag (already being called Salem). Central to all these villages were the stark meetinghouses, most of them of the blockhouse type, cubical, with pyramidal thatched roofs, like that of Boston, only lacking the belfry and bell that adorned the central temple of the capital.

Within this physical body of the Holy Commonwealth, the general holiness was supported by two institutions, one the personality of John Winthrop, Esquire, usually the governor, the other the limitation of the freemanship, including the suffrage, to the "saints" or church members. In Winthrop, intolerance of what he believed to be false religious doctrine could hardly go farther; and at the same time and in the same soul, extreme generosity, Christian charity and universal love qualified him for high station among the blessed of mankind. Born to power as Lord of the Manor of Groton in Essex, he took no pleasure in its exercise nor any in his station. Uncompromising against false dogma, he was humane to the individual false dogmatist; and he surely never took pleasure in anybody's discomfort. It was part of his Christian humility, and the dangerous fault of it, that he was utterly under the will of the clergy. Very early he set down that he so honored a faithful minister that he "could have kissed his feet."[9] Unfortunately, the feet that were most immediately his to kiss were those of Master John Wilson, physical minister of the Boston church and spiritual minister of the Devil, destined in due course to be the twin of John Endicott of Salem in bigoted cruelty, Wilson being less excusable than Endicott for he was a learned man and aspired to be a poet. Winthrop could fetch Endicott to heel. But to Wilson he deferred, and so galvanized in authority a man who ultimately was going to disgrace him and hasten the decline of the Holy Commonwealth.

For an understanding of the limitation of the suffrage to church members, which was adopted by Massachusetts Bay in the spring of 1631, and in New Haven equivalently soon after settlement, in the spring of 1639, for an understanding of this curious device of "intolerance" it is necessary to understand—what few of us nowadays can understand—that a people's religion, their relation to the mysterious Cosmos, could be more important to them than politics, even than life, more important than all other interests combined. There was, to be sure, a strong political element in the motive of the Puritans for leaving England, namely the necessity to escape from the repressive measures of Charles and influential Bishop—now Archbishop—Laud. But there was involved no profession of political theory, let alone of political rights. The whole object was to be able to worship God in their own fashion, without interference by government or by other emigrants who might subsequently come over and try to confuse them with other forms of worship. It seemed to the Massachusetts people "to be a divine ordinance . . . that none should be appointed and chosen by the people of God, magistrates over them, but men fearing God . . . chosen out of their brethren. . . . For, the liberties of the freemen of this commonwealth are such, as require men of faith-ful integrity to God and the state, to preserve the same . . . in case worldly men should prove the major part, as soon they might do. . . ."[10] Or, as the New Haven planters put it unanimously and more succinctly, "they held themselves bound to establish such civil order as might best conduce to the securing of the purity and peace of the ordinances to themselves and their posterity according to God."[11] Here, in other words, was a people whose imaginative Sky was large and who proposed to keep it so, at the sacrifice of all other interests if necessary.

But even in political terms, the limitation of the suffrage to the saints was not remarkable in the seventeenth century. The object of plantation being religious, it was reasonable that the religiously concerned should have the run of it. The number of them was large. Among the men of voting age, the saints in most communities in the 1630's were a little more or less than half, and they had the general support of another large fraction of pious Puritans who were outside the church membership. The method of qualification did not limit authority to any social class, but it made a vertical division representing all classes. While there was in all things a traditional tendency to defer to the educated and the well born, the ignorant and the lowly were numerically well represented among the saints, and the semi-educated group, the yeomen, were everywhere a majority. The notion of universal male suffrage was then a wild and "democratical" idea advocated, so far as appears, by no one in America. Men were accustomed to be ruled, and a fair proportion did not want the responsibility of the suffrage. A point not often emphasized is that in the fall of 1630, before the saintly suffrage was adopted, only 109 desired to be made Freemen out of an adult male population that probably doubled that.[12] The problem of the voting base in Massachusetts was not to keep the unenfranchised in subjection but to get those entitled to the franchise to exercise it. In 1643 things were at a pass where the General Court asked the churches to deal with saints who would not take the Freeman's Oath of responsible citizenship.[13] The pettier political duties were ducked by all. In May 1647 the General Court permitted non-freemen to be chosen for jury duty and other local offices, and to vote in local matters decided at the town meeting. Towns sometimes put non-freemen into office, including militia offices, without waiting for permission from the General Court. In November the Court made those church members "who, to exempt themselves from all publicke service . . . (had) not come in to be made freemen" liable to the same fine as freemen for refusing local offices.[14]

The tragedy of this so-called "theocracy," this democracy of church members, was not that it was itself oligarchy, but that in the long run it failed to exercise its own full popular power to forestall government by a true oligarchy. In the beginning, the Freemen did largely exercise their civic responsibility, and that at the very time when the gentry who were the magistrates were a true aristocracy whose untrammelled rule could have been trusted. Subsequently, the increasing indifference of the saints to their political privileges unhappily coincided with the deaths of the first leaders, and the consequent rise of a dominantly egoistical or self-aggrandizing oligarchy of smaller men. We have yet to know what might eventuate for mankind if a holy democracy, that is a commonwealth democratic within the limits of its holiness, should remain both holy and democratic, without withering into the evils of either decadent holiness or decadent democracy.

But in 1634 and for many years thereafter the experiment of government by the saints was promising. Throughout the empire of Massachusetts or The Bay, as in the lesser one of Plymouth, the social air was charged with religion, with awareness of God's business which was as ubiquitously in the warehouse, the counting house, the field and the military campaign as in the meetinghouse and the home. Every life was turned outward in activity in God's business and inward in ruthless self-questioning as to the purity of its

Faith, and the purity of its Faith depended upon the purity of its current of consciousness between the contaminating streams of Error that flanked it. Am I standing too far on the side of Reason, Moralism and Self-righteousness, toward Sin or Separation from God in the Arminian sense? Am I revelling too self-indulgently in the emotional conviction of Grace, leaning toward Separation from God or Sin in the Antinomian sense? Every person, every child, in New England knew these problems, and could recognize the common signs of one heretical tendency or the other. To walk the line of Moderation and either be in Grace or be prepared for Grace was the reason for their being there, the only reason for living. Every Puritan was a better psychologist than most who rely consciously on psychology, quick to detect the rationalizations and self-emphases by which he kept himself out of Grace or, if he was presumably in Grace, slipped toward "hypocrisy." And all the time the God of Grace was around him in every phenomenon of nature, including the doings of man and his society. Every act of the working week was a step toward truth or a step toward error. On the Sabbath there were no outward steps. At sundown on Saturday "a hush fell over New England." All walked solemnly, or knelt, and listened for the moderate whisper of God's grace, which was not different in quality from the classical whisper of the Good, the Beautiful and the True.

The year 1634 was one of gathering suspense and omen. In January one Captain Stone was murdered by the violent Pequots to the southwest. He had already been tried for "lying in adultery" with a Boston woman and discharged because he had been "in drink" and no act was proved and the woman got off with a censure.[15] It appeared that the Pequots had had provocation, and the dangerous negotiations went on through the year, to the great concern of the friendly Indians and their particular missionary Master John Eliot the minister at Roxbury. Also of the order of foreign affairs, the French were making plausible claims to much of the Bay Territory. Of critical importance locally, at the May Court of Election, the Freemen went on a democratical rampage, assuming to themselves unprecedented political functions which are not our present concern, and further flaunting their power by throwing John Winthrop out of the governorship because he had been too mild in his judicial capacities, and inconsistently substituting Thomas Dudley of Newtown who would be less merciful toward criminals but also more arbitrary in government generally. In the same month of May the four other leading men of Newtown—namely Thomas Hooker the minister,

Samuel Stone the teacher, William Goodwin the Elder, and John Haynes—"that heavenly man"[16]—the wealthiest parishioner, began the agitation that was going to found Connecticut, in which migratory restlessness they were to be joined presently by Roger Ludlow of Dorchester, lawyer of the Inner Temple and now Deputy Governor, and William Pynchon of Roxbury, late squire of Springfield, Essex, and forthcoming founder of Springfield, Massachusetts.

Most immediately ominous, at the court of Charles powerful enemies of the Puritans, and of the Massachusetts Bay Company in particular, were maturing plans for the reduction of the Holy Commonwealth under royal and clerical control. Semi-officially, even high members of the company at home wrote asking that the charter be returned, and there was the savour of sedition in the magistrates' failure to do so and the never-accounted-for disappearance of the charter afterwards. News came of a military expedition preparing in England, supposedly to impose a royal governor on New England, and the response of the Colony was to hasten the fortifications in Boston Harbor and elsewhere. At the height of these tensions, John Endicott, magistrate from Salem, took occasion to vent his chronic insolence upon the royal standard, slicing out of it with his sword the red cross as an emblem of popery—for which he was duly censured by his colleagues, committed to custody, and disqualified for public office for a year.

Seemingly insignificant among these political crises that faintly foreshadow the Revolution of a century and a half later were events of a religious complexion that in the long cultural run overshadow even the Revolution. Early in 1634 a brilliant and truculent young minister Roger Williams, recent graduate of Pembroke College, Cambridge, returned from a session as minister in Plymouth to resume his post of assistant minister in Salem, and in August took over the pastorate there, meanwhile launching vicious attacks against the government which were sure to strengthen its enemies in London. In September, there arrived into residence William and Anne Hutchinson, late parishioners of Master Cotton in Boston, Lincolnshire. On the way over on that memorable voyage of the *Griffin* which also carried Cotton and Hooker, Mistress Hutchinson had an ominous conversation in the great cabin with Master Zecchariah Symmes who was presently to be ordained pastor of the church in Charlestown. She confided to him that nothing of importance ever happened to her but God first warned her of it personally. This had the authentic reek of emotional, self-centered Antinomianism. Master Symmes told on her, and the Boston church, Master Wilson pastor, delayed her admission two months until she gave evidence of respect for objective or biblically legal standards of conduct.

Roger Williams based his war against Massachusetts in religious principles and texts, but neither here nor in his later great debate with Cotton was there any question of religious doctrine or of any intolerance of Williams himself for religious "conscience's sake." His significance at the outset, as in the long run, was political, and if ever a government is entitled to protect itself his banishment was just. When the Massachusetts Bay Company was fighting for its life diplomatically, was preparing to fight for it militarily, and was undoubtedly guilty of at least strong trends in the secessionist direction, this young pietist and perfectionist, absolutely without practical political sense, rose up to throw reckless and irresponsible oil on the flames, charges that were all the more incendiary for being mostly true. On several grounds and loudly he proclaimed that his late sovereign, James by the Grace of God defender of the Faith, had been a liar.[17] Furthermore he had been an Antichristian thief, and the whole charter of Massachusetts was void, because the Monarch had never bought the land from the Indians. Moreover, Massachusetts, The Bay, was prosecuting a work of Antichrist in having in fact separated from the Church of England—something they all desperately denied—without having the courage to go all the way and proclaim the separation. (Even Plymouth, which did proclaim its separation, had not separated unequivocally enough to suit Williams!) He was especially provoking in that, while content to stay in Massachusetts, he refused to take the freeman's oath and assume —in so devilish a community—a freeman's responsibility. At two points Williams at this time foreshadowed the great doctrines which in his maturity he was going to give the world. Massachusetts, he charged, had revolted against a national church in England only to set up one of its own. This foreshadowed the doctrine of liberty of religion—it is typical of Williams's stickling nicety that he never admitted to "tolerance," because tolerance implied a superiority and a condescension. Even more closely to his other great principle of the future, he denied that the magistrates had the right to enforce the First Table of the Law, that is the First Four Commandments, having to do with the worship of God. Here was germinating the doctrine of the separation of church and state.

For two years the General Court debated and pled with this naughty and contentious genius whom Winthrop obviously admired, as did Cotton and Hooker. But his charges got worse, his disaffected following in Salem more numerous, and the astonished inquiries about him from England more ominous. In the vocabulary of the day, a minister of one of the leading churches was in a state of revolt against the Commonwealth. Winthrop had previously recommended to him the Narragansett country. In September of 1635 the Court gave him six weeks to get out of the jurisdiction. When frost arrived and he had made no move, his period of grace was extended till spring, on condition that he hold his dangerous tongue. His attacks grew more extreme. In early January they sent a warrant for him to report at Boston to take a ship then about to sail for England. When he returned a refusal, they sent Captain Underhill, the commander of the military, in a pinnace to apprehend him and put him on the ocean-going vessel. But, while Underhill and the pinnace were on the way, as Williams wrote thirty-four years later, "that ever-honored Governor, Mr. Winthrop, privately wrote to me to steer my course to Narragansett Bay and Indians, for many high and heavenly public ends, encouraging me, from the freeness of the place from English claims and patents."[18] When Underhill reached Salem, Williams was three days away in the snow-deep forest, and Rhode Island and two great democratic principles were just around the corner.

Between Rhode Island and the other New England colonies there was here inaugurated a long disagreement between the principle of the primacy of the individual, whether religious or not, and the principle of the primacy of God. For on the famous ship of Williams's ideal commonwealth, though explicitly his liberty of conscience was limited to all kinds of religionists—"papists and protestants, Jews and Turks,"[19] yet the actual interpretation was and is to accredit equally materialists, atheists and all kinds of infidels. What began as a debate between religious intolerance and religious liberty ended as a struggle between Religion, with its condition of Humility, and secular Individualism. It is to be observed that between two such great principles there has yet been found no moderate, reconciling mean. For the doctrine of political liberty which stems from Williams became, after three centuries, as supreme, as absolute and as intolerant of all religion as was the doctrine of religious conformity in the Massachusetts he so eloquently decried.

The banishment of Roger Williams involved religion only in its political or external relations. But the Anne Hutchinson affair was a disturbance in the main current, the fine balance between Reason and Emotion. Arriving with eleven children in September of 1634, Mrs. Hutchinson and her husband William took a house in the heart of Boston, on the north corner of Sentry Lane (School Street) and

Market (Washington) Street.[20] Diagonally across Market Street on the corner of Milk—doubtless too near for mutual comfort—was the new house of John Winthrop. William Hutchinson was a wealthy tradesman and, though called "a man of a very mild temper and weak parts,"[21] was sufficiently strong for Boston to send him as a Deputy to the General Court the following spring, and presently to make him a Judge. Anne was a lady, a Marbury, on her mother's side a Dryden and a cousin of the poet. As mentioned before, her admission to the Boston church was delayed until November because of suspicions of her Antinomianism. By that time she was already proving herself a lady bountiful to the overworked and overfertile women of Boston, visiting, advising and nursing them. Presently they were assembling in small gatherings in her house, which became regularized, first into a Thursday meeting to discuss today's Lecture, and later into a Monday meeting also, to discuss yesterday's Sermon. For two years these meetings increased in popularity, men attending one of them along with women, until in '36 between seventy and eighty were gathering semi-weekly in the Hutchinson's big "keeping" or living room with the great fire at one end.

Mrs. Hutchinson denied addressing the men's meeting, but she habitually addressed the women, and she had many semi-private conferences with the leading men of the Town. She was theologically literate, eloquent, quick-witted in debate, fearless, of unquestionably pure conduct, not attractive in person but imperious in manner, aggressive, domineering, and probably magnetic in personality. Almost from the start she accused her pastor Master John Wilson of the Boston church, and after him all the ministers of The Bay—except only John Cotton—of preaching not the orthodox Covenant of Grace, but a Covenant of Works, which meant Arminianism, or the Error of Reason, a return toward "popery" and, by implication, the failure of the minister himself to be in Grace. In reply the ministers charged Mrs. Hutchinson with Antinomianism or the Error of Emotion, her identification of her will with God's Will, thereby setting herself above the law and likening herself to the German Antinomians who for three years had enjoyed a reign of bloody licentiousness in the city of Munster. As we have seen, these charges were, in their opposite directions, the two darkest that could be laid against a professing Puritan. Both were in the premises technically false. But there was enough color of truth in each so that we may date from this controversy the instance of both of these generic heresies which, throughout the history of Greater New England, have swayed the median line of Puritanism and Yankeeism, now on one side, now on the other.

In order to understand the contemporary import of this Hutchinsonian or "Antinomian" affair, it is necessary to remind ourselves once more that here was a people it is probably impossible for the contemporary, naïve, materialistic skeptic or agnostic to understand. Here was a people whose whole concern was with the immeasurable things of the Imagination as distinguished from the things of Natural or Scientific Reason. In our irreligious civilization there are few interests, perhaps none, that distil the intensity which all Puritans directed upon the mystery of Being in an incomprehensible Cosmos. An analogy might be posed between the Puritan ministers and our contemporary doctors. Suppose hypothetically that a person, self-educated upon medical surveys and a few special treatises, charged that all of the thirty-odd doctors in his community were destroying more life than they were prolonging by the use of penicillin, thus attacking them at the level, not merely of their competence and integrity, but of the meaning and purpose of their lives. And suppose the charge was just against one, possibly two, of them, in the accuser's neighborhood, but unfounded as to all the rest. Suppose, then, this person set out, with the noblest intentions, to cure miscellaneous infections with some kind of psychic treatment. Suppose that because of the unpopularity of the doctor in his neighborhood, which was central and populous, this layman built up a considerable practice, and that in spite of many deaths there gathered, after a few apparent cures, a menacing public opinion that attacked the professional research of years and spread discontent through the almost wholly successful, legitimate practices of the other doctors. Suppose, then, that instead of repudiating their one or two incompetent colleagues in the neighborhood involved, the doctors all hung together, and by a slightly shady invocation of licensing laws, but with the support of the great majority in the whole community, were able to compel their assailant to leave town. Such would be a fair factual analogy to the Anne Hutchinson affair.

A closer emotional analogy we might find in terms of Radicalism. Suppose that a popular and sincere Communist, or other advocate of change by planned violence, actually captured, say, the states of New York and Pennsylvania. And suppose that the Federal Court, fearing the New York mob, arbitrarily and dubiously changed the venue from that city to Washington, where the defendant was tried, sentenced and whence he was legally deported. As passionate as would be the clash of feelings over such proceedings in the United States today, so passionate were the feelings involved in Massachusetts Bay of 1636-38 in the charges of preaching a Covenant of Works or Arminianism, the counter-charge of Antinomianism, and the ensuing legally questionable "trial" and banishment of Mrs. Hutchinson. As tolerant as we today should be of a Communist who had captured a small but critical minority of the nation, so tolerant should Massachusetts have been three centuries ago of a Heretic who had captured the capital township of Boston.

As in the contrast between their religious culture and our irreligious civilization, so in considering the procedural irregularities of the trial it is well to remember that the seventeenth century was not the twentieth, the nineteenth or even the eighteenth. Constitutional right as against settled authority, like other forms of individualism, was still only emergent out of the Middle Ages. The aristocracy still felt themselves under the code of chivalry with respect to their duty to take care of their people—as had been illustrated in the deadly famine of 1630 by Winthrop's giving without hesitation his last food to a poor man. But in their dealings with each other they tended also to hold to the ancient technique which was that of the court, namely the technique of intrigue, ruthlessness and the coup. There was much complaint against Winthrop and the majority of the General Court for supporting Wilson. But there was no complaint against the shenanigans by which, as we shall see, he simplified and hastened his victory.

As to Mrs. Hutchinson's charges against the ministers that started the trouble, it would be impossible to discover with certainty to what extent some of the less celebrated ones may have in effect been preaching a Covenant of Works. Certainly they all denied it, and sincerely believed they were preaching the Covenant of Grace, in other words that they were living in the large world of imaginative perception that was orthodox Puritanism. But Mrs. Hutchinson's charge went deeper than their theological profession to their personal qualification. She claimed that all of them—except only Cotton—had themselves failed to receive Grace, that they therefore did not understand it, and so, whatever their parroting of doctrine, lived and preached in a small and self-centered world of Works and self-righteousness. We can say with certainty that this was not true of the great leaders who have left their mark on America—besides Cotton, Hooker, Shepard and Davenport. Mrs. Hutchinson said of Hooker that she "liked not his spirit,"[22] but his "spirit" was surely the subtlest and probably the truest of the age, being precisely on the aesthetic line that was Puritanism, running between the emotionalism of Mrs. Hutchinson and the rationality of Arminianism, partaking of both but remaining distinct from both. Of the other ministers of the Bay, it is not easy to believe that Eliot of Roxbury, Richard (the first) Mather of Dorchester, Phillips of Watertown, Symmes of Charlestown, Bulkeley of Concord, all English university men and almost all M.A.'s, were virgin to the emotional experience they professed, and ignorant of the central purport of the doctrine for which they had left their homes for a wilderness and to which they were consecrating their lives. We may look with some suspicion on Hugh Peter, who had replaced Williams at Salem, for he was a fighter and rabble rouser with the ostentation that goes with the latter talent; he returned to England to be a great organizer and chaplain in the Civil War and to lose his head at the Restoration. We may look with more suspicion on Thomas Weld of Roxbury who, like John Wilson of Boston, was a poet, being the author of the *Bay Psalm Book*. There is not evidence enough in the full record of the Hutchinson trial or in the scanty record of his conduct in the year following it to brand him as a self-centered Arminian and persecutor at that time. But his *Preface,* written later in England, to the account of the trial called *A Short Story,* and some passages in the main text of it, which is very questionably attributed to Winthrop, have the harsh ring of the true addict of the doctrine of Works.

Mrs. Hutchinson's inference that the ministers generally were not in Grace was possibly true of Peter, and probably of Weld. But we can agree with her unreservedly only in the case of John Wilson, her own minister and that of all Boston, who was the cause of her first embarking on her campaign of defamation, who by all the plentiful evidence was a small man, a dull and stubborn man, an egoist and always an Arminian of the most legalistic and bigoted sort. Because of his powerful position, and because of Winthrop's childlike loyalty to him, he was the devil in The Bay. Without his presence it is highly unlikely that Mrs. Hutchinson would ever have made trouble. Without his unpopularity with his parishioners it is certain that she would have been unable to arouse them into a state of revolt against him and the authority of the government that backed him. Without that state of revolt in Boston there would have been no apprehension on the part of the Magistrates of physical trouble, for Mrs. Hutchinson had no influence whatever in the main body of the Commonwealth which was outside of Boston. And without that apprehension there would probably have been no trials, and certainly no banishments.

The reason that Mrs. Hutchinson charged the ministers at The Bay—all except Cotton—with preaching a Covenant of Works was probably not that it was true but that to her uncompromising and immoderate Antinomian or Emotional point of view it seemed true. To her the orthodox Puritan line, which admitted works both as a Preparation for and as a sign of Grace, was itself a doctrine of Works. She herself preached that conformance to the law, or "Sanctification," was meaningless, whether as a preparation or as a sign; that a person in Grace could do no wrong, and that if he was troubled in conscience, even for the grossest crimes, this meant simply that he never had been in Grace; that the State of Grace was not a communication from the Holy Spirit of God, but an actual union of the individual with God so that his acts were God's acts; that she herself enjoyed such union and consequent prophetic revelations of everything of importance that was going to happen to her.[23] She went all the way with Antinomian doctrine, and differed from the complete German Antinomians only in that she neither practiced nor advocated any actual infraction of either Biblical or Civil Law. Also, she did a great deal of Christian good among the women of Boston. But she herself would have been the last to claim that good works were any palliative for false doctrine—and in matters of purity of doctrine all the Puritans—none more than herself—were addicted to all the scholastic, essentially the aesthetic, nicety and intolerance that is falsely ascribed to them in matters of conduct.*

The basis of Mrs. Huchinson's quarrel with New England was in doctrine that was not only heretical against the Puritan line of Moderation, but in her claim of emotional identification with God ran close to the mortal sin—the capital crime—of Blasphemy. The basis was in doctrine; yet it would also be externally dangerous in application. It need only be extended to irresponsible people—which the members of Wilson's church for the most part were not, but which some of Boston were—to release a deadly anarchy within the Commonwealth. Mrs. Hutchinson's charges against the ministers were much farther from being justified than their charges against her. It is important to remember that she was not tried and banished for her heretical opinions per se. She was tried and banished for a civil not a religious crime, for what Charles Francis Adams calls "constructive sedition,"[24] the factiousness which her opinions aroused in Boston, the real fear of an uprising by her following, not only the members of Wilson's church but outside the church that famous, enlightened and eventually world-shaking Boston Mob of which she was in fact the first leader.

The details of the "Antinomian affair" concern us here for their revelation of the scope, great or small, of the imaginative or religious landscape of the people of the early "Bay." The trouble brewed, as we have seen, in Mrs. Hutchinson's semi-weekly soirées, beginning in the winter of 1635, in her house at the corner of Sentry Lane and Market Street. In the fall of that year arrived Harry Vane, aged twenty-three, and at the next Court of Election—May '36—because of his rank as the son of a baronet and Privy Councillor, and his "grave deportment," they made him Governor. Meanwhile he

---

* "Yor Mother," said John Cotton to Mrs. Hutchinson's son-in-law during the church trial, "though she be not accused of any thinge in poynt of fact or practice . . . yet she may hould Errors as dayngerous and of worse Consequence than matters of practice cane be. . . ." (Adams, *Antinomianism*, 306.)

joined Mrs. Hutchinson's discussion group, which already included, but for Wilson and Winthrop, all of the top level of the Boston church—Cotton, Humfry, Coddington, Coggeshall, Aspinwall and Captain Underhill, the leader of the military. In the long run the last did the cause much more harm than good. Having, as he supposed, come into Grace one day "while smoking his pipe," he thereupon proclaimed himself outside the law in true Antinomian fashion, and gave both church and magistrates years of petty annoyance—"Adultery—Reviling the Governor—writing slanderous letters to England—enticing some to folly and lewdness upon pretence to knock them off from their owne Righteousnesse"[25]—until at long last he and his courage went off to serve Connecticut, and afterwards the Dutch.[26] Captain Underhill, rather than the virtuous Anne Hutchinson herself, was the true Antinomian in action as Pastor Wilson was the Arminian. Between them ran the true Puritanism of Cotton and Winthrop, Hooker and Haynes, Davenport and Williams, Shepard, Dudley, Bradstreet and the great majority of the people including most of the followers of Mrs. Hutchinson.

The year 1636 was the high tide of Mrs. Hutchinson's influence —and it may be significant that in that spring the pacific Thomas Hooker led away his congregation to found Connecticut, partly because of certain theological differences with John Cotton. Mrs. Hutchinson now had the overwhelming majority of the Boston church, including the titled Governor of the Commonwealth, and a large and militant following in the unchurched town which was doubtless more opposed to authority in general than in favor of any particular doctrine. She and some of her friends now made a practice of leaving meeting when Wilson's sermon began. In the summer came William Hutchinson's brother-in-law, Reverend Master John Wheelwright, who had been popular at Cambridge as an athlete and was with the so-called Antinomians in opposing the preaching of Works in any form, or at the least in opposing Wilson. She proposed him for assistant teacher of the church. In the congregation Winthrop alone stood against the appointment, and his prestige blocked it. Wheelwright took the pulpit at Mt. Wollaston across the Bay, and Winthrop took the warpath. On January 16, 1637, Wheelwright preached a guest sermon in Wilson's pulpit, in which he applied some unattractive epithets to those who walked in a Covenant of Works, though not specifically naming Wilson. The disaffection of Boston from Wilson was already threatening and it raised in the minds of the magistrates the specter of bloody Munster. They proceeded to try Wheelwright for sedition—"constructive sedition"—not for his erroneous opinions but for their tendency to foment an actual uprising. Through the machination of the "priests,"[27] he was convicted on a close vote, but the Boston mob was so menacing that the magistrates suspended sentence. Mrs. Hutchinson's power was still great, but the tide had turned.

The campaign for the spring election of magistrates and deputies was one of unprecedented acerbity, between Winthrop and those allegedly supporting the Covenant of Works, the "Whitecoats," and Vane and those allegedly supporting the Covenant of Grace, the "Bluecoats." It was the first and one of the most spectacular of many elections in New England that turned upon theological questions with all the bitterness that we have come to associate with more "realistic" political and economic issues.

The Whitecoats won the election, partly by the shady shift of moving the Court out of Boston to Cambridge. Winthrop resumed the governorship, but the bodyguard of halberdiers that had accompanied Vane, being Boston men, refused to march with Winthrop, and he went back to Boston from the election alone. The Pequot war ensued immediately, and not a member of the Boston church enlisted, partly because the party of their minister had defeated them, partly because their same hated minister was Chaplain of the Massachusetts contingent. The continuing state of the public mind appeared when the extra-Bostonian Massachusetts detachment, on the way through the woods to join the Connecticut force, required their officers to halt while they debated whether they were proceeding under a Covenant of Works or a Covenant of Grace.[28] Later that summer, after much boyish fulmination, Harry Vane returned to England to mature, to play a noble part in the Civil Wars, and at the Restoration to lose his head as a hero.

Winthrop and Wilson now proceeded to purge the state. In September they assembled a synod which found the famous eighty-two errors in the Antinomian position. In defiance of the charter, Winthrop dissolved the General Court and held a special election. The government had been strengthened by the destruction of the Pequots, and the new court was even more completely his than the last one. Again the deputies and magistrates assembled in the safe province of Cambridge, in the square, thatched meetinghouse on the corner of modern Dunster and Mt. Auburn Streets. The first acts of the Court were to unseat Aspinwall and Coggeshall and to disenfranchise the latter, they being two of the three Boston deputies and good members of the faction—so was the third, William Coddington, but he was too strong for the court to attack. Then they protected the state by disarming sixty-odd Hutchinsonians, presumably all Bostonians, who had signed a petition in the interest of Master Wheelwright, still awaiting sentence. This unpolitic piece of violence reveals the tension of the times, for it is incredible that

these experienced and hardly timid rulers would have had recourse
to such a measure if there had not been real danger of an uprising.
The seditious minority being relieved of their pistols, blunderbusses
and pikes, the court proceeded to sentence Wheelwright to banishment. And after him a dozen other Hutchinsonian leaders, including
Aspinwall, were disenfranchised or banished.

The chief defendant, of course, was Mrs. Hutchinson herself, the
one for whose banishment Winthrop had now for almost a year
been laying and testing the skids. Although her trial violated legal
procedure in many respects, the actual charge against her, if somewhat differently phrased and prosecuted, was one the law would
recognize. It was not that of "traducing the ministers" nor of holding unorthodox opinions, but, as in the case of Wheelwright, was
that of "constructive sedition," fomenting armed rebellion. Here,
according to *A Short Story*—surely the report of one present at the
trial—are Governor Winthrop's first words to the defendant (the
italics are mine):

> Mistris Hutchinson. You are called hither as one of those
> who have had *a great share in the causes of our publick dis-
> turbances,* partly by those erroneous opinions which you have
> broached and divulged amongst us, and maintaining them,
> partly by *countenancing* and *incouraging such as have sowed
> seditions amongst us,* partly by casting reproach upon the faith-
> ful Ministers of this Countrey, . . . and so weakening their
> hands in the work of the Lord, and raising prejudice against
> them, in the hearts of their people, and partly by maintaining
> weekly and publick meetings in your house, to the offence of all
> the Countrey. . . .

Although, throughout the trial, the ministers, who were there not
as judges but as both factual witnesses and expert witnesses on questions of doctrine, naturally showed a dominant concern for their particular interest, yet it is to be remembered that Winthrop and
Lieutenant Governor Thomas Dudley—father of Anne Bradstreet
the poet—and at least the great majority of the Court, kept their
eye on this central matter, the threat to the public peace. Errors of
doctrine were noted, not for their own sake, but for their possible
tendency to stir up armed sedition.

Although it is true that the Court, by the exclusion of Coggeshall
and Aspinwall, was well rigged against Boston and Mrs. Hutchinson,
it is not true that the end was foregone. For in fact the defendant
almost got off. With the adroit support of Cotton, but facing the
prejudice of all of the other ministers and most of the Court, she
actually came near to proving, by theological fencing, that she was
sound in doctrine. More important, they nearly found themselves

compelled to hold her innocent on the central charge, that of having "a great share in the causes of our publick disturbances." It was proven without denial, indeed it was common knowledge, that she had charged the ministers with preaching a Covenant of Works, with being not "sealed"—that is, not themselves in Grace—and with being "unable ministers." It was also assumed without argument that these charges had in fact contributed to the "publick disturbances." But what was not proven was that Mrs. Hutchinson's charges had themselves been "publick," and if they had not been "publick" she could not be held legally for any seditious results of them. One important occasion of the charges was a conference between her and the ministers which the latter had sought in order to test her views. Though they afterwards broadcast her statements, yet the court held that the meeting itself was confidential, and nothing said at it was "publick." Furthermore, after almost two hours of debate, on and off this main point, there remained a seemingly ineradicable doubt whether the open meetings in her house were not also technically private in the eyes of the law.

The hour was late. The Court reached a quandary and a pause, and there were those among the magistrates who were showing restlessness to have done and start home on their long rides through the woods in the November evening. It looked as if Mistress Hutchinson were going to be let off with an admonition, when something occurred which Winthrop called a Providence of God. The defendant herself did something which, being paralleled by similar behavior at other times, seems to indicate a highly emotional, self-assertive compulsiveness in her character, the essential quality of Antinomianism. To the consternation of her friends, while the Court was engaged in its asides, she rose and gave it a piece of her defiant mind. She told them that God had revealed to her in England that she should go to New England where she would be persecuted as she was now being persecuted, that New England would be ruined for it, but that God would deliver her as he had delivered Daniel from the lions' den—

> Therefore I desire you to look to it, for you see this scripture fulfilled this day. . . . You have power over my body but the Lord Jesus hath power over my body and soul, and assure yourselves thus much, you do as much as in you lies to put the Lord Jesus from you, and if you go on in this course you begin you will bring a curse upon you and your posterity, and the mouth of the Lord hath spoken it.

Instantly there was tremor and a change in the atmosphere of the Court and the audience crowded in the little meetinghouse. At the religious foundation, her open and ecstatic assertion of personal revelation by God was a shameless declaration of a heresy which in 1637 was as shocking as an open declaration of Communism in 1954. Furthermore, on the main issue, here, in open court before the whole Commonwealth, was a pronouncement of the same inflammatory attacks on the ministers and government which, made previously in technical private, had been the cause of the "disturbances." And now, what could be more "publick"! Immediately, in legal language, her previous statements were clothed with this present publicity. The members of the Court who had before been merely skeptical or at most inquisitorial now turned with certitude against her. Cotton was silent, Winthrop breathed a sigh of relief audible in the record:

> . . . Now the mercy of God by a providence hath answered our desires and made her to lay open her self and *the ground of all these disturbances* to be by revelations. . . . There is no use of the ministry of the word or of any clear call of God by his word, but the ground work of her revelations is the immediate revelation of the spirit and not by the ministry of the word, and that is the means by which she hath very much abused the country that they . . . are not bound to the ministry of the word, but God will teach them by immediate revelations and *this hath been the ground of all these tumults and troubles.* . . .

Thomas Dudley, the rough-handed Deputy Governor, struck the frightening note of the Antinomian anarchy in Munster:

> These disturbances that have come among the Germans have been all grounded in revelations, and so they that have vented them have stirred up their hearers to take up arms against their prince and to cut the throats of one another, and these have been the fruits of them, and whether the devil may inspire the same into their hearts here I know not, for I am fully persuaded that Mrs. Hutchinson is deluded by the devil. . . .[29]

And so it went around the Court with unanimity, except for William Coddington, the remaining deputy from Boston, who in a last effort courageously denied that she had broken any law of God or of the country.

And so Mrs. Hutchinson was banished. But because winter was at hand, and because she was pregnant—though not yet evidently so—execution of the sentence was postponed until spring, she being meanwhile partially banished to the house of Joseph Weld in Roxbury (brother of the Roxbury minister Thomas Weld) where most of the ministers, notably Davenport and Shepard, labored with her all winter, aiming to turn her from her self-centered theology. Meanwhile, even the public opinion of Boston was taking a conservative turn. In March Wilson dared summon her for an "examination" in their own meetinghouse.[30] In this last ordeal of Anne Hutchinson in Boston, it is noteworthy that Cotton had now turned against her on doctrine, while Winthrop, who in the church had no official authority, generally defended her. Here only doctrine was in issue, and Winthrop's first concern was for the public peace. She was already banished, the Boston mob had quieted down, and the veteran governor was not one for vindictiveness or gratuitous cruelty.

The first hearing passed off in theological dispute about the resurrection of the body, a point which did have a relation to the Antinomian and Mrs. Hutchinson's position. At the second hearing Mrs. Hutchinson at first made a blanket recantation of all her offensive views, professing that overnight Master Davenport had shown her the light. It looked as if Master Wilson were going to be frustrated in his eagerness further to torture her. Then, as the previous November, at the critical moment she forestalled the clemency and the discharge that were imminent. Proudly she informed the church that in spite of the words of her recantation, her opinions were unchanged.

Wilson proposed the excommunication, and there was not a dissenting voice in the congregation, even on the part of her son and son-in-law, who before had been taking her side. We can presume that it was with relish that the brutal little pastor stood up in his great robe in the high pulpit of the Boston meetinghouse on modern State Street and pronounced the dreadful words:

> Forasmuch as yow, Mrs. Hutchinson, have highly transgressed & offended, forasmuch as yow have soe many ways troubled the Church with yor Eror & have drawen away many a porr soule, & have upheld yor Revelations: & forasmuch as yow have made a Lye, &c. Therefor in the name of our Lord Je: Ch: & in the name of the Church I doe not only pronownce yow worthy to be cast owt, but I doe cast yow out & in the name of Ch. I doe deliver yow up to Sathan, that yow may learne no more to blaspheme, to seduce & to lye, & I doe account yow from this time forth to be a Heathen & a Publican & soe to be held of all the Bretheren & Sisters, of this Congregation, & of others: therefor I command yow in the name of Ch: Je: & of this Church as a Leper to withdraw your selfe owt of the Congregation; that as formerly yow have dispised & contemned the Holy Ordinances of God, & turned your Backe one them, soe yow may now have no part in them nor benefit by them.

Mrs. Hutchinson walked out of the crowded meetinghouse with her friend and disciple, the young and "comely" Mary Dyer, and so into King Street just below the Town House where one day the riot called the Boston Massacre was going to occur. As they left the meetinghouse someone said to Mrs. Hutchinson, "The Lord sanctify this unto you." And she replied, "The Lord judgeth not as man judgeth. Better to be cast out of the church than to deny Christ."[31]

Within a few weeks the Hutchinsons, Aspinwall, likewise banished, Coddington, self-banished, and followed later by Coggeshall and the Dyers, self-banished, set out by different routes for Aquidneck, afterwards named Rhode Island, where they founded Portsmouth. Meanwhile Master Wheelwright had gone northward to share in the founding of Exeter, New Hampshire, moved thence into Maine, and was eventually recalled to full honor in Massachusetts. Four years after the banishment, William Hutchinson died and his widow left Rhode Island for no apparent reason, and until the contrary appears it must be presumed that she was bored with a state of affairs that gave her no prominence.[32] With part of her large family, she went to modern Westchester, then subject to the Dutch. There, in August, 1642, she and all but one of the children with her were murdered by the Indians. In Boston it was recalled that she had proclaimed that the Lord would save her from harm by a miracle, and that Massachusetts would be destroyed for its treatment of her. She is commemorated by a small river and by a large highway that knows no repose.

The importance of the Hutchinson affair to the present consideration is in the question whether, in the conditions of the seventeenth century, it tends to support the position taken here, that the Puritans were on the whole an exhibit in Christianity, trying to live in eternity along the selfless line of Grace between the self-indulgence of Emotion and the self-indulgence of Reason, or whether it supports the position usually taken that they were already far gone in the pinched Arminian, self-righteous, unchristian bigotry that awaits those whose approach to religion is too moralistic or too rational. In support of the popular view, five allegations are presented: first, that Mrs. Hutchinson was brutally treated at the trial, that, being evidently pregnant, she was required to stand for the two hours more or less of her examination; second, that she was mentally bullied, browbeaten by the ministers and the members of the court in a cruel, essentially sadistic manner; third, that the ministers and members of the Court behaved patently as small, self-preoccupied men, concerned mainly with their personal interests and their petty authority; fourth, that the "trial" was a legal farce, both in procedure and in the trumped up charge of sedition on which it turned; fifth, that even if the judgment had a technical legal justification, yet in actuality it was based on religious intolerance.

First, as to the supposed physical brutality to Mrs. Hutchinson, there is no evidence of any. If she was pregnant at the time of the trial, in November 1637, it could not have been observed, for the ensuing miscarriage did not occur until the following July or August.[33] Prisoners, male or female, always stood throughout their trials, and she did so at the outset in accordance with the practice. But, "After she had stood a short time"—one account would make it enough of the trial to fill five large-type pages, perhaps ten minutes—Winthrop did observe that she looked ill, and promptly had a chair brought for her.[34] At her church trial the following March she was obviously in a frail condition,[35] but not the most ardent Puritan-baiter, so far as I know, has asserted that she stood during its two sessions, or that she stood at all.

Secondly, one looks in vain in the two full accounts of the court trial[36] to find evidence of the famous mental bullying of the frail defendant. It is of course impossible to say what fierce looks and sarcastic accents might have marked the expressions addressed to her by habitually correct gentlemen, for these are not preserved in the words of the record. Throughout the trial she was referred to as "Mistress" or "Sister" Hutchinson or "this gentlewoman," but for one instance when Mr. Symmes, the minister of Charlestown, slipped and called her "this person." Nowhere is there any hint of nastiness or even of the healthy bawdiness which was typical of the age. The one protest of the defendant—who was a fiery creature on occasion—when she flared up to cry, "My name is precious!," was not against any impugnment of her purity but merely against a questioning of her statement upon a disputed piece of evidence. There was plenty of sarcasm of a healthy nature, such as characterizes any serious trial. There was some browbeating of weaker by stronger men—

> Mr. Coggeshall. Yes I dare say that she did not say all that which they lay against her.
> Mr. Peters. How dare you look into the court to say such a word.
> Mr. Coggeshall. Mr. Peters takes upon him to forbid me. I shall be silent.

But there was very little of this impropriety, and probably none that bore on the result.

Certainly there was no browbeating of Mrs. Hutchinson at all. In the court trial Wilson and Weld, both of whom hated her exquisitely and at least the first of whom was a vicious Arminian, behaved themselves with an excess of dignity, though Wilson in the church trial four months later did indulge in a rhetoric of "loathings" and "rendings of garments," of "Saducism & Athiism." This

is the only recorded effort to bully Mrs. Hutchinson—and, in view
of her contempt for Wilson, this was too absurd to hurt. Considering
that here were a dozen professional men of God whom the defendant
had most dreadfully affronted, considering that she had at least
stirred up a revolt of insolence against Wilson, and that this had
grown into something we know not how close to a violent uprising,
considering also that the fomenter of this menace was a woman who
sat sassily before them giving them a merry chase of evasiveness and
equivocation, and that this was the year 1637 when a woman was
supposed to get her ideas from the "contemplation of her husband's
excellencies," considering all of these things, Mrs. Hutchinson got a
wonderfully polite and dignified hearing. She was treated neither
with special cruelty nor with special consideration, but with the
minimal courtesy due a lady by gentlemen in the seventeenth
century.

Thirdly, the charge of littleness of soul and primary self-concern
against the generality of the ministers in the trials finds possible support in their obvious concern over Mrs. Hutchinson's assertion that
they were men not in Grace, and that they were "unable ministers."
We must have been present to interpret their remarks in these matters. Basically, of course, these assertions of hers were what they were
there to bear witness to, for it was this attack on the ministers that
was supposed to have stirred up the "disturbances" for which she was
being tried. But most of them did return at least once unnecessarily
to the incredible charge—"She said we were unable ministers! She
said we were unable ministers!" And the context permits the interpretation that these were the whimperings of infants who had had
their sweets taken away. Actually, these were all men of education,
worldly experience and proven courage, men of recognized distinction in England who had stood up to worse vilification there when
the shadow of the torturer and hangman was visible behind the
vilifier. If any of them had been small and vanity-ridden men they
would hardly have confessed their hurt by whimpering of it. Rather
they would have covered it under bluster or, more likely, under im-
peccable suavity; and it is noticeable in the record that Wilson and
Weld, probably both Arminians and indeed small men, were the
only two who spoke in elegant phrases and with considered unction.
For the rest, we must presume that the expression, "She said we
were unable ministers!," was either ejaculated in angry disgust or
that it was said wonderingly by men of sufficient caliber to be humble, men who knew they were less than perfect, and who wanted to
elicit any truth there might be in the charge of failing to do their job.

There was not much that we would recognize as affirmative generosity shown the defendant—there was Cotton's strong defense of

his disciple, Coddington's brave and prophetic plea for toleration, scattering expressions of friendliness from half a dozen of the deputies, Shepard's compassionate comment on one of Mrs. Hutchinson's outbursts—"It may be but a slip of her tongue, and I hope she will be sorry for it, and then we shall be glad. . . ."[37] Generally the attitude of the ministers and the magistrates was impersonal toward the defendant, their real concern being whether she was or was not a threat to the Holy Commonwealth to whose founding and development they had dedicated their lives. Hugh Peters spoke for all of them, except Wilson and probably Weld: "We . . . desire that we may not be thought to come as informers against this gentlewoman, but as it may be serviceable for the country and posterity to give you a brief account."[38] On the personal side, their concern was whether they were being thus "serviceable for the country and posterity." And upon this question bore immediately the charge that they were "unable ministers."

The fourth charge of the debunkers respecting the trial is that it was legal farce. On the side of legal procedure, it is in the main a true charge. Winthrop the Governor was at once the chief prosecutor and the presiding judge. Throughout the proceedings the Magistrates or Assistants and the Deputies who were sitting in judgment gave evidence and bickered with each other. The ministers, who were there as witnesses, broke in to question the defendant and other witnesses, and it was with great reluctance that the Court was persuaded to put them under oath. It was, as entitled in Hutchinson, an "Examination"[39]—an "Inquisition," if you prefer—rather than a trial, and an examination is not sufficient basis for serious adjudication. The only excuse for the proceedings, and that insufficient, was that their informality was usual in that embryonic government where legislative, executive and judicial functions were combined in the Magistrates or Assistants, and that Mrs. Hutchinson's procedural rights were given at least as much regard as those of common felons.

Winthrop's handling of the central question, whether the defendant's charges against the ministers were "publick" or not, would be amusing to a modern lawyer. Throughout the body of the trial he was unable to persuade himself that her statements made privately in her home were sufficiently "publick" to justify a conviction for the seditious "disturbances," though all Boston had heard them and there was no doubt that they were one of the causes of the disturbances. Yet when in the trial she publicly repeated the more inflammatory of her Antinomian views and charged both ministers and magistrates not simply with error but with sacrilege, though these present charges had as yet *caused* nothing of external action, yet he did not hesitate to impute the publicity of them to the earlier ones that must have had it to justify a conviction. A legalistic argument could be made in support of Winthrop's procedure, but no modern judge would as readily and with such evident relief leap to so dubious a ruling that involved immediately the final disposition of the case. In defense of Winthrop's procedural short-cuts it may be said only that as Justice of the Peace in his home manor of Groton in England, he was doubtless long accustomed to dispose thus peremptorily of local issues where he took judicial notice of all matters of local knowledge and proceeded to what seemed to him a just solution without clogging the course of justice with a lot of legalistic impedimenta.

More difficult of proof than the procedural complaint against the trial is the substantial charge that Coddington made, that Mrs. Hutchinson had broken no law. She was charged with "having a great share in the causes of our publick disturbances," and with "incouraging such as have sowed seditions." Punishable "sedition" was a word as controversial in law in 1637 as it is today. For this brief glance we can do no better than to cite a common definition which is a formulation of precisely what the court charged: Sedition is "conduct or language inciting to rebellion against the constituted authority of a state."[40] It seems to have been agreed by all that Mrs. Hutchinson's Antinomian expressions and her charges against the ministers had "incited," had had "a great share in the causes" of "our publick disturbances." Yet it is not so clear that these disturbances, both in intent and in action, had been truly of the order of "rebellion." If they had, judgment of the Court would seem to have been sound. But if they had not been truly and overtly rebellious, if they had been a mere "sowing" without yet any sprouting of sedition, then the Court's judgment was undoubtedly error.

The members of the Court and the ministers both recognized this, and were always zealous, during and after the trial, in insisting that the banishment was for instigating overt seditious action. Referring to the banishment of Mrs. Hutchinson and the other "Antinomians," Master Weld, writing later in England, denied that they were delivered "up to Satan" "for their opinions (for which I find we have become slanderously traduced) but the chiefest cause of their censure was their miscarriages . . . persisted in with great obstinacy."[41] And either Winthrop or Weld,[42] writing of Coggeshall's banishment, said that if he "had kept his judgement to himself, so as the public peace had not been troubled or endangered by it, we should have left him to himself, for we do not challenge power over men's conscience, but when seditious speeches and practices discover such a corrupt conscience, it is our duty to use authority to reform both."

So long as the state was not threatened—as it had been unquestionably by the attacks of Roger Williams—Winthrop, who disliked "unloving" controversy, tended to give any sinner the benefit of a long and patient doubt. It is remarkable that during his life, and even after his death in '49 and in the ensuing reign of Bloody Wilson and Bloody Endicott, there were still plenty of discreet Baptists, Quakers and other Antinomians who minded their own business, and held unobtrusive meetings, and never ran foul of the law.

The ultimate and substantial question in the Hutchinson case, then, was whether the "disturbances" which the defendant had incited were, both in intent and in action, of the order of rebellion, and this central question is precisely what we are unable to conclude from the record. It was a grave defect of the trial, at least as reported, that these "disturbances" and "troubles" of the Commonwealth which Mrs. Hutchinson was charged with inciting were not even specifically alleged. On the other hand, not even Coddington or Mrs. Hutchinson herself denied them to be fact, and we may assume that the court took something like judicial notice of them. What we do have is extraneous and inadequate references to at least seven "disturbances" in Boston during the two years preceding the trial, one or more of which may have been of a rebellious nature.

First, in January, 1637, there was a noisy meeting in the Boston church when the saints almost unanimously demanded the formal admonition of Wilson, and he was saved only by the moderation of Cotton the teacher who, when ordered by the Congregation to deliver the admonition, begged off and got momentary peace by delivering his colleague a humiliating rebuke.[43]

Second. There was the practice of Mrs. Hutchinson and some of her following of walking out of church when Wilson began the sermon.

Third. After Wheelwright's conviction of "constructive sedition," the mood of the Boston mob was so threatening that the General Court abstained from sentencing him.

Fourth. The removal of the Court from Boston to Cambridge for the election in the spring of '37 implied a state of lawlessness in the capital, as when the Roman imperial government surrendered Rome to the barbarians and crept off to Byzantium.

Fifth. Of a seemingly revolutionary savour was the refusal of the Governor's official Bodyguard to march with Winthrop after his victory over Vane.

Sixth. Of at least equal seriousness was the refusal of all the eligible men of Wilson's church to enlist for the Pequot War.

Seventh. The "Remonstrance" or petition on Wheelwright's behalf which integrated the Antinomian opposition, the Court took seriously enough to adopt the highly impolitic measure of disarming the signers.[44]

Adams finds in none of this any evidence of sedition, of revolutionary action combined with revolutionary intent.[45] A fairer opinion would seem to be that there is here some. though inconclusive, evidence of both revolutionary intent and revolutionary action implementing the intent. As to the first two instances cited, it must be borne in mind that in a commonwealth where the state ran the church, unseemly brawls in prominent churches may well have carried revolutionary intimations. The other six instances might undoubtedly have involved revolutionary possibilities, and there is some weight in the fact that the magistrates, who were hardly hysterical men, believed these possibilities to be real.

Ultimately, on the question whether Mrs. Hutchinson had stirred up legally seditious "disturbances," we can only say that the evidence for it is at least as weighty as the evidence against it, but that the existing proof is not conclusive either way. Meanwhile, irreligious persons will tend to follow Adams and condemn the magistrates of the Bay simply because they were Puritans. On the other hand, persons who favor both religion and the Puritans will presume in favor of the judgment of the magistrates, pending further evidence.

Pending further evidence, it would be gratuitous to assert categorically that Mrs. Hutchinson, John Wheelwright and William Aspinwall were justly banished for infringement of the established British law of sedition. It is at least as gratuitous to charge, following Coddington at the trial and Adams in his report of it, that she had broken no law, that the "disturbances" were fictitious, trumped up by the clergy and the magistrates to give a color of legality to their action, that actually the "Antinomians" were banished for nothing but "conscience's sake," that the whole performance was simply an exercise in arbitary intolerance.

In view of the singleness of religious intention on the part of the Puritans, in view of the intolerance in England from which they had fled, and generally of the hardly yet questioned condition of intolerance throughout all of seventeenth-century Christendom, it is remarkable that people of Antinomian tendencies, beginning with Anne Hutchinson in the 1630's and ending with the Quakers in the 1650's, got even a pretense of legal treatment. Indeed, under the policy of the Massachusetts Bay Company during the first few years of settlement, they would have been handled much more summarily than they were. From the time of landing in 1630 until tolerance was forced on Massachusetts by the Charter of 1692, there were three successive policies with respect to alleged heresy.

During the first three years, when the only too evident issue was simple survival, the Magistrates behaved with the arbitrariness commonly allowed the Directors or Assistants of a Company, which indeed they were, rather than with the more circumscribed responsibility of political officials. They threw out anybody they conceived to be a menace to the public stability, and this included three who merely defamed the government or the magistrates.[47] Of these, Captain Stone would have been a brawling trial to any village, but he was banished in 1633 merely "for his outrage committed in confronting auethority abuseing Mr. Ludlowe both in words and behavior assalting him and calling him a just as. . . ." (The pun on "justice" was not original with Stone!)

But after Captain Stone no more people were banished summarily. The Bay came into its second phase, that of government under law. In 1632 Winthrop had informed the Freemen that they were no longer a company but a commonwealth—truly the first declaration of American independence. Furthermore, there had come chastening complaints from home about arbitrary justice. Also, the little state was beginning to prosper, and no longer trembled under any blackguard's vocabulary. After 1633, the Bay went politically respectable. Respectability meant among other things that nobody should be punished except under legal procedure. And this meant, under the then state of the laws, that no one should be banished for his religious opinions alone. It was in this early phase of constitutional government that the "Antinomian Affair" occurred, and much as all of the Magistrates would have preferred to toss out the offending heretics without ado, we have seen that they found it necessary to associate some legal misfeasance with the Error of theology. This jurisprudential respectability was formalized in the Massachusetts Bodie of Liberties of 1641, whose first section declares in effect that no man shall be deprived of life, liberty or property without due process of law.

The third phase of Massachusetts policy with respect to heretical opinion began in 1644 with a law which at once eliminated the recent necessity of associating heresy with some other kind of misfeasance, as sedition, and yet did not leave the matter to the arbitrary will of the Magistrates, which had been the case in the first phase. The preamble to the later Law of 1646[48] expressly declared that no human power can be "Lord over the Faith and the Consciences of men," but went on to provide punishment for any who were guilty of "broaching and maintaining any damnable heresy." In other words every man was free to hold any opinions he chose so long as he didn't go about publicly preaching them and trying to subvert this particular Holy Commonwealth which had been founded upon certain specific doctrine. This became the mature legal position of Massachusetts with respect to intolerance, as it did of both Connecticut and New Haven, though in these latter its application was much milder. Said John Cotton:

> . . . If a man hold forthe, or professe any errour, or false way, with a boisterous and arrogant spirit, to the disturbance of the civill peace, he may justly be punished according to the quality and measure of his disturbance caused by him.[49]

Even Roger Williams took the same view in theory, holding:

> That the Civill Peace may be broken by holding forth a Doctrine or practice, with rayling or reviling, daring or challenging speeches (which is a way of Arrogancy:) or with force of Arms, Swords, Guns, etc.; which is a way of Impetuousnesse.[50]

As we shall see, Massachusetts used the heresy laws freely against recent immigrants, but there was a memorable element of leniency in the fact that I have found but one case where its extreme penalty of banishment on pain of death was used against any settled resident of the jurisdiction.*

The Massachusetts Puritans of 1637 were about normal, average for the age, in their "persecution for conscience's sake." Religious liberty was hardly yet a perceptible whisper in the English air. In America, only the genius Williams had caught the pitch of it, and not even he had yet set it down. In Rhode Island they were putting it into amorphous practice, to the accompaniment of high political individualism and anarchy. In 1650 Portsmouth passed a Blue Law forbidding any man to "harbor another man's wife" after warning, "and in case of offence, he should forfeit £5 sterling for every night."[51] Between 1634 and 1637 more than 800 people,[52] including Hooker, Haynes, Ludlow and Pynchon, had left The Bay for Connecticut—"The River"—and prominent among the motives of most of them was a still shadowy dislike of The Bay's arbitrary government in church, state or both. In '38 Davenport was going to lead about 300 more to New Haven,[53] and, though they did set up "theocracy" there, the record shows that it was done hesitantly and with the considered

---

* On May 11, 1659 six residents of Salem, Laurence and Cassandra Southwick, Josiah Southwick, William Shattuck, Joshua Buffun and Nicholas Phelps, were banished by the General Court under pain of death. All were of old Salem families, Laurence Southwick being a freeman and having joined the Church with his wife. They went to Long Island and soon died. The other four returned eventually. (James Duncan Phillips, *Salem in the Seventeenth Century* [Boston, 1933], 197-99, 204, 296, Appendices B and C; Sidney Perley, *The History of Salem, Massachusetts* [Salem, 1924-26] II, 254-57, 260, 262-63, 268-69, 402; *Mass. Col. Rec.*, IV, pt. 1, 349, 366, 367.

consent of all. Already, beginning at Plymouth, running round the corner and westward along the Sound to Westchester, up the Connecticut River to Springfield, and northeastward again to Exeter, already a dimly marked arc that was going to be true New England was widening back like a huge, uncomprehending ripple from the bubbling of medievalism of Boston. But, outside of Rhode Island, no segment of that semicircle was as yet even debating religious tolerance.

In England a similar ripple of revolt was widening away from the arbitrariness of both Anglicans and Presbyterians. In the long Parliament of 1640 tolerance "rushed into the air,"[54] and the two who had lately been antagonists in the Antinomian controversy in New England were going to unite for it in Old England, Vane in the House and Peters stumping the countryside. In 1644 Williams, who remained always an American Puritan, was going to publish in London the *Bloudy Tenent of Persecution,* and Parliament was going to have it burned by the Hangman. But Harry Vane, with whom Williams was living, was going to use it as a weapon in the long fight. At the height of that fight for religious liberty, during the Protectorate, Cromwell the Puritan was going to put the epic question to an intolerant opponent, "Had you considered that, by the bowels of Jesus Christ, ye might be wrong?" And after the Restoration, which was going to cost Vane and Peters their heads, the toleration they had fought for was going to become the wave of the future. Then, and not till then, Massachusetts Bay was going to lag behind England, specifically from 1661 until the New Charter of 1692 forced toleration on the already decadent Puritans. But in 1637 there was no lagging. At the time of the Hutchinson affair they simply failed to grasp a faint whisper that only the gifted and the unsound could even hear, and that none could interpret, the whisper that was going to be the future world. Down one aisle of its history, the social rather than the religious aisle, The Bay has not yet heard that whisper.

The Massachusetts Bay Puritans of 1637 were men of the not yet old school of Medievalism within which religion, being fundamental, must be single. It was either this way or that way. It could not be both ways. Religion still had the dignity of art. God's Will or truth was as absolute as Beauty. Almost right religion, along with almost right poetry, was like an almost right egg. Winthrop, Dudley, Bradstreet and, for that matter, Cotton and Mrs. Hutchinson, could not conceive that there could be more than one right doctrine, more than one perception of Right Reason. If the doctrine of the Magis-

trates and Ministers of The Bay was right—and they were gambling
their lives, their families, their property and their honor that it was
—then every other doctrine must be wrong, and it was their duty as
custodians of Christ's City to see that no such erroneous doctrine
should prevail. To the Puritans, as to almost all humanity through
the first half of the seventeenth century, this singleness of truth and
necessary uniformity in its implementation were self-evident in matters of religion, as they had been two centuries earlier in matters of
government—and, incidentally, as they remain today in matters of
government for the bulk of humanity east of the Rhine.

To the Puritans, as to the Catholics and Anglicans before them,
Error was primarily ignorance. The errorrist was prima facie unin-
structed, and the truth should be lovingly and patiently "opened"
to him. If, after long sufferance, he failed to see the truth, then there
was some inherent "sinne" in him, some break in his potential line
of communication with the Holy Ghost. "For an erroneous and
blind conscience," said Cotton, "it is not lawful to persecute any
untill after admonition once or twice. . . ." The Word of God is
clear, and one in error "cannot but be convinced in conscience of
the dangerous error of his way, after once and twice admonition
wisely and faithfully dispensed. And then if any persist it is not out
of conscience, but against his conscience, as the Apostle saith [3
Titus, 10, 11] he is subverted and sinneth. . . . So that if such a
man . . . be therefore punished, he is not persecuted for cause
of conscience, but for sinning against his own conscience."[55] Master
Thomas Shepard of Cambridge, whose candor never suffered the
shadow of suspicion that eventually fell on Cotton's, used the same
language: "We never banished any for their consciences, but for
sinning against conscience, after the due means of conviction."[56]
There is pathos in Cotton's plea, at the height of his pamphlet war
with Williams, for understanding of this position which is to him
beyond question: "I should stand amazed how a man of understanding could out of such Conclusions make up this Inference. . . .
*That I doe professedly maintaine Persecution for Cause of Con-
science.* I that doe expresly, professedly deny Persecution of any, even
of Hereticks, unless it be when they come to persist in heresie, after
conviction, against conscience: how can I be said to maintaine Persecution for Cause of Conscience? But oh the wofull perversenesse and
blindnesse of a Conscience, when it is left of God, to be so farre trans-
ported with prejudice, as to judge a Cause of Conscience, and a cause
against Conscience to be all one."[57] Perry Miller after pointing out
how Cotton and Williams "debated the question of 'persecution'
through several hundred pages," concludes, "After they had finished,
I think it is very doubtful whether Cotton had even begun to see his
adversary's point."[58]

If from these expressions—and they fill the record—we are able for a moment to conceive of a world in which religious doctrine was as absolute and inviolable as, say, our doctrines of physical health and civil rights, if, in other words, we are able for a moment to tolerate religion, then we may be able to perceive that, even if the spectacular banishments were indeed based in intolerance, yet their perpetrators were not for that selfish and evil men. We may even conceive that it might have been necessary that Mrs. Hutchinson be banished from the Holy Commonwealth on account of her control of Boston. But beyond her political banishment it was unnecessary to go—although the Boston church would have found itself embarrassed if she had left in good standing and afterwards had asked recommendation to another church. The excommunication was Wilson's enterprise, and it is the only part of the proceeding that smacks certainly of arbitrary, self-indulgent tyranny. As already suggested, we find in each of the extremists pitted against each other in 1637 an intimation of one of the great Errors of the future. In the vituperation of Wilson in the church trial we get the tone of true Legal Arminianism, the Error of Moralistic Reason, the accent of William Lloyd Garrison. And in the ecstatic certitude of Mrs. Hutchinson we get a hint of that Antinomianism, that Error of Emotion, which was going to break out in the Great Awakening a century later, and in the barks and howls of camp meetings two centuries later, generally in the exhortings of all the evangelists who ever called poor souls to glory down the sawdust trail.

John Wilson and Anne Hutchinson were each far enough gone in their respective Errors so that in a religious age they could hardly live together in the same community. Even today, churches that profess any kind of doctrine would have trouble embracing them both, let alone Mrs. Hutchinson's disciple Captain Underhill who sinned cheerfully at the orders of the Holy Ghost. What we know today that Winthrop and Cotton and Shepard did not know is that the churches of Wilson and of Mrs. Hutchinson could in a mature polity stand beside each other in the same city block, and each could maintain such arbitrary doctrine and internal intolerance as it saw fit. To Winthrop his religion, being right, must perforce be the religion of the whole jurisdiction. To him the "countrey" of all New England was the single Holy Commonwealth, essentially a single church rather than a civil polity which, in Williams' idea and ours, might tolerate many churches and maintain its own integrity.

Where our churches are at their best, Williams and we are right. But few of our churches are at their best, and for the most part our tolerance is the tolerance of indifference. The price we have surrendered up in payment for our tolerance has been singleness, seriousness, intensity. We have learned to know that the other fellow might be right, and to laugh off our own possible errors as we laugh off defeat in politics. Which means that the price of our peace is flippancy. We are not quite serious any more. In the direction taken in the beginning by Massachusetts Bay there probably lay annihilation, but it would have been annihilation with all the stars in the sky of imagination burning. Our way may lead to annihilation also, the dull annihilation of the candles flickering out one by one. It may not be so. If it does not come it will be because once more we are able to feel intensely and selflessly, as Winthrop did and Shepard and Eliot and Warham and Hooker and Davenport and Eaton and Ludlow and Haynes; and Wheelwright and Vane and Peters and Williams and Coddington and Gorton and the Hutchinsons and Coggeshall and the Dyers. We can admire all these people for their spirit, of whichever persuasion. But what to us is the human cost of this catholicity of tolerant admiration? This putting of human value above Godly value?

In spite of the Antinomian trouble, and the temporary Alien Law that grew out of it, permitting any Magistrate to exclude an immigrant, the great migration continued at flood. Most of the new "planting" was under religious motivation, some by schism from older churches, some by groups that brought over their ministers from England and wanted to stay with them, some through divers scarcely Christian quarrels within the churches. By 1655 Massachusetts had edged back into the woods five, ten, fifteen miles above navigation and the metallic, oligarchical flavor of The Bay: Concord—their pastor the generally orthodox Peter Bulkeley; Hingham—their pastor the always revolutionary Peter Hobart; Dedham, Gloucester, Lynn, Longmeadow, Westfield, Northampton, Newbury, Haverhill, Topsfield, Groton, Nashua, Stow, Woburn, Sudbury, Medfield, Rowley, Reading, Billerica, Salisbury, Andover. And likewise by 1660 within and around Plymouth's jurisdiction, Scituate, Duxbury, Freetown, Sandwich, Bridgewater, Rehoboth, Taunton, Swansea, Eastham, Harwich, Yarmouth, Barnstable, Falmouth, Nausett, Edgartown, Middleborough and Nantucket became tiny outposts carrying God's business back among the Indians of the measureless forest and out among the great whales of the measureless sea.[59]

Rhode Island had got started in the spring of 1636 when Roger Williams, having spent most of the winter in the "filthy smoke holes" of the Narragansetts, had paddled down the Seekonk River, rounded Fox Hill, and presently settled in the woods of modern Main Street just above the spring that is the Plymouth Rock of Providence. In

'38 Mrs. Hutchinson and her family likewise went overland southerly and settled Portsmouth, and a distinguished group of banished Boston "Antinomians" came by sea.[60] The next year Coddington broke from them in a political quarrel and, with Dr. John Clark, founded Newport. Samuel Gorton, an original and truculent humanitarian, being long banished from Plymouth for denying the jurisdiction of their court to punish his wife's maid for smiling in church, and being afterwards banished from Portsmouth for denying the jurisdiction of their court to punish his servant for beating an old woman and her cow for trespassing on his land, and having quarrelled with Williams and Providence, finally settled Shawomet (Warwick) in 1643, thus completing the outline of the chaotic little Commonwealth.

Meanwhile, in '34, '35, and '36, secession from Massachusetts had put down schismatic roots along the Connecticut River: Windsor mostly from Dorchester on political motivation, under the leadership of Roger Ludlow, solicitor of the Inner Temple and late Deputy Governor of Massachusetts; Wethersfield by a church schism from Watertown; Hartford by a transference of the entire Newtown (Cambridge) church, complete with Thomas Hooker and the Teacher Samuel Stone whose home town in England had been Hertford, Elder William Goodwin and John Haynes, the richest man in rich Newtown. The cause of the Newtown-Hartford break was partly economic—a matter of more and better pasture for cows—partly religious—between Hooker and Cotton—and partly political—between Hooker and Haynes together against Winthrop—and it was a hegira of importance in the social and political evolution of America. Besides, there was Agawam* (Springfield), at first part of Connecticut and settled chiefly on economic motives under William Pynchon, late lord of the manor of Springfield in Essex; also Saybrook at the mouth of the River under the leadership of John Winthrop, Jr., planted as a refuge if need be for Lords Saye and Brooke, the latter the Earl of Lincoln.

Connecticut, as Windsor, Wethersfield and Hartford were collectively called, though it lost Springfield through an exchange of insolences with Pynchon about some corn for the Pequot War ('37), otherwise extended its jurisdiction rapidly. By 1660 it had expanded southward, to settle or absorb Middletown ('47) and Saybrook on the River, Southampton ('44) and Easthampton ('49) on Long Island, Stratford ('39), Fairfield ('39) and Norwalk ('49) on Long Island Sound, Derby ('54) on the Housatonic, and had moved northward to Hadley ('59) in Massachusetts, all of these settled chiefly for religious reasons. Only the two westward plantations of Farmington ('45) and

---

* "Agawam" means simply river, or the place on the river. It was first adopted for Ipswich, and there are a few other adoptions of it.

Simsbury ('47) were dominantly economic ventures, aiming at the Indian trade and certain local industries.

New Haven, founded in '38 by John Davenport and the rich merchant Theophilus Eaton because of dislike of the government of The Bay, was swiftly expanding its empire: Guilford ('38), Milford ('39), Southhold on Long Island and Greenwich ('40), Stamford ('41), and Branford ('44), all but the last planted chiefly for religion. Eastward grew up New London ('46) and Norwich ('60), the motives of these plantations partly religious, and Stonington whose motive was not religious. At least twenty-seven townships were settled by 1660 in the general jurisdictions of Massachusetts, Plymouth, Rhode Island, Connecticut and New Haven. And around the parent "Center" of each of these towns there sprouted, long before 1660, a little entourage of hamlets, typically bearing the name of the town with a directional or topographical qualification, as "North," "East," "South," "West," "Upper," "Lower," "Plains," or "Hollow."

By 1660 New England was well settled, and was divided between the inner and outer of two arcs concentric at Boston, the original port of entry and directly or indirectly the parent of all the other plantations except Plymouth. Close around the metropolis and suburban to it, the smaller arc cut inward from Salem far enough to include Lynn but not so far as to touch Groton or even Concord, and curved back to the ocean at Weymouth. This was the original Empire of Massachusetts Bay, always sturdy, pompous and intellectually distinguished, always hybrid between Europe and America. And standing back from Boston outside its empire of satellites, beginning at Plymouth, running southward and westward along the Sound to Greenwich, thence up along the frontier northeastward through Derby, Farmington, Simsbury, Westfield, Northampton, Hadley, Nashua, Groton, Exeter in New Hampshire, back to the coast at Hampton, and so up the coast of Maine to Damariscotta, was the great crooked arc which already was truly New England and which, from its geographical and cultural spine, was then and still might properly be called The River.

Of the four jurisdictions of The River, New Haven was alien, being "theocratic" and essentially oligarchical after the manner of Boston. Plymouth was already lapsing into snobbish mediocrity under the heavy shadow of the Bay, and Rhode Island was a brawling shambles of individualism. More populous, distinguished in leadership and prophetic of America than any of these, Connecticut was truly The River, together with all of its outposts, culturally most of those of New Haven, and many in the jurisdiction of Massachusetts outside the semicircle of The Bay. Here in Windsor, Wethersfield and Hartford, born in revolt against The Bay, was the center and source of what was going to be truly New England and Greater New England westward to the Pacific.

In formal religion the revolt of The River against The Bay was of no great importance, being based in disapproval partly of Cotton's near-Antinomian leanings, and partly of the limitations he put on the powers of the Congregation.[61] But in Political terms it was a move of significance, being a secular extension of the Equalitarian aspect of Congregationalism and, conformably to that, an Individualistic revolt against Winthrop's doctrine of arbitrary power in the Magistrates. This early proto-democratic tendency in Connecticut is recorded chiefly in three documents.

The first is a *Sermon* preached by Thomas Hooker to the Connecticut General Court in May, 1638, in which he makes an important point that was in contrast to the practice in Massachusetts: The People who choose their governing officials should also have the power to limit their authority by law.

The second pertinent document is a *Letter* of Hooker's to Winthrop in September, 1638, replying to one of the Massachusetts Governor in which he had asserted his well-known view that the smaller the number of people governing a state—he had in mind the Magistrates—the more efficient would be the government. Hooker's reply makes, among others, two major points: 1) Government should be by law, not by men—a broadening of the doctrine announced in the Sermon; 2) The best government is a representative one chosen by "all." (By "all," Hooker may have meant the large aristocracy of the Freemen, about a quarter of the mature males, who had the suffrage in Colony matters, or he may have meant the "Inhabitants" who were virtually all of the adult males and had the vote in local matters.)

The third document recording Connecticut's early democratic tendency is the Fundamental Orders adopted by the Connecticut General Court in 1639, about four months after Hooker's letter to Winthrop. They include five measures of a seeming democratic tendency away from the system of government at The Bay:

1) The Freemen were to be elected by the General Court, without the condition of church membership which was imposed at The Bay.

2) The Inhabitants were to be elected by their towns upon no qualification except that they be "of honest conversation."

3) The Inhabitants were to elect the Deputies or Representatives to the General Court, though the Deputies themselves must be Freemen.

4) If the Governor or Magistrates failed to assemble the Genral Court in emergency, the Freemen might do so.

5) No one could hold successive terms as Governor.

These eight "democratical" measures in these three documents have been the subject of much controversy, and it is not the present purpose to add to it.* All but the third of the "Fundamentals" quoted was somewhat dedemocratized in the reaction which Connecticut suffered in the 1650's and '60's. Our concern here is not directly with the Political meaning of these things but with their Religious origins. In each of the measures mentioned we can feel a quality of Individualism, of the self-assertion of the Connecticut emigrés against the oligarchical practices at The Bay. But, also, in every one of them we can sense the Equalitarian trend of which we find some evidences

* The recognized statement upon the democratic trend in early Connecticut is that of Perry Miller in "Hooker and Connecticut Democracy" (*The New England Quarterly*, IV, 4 [October, 1931], 663-712). The article is directed chiefly at the absurd conclusions of earlier historians that Hooker and others were motivated by consciously democratic doctrine. With this aim in view, most of it is devoted to showing that Hooker and everybody else in the seventeenth century was aristocratic in social assumptions, and that he was spotlessly orthodox in religion. Professor Miller concedes in the last few pages that the *Fundamental Articles* did in fact contain important advances in the democratic direction, but he seems to minimize their importance because they evolved out of clerical rather than secular political doctrine. The effect of his article, whether intended or not, has been the deprecation of the very great importance of Hooker and the *Fundamental Orders* in American political and social evolution. He barely hints at what was perhaps the basically significant point, namely the equalitarian *feeling* in Connecticut of which the three pertinent documents were outward expressions.

Elsewhere (*The New England Mind—The Seventeenth Century* [New York, 1939], 439-40) Professor Miller makes without citation a statement for which I have been able to find no support. Referring to the theocratic franchise of Massachusetts and New Haven, he says: ". . . The Connecticut settlements did not expressly confine the vote to church members, but provided for a ministerial supervision of the electorate that achieved by less obvious means the same control." From this I must dissent. In the beginning the "Inhabitants" were chosen by majority vote in town meeting. During the reaction of the 1650's and '60's a property qualification was imposed, and a candidate for the freemanship had to bring to the General Court a certificate of good character, not from the Minister but from the Deputies of his town. Other limitations were put both on the local and the "free" suffrage, but they had nothing to do with religion. The Connecticut government was notoriously free of that meddling by the ministers which was the practice at The Bay. The ministers were doubtless the most influential citizens at The River, as elsewhere, but there was no "provision" for a "ministerial supervision of the electorate."

It is also sometimes stated that the freemanship in Connecticut was restricted to the church members in practice, if not by law. Because the early records of all three of the first towns have been lost, there is available scarcely more evidence to rebut such a charge than there is to support it. There is no space here for a detailing of such evidence as there is; but the inference to be drawn from it is, first, that the male membership in the churches was very small, though the attendance was large, and, second, that the magistrates and deputies, which is to say the leading freemen, were often not members of any church.

The emergence of equalitarian and possibly "democratical" tendencies in early Connecticut is an intriguing topic because of the initial difficulty of putting ourselves in the social posture of the Puritans and those particular Puritans. But it is an important transition withal, and doubtless much more inquiry will be directed to it. A possibly new approach is made by B. Katherine Brown in "A Note on the Puritan Concept of Aristocracy" in the *Mississippi Valley Historical Review* for June, 1954. At the State University of Iowa, Douglas Shepard is at work translating out of shorthand notes certain unpublished sermons of Hooker during 1638 which may or may not throw further light on his attitude.

elsewhere both in Hooker and in John Haynes the first Governor. In Connecticut from the very beginning, the Congregational fellowship in which all were equal before God was extended to embrace many, indeed most, outside the church in an equivalent secular fellowship. Thus there was established early along The River a special social atmosphere which was in contrast to the Oligarchical tension at The Bay, the equality of Mediocrity at Plymouth, and the belligerent Individualism of Rhode Island. In the midst of a society that was and for a long time remained formally aristocratic, the *Fundamental Orders* secularized a religious principle which became the focus of the formative culture of The River and eventually of most of America.

By the time of the passage of the *Fundamental Orders*, the population that was going to mature that culture and carry it into the fu-ure was already appreciable. Having started from the pathetic 400 of Plymouth in 1634 when the Bay was far over 4,000, the population of the great arc had grown steadily to overhaul that of the more European culture. In 1640, The Bay, including Maine but not New Hampshire, had about 16,000 souls, The River about 8,000. By 1660, one was a little above and the other a little below 20,000.[62] From then on The River moved into the majority of New England, and much later into the major influence upon America.

The quality of the immigration after the 1630's was, from the Puritan point of view, decreasingly savory. It was what might be expected to flock to now successful settlements out of a crowded and revolutionary England—wastrels, criminals, adventur-ers, Baptists, Presbyterians, Quakers and, during the Commonwealth, even Anglicans. The court records proclaim the wastrels and the criminals with their multiplying charges of pilfering, of being taken "disguised with drink," of "threatening and tumultuous carriage," of divers assaults and "profane swearing," and the excess of men in the population is apparent in the cases of "lascivious carriage," lewd be-havior, "bestial carriage" and the official watchfulness for professional and semi-professional brothels. In Hartford Walter Gray was "publiquely corrected"—that is, whipped—"for his misdemeanor in laboring to inveagle the affections of Mr. Hoockers mayde." Boggett Egleston was fined 20s "for bequeathing his wife to a young man."[63] The pillory, stocks, whipping-post, the placard, the forked stick on the tongue, the ducking stool were all well patronized in the larger villages, as they were in large villages everywhere.

In 1640 and '50 Massachusetts, New Haven and Connecticut pub-

lished their criminal codes[64] whose chief object was the maintenance
of the public peace. In an age of religion and state socialism, there was
nothing peculiarly "blue" in a five shilling fine—rarely enforced—for
failure to go to church, and in larger penalties for profaning the
Sabbath. One finds less of the savor of Arminianism or "Puritanism"
than of bourgeois respectability in the limitation upon sales of
liquor calculated to reduce the tavern brawls, and in the prohibition
of "drinking"— that is, smoking—tobacco on the street, a notoriously
vulgar practice. There was everywhere great concern over and legislation against the use of lace and fancy ribbands by those of low
station,[65] but this was aimed not at the denial of pleasure but at the
maintenance of social stratification, a conservative ruling class repressing the lower orders who were thought to be making too much
money and forgetting their place—for American social climbing and
shortage of labor were chronic from the beginning.

As in the matter of ordinary police court criminology, so in the
suppression of heresy, "persecution for conscience's sake," there was
more of it between 1640 and 1660 because the population was greater
and there was proportionately more offense. In 1644 and 1646 Massachusetts, as we have seen, made specifically criminal the promulgation of the heresies that it had already found to be a menace to the
Holy Commonwealth, thus avoiding the former need of finding them
seditious. The preamble of the '46 statute is noteworthy as stating the
basis of religious tolerance, and it is to be observed in this, as in most
statutes of orthodoxy, that heresies were not punishable until they
were "broached" or preached. The two statutes of '44 and '46 were
combined in the *Lawes and Libertyes* of 1660:[66]

> *Although no human Power, be Lord over the Faith and Con-*
> *sciences of men, yet because such as bring in damnable Heresies,*
> *tending to the subversion of the Christian Faith and destruc-*
> *tions of the soules of men, ought surely to be restrained from*
> *such notorious impieties.* It is therefore Ordered and declared
> by the Court. That if any *Christian* within this Iurisdiction,
> shall go about to subvert and destroy the *Christian Faith and*
> *Religion,* by broaching and maintaining any *damnable Here-*
> *sies:* as denying the immortality of the soule [this a reference to
> Mrs. Hutchinson in her Examination] or the resurrection of
> the body [the same], . . . or . . . that Christ gave himselfe a
> ransom for our sins, or shall affirm that we are not justifyed by
> his death and righteousnes, but by the perfections of our own
> works [This asserts the Covenant of Grace as the law of the
> land, and makes criminal Arminianism and the doctrine of
> the Covenant of Works, but for the slight hedge in the word
> "righteousnes"], or shall deny the morallity of the Fourth
> Commandement [This probably directed against the Seventh

Day Baptists], or shall openly Condemn or oppose the Baptizing of Infants [this, of course, for all the Baptists] . . . or shall deny the ordinance of the Magistracy [this taking care of Williams' charges], or their Lawfull Authority to make war [this meeting an old complaint of John Eliot against the magistrates' dealing with the Pequots], or to punish the outward breaches of the first Table* [this for Williams again], or shall endeavour to seduce others to any of the errors or heresies above mentioned, every such person continuing obstinate therein, after due means of Conviction, shall be sentenced to Banishment.

New Haven had a similar law with a nearly identical preamble, but it was much milder in scope and punishment.[67] Connecticut and Rhode Island had no laws against heresy at all, though both Connecticut and New Haven had laws aimed at the Quakers, forbidding the interruption of church meetings.[68] Even in Massachusetts, there were numerous Quaker meetings and Baptist congregations that met discreetly and were never disturbed.

A much publicized case of persecution in this period is that of the blazing humanitarian Samuel Gorton who, having quarrelled with every leader in Plymouth and Rhode Island, founded Warwick on Narragansett Bay and built a blockhouse there. The land was within the patent of Massachusetts Bay, whose authorities in 1643 demanded that Gorton come to Boston to account for his unauthorized and so illegal behavior. His reply was in rich Elizabethan prose, so they sent a posse to take him and nine friends who comprised his garrison. After resisting the law with military force for twenty-four hours, they surrendered and were marched to Boston. Their highly original heresies were investigated, and Gorton's biographer[69] says they were tried for blasphemy while Winthrop[70] has it that they were tried for blasphemy and treason which very nearly cost Gorton his life. They were all put to work on farms, with a shackle on one leg, and after a few months were released upon the insistence of the Deputies, the Lower House of the General Court. Gorton went to England and got an order of free passage across Massachusetts, for in the Long Parliament tolerance had already "rushed into the air." Nine years later, in 1652, he was moderator of the Rhode Island Assembly that passed, and he is supposed to have written, the first Abolition Law in America, freeing slaves and indentured servants who had worked ten years.[71] (Needless to say, the law was not enforced and ultimately Rhode Island had more slaves per capita than any other Commonwealth in New England.)

A more important heresy of the 1640's was that of the "Remonstrance and Humble Petition," in which seven gentlemen, residents

---

* The First Table of the Law, being the first four Commandments, the only truly religious commandments.

of Massachusetts—including Dr. Robert Child, a friend of John Winthrop, Jr., William Vassal, original governor of the Massachusetts Bay Company in England, Samuel Maverick, for long a barely tolerated Anglican on Noddle's Island in Massachusetts Bay and the donator of his surname to American slang, and David Yale, the father of Elihu, tried both openly and by intrigue, to oust the Puritan government, seat a royal governor, and set up English law and Presbyterian church polity. Doubtless because of the high station of these people—for gentlemen must not suffer ignominious "correction" —their very real and dangerous sedition brought on them only heavy fines.

In 1648 as part of the general religious ferment, especially the tension between the Independents or Puritans and the Presbyterians in England which had produced the Westminster Confession, the first of New England's great synods assembled and passed the Cambridge Platform,[72] being the composition of Richard Mather. Two established practices of Massachusetts were confirmed. On the side of religious intolerance it was declared by the ministers that "Idolatry, Blasphemy, Heresy, venting corrupt and pernicious opinions . . . are to be restrayned; and punished by civil authority."[73] And on the more permanently American side, the congregational polity, the "New England way" as it was called, was reasserted as against the Presbyterians.[74]

In the years surrounding the promulgation of the Cambridge Platform by the synod of 1648, and its adoption two years later, the three personal pillars of the Holy Commonwealth fell, two of them accredited with appropriate death-bed speeches. We have already noticed that of Hooker, dying in Hartford in the flu epidemic of 1647, when one of his parishioners said, "Sir, you are going to receive your reward," and he replied, "Brother, I am going to receive mercy."[75] At Winthrop's death in 1649, it was fitting that, as at the first settlement of The Bay, he was the Governor and Thomas Dudley was Deputy Governor. As he lay in bed, the Deputy brought him to sign a routine order for the expulsion of some Heretic. Wearily Winthrop pushed it away, saying he had done too much of that work already.[76] We read with relief that at the end this great man at least glimpsed the modern light. But for him it probably was not a light. For him it was a confession that the integrated Holy Commonwealth could not be, that the work of his life was a failure. His death removed the personal bulwark of the Massachusetts "theocracy." Its artificial support of the "sanctified" suffrage remained for fifteen years more.

Three years later, in '52, the death of John Cotton was the fall of a pillar that in our view had shrunk smaller than the diameter of either Hooker or Winthrop, for rightly or wrongly Cotton had turned his coat, during the "Antinomian" trouble, to the uniform of the strongest legions. But he was for all that a great reputation throughout New England, and his name alone was a support to the Holy Commonwealth. Even before Cotton's death, Endicott as governor was embarking on the course that was going to weaken the state and hurt religion in America, both then and for centuries to come.

Until 1650 and the death of the great leaders, there is no real sign of any decline in religion. No doubt the general intensity was diluted a little toward worldliness by the invasion of thousands of irresponsibles with their brawls and their brothels. Possibly there was among the merchants an increasing tendency to practice "Diligence" with an eye to its profitability rather than as a compliance with God's command to exercise in one's calling. But in the records of the colonies there is no sign of the narrowing of the Current of Religion through the intrusion of Arminianism and its bigotry, or of any contraction or dimming of the sky of eternity which the current through Faith reflected. In 1647, the *Diary* of John Hull,[77] then still a young man, son of a yeoman, destined to become the Mintmaster, probably the richest citizen of Boston, no intellectual, perhaps the first "proper Bostonian," shows the simple piety of the old Orthodoxy under the doctrine of the Covenant of Grace, with never a thought of Works:

> It pleased God not to let me run on always in my sinful way, the end of which is hell: but, as he brought me to this good land, so he planted me under choice means—viz. in Boston, under the ministry of Mr. John Cotton,—and, in the end, did make his ministry effectual (by the breathings of his own good Spirit) to beget me to God, and in some measure to increase and build me up in holy fellowship with him. Through his abundant grace, he gave me room in the hearts of his people, so that I was accepted to fellowship with his church, about the 15th of October, 1648.

The old faith continued healthy through the 1640's, and it declines less in the 1650's than might be implied from the notorious activities of the self-centered Arminians: John Endicott, henceforth perennial Governor, John Wilson, still reigning in the Boston pulpit from which Mrs. Hutchinson had failed to dislodge him, and John Norton, imported from Ipswich to take Cotton's place as teacher and complete the bloody triumvirate. These were perverted men in whom the light of Religion had turned to the fire of self-assertiveness and who, in their mistaken efforts to maintain the old order, went to excesses which Winthrop at his least tolerant would not have permitted. The strongest point against Massachusetts in the anti-Puritan indictment is that in the face of a trend toward tolerance in England, it so far submitted to the prestige of these small and single-minded men as to keep them in power.

In alleviation of the reputation that has been spread over New England, it may be pointed out that the persecution of Quakers in England exceeded that of Massachusetts in scope if not in intensity, and that in New England generally, that is in what I call The River, the persecution of heretics varied from slight in New Haven to non-existent in Rhode Island. Connecticut disliked Baptists[78] and Quakers[79] as sincerely as Massachusetts did. Yet it handled them with relative gentleness, easing them out under threats of imprisonment and laws of banishment, not under pain of death. Theocratic New Haven appears to have been the only community in all The River to apply even the traditionally routine "corrections" of branding or light whipping, and then only when Quakers held meetings or interrupted orthodox ones. It has been the efforts of the debunkers, not the facts, that in the popular mind have attributed to all Puritans the practices of three leaders of The Bay.

The Massachusetts persecution got under way in 1651 when three Rhode Island Baptists, including that rival of Winthrop for selflessness, Dr. John Clark, coming to visit in Lynn a sick former member of their Newport church, committed contemptuous indecorum by keeping their hats on in a Puritan meeting, and violated the Law of 1644 by holding small Baptist services. They were arrested, carried to Boston, hailed before a Particular Court—the Magistrates in their judicial capacity—and fined, with an alternative of whipping. During the trial, according to Obadiah Holmes, one of the defendants,[80] "I exprest myself in these words; I blesse God I am counted worthy to suffer for the name of Iesus; whereupon Iohn Wilson (their pastor as they call him) strook me before the Judgement Seat, and cursed me, saying, The Curse of God, or Iesus goe with thee. . . ."

Protesting against their trial, the Baptists would not pay their fines, so their sentence was virtually of whipping. Surreptitiously, someone paid Clark's fine and the bail of the third prisoner, Crandall, to the chagrin of both. Holmes took his whipping. He reported that as he left the whipping post two local Baptists expressed sympathy for him, and that for this sacrilege they were themselves sentenced to an alternative of a fine or a whipping. As in the cases of Clark and Crandall, their fines were clandestinely paid. Immediately out of jail Holmes preached again, and a new warrant was issued for his arrest.

This time he fled, and escaped into Rhode Island from hot pursuit. The Quakers were an entirely different kettle of heresy. The Baptists were essentially as good Calvinists as the Puritans, but the Quakers, with their doctrine of the Inner Light, were close to true and irresponsible Antinomianism. Furthermore, they—or some of them, especially their missionaries—supported the suspicion by their conduct, which was intolerably offensive, even in that coarse age. By the religious criminology of the day, anywhere in Christendom, they gave Massachusetts provocation and got what they deserved.* With the exception of Mary Dyer, those who suffered in New England were ignorant, filthy, psychopathic and shrill, having no moral relation to the later Quakers of quietism and Christian service. And even Mary Dyer is supposed by good authority to have been of unsound mind.[81] They were the radicals of the seventeenth-century religious world, and their purposes, like those of all radicals, were primarily destructive, especially to spoil the efforts of the Liberals, the Puritans. It was the practice of their missionaries to go about the streets and enter Puritan meetings either naked or swathed in ghostly sheets,[82] their faces smeared with black paint which was associated with prophetic powers, and to disrupt the services by screams and dismal prophecies of fire and pestilence to fall upon Massachusetts, along with filthy vilification of the ministers. At one Thursday lecture in Boston two Quaker women left relieving signs of humor in the record by breaking each a bottle over Norton's head "as a sign of his emptiness."[83]

This behavior of the Quakers was comprehensibly unpopular and probably was perpetrated with the deliberate purpose of winning torture and in some cases martyrdom. It is to the eternal credit of

* The persecution of Quakers in England lasted longer and was larger per capita of the population. A conservative estimate of Quakers jailed in England between 1660 and 1685 would be 10,000 (combined from the figures for the separate persecutions in Elbert Russell, *The History of Quakerism,* [New York, 1942] 107) out of a mean population of 5,000,000 (estimate combined from Godfrey Davies, *The Early Stuarts* [Oxford, 1937] 259, and *An Historical Geography of England before A.D. 1800,* H. C. Darby, ed., [Cambridge, 1836], 435-6.)—that is, one in 500. In the same period about 50 Quakers were jailed in New England out of an estimated mean population of 75,000 (Greene and Harrington, *Population before 1790,* 9—one in 1,500. These estimates which ignore duplications and the total Quaker population on both sides, for which no figures seem to exist, are guesses. There are no data on which to base a comparison of whippings and mutilations, but the former were common and the latter rare in both jurisdictions. In the matter of fatalities, New England comes off badly. The laws permitted banishment upon pain of death under certain conditions in both countries, but the extreme penalty was not applied in England. Out of 10,000 jailed there, perhaps 100 died through the unbribed malice or deliberate neglect of the jailers—one in 100. Out of perhaps 50 jailed in New England, four were executed—one in twelve. Russell's *Quakerism,* 65, calls the sufferings in New England "on the whole light" compared with those in England after 1660.

Rhode Island that, while the Quakers—or their missionaries—behaved as badly there, and everyone, including Williams,[84] openly despised them, they were treated with no more violence than was necessary to eject them from the meetings of the Puritans, the Baptists and other Christians. In '57, when a "band of Quaker missionaries" landed in Rhode Island, and commissioners of the United Colonies—Massachusetts, Plymouth, Connecticut and New Haven—wrote asking that they send them away, the classic reply is supposed by some to have been written by the same Samuel Gorton whom the Massachusetts Magistrates had manhandled ten years before, and who was now secretary of the united Plantations. According to this letter,[85] the Quakers in Rhode Island were coming "to loath this place, for that they are not opposed by the civill authority. . . ; they delight to be persecuted by civill powers, and when they are soe, they are like to gain more adherents by the conseyte of their patient sufferings, than by consent to their pernicious sayings."

The first Quakers of record to enter Massachusetts were ten missionaries in 1656 who were deported—in the salutary method used in Virginia—under a series of laws passed quickly for their benefit. After several less drastic laws failed to keep out the "pernitious sect," in 1658 the General Court passed the famous severe one providing banishment on pain of death for non-resident Quakers who came in, and the same dreadful penalty for "Inhabitants"—that is, residents—who, after a session in jail and plenty of opportunity to recant, refused to do so. As already observed, the law seems to have been invoked against Inhabitants in only one trial, though there were six defendants.

This was the first of the laws of intolerance that did not make "broaching" or preaching the condition of the penalty of banishment. But the four executed under it were plentifully guilty of preaching; and all came in from Rhode Island intentionally seeking martyrdom. Mary Dyer, the friend of Anne Hutchinson, was a decent and beautiful woman who greatly embarrassed Massachusetts by insisting that they apply the law to her. In October, '59, when two of her companions were hanged, she was reprieved on the scaffold, the hood already on and the noose around her neck, and carried back to Rhode Island by her family. All winter her friends and relations pled with her, including some who came down from Massachusetts. But in the spring of '60, she insisted on returning to bear witness, as she told the Massachusetts magistrates, against the unjust law. There is much legend about her last twenty-four hours. One—so probable as to be self-evident—was that she was offered a reprieve at the scaffold if she would recant.[86] The other, wholly apocryphal though possible, is that, as in the case of Socrates, her jail door was left unlocked the night before her execution, and a ship lay waiting in the Harbor. All we know for certain is that she refused all shifts.

After one more execution, in the spring of '61, the Massachusetts capital penalty was repealed, under both popular pressure and a royal order. A substitute law required the leading of Quakers at a cart's tail to the boundary of the jurisdiction, ten stripes to be given them in every town through which they passed. In 1662 the number of towns required to whip them was reduced to three.

Like the first and great triumvirate of New England, the second and evil one of Boston finished their work within a few years of each other. Norton died in '63, Endicott in '65, and Wilson in '67. Appropriately, in the year of Endicott's death a royal commission ordered Massachusetts to stop persecuting the Quakers.[87] It is refreshing to read in the Journal of the *Life and Gospel Labours of John Burnyeat*,[88] Quaker, the following account of a casual trip in '66—the year between the deaths of Endicott and Wilson—through what in their active lives would have been the Valley of Death for him:

> About the latter end of the sixth month, I took my journey [from Rhode Island] towards Sandwich; and when I was clear there, I took my journey by Plymouth to Tewkesbury, and so to Marshfield and Scituate, and to Boston, and I visited Friends and had meetings. From Boston I went to Salem, and so on to Piscataqua. When I was clear there, I returned back through the meetings, and came to Hampton, Salem, Boston, Scituate, Marshfield, and so by Tewkesbury and Plymouth to Sandwich, and from thence through the woods to Ponyganset, and from thence over into Rhode Island.

Thus ended the bloody 50's of Puritanism, the reign of three cruel, un-Christian, self-assertive old men who, through their prestige as survivors, however perverted, of the first generation, were able to browbeat a bare majority of the Magistrates and a minority of the Deputies. And paradoxically, during this same decade, the actual drift of public feeling was toward tolerance, like that of England, so that by 1660 the senile triumvirate was ruling in the face of a preponderant popular disapproval. Even in Winthrop's time, the punishment of Samuel Gorton and his friends is claimed to have been suspended because of popular pressure. Because the Cambridge Platform confirmed clerical authority to the Civil Courts, the Deputies refused for two years to pass the whole Platform and in the final vote fourteen deputies from thirteen towns, including Boston and Salem, voted against it.[89] The capital law against Quakers passed the Deputies against opposition. In '58 the people of Boston were so angered at the particularly brutal treatment of William Brend—"His Back and Arms were bruised, and black, and the

Blood hanging as it were in Bags under his Arms . . ." that the
Governor sent "his Surgeion" to prison to treat him. The doctor's
report that "His Flesh would rot from off his Bones" so "exas-
perated" the crowd that the Magistrates were forced to post on the
Meeting House door a notice that the jailer would be "dealt withal
at the next Court."[90]

Besides these specific evidences of emergent tolerance there was a
general and practical form of it which began to show itself in this
period and was related to the growth of local democracy. This was
the internal tolerance of the townships, of people involved in a
common religious, social and economic enterprise, who asked no more
of each other than a God-fearing external decency, to whom neigh-
borliness and cooperation were more essential than uniform dogma.
While the minority of the hairline orthodox, backed by the distant
central government, held the community integrated round the
church, the majority of the slightly heterodox, some in the church
and some outside it, knew each in his heart that he deviated from
the line of pure doctrine, and that most of his neighbors did also.
So there grew up a mutual tolerance conformable to the already
settled habit of reticence, each Inhabitant or local voter minding
his own business and asking that his neighbors mind theirs. Behind
this solid, interlocked local wall, unrecorded numbers of Baptists
and Quakers flourished and even convened, in Massachusetts as in
Connecticut and New Haven, without being informed upon. Of the
Baptists we know only that there were enough in Lynn to assemble
a meeting under Clark, Holmes and Crandall, and that of these
only the three "foreigners" were troubled; that others appeared out
of the ground in Boston to sympathize with Holmes, and still others
to pay the fines of these sympathizers as well as those of Clark and
Crandall;[91] that a party came from Rhode Island to visit Holmes,
Clark and Crandall, and returned without being molested.[92] Likewise, divers Quakers appeared from nowhere to take over, swathe,
and bury under Boston Common the bodies of the four of their
bretheren who were hung on the scaffold at the North End.[93] All of
these people lived in their communities by virtue of a wall of outward uniformity and local solidarity behind which there developed
a passionate independence or individualism of opinion—one of
the happy by-products of oppressive orthodoxy. What the more or
less heterodox Puritan could not express openly boiled in him
privately; and he knew that his neighbors boiled also. And they convened at town affairs, and drank rum together at raisings and train-

ing days, and cooperated for the general good, and knew intimately each other's habits and opinions, and in the presence of the orthodox and of strangers were ignorant of all these things.

But the increasing tolerance of religious difference may have marked less a trend toward a more genial Christianity than a drift toward indifference to all religion. There was evidence of this in decreasing crops of saints during the '50's, especially in the failure of many regular church attendants of the new generation to qualify for membership by an experience of Grace and recitation thereof before the local Congregation. Among the causes of this ominous reticence one of the strongest was of a personal nature, a decline in reverence, if not for God, then certainly for their neighbors, a perhaps excusable doubt of the complete saintliness of the Elected congregations whom they knew intimately, even including the Minister. You couldn't grow up in the palisaded or fortified village with John and Thomas, Priscilla and Abigail without knowing both the gossip and the truth about them. Under the reticence of village life you tolerated and concealed their moral errors, just as you did their doctrinal errors. But as to their special sanctification, even after the church recognized it by admitting them, and especially as to their qualification to pass on your qualification for admission, you must have your reservations. A little later, in 1665, John Farnam, under the gravest doctrinal charges by his brethren in the Second Church of Christ in Boston, told them defiantly that they "must not expect that he should whine & Blubber & keep a stiew" because they were threatening to excommunicate him, that he "did not come here to be snapt & snubd & snarled at by every one."[94]

This social sophistication began seriously to clog the machinery of the churches after 1647. In that year Thomas Hooker died, and, freed of the moderating effect of his large humanity, Connecticut "burst into flames." The first quarrel broke in his own church in Hartford, between the liberal faction, led by Master Samuel Stone, for fourteen years the teacher and Hooker's associate, and the conservative faction, led by William Goodwin who had been Ruling Elder somewhat longer. The division in the beginning was over a complaint by the powerful Goodwin minority that Master Stone had not consulted the Congregation before rejecting, as a candidate for Hooker's successor, the distinguished dyspeptic Michael Wigglesworth, afterwards author of *The Day of Doom*. Here Stone's position was partly that of ancient aristocracy that he had brought from England which many still shared and which he revealed in his famous description of congregational polity as a "speaking aristocracy before a silent democracy." And he was also suspect, in application of this view, of leanings toward that Presbyterianism which, in this time of the *Remonstrance* in Massachusetts, was inflammable matter.[95] The controversy presently took other forms, and when it had gone on for many years, and several councils in Connecticut had failed to accomplish a reconciliation, five of the chief ministers of Massachusetts wrote in great concern over "so famous a sister church and mother in Israel still bleeding, if not ulcerating. . . . Our bowels! Our bowels! we are payned at the very hearts, we cannot hold our penn."[96]

Meanwhile there were other churches "in flames" in the Connecticut Valley, including those of the two other original towns, Windsor[97] and Wethersfield.[98] In all of them, as in Hartford and in many in Massachusetts, whatever the instance of controversy might have been, it eventually gathered around the question of church admissions. Many of the children of the first generation, although they were baptized Puritans, pious and regular church attendants, either could not or would not pass the inquisition by their familiar neighbors required to admit them to the congregations. By the '50's their children were numerous, and they wanted to have them baptized. But persons who were not themselves in full membership could not have their children baptized, wherefore the little ones in increasing thousands were in danger of, and many of the them yearly were entering through infant mortality, "the easiest room in hell."[99] The aggrieved second-generation Puritans were reinforced by the respectable elements in the continuing immigration, church-goers and valuable citizens, some of them Anglicans, some English Puritans of moderate churches from whom the American Puritans would not receive transfers. All demanded baptism for their children, and in some places also they demanded a voice in the affairs of the churches they attended and for whose support they were taxed.[100]

The result of the controversy was the famous Halfway Covenant, adopted in 1657 by a conference attended by the elders of Massachusetts and Connecticut, New Haven sending its opinion, and Plymouth not responding to the invitation. The central finding of the conference, respecting a baptized person who had not enjoyed and revealed to a congregation a full experience of Grace, was that, "In case they understand the ground of Religion, are not scandalous, and solemnly own the Covenant" (that is, the contract of membership of the church they attended) "in their own persons, wherein they give up both themselves and their children unto the Lord, and desire Baptism for them, we . . . see not sufficient cause to deny Baptism unto their children——."[101] Such parents, such baptized persons who could not or would not give such a public account of religious experience as would qualify them for full communion, such persons who had taken one but not the other of the two sacraments (Baptism and Communion), that is to say they had taken half of them, were called colloquially Halfway Members of the churches. And their contract with the church was called the Halfway Covenant.

The Connecticut General Court promptly recommended the findings of the Conference to the churches, and later—1662—the Massachusetts Court did the same. The immediate effect of the recommendation in Connecticut was to increase the scope and violence of the religious civil war, now aligned along the question whether they should or should not accept it. Things got worse in Wethersfield and Windsor, but especially in Hartford where the Goodwin group withdrew from the church though Stone would not grant them an official dismission. The churches of Stratford, Norwalk, New Haven, Branford and Guilford—the last three still independent of Connecticut—all rocked and split in varying degrees.[102] Generally, the ministers favored the Halfway Covenant, because it offered the best hope of increasing their attendance. Master Stow of Middletown was an exception, a conservative minister. He was described by several as a contentious, pestilent person, one of them charging him with stating that those that were not in the full church covenant were "dogs and among dogs and in the Kingdom of Sathan and at Sathan's command."[103]

The central and parent struggle in Hartford was resolved in 1659 when a new church Council advised the granting of a dismission to Goodwin and his "withdrawers." This was done, and some sixty of them "speedily removed to Hadley," Massachusetts,[104] where they took for pastor of their new church the Reverend John Russell who had just been ousted from his former one in Wethersfield.[105] The end of the season of strife came in 1666 when Connecticut passed its "first toleration act." It was sorry toleration, admitting no heretical sects, but permitting "persons of worth for prudence and piety" who were "approved . . . as orthodox and sound in the fundamentals of Christian religion" to found separate churches.[106] It was a long way yet to religious liberty, but the wall was minutely breached. At least in one of the two strong colonies of New England the Holy Experiment of orthodoxy supported by government to the last comma was over.

Actually, the whole struggle that centered around the Halfway Covenant throughout New England evinced a confusion of godly and worldy motives, of piety and social snobbery, which were the

death throes of the hope of the Holy Commonwealth, and the recommendation of the Covenant by the Conference of 1657 was the first
unmistakable confession of mortality. Thereafter death gathered in
from different directions. The Restoration in 1660 was a guarantee
of the end of the Puritan state, sooner or later. In 1664 and '65 the
artificial bulwark of electoral "theocracy" fell in the two colonies
that practiced it, completing the collapse that had begun when
Massachusetts lost its personal support in the deaths of Winthrop
and Cotton. In 1664 The Bay, under great pressure from England,
repealed its saintly qualification for the vote. In 1665 the other
"theocracy," New Haven, was devoured by Connecticut, which had
never presumed to such saintliness in its politics. In Hooker's community from the beginning, whether derived from his personality
or from some other source, there had been an un-Bay-like suspicion
that true religion implied a humane catholicity in government. With
the collapse of the theocracies of Massachusetts and New Haven, this
more genial Puritanism of The River, more conformable as it was
to the Liberalism of the Halfway Covenant, became the pattern for
future New England.

In the religious wars of the 1650's and '60's there was plenty of
genuine piety mixed with a multiplicity of special interests. There
is much to be said for the conservative side which, after all, was
holding out for the tradition that the churches were for religious
people, not simply for respectable people, people whose religion was
an experience and not a badge of social standing. The ministers who
favored the Halfway Covenant must be suspect of the shift that has
marked the Christian church down the ages, the dilution of Religion
by compromise in order to preserve the institution of the Church.
And likewise the laymen who demanded and accepted Halfway
Membership were in the main guilty of Halfway Religion. Either
they had had no experience of Grace and were not greatly troubled
by the lack so long as they could present a decent front to the
community, or, having had such an experience, it weighed less with
them than would the humiliation of parading their private affairs
before their neighbors.

One reason for this cooling of religion to lukewarmth was, as we
have seen, personal, the state of over-familiarity between the actual
and the potential Elect. Another and probably more fundamental
reason was economic. In the 1650's there is not yet much evidence
of that Greed, the perversion of Calvin's injunction to practice the
Economic Virtues, which in the long run was going to replace religion in America. But there is plenty of evidence of a general economic condition which, perhaps even more than Greed, is a common cause of a dimming of the religious sky. This deadly infection

was Complacency. The clouding of the Puritan Cosmos that threatened in the 1650's was based less in the effort to attain material prosperity than in the attained fact of it. The second generation, those whom the first immigrants had carried off the ships as children, or who were born in the new settlements in the '30's and '40's, were brought up in the Faith and the Doctrine, and for the most part were as familiar with the meaning of both as were their parents. But in them, especially in the large and prospering villages like Boston, Hartford and New Haven, the essential humility had been weakened by economic security. The founders as a matter of course had sacrificed their comfort and their property, and had momently risked their lives and seen their friends lose theirs, for the glory of God. The new generation had been brought up in substantial houses with the basic comforts, some of them in wealth. By the '40's, the fear of the Indians was past, and in some plantations the people rarely saw bear or even heard the sound of wolves. In their doctrine they were still utterly in God's hands, but practically they were taking very good care of themselves, and there was earthly self-sufficiency mixed with their heavenly faith. It was in the complacency of economic assurance or social importance or both that they dared let their familiarity with and contempt for their neighbors interfere with their anxiety to make a public avowal of religion and to be accepted as a Saint in the Visible Church of Christ.

The fact was that in 1660 New England was no longer a remote and bizarre Holy Experiment but an established community and part of the world. The big and metropolitan village of Boston, with its two thousand inhabitants, and its houses, wharfs and ships pretentious beyond its size,[107] the comparably rich ports of Newport, Providence, New London, New Haven, Wethersfield and Hartford, together with the scores of smaller prosperous villages along the coast and the streams, none of these were the same places as the saintly nucleii of 1634 when everything was still precarious and no man, no matter how rich he was, suspected for a moment that he could get on without God's help. In comparison to the actual decline of religion during the next forty years, that before 1660 was hardly noticeable. No visible tendency was yet threatening religion's primacy in the public mind. The charges of worldliness against New England were not yet impressive. By dint of the Halfway Covenant the churches were flourishing, still casting off centrifugal schisms into the woods in the way of healthy Protestantism. As in this middle of the twentieth century, statistics of church membership

and church activity, including work among the Indians, would have
been impressive. There was not so much a contraction of the current of religion as a dimming of the Sky that the River reflected.
With the Halfway Covenant the principle of tolerance and hetero-
doxy triumphed, and sectarianism was just around the corner. The
senile performances of Endicott and Wilson had been the last
desperately and perversely consistent efforts to preserve and perpetuate the hope of the Kingdom of God on earth as it had been
conceived, fought for and died for by a large minority of the best
minds in England. After 1660 New England was no longer an absolutely unique Holy Commonwealth, but a culture already mature
and distinct among the other cultures of western Christendom, a
culture alive in the political frames of the strong and disparate
commonwealths: Massachusetts, about to relax from its intense
purity by recommending the Halfway Covenant to the towns, and
shortly to relax further by repealing the "theocratic" suffrage; Connecticut about to embalm its security in the Charter of 1662 under
which it would absorb New Haven; Rhode Island about to emerge
from anarchy in its Charter of 1664 which engrossed the new virtue
of Religious Tolerance. In any of these commonwealths religion
might decline and vanish, but life in externals would continue.

At approximately 1660 we may conveniently date the end of First
Puritanism, which had been dominated on the whole by the conservative theology of Hooker and the conservative politics of Winthrop. The culture of 1660 was no longer Puritan culture but a tension of three Forces each emergent out of original Puritanism. In the
forces favoring the Halfway Covenant we see the beginning of
Liberalism or Intellectual Arminianism which in divers religious
and secular expressions was going to become an increasing force in
the eighteenth century. And resisting this Liberalism there were two
separate forces hardly yet differentiated. There was sheer Conservatism or Old Guardism which, combining Legal Arminianism with
the outward forms of original Puritanism, was eventually to be called
Old Calvinism. And there was True Puritanism, the original
Religion of Grace which persisted and persists today and is never
quite lost. Out of the decline of its original experiment, New England culture matured as a state of civilized conflict between Puritanism, Old Calvinism comprising Moralistic or Legal Arminianism,
and Liberalism comprising Intellectual Arminianism.

Of the great changes that gathered around the year 1660, the
Halfway Covenant was perhaps the most significant for America. But

the repeal by Massachusetts in 1664 of the churchly qualification for the vote, the end of the experiment in "theocracy" or centralized religion, was more significant philosophically for mankind. In that repeal of the paradox of Orthodoxy within Protestantism we can see the beginning of the victory of Roger Williams and Individualism in both religion and politics, that Individualism which in the long run, and in divers economic, political and philosophical forms, was going to steal America from God. And it was also the beginning of the victory of Samuel Gorton and Humanitarianism which was going to make its contribution to the Individualism.

Not that we can trace an unbroken line of connection from Gorton to the nineteenth-century Humanitarians, or from Williams to the Individualists of the eighteenth, nineteenth and twentieth centuries. In fact, Williams would be astonished to find himself admired by materialists and skeptics, admired above all other Puritans not for his piety but for his politics. Especially in his great and original doctrine of the separation of Church and State, which he promulgated in the desire that the Church be free from the predatory power of the State, he would be appalled to find himself honored by persons who desire to keep the State free from the predatory power of the Church. And yet, as there is in Gorton an intimation of Garrison, Mann, Barnard, Dorothea Dix, even of Noyes and Joseph Smith, so in Williams there is the promise of John Wise and Ethan Allen, of Sam Adams and Hancock. Indeed, even in Rhode Island and Providence in his own day we see individualism carried beyond sane doctrine into insane self-assertion. There religious liberty had led immediately to so much irreligious acrimony between sects and interests as involved more people in un-Christian hatred than were ever involved in all of the persecutions in the rest of New England combined. As we read of the continuing battle royal between Williams, Coddington, Gorton, Harris and their followers, between the simple Congregationalists, the Baptists, the Seventh Day Baptists, the Quakers, the Seekers, the Ranters, the Familists, the Presbyterians and the Anglicans, one wonders whether there was as much religion anywhere in Rhode Island as burned silently in any village of Massachusetts or Connecticut under the restraint of the general orthodoxy and the local tolerance and reserve.

In dismissing the Theocracy for its imperfections and its evils, let us not forget also its possibilities, the essential idea behind it. Let us try for a moment to put ourselves in a religious frame of imagination wherein every embodiment and manifestation has some relation to the actual, external Cosmos with its Meaning and purpose called God. In such a Cosmos the presence and activity of each individual, alongside his neighbors, in relation to that Central

Meaning, comprises the whole meaning of his own being. If for a moment we can accept this concept, we can then see mankind as a unit, one family, the "bride" of God, the individual's rights in and obligations to that family being very much more important than his rights in and obligations to his own separate self. In such a concept there is only one church, identical with that human family, and both in the whole family and in its subdivisions or localities the church contains all other social units. There is no difference between the ecclesiastical and political community. The common building is neither the "church" nor the "town hall," but both of these in one. It is the Meetinghouse where the community assembles in any of its aspects, political, recreational, military, each of them being contained within its single religious significance. This, of course, is the concept of the universal Catholic Church which has been professed by all sects that have long survived. It has not yet proved applicable in its universality, because it involves the seeming paradox of unity and separateness. The Roman church is the attempt to embody the concept putting prime emphasis upon the unity, and so far it has seemed that true separateness is not possible for the generality within it. The Puritan orthodoxy of Massachusetts was an attempt to embody the concept putting prime emphasis upon separateness, and its attempt to impose unity upon its separate individuals proved impractical, and to us ridiculous. But its essential concept and intention had the same catholicity, the same magnitude, as that of Rome. It is worth the attention and the honor of those who in their several ways derive from it.

The passing of intolerance—other than within separate churches, all equally protected by the state—we must recognize as progress. But that is because we have not yet learned to organize the church universal within whose orthodox unity each group, each sect, each individual, yet enjoys his separateness. As today we move once more out of Materialism toward Religion, it might be well to remember the defeated "theocracy," or the intentions of theocracy, with a tolerance of our own. If we are again to live together in a Cosmos that is larger than our separate importances, then again it will be a cosmos containing and assimilating church and state, the spiritual and the material. In such a cosmos a vote for a sewer or a president is as much God's business as a vote to buy hymn books or call a minister or adopt an article of doctrine. The qualifications for one are the same as those for the other, namely, residence in a place and in time and also residence in God's Cosmos and in eternity, residence, so to speak, in God's family or "bride." If again we come back to value the meaning of Being above any of its incidental expressions, we might well once more limit the suffrage upon cosmic matters—which are all matters—to those who have taken up this timeless residence in God's spaceless city. We might well again limit the suffrage to church members, only recognizing, with Roger Williams, that the churches, in the local sense, include those of Turk, Jew, Infidel, "Papist," Arminian, Antinomian and wholly separate Seeker. If then we were to practice intolerance upon materialists by disenfranchising them, not banishing them, not punishing them in any way, not depriving them of any other rights, would we be taking a step back toward barbarism? If we were to go a step beyond Williams, recognizing as in some "church" and uniting in Equality all who in any way have a claim to having enjoyed the Grace of God, might we not then be moving an inch forward toward the Church Universal, with its combined unity and separateness? Might we not then again limit the vote, in the words of the Massachusetts Law of 1631, to "those who shall be members of some of the churches of this jurisdiction"?

2. FIRST DECLINE (1660-1700)

IN CONSIDERING the Decline and moralistic Perversion of Religion in New England after 1660, it is difficult to disentangle causes from results. The increasing worldliness of society, both in moral and financial terms, was no doubt an influence on the young and so a cause of the continuing Decline. But at the outset it was itself a result of the dimming of the Sky of religion, a surrender to common shadows previously forestalled by the light of Faith. The Perversion itself, which we have already seen beginning in the ascendancy in the '50's of the Arminian and Self-centered Endicott and Wilson, was perhaps a cause of increasing aversion to a "religion" so expressed. In the main, however, this also was not a cause but a result of the Decline, a desperate and last effort on the part of the lesser remnants of the First Generation to preserve by force the Holy Commonwealth which was already moribund in spirit. It was, after all, the common vicissitude of all imaginative and worldless enterprises which enjoy an unintended material and worldly success: the founders proceed to resist the materialism and worldliness by means more depraved than these qualities themselves. From the whole tragic failure of the Puritan Holy Experiment we might infer a cynical principle that no large-scale human enterprise can be at once dominantly idealistic, materially successful, and long-lived.

The twilight of First Puritanism that we saw starting to fall in the '50's was caused chiefly by the Complacency that came in the second and third generations with economic security, resulting in the beginning of Tolerance and Liberalism expressed in the promulgation of the Halfway Covenant in 1657, and in the repeal by The Bay in 1664 of its absolute theocratic or saintly qualification for the vote.* Contributory also was the continuing immigration of non-Puritans, many of them respectable financial "adventurers," many others more colorful adventurers of the usual dissolute sort. Similar to the influence of the latter was that of the debauched Restoration court: witness the censorship of the salacious drama, and the lengthy and solemn "thoughts" by first-rate minds concerning the "abundance of sin . . . in wearing *Periwigs.* . . ."

> It is an *Uncontentedness* with that Provision God has made. . . . It is *Wastefullness.* . . . It is Pride . . . a great *Shew* . . . swaggering . . . an Affecting of Finery. . . . It is contrary to *Gravity* . . . is *Light,* and *Effeminat* . . . *Vanity.* . . .[1]

There was, as we have seen, the death of the leaders of the first generation, and the replacement of them by smaller men. There was also, at least in the more remote settlements, a decline in the level of that Education which was essential to the understanding and maintenance of Calvinist Christianity; witness the appeal of Groton, ironic of its future, to a schoolmaster to come up and teach us to "reed and right";[2] witness the complaint of the teacher of Roxbury's Grammar School in 1681 that it "was not fitting for to reside in; the glass broken, and thereupon very raw and cold, the floor very much broken and torn up to kindle fires, the hearth spoiled, the seats, some burnt and others out of kilter, that one had as well nigh as goods (sic) keep school in a hog stie as in it."[3]

It can hardly be said, however, that the early graduates of Harvard —men such as Samuel Willard, Solomon Stoddard and Cotton Mather—themselves represented any lapse of learning in comparison with their predecessors of Cambridge, Oxford or Dublin. Among the intellectuals it was not a lapse but an expansion of learning that was significant. The current rise of Experimental Science, which most of these men followed and to which some of them contributed, had, as we shall see presently, important effects not so much on their theology as on their application of religion. And these changes in religious practice they passed on to the mass of the people, few of whom had themselves yet heard of Newton or even Bacon or Galileo.

---

* This act did require that the local ministers certify the applicants for the Freemanship as "orthodox in religion and not vitious in theire lives"; but the wall was down and the way open to local discretion. (Massachusetts Colonial Records, IV, pt 2, 118)

Of greater influence than any of the causes of Decline, except only the general economic Complacency, was the series of Calamities that descended upon New England, especially The Bay, between 1660 and 1700. It was like a barrage of divine blows, visitations which were in contrast to the remarkable state of health and peace which New England had enjoyed since the Pequot war of '37. In '60, besides the news of the Restoration, Boston suffered an "epidemical cold."[4] In '67, a smallpox epidemic.[5] In '72, the "great fire," although there were greater coming—John Hull, diarist and later Mintmaster, almost lost his warehouse, for "none durst to cool it with water, because of the powder that was in it . . . until we had cut through the roof, and taken out the powder." The same year he lost three shiploads to the Dutch, worth £640,[6] a common misfortune of all merchants in the current Dutch war. In '75 and '76 occurred the dreadful scourge of King Philip's War, in which at least a dozen villages were destroyed, another dozen abandoned, a half dozen partially burned, not far from a tenth of the 15,000 men of military age killed, a considerable population of noncombatants massacred, and the frontier pushed back twenty-five or more miles, from which line it was not to be restored for twenty-five years.[7] In '76, when the war was just over, Boston suffered its "greatest Fire" which took forty-six houses including that of Increase Mather, the chief man of God of the Commonwealth, together with his Second or North Church. In '79, a still greater fire, destroyed more than 80 houses and 70 warehouses, most of the business section.[8]

In '84, the charter of Massachusetts was revoked and it became a Crown Colony. The Boston Mob, led by Liberals of the Gentry, enjoyed more or less continuous hegemony for five years, which included the coming of James II's governor, Sir William Andros, and in '89 the "Revolution" of his expulsion. In '88 there was an epidemic of measles,[9] and the same year King's Chapel was built in Boston, New England's first temple of the Anglican "Anti-christ." In '89 war broke out with France on the sea and along the northern and western frontier, and remained, with brief respites, the chronic state of the country for seventy years, incidentally closing the doors against northern and western expansion and accomplishing that overpopulation and compression of New England which hastened the culture toward inbred maturity. In '90 there were four fires in Boston.[10] In '92 came the new charter for Massachusetts, prescribing a property qualification for the vote and toleration for Quakers, Baptists, Anabaptists and Anglicans—though they could still be taxed for the Establishment. Under this charter Plymouth was merged into Massachusetts and ceased to exist as an independent empire. The witch scare of '92 was not then considered as an imposed visitation or Divine Providence, and it will be noticed later.

In this year a fire destroyed about twenty homes and warehouses, and in '93 there was another conflagration, a paltry matter of five houses of which two were blown up to stop the spread of it.[11] And from then on, while fires and epidemics continue, they seem to reduce in ferocity.

From any or all of these causes—Economic Complacency, Godless Immigration, the Restoration, the Deterioration of Leadership, the Lapse of Learning, the Rise of Modern Science, the Series of Calamities—from any and all of these causes there is no doubt that after 1660 there was in fact a noticeable Decline in the religious tenor of society, a clouding of the Faith of these late Puritans. "A little after 1660," wrote Thomas Prince within living memory of the period,[12] "there began to appear a *Decay:* And this increased to 1670, when it grew very visible and threatening, and was generally complained of and bewailed bitterly by the Pious among them: And yet much more to 1680, when but few of the first Generation remained."

The bitter bewailing of the pious is in the sermons of the day, the titles sometimes revealing the generic subject of the Decline—*New England Pleaded With* (Urian Oakes, 1673), *The Day of Trouble is Near* (Increase Mather, 1673), *A Discourse Concerning the Danger of Apostacy* (Increase Mather, 1677), *The Only Sure Way to Prevent Threatened Calamity* (Samuel Willard, 1682), *A Plea for the Life of Dying Religion* (Samuel Torrey, 1683). According to the findings of the Synod of 1679, heresy was rampant, not only the common Antinomian tendencies but all kinds of private "fancyes and Satans delusions." In contrast to the course most of the ministers were going to take after that famous Reforming Synod, numbers of them before it were found still hewing to the old, pure line of Salvation by Grace, complaining not so much of immorality as of respectability on the surface of an inward emptiness of religion, "drudging and plodding on in a visible regular course of Obedience and Profession," while inwardly in "a careless, rimiss, flat dry cold dead frame of spirit." They go "a great way by civill honesty and morality, and if one be gone so far, he is accounted to be in a state of salvation.[13] Many have grown "Sermon-proof":

> We had as good preach to the Heavens and Earth, and direct our discourse to the Walls and Seats and Pillars of the meeting house, and say, Hear, O ye Walls, give ear, O ye Seats and Pillars, as to many men in these Churches, that are deaf to all that is cried in their ears by the Lords Messengers, and are indeed like Rocks in the Sea, not to be stirred and moved by the beating and dashing of these waters of Sanctuary, or by the strongest gust of rational and affectionate discourse that can blow upon them.

Even Increase Mather, who in a few years was going to lead the turn into Good Works and Arminianism, was complaining in 1674 of those "who give out, as if saving Grace and Morality were the same."[14]

Evidence of the general decline is found also in the decrease in both church membership and church attendance. It was for 1670, after the religious qualification for the vote had been repealed in Massachusetts, that Palfrey achieved his inference, so cherished by the Puritan-baiters, that only a fifth of the adult males of The Bay were Freemen.[15] After 1657 in Connecticut and '62 in Massachusetts, when the General Courts recommended the Halfway Covenant, probably another fifth or more were coasting in the part membership it provided, and many churches, especially at The River, allowed baptism to adults so freely that it lost its significance as a sacrament and earnest of eternal Election, and the nominal membership that went with it was treated with indifference.[16] Outside the double church membership and including it was the Town which paid the minister's salary and of which variously a small majority or large minority was wholly unchurched and for the most part didn't go to service at all. We wonder what has become of the old 5s fine for failing to attend church, if indeed it was ever seriously enforced.[17]

However these causes may have contributed to the Decline of Religion, there were four noticeable results of which three were fraught with much of the future of America. There was *Licentiousness,* which was of small consequence in itself, and there was almost none of that Antinominianism or emotionally self-indulgent religion of which Licentiousness is a secular analogue. There was *Greed* which, after various vicissitudes, became the commonest substitute for Religion in the definitive Decline two centuries later. There was *Liberalism,* which we have seen appearing, chiefly in the Halfway Covenant, and which as Intellectual Arminianism with its Common Sense or Natural Reason, rises steadily from this period into Political Liberalism, Unitarianism, Reform, Laissez-faire and, at the end of the Nineteenth Century, the Social Gospel. And, fourthly, there emerged Reaction, or *Old Calvinism,* whose tenor was Legal Arminian and Self-righteous, and whose instance was the impulse to resist the other three results of Decline. As so-called "Puritanism," it enjoys a brief ascendance at this time, lapses into obstructionism in the eighteenth century, rises again in the nineteenth century as Victorianism and Fundamentalism, and flourishes today in the souls of the D.A.R., the great Veterans' Organizations and divers Congressional Committees that identify thought with the Devil. From now on *Liberalism* and *Old Calvinism* are strong forces intruding upon True and Gracious Puritanism. As the light of Objective Faith or Imagination fails and Sky over the River of Religion contracts or grows dim, then one or both of these forms of Arminianism edge in upon the central stream with their self-muddied current that reflects no Sky.

The Licentiousness of this Decline at the end of the seventeenth century was significant only as the most overt sign of the general impiety, that evidence of it which "the pious" could and did most readily attack. Bitterly the ministers "bewailed" the widespread fornication and adultery, which they attributed to divers causes, viz., immodest dress, "Laying out of hair"—that is, ornate wigs, "Borders, naked Neck and Arms, or which is more abominable, naked Breasts," "mixed Dancings, light behavior and expressions, sinful Company-keeping with light and vain persons, unlawful Gaming, an abundance of Idleness. . . ."[18] In 1672 one Alice Thomas of Boston was apprehended and whipped for operating "a stewe, whore house, or brothell house,"[19] and there was much watchfulness by magistrates and ministers for recurrences on either the professional or amateur level. Intemperance was also bewailed:

> Every Farmers Son, when he goes to the Market-Town, must have money in his purse; and when he meets with his Companions, they goe to the Tavern or Ale-house, and seldome away before Drunk, or well tipled.[20]

There was an increase in insolence and naughtiness at Harvard.[21] In 1677 Increase Mather said, "People are ready to run wild into the woods again and be as Heathenish as ever, if you do not prevent it."[22]

More significant than the emergence of licentiousness out of declining Religion was that of Greed, for this marked the beginning of what became two centuries later the most destructive kind of self-assertion in American History. Not that there had not been early, scattering instances of it breaking through the restraints of religion. Captain Robert Keayne, wealthy shopkeeper and founder of the Ancient and Honorable Artillery, got fined for selling above the market price "to the Dishonor of God's name, the Offense of the Generall Court & the Publique Scandall of the Country";[23] and on another occasion he was accused of cheating a laborer by paying him in a cloth which he represented as of better quality than was the case.[24] With less semblance of justice William Pynchon, gent., founder of Springfield, was fined by Connecticut for alleged niggardliness in meeting certain obligations of his plantation to supply corn for the Pequot War in '37. In 1640 Temperance Sweet of Boston was churched for cheating in the sale of wine and strong waters, and Goody Webb of Roxbury for selling short loaves in her business as baker.[25] But by and large Calvin's injunction to prosecute your calling because God assigned it to you and not because of the benefits that might ensue was followed in the early years. No candid inquiry could find the profit motive characteristic of the Puritans of the first generation, nor any general realization of Winthrop's original concern lest we "fall to embrace this present world and prosecute our carnall intencions, seekeing greate things for our selves and our posterity. . . ."[26]

The flavor of early Puritan society was that of what I have called the Grand Hypocrisy, wherein diligence had the appearance and pretense of cupidity, but the actual motivation was to exercise as God willed in the God-given calling. Doubtless in some cases this hypocrisy was reversed into Common Hypocrisy, which professes to serve God while inwardly concerned for the aggrandizement of self. But every Puritan was on the watch for this kind of self-deception. The typical Boston citizen of the first period was John Hull, goldsmith, rich merchant, mintmaster of the famous pine tree shilling, and eventual Magistrate. Indeed his concern lest his motive in business be profit instead of God's service was—but for two lapses, of which that between 1660 and 1700 was the first—typical of all Puritans and most Yankees right down to the middle of the nineteenth century. In 1653, when he was twenty-nine years old, he lost £120 worth of beaver in a shipwreck, and recorded the misadventure in the more intimate or "Private" of his two diaries:

> The loss of my estate will be nothing, if the Lord please to join my soul nearer to himself, and loose it more from creature comforts: my loss will be repaid with advantage.[27]

And then he sets down in two sentences the whole Calvinist, economic attitude which could so easily slip over into Common Hypocrisy if and when the original piety should fail:

> The Lord also hath made up my loss in outward estate. To him be all praise.

Five years later he again lost £120 in two shipwrecks, and was obviously deeply suspicious of his concern over the loss—

> The Lord wean my heart more from these outward things, and fix it more upon himself! The loss will then be gain.

And again the next year, the Lord's restitution that he is afraid he will value for the wrong reasons:

> The Lord made up my lost goods in the two vessels last year by his own secret blessing, though I know not which way.

In '62 there is an entry in which cynicism can find conventional unction and common hypocrisy:

> We heard of the safe arrival of all the ships that' sailed hence for England last year, and therein the Lord's Gracious preservation of the estates of his poor, despised people.

But it is well to remember that at this time all but the hopelessly stubborn were recognizing the failure of the Holy Commonwealth. During the recent Protectorate in England, the new tolerance had spelled the end of that purity of doctrine for whose maintenance, and with the hope of sending it back again to the mother country, the fathers had settled New England. The financial state of Massachusetts was at its lowest, and Hull was helping support the general credit out of his personal fortune. Also, in 1662 the Restoration was well away, and the Puritan colonies, especially Massachusetts, were a-tremble before the Anglican and Catholic possibilities. There was more than false humility in Hull's reference to his "despised people."

In '72, at the height of the Dutch war, he is back again in affirmative Faith. Being now a rich man and full of honor, he had just lost three shiploads to the Dutch, totalling £640—

> God mixeth his mercies and chastisements, that we may neither be tempted to faint or to despise.

In a letter of instructions to one of his ship captains we again see the remarkable fusion of religious and economic motives, here made humorous by the omission of punctuation. Having just given his skipper large latitude in disposing of the cargo, he continues:

> . . . But indeed it is hard to foresee what will be and therfore it is best willing to submit to the great governing hand of the great Governor of all the greater and lesser revolutions that wee the poore sons of men are invoved in   by the invoyce you see the whole amounteth to £405:16:3.[28]

John Hull, having been brought in in 1630 at six years of age, was of the second generation, but he maintained the tradition of the first until his death in 1683. He left a fair estate of £6,000, but more than one-third of it was in bonds due for money loaned to the Colony treasury in its financial straits.[29]

The gradual shift from Hull's financial humility to either Common Hypocrisy or shameless Greed is more clearly evinced by external than by internal evidence. Probably the first common form of unabashed cupidity was that for land. John Cotton noticed it as early as 1642, when he complained that many wanted more "elbowe-roome" that they might "live like lambs in a large place"; and by the '70's Increase Mather was declaring that land had been the Idol of many, that they would leave "Churches, and Ordinances, and all for land and elbowroom enough in the World."[30] Another early evidence of greed as stronger than religion was in Captain Edward Johnson's disgust in 1650[31] that some merchants, desiring more immigration and so more "coyne" for themselves, were opposing the alien laws that excluded heretics. Perhaps the first candid evidence of a shift toward economic motivation in the main undercurrent of society was in a sermon which the gentle and always moderate Richard Mather preached to his congregation in Dorchester in '57, the year when the adoption of the Halfway Covenant by the Conference of ministers implied a generic decline in godliness:

> It is true the condition of many amongst you . . . is such as necessarily puts you on to have much imployment about the things of this life, . . . the Lord having laid this burden on man . . . and experience shews that it is an easy thing in the middest of worldly business to lose the life and power of Religion, that nothing thereof should be left but only the external form, as it were the carcass or shell, worldliness having eaten out the kernell, and having consumed the very soul and life of godliness.[32]

Probably the surest index of the shrivelling away of "the very soul & life of godliness" was in the decline of the old godly-mercantilist socialism into what was in commercial terms the beginning of "free enterprise." John Cotton was a great bulwark of the "just price," and after his death in 1652, though the ministers continued to preach the old ceremony and most of the regulations remained law, they passed into dead letters. In '55 Charles Chauncey complained that the merchants habitually gouged the poor. In '73 and '74 Urian Oakes and Increase Mather were making the same complaint with the greater eloquence.[33] In the '30's and '40's, a profit above 33% had been criminal. By the '70's the regulation had not been repealed, but it was no longer or rarely enforced, and profits of 60 and 70% were not rare.[34] In '74 Increase Mather preached against cards and dice, not, it is to be observed, because gambling itself was any sin, but because the winner got the loser's goods at too small a price.[35] In '76 he was attacking the sin of Usury which was becoming common practice at The Bay.[36]

Among the records for the year 1686 there are two items which show that Massachusetts was well gone in greed as the dominant impulse in society. From the beginning Puritan ministers, assuming religion to be the foundation of life, had used figures of commerce and industry to illustrate aspects and expressions of it; now Samuel Willard of Boston's Third Church—presently Old South—reversed the process; assuming the principles of business to be fundamental, and religion a possible application of them, he preached in effect that Christ was a good investment, that you would get a return far beyond what contributions in thought, conduct and money you put into Him.[37] And in the same year John Dunton reported a condition of affairs which, recurring two centuries later, would be perhaps the ultimate depravity in the Decline of Religion. Cheating, he said, the sharp deal, had become fashionable and admired as "a commendable Piece of Ingenuity."[38]

By 1686 a revolution had been completed, both in principles and in population. Persons named Winthrop, Dudley, Saltonstall, Bellingham and Legg were still given the front pews in "dignifying" the meetings. But the real power was in new people, either those who had risen from initial poverty there, or immigrants whose fathers had never known the Holy Experiment in its pristine, approximate purity, great merchants, probably forty of them, worth over £10,000, weighty new names such as Belcher, Brattle, Clarke, Dummer, Fanueil, Foster, Hutchinson—the children of Anne, returned to the fold—, Lillie, Oliver, Phillips, Sargent, Sewall, Wharton. They occupied "stately" houses on the High or Chief—modern Washington —Street worth two or three thousand pounds apiece. Among most of them the Holy Commonwealth was a matter of respectable tradition, to be given lip service. Piety was well enough, provided that Religious and Social Election were recognized as the same. The Kingdom of God that had been hoped for got confused with Boston as it was.

By 1686, indeed by 1684, most of these rich merchants saw the loss, in the earlier year, of the old religious Charter not as a piece of Stuart despotism but as a desirable change which did away with the tiresome dominance of religion and admitted tolerance, not only in matters of worship, but in matters of business. Under the new Government, a man might pick up what he chose, by any method he chose, and at least the local authorities would recognize his action as his private affair. Religion of sorts remained powerful among the merchants of The Bay. But it was no longer pure religion. It was no longer Puritanism. In some, especially after the receipt of the new Charter of 1692, it became the Pseudo-religion of Reaction, of Old Calvinism. In others it became the more enterprising Pseudo-religion of Liberalism. In both cases the Cosmos of the fathers was clouded over and forgotten.

Of the four Results of the Decline, Old Calvinism was the last to formulate, and its purpose was to attack the other three in the interest of the Old Order. During its ascendancy of twenty years— 1679-99—it took on three elements which characterized it thereafter in its long role of obstructionism, and again its reascendancy into power in the nineteenth century. These were, first, Legal Arminianism, the insistence upon conduct and the Moral Law; second, the preaching of Hell Fire and Terror, a luxury in which the true Puritans had rarely indulged; and third, since it had lost the inward and Gracious spirit of Puritanism, a grim insistence on its outward forms, the simplicity of the liturgy, the purity of the sacraments of Baptism and Communion, the old vocabulary of Justification by Grace which its Arminianism falsified, and, for at least a half-century yet, a pretence of requiring a recital of an Experience of Grace as a condition of admission to the church. The essential inner quality of Old Calvinism was Reaction. Its outward mark was Legal Arminianism, Moralism. Now at last Anne Hutchinson was vindicated. The Covenant of Works which she had charged—on the whole falsely—against the early ministers was now in effect preached, although still not professed, by most of the ministers of The Bay. In the emergence of Old Calvinism we have the irony that, while professing the old Covenant of Grace and Salvation by unpredictable Predestination, these ministers concluded that in the parlous state of the country an insistence upon Works, if need be a frightening insistence, was the only way to induce a return to True Religion. Dubious means were thought justified by a worthy end. A sincere enough effort to revive the Holy Commonwealth degenerated into a campaign to lift moral faces of existing Villages.

In the days of Anne Hutchinson John Wilson was the only sure apostle of Moralism. But starting in the '50's with Hooker's old rule of Works as a Preparation for Grace, we can watch, notable in the expressions of Thomas Shepard, John Norton and Peter Bulkeley, a gradual submergence of the original delicate doctrine of the Holy Mean under a simple Arminianism of Works as inducing Grace.[39] It is easy to suspect that it was with relief that the ministers recognized in the crisis of The Decline a valid pretext for going all the way and, while still giving lip service to God's Free Grace, yet putting the emphasis on man's voluntary Works as the way to Salvation.

Also, in the profession of fidelity to the Holy Commonwealth

we may recognize perhaps an unconscious hypocrisy. Since the days
of Winthrop, Cotton and Hooker, New England had grown from an
exotic Experiment to a mature Culture with its own standards, including normal standards of respectability. To the ministers of the
1660's and '70's, Boston, Cambridge, Concord, Hartford, New Haven
and Northampton were not precarious outposts whose only meaning
was freedom from Anglican surveillance. To the ministers of the
last half of the century these prosperous villages were places where
one had been born. They were home. One had a sense of responsibility for them that had nothing to do with religion. Increase Mather
in the '70's was of course concerned as a minister with the Godlessness of the country. But as a leading citizen he was also mightily
aware of the need of a clean-up campaign in Boston. It was desirable to do something to appease God's evident anger at New England. But it was also necessary to attack directly the disgraceful conditions of his home town. Happily the same procedure suited both
aims.

We have seen as high among the causes of Decline after 1660 the
series of calamities which New England suffered during the period.
To our materialistic assumptions it seems obvious enough that these
disasters should lead to cynicism and loss of religion, and especially
to disillusion of the millennial hope of the Holy Commonwealth.
And among those already of little faith, this was indeed the interpretation. But the leadership and probably still the majority of the
people, whether churched or not, yet professed the ancient theology.
And this taught them to read the calamities in the opposite sense.
To them they were not causes but results of "sliding off" or Sin.
They were punishments laid on by God for the wickedness of His
people.

God was evidently "in controversy" with New England. It was
not His practice to punish here and now the misfeasances of individuals, for there was Eternity in which to take care of that. But
communities are exclusively earthly and mortal affairs, and they must
be dealt with in their present carnal form. Consequently God sends
upon those which are in Covenant with Him—that is, Holy Commonwealths that have undertaken to be His People—such corrections as
he deems necessary to remind them of their backsliding and to
compel them to return to His worship. None doubted, not even the
Greedy and the Liberal, that the fires, pestilences and wars were
Providences of God sent upon New England for its evil conduct as
a Commonwealth. Numerous fast days of humiliation, with whole
townships gathered in the churches for daylong prayer, were only
momentarily efficacious. As fast as the Commonwealth rededicated
itself to God, it slid off again into every kind of wordliness.

In the '70's The Bay and The River passed a few "blue" laws aiming at reform. But they were "little regarded by the People, so at least as to make 'em better, or cause 'em to mend their manners."[40] The war with Philip did at long last end in '76, but the fires and epidemics continued. Something more radical must be done. In 1679 Increase Mather, the strongest minister of The Bay, induced the General Court to assemble the ministers in synod to conclude why God was angry, and what might be done to appease Him. Indicative perhaps of the change in the times was the fact that now the General Court issued its "order" to the ministers to convene, in contrast to the deference it used to show them.[41] But indicative, contrariwise, of the continuing prestige, or perhaps the solidarity, of the divines was the neglect of anyone, in this inquiry into God's anger manifested in pestilence, war, and holocaust, to raise the point that in the Great Fire of '76 the great Dr. Mather himself had lost both his house and his Second Church—the one whose replacement later became Old North.*

The "Reforming Synod" of 1679, assembling in Boston, was attended by Massachusetts divines only, though Connecticut and Plymouth approved it and its results.[42] With amazing alacrity, involving the appointment, brief deliberation and full and methodical report of a committee in twenty-four hours, these learned vicars of the Lord got at the bottom of His wrath. It was because of the following sins, some of which we have noticed: Loss of godliness among church members; Pride (especially the vanity of the lower classes in dressing above their station); Profanity; Sabbath-breaking; Lapse of family prayers; Hatred, backbiting and lawsuits; Intemperance; Fornication and Adultery, deriving from divers causes, viz., immodest dress, "mixed Dancings, light behavior and expressions, sinful Company-keeping, unlawful Gaming, an abundance of Idleness, which brought ruinating Judgement upon Sodom. . . ."; Lying; Business interests above religion, including the imposition of excessive prices; Niggardliness in contribution to public purposes.[43]

The published *Result* of the Synod proposed a program of Reform, and in its enactment by the General Courts the ministers got less than they probably hoped for. The Massachusetts General Court recommended the report to the churches.[44] Also it promptly passed an act "for the prevention of the profanation of the Sabbath" through disorders on Saturday night by forbidding carts and horsemen to leave Boston without cause after sundown on that day. It passed a very blue Law requiring the tithing men of the churches to enter houses suspected of selling liquor without license and, with certain safeguards, to seize and dispose of any "wines, strong beere, ale,

* Not to be confused with the present Old North.

cider, perry, matheglin, rumn, brandy, &c." that they might find
there.[45] The Connecticut General Court, taking note of the findings
and recommendations of the Massachusetts Synod, did not add to
its statutes but it did order "the selectmen constables and grand-
jury men in their several plantations" to take "special care" to
enforce certain "laws for the suppressing of some provoaking evils"
which had been passed during "the calamitous times of '75 and '76"
and—like most such laws—had "little prevailed."[46] Also, the Connecticut Court ordered a day of humiliation, and later took occasion
to thank God a little smugly for His tenderness in that, in view of
their sins, "he hath not consumed us."[47]

Besides asking the Legislatures for action, the good ministers of
'79 stirred up the churches to greater diligence in their own judicial
proceedings where the penalties were Admonition and Excommunication. Although generalization is precarious, it would seem that
from about this time the number of church trials increased in number and declined in quality. In the earlier period the congregations
were specially attentive to irreverence, blasphemy, lying, heresy—
the straight religious crimes—and tended to leave scandal to the civil
courts. We saw Anne Hutchinson first admonished and then excommunicated for heresy in two successive church sessions. Other typical
early trials included one before Cotton where a woman—considered
insane and twenty-six years later hung as a witch—was obviously
impairing the peace and tenor of the congregation,[48] and the famous
trial of Mrs. Eaton, wife of the Governor of New Haven and grand-
mother of Elihu Yale, which gathered much pettiness in proceeding,
but was based in a doctrinal difference, Mrs. Eaton's denial of the
efficacy of infant baptism.[49]

Of the church trials in the period we are now considering, Charles
Francis Adams collected a number from the records of Quincy, some
involving properly churchly matters, such as attacks on the minister,
but mostly involving sexual irregularities.[50] A richer and more diverting field is that of Plymouth where John Cotton, son of the
original John, was minister, and where there were thirty-two trials
in the church between 1671 and 1695.[51] Most of the accounts are
brief, laconic and wear a kind of Victorian blush of naughty-niceness
which is perhaps the inevitable result of moralism. The culprit is
always called a "chh-child" (church-child), and is treated with great
tenderness by the recorder. Three of the trials are frankly for pre-
marital relations, which always get an admonition and very much
later a forgiveness; one is for selling liquor to Indians; three for intemperance; one for "evil words against the church," and in one the
pastor had been "scandalized." As for the rest, the chaste recorder
cannot bring himself to signify them by their horrid names—which

were of course well enough understood by his contemporary readers. There is one case of "evil words," one of "scandalous words," one of "giving offense," one of "inordinate walking," one of "unsuitable walking," one of "morall scandall," fifteen that are named with the awful simplicity of "sinne," and two are too dreadful to be named at all. The results depend always on the degree of penitence of the accused, and the recorder, who is sometimes the minister, wants us to understand how peacefully and lovingly everything is always resolved. From these and similar records we may infer any of three things: that sexual irregularity was getting more frequent in New England; that, in conformance to the Arminian flavor of the Synod of 1679, all kinds of misfeasance were being given closer public scrutiny; and that, in such a time of moralism there was an unusually strong temptation for villagers to exult in "self love" over one another by informing and sitting in judgment on each other. Doubtless all three conditions of decadence were coexisting.

But more important than the campaigns against Sin which the leading ministers stirred up in the legislatures and among their humbler colleagues was the completion of their own drift into Arminianism and a preachment of Works. As late as 1674, Increase Mather was still preaching the pure Covenant of Grace, holding that men were utterly helpless in their Justification,[52] and he was still opposing the Halfway Covenant as a violation of Congregational doctrine. But by the time of the Synod of 1679 he had switched to support the Halfway Covenant, and shortly thereafter he was preaching that people should "do things as have a tendency to cause them to believe."[53] Since Belief was the surest sign of acceptance within the Covenant, this was in effect to preach that men should do such things as would win them Salvation. Samuel Willard of the Third Church, and almost as weighty as Mather at The Bay, was preaching in the early '80's that men of their own wills could prepare themselves for regeneration—"It is one of Satan's cheats, to tell us we must wait before we resolve."[54] And ten years later he declared straight out, "The Gospel Promises are exhibited on terms; and these . . . do not only tell us what it is that God requires of Sinners . . . but they also do give us to understand after what manner God will by his Grace convey a pardon to Sinners."[55] Said Samuel Mather, the older brother of Increase, "As is the preparation work, such is the closing with Christ."[56]

In 1690 a committee of ministers, issuing a manifesto of the creed of New England, announced that, while men were saved entirely by God's will, yet "some previous and preparatory common works" are required.[57] And in Cotton Mather, grandson of the two true and Gracious Puritans John Cotton and Richard Mather, we find the

Covenant of Grace relegated to a dead recital and the reality of religion related to Works: "You may make a Tryal. . . . Never, I am perswaded, never any Soul miscarried, that made such Applications."[58] " 'Tis many ways advantageous, for an *Unregenerate Man*, to Do as much as he *can* . . . there is a probability that God intends to help him, so that he shall *do* more than he can." If a man makes his "*Impotency* a cloak for his *Obstinacy*, it will Aggravate his Condemnation at the Last. . . . The way of the *New-Covenant*" is, "*Try* whether you can't give that Consent; if you *can*, 'tis done!"[59] Here is complete Arminianism; every man to be saved or damned by his own acts as freely determined by his own will, while God humbly awaits the determination.

As a natural consequence of the Individualism or Self-Concern that is central to Arminianism, we find throughout the '60's, '70's, '80's, and '90's an increasing rumble of Hell Fire in the sermons. Since men were to be saved by their own efforts, it was well to remind them of the rewards of their efforts, and especially the distresses that awaited the failure to exercise them. In 1659 Charles Chauncey was still moderate in his warning to men who say,

> If I go to Hell, I shall have company,—and will bear it as well as I can. Wilt thou bear it, O heap of dust? Hast thou an arm like God?[60]

Beginning in the '60's the threat was getting more grave.

> Hasten you after your lecherous Kindred into the stinking Lake: . . . Let thy lustful Body be everlasting Fuel for the unquenchable fire: Let thy lascivious Soul be eternal Food for the never-dying Worm. Let Indignation and Wrath, Tribulation and Anguish be thy portion world without end.[61]

> Eternity will fasten its iron teeth upon thy soul . . . after thou hast been in misery as many millions of ages as there have been days and minutes since the world began, thou art no nearer to an end of thy misery than thou wast the first hour that the Son of God passed on thee a sentence of eternal death.[62]

By the next century we have the Hell that since that day has been a convention:

> Suppose the Water of some Large and Deep Pond were turned into Boiling, Flaming Brimstone; (and devils dragged thither your neighbors) and cast them Alive into that Boiling Pond, . . . And suppose further, that God should keep them Alive in this Fiery Pond, from one Year and Age to another. . . .[63]

After 1679, in the concerted effort to frighten the people back into

the old faith, children were taught in their catechising that this kind
of hell awaited them, and that the Devil was forever near them and
watchful to snatch them and involve them hopelessly in his toils.
Thus an originally honest Conservatism violated the religion it
aimed to conserve, and made a joke of the Puritanism it professed.

Actually, in these last decades of the seventeenth century emergent
Conservatism or Old Calvinism and Liberalism were both as yet
amorphous and not yet as sharply distinguished from each other as
each was from the Puritanism whence both emerged. Increase Mather,
who rates as the first pure Reactionary, the First Old Calvinist, yet was
persuaded to accept the Halfway Covenant—though intending to
limit its benefits, if not to the children, then certainly to the grandchildren, of saints. Samuel Willard went as far toward Arminianism
as any. Yet he went just as far in Liberalism, keeping up his church
membership by surrendering the last pretense of requiring a true
religious experience as a condition of admission, and virtually accepting in full communion anyone who met the genial requirements
of the Halfway Covenant. Solomon Stoddard of Northampton, the
"Pope" of The River and grandfather of Jonathan Edwards, imposed
up and down the Connecticut Valley his revolutionary system called
Stoddardeanism, under which he not only would Baptize anybody
with a decent record but served Communion to all and sundry unregenerate in the hope that it might prove to be a "converting ordinance" and a Means to lead them to Grace. In all this he was deeply
Arminian, making Salvation depend on divers acts of the human will.
In general the Halfway position and the Liberal and popular trend
were at this time prevalent at The River, while Conservatism was in
the ascendant at The Bay[64] where the western "Pope" was not popular. In the Synod of 1679 he went so far as to call a lay member a liar,
and the Deputy Governor, Thomas Danforth, told Stoddard he "deserved to be laid by the heels"—though His Honor later apologized.[65]

At this time Liberalism and Old Calvinism were not yet clearly
differentiated, and in fact the former was, as it continued to be, as
Arminian as the latter. The heart of Arminianism is man's Free Will
applying his Reason to problems of Theology and Morality. Man
voluntarily figures out the right thing to do, and then just as voluntarily goes and does it, while God stands by, awaiting the pleasure
of His Creature. One distinction from Puritanism is in the concept
of Trustworthy Reason. The Reason of Arminian procedure is what
the Puritans called Natural Reason, which is possessed by everybody,
as distinguished from Right Reason which comes only with Grace,

Grace operating entirely under God's Predestination, unpredictably and independently of Man's will. The difference between the Liberals and the Old Calvinists was not in their concept of Reason but in the data to which they applied that Reason. The Liberals of the Halfway Covenant and the subsequent prostitution of the Sacraments implemented Natural Reason with Outward Experience, Scientific Observation, Practicality and Common Sense. They saw that if religion were to be kept alive and powerful in the community, it must be simplified, popularized and conformed to Social Reality, as in the Halfway Covenant. The Old Calvinists, on the other hand, implemented Natural Reason with Law, the Law of the Bible and established Puritan Theology and Practice, with such nice inferences as scholars and lawyers must always draw in particular cases. Their Arminianism was *Legal Arminianism,* while that of the Liberals was *Intellectual Arminianism.* They were shortly to become as widely separated and antagonistic as each was toward the Puritanism of Free Grace. But in the 1680's this divergence was hardly yet intimated.

The proceedings of the Synod of 1679—the call, the findings, and the recommendations—were expressive of the generic Rationalism of the day, at once Legalistic and Scientific. The behavior of the Ministers was as systematic as that of any group of specialists convened by a legislature today. As experts on the attributes and habits of God, called in to make suggestions for putting an end to His Controversy with New England, they first analyzed with Biblical and Calvinist learning the causes of His anger, and proceeded with confidence to propose measures that would be likely to remove these causes. The assumption, whether conscious or not, was that God and His morality were as subject to discoverable Law as His universe and His physics that were in those days becoming matters of knowledge to the enlightened. God was as mechanical as a harpsichord. Hit the right keys and you get a harmony between yourself and eternity. Hit the wrong keys and you get a discord.

Not only in the larger patterns of religion but also in its detailed applications, Natural Reason and Common Sense were becoming the common methods of procedure. Prayer that was traditionally an effort to establish or maintain the current of Faith and Grace with God, now becomes practical and businesslike. We find educated adults asking God for specific favors, using good arguments and diplomacy. Much could be made of Him if you knew how to approach Him. Often the matter of prayers was of import, and the results obtained were impressive. The Reverend Jonathan Pierpont of Reading, Massachusetts, with two of his parishioners, cured a girl of insanity by praying for her all day; also he records with great satisfaction that in a certain skirmish in the war in Canada in '90, the

Reading contingent came through unscathed—inferentially the only one to do so—because happily he and his congregation, under his urgence, were praying for them at the moment of the action.[66] Sometimes God was given very specific instructions how to proceed in favoring His children: with great confidence one minister, praying in a drought, directed God not to send them a piddling shower to tease them, nor yet a cloudburst to wash away their gardens, but "Oh God, bless us with a steady and comforting drizzle-drozzle to make the seeds grow."

The first generation had been humble before God. He was the Father of the Universe; His ways were inscrutable; one could ask favors of Him but piously and with awe, not presuming to inquire whether His will and His justice would provide the thing His foolish children might desire. The Third generation, though they still spoke the language of humility as they did the language of Grace, approached God as scheming children approach an earthly father toward whom their dominant feeling is not love or respect but the hope of tangible benefits in their visible world. The muddy current of Arminian Reasonableness was intruding widely upon the Central Stream of Religion.

For the same Natural Reason which provided Increase Mather and the Synod of '79 with their doctrine of Works and Damnation, and Solomon Stoddard with his common sense prostitution of the Communion, was really the method of dawning Experimental Science. In this coming on of the modern spirit, from Copernicus up through Bacon, Galileo and Descartes, New England played a distinguished part.* John Winthrop, Jr., the founder of Ipswich and New London, builder of the first iron furnaces in America, and perennial governor of Connecticut, was in England the intimate of Newton, Wren, Boyle, Stirk and Digby. In 1663 he was elected a member of the Royal Society. The same year he brought to America, and in '72 presented to Harvard, a three-and-a-half-foot telescope, and observations made with it, being sent to Newton, helped him in arriving at the laws of gravitation.[67] Subsequently he provided the Society with valuable notes on plants and minerals in America. Two other Winthrops became members of the Royal Society, a third John carrying out experiments in electricity.[68] Increase Mather was

---

* The new method and its results reached the students at Harvard through Robert Boyle's *Usefulness of Experimental Philosophy* (1663), Charles Morton's *Compendium Physics*, the works of Vincent Wing and Arian Heereboord, and presently the world-shaking news from Newton and Halley. (Miller and Johnson, 733.)

a weighty man in England, and he was in London in '87 when Newton read before the Royal Society and published his *Principia*. Increase did not himself make the Society, but his eccentric son Cotton did. Of their many scientific activities, their joint fight for smallpox inoculation in 1721, against the mass of public opinion, was specially spectacular. Of the nine colonials who were elected to the Royal Society before 1740, only William Byrd of Virginia was not of New England.[69] During the Civil War, before the formation of the Society, its potential charter members seem to have considered emigrating to Connecticut "out of esteem for the most excellent and valuable Governor John Winthrop," and if they had done so the society would have been established there.[70]

The experimental method and inductive reason which, by way of materialism, were one day going to attack religion directly, were in this age already undermining it indirectly while trying to help it. Time out of mind it had been believed that every smallest and greatest phenomenon was the work of either of two superhuman wills, that of God or that of the Devil, and in this belief alone there lurked no danger. But also time out of mind Religion and Science had been identified, and while this did no harm in early Puritanism when the "reason" involved was Right Reason, the Imagination or Religious Perception that comes with Grace, it was a dangerous identification in the last half of the seventeenth century when the Experimental Reason involved was merely a new and clearer kind of Natural Reason and so had no relation to Religion. No immediate harm was done by cautious people who did not make the complete identification, as when the Reverend Samuel Danforth recognized the comet of 1664 both as a divine portent and as under natural law.[71] But most of the best minds were not content with such dualism, and did not hesitate to attack the most recondite subjects with the scientific method.

These attempts were the more perilous when, as was usually the case, the new method was not mastered, so that at critical points we often get a combination of curious observation and deductive reasoning drawn from medieval assumptions. The *Journal*[72] of Simon Bradstreet the younger, son of the Massachusetts governor and his wife Ann the poet, is a relatively harmless piece of morbidity, listing, to illustrate the "Kindnesse of the Lord," every disaster and violent death that came to his attention between 1664 and 1683. More ominous were the proposals, in 1681, of Increase Mather and a group of the most distinguished ministers of Massachusetts for the systematic recording of "illustrious providences," which were described as "such Divine judgements, tempests, floods, earthquakes, thunders as are unusual, strange apparitions, or whatever else shall happen that is

prodigious, witchcraft, diabolical possessions, remarkable judgements upon noted sinners, eminent deliverances, and answers of
prayer. . . ."[73] There ensued such findings as those of Tutor Noadiah
Russell who recorded the case of "a man in Connecticut" who was
taken with a sudden shivering after which he heard a voice saying
that "four dreadful judgements should come speedily upon the whole
world viz: sword, famine, fire and sickness which should, without
speedy reformation prevented, begin at New England. . . ."[74] A step
beyond this was the suggested inquiry into "witchcraft, diabolical
possessions," the Invisible World of the Devil, and hell let loose at
The Bay.

Before glancing at the Salem witch scare, it is well to recall one of
the exaggerations of it on the part of the Puritan-burners which even
the honest historians rarely point out. The debunkers ascribe the
phenomenon of 1692 to "New England" and conjure up the general
impression of all Puritans as "witch-hunters." Actually, the epidemic
extended very little beyond Salem and its vicinity, and it was entirely
confined to The Bay, that strip lying a dozen miles in from the coast
from Cape Anne to Weymouth and acknowledging Boston for its
capital and pattern. While there had been witch executions, ten of
them, in the larger arc of Greater New England or The River, including a scare in Hartford in 1656 when four were hung, all of that was
long past in 1692. Already the Connecticut Valley was building its
"steadier" type, pervaded by an easier, more realistic humanity. In
all the calamities and excesses that befell between 1660 and 1700, the
behavior of Connecticut and Middle and Western Massachusetts was
more moderate than that of The Bay. Possibly this derived from the
Equalitarianism we saw early at The River, in contrast to the tension
and explosiveness of Boston and its Mob, based in its English
stratification, class-consciousness and consequent Individualism.

The contrast was strikingly apparent in this age of change, as
epitomized in the personalities of Solomon Stoddard and Increase
Mather. Stoddard of Northampton was interested in People, and his
life was a protest against the scholastic rigidity which he had seen
growing in Boston when he was studying and teaching at Harvard.
His unsystematic emotionalism produced the first revivals in New
England, four gatherings of the harvest, mostly in his own parish, in
1680, '84, 1713 and '18, noisy, crude, but relaxed, released. In contrast to Stoddard, Mather was interested in Intellectual Truth, involving both sound science and right conduct according to law. And
after Mather, though he had not the slightest direct responsibility

for it, came the sad little epidemic at The Bay for six months in 1692.

The background for the hysteria was the state of anxiety blended of the spectacle of pestilence, war, godlessness and disillusion, and Matherian moralism which saw these visitations as God's punishment for the wickedness of the people. Puritanism at its best had always been an introspective business, requiring ruthless self-examination for any signs of Grace, and producing in every life at least one critical period, usually in adolescence.[75] But under the old orthodoxy there was a relief for anxiety in Predestination and Humility. It was refreshing to realize in moments of discouragement that you still might be on the list for good and all. Also it was easier to prove, at least to your own satisfaction, by a combination of Belief and Diligence in the Lord's business, that you were already Elected than it was to continue piling up good works to what requisite height no one had specified. After all, it was indeed settled ahead of time, and the question of whether you took another drink, or even if you did a little bowling on the Sabbath, was not going to alter the script of the play that had been written before the beginning of the world. Also, while it was desirable and comforting to persuade the Minister and the Congregation that you were duly Sanctified, they might after all be wrong. Anybody might be in Grace any time, for all any mortal could say to the contrary; and in the secret Central Idea which each of those pre-Yankees carried inside his reticence, most of them did suspect that they were elected right now. Furthermore, the old ministers—Cotton, Shepard, Eliot, Richard (the first) Mather and the rest—rarely talked about the fiery pit of hell. The problem was to get into cosmic equipoise here, and the punishment for failing to do it was an unhappy existence now. The "rewards" and "punishments" to be distributed at the Last Judgement were a dramatization, a metaphor, of the actual psychic present.

But in the time of God's Controversy with New England, the old comforts were being withdrawn. As the habit of inductive or Experimental Thinking grew, the old principle of Predestined Election, evinced mostly by Belief, shrivelled to a cliché. The locale and significance of religion shifted from a psychological present to a material hereafter. You were going presently to a physical Heaven or a physical Hell, and your final location in the one or the other would depend largely on your free choices and free actions here. Furthermore, since you started out in a state of condemnation or Reprobation, your chances of working yourself up to Salvation were desperately slim. Compare the sufferings of young Thomas Shepard at Cambridge during his ordeal of conversion in the 1620's with the continuous desperate plight of Michael Wigglesworth during his equivalent period in Harvard in the 1650's. Shepard, after several approaches and back-slippings, finally got good and drunk, and in his dreadful hangover the next day God "who might justly have cut me off in the mids of my sin; did meet me with much sadnes of hart," and so presently fetched him round.[76] And here is Wigglesworth at about the same age:

> January 11, 1656. Sabbath. Lord I am not worthy to be owned or pittied by the, a sink of sin! so frowardly passionate, so earthly and carnal as I have bin this week past. for the Lords sake hide not away they face this day. oh! . . . when wilt thou mortify these lusts . . .?[77]

Wigglesworth in the '50's was a little ahead of the times, but the agonies in which he was extreme among his fellows were everybody's agonies ten years later when his *Day of Doom* became the second best seller in America—Richard Mather's *Bay Psalm Book* having been the first.

Especially after the Reforming Synod of 1679, when the ministers of the Bay were attributing God's anger to the wickedness of His People which would lead to The Fiery Pit, there seemed but slight chance of escaping the conflagration through the small door of Good Works. From their earliest catechizing, children lived in the assurance of eternity in burning oil that yet never consumed them, of the fiery jaws of hell gaped even now to swallow them, their only hope in a succession of paltry good deeds that apparently were never enough, that were as a breath of air against the massed weight of racial depravity in which they were born, and which they momently recognized in their evil thoughts. The records of children after 1660 are usually pathetic and often pathological. There could hardly have been a more stable environment in Boston than the house of Judge Samuel Sewall the great diarist and his wife the daughter of John Hull. Yet here is his entry for January 13, 1696, respecting his fourteen-year-old daughter:

> When I came in, past 7, at night, my wife met me in the Entry and told me Betty had surprised them. I was surprised at the abruptness of the Relation. It seems Betty Sewall had given some signs of dejection and sorrow; but a little after dinner she burst out into an amazing cry, which caus'd all the family to cry too; Her Mother ask'd the reason; she gave none; at last said she was afraid she would goe to Hell, her Sins were not pardon'd. She was first wounded by my reading a Sermon of Mr. Norton's, about the 5th of Jan. Text Jno 7. 34. Ye shall seek me and shall not find me. And those words in the Sermon Jno 8. 21 Ye shall seek me and die in your sins, ran in her mind, and terrified her greatly. And staying at home Jan. 12 she read out

of her Cotton Mather—Why hath Satan filled thy heart, which increas'd her Fear. Her Mother ask'd her whether she pray'd. She answer'd Yes; but feared her prayers were not heard because her Sins not pardon'd. Mr. Willard . . . came . . . after I came home. He discoursed with Betty who could not give a distinct account, but was confused as his phrase was, and as had experienced in himself. Mr. Willard pray'd excellently. The Lord bring Light and Comfort out of this dark and dreadful Cloud, and Grant that Christ's being formed in my dear child, may be the issue of these painful pangs.[78]

It is comforting to recall that externally at least the prayers of pastor and father were answered. For some four years later Betty married Grove Hirst and became the ancestor of a good share of Greater New England.

But there were not many children in Boston and The Bay who had in them the solid and fused metal of two such families as the Sewalls and the Hulls. The mass result of hell fire teaching to little ones was the pathological behavior of the "bad girls" of Salem, the six or eight little things who by their screams and writhings brought death to a score of wretches. One or two of them may have been "bad," but mostly they were frightened babies who believed the absurdities they reported and suffered the hysteria they have been suspected of simulating. In the most complete study of the Salem tragedy, the author takes this view and supports it in a semi-fictionalized account which is convincing.[79] More authoritative is the report of a psycho-pediatrician who, after a study of all available evidence, concludes quite simply that the whole ordeal was the direct result of the morbid training and environment of the little girls.[80] It would not seem unreasonable to expand the area of application of that professional opinion to much of the grown-up society of Salem at the time.

So much nonsense has been concocted about the Mathers that it is difficult at once to acknowledge their considerable responsibility as leaders in the first decline of Puritanism into Old Calvinism and to do justice to them as minds of the first distinction and important pioneers of the modern, rationalistic civilization which denies them. Among their contribution to the investigation of "Illustrious Providences" undertaken by the ministers in 1681, both Increase and his son Cotton embarked into the esoteric but perfectly healthy field of witchcraft, roughly the doings of the Devil in his capacity as the preserver of Paganism. And because they happened to choose this subject—among many others—and because their ensuing publications happened to fall within a decade of the outbreak in Salem in 1692, the absurd assumption has become general that the Mathers were intentionally influential in stirring up the business because they had a psychopathic interest in getting pathetic crones violently killed.

The conclusions of Increase in the matter formed a part of his *Essay for the Recording of Illustrious Providences,* published in 1684, and containing besides much other valuable scientific data, some of it exposing divers other superstitions. This scholarly work may or may not have drawn some attention to witchcraft on the educated level, and may or may not have had some minute influence on the tragedy eight years later—during the last four of which Increase Mather was in England, his return in the fall of '92 coinciding with the beginning of the decline of the witch epidemic.

Cotton was both less discreet and less fortunate than his father, for his *Memorable Providences, Relating to Witchcrafts and Possessions* appeared in 1689, was popular, and undoubtedly helped to focus the public mind on the subject. Its author's object, however, was not to accomplish a brutal purge of possible witches. Rather it was a sincere though wonderfully naïve attempt to find a means of getting rid of satanic influences without having recourse to the violence of the law. One of the objects of the book was to boast of how he had cured four children on whose testimony of bewitchedness an old woman had been executed, and to imply that he might do as much for others if they would put themselves in his care. Mather had a genuine interest in the matter, partly scientific, partly aesthetic—for he always had a nose for a dramatic story. But in the apprehensive state of the public mind, nervous persons were able to translate the book into a "manual for the practice of witchcraft"[81] and so bring the public psyche a little nearer to boiling.

Doubtless Cotton Mather, before the horror began, enjoyed the notoriety, and he did get quite a string of patients. He was a complicated character, at once less sound and more original than his father, undoubtedly a spoiled brat at bottom, and at the same bottom essentially an artist who—in Wordsworth's definition of a poet—was "pleased with his own passions." It is quite possible—though no one has ever troubled to offer proof—that he had more than a scientific concern for the suspected, and often pretty, girls he entertained from time to time in his house for observation*—and always gave a clean bill of devillessness. Doubtless he had some of the complexes which eager people have enjoyed sniffing into. But murderous sadism was hardly one of them. He made a tragic but hardly foreseeable mistake

---

* Robert Calef's account of the Margaret Rule case, (*More Wonders of the Invisible World* 1700) intended to give the reader this impression, and seemed to charge specific acts, "rubb'd her stomach (her breast not covered with the Bed-cloaths)" and shortly thereafter, "he again rub'd her Breast, etc." When Mather denied rubbing her uncovered breast, Calef said he had not accused him of that. George Burr, ed, *Narratives of the Witchcraft Cases* (New York, 1914) prints the documents, 325-26, 335, 339.

in issuing his too lurid publication of 1689. He made an egregious fool of himself, after the hangings were over, by publishing his *Wonders of the Invisible World.* But his most positive and intentional effect on the trials was as the writer of a pamphlet of advice to the judges, signed by most of the Massachusetts ministers, including his father, which was probably the first voice to be raised to caution the court against the use of "spectral evidence." This consisted of reports by "afflicted" persons of events invisible to others, such as seeing the accused, sometimes in natural shape, sometimes in a fantastic shape, as of an animal, engaged in some abnormal activity such as "attacking" the accusers.[82]

Such evidence was admissible under traditional English law, though it was at this very time being questioned by European jurists,[83] probably without the knowledge of the colonial court. It was responsible for all the Salem executions. When other opinion confirmed Mather's advice, the Governor ordered the elimination of spectral evidence. And with that the executions ended. Presently the governor pardoned those condemned and awaiting execution. In early 1693, after the trials had been stopped, Increase Mather published his powerful pamphlet, *Cases of Conscience concerning Evil Spirits,* in which he said, "It were better that ten suspected witches should escape, than that one innocent person should be condemned." It is not known whether this pamphlet circulated in manuscript in the fall of 1692 just before Governor Phipps stopped the executions. But it is known that Increase Mather had got Phipps his appointment and was his intimate adviser.

Of the witchcraft epidemic itself, the only significance here is as an expression of the state of small-minded, self-concerned and apprehensive rationalism into which the people of The Bay had fallen. What proportion kept their balance can not be known. But we may hope that a letter of Joseph Wolcott, merchant of Salem, to his brother Henry of Windsor, written July 25, 1692,[84] at the height of the scare, represents the common attitude of the adult public. Certainly we can detect in it the beginnings of that unsmiling humor which presently will remodel the Puritans into Yankees—incidentally a humor of the skeptical kind that might not be inappropriate in our modern witch hunts for communists in liberal places. It is a news letter, and the first news is that the local smallpox epidemic is over and the general health is good. Then he goes into the "unheard of calamity of the witchcraft," how six have been executed, and how those about to be condemned as "confessors" include "a Comely Ingeinous young woman of about 17 years old, and two brothers one about 19 years old and the other near sixteen—both likely Ingenious, manly and hardy, Young men." Among the "confessors" also is "good Mr. Higginson's daughter, who has long been melancholy, and seemed crazed. It appears that the Devill has not (as formerly) gained a few discontented and revengefull persons, but was making a Collony to set up his kingdom by force of Armes." Just as he seems to have been doing recently in the State Department!

However prevalent may have been men of the solid stamp of Merchant Wolcott, the epidemic did smirch the otherwise relatively clean record of New England in an age when witchcraft was still universally believed in and prosecuted as a capital crime. The Salem affair took care of twenty-three unfortunates including two dogs; and between 1630 and 1692 twenty others had been done away with in all of New England. Forty-three in sixty-two years seems an abstemious record, especially as none were burned in the common European fashion. It is estimated that 500,000 witches were executed in Europe between 1500 and 1700.[85] If we reduce that to an average of 2,500 a year, and, taking a probably high estimate of 50,000,000 for the mean population, we get an annual execution of one in 20,-000. If we reduce New England's 43 in 62 years to an approximate two-thirds of a witch a year, and take the mean population as 50,000, we get a ratio of one in 75,000. Similar calculations with similarly unreliable figures for Great Britain indicate approximately the same relatively advanced state as New England. As between the American colonies, New England comes off worst, possibly because its records are preserved. Virginia may or may not be fortunate in that, while many trials are intimated in the records, the results of only two are preserved.[86]

What appears to be the first general revulsion against and condemnation of witchcraft in western Christendom followed closely at The Bay upon the Salem epidemic. Five years after the trials, on a day of fasting called by the General Court for general repentance for "the late tragedy," Samuel Sewall, prominent magistrate and member of the special witch court, publicly confessed in church that he had been the victim of bad law and had shed innocent blood. The same day twelve jurors made similar efforts to purge their consciences.[87] Later, the attainders were removed from the estates of most of the victims, and compensation was paid to their families. So ended the ancient delusion in New England. There are no known executions in America after 1692. The last of record in England had been of three in 1682, but in 1722 an old woman was burned at the stake in Scotland.[88] The last fling of witchcraft in the 1690's is of interest here as showing the extremities to which Legal Arminianism can lead a people, the contraction of the general vision from that of

God's Cosmos to one ruled by a Human Code, and the commensurate enlargement of the common self-concern in terms of fear.

The contracted Cosmos of the late Puritans of the 1690's was in some respects an Earthly Paradise which took the place of the Kingdom of God their fathers and grandfathers had expected presently to descend upon the undeveloped and waiting land. The hoped for New Jerusalem had now faded into actual, existing Commonwealths where—and notably in their metropolitan little capitals of Boston, Providence, Newport, New Haven and Hartford, the houses of whose merchants were "as handsomely equipped as most in London,"[89]—the residents were no longer pure idealists immigrant from a far country and carrying their boundless idea into an equally boundless land. Their actual ideas are now framed by known and beloved places, and are mostly of decorum appropriate within those frames. Basic to the code of decorum in all of them is an imported English Puritan perversion of Calvin's doctrine of The Calling into a financial dogma to the effect that wealth is a sign of God's favor and so a reward of virtue.[90] The holy stratification by Justification has blurred into the social stratification of Boston and Providence and Hartford. Although there are local differences in the limitation of and admission to the ruling classes, yet in general the religiously Elect have merged into the socially Elite. The little capitals of the little empires have become each its own Cosmos with its own cosmology and Cosmic Drama, its own Angels, Principalities and Powers comprising a larger committee for handing down divine commands than the ministers had been before, each committee declaring its own socially sanctifying virtues, its deadly sins, its conditions of Reprobation and its conditions of the receipt of Justification and Grace.

As Boston with its population of over 10,000[91] was the largest of the capitals, its independence and maturity were more absolute. Already in Boston, the criteria of Election were refined beyond that of mere wealth, providing a surer tenure in worldly consequence than did the vicissitudes of commerce in an age of almost perpetual war with other maritime powers. One reads a good deal more than theological snobbery in Increase Mather's dictum that the "vein of Election" runs only "through the loyns of godly Parents," for "God hath seen meet to cast the line of election so, as that generally elect Children are cast upon elect Parents."[92] Officially, the young were warned to be worthy of their noble ancestors who had settled the country in God's interest, but the same warning served to remind them that they did indeed have noble ancestors. In 1668 William Stoughton—later chief judge of the witch trials and deputy governor—issued this caution: "Consider and remember always that the *Books* that shall be opened at the last day will contain *Geneologies* in them. There shall then be brought forth a Register of the *Geneologies* of *New England's sons and daughters*. How shall we many of us hold up our faces then, when there shall be a solemn rehearsal of our *descent*, as well as our degeneracies?"[93]

But of course the same noble descent, the same custody of names like Winthrop and Saltonstall, that would make it impossible for shamed sinners to hold up their faces at the Last Judgement made them hold them shamelessly high on King or School or High or Beacon Street. After 1660 Boston was already looking back to "ancient" beginnings. Dynasties were established that would suitably support self-important people whose ancestors God had supported without any need of the trappings of vanity and self-concern. In a New England already going democratic, this settlement into hereditary aristocracy was going to keep Boston forever in a state of transition between the old world and the new. And in this anomalous state Boston was going to perform the very great service of keeping up standards of excellence, social, political and intellectual, that might otherwhere be impaired or lost.

Boston, besides being by 1700 more maturely integrated than the other capitals, was a physical World whose limits were more precisely defined. It was still the old peninsula of Shawmut, but now expanded far into the Outer and Back Bays by fill from excavation and other sources, for the Proper Bostonians had already established their traditional preference to live on their own surplus rather than to risk their sainthood on less stable ground. The outmost gates of Heaven were securely on Roxbury Neck, and the highest firmament was the comfortably smoky sky not far over the steep roofs and the heavy chimneys.

The outward opulence of this Paradise was in keeping with its inward sufficiency. The public buildings, still close around King (State) Street, and the houses of the rich, spreading south alongside the Common, westward well up Beacon Hill and to present Scollay and Adams Squares, northward to cover most of the North End, were of solid brick and stone, the outlying bulk of the city still of "timber."[94] There were now three large Meetinghouses: the First Church having its new edifice across Market (Washington) Street and facing past the Town (Old State) House down King (State) Street; Increase Mather's Second Church, having burned down in the Great Fire of '76, now replaced and its next successor to be known as Old North; Samuel Willard's Third Church about to enjoy a new edifice at the corner of Market and Milk Streets—the site of Governor John Winthrop's second house and diagonally across from the Hutchinsons'—and to be known as Old South. Besides, there was Robert Colman's Brattle Street Church, of which more presently. All the implications of contemporary reports are of a rich and proud society. African slaves were sold on the wharfs for domestic service. Incessantly the ministers thundered against the non-enforcement of the Blue Laws, and bewailed the luxuries of the people, the sumptuous wigs, plumed hats, slashed jackets, costly boots and gauntlets,[95] all the extravagances of lace, silk and hedonism that marked the Restoration.

Within this celestial capital there were set up those patterns of balanced self-interests by means of which all live and let live, those routines of the initiated which provide the charm and the squalor of the crowded metropolises of all ages. Epitomizing these patterns, there is an ideal Sophistication which, being far more complicated than the Truth of Eternity, is enough to engage every man's best efforts for a lifetime. By 1690 the gentry of Boston were fully occupied in running the city and the province, in maintaining their own code of civility, in taking care of the poor and keeping them in their place. Likewise that powerful middling class of small tradesmen and artisans, who were always potentially the enlightened and dangerous Boston Mob, were sufficiently engaged in their private affairs and in guarding their rights and in reaching for more, alternately cheering new governors and deposing them with as much violence as was required. Among all these people religion was of very great importance, but it could be no more than the first consideration within the all-inclusive frame of the interests of the Town. In fact, if religion, or other virtue, were to be preserved at all, The Town must be kept stable as its base and frame. Boston was grown a very long way from the original Shawmut which God had formed to support His People, where He had opened a sweet spring for their comfort, and where they were utterly within His care. Now it was He who was within their care.

Typical of this society at its highest and most responsible level walked Samuel Sewall, only moderately rich but of the company of the richest, son of a yeoman-merchant, son-in-law of Mintmaster Hull, Magistrate, member of the special court of oyer and terminer that tried the Salem witches, member of the Council under the Crown Government, and perhaps America's most engaging diarist. His entry for April 29, 1695, tells much of the outward aspect and the inward flavor of Boston. He records a hailstorm that broke 480 panes in his unfinished house, which meant the equivalent of at least fifteen full windows, and *this was only on the front and not all the windows there.* The same storm did damage to "Mr. Sergeant's about as much; Col. Shrimpton, Major General, Gov'r Bradstreet, New Meetinghouse, Mr. Willard." During the storm Master Cotton Mather happened to be dining with the Sewalls, and the Judge got him to do a little praying after the "awfull providence." Sewall did not like the Mathers, and the edge of sarcasm, like the edge of his deadpan humor elsewhere, is perceptible in his record of the prayer —"He told God he had broken the brittle part of our house, and prayd that we might be ready for the time when our Clay-Tabernacles should be broken."[96]

It is not fair to spunky, conscientious, generous and puttering little Samuel Sewall, who was only a first-rate man, to compare him with John Winthrop, the dark and passionate first governor of The Bay, who was of the order of saints and the world's great men. Yet, as each stood for the best in his time, we may see in them how the landscape of New England has shrunk from the City of God to the City of Man, from the Cosmos to Boston. Here are two passages from those lyric love letters of Winthrop to his third wife which are of universal humanity and have no place or time. The first was written in 1629, the year before the departure for America:

> The largnesse and trueth of my love to thee makes me allwayes mindfull of thy wellfare . . .: the verye thought of thee affordes me many a kynde refreshinge, what will then be the enjoyinge of they sweet societye, which I prize above all worldly comfortes?

And here he is writing her from Cowes in late March, 1630, when he is already aboard the *Arbella,* about to weigh for America:

> And now (my sweet soule) I must once againe take my last farewell of thee in old England, it goeth verye neere to my heart to leave thee, but I know to whom I have committed thee, even to him, who loves the[e] much better than any husband can, who hath taken account of the haires of thy head, and putts all thy teares in his bottle, who can, and (if it be for his glorie) will bringe us togither againe with peace and comfort.[97]

(It is good to recall that God did indeed "bring us togither againe with peace and comfort"—and also with the greatest feast the early colonists are recorded to have put on, with every yeoman fetching in something from far off Roxbury and Dorchester, from far off Newtown and Watertown—in that new England of which this lover, more than any other, was the artificer.)

And here, in contrast, are a few entries in Sewall's diary, recording those courtships that began after a discreet interval following the death of his first wife who had been Hannah Hull, entries which, for all the delicate feelings they sometimes show, could not have been

made, as the courtships could not have occurred, anywhere in God's
universe but Boston:[98]

> June 17, 1718. (Sewall in his late '60's) Went to Roxbury
> Lecture, visited Mr. Walter. Mr. Webb preach'd. Visited Govr
> Dudley, Mrs. Denison, gave her Dr. Mather's Sermons very well
> bound; told her we were in it invited to a Wedding. She gave
> me very good Curds.
> July 25, 1718. I go in the Hackny Coach to Roxbury. Call at
> Mr. Walter's who is not at home; nor Govr Dudley, nor his
> Lady. Visit Mrs. Denison: she invites me to eat. I give her two
> Cases with a knife and fork in each; one Turtle shell tackling;
> the other long, with Ivory handles, Squar'd, cost 4s6d; Pound of
> Raisins with proportionable Almonds.

Four months later:

> My bowels yern towards Mrs. Denison; but I think God di-
> rects me in his Providence to desist.

Presently he married the widow Abigail Tilly, and a few months
later, in May, 1720, he recorded:

> About midnight my dear wife expired to our great astonish-
> ment, especially mine.

Again, after a passage of a few months, there began the hilarious
and pathetic courtship of the arch widow Madame Winthrop, of
whose record two passages will suffice to show Judge Sewall's combined snobbery and tenderness. The "Fore-seat" in the Meetinghouse
amounted to a kind of Social Register, the seats being assigned by
rank:

> Oct 1, 1720. Satterday, I dine at Mr. Stoddard's: from thence
> I went to Madame Winthrop's just at 3. Spake to her, saying my
> loving wife died so soon and suddenly, 'twas hardly convenient
> for me to think of Marrying again; however I came to this Reso-
> lution, that I would not make my Court to any person without
> first Consulting with her. Had a pleasant discourse about 7
> Single persons sitting in the Fore-seat 7r 29th, viz. Madm. Re-
> bekah Dudley, Catharine Winthrop, Bridget Usher, Deliverance
> Legg, Rebekah Loyd, Lydia Colman, Elizabeth Bellingham.
> She propounded one and another to me; but none would do,
> said Mrs. Loyd was about her Age.

And here is the eloquent ending, the final call after five weeks
whirlwind courtship in which the old gentleman had been obviously
touched, had expended and carefully recorded a great deal on
sweets, local literature, and divers other presents, and on the
whole was shamefully flirted with by the lady. Here he attains

the human universality of Winthrop in his love passages, the difference being between ecstatic writing and merely excellent writing:

> Novr. 7. . . . The Fire was come to one short Brand besides the Block, which Brand was set up in end; at last it fell to pieces, and no Recruit was made: She gave me a Glass of Wine. I think I repeated again that I would go home and bewail my Rashness in making more haste than good Speed. I would endeavour to contain myself, and not go on to sollicit her to do that which she could not Consent to. Took leave of her. As came down the steps she bid me have a Care. Treated me Courteously. Told her she had enter'd the 4th year of her Widowhood. I had given her the News-Letter before: I did not bid her draw off her Glove as sometime I had done. Her dress was not as clean as sometime it had been. Jehovah jireh!

In their religious expressions, we see even more clearly the contrast between Winthrop and Sewall, between the Fathers and the Children and Grandchildren. Here is Winthrop:

> O: the riches of Christ! O: the sweetnesse of the worde of Grace! it ravisheth my soule in the thought heerof, so as when I apprehende but a glimpse of the dignitye and felicitye of a Christian, I can hardly perswade my heart to hope for so great happynesse: let men talke what they will of riches, honors pleasures etc.; let us have Christ crucified, and let them take all besides. . . .[99]

In transition between this unqualified religion of Winthrop's and the constricted religion of Sewall, we can notice the intermediate station of John Hull who, in his Diary is not yet dominantly self-concerned but is apprehensive lest he become so. In the following passage, written in 1648, when Hull was twenty-four, he records how the Lord

> made me also, according to the talent he betrusted me with, in some small sense serviceable to his people, and . . . as a fruit thereof, advancement (I must needs say) above my desert. I was chosen and accepted a corporal——.

Eleven years later, in 1657, he is made a Selectman of Boston, and his diary fairly cries out:

> The Lord make me sensible of the new debt I am obliged in, and give me answerable grace![100]

And in contrast to both Winthrop and Hull, we have good Samuel Sewall of the end of the century, no longer primarily concerned with God's Glory but with his own deserts to have a share in it through Eternity, while in passing holding his position of importance in Boston. Sewall's most famous, and possibly his purest religious expression, is in his confession of guilt in the Salem Witch Trials, which he posted on the Church Door on a Fast Day in January, 1697, and in the service had the minister Samuel Willard read it as Sewall stood bowed in the Mourner's Seat:

> Samuel Sewall, sensible of the reiterated strokes of God upon himself and family; and being sensible, that as to the Guilt contracted upon the opening of the late Commission of Oyer and Terminer at Salem . . . he is, upon many accounts, more concerned than any that he knows of, Desires to take the Blame and shame of it, Asking pardon of men, And especially desiring prayers that God, who has an Unlimited Authority, would pardon that sin and all other his sins; personal and Relative: And according to his infinite Benignity, and Sovereignty, Not Visit the sin of him, or of any other, upon himself or any of his, nor upon the Land. . . .[101]

This entry was on January 15, 1697. Eleven days later we have this piece of complacent Bostonese:

> Jany 26, 1696/7. I lodged at Charlestown, at Mrs. Shepards, who tells me Mr. Harvard built that house. . . . As I lay awake past midnight, In my Meditation, I was affected to consider how long agoe God had made provision for my comfortable Lodging that night; seeing that was Mr. Harvards house; And that led me to think of Heaven the House not made with hands, which God for many Thousands of years has been storing with the richest furniture (saints that are from time to time placed there), and that I had some hopes of being entertain'd in that Magnificent Convenient Palace, every way finished and furnished. These thoughts were very refereshing to me.

And here, a few months before beginning his courtship of the Widow Denison, it occurs to him that after all Christ was as well connected as most in Boston:

> Feby 6, [1718.] This morning wandering in my mind whether to live a Single or a Married Life; I had a sweet and very affectionat Meditation Concerning the Lord Jesus; Nothing was to be objected against his Person, Parentage, Relations, Estate, House, Home! Why did I not resolutely, presently close with Him! And I cried mightily to God that He would help me so to doe!

And here, in his seventy-seventh year, he is evidently as sure of his place in the Ultimate Boston as he is in the present one. He has just buried one of his three surviving Harvard classmates:

> Dec. 22, [1727] Now I can go to no more Funerals of my Classmates; nor none be at mine; for the survivors, the Rev'd

Mr. Samuel Mather at Windsor, and the Rev'd Mr. Taylor*
at Westfield, [are] one Hundred Miles off, and are entirely en-
feebled. I humbly pray that Christ may be graciously present
with us all Three both in Life, and in Death, and then we shall
safely and Comfortably walk through the shady valley that leads
to Glory.

Sewall's complacency in the Cosmos of Boston can be matched
by other less engaging diarists in other New England towns, and in
compensation for their loss of profundity in religion we see them
enjoying a cultural adjustment which represents a radical break
with Puritanism. The Second and Third Generations have finally
despaired of the Millennial hope of the Founders. They know that
New England is not to become Heaven, that it is and will remain
a place among other places on the earth. This is a tragic admission,
but it was not of the nature of Puritan realism to waste time in sad-
ness, let alone confess it by word or sign. Instead, the Puritan mind,
beginning at about this time, experienced a kind of sublimation of
the old Hope, and of so much of the old Faith as was now contracted, qualified or lost. Since things were as they were, and nothing could be done about it, the Puritan learned to take a wry
pleasure in the incongruity between this actuality and the Millennial
Idea his fathers had and which he inherited in some new form,
some contracted Idea of his own fabrication. Only now he secreted
his private idea, whatever it might be, within his reticence and enjoyed the absurdity of it in contrast to the outer and worldly disillusionment that he knew awaited all ideas. When he uttered, in the
deadpan Plain Style of the Puritans, an observation upon that outer
world, he was sometimes tragically aware of the disparity between
the stated outward fact and the unstated truth within. This sense of
tragedy in the necessary failure of human perfectionism flipped over
into an equally profound pleasure in the spectacle of human absurdity in clinging, as he did himself, to that impossible perfectionism.

Thus at the end of the first century the Puritans were old, and the
marks of their antiquity were the first intimations of Yankee Humor.
Here we begin to see the transformation of the humorless Puritan
into the humorous Yankee. The individual who had lived entirely in
God's world, had been content in it, and had not compromised it, or
compensated for its failures, was changed into the individual who
knew he had compromised with Truth and had compensated for the
loss by an inward and secret joy at his own and all men's incongruity
and absurdity. This realization sprinkles Sewall's Diary and livens it.
For all his moralism and sincerely attempted piety, the brave little

* The poet.

judge knew well enough that Boston was not a sufficient substitute for the Grace and the Eternity of his father the farmer. We can not know surely, for he did not know himself—no true Yankee ever does—in just which of his flat, literal entries he was intentionally humorous. But it is hardly credible of a man of his learning and astuteness that in those minute accountings of the costs of his courtships, and certainly in his recitation of Christ's social qualifications, we are not laughing with him as well as at him. And surely he is chuckling as he makes this hilarious entry during the courtship of the cruel Madame Winthrop:[102]

> 8ʳ 12, [1720.] . . . Madam Winthrop's countenance was much changed from what 'twas on Monday, look'd dark and lowering. At last the work, (black stuff or Silk) was taken away, I got my Chair in place, had Some Converse, but very Cold and indifferent to what 'twas before. Ask'd her to acquit me of Rudeness if I drew off her Glove. Enquiring the reason, I told her twas great odds between handling a dead Goat, and a living Lady. Got it off.

In Samuel Sewall we can recognize the first Yankee, who recorded the shrinking of his God, and the compensation for the shrinkage partly in vanity, partly in humor. In him we have a new type, less noble than the Puritan, but representing an adjustment of the Puritan to the social and carnal realities of the world, an adjustment which, as Yankee culture, was going to last two centuries and a half and we know not how much longer. It was still the Puritan House, but the Idea embodied in the Frame was no longer that of the timeless and dimensionless Christian Drama. The Central Current of the River was still of Idealism, but the outward Sky it reflected was smaller than the whole Cosmos. Within the Frame, within the Central Current of the River, True Religion, Puritanism, will revive from time to time. But whenever it declines and fades out, from this time forward, its close derivative Yankee culture will be found standing, or flowing on, without change.

The end of the seventeenth century represented the first Decline of Religion, the first shrinkage of the River by Heresy between the wide clear flow of the First Puritanism of two generations earlier and the wide clear flow of the Second Puritanism in the new century to come. It was not itself a historical age, with an integrated state of Faith and Theology, but it was a time of transition, preserving much of the past and showing still random sallies toward the future. The Cosmos of Cotton, Hooker and Williams, of Winthrop, Coddington and Ludlow, had been a real world. So would be the forthcoming Cosmos of Edwards, Bellamy and their followers. But the world of the Mathers and Willard and Stoddard, with its confusion of medieval and modern scientific method, of experimental inquiry into "illustrious providences," its mixture of Puritanism, Old Calvinist or Legal Arminianism and Liberal or Intellectual Arminianism, was a world of Bizarrity. Its leaders were like the uncouth, primitive mammals of the Eocene Age who remembered the integrated power of the dinosaurs, who in experimenting toward the future became absurd with horny excrescences, yet within them already stirred the promises of the Horse and the Dog, the Sabre-toothed tiger, the Mastodon and Man. At a remove of two decades from the chaos of the 1690's, the Puritanism it distorted will revive in a slightly altered form. But before that, the other two elements struggling toward reality in the mist will attain formulation, Old Calvinism now most nearly represented by the Mathers, and Liberalism, now most nearly represented by Willard and Stoddard. The collision and clarification of these forces will be the next action of importance in the history of New England. It begins when the last echoes of the "late commission of Oyer and Terminer at Salem" are not yet quiet. And it introduces the new century.

II. The World of Man (1700-1800)

1. SECOND PURITANISM (1700-1760)

ALTHOUGH THE CHARTER OF 1692 made Massachusetts politically a province with a royal governor, New England by that time was an integrated little nation of about 90,000 people[1] independent of Old England in the essentials of its culture. Its provinciality was no longer the singleness of a company of fanatics, emigrant from somewhere else, who had staked everything on an idea. It was the provinciality of people who live in a place and who have lost interest in their remote origins except for those purposes of genealogical snobbery which bespangle any established culture. Samuel Sewall and his first flight of Brahmins differed from the bulk of New England in their European class consciousness; but for all that they resembled more nearly the Yankees of The River than they did Pepys' metropolitan gentry or Sterne's burghers. The saucy yokels whom Sarah Kemble Knight described during her land journey from Boston to New York in 1704,[2] notably "Bumpkin Simpers" with his cheeks full of tobacco and his "Tawdry Jone" who came into the Connecticut merchant's house "dropping about 50 curtsees," these do recall Shakespeare's clods; yet their determination to buy Jone "Ribenen for Hatbands" that were "Gent"—that is, above their station—and their insolent deliberation in making up their mind to the purchase, here we have already both the Equalitarian best and the Individualistic worst of New England and America.

More typical of the whole Puritan-Yankee world than these representatives of the "Upper" and "Lower" classes was One-Class Joshua Hempsted of New London—farmer, surveyor, carpenter, shipbuilder, furniture and coffin maker, attorney, stonecutter, sailor, trader, cooper, shoemaker, Justice of the Peace, Judge of Probate, School Committeeman, Selectman, Steward to the second Governor John Winthrop of Connecticut, the third Governor John Winthrop in New England. Steady Joshua Hempsted, keeping his detailed and uninspired Diary from 1711 till 1758, has reached the point where, while he is quite aware of social differences, he yet moves through forty-seven years quite naturally from one level to another, from the cowshed to the Winthrops' parlor and the company of visiting celebrities, without revealing any sense of change.[3] Early in the Diary there is no deference when one day he "went to Winthrop to do a neighborly act in turning out a great stone"; nor is there any sense of triumph when in 1749 he

> was out to the cornfield & in the afternoon att Mr Winthrops to Dinner. a great Entertainment. Mr. Wanton Colln Sergeant, Coll Saltonstall, Mr adams & mr Lechmere & their wives, Mr Graves, Mr Stewar & my self, all the afternoon . . . ,

—these people all of the high gentry. Joshua Hempsted in the first half of the eighteenth century embodies in completed form that expansion of Congregational Equality into Secular Equality which we saw intimated at the foundation of Connecticut. It would be hard to conceive between his type and the type of the second Governor Winthrop of Connecticut an altercation such as occurred at The Bay one December day in 1705 when Governor Joseph Dudley was being driven along a country road between high snowdrifts and encountered two carters with two loads of wood. When he looked out of his chariot and told them to make way, they refused, and one of them shouted the cry of Individualism, "I am as good flesh and blood as you . . . you may go out of the way." At this the Governor descended and made a pass with his sword at one of the men who caught it and broke it; and so Dudley arrested both of them.* This was the way of the stratification and individualism of the Old World, while at The River, across equal disparities in education, training and vocation, there was already essential Yankee Equality.

In 1700, although religion and education are at a very low ebb in New England, yet the culture as a whole is long mature. The young nation need no longer look with jealous deference at its parent English culture and its collateral relations on the continent of Europe. At the beginning of the Great Revolutionary Century it can afford to stand on its own feet and rub shoulders and ideas with the world around it. The rubbing of shoulders is to be in terms of War which, having begun in 1693, is to be the continuous condition of life until 1815. Fifty-three of those hundred and twenty-three years will be of "hot" war, all but one of the struggles being foreign.[4] And the years between will be of tensely apprehensive "cold" war when every moment along the maritime and inland frontiers will be a listening by the Militia—

---

* Paraphrased from the account in Parrington's *Colonial Mind* (New York, 1929) 126. The farmers were kept in jail some time and under bond for a year, being released then only through the efforts of Samuel Sewall.

all the able-bodied men from 16 to 60—and their women and children for the signal gun or the roll of the drum from the fort or the watch-house or the church step where the messenger from the capital has dismounted.

Henceforth war will keep all the people aware of the outer world, and at the same time it will compress the culture into carica-ture. The enemy French and their Algonquin allies will block ex-pansion to the north, and the diplomatically friendly Iroquois, es-pecially the powerful Mohawks, will block it to the west. Settlement will edge out in the latter direction to occupy about half of the modern western boundary of New England, the Housatonic Valley, solidly north to Great Barrington, nervously to Pittsfield which, con-secutively settled and abandoned, will stand as the northwest corner of the Yankee world. Deerfield, erased by the tomahawk and prison train in 1675 and again in 1704, will build the third time to stand as the northern limit at the center. Until 1760, there will be nothing north and west of these points but a few log forts with inadequate and heroic garrisons, and beyond them the Enemy and War and Outer Chaos. Almost as dangerous will be the open water beyond the Atlantic frontier. But the difference there will be that through the cruising danger and in spite of it will come those ideas against which New England will rub its native ones, with even more impor-tant results than those of the shoulder-rubbing in the wars.

For now in the Great Century the Renaissance that was the transi-tion out of Middle into Modern time is to complete its Humanistic change. Every idea that will be fundamental in society two centuries later is now to be broached and variously developed. The basic doc-trines of *A Posteriori*, Experimental or Natural Reason, Natural Law and the Rights of Natural Man, which New England is al-ready receiving across the frontier of the Sea, she will adapt to her own conditions and will send them back to Europe in counter-in-fluence. Among these adaptations, the category of Liberal Religion or Intellectual Arminianism will show theological developments of consequence, but its chief importance will be secondary, as the cradle and support of Liberal Politics.* Its primary concern will be with Man, and the effort to adapt the realities of the Cosmos to the reali-ties of Human Life, rather than to discipline physical and social ex-istence into conformance with the nature of Being. In the eighteenth century, the affirmative contribution of the liberal ministry and its so-called religion will be that it will first introduce Libertarian ideas into New England, will identify them with the Will of God, and will make of its pulpits the political forums from which the

* Of the great developments of the Eighteenth Century, only those of Liberal Religion and Liberal Politics will be much noticed here, because other great categories, such as Physical Science, Materialistic Philosophy and the Doctrine of Laissez-faire, while broached at this time, will not be matured until later.

great Secular Revolutions will be fomented and, on the local and personal level, actually led. Incidentally, though the wholly religious Puritan Revival will be the strongest movement in the first half of the century, and though in its Antinomian Decline it will help to settle Revivalism permanently on America, yet in that same Decline its Religious individualism will turn into Social and Political individualism, wherefore it also will contribute to the great tide of Humanistic self-assertion.

Until 1760, Religion was probably the strongest force in the Great Century, but on the whole the trend was Humanistic. On the whole the Puritan Idea of the mysterious Cosmos contracted to a still large but withal a reduced Idea called Man, Natural Man, Man on the earth. As the stage setting of the seventeenth century had been the World of The Cosmos, so that of the eighteenth century was the World of Man. Carl Becker points out that the Eighteenth Century retained more of the "superstitious" Imagination of the seventeenth than it liked to admit.[5] It dismissed God but replaced Him with a "Supreme Being," "Prime Mover" or "First Cause." It eschewed the hocus-pocus of Christian Grace, yet its Natural Reason was often as intuitive and mysterious as the Puritans' Right Reason which was the application of Grace. It laughed at the Creation and at Eden, but accredited a lost Golden Age, and professed that the Universe was a perfect Mechanism designed by a Rational Supreme Being. It denied Heaven, but apostrophized Posterity and generally clung to the notion of a Future Life. In all of this Becker is probably right that the eighteenth century did not purge itself of "superstition" as fully as its philosophers thought it did. But it did substitute Abstraction for Imagination, Natural Reason for Right Reason, and it did open the way for the next great Scientific Century. Both in theory and in practice it occupied a smaller landscape than the seventeenth century had done. Yet undimmed by the brutalities of mature Materialism, the Light of Liberalism was then a clear, vivid and exciting light, and the scope of its world opening before the still young dawn of Natural Law seemed at least as great as that of true Puritan, Gracious or Aesthetic Religion. Yet, in the eighteenth century as today, the light of liberalism showed only the lower and superficial reaches of the Universe, the reaches inhabited and seen by Man. It widened the horizontal vistas, but it shallowed the Puritan sky.

True or Gracious Puritanism and Liberalism are the two Affirmative Religious forces of the eighteenth century. At the beginning of the period, however, Old Calvinism, with its Legal Arminian or Moralistic Theology, is the best integrated out of the transitional chaos of the end of the previous age. Old Calvinism in New England is not different from Conservatism in any other form. It is a point of view rather than a dogma—though the Conservative must of course wear an outward profession of "principle" in order to appear human to the world and to himself. The Central Ideas to which the Old Calvinist clings for his security are the habits and prejudices in which he was raised. In him the boundless Cosmos of the Puritan imagination has shrunk to the horizons of the township; Grace is Social Self-Assurance; and the meaning of the Sky is the Weather. The New England Old Calvinists generally miscalled themselves "orthodox," for they claimed Puritan dogma for their prerogative. But they failed progressively to understand the true meaning of the "Grace" and "Regeneration" they professed, and their ministers ignored the meaning. Neither ministers nor people were orthodox in the sense that they seriously adopted and tried to apply the orthodoxy of their background. They were—and still are—orthodoxians, people for whom any orthodoxy will do so long as the profession of it is a mark of respectable status, and so long as the minister can profess it for them without their having to tire their minds in trying to understand it. The multitudinous and admirable get of Increase Mather today might as well be Catholics, Roman or Anglican, would be at home in any liturgy into which they were born and where their thinking might safely be done for them, where they can be assured of Salvation without having to inconvenience themselves by trying, in the phrase of Jonathan Edwards, "to live as hard as I can."

The scope of Old Calvinism is large, embracing most pillars and all snobs of all communities. Its leaders are Legal Arminians, Moralists, Fundamentalists, Anti-Intellectuals, Witch Hunters, persons whom theologically illiterate historians delight to call "Puritans." Its multitude is a lukewarm broth of all these, all assuming together that if you make a discreet effort to behave yourself according to the acceptable suggestions laid down as Moral Law by the minister of your hiring, and occasionally boil a little with the warmth of those suggestions, all will somehow come well for you in a far off disposal called "Heaven." First numerously recognizable at the end of the seventeenth century, Old Calvinism, or New England Conservatism, will not come to full flower until the nineteenth century when, in the form we call Victorianism, it will roll into one ball a hypocritical morality, a new-rich respectability, a sentimentality pretending to religion, and an enamelled cruelty. After 1700 it will always comprise a large minority or a small majority of the people, the solid lump, resistant alike to Religion and to Liberalism, whose eventual slow stir, goaded by either of the affirmative forces, will be the advance of history.

Of all the great names in New England religion, I know of only

the Mathers and the Beechers who attained at once to Conservatism
and to Distinction. Among the Old Calvinists at the opening of
the eighteenth century, whose function it will be to oppose the
affirmative work both of the Liberals and of the Puritans, popular
"Johnnie" Barnard, minister at Marblehead from 1716 till his death
in 1770, sets a pattern for the rest. Graduating from Harvard in
1700, he became a protegé of the Mathers and was involved with
Cotton in much small, ecclesiastical politics. At the beginning of his
Autobiography,[6] he informs us modestly that he wrote it under the
pressure of friends. Composing in a style of stock humility, he records with zest what good use the Lord made of him in the material
advancement of Marblehead during his long incumbency, notably in
the growth of its commerce and the expansion of the train band (the
militia) from a ragged company into a well-equipped regiment. In
the interest of the only True Religion, he is critically watchful of the
Anglican ministers after their church was founded in town: the first,
he tells us, was "neither a scholar nor a gentleman"; the second was
tolerable but absurdly shy; the third was ignorant and worthless;
the fourth was a good Scotchman; the fifth, being from Rhode Island
and Harvard, was the best of the lot. Barnard's consummate achievement was as the spokesman for the opposition to the Great Awakening of Edwards and Whitefield, which was the most important religious event of the century:[7]

> In the time of the Whitefieldian ferment, in 1741, I was en-
> abled, by the Grace of God, so to conduct, as not only to pre-
> serve my own flock in peace and quietness, but to prevent the
> other church in town, and their minister, from being thrown
> into the like disorders and confusions, in which so many towns
> and churches in the country were involved; and when the min-
> isters of the Convention proposed to draw up a public Testi-
> mony against several errors and bad practices prevalent among
> us, they made use of my hand for the draught.

This testimony against the Revival was signed by 38 Conservative
ministers of Massachusetts, and was countered by another signed by
113 Puritanical ones of Massachusetts, New Hampshire, Maine and
Connecticut.[8]

Where the Old Calvinists were Legal Arminians, the Religious
Liberals who, as we have seen, characterized the century as a whole,
were Intellectual Arminians. They were the American priests of The
Enlightenment, that rising of the sun of combined Reason and Humanism by which we still guide our way. Like the Old Calvinists,
they believed that each man could and should figure out his course
by the use of Natural Reason, in contrast to the Right Reason of the

Puritans which was a function of Grace. But where the Old Calvinists conceived Reason as a scholastic implement for analyzing and applying the established Divine or Social Law, the Liberals used it, or professed to, as an Experimental method, the new Scientific method, for examining and applying the principles of new and unfolding Natural Law, especially the supposed laws governing the Nature and the Rights of Man. Both Liberals and Conservatives saw every man as "his own cause," accredited to make his choices by his own Natural Reason and to apply them with his own unpredestined will. The Liberals scorned equally the Old Calvinists and the Puritans, but they aligned themselves with the former in the central struggle of the century, and provided better leadership than Johnnie Barnard against the great Puritan Jonathan Edwards and the Revival of Religion. They were altogether more effective and attractive, indeed vastly more selfless and heroic, than the Old Calvinists were, standing somewhere between the latter's dependence on social sanction and the Puritan's independence of it. Through the eighteenth century and longer, the Liberals were more tolerant than either of the other two religious parties. But in the twentieth century Liberalism itself has become a conventional posture, a Neo-Conservatism, and today our typical Liberals are as intolerant of Religion as, say, Increase Mather was of "Popish" innovations in the Liberal Churches of his time.

Of the many trends that comprised the eighteenth century, perhaps the one to notice first is the drift into Tolerance, not because it was itself a substantial development, but because it provided a wider frame than that of the seventeenth century, a freer stage for the less trammelled exercise of the substantial and generally conflicting tendencies. There were two currents, more or less reinforcing each other, in the trend into tolerance. Of these the deeper current was the Popular one, and we shall consider it later as related to the Revival of Religion. At present we shall notice only the rise of Official Tolerance which, while it gathered strength from awakening Religion, was in the main a political and involuntary adjustment, being forced upon Massachusetts by the Charter of 1692 and its consequences, and adopted by Connecticut under an expediency that was almost as compelling.

It is interesting to observe that in inverse ratio as Massachusetts grew powerful she submitted to imperial authority imposing Toleration. In the 1630's when she was tiny with a population of scarcely 8,000, and was threatened with a Royal Governor and the Anglican establishment, then her answer was to strengthen the fortifications at Boston and Salem. A generation later, in 1661, at the beginning of the Decline of Religion, when the population was nearly 25,000 and she was the strongest voice in the New England Confederation which could put in the field a military force of perhaps 12,000, then at the King's order she stopped persecuting Quakers and permitted them to hold meetings. In 1664, under continuing royal pressure, the qualifications of church membership for the suffrage were diplomatically repealed. In 1665 the Baptists, and in '74 the Quakers, openly established regular meetings contrary to law, and although they suffered some official persecution, both survived, and presently built churches.

The more Massachusetts deferred to the Stuarts, the stronger became the royal determination to bring to heel this always secessionist and recalcitrant colony. The great blow fell in 1684 when the charter was annulled. In 1686 arrived Sir Edmund Andros with dictatorial authority who, when the Third or Old South Church refused him its building for the dreaded Anglican services, took it part time by force. In 1688 King's Chapel was begun at the corner of School Street and Tremont Street, the first Episcopal Church in New England—its completion and occupation were delayed by the ascension of Protestant William and Mary in the same year, and Boston's own Glorious Revolution that threw out Andros. Increase Mather went to England and spent four years trying to get back the ancient charter and the ancient Rights of Intolerance.

But toleration was now the way of the Mother Country, whoever was on the throne, and the new Charter that went into effect in 1692 expressly abolished the religious qualifications for the vote. In 1727 the Anglicans got the privilege of having their ecclesiastical taxes diverted to the use of their own churches, and the Quakers and Baptists got the same right in 1731 and '35 respectively. The ancient Purity of Massachusetts was compromised after 1664, and in 1718 when Increase and Cotton Mather assisted at a Baptist ordination it was acknowledged as lost. By the 1720's the Anglicans were flourishing. In 1722 King's Chapel overflowed, and Christ Church was founded under the rectorship of Timothy Cutler, a prominent renegade from the Connecticut Establishment, one of the first three Yankees to go to England for Episcopal ordination. Presently Christ Church had a membership of over 700, and so in 1729 Trinty Church was founded, the third Anglican parish in Boston. By the early 1730's Episcopalianism, potential Toryism, was powerful in Boston, and the once scorned Quakers and Baptists were free and almost respectable.

As Intolerance had been less extreme in Connecticut than in Boston, so Tolerance arrived by less spectacular means. But it was hardly less compulsory for being more subtly so. The first heretical victory was on the part of the Quakers, with probably necessary support from the Anglicans. Connecticut's persecuting law of 1657 against "Heretics, Infidels and Quakers" had been mild, and after touring the Colony in 1658, the Quaker missionary John Rous had reported that "Among all the colonies found we not moderation like this." In 1675 the General Court, desiring to ingratiate Rhode Island during King Philip's War, had exempted Quakers from the general fine for missing public worship, though still forbidding them to assemble or make disturbances. In 1700 a degree of persecution seems to have been revived.[9] But shortly thereafter the Quakers got an effective advocate at Court in the person of William Penn who was in favor with Queen Anne, and reinforcement of their complaints from other sources.

For after 1700 charges began pouring into England of Connecticut's intolerance of the Anglicans. The Society for the Propagation of the Gospel in Foreign Parts was formed in 1701, and there arose a strong demand for the appointment of a Bishop in America. The Anglican Church in Rye, N.Y., just over the Connecticut border, was operating a base and a propaganda machine, both for conducting converting raids and for reporting to England the crimes of their neighbors. Also, a considerable body of secular charges was accumulating against Connecticut, such as violating the Navigation Laws, failing in military duties, and exceeding the Charter in divers ways including the encouragement of manufactures contrary to law. Most of the charges were false or exaggerated, but they did make a formidable array. To these were now added the various true allegations of religious persecution, and the list was too long for good Queen Anne to bear, with her friend William Penn importunately before her. In October, 1705, in Privy Council she annulled Connecticut's law of 1657 against "Heretics, Infidels and Quakers." Shortly thereafter a bill came up for consideration in Parliament consolidating Connecticut's military under the Governor of New York. The bill was defeated in the Lords through the efforts of Connecticut's agent Sir Henry Ashurst, but privately he wrote to the colony urging them formally to repeal the law of 1657 which the Queen had just annulled. This they graciously did in 1706, but only with respect to the Quakers, who thereby became the first officially tolerated heretics in the Colony, as they had been in Massachusetts forty-five years before.

Meanwhile the Episcopal pressure continued strong, and the threat of a bishop was real. In May, 1708, the General Court passed the famous Toleration Act, in close imitation of the similar Act of William and Mary of 1689, apparently granting the same liberty as that act to worship God "in a way separate from that which is by law established." And in the autumn of the same year the General Court recommended the highly Conservative Saybrook Platform with a proviso "that nothing herein shall be intended or construed to hinder or prevent any Society or Church that is or shall be allowed by the laws of this government, who soberly differ or dissent from the United Churches hereby established from exercising worship and discipline in their own way, according to their conscience."

Practically, Connecticut's Toleration Act of 1708 was a piece of official hypocrisy. To enjoy it, the Dissenters had to take an oath of allegiance, and that eliminated the Quakers and other minor sects whose members would not take oaths. For the Anglicans and the Baptists there was a degree of toleration in it, but they were still subject to taxes for the Establishment, and in practice they usually suffered petty obstruction in their efforts to get the official recognition required by law. Connecticut's Toleration Act was important only as the declaration of a principle, but as such a declaration it was important indeed. On the part of the legislators, or most of them, it was doubtless a concession to expediency. But by 1708 there was an increasing popular minority in the Colony which was concerned about the things of Religion, and concerned in a yet inchoate way to which the idea of toleration would in this early phase be congenial. Like many in their position two centuries and a half later, they did not yet know what they wanted, but they were curious and they didn't like the dominant Conservatism. For all they knew, any of these Heretical Sects might have the Secret.

This was the Popular drift toward a Revival of Religion, which took at first the form of a trend toward Toleration, giving some honest support to the official trend, and finding honest expression in the Toleration Act. Nineteen years later it represented a wide enough sentiment to compel real concessions by the government. In 1727, Episcopalians were permitted, as in Massachusetts, to divert their ecclesiastical taxes to their own churches. And two years later the Quakers and Baptists were permitted to do the same. When in 1731 and 1735, as already recounted, they got the same liberty in Massachusetts, Toleration for almost everybody was complete in New England. It is customary among New England-baiters to assert that Intolerance lasted until 1818 and 1833 when the official churches were disestablished in Connecticut and Massachusetts respectively. This reasoning would hold that private schools are not tolerated today because the states also maintain "established" public schools. After 1734 the heretical sects fared better than the patrons of private schools today, for they were not taxed for the Establishment.

On the widening stage of increasing Toleration during the first third of the Eighteenth Century we can watch the three-cornered wars of the century developing between Old Calvinism, Liberalism and Puritanism at the opening of the period. Religion or Puritanism was so moribund as to be negligible, and the first campaign of the new age, beginning two years before the century opened, was an attack on the Old Calvinism of the Mathers by that inchoate Liberalism which thus far we have associated with Solomon Stoddard and Samuel Willard. The effect of the struggle was to delineate both forces and qualify them for their later Unholy Alliance against Puritanism.

Until the mid-90's the stronghold of Liberalism had been generally The River. But about that time it began dangerously to undermine The Bay, specifically The Holy Foundations of Harvard, where Increase Mather was president. Two of the tutors, the Masters William Brattle and John Leverett, were setting out to teach and to preach the abandonment of the "public relation" of the Experience of Grace as a condition of full church membership, and other dangerous innovations. The Harvard corporation slipped into a state of intramural war wherein it sizzled until 1707.

Meanwhile, the rising power in the premises, and a match even for the Mathers, was William Brattle's big brother Thomas—said to have been then the wealthiest man in Boston—Harvard Trustee and Treasurer after 1693—the resources of the College tripled under his administration. Having taken an extended grand tour between his graduation in '76 and his settling down in '89, he acquired an "inclination toward the forms of the Church of England," at the same time establishing himself as a mathematician and an astronomer who subsequently supplied observations of eclipses to the Royal Society. He was never but a Halfway Member of Willard's Third Church, and in 1698 he was chiefly instrumental in founding the Fourth Church in Boston, the Brattle Street Church which was the first frankly Liberal fort to be erected in Conservative territory. In its construction hardly a formal Puritan beam or post remained. The "public relation" as a condition of full membership was discarded. Baptism, previously limited to the children of Saints and Halfway Saints, was offered to all who had a Christian sponsor who would undertake their training. Almost as heinous, the Lord's Prayer—a piece of obvious popery—was introduced in the liturgy. Likewise, "dumb reading" or reading of the Scriptures without comment, also a piece of Roman formalism, was practiced. The Brattle Street service of 1698 became in most respects the Congregational service of today. On the practical side, all persons who contributed to the minister's salary were permitted to vote in his selection, whether members of the church or not.

The first minister called to this heretical congregation was Benjamin Colman, Harvard '92, M.A. '95, a reputed Liberal who was occupying a pulpit in England at the time of his call back home. Uncertain of what reception he might receive at the hands of his future brother ministers, he committed the Awful Heresy of having himself ordained by the London *Presbytery* before accepting God's summons to Brattle Street. Upon his installation in 1699, the new church had the impudence to ask to be received in fellowship by the other churches, and the Mathers suffered first blood in the war when the request was granted. Increase counter-attacked successfully by obtaining the dismissal from the Harvard Corporation of Thomas Brattle, his brother William, and the other Liberal tutor John Leverett.

But the revolutionary faction soon recaptured control, and in 1701 the Corporation passed a law that no one should at the same time occupy the Presidency and a Pulpit. This forced out the great Increase himself, for he preferred his pastorship of the Second Church to the presidency of the College. His son Cotton received a passing slap in not being invited to succeed his father, as they had assumed he would be. The slight to the Mathers was made the more evident when Samuel Willard was elevated to the position of Vice-President and permitted to perform as president, while retaining his pulpit in the Third Church. In 1703, Leverett and the two Brattles were restored to the Corporation, and in 1707 Liberalism won the victory when Leverett was made President of Harvard. Henceforth "The College" was on the side of dangerous innovation, and not to be trusted by Conservatives. To be sure, even the wildest Liberalism did have its limits. Thomas Brattle had in his house the only organ in Boston, probably the only one in New England. Dying in 1713, he left it to his beloved Brattle Street Church, provided they would "procure a Sober person (to) play skilfully thereon with a loud noise." Regretfully, the Liberal Congregationalists felt forced to decline the bequest though not because of any anti-musical prejudice. The Romish instrument went to King's Chapel, that den of popish Anglicanism.[10]

Meanwhile, the Mathers had lost on a wider field. Still controlling many, perhaps most, of the ministers of The Bay, they assembled in 1705 a Convention which recommended to the churches the *Massachusetts Proposals*. One provision was that the ministerial associations should pass on candidates for the ministry; but the critical feature was the establishment of a Standing Council in each Association which should have authority over the churches in all things, including the right of expulsion from the Association. This was

apparently a concession to the Presbyterian drift which was strong
in the Congregational churches in England and getting stronger in
America. Actually, it was an effort on the part of the Mathers and
their Conservative minions to regain ministerial authority in order
to cope with Liberalism. The convention of Ministers adopted the
Proposals, but it was not until eighty-five years later that the
Churches adopted even the mild one about the supervision of the
Associations over candidates for the ministry. The attempt of the
Mathers to constitute an oligarchy was roundly defeated by the general ministry of The Bay, under the principal leadership of intrepid
John Wise, Harvard, 1673, M.A. '76, of Chebaco Parish, Ipswich. He
was a famous wrestler who, when a certain Captain John Chandler
rode over from Andover and challenged him in his front yard, threw
the challenger over the front wall, at which the courteous Captain
arose and said that if the Parson would throw over his horse also he
would be on his way.[11] Wise had gone to jail in 1687 for opposing an
illegal tax of Royal Governor Andros, and as Chaplain of the un-
successful expedition against Quebec in 1690, was accredited by
several—including himself—with being the only aggressive officer
present. Now his *The Churches Quarrel Espoused,* published in
1710, and *Vindication of the Government of New England Churches,*
1717, throwing Lockian democratic arguments at the Mathers, equat-
ing ecclesiatical and secular Liberty, were the first audible guns of
the American Revolution.

By 1710 Liberalism was triumphant at The Bay, not yet the Quasi-
Religious Political Liberalism of Wise, but that pure and generic
Liberalism whose central quality is Toleration. With the defeat of
the Mathers, Benjamin Colman of the Brattle Street Church became
the leader of clerical and academic thought, and he was characterized by a Tolerance so genial and broad that it is difficult to find in
him enough consistency even to classify him as a Liberal. After the
tensions of the Matherian wars, Boston wanted peace, and Colman
gave it to them. He lapsed into a social or polite conservatism so
urbane that he extended a reconciling hand to the defeated Mathers
of the Right, deferring to them in many things as his seniors though
their power was gone. And after their deaths, Increase in 1723,
Cotton in 1728, he showed himself so "free and catholick"—in his
own favorite phrase—that he extended another reconciling hand to
the Puritan Great Awakening of the Left and had no part in the
Liberal campaign against Edwards. In Boston Colman reigned alone,
gathering many boons for Harvard and always refusing the presidency, dying in 1747 full of peace. Meanwhile more aggressive
Liberals had matured in his shadow and were in action. A new reli-

gious war was raging along The River, where Puritanism had risen
from its ashes for its last great fight.

The drift at The River had been in the opposite direction from
that at The Bay. As the East had gone Liberal, the West had gone at
first Conservative. Solomon Stoddard, the "Pope" of the region, had
rated as Liberal in the period of hybrid transition, using Communion as a Means to Grace rather than as a celebration of Grace
already attained. But he was Illiberal and Matherian in wanting the
churches run by the Ministerial Associations. Although there is no
sign that he ever so far acknowledged the Mathers as to endorse a
measure sponsored by them, yet he and his large following approved
the principle of centralized authority contained in their *Massachusetts Proposals*. And when real Liberals began to breach the walls
at Harvard, and when they founded their Brattle Street Church and
introduced such popery as the Lord's Prayer and Dumb Reading of
the Scriptures, and such democracy as letting every Reprobate vote
for the minister if he had contributed to the church, then the body of
ministerial and lay opinion along the River boiled, compressed and
erupted. There was correspondence between Connecticut leaders
and the Mathers and other Conservatives of Boston. Connecticut
began to remember the need of having "a nearer and less expensive
seat of learning" than Harvard, a project which New Haven Colony
years before had almost realized. In 1700 eleven ministers of the
purest Conservative Blue, being named Trustees, met first at New
Haven and afterwards at Branford, each bringing a few of his choic-
est folios as a contribution. In 1701, the very year that Increase
Mather was virtually ejected from "The College" at The Bay, the
Connecticut Legislature chartered[12] and appropriated £60 a year[13]
for the establishment of a "Collegiate School." The college which
seventeen years later was to be named in gratitude for a large dona-
tion by Merchant Elihu Yale, was set up at Saybrook for the purpose
of holding the Conservative Old Calvinist Line.

Seven years later that Line was clearly drawn when the Saybrook
Synod met at the College—and was dominated by its faculty—for the
purpose of dealing with the problem of Centralized Church Authority
which The Bay was then in process of rejecting in the form of the
Mathers' *Proposals*. In the resultant *Saybrook Platform*, recommended to the churches by the General Court that same year of 1708,
and accepted by most of them, Connecticut virtually adopted the
Proposals, substituting for the Mathers' "Standing Councils" county
Consociations with equivalent power over the separate churches.

Thus Connecticut went, and remained, virtually Presbyterian. And its government, both ecclesiastical and political, went, and remained for a long time, Conservative.

So in the first decade of the seventeenth century The Bay and The River exchanged roles. After the definitive victory of the Boston Liberals in the election of Leverett to the presidency of Harvard in 1707, and the definitive victory of the Connecticut Conservatives in the Saybrook Platform the following year, the quarrel between these two wings of the New England clergy was grudgingly ended. On the local level the war between Liberals and Old Calvinists continued bitter in both regions. But on the level of leadership each group conceded the other authority in its precinct. Each was academically, socially and politically entrenched, unctuously tolerant of the other and ready to join forces in the new war against renascent Puritanism that would know no truce. For the religion of Edwards and the Puritan Reaction was by its nature incapable of both worldly compromise and survival.

But before the opening of the great struggle of the century, the curtain rose for a comic interlude, a continuation on the local level of the Conservative-Liberal fight in the form of a fierce and quarterless War between the addicts of the "Old Way" and the "New Way" of singing in Church. The original Puritans had had some knowledge of orderly psalmody, and the gradual loss of it had been part of the decline in education since about 1660. With a few metropolitan exceptions like Samuel Sewall, no layman in New England knew that there was or could be any order for notes, let alone a notation. The method of singing was the "deaconing" of the psalms which presently was called the "Old Way" or the "Usual Way." The deacon, whose chief qualification for office was a "big and taking voice,"[14] sang a line as seemed to him fit, and the congregation sang it after him, each participant taking the "Run of the Tune" without any concept of either pitch or time and adding "little Slidings and Purrings, raisings and lowerings" as the spirit moved him. The result was an "indecent jargon," or, in Increase Mather's understatement, an "Odd Noise."

The "New Way" was quite suddenly proposed in 1715 by John Tufts, the young minister of Medford, Massachusetts, in a booklet entitled *An Introduction to the Singing of Psalm-Tunes, in a Plain & Easy Method, With a Collection of Tunes in Three Parts*. There ensued fifteen years of alarms and excursions, in every township great and small, local sideshows that barked and rattled while the central wars of the great over points of Theology, Church Polity and Toleration rumbled on the main stage. The "New Way" was nothing other than harmony, Tuft's book a proposal that people learn how to sing. Almost all congregations were split, the advocates of the "New Way" generally the minister and the young, the defenders of the "Old Way" the oldsters who not only resisted change in general but were able to see in this "New Way" a lapse into Popery. It was a reduction to absurdity of the quarrel over the Lord's Prayer and the Dumb Reading of Scripture, for trained singing also was held to be a snare of Rome. At this time the division was in the main that of the recent Conservative-Liberal struggle, though with the New Singers now reinforced by the educated among the Old Calvinists, and inspired also by something of the freshness of the incipient Revival of Religion. Much later the churches were to be again split on similar absurd issues, on a point of "carnality" when it was proposed to violate the winter churches with stoves, on a point of artificiality in the issue between a trained and an untrained ministry.

The "Singing Quarrel" was as bitter as any of the nobler ones that shook New England before and after. Itinerant lecturers taught the New Way to singing clubs that presently were constituted choirs by that part of the congregation—majority or minority—which favored them. The conflict would then be carried into divine service where the conflicting parties would attempt to shout each other down, and on several occasions it is recorded that a deacon left the church in tears. Miss Winslow sees in this long and hilarious quarrel a training in modern democracy, a gradual realization that in a congregation where all were equal in God's eyes unanimity was not always possible, and the only way to solve such problems was by majority vote. However that may be, the Singing Quarrel was an exercise in burlesque form of the new Individualism that was already emergent. First in Boston, and gradually through the rest of New England, the sweet singers of the New Way became the dominant voices in meeting, whether by volume or by weight. By the 1730's the victory of Music as well as that of Toleration was complete, and Yankee Idealism was released to seek implementation in larger terms.

Meanwhile, during that same third of a century while the Singers were screaming in their sideshows, and the Tolerators and the Intolerators, the Liberals and the Old Calvinists, were occupying the center of the main stage, Pure Religion, little compromised by either Music, Prejudice or Reason, was stirring in its corners. As we have intimated, the Revival of Puritanism after 1700 was from what was perhaps New England's all time low, both in education and in reli-

gion.* At the level of higher education, Harvard had a library of
less than 400 volumes, and these were not greatly used by the undergraduates.[15] The College at The Bay was still using textbooks from
the early seventeenth century, and logic from the Middle Ages. Yale's
library, founded with forty folios in 1700, probably did not surpass
200 volumes during the first decade of the new century.[16] Every indication is that primary and secondary education were in equally disgraceful condition. In many towns the great grandchildren of the
original yeomen had lost the power to "rede, right and sypher." A
somewhat overfastidious preacher before the Massachusetts General
Court said that the backwoods towns were "Nurseries of Ignorance,
Prophaneness and Atheism."[17]

Not only had the great body of the people lost the common
literacy, they had also lost the religious literacy of the fathers. We
have seen how at the top the Ministers after 1679 generally pursued
a policy of compelling conformance to the Law, while continuing to
mouth the doctrines of the Gracious Religion of the Puritans. In
some Connecticut towns these Conservative ministers, while still
insisting on the letter of a Public Narration of Conversion for admission to church membership, would yet accept such a narrative
written for the supposed Elect by others.[18] Jonathan Edwards, the
implacable enemy of Arminianism, made even more scathing
charges:

> It is a great mistake if anyone imagines that all these external
> performances (owning the covenant, accepting the sacraments,
> observing the Sabbath and attending the ministry), are of the
> nature of a *profession* of anything that belongs to *saving grace,*
> as they are commonly used and understood. . . . People are
> taught that they may use them all, and not so much as make any
> pretence of the least degree of *sanctifying grace;* . . . It is not
> unusual . . . for persons, at the same time they come into
> church and pretend to own the covenant, freely to declare to
> their neighbors, that they have no imagination that they have
> any true faith in Christ or love for him.[19]

New England of 1700 was an intellectually empty world, a society
as blank as the *tabula rasa,* the blank sheet of paper, of the Lockian
psychology which its greatest leader was about to espouse, the blank
sheet of paper that is every mind at birth, unmarked by inheritance,
upon which all ideas are to be impressed by outward experience. It
was an amorphous world, a little chaos in which formless ideas
were stirring in the mist, struggling for being, coalescing and again

* "The general level of culture in the colonies was lower than it had been at
any time since the founding and lower than it has been ever since." (Winslow,
Meetinghouse Hill, 153.)

dissolving, shapes of blind curiosity, small collisions of petty notions, but all tending gradually toward the alignments of the '40's that were to have in them the future of the Nation.

Among the random gestures of this society the Singing War was probably the best caricature of this its second infancy. Other yearnings and experiments after 1700 were less organized and, in the noise of the Battle of the Divines and the Battle of the Songsters, less audible. The trend into Official Toleration which we have seen was doubtless encouraged in part by popular indifference to Religion, but it was encouraged also by an emergent suspicion that the Truth might be found in any of the barred sects if only one were permitted to run up the by-way and look at them. What turned out presently to be the bulk of the people were in that formless state, that state of religious susceptibility without religion, to which the idea of Toleration is congenial. Like many in their position two centuries and a half later, they did not yet know what they wanted, but they were curious. They didn't like the current Conservatism, and they wanted something meatier than the current Liberalism. In 1711 the Hartford North Association asked for a change in the Halfway Covenant practice because under it irreligious people were being admitted to church membership. The curiosity that had always turned out to hear Quakers and Baptists when they were permitted to preach increased in quantity and intensity, and conversions to Heresy began to reach impressive numbers. After the Quakers were permitted to substitute affirmation for the oath of allegiance, and to have their ecclesiastical taxes diverted to their own use, their meetings—usually without meetinghouses—began to dot New England. In New Milford nineteen, mostly young people, "fell away" into Quakerism, and the beloved minister of the town, Daniel Boardman, used to attend the meetings of the Friends who were stealing his parishioners; but at the same time the number of Conversions into his own church approached revivalistic proportions. In Northampton the aged Solomon Stoddard, who had staged revivals before, effected two more in 1713 and 1719.[20] The Baptist conversions after 1727 ran into increasing thousands, but as they were part of the general upheaval of the Great Awakening, we shall notice them in more detail later.

Anomalous and spectacular in the random unrest of the early part of the century was the rise of Episcopalianism. In spite of the persecutions that had forced the American Puritans out of England, there was, after the middle of the seventeenth century, a disposition in favor of Anglicans on the part of some of the New Englanders, in-

cluding some members of the Establishment. When two Church of
England scouts, John Talbot and George Keith, toured Connecticut
in 1702 for the Society of the Propagation of the Gospel, the Reverend Saltonstall of New London, subsequently Governor, entertained
them at his house and invited them to preach in his church. He was
a good deal disillusioned when it appeared subsequently that they
were no sooner back in New York than they wrote to London
strongly urging the placing of a bishop over New England. The
southwest corner of Connecticut was under seige by the Anglican
church of Rye, N.Y., which was sending its Rector Muirson upon
itinerating forays across the border where he addressed increasingly
large and curious audiences. In some of the towns the civil officers
felt compelled to go about pleading with the people not to listen to
these apostles of Antichrist, and at Fairfield they closed the Meetinghouse lest it be "defiled by idolatrous worship and superstitious
ceremonies."[21] In spite of these precautions the invaders made numerous converts, especially around Stratford. After the Toleration
Act of 1708, these immediately founded Stratford Church which soon
built up a congregation of around two hundred and fifty, including
a hundred baptized persons and thirty-six communicants.

But the great victory for Anglicanism, and the best evidence that
the age was weary with Conservative domination and was looking
toward some new Truth, was the "Great Apostasy" at Yale in 1722.
At Commencement in September of that year, the Rector or President Timothy Cutler, one tutor, a former tutor Samuel Johnson,
then minister at West Haven, and the minister of North Haven declared for Episcopacy. Presently they sailed for England and were
ordained, Cutler and Johnson being besides decorated for their
treason by both Oxford and Cambridge. Cutler returned, as we have
seen, to be minister of the new Christ's Church in Boston. Johnson
in England became the intimate friend of Bishop Berkley, and persuaded him to make his later gift to Yale's library. Returning to
America, Johnson accepted the Episcopal Pulpit in his native Stratford. In 1752 he refused the presidency of a new college—later the
University of Pennsylvania—then being founded under Benjamin
Franklin's auspices in Philadelphia. But in 1754 he became the first
President of King's College—later Columbia—in New York.

Cutler was rated by many the best orator in New England, and his
conversion resulted in part as a backfire from his having been sent
to Stratford to do forensic battle with the Anglican priest there and
being himself overcome. Johnson's apostasy seems to have had some
secular basis in his awakening to the inadequacy of the libraries of
New England's two colleges. He feared that if closer intellectual relations were not established with England, the country would con-

tinue its descent into savagery. Both Cutler and Johnson were finally persuaded of the superiority of the Anglican polity by a study of books on the subject which were new to them and were included in Jeremy Dummer's gift to Yale in 1714 of a thousand volumes collected in England. The backsliding of Cutler and Johnson, eventually four or five other ministers and large numbers from the student body at Yale, might be noted by today's Guardians of Prejudice as the first, and probably still the greatest, victory of Subversive Propaganda in America. Before long, nearly every town in Connecticut and Massachusetts had its Episcopal minister and his flock with their primary loyalty to an Alien Bishop, an Alien Archbishop and an Alien King.

But in spite of its spectacular rise, the Anglican apostasy had less relevance to the main current of religion in New England than did the rise of the other sects that won Toleration about the same time. It comprised a few consecrated men, like Cutler and Johnson and most of their first colleagues. It produced in the second generation at least two laymen of distinction, namely Lieutenant Governor Thomas Hutchinson of Massachusetts and William Samuel Johnson, son of Johnson the apostate. It contained a nucleus of honest Englishmen, immigrated during the last two or three generations, who never had any understanding of or interest in either New England or its Separatism. But of the Yankees who made the shift, the bulk were of the small snobs whose children found themselves in the pathetic pass of being Tories in the great conflict, little people who must borrow their strength from an institution of pomp and power that held them in contempt. As they were alien to the epic surge of Political and Social Individualism that was the central current of the Eighteenth Century, so they had no understanding of the revived Protestantism or Religious Individualism which was part of the same tide. Their concern was faintly if at all with religion, but was chiefly with their worldly status. As in their social life they must look up to the glitter of a hereditary aristocracy, so in their religious life they must look up to invested authority to relieve them of the fatigue of thinking, and they must rest in a sweet rhetoric and a kindly complacency. The New England Episcopalians were incapable of the passionate private Idealism of the Puritans, let alone their Equalitarianism. The Anglican apostasy, like the Tory backsliding which it portended, was not a development within New England culture but a sloughing from the culture of those not qualified to bear their part in it.

For even while the thousands were setting up their Episcopal

Parishes throughout New England, and other thousands of purer Yankees were moving out of the Legal Arminianism of the Conservatives into the Intellectual Arminianism of the Liberals, the definitive tens of thousands were stirring in their dormant Puritanism to break from their cocoons of Human Law and Reason into a Religion of Cosmic Scope and Free Imagination. During the first thirty years of the century we have seen them exercising in divers trials of Toleration and Liberalism, experimenting with strange sects that were outside the traditional pale, scurrying this way and that in small revivals and apostasies like last year's leaves whirled by the unsure wind of early spring. And, as in all great human movements, throughout these same uncertain thirty years Destiny—or Predestiny—was preparing for them the Leadership they must have to integrate their restlessness into Direction.

In 1703 Jonathan Edwards had been born in East Windsor, Connecticut, all brilliance on his mother's side, a possible spark of madness through his father the minister. In 1720 he graduated and in '22 got his M.A., from the Collegiate School recently settled in New Haven and rechristened Yale College. In 1727, the year before Cotton Mather died, this tall, fastidious, solemn, pale, long-faced youngster, with the blazing beauty of absolutely disciplined absolute idealism, went to Northampton as Assistant Minister under his failing grandfather Solomon Stoddard. He did not go alone, but was fortunate in the companionship of a new wife Sarah Pierpont who rates with Abigail Adams among the great wives of great Americans. His famous love letter to her, written when he was an undergraduate, defines the tenderness and spiritual plane of their lifelong relationship:

> They say there is a young lady in [New Haven] who is beloved of that Great Being, who made and rules the world, and that there are certain seasons in which this Great Being, in some way or other invisible, comes to her and fills her mind with exceeding sweet delight, and that she hardly cares for any thing, except to meditate on him—that she expects after a while to be received up where he is, to be raised up out of the world and caught up into heaven; being assured that he loves her too well to let her remain at a distance from him always. . . . She has a strange sweetness in her mind, and singular purity in her affections; is most just and conscientious in all her conduct; and you could not persuade her to do any thing wrong or sinful, if you would give her all the world, lest she should offend this Great Being. . . . She will sometimes go about from place to place, singing sweetly; and seems to be always full of joy and pleasure; and no one knows for what. She loves to be alone . . . in the fields and groves, and seems to have some one invisible always conversing with her.[22]

In spite of Northampton's fortified houses and the surviving port-holes in the crude square Meetinghouse, it was long past its frontier phase. With its population of about 1,000, its congregation of 600, and its record of revivals, it had become, under Pope Stoddard and his Stoddardeanism, the Ecclesiastical Capital of The River, rivalled only recently by New Haven with the Collegiate School. But in the late 1720's and early '30's prosperous Northampton was not support-ing its reputation. Young Edwards found much licentiousness among the young, and he first addressed himself to them, encouraging them to form discussion and singing groups. He offered them and the rest of the congregation the orthodox Puritan doctrine of Grace as an aesthetic and wholly God-given experience, as distinguished equally from the Half-Liberal–Half-Conservative Arminianism of his grand-father, the pure Legal Arminianism of the late Mathers, and the pure Intellectual Arminianism of Colman and the younger Liberals of Edwards's own generation who were rising in Boston. He revital-ized out of passionate, personal experience The Christian Truths which the ministers of all other schools were repeating as platitudes: the Boundless Omnipotence and Goodness of God, the Perversity and Absolute Helplessness of Man, the Loveliness of Grace, the Aw-fulness of Perdition. And he preached these things out of a simple and solemn sincerity, with a sensitive precision of diction, and in a wholly unadorned and little modulated style, which were inescapably magnetic to all ages and both sexes.

In 1729 Solomon Stoddard died, and Edwards succeeded him in full authority. Two years later, in a famous guest sermon in the First Church in Boston, he threw down the gauntlet to the Armin-ians, whether Conservative or Liberal, whether Legal or Intellectual, and put the best of them on notice that here was an opponent worth their watching. Here without compromise was that actual Puritan-ism which all of them professed, and none of them practiced, in their pulpits. Young Edwards went home leaving New England shaken as by a premonitory earthquake. A fault, a line of cleavage, had opened which none but the great and imperturbable Benjamin Colman would be able to straddle. The ministry of New England began to take sides for the War that would open ten years later.

Back in his own parish, the interest Edwards had aroused among the young spread for three years more among their elders. In '34 he began the scathing attacks on local hypocrisy which at once alienated the powerful—most of whom were his kin—and struck the first sparks of the Great Awakening. Edwards' own account of the early results, some of which was quoted earlier, can hardly be improved upon:

> . . . Upon this a great and earnest concern about the great
> things of religion and the eternal world became universal in all

parts of the town, and among persons of all degrees and all ages; the noise among the dry bones waxed louder and louder; all other talk about spiritual and eternal things was soon thrown by; all the conversation in all companies, and upon all occasions, was upon these things only. . . .[23]

It was like a rushing wind, a storm of God's will, rising through Northampton where early revivals had not had this quality. Beginning in December, 1734, the Parsonage on King Street was besieged by the citizens night and day, some to declare their Conversion, some to implore help as to how they might be saved. "I never saw the Christian Spirit in Love to Enemies so Exemplified." "The world was a thing only by the bye." On a single Sunday in the spring of '35 Edwards received a hundred into membership in the church. Altogether three hundred joined in this six months' "rehersal for the Great Awakening," and it seems that a greater proportion of these converts stayed converted than is common in revivals.

Although the nervous tension, especially of the unconverted, was great, there was very little of the extravagance that marked the later full scale revival when less careful ministers than Edwards were exhorting many more people. However, the curtain-raiser of '35 had its tragedy in at least one suicide in the late spring, that of Joseph Hawley the leading merchant of Northampton. With that the graph of enthusiasm turned down, and many began to question the validity of the emotional extremities they had suffered and enjoyed.

Meanwhile, visitors had come to investigate the bruited uproar and had scattered reports of the reality of it up and down The River. Especially in Connecticut the results were comparable to those in Northampton. Bolton, Coventry, Durham, Groton, Guilford, Hebron, Lebanon, New Haven, Preston, Ripton, Stratford, Tolland, Windsor, East Windsor—Edwards' birthplace—and Woodbury, all rose in local "rehersals."[24] The great "free and catholick" Colman wrote Edwards for a report on the phenomenon. In reply Edwards composed *A Faithful Narrative of the Surprizing Work of God*, which powerful piece of eloquence, being published in 1737, was a contributing cause of the tidal wave of 1740. In the fall of '35 and through '36, the first premonitory surge of religious enthusiasm receded. The Pundits, Conservative, Liberal and Puritan, debated its validity. And the inarticulate thousands waited.

Before discussing the full tide of the early 1740's, it is perhaps desirable to review the salient features of Edwards' Theology, though some repetition is involved.* Both in philosophic scope and in psychological profundity he exceeded his great seventeenth-cen-

---

* Some of Edwards' theology, especially his views on Predestination and Grace, was discussed in the section called Architecture.

tury predecessors, Cotton and Hooker, and his great nineteenth-century successors, Channing, Emerson and Melville. Accepting without a tremor the Materialism of Newton and the Sensational Psychology of Locke, he was America's first major modern mind, and his Creative Aesthetic still speaks to our condition. If we were to select America's contribution to the gallery of the world's indispensible thinkers, we must mention James, and we must mention Edwards, and after that we must hesitate and weigh. Standing on his lonely pinnacle, with the Antinomians screaming at him from one side and the Arminians sneering at him from the other, both biding the moment to crucify him, Edwards, more than any other of record, portrayed in his life and his expressions that delicate line of Truth, running between Emotion and Reason, which is Puritanism. As Professor Miller says, the simplest way to define Puritanism is to say it is what Edwards was.

The Debunkers of the Puritans, being intent only on belittling that Religion which they can not understand, discovered Edwards' significance in the so-called Enfield Sermon—"Sinners in the Hands of an Angry God"—in which he portrays God, "very angry" at every man's Sin or Self-concern, holding him by a spider-thread over a luridly portrayed eternal hell. The fact is that outside of being a fine example of Edwards' very modern critical theory of exact, sensuous imagery as the best means of conveying ideas, there is not much of Edwards in the Enfield Sermon. At the height of the Great Awakening—July, 1741—he had been invited by the local minister to come and try to stir up his uniquely dead congregation. Edwards had not much interest in either Post-Mortal Hell or Post-Mortal Heaven, for he lived outside of time and saw the Cosmos and Life as a finished mural of things as they are in four dimensions rather than as a succession of three-dimensional developments. His concern was to relieve people from the present Hell of Blindness or Self, and if it happened to be in the destinies of some or all of this congregation that he was to be the means of helping them to this escape, it was fitting that he do the best job possible. The subject of the sermon is not God's delight to drop helpless insects into fire and watch them glow, but God's Mercy in holding them from dropping into the fire of Self-indulgence by the thread of Grace or Imagination or Perception, by means of which they can, if they "will," climb to Understanding which is Salvation.

Likewise, a great deal has been made of Edwards' orthodox Calvinist Predestination, as implying a belief in and sympathy with this same cruel God who persecutes people without giving them any hope of escape. Edwards' Predestination is indeed a necessary part of him. It is essential to his concept of the Grandeur of the Universe, its Omnipotent Meaning or Control, and the tragedy of Man's Self-Concern, Blindness or Sin. In application his Determinism was a little more liberal than common modern psychology. In vocabulary he equated "Will" with "Desire," and he believed, as we do, that a combination of heredity and environment predetermines the successions of choices by which we build up our dominant Inclinations or Desires. But the individual, being helpless to refuse this bequest of the past to his Desires, his "Will," is not at all helpless when it comes to expressing them. He has a power of choice to "do what he wills," *or not to do it.* If he is predestined dominantly to Will or Desire that Perception, that Understanding, which is Grace and Election, and which the Atonement has made available to him, he may yet refuse it. Edwards does not, so far as I know, say expressly that if a man is predestined—what we would call Conditioned—chiefly to Will or Desire the Hell—what we could call the Neurosis—of Blindness or Self-concern, he may likewise reject or accept it. Nor does he, so far as I know, deny that all men may be born with the capacity, by a succession of choices, to build themselves into a dominant Desire or Will to perceive Truth and so to attain Salvation. Edwards does not express himself in these refinements of theory, for even to consider them would be to diminish the larger concept of the Self. To be concerned at all with the future comfort or discomfort of that self would be to reject the saving Desire for the Objective Perception of the Meaning or Excellency of the Cosmos. For all Edwards knew to the contrary, this Desire for Perception might be potential in all men. All he affirmed was that if a man truly desires to obtain Grace—that is to be "Saved"—he has the power to do so.

Edwards' Science and his Philosophy are not in themselves our concern, but they are pertinent in two respects. First, and less important, they show Edwards as exceptional among Puritans in that he did go all the analytical way and address Reality in secular terms, instead of resting in the acknowledgement that Truth is in the hands of an inscrutable God, and that for the human mind to inquire too far into His Nature is to skirt uncomfortably close to the sinful or self-centered notion of a Man-Centered Cosmos. Edwards not only entered into the arena of the philosophers, he went all the way with the most modern and materialistic of them.

Secondly, Edwards' philosophy itself is of interest to us both as America's first modern expression and as the abstract continuum of his theology. He accepted Newton's Materialism, his Universe composed of atoms of Matter, and went farther than Newton did in facing its implications. Newton, after the publication of the *Principia* in 1687, seems to have fled to a hobby in order to escape from the inference that there was no God but soulless and inexorable Law.

Edwards—though there is no evidence that he preached such star-tling doctrine to his Congregation—faced it with his usual candor in his private Notes. To him God was the Meaning of things as they are and however constituted, and the problem of religion, as of phi-losophy, was simply to perceive that Meaning, pleasant or unpleasant.

To Edwards the building stones of the Universe were Newton's objective atoms. But they were by themselves not yet living building stones. They qualified for reality by way of Locke's sensational psychology: the mind at birth is a blank sheet of paper, and all knowledge is received through the senses. From this point Edwards, having paid full respect to the Materialists, leaves them in favor of Idealism. The Images which the senses bring in have no Meaning, no Reality, no Life, until the Mind, Perceiving them, translates them into Ideas. This gesture of the Aesthetic or Creative Imagina-tion is precisely the Experience of Grace. It is also the prerogative of God by means of which he "creates" or gives significance to the Cosmos and which He projects into Man when He makes him in His "Image." This interpretation of the Meaning of Reality as aesthetic Perception—usually portrayed as Light—is the center of Puritanism. "Unless this is seen," said Edwards,

> nothing is seen that is worth the seeing; for there is no other true excellency or beauty. . . . This is the beauty of the Godhead, and the divinity of divinity. . . , the good of the infinite foun-tain of good; without which, God himself (if that were possible) would be an infinite evil; without which we ourselves had better never have been; without which there had better have been no being.[25]

More than any other Puritan, Edwards relates to this central qual-ity of Perception the various doctrines which we saw as the chief members of the Puritan House. *Original Sin,* the divorce from God, was simply the "stupidity of mind," the "sottish insensibility," that through attending to "immediate pleasures and pains," let the fire of Imagination burn out and so lost the Perception of Being with its accompanying joy which "sweetly entertains and strongly holds the mind." The continuity of Original Sin throughout the race fol-lowed from Edwards' percept of humanity as all one body, with its numerous members, perceivable either as extended in time or as now and timeless. From his own observation and from the historical record, Edwards the scientist concluded that this body as a whole was motivated largely by self-interest that blinded it to the offerings of the imagination. In the *Atonement* God submitted to this human blindness and escaped from it, that those who could identify them-selves with the sacrifice by perceiving it might thereby likewise es-cape from it. God's Love that was central to the Atonement, like the love that motivates every act of human *self-loss* that takes advantage of the Atonement, was simply the perception of the beloved, the object of sacrifice. With Edwards, to love is to perceive, in divine as in human things. Love is the "disinterested" objectivity which is essential at once to the lover, the neighbor, the devotee and the artist. *Grace* is the gift to individuals of this Love, this Objectivity, this Perceptiveness. The meaning of the Intellectual Tradition is that Grace is a mental experience, and Education sharpens the mind to recognize it when it offers. At the same time all men are absolutely *Equal* in Depravity, in being objects of God's compassion, and in the capacity to attain Perception if they Will.

Of a piece with his philosophy and theology, Edwards' literary theory was based in the need to convey Beauty or "Excellency" to the perceptions of his readers. He adhered to the *Plain Style* of the Puritans in eschewing rhetorical ornament in his speaking and writing, and he elaborated in a modern direction the traditional use of homely and exact figures of speech. Applying the doctrine that all knowledge enters the mind as images through the channels of the senses and thereafter takes the form of ideas, he conceived the function of words to be the projection into the listener's mind of the clearest possible images. Thus his sermons glowed with a Keatsian richness which was the more effective for the imposing simplicity of his delivery. Leaning on one elbow on the pulpit, his long chin in his hand, his burning eyes fixed on one point—in his own church, "the bellrope" in the vestibule—he dispensed without gesture or modulation words with an awful precision which straightway had his listeners exulting in an actual Heaven or writhing in an actual Hell. His biographer Ola Winslow quotes Timothy Dwight's account of the effect on Nehemiah Strong, one of Edwards' Northampton parishioners, of his portrayal of the Last Judgement in a sermon on *The History of Redemption*. Mr. Strong says that he expected

> without one thought to the contrary, the awful scene to be unfolded on that day, and in that place. . . . Accordingly, he waited with the deepest and most solemn solicitude to hear the trumpet sound and the archangel call; to see the graves open, the dead arise, and the Judge descend in the glory of his Father, with all his holy angels; and was deeply disappointed, when the day terminated, and left the world in the usual state of tranquility.[26]

Like most of Edwards' listeners and readers, good Mr. Strong received his vivid images but failed to translate them into the Ideas of which Edwards intended them to be merely the instigation. Edwards' tragedy, like that of most great Americans, was that he sought from the common man an expression of Imaginative Energy which the common man was too indolent, too "sottish," to release.

Edwards, like the other Puritans, was chary of affirming directly what I called the Holy Ratio, the fine line between the opposing Errors or Heresies of Emotion and Reason, possibly because the implicit standard of Moderation would smack too much of a classical Humanism. Yet in fact the chief work of the controversial part of Edwards' life was the maintenance of that Central Line against extremists of the Right and of the Left.* Because some of the extraordinary manifestations of the Great Awakening were new and "surprizing" to Edwards, and perhaps also because their highly emotional quality was alien and offensive to his own fastidiousness, he did give them more respect and toleration than the doctrine of the Holy Mean justified. Also, without referring to the religious debauchery committed by some of his successors, it must be observed that Edwards himself, if not personally then at least in the effects of his preaching, was farther on the emotional side than his great seventeenth century predecessors. Wherefore, we may distinguish between the *First Puritanism* of the seventeenth century with its slight Arminian leaning under Hooker's doctrine of Works as voluntary Preparation for Grace, and the *Second Puritanism* of the eighteenth century with its slight Antinomian leaning under Edwards' pure Calvinism of Total Depravity and Predestination and the emotional effects of his preaching. Correspondingly, the Decline of First Puritanism, as we have seen, was into Legal Arminianism, and the Decline of Second Puritanism, as we shall see, was into Antinomianism. After 1740 both Heresies walked openly, hateful alike to each other and to the Central Current of Puritanism which ran and continues to run between them.

Finally, Edwards restored the immeasurable grandeur of the Puritan universe, after the diminution it had suffered in the fussy, local minds of such as Samuel Sewall, Cotton Mather and the founders of Yale and the Saybrook Platform. Accepting Materialism and Sensationalism in his stride, he reproclaimed in his Idealism a Cosmos that was more than three-dimensional and was consequently the realm of a God incomprehensible to Natural Reason. From the time of his conversion when he was seventeen, while reading the seventeenth verse of the first chapter of First Timothy—"Now unto the King eternal, immortal, invisible, the only wise God, be honour and glory for ever and ever. Amen"—from the time of that early re-

---

* The *Religious Affections* is probably Edwards' clearest statement of the true line between Arminianism and Antinomianism. He complains of the error both of Heat without Light and of Light without Heat, but I find no direct statement of what he everywhere infers, that true religious experience contains something of both, drawing at once upon the "Affections" and the discipline of the Mind.

sponse to large and inclusive concepts, the notion of the greatness, the size, the Grandeur of the God who was the Ruler or the Fact of Being was dynamic in the leap of his perception. He desired only to be "rapt up to God" in Heaven, and be as it were swallowed up in him forever. He knew the familar sensations of the mystic:

> . . . a calm, sweet abstraction of soul from all the concerns of the world; and sometimes a kind of vision, or fixed ideas and imaginations, of being alone in the mountains, or some solitary wilderness, far from all mankind, sweetly conversing with Christ, and wrapt and swallowed up in God.[27]

After the premonitory storm that Edwards sent down the Connecticut River from Northampton in 1735, New England lapsed into a laden hush before the hurricane. The new clouds began gathering on September 14, 1740, when twenty-six year-old George Whitefield, semi-educated oratorical genius, debarked at Newport, fresh from the Wesleys' new school of evangelical exhortation, and still fresher from well publicized triumphs in the Middle Colonies. The storm rustled as he brought big audiences to their knees in Newport, and so moved toward Boston levelling the little towns as he passed. It broke and whirled cyclonic in Boston where he spent four weeks thundering from the pulpits of the churches, from perches on the Common, and in the assemblies at Harvard. New England had never seen anything like this man, unprepossessing in his appearance with his crossed eyes, unrestrained, short on doctrine, long on weeping and shouting, and possessed of unique magnetism of voice. One of his enemies said that he could bring an audience to its knees by merely pronouncing the word "Mesopotamia." Most of the Boston ministers, both Conservative and Liberal, rallied against him, especially after he began to tell the people that their pastors were not themselves saved. The great Jonathan Mayhew, just now emerging into prominence, said Whitefield's histrionics were "low, confused, puerile, conceited, ill-natured, enthusiastic"—all deadly adjectives in the armory of the eighteenth century. The few leading ministers who were for him were those who were also for Edwards against the Arminians—William Cooper, Joseph Sewall, son of the late Judge Sewall, and Thomas Prince—with the reigning Benjamin Colman tolerant to favorable. But it made small difference what leaders were for or against Whitefield. This was a movement of the people, a release of that hunger for religion that had been growing for forty years, an uplift of the dry leaves that had been lying restless over New England during the autumn of Puritanism's year. Five years before, Edwards had stirred them in their corners. Now they rose to Whitefield from every forest and field.

Having saved everyone in Boston who could be saved, the evangelist moved through Concord, Sudbury, Marlborough and Leicester, and everywhere the people "sweetly melted" before him. On Friday, October 17, he reached Northampton and spent the week-end with the Edwardses, preaching four times in the local pulpit. Although Whitefield wrote in his diary that "dear Mr. Edwards wept" under his oratory, the two men had nothing in common beyond the deep bond of recognition of each other's godliness. Edwards politely complained of his guest for succumbing to emotion in his sermons, and of speaking openly of "unconverted ministers." Poor, cross-eyed Whitefield seems himself to have been "sweetly melted" by Sarah Pierpont Edwards, for he wrote in his diary that she caused him "to renew those Prayers . . . to God, that he would send me a Daughter of Abraham to be my wife."

From Northampton the cyclone of the Awakening, with Whitefield at its center, moved down the Connecticut Valley. Edwards rode with his guest to his home town of East Windsor and saw the evangelist mow down his father's congregation. And so to Suffield. And on down to Wethersfield, where he met the Reverends Seth Pomeroy and Eleazer Wheelock who joined up with the revival. Thence to Middletown, where his visit left what is perhaps the best report of the Great Awakening, its essentially popular aspect, its sense of breathless urgency as of a pentecostal wind gathering up everyone in its path. The account is in the diary of Nathan Cole,[28] semi-literate farmer and carpenter of Kensington, Middletown township, whose life was in due course happily integrated as a result of this experience. Cole was probably typical of the great bulk of New Englanders who were "stricken" or "wounded." He was possessed by a power outside himself that he eventually recognized as Grace. Yet neither here nor in the rest of his consecrated life did he approach idiocy in either expression or behavior. ,

Cole, who theretofore had been a Legal Arminian, had heard of Whitefield's ". . . preaching at Philadelphia like one of the old apostles, & many thousands of people flocking after him to hear the gospel & great numbers were converted to Christ i felt the spirit of god drawing me by conviction i longed to see and hear him & wished he would come this way."

He had heard of his coming to the Jerseys and New York and of the great multitudes flocking after him. He had heard of his coming to Boston—then to Northampton and—

> Then one morning all on a suding about 8 or 9 o'clock thare came a messinger & said mr. whitfield preached at hartford and

weathersfield yesterday & is to preach at middletown this morning at 10 o'clock i was in my feld at work i dropt my tool that i
had in my hand & run home & run thru my house & bad my
wife get ready quick to goo and hear mr. whitfield preach at
middletown & run to my pasture for my hors with all my might
fearing that i should be too late to hear him i brought my hors
home & soon mounted & took my wife up & went forward as fast
as i thought the hors could bear it & when my hors began to be
out of breath i would get down & put my wife on the saddel and
bid her ride as fast as she could & not stop or slack for me except
i bad her & so i would run untill i was allmost out of breath and
then mount my hors again and so i did several times to favour
my hors we improved every moment to get along as if we was
fleeing for our lives all the while fearing we should be too late
to hear the sarmon for we had twelve miles to ride dubble in
littel more than an hour. . . . & when we came within about
half a mile or a mile of the road that comes down from hartford
. . . on high land i saw before me a cloud or fog rising i first
thought off from the great river but as i came nearer the road i
heard a noise something like a low rumbling thunder i presently
found it was the rumbling of horses feet . . . & this cloud was
a cloud of dust made by the runing of horses feet . . . & when
i came within about twenty rods of the road i could see men
& horses sliping along in the cloud like shadows & when i came
near it was like a stedy streem of horses & their riders scarcely a
horse more than his length behind an other all of a lather &
fome with sweat ther breath rooling out of their noistrels in
the cloud of dust every jump every hors seemed to go with all
his might to carry his rider to hear the news from heaven for the
saveing of their souls it made me trembel to see the sight how
the world was in a strugle i found a vaconce between two horses
to slip in my hors & my wife said law our cloases will all be
spilt . . . they was so covered with Dust that thay looked allmost all of a coler. . . . i heard no man speak a word all the
way three mils out every one presing forward in great heast &
when we gat down to the old meating house thare was a great
multitude of people asembled . . . i turned & looked to wards
the great river & saw the fery boats runing swift forward &
backward bringing over loads of people the ors roed nimble &
quick every thing men horses & boats all seamed to be Struglin
for life all along the twelve mils i see no man at work in his
field but all seamed to be gone—when i see mr whitfield come
up upon the Scaffil he looked almost angellical a yong slim
slender youth before some thousands of people & with a bold
undainted Countinance & my hearing how god was with him
every where as he came along it solomnized my mind & put me
into a trembleing fear before he began to preach for he looked
as if he was clothed with athority from god & a sweet sollome

. . . solemnity sat upon his brow and my hearing him preach gave me a heart wound; By Gods blessing: . . . my old Foundation was broken up and i saw that my righteousness would not save me. . . .

Although here "wounded" and turned from Arminianism, Cole went through two years of torture before he was sure of Grace. He then became part of the Separatist Movement, and in that connection we shall see him again.

In Cole's report we may find "mob psychology" covering a radius of twelve, if not hundreds of miles, or we may find, as at Pentecost, "the sound . . . as of a rushing mighty wind." We may describe the Great Awakening in physical or metaphysical terms according to our prejudices. But what we cannot deny is that it was a definitive event in the lives of many thousands, an event on a psychological plane other than that of their usual experience, a plane which all of them, ignorant and educated alike, recognized as in the region of eternal, absolute and happy values. To deny that is to value private and unconfirmable opinion above a large body of precise and positive evidence. The number of people who were permanently converted in the Great Awakening can only be guessed. But that there were enough permanently to change the complexion of New England can not be questioned. After the passage of Whitefield in the fall of 1740 the general trend of the movement was downward into an emotional "shambles." But even in that shambles many souls found God and clung to Him and held on against persecution by Arminians and Antinomians alike.

From Middletown, Whitefield progressed to New Haven where he gathered a harvest among the students, troubled the college authorities, and so moved out of New England into the Middle States where a concurrent Awakening was raging. In Philadelphia the deist Ben Franklin—always watchful for any kind of anchor to windward—became his admirer and lifelong friend. As if in exchange for Whitefield, Gilbert Tennent, the leader of the revival in Pennsylvania and New Jersey who had been in correspondence with Edwards, moved up into New England and seems to have done even greater execution than his predecessor. Where Whitefield had intoned and wept, Tennent roared and stamped, and instead of emphasizing love and peace he preached hell and damnation. In dress and manner he was more of a boor than Whitefield, and he increased the harvest of the Awakening in the pews. But, through his habit of stigmatizing the established ministers with such titles as "hirelings," "caterpillars," "hypocrites," "varlets," "dead dogs" and "enemies of God," he consolidated against the movement the opposition of all schools of Arminians, both the basically tolerant Liberals and the basically intolerant Old Calvinists.

The storms of Whitefield and Tennent having filled the air of New England with despair and hope and joy, they moved out of the region and left the Puritans to the Puritans. There ensued, through the winter, spring and early summer of 1741, the full and ubiquitous hurricane of the Awakening, with no such star performers, no such cyclonic centers, as the foreign invaders had been. In place of them, the local leaders were the theologians Edwards and his friend Joseph Bellamy of Bethlehem, Connecticut, founder of America's first divinity school and, like Edwards, honored more in Britain than in America. And high in the second rank of revivalists were Wheelock and Pomeroy of Connecticut and Sewall and Cooper of Boston. Worthy of Edwards and Bellamy's metal, the opposition now moved into action, chiefly the great Liberals of Boston, Charles Chauncey who had Cotton's old place as teacher of the First Church, and Jonathan Mayhew, virtual Unitarian and forthcoming Revolutionary leader. With them were aligned against Edwards the Conservatives, notably Johnny Barnard of Marblehead, and in Connecticut Elisha Williams, Edwards' cousin and former Rector of Yale, together with Samuel Whittlesy and other dignitaries of the College.

With other revivalists, Edwards itinerated up and down The River, and in July as a guest preacher at Enfield delivered himself into the hands of the Puritan-burners forever. In his most famous sermon he applied his sensuous literary theory so successfully as to rival Dante in the portrayal of Hell. There we see Edwards standing tall, cool, motionless, outwardly dispassionate, his long chin in his hand, his eyes straight before him or dropping to his microscopic notes on tiny pieces of paper, saying carefully selected words that penetrated to the deepest emotions of the people. The delivery lacked all of the acrobatics of Whitefield and Tennent, and the "exercises" it drew from the people were milder than those that more extravagant evangelists had elicited and presently would elicit again. But the results were probably the more permanent for this moderation. The account is from the diary of the Reverend Stephen Williams of Longmeadow, who as a boy had been carried prisoner to Quebec from the Deerfield Massacre of 1704:

> We went over to Enfl—where we met dear Mr E- of N-H- who preachd a most awakening sermon from these words—Deut. 32-35 and before the sermon was done—there was a great moaning & crying out through the whole house—What Shall I do to

be savd—oh I am going to Hell—Oh what shall I do for Christ
&c &c. So that the minister was obliged to desist—the shrieks and
crys were piercing & Amazing—after Some time of waiting the
Congregation were Still so that a prayer was made by Mr. W
& after that we descend from the pulpitt and discoursd with the
people—Some in one place and Some in another—and Amazing
and Astonishing the power God was seen—& Several Souls were
hopefully wrought upon that night. & oh the cheerfulness and
pleasantness of their countenances that received comfort. . . .[29]

If the Great Awakening had been left after 1740 in the hands of
Edwards, Bellamy, even Pomeroy and Wheelock, there would have
been a better chance that Puritanism would have survived against
the powerful forces of Reason and Materialism that eventually captured the century. But in 1742 the defeat of the Awakening was assured when James Davenport of Long Island, descendant of John
Davenport of New Haven, and after him other similarly extravagant
ignoramuses, most of them unlicensed, began itinerating through
New England, making of Religion a travesty as extreme on the Emotional side as the Arminians had made and were making of it on the
Rational side. As Tennent's method had been more ecstatic and less
sane than Whitefield's, so Davenport's yawping and snorting and
his charges against the ministry, were wilder than Tennent's. In
Boston he escaped a jail sentence for breach of the peace only by
being found *non compos mentis* by the grand jury and sent out of
the jurisdiction. He strengthened Chauncey and alienated the previously friendly and now ancient Colman by marching into their
studies and demanding whether they were saved. He encouraged
ignorant and excitable young yokels to become itinerant exhorters,
and they responded by scores. A kind of Seminary, known as the
Shepherd's Tent, was set up in New London for the training of
these naive voices in Wesleyan, and especially Davenportian,
methods of exhortation. They invaded established ministers' pulpits
without invitation and without preaching licenses and told the
people their educated pastors were reprobate.

New England rumbled with controversy. Especially in Connecticut, where the Awakening had been strong from the beginning, Congregations were acrimoniously divided between the Emotionalists,
known as New Lights, and the Conservatives and Liberals, known
as Old Lights. Often the New Lights withdrew and, under the protection of the Toleration Act of 1708 and the toleration proviso of
the Saybrook Platform, set up what were known as Separatist
Churches. Most of the Second Churches of Christ in most of the

towns date from this War. Especially vicious were the schisms in New Haven, Canterbury, Enfield, and Windham County, Connecticut.[30] During '40 and '41 the conversions, though often overemotional, had pretended to no motivation other than religious. Now churches and towns, or the more excitable members of them, competed as to which could put on the most extravagant shows by none but melodramatic standards. The attacks of the Arminians that had been exaggerated against Edwards, Bellamy and the literate revivalists, were now justified against many of the itinerant preachers and the orgies, sometimes sexual, of their converts. The Great Awakening degenerated, in Professor Miller's phrase, into an Antinomian "shambles." Not even Mrs. Hutchinson in her loftiest ecstasies would have condoned the idiotic anarchy the Itinerants released.

The Conservatives or Old Calvinists of Connecticut, where they had all the time controlled the Government, were not content to let the New Lights burn out in their own folly, but proceeded to disgrace themselves by the injustice of their reaction. In 1742 they passed a series of laws forbidding anyone to preach anywhere in a parish without the invitation of the minister and his congregation, abolishing the Shepherd's Tent in New London, and finally putting most of the itinerants out of action by requiring degrees from Yale, Harvard or other approved Protestant colleges for incumbents of established pulpits.[31] Thus they quashed the ignorant exhorters. But the policy of persecution also drove out of the Colony the enlightened among the New Light ministers, notably Dr. Samuel Finley who later became president of Princeton. In 1742, also, the General Court excepted the Separating Congregational or Presbyterian churches from the protection of the Saybrook proviso. When the dissenters looked for the right to form their own churches under the general provisions of the Toleration Act, they found themselves excepted from that also. Finally, when Separating Groups began in some numbers to adopt the shift of forming Baptist churches, which differed from the Congregationalist only in the point of baptism, the General Court went all the way into reaction and repealed the Toleration Act entirely.[32]

Thus, while Episcopalians, Quakers, and original Baptists were in practice unmolested, the Separatists whose sane majority were in the direct Puritan tradition, were forbidden religious observance. The Reverend Isaac Backus of Norwich and vicinity, Yale graduate and subsequently member of the Continental Congress, much beloved, and much in demand among the Separatists, was first forced into the Baptist church, and then in effect debarred from preaching. Yale College was as always in the forefront of reaction. It refused a degree to David Brainard, presently one of America's greatest missionaries to the Indians, because he said one of the tutors had "no more piety than a chair," and in 1743 it expelled two boys for attending a Separatist meeting while at home with their parents. Not only were the New Lights and the Separatists denied what had become normal freedom of worship, they were also discriminated against in the government. The General Court refused to seat Deputies or to confirm Sheriffs and other local officers who were of their persuasion.

For eight years Connecticut lived in a state of majority tyranny such as made the Endicott-Wilson tyranny in Massachusetts ninety years before seem trivial. But as oppression grew its extremism was correcting itself, and the forces of moderation were gathering in the quiet and unlegislated order of things. The New Lights matured out of the more extravagant practices of Revivalism, and rested upon their Edwardsian or Puritan foundation of God's omnipotence, man's helplessness, and Grace as a disciplined emotional experience. In several foolish measures the Old Lights overreached themselves and lost their majority in the Government. In a new edition of the laws, issued in 1750, none of the persecuting measures were inscribed. In 1758 the New Lights captured the General Court, and controlled it thereafter. Connecticut's one spree in persecution was over.

And in the meantime, through those same 1740's, Jonathan Edwards, in America's greatest theological debate, was trying to hold the line of the Holy Ratio on the ministerial and intellectual level. On the one side were the Antinomian supporters of Whitefield and Tennent, of whom Sewall and Cooper at The Bay and Pomeroy and Wheelock at The River were the strongest native ministers, and with whom Edwards was entirely identified by his enemies. On the other side was the Coalition of the Old Calvinists or Legal Arminians, notably the Yale authorities, and the Liberals or Intellectual Arminians, who included the Harvard authorities and provided the effective leadership against Edwards in the persons of Charles Chauncey of the Boston First Church, and Jonathan Mayhew of the West Church. It was at this time that Liberalism, emerging from the meaninglessly broad tolerance of Colman, entered upon the aggressive course which has continued triumphantly to date. Edwards was under the eternal handicap of the Moderate, that of having to fight on two fronts. With one hand, he fenced with the Arminians, and with the other he bludgeoned his own over-exuberant, Antinomian followers.

In the summer of 1741 Chauncey and Edwards took their stations
for their duel in two famous sermons, Chauncey's in June under the
title *The New Creature,* in which he attacked Whitefield, extolled
sound Reason and human freedom, Edwards' in July in *Sinners in
the Hands of an Angry God* in which he stated the helplessness of
man and his devices. The following September, at the Yale Commencement, Edwards made the first major thrust in a sermon whose
printed form, entitled *The Distinguishing Marks of a Work of the
Spirit of God,* went through many editions in America and Great
Britain. Here he revealed his moderate position by listing a number
of extravagant manifestations, common in revival meetings, as being
more likely of natural than of divine origin. He had observed in his
own Northampton a tendency toward the extreme emotionalism
that was presently to characterize the itinerants, and the work as a
whole was aimed more against the Antinomians than against the
Arminians. It was the following spring that James Davenport began
seriously to debase the Awakening, alienating Colman and supplying Chauncey with ammunition for a series of powerful pamphlets
in which he portrayed justly the bathos to which the revival had
sunk.

In the autumn of '42 Edwards published a reworked version of
The Distinguishing Marks, under the new title *Some Thoughts
Concerning the Present Revival of Religion in New England.* But
intelligent public opinion was now identifying the Awakening,
including Edwards, with the Itinerants, and was turning against the
whole movement. Connecticut swung into its official reaction which
we have seen. In the spring of 1743 Chauncey felt strong enough
to attack Edwards directly in *The Late Religious Commotions in
New England Considered.* In May the convention of Massachusetts
ministers condemned the Revival in Johnny Barnard's *Manifesto,*
and in July Chauncey published his carefully documented and
crushing *Seasonable Thoughts on the State of Religion.* Actually,
Chauncey's psychology was medieval, whereas Edwards in his
Thoughts of the previous year had embodied a psychology advanced
beyond the age. But Chauncey spoke with the clarity and assurance
of the rising Enlightenment, whereas Edwards' Calvinistic Theology,
and especially the emotional caricature of it presented by the Itinerants, was now outmoded.

Edwards and Puritanism were beaten by the *Seasonable Thoughts.*
When Whitefield attempted a second tour in '44 he was excluded
from most pulpits, and in the same year young Jonathan Mayhew
emerged from Harvard fulminating against "these enlightened
Ideots" who "make inspiration, and the spirit of truth and wisdom,
the vehicle of nonsense and contradiction." In '46 Edwards issued

A Treatise Concerning Religious Affections, certainly the most profound document of the Great Debate and probably the finest analysis
of religious psychology in American literature. It was the work in
which he set out his aesthetic interpretation of Grace which we have
noticed. Yet it fell unnoticed at the time, and neither Chauncey nor
Mayhew found it worth direct reply. In '47 Mayhew was ordained in
the West Church, the only one of the Liberals to admit himself an
Arminian and to defy Puritanism all along the line. Though Chauncey and the rest agreed with Mayhew, his unorthodoxy was so frank
that he had difficulty finding a minister honest enough to preach his
ordination sermon. High among his heresies was his denial of the
Trinity, which caused him to be excluded from the ministerial Association of Boston and placed him prominently in the special current
of Liberalism which became Unitarianism.

And while Edwards was losing the war on the intellectual stage,
he was drawing down on himself his personal tragedy in Northampton through his attacks on his rich kinsmen, chiefly the Williamses,
among the "River Gods" of Hamden and Berkshire Counties, and
through a series of uncompromising indiscretions toward his Congregation. In '42 and '43 he asked for salary increases, though he was
already the highest paid minister in New England outside of Boston,
and his wife Sarah was reputed the best dresser in Northampton.
In '44 there occurred the absurd scandal of the "bad book" which
was a "granny book" or set of instructions to midwives. The children
of some of Edwards' influential parishioners were caught enjoying
the book with normal infantile prurience, and Edwards insisted on
disgracing them publicly. About this time, also, consistently with his
doctrine of free and emotional Grace, he began to revive the long
abandoned requirement of a public narration of an Experience of
Grace as a condition of admission to the church. It is perhaps significant that between '44 and '48 none applied for membership in his
flock. When in '48 one did, and another in '49, Edwards in each case
required the ancient narration, and in each case the applicant, incited by the antagonistic majority in the congregation, refused to
give it. This majority, which was now for his dismissal on any pretext, suspended Communion altogether. Edwards, with his usual cool
and infuriating candor, published his powerful *Humble Inquiry Into
the Rules of the Word of God Concerning the Qualification Requisite to a Compleat Standing and Full Communion,* and said that he
would submit to dismissal, without calling a church council, upon
the vote of those of the congregation who had read the book.

But almost no one bothered to read Edwards' peace offering. In
June, 1750, a Council packed with his enemies recommended a sever-
ance of his relationship to the church. This was official dismissal. A

month later he preached his confession of failure, his withering
Farewell Sermon. At the last judgment,

> . . . it will appear, whether my people have done their duty to
> their pastor, with respect to this matter. . . . Then every step
> of the conduct of each of us, . . . and the spirit we have exer-
> cised in all, shall be examined . . . and our own consciences
> shall speak plain and loud, and each of us shall be convinced
> . . . ; and never shall there be any more mistake, misrepresenta-
> tion or misapprehension of the affair, to eternity.[33]

Here, as always in extremity, was his aesthetic criterion, his standards of reality as perception.

And at the same time that Edwards was speaking quiet truth to
galvanized pews in Northampton, Mayhew in Boston was preaching
what intellectual New England now wanted to hear. To try to bring
a people to emotional conversion, he said, was like "a blow with a
club" which "may fracture a man's skull; but I suppose he will not
think or reason more clearly for that; though he may possibly believe more *orthodoxly* according to the opinion of some, . . . for their
doctrines are generally such as are more readily embraced by a man
after his brains are knocked out. . . ."[34] And with the ascendancy of
this vulgarity, together with the banishment of Edwards, we might
date at 1750 the technical end of the Great Awakening and the end
of Edwardsean or Second Puritanism, as a century before we might
have identified the end of First Puritanism with the deaths, all close
to 1650, of Winthrop, Hooker and Cotton. But after 1750, as after
1650, religion had still a decade to go as the dominant force among
most of the people, before the whole culture stampeded into Reason
and Arminianism.

Edwards spent the rest of his life as the almost wholly unqualified
missionary to the Housatonic Indians in Stockbridge, and his biographer has left us the hilarious picture of him, standing tall and
solemn in the pulpit before them, cautioning them out of one of the
world's great minds that it is not good to get drunk.[35] But there in
banishment, in the quiet of defeat by his own time, he made in compensation most of his timeless contributions, the works in theology
which will survive the combined contributions of his destroyers. As
often happens to distinguished Americans, his British public was
faithful to him after his own people rejected him, and even in America outside of New England he continued a great light in the Calvinist world. In 1757 he was invited to succeed his son-in-law Aaron Burr
as president of the College of New Jersey (Princeton), and, reporting
for duty there in the winter of '58, he died of smallpox inoculation in
the spring. His daughter Esther, the mother of Aaron Burr, Jr., died
two weeks later, and his wife Sarah followed in October. Samuel

Hopkins of Newport, after Bellamy the greatest of Edwards' students and followers, said, "Surely America is greatly emptied by these deaths." So ended Second Puritanism in 1758, the year approximating the centennial of the ministerial adoption of the Halfway Covenant (1657) which had been the end of First Puritanism.

With the death of Edwards and, two years later, the final defeat of the French at Quebec, the dominantly religious part of the eighteenth century closes. The Great Awakening, which may be identified either exclusively with the peak years 1740-1742 or more largely with the whole surge and recession from the beginning of the century till 1760, had brought in converts estimated as low as 20,000 and as high as 50,000, including those who joined the Baptists, the Episcopalians and the Quakers as well as either the Separatist or the Old Calvinist Congregationalists. If we also consider the incalculable number who, being already church members, were yet quickened into new religious awareness, it became plain that an appreciable part of New England's current population of 300,000 was involved. For the great majority, the effects were probably transitory, though there must have been many, like Nathan Cole the farmer of Middletown, who entertained the experience with moderation and whose lives were permanently steadied by it.

Outside of religion, there were perhaps two important and related effects of the Awakening. For one, the people for the first time debated and decided great theological questions whose solution they had previously tended to accept from the learned. For another, the doctrine of Religious Individualism, that is emotional Grace to be recognized primarily by the person involved, fed directly, as religion declined, into the swelling current of Political Individualism.* The farmer who before 1760 had found himself important before the Idea of God tended thereafter to find himself and his rights important before the Idea of Man, and his primary concern became the assertion of those rights, first against the local gentry, and afterwards against the

---

* ". . . The language of the meetinghouse had been translated into the vernacular, somewhat too suddenly. Man's notion of his own individual dignity and importance had been greatly increased, also too suddenly. Whitefield . . . by his deference to men and women as individual human beings . . . had added a timely potency to his words of entreaty; he had also planted seeds that would bear fruit in later independence of action which had nothing to do with life in the meetinghouse. That religion was to emerge from this, its . . . hour of triumph . . ., to take henceforth a secondary place, was therefore of all results of the Great Awakening the most ironic. Prior to 1740, there was already a cleavage between religion and the broader stream of American thought. The Great Awakening made the rift wider." (Winslow, *Edwards*, 212-13.) Religious excesses led to "patriotic excesses" . . . (*Ibid.*, 197).

British tyrants. Before 1760, the Sky of Religion, reflected in the River of New England history, though narrowed between the opposite egoisms of Antinomian emotion and Arminian rationality, had yet been a large Sky with a large God. After 1760, even more than in the First Decline after 1660, the light of Faith failed. Intellectual Arminianism preëmpted most of the Central Stream and reflected its own special Sky that was an Abstraction called Man. It was a lower Sky than that of the Cosmos of the First and Second Puritanism. And it had a special rational shine, a peculiarly bright and shadowless shine.

2. SECOND DECLINE (1760-1800)

Like the year 1660, the year 1760 marked major turns in several trends. It marked the end of the Great Awakening and the beginning of the Second Decline of Religion in New England. It marked the final defeat of the French at Quebec and the turn of worldly attention from foreign war to domestic questions, from the offenses of the alien French to those of the increasingly alien British. And it marked the beginning of the expansion that was to create Greater New England. Ever since King Philip's War the culture had inbred within the cordon of the French and their Algonquins on the north, and the Iroquois and their watchful friendliness on the west. After 1760 the northern barrier withdrew almost to the St. Lawrence, and New England, especially western Massachusetts and badly compressed Connecticut, exploded northward to settle in fifteen years a hundred towns in New Hampshire and seventy-four in Vermont, the immediate motive of migration in many, and probably most, cases being still religious schism, the aftermath of the yet smouldering New Light-Old Light controversy. After the Revolution, when the Iroquois had made the bad guess of siding with the British and so had suffered immolation, Connecticut, western Massachusetts and Vermont—that is to say, The River—overflowed westward in the beginning of a century of pulsations that filled immediately a strip of northern Pennsylvania, all of Upstate New York and the old Northwest, and afterwards the northern half of the national domain. After 1760 the Yankees for the first time since 1675 saw large horizons that might be occupied and fenced into the culture. For a while yet the central intellectual and spiritual drama continued to be played on the old stage of Old New England. But now the exits began to open, and those who didn't like the current production could slip out, if they wished, and try a new one in a new scene.

Each of the four main currents of religion declined in its fashion. Old Calvinism cast up no leader of consequence until the dawn of the next age, and can be ignored here. Antinomianism, Emotional Religion, having accomplished its "shambles," moved out of Old New England. Whitefield, making return tours in 1744, '54, '64 and '70, spoke to still enthusiastic but decreasing audiences. The Religion of Excitement flourished for a while in Vermont whose settlers were drawn chiefly from The River where the Awakening had been strongest. But after 1780 its center moved out into New York, and later into the Old Northwest.

The purest fragment of Puritanism, the one which carried the aesthetic tradition of Edwards, was the extension of his theology developed by his more distinguished disciples and christened abroad *The New England Theology*. In his assertion of private and emotional criteria, Edwards had not expressly moved out of the orthodox Calvinist doctrine of the Limited Atonement, the doctrine that God would in his pleasure impute the Atonement to some and not to others. But after Edwards, Joseph Bellamy of Bethlehem, Connecticut, his chief disciple and second in command in the Great Awakening, went all the way to Universal Atonement in his *True Religion Delineated* (1750). Here Bellamy asserted—with Edwards' consent, for he wrote an approving preface to the book—that Christ died for everybody; but, like Edwards, he allowed every individual the power to accept or refuse the proffered Grace, leaving God the inscrutable Judge as to whether the offer had been accepted. Samuel Hopkins, first minister of Great Barrington, Massachusetts, and afterwards, and for most of his life, the leading divine of Newport, devoted student, disciple, and first publisher of Edwards, extended Bellamy's theology less in terms of doctrine than in concrete application. He startled New England by proclaiming that Christ died for unregenerate Indians and Negroes as well as for Yankee Congregationalists. And he confirmed his sincerity by freeing his own slaves and promoting in Rhode Island a successful Abolition movement, culminating in a statute that freed all born after 1785.

Bellamy and Hopkins were both large, Edwardsean souls, but their New England Theology opened two ways into narrowing vistas. In their doctrine of Universal Atonement they avoided Universalism or Universal Salvation, by holding, even more aggressively than Edwards had, that individuals might choose to rest Unregenerate in their state of Depravity, and that God was a "vindictive" Judge who would decide by his own unpredictable standards whether or not they had done so. By this emphasis upon God's Judicial function they suggested Legal Arminianism to the unwary, though they were clear enough in holding, with Edwards, that Grace, the complete

Love of God, was an achieved state of mind, not a reward for a course of conduct.

At the other theological extreme, in the doctrine of Universal Atonement, and especially in Hopkins' practical concern for Negroes and Indians, he and Bellamy suggested that Humanitarianism which in the next century was going to be at once the quality of Third Puritanism and a substitute for Puritanism. By and large Bellamy and Hopkins carried the Puritan torch through a time that wanted none of its light. So did their somewhat less distinguished successors, Jonathan Edwards, Jr., Nathaniel Emmons and Nathaniel Whitaker. At least until the War, Puritanism dominated the pulpits of The River, and Intellectual Arminianism those of The Bay.

Intellectual Arminianism or Religious Liberalism was no more than the clerical fringe on the Secular Liberalism which dominated the age after 1760 and provided the historical significance of the whole century. Indeed, when we find Intellectual Arminianism talking the language of Natural Reason and Natural Law, we may wonder whether there was any real difference between Religious and Secular Liberalism. Among the several shades of Rationalistic Theology the religious pretence was strong in at least two of its subdivisions, namely in the Unitarian trend and in Universalism.

We saw Jonathan Mayhew denying the Trinity, and so putting himself in the line of Unitarian descent. Paradoxically, however, the first organized step toward this Heresy of Congregationalism was taken by the Episcopalians. King's Chapel in Boston, the oldest Anglican church in New England, lost its Rector and most of its Congregation in the exodus of Tories that accompanied the evacuation by the British in 1776. The remnant of the parish chose James Freeman, a recent Harvard graduate, as lay reader, and shortly gave him lay ordination, no bishop being available. He was disposed against the doctrine of the Trinity and in 1785 persuaded his congregation to strike from their liturgy all reference to it. Thus King's Chapel became the first Unitarian Church in America. The doctrine was already widely bruited in Eastern Massachusetts, but before 1800 only two other congregations adopted it, those in Saco and Portland, Maine.

The second presumably religious offshoot of Liberalism was Universalism. Where the New England Theologians, the heirs of Edwards, postulated the universal Benevolence of God and a universal Atonement, the Universalists went all the logical way and affirmed universal Salvation, whether the individual willed it or not, and with or without an intermediate passage of purgation in Hell. Though never numerous, the sect was earlier in New England outside of Boston than organized Unitarianism, having a few converts in Connecticut before the Revolution. No less a personage than the great Charles Chauncey came out for Universalism in 1782, five years before his death, but in the "free and catholick" spirit of the time that did not require him to withdraw from John Cotton's chair as Teacher of the First Church of Christ in Boston.

In general, religion after 1760 was eclipsed by the full shine of the Enlightenment, that metallic light of Reason over the surface of humanity which had been growing in intensity as more and more people absorbed smatterings of Locke and Newton, with their European and American interpreters. After 1760, the eighteenth century was like a strait of this Intellectual Ice that lay between the hard ground of the seventeenth, Actual God, and the hard ground of the nineteenth, Actual Man. While the throng was not too great the cool crossing upon Abstract Theory could be made. But when too many real people set out to follow, the ice tended to break into French Revolution, Jacksonian Revolutions, and similar violences and anarchies. In the American Revolution most of the people crossed upon solid bridges, the northern merchants and the southern planters on the bridge of Greed, the Yankee Farmers on the bridges of Equality and Local Independence. But the atmosphere, especially as the Revolution gathered in the '70's, of the age, was in the doctrines of cool and abstract Natural Reason, the reason of Franklin and Jefferson. Instead of God, they acknowledged a Prime Mover or First Cause, instead of the immeasurable Cosmos, measurable Nature, instead of the Will of God, Natural Law, instead of particular Men, Natural Man, instead of Eden, the Golden Age, instead of the Bible or the Church, the Book of Nature, Philosophers instead of Priests, the State of Reason instead of Grace, Posterity instead of the Last Judgment, the Future State, Progress or Perfectability instead of Heaven.[1]

Prominent among the symptoms of this cool plague of rationalistic unreality after 1760 was the imitation of religion called Deism. It substituted intellection for either Imaginative Perception or biblical interpretation as the source of knowledge, postulating a Benevolent though not a technically Christian God, and advocating the doing of good, not because it is enjoined by divine law, but because it is expedient and solidly satisfying here and may conceivably be rewarded in an after life. Early in the century Cotton Mather, always experimental and puttering, expressed a deistic kind of moralism in his Essays to *Do Good,* and in his practice of going from house to house trying to find kindnesses to perform, a practice which the then young Franklin satired in the *Do-Good Papers.* The rambunctious Ethan Allen, who got his learning during his period of chastening quiet as a prisoner of war in England, rates high among American deists in terms of philosophical inquiry and publication. His *Reason the Only Oracle of Man* (1784) is the first real attack on revealed religion in America, and at the same time is an attempted rational proof of the existence of God and immortality. His Essay on the *Universal Plenitude of Being* is a philosophical argument for the existence of God as "infinite intelligent substance" omnipresent in human souls. By the end of the War there were deistic societies all over New England. Distinguished Yankee Deists, more subtly if less volubly articulate than Allen and Franklin, were Elihu Palmer (*Principles of Nature,* 1801) and Joel Barlow the epic poet of the *Columbiad.*

However much Franklin may have become a Pennsylvanian, he remained also a Yankee, and, though raised in Boston, yet a Yankee of the homespun and genial soil, more typical of the wide culture of The River than of the special one of The Bay. With his genius for being and prophesying what was to be the America of the distant future, he was historically the most significant of the Yankee Deists. His Puritan Central Idealism, where religion had been in his native maternal and English Presbyterian paternal ancestors, was occupied by his passion for Science, an interest as large as the Explorable World but not as large as the Unexplorable one. This was "the one mistress to whom he gave himself without reserve," the one interest in which "he emits a light quite unclouded." In the rest of his multifarious interests and activities—his devoted public service, his genuine benevolence, his belief in a reasoned God who ought to be worshipped and who will reward virtue and punish vice, his dedication to the advancement of human welfare, in all these things he seems never to be wholly absorbed. Even "at the signing of the great Declaration," he has the placid countenance, wearing "the bland smile which seems to say: This is an interesting, alas, even a necessary, game; and we are playing it well . . .; but men being what they are it is perhaps best not to inquire too curiously what its ultimate significance may be."[2] Outside of his scientific work, in terms of which he retained the Puritan dedication and demand for truth, his life was on the plane of that superficial Natural Reason, that Common Sense concern with seen surfaces, which was the quality of his age. And in this genial semi-indifference, in which ultimate values are private and shared with no one, in which active concern is at best with expediency and is generally with means not ends, Franklin is the mature Yankee whom we saw intimated in Samuel Sewall. In Franklin, as in later godless Yankees, final or spiritual values are rather assumed than envisaged, as children accept them from their parents.[3] The practical import of life is not in its Meaning but in its activity, not in the goal but in having a comfortable and profitable journey.

Franklin's place in Puritan decadence is generally in that contracted Sky of Man and Natural Reason which he shared with other Deists and Rationalists of divers complexions. But his motives for virtue contract his landscapes even farther, from even a rationalized social Idea of Man to the confines of Rationalized Self. "In the Affairs of this World, men are saved, not by Faith, but by the Want of it." "If you would have a faithful servant, . . . serve yourself." "God helps them that help themselves."[4] He was the first great Utilitarian who, whatever his genuinely benevolent impulses may have been, yet advocated virtue because it worked, because it was wise to be on the safe side. Actions are not bad because they are forbidden, but they are forbidden because they have bad effects. The only ultimate values Poor Richard professed were those of comfort, to be "free and easy," to be healthy, free from pain and free from anybody else's legal or social control. Franklin's personal determinations were always impelled by the anxiety to miss no trick that might be of benefit to him, either in his worldly affairs or in his busy and absurd plans to "arrive at moral perfection." When in his systematic effort to accomplish the latter he felt he wasn't doing as well as he should, he introduced, as an after-thought, a "little prayer" whose first and principal appeal was "Increase in me that wisdom which discovers my truest interest."

Calvin recommended the Economic Virtues of Industry, Frugality and Prudence, not because he held wealth to be a virtue or even a reward of virtue, but because he wanted to recognize the merchant class which had these qualities and was generally snubbed for them by medieval Society. To be sure, they did comprise a temptation to greed, and they were so interpreted and applied by some English Puritans. But until Franklin's time the Piety had been strong enough in America so that even in the First Decline after 1660 they had led no man of record farther than Common Hypocrisy. In Franklin for the first time they are frankly celebrated, not because they are virtues, but because they will make you rich. "Without industry and frugality nothing will do, and with them every thing. He that gets all he can honestly, and saves all he gets (necessary expenses excepted), will certainly beome *rich* . . ."[5] The Materialism of Copernicus, Galileo, Descartes, Newton and Locke which his contemporary Jonathan Edwards still expanded to fill a Cosmos as large as human

Imagination, Franklin contracted to the measure of the meanest of immediate comforts and the pettiest of bourgeois complacencies. For himself, perhaps because of the novelty of these utilitarian professions, perhaps because of his honest kindliness, and certainly because of his scientific idealism which was indifferent to wealth, Franklin's express perversion of Calvin's economic virtues did not lead him personally into the predatoriness which he recommended. But a century later, when the religious foundations were crumbled into clichés, and when great wealth was visible as an attainable lure, these "sage" "virtures" tended to "harden into the stuff of unbridled competition and sordid business,"[6] the acme of self-concern and the antithesis of Christian or any other virtue.

Although Franklin's humor is too witty, too self-conscious in its artistic artlessness, to be true Yankee deadpan humor, yet in terms of it also we can conveniently identify him as the first true Yankee. The Puritan becomes a Yankee when the Faith and the God it used to reach are no longer matters of certainty, and in compensation for this tragic loss, Providence or his own capacity for psychic adjustment provides him with this strange compensation which we call humor, this pleasure in incongruity, this pleasure ultimately in the incongruity and absurdity which he finds in himself. The Puritan puts off his solemn certitude, and substitutes for it "salty" wisdom. We saw intimations of the change in the diary of Samuel Sewall whose old age overlapped Franklin's youth. In Franklin the change is far advanced, the ironic attitude revealed rather than concealed by the "placid countenance" and the "bland smile," the result short of mature Yankee humor only in that it is too courtly, too pat, instead of being naive. "We must indeed all hang together, or, most assuredly we shall hang separately." It has the Yankee flavor, but the pun keeps it from being the true article.

An application of the pseudo-religion of Reason equally characteristic with Deism, but esoteric and less widespread, was the new Rational Aesthetic, the conscious literary craftsmanship that came across the water from Dryden, Pope, Gray and the English Dr. Johnson. Substituting Verbal Excellence for the Puritans' Cosmic Order as standard, it produced the first school of Criticism and of Art for Art's sake in America. It was intimated early in the century by an insignificant group of "wits" who published in *The New England Courant* of Boston, edited by Franklin's brother James. Edwards showed awareness of it in his admiration of the style of Richardson. Franklin touches it in his principles of succinctness and clarity—"The words used should be the most expressive the language affords, provided they are the most generally understood. Nothing should be expressed in two words that can be as well expressed in one; . . . the whole should be as short as possible, consistent with clearness. . . ." But here Franklin relates not only to his Contemporaries but at once back to the solid reality of the Puritan Plain Style and forward to the shallow reality of twentieth century journalism. For the pure Standard of Reason, and the pseudo-realistic glitter of its Style as laid down by Pope and epitomized in the seesaw of his couplet, we must look to the professional poets, the effete Hartford Wits who flourished during and after the Revolution.

This group, although with one exception they were of little influence in their period, yet in their theories and practices provide perhaps the best caricature of it that we have. Adopting for slogan the principle that things must be presented "as they are"—what the political philosophers called "Nature"—their method of so presenting them was to devote themselves to the most artificial and excruciatingly complicated rules of expression as laid down by contemporary works of criticism and rhetoric. Under these rules they did not even accredit originality as a virtue, but as they adjusted their private lives to the current fashions of snobbery, so in their verse they indulged in frank imitation not only of the classics but also of Milton, Butler, Pope, Swift, Prior, Thomson, Shenstone and Gray.

Of this considerable group, at least four were men of native talent who would have made permanent contributions to literature in an age of emotional honesty. There was John Trumbull, satirist, who in his youth pilloried Whitefield, Bellamy and the New Lights in *The Art of Second Sight,* and later did the same to both Whigs and Tories in *M'Fingal,* his imitation of the *Hudibras* written during the Revolution and published in 1782. But he lacked the courage to jeopardize his social position by carrying through major attacks on contemporaries, and "as he gradually increased his girth and his influence in Hartford, the semblance of original force faded away."[7] There was David Humphries, able aide to Washington and post-war diplomat, Shenstonesque lyricist, most notably to the Army (*An Address to the Armies of the United States,* 1782), extraordinary snob who valued his talent only as the ornament of a gentleman, and who found the rustic atmosphere of his native Derby, Connecticut, insufferably hard to bear. There was Joel Barlow, probably the biggest and most honest imagination, as he was the most versatile, of the lot, soldier, lawyer, minister, merchant, politician, diplomat who died while with Napoleon in the retreat from Moscow, and whose epic, *The Vision of Columbus* (1787), revised and republished as *The Columbiad* (1805), is the one work of the Wits which literary historians can not quite dismiss. And there was Timothy Dwight, grandson of Jonathan Edwards, convinced from infancy of his greatness and superiority to Pope—and handicapped by this self-consciousness—author of the Pope-derived epic *The Conquest of Canaan* which lacks the power, the sweep and the dashes of originality that distinguish *The Columbiad,* in later life the able president of Yale. Dwight was the only one of the Wits who stands as a link in the chain of history, the reed that harbored the fire of the New England Theology through the post-war debauch of the 1780's and '90's and, in a famous series of sermons at Yale near the end of the latter decade, released it into the Revival of 1800 and the New Age.

Related to the Enlightenment during the last forty years of the eighteenth century was a spectacular improvement and expansion in education. In 1700, as we saw, the ancient statutes of compulsory education, left as they were to the enforcement of the local selectmen, had become so little compulsory that literacy was at an all-time low. But from that time and throughout the century there was a rise. At the elementary level, the ministers became School Visitors, and generally did their jobs well. After 1720, each new town settled in western Connecticut was required to reserve a lot for the support of the school. There had been public and quasi-public secondary schools from the beginning, but only the Boston Latin School and the two Hopkins Grammar Schools of New Haven and Hartford had achieved distinction. Throughout the eighteenth century, especially after 1760, the number of good ones increased, and after the Revolution the justly famous New England semi-private Academies began to sprout by scores, including Andover and Exeter and thirteen reported as founded in Connecticut between 1780 and 1786. New colleges during the same period were Brown (Baptist, 1764), Dartmouth (Indian, 1769) Bowdoin, (1794) and Williams, (founded in 1795, having been provided for out of bad conscience by Ephraim, the son of Ephraim Williams, the great grafter and chief persecutor of Edwards and the Indians in Stockbridge).

But the essential quality of the Age of Reason and Religious Decline after 1760, was neither in education, nor the pseudo-art of the Wits, nor in the pseudo-religion of the Deists, nor in the Scientific advances of the century, nor even in the general Intellectual Arminianism or Religious Liberalism which we saw emergent at the end of the seventeenth century, and have watched developing through the first half of the eighteenth century. The essential and important quality of the Age of Reason was the political parallel to this Intellectual Arminianism, the Political Liberalism which, closely intertwined with Religious Liberalism, replaced the concrete Cosmos of Puritanism with the humanistically limited abstraction called Nature, the World of Man. Unlike Religion, which had seen human relations in personal and individual terms, Natural Reason—like Marxian and modern Communism which are among its late products—saw them in mass terms. Wherefore the language of the time of Decline after the middle of the eighteenth century was a socio-political language, a language of Law and Government and Rights. And personal relations, insofar as they were not imposed by these, were relegated, as we saw in Franklin, to the direction of common sense and expediency.

The basic political ideas and some of the phraseology which eventually found their way into the great documents of the 1770's and '80's were not new, even at the emergence of Intellectual Arminianism in the 1690's. In more or less rudimentary form they had been brought over by the Puritans sixty years before as the stock of their current revolt against Charles I. Conveniently these ideas or principles may be grouped under six headings:

1) *Equality.* In Massachusetts in the seventeenth century this idea was applied only as among the Church Members or Saints and the Freemen who were approximately the same group and included from a third to a half of the population. The spiritual Equality within this group, however, was still far from producing practical democracy. The voters were not conceived equal as individuals with equally valuable individual opinions, but as equal channels for the Will of God who expressed Himself through the Electorate. Because of this saintly Equality, unanimity should always be possible. Wherefore, unanimity was sought, a requirement which played into the hands of the leaders, as did the traditional deference of the yeomen and the artisans both to the ministers and the gentry. Normally, the Magistrates presented proposals and asked for objections. Rarely were any heard. In Connecticut, the extension of the qualification for the Freemanship beyond the church membership, and the increase in the number and prerogatives of the local voters or Inhabitants began a practical and untheoretical secularization of Equality which was well advanced by the middle of the eighteenth century.

2) *Fundamental Rights.* In the seventeenth century, this idea also was rudimentary, being implicit in the idea of a basic Constitution or "The Law of Nature" which together with the Bible comprised God's Law, applicable to everybody.[8]

3) *The Foundation of Government in the People.* "The People," said John Cotton, "in whom fundamentally all power lyes . . ."[9] And there were those foundation stones of democracy laid by Thomas Hooker: "In matters of greater consequence, which concern the common good, a general counsell, chosen by all, to transact businesses which concerne all, I conceve, under favour, most suitable to rule and most safe for relief of the whol . . ."[10]; and again: . . . "The foundation of authority is laid, firstly, in the free consent of the people."[11] And Roger Williams: "The Soveraigne, original, and foundation of civill power lies in the people; . . . such Governments as are by them . . . established, have no more power, nor for no longer time, then the civill power of people consenting and agreeing shall betrust them with."[12]

4) *Government by Contract Freely Entered Into.* The doctrine of the Social Covenant or contract between citizens among themselves and with their Rulers and with God was essential in political thinking in the seventeenth century and easily became the doctrine of the Social Compact in the eighteenth. "No common weale can be founded but by free consent," said John Winthrop.[13] And there is John Cotton's famous statement, "It is necessary . . . that all power that is on earth be limited."[14] And again Cotton: "All civill Relations are founded in Covenant . . . there is no other way given whereby a people free from naturall and compulsory engagements, can be united or combined together into one visible body."[15]

5) *The Aim of Government the Common Good and the Protection of Basic Rights.* John Davenport: ". . . The end of all Civil Government and Administrations . . . is the publick and common good."[16] Here is Jonathan Mitchell in the Massachusetts Election Sermon of 1667: ". . . All that are set in place of Rule and Government . . . do stand charged with the welfare of that people, whom they are Rulers over. . . . The things wherein the welfare of a people does consist" are "Religion . . ., Safety, or the Preservation of their Being, both Personal and Political, and their participation in the Rules and Fruits of Righteousness, Equity, Order and Peace."[17]

6) *The Right of Revolution When the Contract is Broken.* John Davenport, in his famous Election Sermon of 1669: The People, in whom "the Power of Government is originally, . . . give it out conditionally; so as, if the condition is violated, they may resume their power of chusing another."[18] And Jonathan Mitchell in the above Massachusetts Election Sermon of 1667: If "a people or their Rulers . . . do any thing that is really and evidently . . . contrary or destructive to the welfare of the people, . . . it is impossible they should be bound in Conscience to do it."[19] And in 1692 Gershom Bulkeley of Hartford, though he was a Conservative and an opponent of the

current "revolution" against Governor Andros, spoke the revolutionary language of the eighteenth century when he held that no human law can be contrary to the law of nature and right—that is natural—reason, for an unreasonable law is a law against law and unlawful authority is no authority.

But these early political theories were all subject to the rule that government was by Christ and not at all by men, who were no more than instruments, "means," in His hands. Also, these expressions of political doctrine were mostly by way of discussion and debate among the leaders and did not greatly engage the understanding, let alone the actions, of the people. In 1632 the group of Freemen of Watertown, Massachusetts, staged a small uprising in order to see the Charter, but the revolt was aimed merely at the determination of practical, legal rights, and there was no evidence of any conscious, general political theory behind it. The people of early Rhode Island lived in a turmoil of conflicting, individualistic self-assertivenesses. But there too there was little doctrine involved, beyond Williams' principle of religious freedom which, with his characteristic political naïveté, he felt might have an analogy in the freedom to squabble for property and power. Even the systematic, democratic advances in early Connecticut were not accompanied, so far as we know, by any profession of political theory except on the part of two or three leaders.

It is not until the eighteenth century, following upon the importation of the works of Puffendorf, Sydney and Locke, that we begin to get expressions from the pulpits of humanistic political doctrine intended for popular understanding and actual application. Religion remained dominant until about 1760. But in the meantime the emergence and maturing in the first quarter of the century of a comprehensive Rational System celebrating the Rights of Man and masquerading as Religion, had been so abrupt in history as to be analogous to a mutation in biology. By 1725 all of the social and political rationalizations of the Revolution were audible, and with the decline of religion and the sharpening of political issues after 1760 these ideas became the common idiom of thought of the entire population.

Far more than the better accredited Benjamin Colman whom we saw setting up Liberal Religion in the Brattle Street Church in 1698, America's John the Baptist preparing the way for Reason and Independence was, as we have seen, John Wise, son of an indentured servant, Harvard 1673, minister of a parish in Ipswich, defier of Governor Andros, Chaplain in King Philip's War, and in the expedition against Quebec in 1690, and active in the movement of ministers that stopped the witch trials in 1692. His first major service was the defeat of the "Massachusetts Proposals" of 1705, whereby the Mathers tried to take control of the Congregational churches under a Standing Council which approximated the Presbyterian polity. Wise beat the plan in his *The Churches Quarrel Espoused* (1710—probably not published till 1715) partly by ridicule and partly by a deluge of Biblical quotations and New England precedents of democratic principles which he transferred from civil to ecclesiastical application. In his *Vindication of the Government of New England Churches* (1717),[20] he better systematized his argument, and so set the scene and raised the curtain on the stage of eighteenth-century political thought. Government and law were not, as the seventeenth-century divines had held, tendered to men directly by God, for their acceptance or refusal in the "Social Covenant," but "Wise and Provident Nature by the Dictates of Right Reason"—he means Natural Reason, the reason of Man, as he shows elsewhere—"Originally drew up the Scheme, and then obtained the Royal"—that is, the Godly—"approbation." Here came Nature and Reason, or Natural Reason, as senior to God, and, emanating from this man-made wisdom, every fundamental principle but one of the Declaration of Independence, at a time when Franklin was eleven years old, Jefferson, Adams and Sherman were not born, and the French Encyclopedists had not been heard of. Here we find a sudden crystallization of five of the six political ideas which we saw more or less inchoate in the seventeenth century:

1) *Equality.* "The Third Capital Immunity belonging to Mans Nature"—the first being identification with the Law of Nature or Reason, and the second Liberty—"is an equality amongst Men." "Let us conceive in our Mind a multitude of Men, all Naturally Free & Equal; going about voluntarily, to Erect themselves into a new Common-Wealth." (Later Wise argues combined Democracy and Republicanism as the best form of government.)

2) *Fundamental Rights.* Besides the "Capital Immunities," a man's basic Rights include "Life, Liberty, Estate. . . ."

3) *The Foundation of Government in the People.* "The first Humane Subject and Original of Civil Power is the People. For as they have a Power every Man over himself in a Natural State, so upon a Combination they can and do bequeath this Power unto others. . . ."

4) *Government by Contract Freely Entered Into.* "Civil Government . . . must needs be acknowledged to be the Effect of Humane Free-Compacts and not of Divine Institution; it is the Produce of Mans Reason, of Humane and Rational Combinations . . ." "Now

their Condition being such, to bring themselves into a Politick Body, they must needs Enter into divers Covenants."

5) *The Aim of Government the Common Good and the Protection of Basic Rights.* "It is certainly a great Truth, *scil.* That Mans Original Liberty after it is Resigned, (yet under due Restrictions) ought to be Cherished in all wise Governments; or otherwise a man in making himself a Subject, he alters himself from a Freeman, into a Slave, which to do is repugnant to the Law of Nature. Also the Natural Equality of Men amongst Men must be duly favoured; in that Government was never Established by God or Nature, to give one Man a Prerogative to insult over another; . . . a just Equality is to be indulged so far that every Man is bound to Honour every Man . . . The End of all good Government is to Cultivate Humanity, and Promote the happiness of all, and the good of every Man in all his Rights, his Life, Liberty, Estate, Honour, &c without injury or abuse done to any. . . . The main Point" of government is to attain the "peculiar good, and benefit of the whole, and every particular Member fairly and sincerely."

6) *The Right of Revolution When the Contract is Broken.* This is one fundamental principle of the Declaration which Wise did not assert, even as clearly as it had been asserted in the seventeenth century. He does say that "when the Subject of Sovereign Power is quite Extinct, that Power returns to the People again"; but that is not to declare the right of the people to void the delegated power when the Compact of Government is broken. We can say for Wise's omission only that he had himself illustrated the Right of Revolution by refusing to pay the illegal tax levied in 1687 by Governor Andros without any Act of the popular Assembly, and going to jail for his convictions; also that he had a leading part in the formulation and passage of Ipswich's resolution of refusal to collect the same tax, which refusal lends support to the claim, made on the Town Seal, that Ipswich is "The Birthplace of American Independence, 1687":

At a Legall Town Meeting Augst; 23 assembled by Vertue of an order from Jno Usher Esqr Treasurr; for choosing a Commissionr; to Joyne wt the Selectmen to Assesse the Inhabitants, according to an act of His Excellie; the Govrnr & Councill fr; Laying of Rates; the Towne thn considring tht the Sd act doth Infringe thr Libertie as free-borne English Subjects of his Majestie by Interfeiring wt the Statute Lawes of the Land, by wch it was Enacted tht no taxes Should be Levyed on the Subjects wtout Consent of an Assembly Choasen by the free-holders, for Assessing of the Same, they Do therfore Vote tht they are not willing to Choose a Commissionr for Such an End wtout Sd Previledge; & more over Consent not tht the Selectmen do proceed to Lay any Such Rate untill it be appointed by a Genll; Assembly Concurring wt the Govrnr & Councill.[21]

At the time Wise wrote the *Vindication* the only revolution in contemplation was Increase Mather's proposed centralization of clerical authority, and as against that Wise was in the conservative or anti-revolutionary position.

In Wise's *Vindication* the substitution for God's Will of Man's Natural Rights as interpreted by his Natural Reason is first seriously broached in America. And following Wise, along with the European models Puffendorf, Sydney, Locke, and presently Hoadley, the New England clergy fell into this stream of Intellectual Arminianism at a rate that accelerated through the century.[22] Even before the *Vindication*, John Bulkeley in 1713 was preaching in a Connecticut Election Sermon—the sermon to the newly elected Legislature—that "As for Mens Civil Rights, as Life, Liberty, Estate, &c. God has not subjected these to the Will and Pleasure of Rulers." And two years later Joseph Moss on the same annual occasion was preaching the compact theory of government, the powers of the authorities being limited by agreement entered into with the people.[23]

Outstanding among the political sermons that multiply after 1717 was a Massachusetts Election Sermon in 1734 by popular "Johnnie" Barnard of Marblehead who was presently to stand conservative against Edwards in religion but here went liberal in politics, preaching government under constitutions that can be amended only by the people—"Vox populi est vox Dei." In 1738 Reverend Jared Eliot of Killingsworth, Connecticut, the friend of Franklin, praised the British government as a constituted one under which "no man's Life, limb, Name or Estate, shall be taken away but by his Peers, and the known Law of the Land."[24]

In 1744 appeared a pamphlet, attributed to Elisha Williams, Rector of Yale, and entitled *The Essential Rights and Liberties of Protestants, a Seasonable Plea for Liberty of Conscience and the Right of Private Judgement in matter of Religion*, etc., which illustrates thoroughly the fashion in which the ministers, following Wise, found the same Natural Rights underlying Religious and Civil Liberty, and so encouraged the substitution of a Natural or Human World for a Supernatural or Godly one in the minds of their readers and listeners. Williams touches on most of the principles already stated as typical of the century: "As Reason tells us, all are born thus naturally *Equal*, i.e. with an equal Right to their Person" (that is, *Liberty*); "so also with an equal Right to their Preservation" (that is, *Life*); "and therefore to such Things as Nature affords for their Subsistence" (that is, *Property*); and he goes on to define property as that which a man appropriates from the common pool of Nature by adding his labor to it. And he adds the right of Revolution: "If every Man has a Right to his Person and Property; he has also a Right to defend them. . . ."[25]

Among the political sermons that in the 1740's are everywhere proclaiming the Natural Rights of Life, Liberty and Property, and government by Compact between people and rulers, one of Charles Chauncey's in 1747 sounds the usual notes, scolds the General Court of Massachusetts for venality, and goes on to utter phrases that look even beyond the *Declaration* of 1776 to the *Constitution* of 1787: Rulers must confine themselves within the limits of the *constitution* by which their power is *delegated* to them, "Especially . . . where the constitution is *branched* into severall parts . . . in order to preserve a *ballance* in the whole . . ."; he also mentions the rights *reserved* by the people in setting up their government. The next year, 1748, we find Jonathan Mayhew speaking of Natural Rights as "unailienable." In 1750, in response to a royal order to celebrate the birthday of Charles I, he preached the first of those fiery sermons on Liberty and the Right of Revolution that prepared the way for Sam Adams and Hancock: "Neither God nor nature has given any man a right of dominion over any society independently of that society's approbation and consent . . ." "Disobedience is not only lawful but glorious" to those that "enjoin things that are inconsistant with the demands of God." The people themselves have the right to judge when the social compact is broken and resistance is proper. And here is Mayhew in the Massachusetts Election Sermon of '54, when the final war with the French was beginning:

> . . . What horrid scene is this, which restles, roving fancy, or something of an higher nature, presents to me, and so chills my blood! Do I behold these territories of Freedom, become the prey of arbitrary power? . . . Do I see the slaves of Lewis with their Indian allies, dispossessing the freeborn subjects of King George, and of the inheritance received from their fore-fathers, and purchased by them at the expense of their ease, their treasure, their blood! . . . Do I see all liberty, property, religion, happiness, changed, or rather transsubstantiated, into slavery, poverty, superstition, wretchedness!

And he goes on to show death better than submission to the French.[26] In the same way hundreds of other ministers used their pulpits to urge the people to bloodshed in defense of their political privileges. Wherefore, when trouble with England began to gather,

they had a vocabulary and sympathetic congregations trained and
ready for revolt.

Meanwhile there was more than pulpit oratory and leadership
shrinking the Sky over New England from the religious and godly
one of the Puritans to the political and humanistic one of the
Yankees. Especially in Connecticut, after the enactment of the Saybrook Platform by an "Ambitious and Designing Clergy,"[27] a popular
counter-reaction gathered and found individualistic confirmation
in the Great Awakening. In its terminal excesses the Itinerant
Preachers told the people that they should not defer to their
educated ministers, that all men were capable of religious understanding; and it was an easy transfer from that to a suspicion on the
part of the poor and ignorant that they were in *All Things* the equals
of the rich and enlightened.

After Connecticut's oppression of the New Lights in 1742, the
counter-reaction integrated in widespread resistance, becoming at
the same time a religious and a social uprising, an awakening of the
lower classes to political self-consciousness. Strengthening the movement was the tax upon the Separatists for the support of the Establishment, though the Episcopalians, Quakers and the real Baptists
were still permitted in effect to enjoy the repealed Toleration Act.
Also, throughout the whole of the period the condition of life was
actual or threatened war, and to finance it there was currency infla-
tion and hard times, and more suffering than New England had
known since King Philip's War. In the ensuing unrest, the same masses
whom the great liberals excoriated for Antinomian Individualism in
religion, became the natural exemplars of their Liberal Individualism in politics. Among the people, as among their leaders, religious
and political freedom became interchangeable and indistinguishable.

After 1742 God was if anything more concerned with Liberty and
Property than he was with Grace, or perhaps Liberty and Property
were identified with Grace. The ministers of Eastern Connecticut—
dominantly New Light—petitioned the Assembly against the laws of
1742 on the ground that they infringed their "Natural and Lawfull
Right." In '47 Daniel Hovey, layman of Mansfield, was imprisoned
for refusal to pay the church tax, and petitioned the Assembly for
relief on the ground that liberty of conscience in religion was an
"unalienable Right of Every Rational Creature. . . ." And he said
he would continue his resistance though stripped of all his worldly
goods. Although Massachusetts and New Hampshire did not suffer
under the oppressive laws of Connecticut, yet in 1749 the Separatists

in nineteen of the towns in those colonies appealed against miscellaneous discriminations as violations of their "Unalienable Right" of Liberty of Conscience. In '53 the request of nine Connecticut towns for exemption from the taxes for the Establishment was rejected by the Assembly.[28]

Meanwhile, in '52 Solomon Paine, layman of Canterbury, had published an eloquent pamphlet on behalf of the Separatists—

> The Word of the Lord was like a Fire shut up in my Bones, and the Cry of the Poor Innocents, who are some of them shut up in Prisons, and others with their little Children crying for Milk, and could get none, for the Collector had taken their Cow for the Minister; and the very grey-headed stript of their necessary Household-stuff; And poor weakly Women, their's taken away, even to their Warming-Pan. Men's Oxen taken out of their Teams; Horses stript of their Tackling; All the Meat taken away from some, just at the setting-in of Winter . . .

and what the Word of the Lord really told Paine was that Connecticut's repeal of its Toleration Act in 1743 was contrary to God's Law, that to take away men's estates without their consent was a sin which God would punish "with publick Judgements."[29]

Another layman declared in 1757, respecting the diminishing persecution of the New Lights:

> These things will never go down in a free State, where People are bred in, and breathe a free Air, and are formed upon Principles of Liberty; they might Answer in a Popish Country, or in Turkey, where the common People are sunk and degraded almost to the State of Brutes, by Poverty, Chains and absolute Tyranny, and have no more Sense of Liberty and Property, than so many Jack-Asses. . . . 'Tis too late in the Day for these Things, these Gentlemen should have lived 12 or 13 Hundred Years ago. . . . But as to Us in this Country, we are Freeborn, and have the keenest Sense of Liberty, and han't the least Notion of pampering and making a Few great, at the Expense of our own Liberty and Property.[30]

In addition to the identification of political principles with religion, there is, in this quotation, the note of swaggering individualism which might be expected in such a complaint, the assertion of Equality not as a general idea but as a basis for that personal self-aggrandizement which is in fact contrary to the idea of equality. What is remarkable is that in this age of unrest we find very little of this truculence on the part of the Lower Classes who were in angry revolt against the gentry.

Soon after the above statement we pass our approximate, divisive date of 1760, after which Religion was everywhere in decline. The

surge of the Great Awakening had receded, and the defeat of the
French—the fall of Quebec late in '59 and the Peace of Paris in '63—
was ending seventy years of partial diversion from domestic secular
issues. The New Light—Old Light War was dwindling into fatigue
and mutual concessions, and it is refreshing to see the New Lights
now offering the Old Lights the Toleration which they had themselves been refused. Here is the generous advocacy of "Joseph
Marshl," semi-literate Separatist pastor, writing in 1763 to "Brother
Morse" upon the assumption that they, the New Lights, were now
in local Control:

> Now there is Parte of Said in habitants That Like Siad Constitu-
> tion" [By the "Constitution" in this controversy they meant
> the Saybrook Platform and the body of oppressive laws in Con-
> necticut] "& Chuse to be undere it, & Part that Dount But Chuse
> to be at free Liberty to maintain the Gospel a thay thinke best
> the question being Put to the wholle whether they all are agree
> and are willing Said Disattisfied bretherin Should be Releast
> and wee all Say in the affermitive—as we think . . . they have as
> Good natrel Right to act for thamself as we have therefore for
> us to Say that we wont have freedom unless they Destroy that
> they Jdgue to be agreble to the word of God . . . we thike
> Conterary to natrel Right and Christone Libbert, for us to
> Say that they hant Libberty to act for themselfe Ceme to Con-
> tredect what wee have Bene Contending for to wet that we
> have unalienable Right to Judge in matters of Faith and Prac-
> tices for our Selves.[31]

In '63, the same year as the letter of "Joseph Marshl," we find a
petition of Nathan Cole of Middletown, Connecticut, whom we
saw in 1741 hurrying on the wind of the spirit to hear Whitefield. He
has since become both a Separatist and an important man in his
town. Now he asks the legislature to be freed of church taxes on the
ground that he could not in conscience agree with the Saybrook
"Constitution":[32]

> Now see, we are free born as much as you be & have as good a
> right to liberty as you have every way from God himself. . . .

He goes on to show at once pride and humor in a later part of the
petition:

> Now men have been at work to hew down this Constitution tree
> of Connecticut & i am quit willing to doo my part & it seemeth
> allmost as if I see people very desireous to have this constitu-
> tion tree cut down . . . as if it were see me a comeing with a
> battel axe or eternal truth to help hew down this tree say to
> those about them pointing at me

1   Oh he was once a lump of sin
    but he's now just a enter'g in
    & here he comes a willing soul
    I say to yo make room for Cole

2   See now paine, frothingham & Cole
    have labour'd with a willing soul
    our harts unite & all agree
    to help in hewing down this tree

Such petitions as Cole's from individuals and from congregations, continue decreasingly through the Revolution until 1784 when the Saybrook platform with its enabling acts taxing Separatists to support the Establishment was repealed.

After 1760 New England enjoyed a brief age approximating one of pure Reason, pure Liberalism. Edwards was dead, Bellamy had moved to Scotland, and Puritanism, the religion of the Holy Ratio between Reason and Emotion, was relegated to the custody of an intellectual minority who were something less than giants. The Emotional or Antinomian elements among the Separatists were disappearing northward into the woods of Vermont and New Hampshire. The bulk of the Separatists remained and went respectable, and instead of swinging all the way into Conservatism they reinforced the Liberals who had also been their religious enemies. Everywhere the idiom of thought was that of Intellectual Arminianism. At The Bay Chauncey and Mayhew were the unrivalled leading ministers. In Rhode Island Edwardsean Samuel Hopkins was being pressed for leadership by the Liberal Ezra Stiles. The politically Liberal ex-rector of Yale, Elisha Williams, was the biggest gun along The River, where Stiles, after a turn in New Hampshire, was going to succeed to his academic laurels and political authority. In 1760 Stiles published his *Discourse on Christian Union,* widely read by the clergy in its exposition of the inalienable right of private judgment and liberty in religion, and of the political rights of the churches.

Though an age of religious decline, it was not a time of either moral or intellectual decadence. The Ignorant were not yet entirely persuaded of their superiority over the Educated, and the enlightened Liberals were not entrenched in smugness. For twenty years between the end of the French War and the end of the Revolution, fused Intellectual Arminianism and Political Liberalism exercised a benign tyranny over New England. Between the masses and the classes there was unanimity and seriousness and a steady elevation of thought in preparation for and then sustaining the great struggle for survival. It has been this political idealism, dramatized by a successful war, that has been taken as the mark of the century rather than the Puritanism of Jonathan Edwards. It is for this reason that we identify the whole century with its time of religious Decline, calling it commonly the Age of Reason or the American Enlightenment, and for our present religious purposes calling its landscape the World of Man.

As the tension with England approached an issue, the Ministers were ready with a vocabulary of thought and expression developed from the time of Wise two generations before, and they took militaristic charge without hesitation. Speaking of the Stamp Act in 1765, the Rev. Stephen Johnson of Lynne said, "It is a flagrant absurdity to suppose a free constitution empowers any to decree or execute its own destruction," and he said that no obedience was due the Act "by the law of God." When it was repealed, Rev. Joseph Emerson of Pepperell, in his Thanksgiving sermon, 1766, said that the happy outcome was such a thing "as our Saviour purchased for us . . . as there are such glorious things, of a spiritual nature, connected with it . . . A deliverance from . . . vile ignominious slavery." If it had not been repealed, he added, then "we should have fought . . . for our children, our wives, our liberty, our religion, for everything near and dear to us; and the issue might have been the disruption of the British empire."[33]

On the Sunday following the Boston Massacre in 1770 Rev. John Lathrop of Old North Church, Boston, preached from the text, "The voice of my brother's blood cryeth unto me from the ground," and argued in the sermon, which was presently printed and widely distributed, that a government which failed to serve the general good should be abolished and a better one established. In 1772, an article attributed to a clergyman held that "the Americans would be justified in the sight of Heaven and before all nations of mankind, in forming an independent government of their own . . . Great Britain has robbed them, sent her armies to enslave them, and totally cancelled all obligations to continue their connection with her another day—I am however for making the King of Great Britain the offer once more, and but once, to renew the compact." A year later, the Reverend Isaac Skillman, of the Second Baptist Church of Boston, published an incendiary pamphlet: ". . . For violating the people's rights, Charles Stewart, King of England, lost his Head, and if another King, who is more solemnly bound than ever Charles Stewart, was, should tread in his steps, what can he expect?" He went on to argue that the king had no more rights in America than the people had invested him with, which were chiefly to defend their rights and to confirm the laws they passed. And he ended with a belligerent flourish—"Where his Majesty has one soldier, who art in general the refuse of the earth, American can produce fifty, free men, and all volunteers, and raise a more potent army in three weeks, than England can in three years."[34]

After hostilities opened, it was the ministry, in larger proportion than any other group, that preached the War and gave help to the recruiting officers. And in all this preachment there was more than the jingoism with which ministers in time of war sometimes disgrace their calling in the interest of their popularity. Behind these eighteenth-century preachments there was always a dream of human rights and happiness, and in some the Utopian concept of America as a great and free nation, the hope of liberty for mankind. There were ostentatious firebrands among them, to be sure, such as the Reverend Thomas Allen of Pittsfield who took down his musket, marched on Saturday with his parishioners to the Battle of Bennington, silenced a Hessian sharpshooter, and was back on duty in his pulpit Sunday morning. But for the most part the chaplains confined themselves to their non-violent duties of solace and kindness, while the ministers who stayed at home preached, as they had been doing for three-quarters of a century, the victory not of violence but of those ideas of liberty and humane and free government which they believed to be of divine origin and to be worth the supreme sacrifice. Although it may be true that the War would not have been undertaken but for the well known economic Acts of the British Parliament, it is also true that in their final form these Acts were no more than a nominal invasion of the actual pocketbooks of the merchants and the farmers. In the final issue it was the principle of the invasion of the Inalienable Rights of Abstract Man upon which the war was sustained. The economic motive as such was negligibly slight. But as translated into a political principle, it was decisive.

As to the attitude of the laymen during the Revolution, almost any interpretation can be supported by plentiful evidence. If we accept the estimate of John Adams that a third of the nation supported the War, then it would seem that at least so much of that third as came from New England had some notion of the ideas they were fighting for. Among the officers there were plenty of sophomoric snobs like Elijah Backus, Jr., who as an undergraduate at Yale in 1777 complained of "the present nocturnal assemblies and the tumultuous and riotous proceedings of the mob of this town" as "sufficient to strike any sensible person with horror and raise his indignation against a set of men that not only disgrace the name of

Whig by being called by it, but human nature."[35] Yet three months after young Backus' irritated entry we find "I carried my gun to Weston's to have a bayonet put on it." If there were airy young officers, distinguishable by a hairline from the unimaginative little people who were the Tories, there were also dedicated men of the temper of Captain Nathan Hale who, while standing by his improvised gallows near present 3d Avenue and 66th Street, New York, not only delivered his famous adaptation of a line from Addison's *Cato*,[36] but also pled with his executioners and the others present to be ready to die any moment for what they believed to be their duty.[37]

The run of the line officers of New England were not as well educated as either Backus or Hale, neither as supercilious as the one nor as noble as the other. Whatever their ideas may have been, they revealed in their behavior an Equalitarianism, now entirely divorced from religion, whose "levelling spirit" "intimidated" the individualistic snobs from the Middle and Southern States.[38] Most of them were elected officers of the local Train Bands or militia who had no understanding of discipline, and generally the Yankees would not enlist unless they could choose their officers. Joseph Reed, Adjutant General of the Army, said that it was "impossible for any one to have an idea of the complete equality" in the New England troops. A Connecticut captain of horse was once seen "shaving one of his men on the parade"; Captain David Dexter of the 2d Rhode Island was discharged from the service for "frequently associating with the Waggon Master of the Brigade"; a certain Lieutenant Whitney was reprimanded before the brigade for "degrading himself by doing the duty of an Orderly Sargeant."[39] At Fort Ticonderoga a Colonel from Western Massachusetts, for sharing his quarters with a shoemaker was first rebuked and then knocked down by a Pennsylvania officer, whereby a brief riot was precipitated, and when it was quelled the two principals sat down to a good dinner of bear steak.[40]

Along with the Yankee equalitarianism there was enough angry individualism to compose such mobs as the 500 from Windham and New London Counties, Connecticut, who in '65 caught the stamp agent on his way to Hartford, forced him to shout "Liberty and Property" and resign his office, or the famous ones of Newport and Boston that gutted many fine houses including that of Tory Deputy Governor Hutchinson of Massachusetts whose library they threw down the well. And there were numerous small mobs such as the group of Liberty Boys who in '74 threatened with tar and feathers the Episcopal Reverend Samuel Peters of Hebron, Connecticut, who thereupon fled to England and wrote his famous fantasy *A General History of Connecticut* which is the source of the peculiar reputation of Connecticut for "Blue Laws."

How many of the members of these mobs presently risked their skins in the War there is no telling. Nor is there any knowing how many of the more than 232,000 who were in and out of the Army during the eight years involved[41] were criminals and miscellaneous wastrels, braggarts and bullies whom their communities were glad to be rid of. But it is certain that in the nucleus that fought the War through from the defeat, nakedness and starvation of '76, through the nakedness, starvation and freezing of '77, to the partially fed and equipped '80 and '81, it is certain that among these the greater part were in their agony aware of the concept of human liberty for which they were fighting. They were the actual realization, the embodiment in action, of the whole Age of Reason, the whole Ideal of Liberalism which had been preparing for them for a century.

"The diaries of officers and privates, written with no thought of publication, show a loyalty and in some cases a religious earnestness that must indicate widespread moral purpose."[42] "Our war is a righteous war," wrote the Rev. Ammi R. Robbins of Norfolk, Connecticut, in his journal. "Our men are called to defend the country; whole congregations turn out, and the ministers of the gospel should go and encourage them when doing duty. . . ."[43] And later he reports a dying Massachusetts youth who "asked me to save him if possible; said he was not fit to die. . . ."[44]

Sometimes the soldiers beat up those who were preparing to take advantage of the end of their enlistments and go home. At Yorktown, where part of the army was still more or less naked, when a shipment of coats arrived from Spain and were found to be red like the British, the soldiers refused to wear them.[45]

One of the finest of the revolutionary diaries is that of Elijah Fisher of Boston who had something of the unrhetorical stability of Captain John Parker who said he led his neighbors to their death on Lexington Green because "we had always run our own affairs and they were trying to stop us." After Fisher had fought through most or all of the war and was discharged in '83, he went back to Boston and found himself alone and a stranger, as Robinson Crusoe or E. A. Robinson's Mr. Flood found themselves alone on returning where once they had been at home:

> The 14th . . . Cross the farray into Boston, but there was so meny that Come from the army and from see that had no homes that would work for little or nothing but there vitels that I Could not find any Employment, so stays in Boston till the seventeenth; in the meenwhile one Day after I had been Inquiring and had ben on bord severel of there Vesels but could git into no bisnes neither by see nor Land.

The 16th. I Com Down by the markett and sits Down all
alone, allmost Descureged, and begun to think over how I had
ben in the army, what ill success I had met with there and all so
how I was ronged by them I worked for at home, and lost all
last winter, and now that I could not get into any besness and
no home, which you may well think how I felt; but then Come
into my mind that there ware thousands in wors sircumstances
then I was, and having food and rament [I ought to] be Content, and that I had nothing to reflect on myself, and I [resolved]
to do my endever and leave the avent to Provedance, and after
that I felt as contented as need to be.[46]

Private Elisha Stevens of Glastonbury and afterwards Salem Bridge
(Naugatuck), Connecticut, was in every major battle of Washington's
own army, and kept a partially legible diary which afterwards he—
or possibly someone else in an almost identical hand—entitled "This
is but a small part of the memoranda of Elisha Stevens services in
the Army of the Revolution of 1776, which planted the tree of Liberty whose branches in my humble opinion will extend in the Course
of 150 or 200 years to Earth's remotest Bounds by which time all
Nations will have tasted the Blessed Fruits Thereof and become
Completely [renovated?]"[47]

From early in the war, while enough Liberal Idealism remained to
finish the fight, morals declined, as they must in every war, in private
conduct, in business, and probably in politics.[48] During and shortly
after the end of hostilities, there was enough fidelity to the principle
of Liberty to accomplish the emancipation of slaves, in Vermont by
statute immediately effective, in Massachusetts by judicial interpretation of the preamble to its new Constitution, "All men are born free
and equal," in Rhode Island and Connecticut by statutes freeing all
born after a certain date. During the years between 1780 and the
end of the century there were faint stirrings of what was to become
the Missionary Movement. In such activities was the beginning of
transition out of the abstract idealism of the eighteenth century into
the practical humanitarianism of the nineteenth.

But all of these more or less generous intimations were small
rustlings against the general cascade into true decadence that followed the war. The soldiers who had been stiffened by danger and
by idealism lapsed into the insolent individualism which is the excess
of Intellectual Arminianism and Liberalism. Licentiousness for a
dozen or more years was on the increase, and commensurately Conservatism or Legal Arminianism rose to combat it, as it had done in
the equivalent period of decline at the end of the seventeenth cen-

tury. As part of this wave of reaction, the same Conservatives rose up to put a check on the very Libertarianism which had fought the war. The new state constitutions raised the property qualification for the suffrage and increased the power of the Upper Houses of the Legislatures. Meanwhile the powerless Confederation was increasingly in debt to the increasingly impoverished soldiers, and there ensued the well-known local rebellions—notably Shays' in Massachusetts—which were based in just causes but defeated themselves by their drunkenness, pilfering, and the foolish fulminations of their leaders—Eli Parsons, one of Shays' colleagues, notified Berkshire County in Massachusetts that he was going to visit upon it "fire, blood and carnage."

The War had been won for great ideas and its immediate result was revolt by the young, frivolity and extravagance in society, increase of crime, strengthening of social stratification and the rise of class hatred, everywhere self-assertion, mutual predatoriness and, central to all these, a deadness of religion.[49] Religion had been absorbed in the '50's into a virtuous intellectual Arminianism, and now the great Ideas of the latter also failed and left both a mental and a spiritual void. The ministers, who up until the War had still been the leaders of the communities, were now underpaid, many of them forced below subsistence, and ignored. "The late contest with Great Britain," complained the Reverend Peter Thacher,

> hath been peculiarly unfortunate for the clergy. Perhaps no set of men, whose hearts were so thoroughly engaged in it, or who contributed in so great a degree to its success, have suffered more for it. The people, having emancipated themselves from Great Britain, . . . have . . . forgotten that they could never be emancipated from the bonds of justice.

The ministers of New England, he says, are in poverty, many of them, especially the aged, thrown "out into the wide world." They are worse off than slaves, because the masters of slaves must at least keep them in old age. Even when ministers are in a fashion supported, yet their poverty "cramps the mind" and "prevents their progress in science, human and divine, which is calculated to make them useful."[50]

In 1791, Rev. Francis Aspinwall of the Methodist Church which was flourishing in the South and West under the new individualism, toured New England, entering it by the southwest on June 4, and recording his progress:

> I rode over rocks and hills, and came to Wilton. . . . My horse is very small, and my carriage is inconvenient in such rocky, uneven, jolting ways. . . . We are now in Connecticut; and never out of sight of a house . . . I do feel as if there had been religion in this country once; and I apprehend there is a little

in form and theory left. There may have been a praying ministry and people here; but I fear they are now spiritually dead.
. . .[51]

A few years later Lyman Beecher, then a student at Yale, reported
the depravity to which the students had descended, liquor in the
rooms, gambling and wenching prevalent, the "French Infidelity"
—that is rational Atheism—almost universal. But at the very time,
the late 1790's, when Beecher as a student reported this paganism,
Timothy Dwight, grandson of Jonathan Edwards, the new Rector of
Yale, was beginning a long series of chapel sermons in Theology
which were going to reverse the trend of the students and comprise
the first voice of a new Awakening and a new age.

III. The World of Men (1800-1900)

1. THIRD PURITANISM (1800-1860)

THIS THIRD CENTURY of New England culture, with its initial Revival or Re-expansion of Puritanism, was also the great century of expansion of population, the spreading of Old New England to become Greater New England, encompassing all of those states north of the Ohio and a waving line from Iowa to northern California wherein Yankee culture was first dominant and remains so. Throughout the century the Yankee population over the whole domain was enriched, and usually outnumbered, by immigrants from the South, from the Middle States, and from Europe. But, with the exception of the cultural islands which were noticed earlier, the people of New England tradition, whatever their ethnic derivation, controlled and stamped their quality on the whole area.

The great "Expansion," the "Yankee Exodus," got under way in the late 1780's, and we shall follow it here until 1860, the approximate date when the psychologically Expansive or Affirmative movement of the culture ended. Between 1790 and 1860, we can guess that about a million of the people born in New England moved westward into the states and future states of Greater New England,[1] a figure approximating the entire population of Old New England at the earlier date and a third of it at the later date.[2] If we make a reasonable assumption that the Yankee population tripled itself by natural increase in seventy years, then we could guess that in 1860 the pure Yankees counted for a quarter of the then 12,000,000 population of Greater New England.

Generally, we can assume that, but for fairly pure cultural islands of Germans, Scandinavians, Bohemians, Poles and others in Wisconsin and Minnesota, the western part of Greater New England was in this period divisible into four approximately equal groups, those derived from Old New England—including Upstate New York, which was of nearly pure New England stock—(29%), those from Pennsylvania, New Jersey and Delaware (18%), those from the South (25%), and those from Europe (28%).[3] The question is whether the local cultures of Ohio, Indiana, Michigan, Illinois, Wisconsin, Minnesota, Iowa, Kansas, Colorado, Utah, California, Oregon and Washington became a blend to which the four parent cultures made each a major contribution, or whether one of them dominated the others everywhere, taking only secondary coloring from them and from the environment.

This is not a question that can be resolved by statistics. From the evidence of the behaviors of these Commonwealths and their individuals in 1790, in 1860 and today, the inference taken here is that in this vast region, later embracing also Wyoming, Montana and Idaho, New England or Yankee culture dominated the other three. It was the most homogeneous, the most aggressive, and the most accustomed to organize and run on a responsible, popular basis the institutions of government, religion, education and the economy of small ownership in agriculture, industry and trade. Also the Yankee culture was qualified by an Idealism and a Millenarianism which easily combined into that optimistic Humanitarianism and Utopianism which chiefly characterized the age. After the original immigrants died, most of the people displayed these and other Yankee qualities, and their original derivations were no longer of importance. By the second generation they are all one people, and they differ from the Yankees of New England only in the results of the nearer experience of hardship and violence. These results included a Fear lest their culture erode into barbarism, and in consequence an extremity in the exercise of its qualities, the Idealism, the Equalitarianism and the respect for Education and the things of the Mind. Long before 1860 the people of the old Northwest were not only Puritans but in some respects the most aggressive exemplars of the whole tradition.

The hardships of pioneering and the extreme fortitude required of millions of people to overcome them in the age before machines, are important to us chiefly in their implication of the strength of the culture that could survive them without serious deterioration. What Perry Miller says of the first Puritans in the wilderness of Old New England—"They made no concession to the forest"[4]—was equally true of their descendants of the sixth and eighth generations in the wilderness of the Old Northwest Territory. By and large the first generation and their children came through the ordeal into settled civilization without having sacrificed imaginative and intellectual values to economic standards beyond that of Necessity. It was not until their grandchildren were maturing after our divisive date of 1860 that degenerating forces quite different from those of the Frontier sapped the culture of these Late Puritans with the temptations of Greed and outward power.

The stories of hardship and courage hardly credible to our decrepitude are in the records of every settlement, and accounts from the beginning and the end of the period will suffice for all. Here are bits from the journal of Seth Hubbell who, like many pioneers, chose the winter for his major move because the going through the unbroken wilderness, whether by sleigh or snowshoes, was easier than in the season of leaves and rocky ground:

> In the latter part of February, 1789, I set out from the town of Norwalk, in Connecticut, on my journey for Wolcott, Vermont, to commence a settlement . . . family consisting of my wife and five children . . . all . . . girls, the eldest nine or ten years old. My team was a yoke of oxen and a horse. After I proceeded on my journey to within about one hundred miles of Wolcott, one of my oxen failed, but I . . . took his end of the yoke myself, and proceeded on in that manner with my load to about fourteen miles of my journey's end. . . . I then proceeded on with some help to Esq. McDaniel's in Hydepark . . . the end of the road. It was now about the 20th of March; and the snow not far from four feet deep. . . . On the 6th of April I set out from Esq. McDaniel's, his being the last house. . . . We had eight miles to travel on snow-shoes, by marked trees. . . . I had now got to the end of my journey, and I may say almost to the end of my property, for I had not a mouthful of meal or kernel of grain for my family, nor had I a cent of money left to buy with, or property that I could apply to that purpose. I however had the good luck to catch a sable. The skin I carried fifty miles, and exchanged for half a bushel of wheat, and backed it home. We now had lived three weeks without bread; though in the time I had bought a moose of an Indian, and backed the meat five miles, which answered to subsist upon. . . . I had to go into New Hampshire, sixty miles for the little (grain) I had for my family, till harvest. . . .

> [His only cow having died] . . . In the fall I had the good fortune to purchase another cow; but . . . in the June following she was killed by a singular accident . . . this last cow left a fine heifer calf that in the next fall I lost by being choaked. . . . I took two cows to double in four years. . . . In June following, one of those . . . was killed while fighting: the other was found dead in the yeard, both of which I had to replace. . . . I was informed that a merchant in Haverhill was

buying snakeroot and sicily . . . with the help of my two oldest
girls, I dug and dried a horse-load, and carried this new commodity to the merchant; but . . . he knew nothing about this
strange article, and would not even venture to make an offer;
but . . . I importuned with the good merchant to give me a
three year old heifer for my roots. . . . I drove her home, and
with joy she was welcomed to my habitation, and it has been
my good fortune to have a cow ever since. Though my faith was
weak; yet being vigilant and persevering, I obtained the object,
and the wilderness produced me a cow.

. . . The first year I cleared about two acres, wholly without any
team, and being short of provision. . . . When too faint to
labor, for want of food, I used to take a fish from the river, broil
it on the coals, and eat it without bread or salt, and then to my
work again. . . . I planted that which I cleared in season with
corn; and an early frost ruined the crop, so that I raised nothing
the first year . . . all were friendly and ready to assist me in
my known distress as far as they had ability.[5]

In the main Mr. Hubbell's experience was typical of that of all
the pioneers. His disasters with cattle were not universal, but could
be matched by equivalent special calamities suffered by each of the
millions. As the frontier moved west to the plains where the forest
no longer supplied sable, fish, timber and a varying environment,
deadly loneliness and more enduring squalor were the common
experience:

Many women were reduced to tears when they first caught
sight of their future dwelling [which would be a dugout or a
sod hut]. One witness tells of a refined woman born in New
York. . . . She settled on the Kansas plains about 1860. She
was found crying—crying because there was nothing beautiful
at which to look; everything was hopelessly ugly.

We are in a state of excitement. . . . The Indians sent word
by the half-breed for us to leave the country forthwith and that
they would be down here . . . and drive us out. . . . We are
on a military footing. . . . All told we number thirty-five for
defense, not including the women who can shoot as well as
anyone. . . . All the troops in this section . . . are on the Mormon expedition, and . . . the settlers are left to protect themselves.

. . . I venture to assert that these men and women did not
spend most of their time dreaming of the empire they were
building, of the splendid civilization that was to grow up on
the plains. No, the truth is . . . that they spent much of their
time "scratching," for they had not only fleas and bedbugs, but
some other parasitic afflictions of a definitely personal character;
and bathing was indulged in only by those of heroic courage.

. . . one resourceful young woman kept a toad in her dugout, which not only cleared the house of fleas, but served as a pet for the children. She called the toad Tilden—her father was a democrat, and it was the time of the Hayes-Tilden campaign.

All kinds of pests, especially snakes, inhabited the layer of straw under the sod roofs of the houses:

> One old lady remembered a dinner with one of the neighbors, in the course of which a snake fell down into the meat platter. It was . . . chasing a mouse, and worked up too much momentum.[6]

The records of the squalor or charm of the frontier settlements, once they were established, vary with the age of the settlements and with the disposition of the narrator, but they also reflect differences in the qualities of different groups of settlers. The eminent and fastidious Reverend Nathan Perkins, D.D., of the Third Church of West Hartford, toured Vermont the same year of 1789 that Seth Hubbell and others settled Wolcott. Through his finicky horror there shines much of the reality of the Frontier, both for better and for worse. His progress was mostly during the month of May:

> . . . Friday entered the State of Vermont—a bad appearance at the entrance, Pownal the first town, poor land—very unpleasant—very uneven*—miserable set of inhabitants—no religion, Rhode Island haters of religion—baptists, quakers, & some presbyterians—no meeting house. . . . Sabbath in May, preached at Sunderland, in a barn, to a considerable audience, very attentive & much affected, received much applause, a raving arminian methodist preached in the Evening; Here lived formerly the awful Deist Ethan Allen. . . . In his house now lives a quaker from Long Island, with a young girl from Seabrook whom he seduced, though a married man, a picture of beauty and elegance. . . . Came to one Deacon Talcotts and he accompanied me to his Excellency's Governor Chittenden's. A low poor house,—a plain family—a low, vulgar man, clownish, excessively parsimonious,—made me welcome,—hard fare, a very great farm. . . . A shrewd cunning man—skilled in human nature & in agriculture . . . —got lost twice in the woods already—heard the horrible howling of the wolves. Far absent in the wilderness . . . among log-huts—people nasty—poor—low-lived—indelicate—and miserable cooks . . . nothing to eat, —to drink,—or wear,—all work, & yet the women quiet,—serene, —peaceable,—contented, loving their husbands,—their home,— wanting never to return,—nor any dressy clothes; I think how strange—I ask myself are these women of the same species with

* Travelers on Route 7 today may recall Pownal Valley as one of the most beautiful in America.

our fine Ladies? tough are they, brawny their limbs,—their
young girls unpolished—& will bear work as well as mules. Woods
made people love one another & kind & obliging and good
natured. They set much more by one another than in the old
settlements. Leave their doors unbarred. Sleep quietly amid flies
—bed-buggs—dirt & rags, O how vile,—how guilty,—how ungrate-
ful to providence are our women! Tell lies about one another—
envy one another—go abroad, dress & enjoy fine roads—carriages
—husbands to wait on them—& are yet uneasy—unaffectionate.
Could my Lady so agreeable & pleasant to me, only see & endure
what I have . . . how thankful would she be![7]

Equivalent squalor, but without a recitation of any redeeming
virtues of the settlers, is reported by Dr. Zerah Hawley who in 1820
came to practice medicine at Harpersfield in Connecticut's Western
Reserve, being northern Ohio, then called New Connecticut, and
soon after published a journal (New Haven, 1822).[8] He said his motive was to "undeceive the community, respecting a portion of the
Western Country, which has been represented as an earthly Paradise. . . . I entered . . . a log house with one room without any
fire-place, the log being laid against the logs of the house and the
fire built in front." There was no chimney, only a hole in the roof
for smoke, and the roof leaked. A few chairs, a bedstead of saplings,
two chests and a set of shelves were all the furniture, and there was
a sick child in another cabin, where the roof leaked so copiously
that there was no dry spot. Dr. Hawley was entertained in another
one-room cabin by a "titled man" or judge "in which all the family,
with their guests, eat, sleep, and perform all domestic operations."
Here there were beds in two corners, a cupboard in a third, and a
swill barrel in the fourth to which the hogs wandered in and out
freely and noisily all night. Generally, the doctor found the older
generation cultivated, the children less so, the grandchildren crude
and ignorant of the world. The schools of the region were make-
shifts, some holding only in summer, and at Madison and Monroe
he found the teachers' salaries six and five barrels of whiskey respectively.

In contrast with these accounts we have reports such as the following on Marietta, Ohio, in 1803, the year Ohio was admitted as
a state, when Marietta was no older than the hamlets described by
the Reverend Doctor Perkins and the Medical Doctor Hawley: (In
the vicinity of Marietta the Ohio River flows more south than west,
so that Ohio is on the west bank and Kentucky on the east.)

The industrious habits and neat improvements of the people
on the west side of the river, are strikingly contrasted with those
on the east. *Here* in Ohio . . . the buildings are neat, though

small, and furnished in many instances with brick chimnies and glass windows; *there* the habitations are miserable cabins. *Here* the grounds are laid out in a regular manner, and inclosed by strong posts and rails; *there* the fields are surrounded by a rough zig-zag log fence. *Here* are thrifty young apple orchards; *there* the only fruit that is raised is the peach, *from which a good brandy is distilled.*[9]

In 1810 we have a more specifically favorable report, this on the village of Warren in the Western Reserve in the north of the state.

At a neat frame school house the learned languages are taught by Mr. Gad H. Towner, who has at present, the charge of several students of the first respectability in that part of the state. There is a public library and a number of genteel persons residing in the neighborhood.[10]

An account prejudiced similarly with that of Marietta above describes the Yankee settlement in Denmark, Iowa (1836), and its effect on the Southerners who had been earlier in the territory:

They called Denmark in derision, a 'Yankee Heaven.' Their neat, painted houses with charming shaded yards in front, and surrounded by neatly trimmed hedges, their church and academy, and all the New England ways and works, excited envy and even alarm. . . . A man of Southern origin . . . declared he would sell out and leave or he would be cheated out of everything. . . . He chanced to call upon one of his new neighbors at their tea hour. For the first time in his life he saw a candle and (had a piece of) mince pie. . . . When soon afterwards, he was burned out, and the Yankees put him up a new house, he concluded it was safe to stay among them.[11]

Analogous to these contrasting accounts of the Frontier settlements is the ancient argument between interested parties, the Yankees who did not emigrate generally charging that the pioneers, at least the first and genuine ones, were the scum of society, while the pioneers themselves, and especially their children, observed that the emigrants were the enterprising and courageous people while those who stayed back in New England were the timid, the feeble and the dull.

The traditionally authoritative statement for the rooted Old New Englanders is that of President Timothy Dwight of Yale who in 1803 made and recorded this tour of Vermont and New York:

In the formation of Colonies, those, who are first inclined to emigrate, are usually such, as have met with difficulties at home. . . . These men cannot live in regular society. They are too idle; too talkative; too passionate, too prodigal; and too shiftless; to acquire either property or character. They are impa-

tient of the restraints of law, religion, and morality; grumble
about the taxes by which Rulers, Ministers, and Schoolmasters,
are supported; and complain incessantly, as well as bitterly, of
the extortions of mechanics, farmers, merchants, and physi-
cians; to whom they are always indebted. At the same time, they
are usually possessed, in their own view, of uncommon wisdom;
understand medical science, politics, and religion, better than
those, who have studied them through life; and, although they
manage their own concerns worse than any other men, feel
perfectly satisfied, that they could manage those of the nation
far better than the agents, to whom they are committed by the
public. After displaying their own talents, and worth; after
censuring the weakness, and wickedness, of their superiors; . . .
in many an eloquent harangue, uttered by many a kitchen fire,
in every blacksmith's shop, and in every corner of the streets;
and finding all their efforts vain; they become at length discouraged: and under the pressure of poverty, the fear of a gaol,
and consciousness of public contempt, leave their native places,
and betake themselves to the wilderness. . . . We have many
troubles even now: but we should have many more, if this body
of foresters had remained at home.[12]

Of equal authority on the side of the virtues of the frontiersman
and his indispensable contribution to our culture, is Frederick Jackson Turner and his famous Frontier Hypothesis:

> . . . To the frontier the American intellect owes its striking
> characteristics. That coarseness and strength combined with
> acuteness and inquisitiveness; that masterful grasp of material
> things, lacking in the artistic but powerful to effect great ends;
> that restless, nervous energy; that dominant individualism,
> working for good and for evil, and withal that buoyancy and
> exuberance which comes with freedom.[13]

And elsewhere in his papers Professor Turner pointed out, as
pioneer virtues, politeness, hospitality and ideals of equality based in
faith in the common man.

Out of the records of one of the great movements of peoples in the
history of the world, with millions on the move, we can find plentiful support for either Dwight's* or Turner's view, and it is equally
an error to espouse either of them exclusively. It is possible, however,
to venture one generality which weighs especially against the wastrel
theory of pioneering. Financially, the bulk of the pioneers belonged
in a medial bracket. At the top, the wealthy did not usually migrate,
because, on the one hand, they were securely comfortable at home

* Dwight had a high opinion of those Yankees who followed the "foresters."
See his *Travels*. (New Haven, 1821-22) III, 529.

and, on the other hand, most of the truly rich were of an age past that of the energies required for survival on the Frontier. At the bottom of the financial scale, on the other hand, the destitute did not pioneer either, except for those individualistic backwoodsmen who were a negligibly small class among Yankees, and whom Dwight overemphasized. For the generality who were of the culture and the civilization, property was required to go west. At the most primitive you must have a wagon or cart whose commodiousness depended on the size of your family, a yoke of oxen, a few tools, firearms and stores for some weeks. Besides you should have, and most did have, a cow, a horse, money enough to buy land—usually before they set out—and a fund of hard cash for emergencies. After 1825 most of them had the fare on the Erie Canal, and afterwards the railroad.

Typically, the emigrants were farmers who sold their farms or at least their stock to make the needful provision, or they were the surplus members of families grown too large for their acres whom their relatives staked for the venture. Among the great majority there was money in the picture, and the deeply channelled responsibility of the class of Yankee farmers. Where cash was not sufficiently available, or where the individual was of an irresponsibly venturesome nature, he was less likely to take part in the movement that settled and civilized the West than he was to be sucked into one of the lurid and atypical gold and silver rushes or, more commonly, to tie his nightshirt and his mittens in a big handkerchief on a stick and trudge into one of the rising cities where the industrial revolution was advertising for hands. There in the factories he usually did find work, and if he was smart he got in on the ground floor of the first flight of industries. Even if he did not rise above the plane of wage-earning, his pay was usually good in this early phase when employers were still mainly responsible, and the growing city was inspiring, especially to his wife. Once he was settled in Lowell or Waltham, in Adams, Springfield, Waterbury, Danbury or Bridgeport, in Glens Falls, Amsterdam, Little Falls, Utica or Watertown, he rarely pulled stakes again to join his cousins out yonder among the Indians and the buffalo.[14]

In the impulsion of the Yankee Westward Movement we can still find plenty of the old religious motive that characterized the expansion of the seventeenth and a good share of that of the eighteenth centuries, the motive of Church Schism, especially along the line of the Old-Light—New-Light controversy which we saw waging in the wake of Edwards. The economic motive of Greed which the debunking historians delight to universalize was now also widespread, both among the usually home-keeping investors in the land companies and among speculators who sometimes actually

settled under the requirements of the law, with the hope of selling
out profitably and moving on. But the dominant motive, the motive
of the preponderance of the emigrants, was the economic one of
Necessity, the anxiety to refound themselves, not in palatial luxury
but in substantial comfort obtainable as the reward of hard labor. It
is true that during this period the ancient Calvinist injunction to
Diligence in the affairs of the world was passing into its hypocritical
phase where Greed was the real motive behind the pretence of cultivating the Lord's garden. But this great change was until 1860
characteristic rather of the urban minority who ran the new factories
than of the agricultural majority which supplied the western
pioneers. They were in the main farmers who retained as the dominant force in their lives either the Puritan piety, currently enjoying
its second Great Revival, or the Yankee Idealism which was the godless form of it. In process of the piety they might well ask the Lord
to reward their labors with a substantial house and clothing, full
bins, and a surplus to send the children to the Academy and the College. But beyond that neither the Puritan nor the Yankee could in
conscience aspire.

Old New England must disgorge a good share of its population
westward on either or all of three scores. In the first place, the long
congestion within the Indian walls north and west had produced a
dangerous over-population, even for good soil—and it had exaggerated the Calvinist parsimony and Yankee "shrewdness" which
were necessary, long before 1800, simply to support life on a subsistence level.

Secondly, and irrespective of either population or soil, New England agriculture in the decades surrounding 1800 was in a bad way
for either foreign or domestic markets. The Napoleonic Wars, including the War of 1812, obstructed foreign trade. The seaports were
impoverished and took little, even for their own consumption. In
consequence the farmers were squeezed down to a hard subsistence
level, with little cash and that having to go a long way. Between 1810
and 1860 the industrial revolution did transfer some of the surplus
farm population to the cities. But the Westward Movement was in
greater flood, and as rapidly as the city markets increased, foodstuffs
came in from the West in quantities that could undersell the products of New England agriculture. Wherefore, the Yankee farmers
were increasingly invited westward, and the more of them that went
the worse the plight of those who remained.[15]

In addition to overpopulation and the failure of markets, the
third and gravest plight of the Yankee farmers was that the earth itself was failing. In the heavily forested times of original settlement,
the soil on the hilltops and the high slopes had been deep and good,

while the valleys were marshy and miasmic. But after the great trees were slaughtered and burned, and the ploughs of the centuries furrowed in whatever imprudent direction was easy, and the rains of the centuries furrowed all down hill, the loam ran slowly down into the river basins. Thus new farms were made but many more farms from the heights ran off like snow in a slow April. By 1800 New England was again showing those "rocky hilltops" which at first had been scraped bare by the Glacier but in the twenty thousand years since had taken on the depth of loam which they could have been made to hold.

Not perceptibly in a lifetime, but dramatically through successions of lifetimes, the bones of the planet rose and edged out of the soil. In Granville, Massachusetts, Alfred Avery, a little boy, went out with his hoe to do what he could to help his father plant corn. Presently he was sobbing, and when his father asked him what was the matter he cried out, "I can't get dirt enough to cover the corn." Not long after, his father joined the company about to set out—1804—to found Granville, Ohio,[16] being 176 persons and taking with them the complete church, pastor, deacons and all the members.[17] From prosperous Dudleytown in Cornwall, Connecticut, the rich Pattersons made the first of three major moves and rebuildings down the hill southward from the high plateau; the last of the Dudleys, reputedly unsavory remnants of the great gubernatorial family of Massachusetts Bay, moved away, reputedly westward, and in three or four decades their house fell. In Connecticut and Massachusetts and Vermont whole hilltop hamlets emptied into ghost towns, where the wind and the streams and the insects survived the sounds of men and cattle, and the lead spout still ran water in the tangle after the watering-trough had rotted, and no human ear heard the crash when the roof trees collapsed in the storm, leaving the stone chimneys stark and startled under the fourth-growth forest that stood tall on the naked rocks where man could no longer stand.

The Westward Movement out of New England became noticeable in the 1780's when Vermonters crossed Lake Champlain to settle among their old enemies in New York. Other companies from Massachusetts and Connecticut likewise injected themselves among the established settlements along the Hudson. Numerous veterans of General Sullivan's army that had destroyed the Iroquois in '78 sought and received grants in the country they had campaigned through in central New York. But the real tide of the Great Exodus began after 1786 when New York ceded to Massachusetts, in settle-

ment of an ancient claim, a vast tract in the west of the state, and
Massachusetts sold the preemptive rights to Oliver Phelps and Nathaniel Gorham. Phelps and Gorham opened a land office at Canan-
daigua, and the "Genesee Fever," running high by 1790, began to
empty Old New England. Travel was preferably by sleigh, and on a
single winter's day in 1795 one observer counted 500 of them passing
through Albany between sunrise and sunset. The following summer
an average of twenty boats daily went up the Mohawk River carrying pioneers. One estimate has it that between 1790 and 1820 alone
800,000 people from New England either settled in or passed through
New York.[18] In new town after new town the arriving companies first
set up their system of worship, in the beginning in the open, then in
someone's cabin* or house, or in the church, whichever was finished
first.

Before 1800 the tide had swept through New York, had narrowed
to cascade across Pennsylvania's northern corridor, and flooded out
into Ohio. There in 1786, under the auspices of the Ohio Company
led by General Rufus Putnam and Reverend Manasseh Cutler,
twelve families,[19] most of them headed by officers and men of the
Massachusetts, Connecticut and Rhode Island line, founded Marietta, at the same time organizing themselves into a Congregational
church with thirty-one members. The post was typical of the remote frontier, where the recent treaty with the Indians was not entirely to be trusted. It was about a hundred by fifty yards in extent,
comprising five log blockhouses, six log dwellings and a schoolhouse,
all enclosed by a "stout" palisade. The schoolteacher was one Joseph
Barker from somewhere in New Hampshire, and he had forty pupils
between four and twenty. Upon an Indian alarm, says a contemporary account,

> the first person for admittance into the central blockhouse was
> Colonel Sproat, with a box of papers. Then came some young
> men with their arms. Then a woman with her bed and children.
> Next old Mr. William Moulton, from Newburyport, aged
> seventy, with his leather apron full of old goldsmith tools and
> tobacco. Close at his heels came his daughter Anna, with the
> china teapot, cups and saucers; Lydia brought the great Bible;
> but when all were in, their mother was missing. Where was
> mother? She must be killed! No, says Lydia, mother said she
> would not leave the house looking so; she would put things a
> little more to rights, and then she would come. Directly, mother
> came, bringing the looking-glass, knives and forks &c.[20]

Although town planning for defense and other practicalities was
as old as New England, Marietta was perhaps the first town to plan

---

* The Yankees had now learned, perhaps from the Swedes along the Delaware,
the art of building cabins with logs laid horizontally.

in detail under an aesthetic motive. In 1791, the date of the above description of the central defensive close, a committee of three citizens "For Leasing and Ornamenting Public Squares" put in a report, presently accepted, for the salient features of a village, or Center of the Town, obviously much larger than the close:

> The mound square to be leased to General Putnam, for twelve years, on these conditions: To surround the whole square with mulberry trees, at suitable distances, with an elm in each corner; the base of the mound to be encircled with weeping willows, and evergreens on the mound; the circular parapet, outside the ditch, to be surrounded with trees; all within this to remain undisturbed by the plow, seeded down to grass, and the whole inclosed with a post and rail fence. The squares Capitolium and Quadranaou to be ornamented in the same way, with different species of forest trees, seeded down to grass, and never disturbed with the plow. Sacra Via, or the covert way, was not leased, but put into the care of General Putnam for its preservation, and seeded down to grass as a public ground. Subsequently, Rufus Putnam, Jabez True, and Paul Fearing, or either of them, were appointed trustees to take charge of these squares, and lease them to suitable persons. . . . The avails of the rents were to be appropriated to the education of indigent orphan children of Marietta.[21]

Ten years after the settling of Marietta and its entourage of smaller hamlets, the Connecticut Land Company, under the leadership of General Moses Cleaveland, of Canterbury, Connecticut, bought three million acres of the Connecticut Reserve in the northern reaches along Lake Erie. In the same year Cleaveland

> . . . led fifty-two other Yankees out of New England and into New Zion. . . . He did his surveying job with dispatch and returned to his home in Canterbury before the harvest of 1796, to report that two towns, with a few settlers in each, had been laid out at Conneaut and Cleveland. . . . Accounts of the founding of Conneaut are conflicting. "With their *tin cups*," says a pious version, "dipping from the broad lake the crystal waters with which to pledge the national honor," the Ohio pilgrims raised the first log cabin there. General Cleaveland himself said that he caused rum to be poured for all the party, and that after salutes had been fired and the toasts drunk, the affair closed "with three cheers. Drank several pails of grog, supped and retired in remarkably good order."[22]

By 1800 Greater New England had bulged westward to include New York state from Plattsburg, Lowville and Rochester in the north to Amenia, Binghamton and the Pennsylvania border on the south, leaving the still small New York City to its own cosmopolitan culture, and northern corners at the eastern and western ends of Lake Ontario to be occupied in the next decade. It had narrowed across the northern isthmus of Pennsylvania, had expanded again to settle the eastern quarter of Ohio, and had sent a long salient down the Great River to found Cincinnati. One estimate for the early nineteenth century derives 60-67% of the people of all New York State from New England.[23] Another estimate locates 60,000 Yankees west of the central counties of Oswego and Oneida.[24] The northern counties of St. Lawrence, Jefferson and Lewis were settled almost purely from Vermont.[25] Of 103 towns laid out in Connecticut's Western Reserve in Ohio, thirty-five had been settled by 1800.[26]

In the new towns the first log structures were already giving way to Yankee saltbox houses and churches with "pretty steeples," and the first squalor of charred stumps was becoming the "sprightliness, thrift and beauty" of New England.[27] In this first wave the emigrants were still exuberant enough in escaping from hardship or church, family or social quarrels at home so that nostalgia not often named the new settlements for the native town—in New York, a Stamford and a New Milford, in the Pennsylvania corridor a Waterford, in Ohio, another Waterford, a Sharon and a Windsor. On the other hand, the characteristic Puritan anxiety that learning should not "lie buried in the graves of our fathers" showed itself in the intellectual pretense of naming frontier hamlets in New York Northumberland, Troy, Rome, Utica, Syracuse, Oxford, Sidney, Ithaca, Geneva, Palmyra and Elmira, and in Ohio, Athens, Cincinnati and Ravenna. More substantially, ten years out of Old New England the great migration had left behind it in New York, Hamilton College, set up originally, in 1793, by Samuel Kirkland as Hamilton Oneida Academy for the instruction of the Indians, and Union College (1795), and in Ohio, Muskingum Academy (later Marietta College); together with scores of those Yankee Academies, those local "poor men's colleges," which were probably the best secondary schools of a public nature that America has had, assuring every bright boy an education, overlapping the first and sometimes the second years of the "liberal" colleges.

The nineteenth century turned, and the Great Tide rolled on, increasing in mass rather than extent. During the next twenty years, Ohio (1803), Indiana (1816) and Illinois (1820) all became states, the first finally absorbed by Greater New England, the second and third seeming to be finally absorbed by the South, the Yankees having in

Indiana only two or three outposts, and in Illinois a small but ornamental Advance Party of Collinses from Collinsville, Connecticut,
as a salient out across the state at Collinsville, Illinois, within four
hoots and a holler of the Mississippi. In the settlement of the Fire
Lands—the western part of Connecticut's Western Reserve given
to the towns mostly on Long Island Sound, that had been burned
in the Revolution—the home names were carried to Greenwich,
Norwalk, New Haven and New London, Ohio, with Boston and
Plymouth thrown in for good measure. In this period generally
the transfer of names from Old New England to the new towns became common practice. Besides those in the Fire Lands, there were
settled elsewhere in the Western Reserve Salem, Andover, Hartford,
Bloomfield, Windsor, Brookfield and Warren, and spreading southwest across the rest of the state Berlin, Danbury, Bristol, Colebrook,
Wooster, Chester, Fairfield, Farmington, Huntington, Litchfield,
Lyme, Saybrook, Southington, Thompson, Trumbull, Windham,
Granville and Monroe. In Indiana there were Guilford and Bennington, and at the Illinois spearhead the still Rebel-dominated
Collinsville. Back in New York settlers from Vermont transplanted
their home names of Rutland and Bennington. Classicism seemed on
the decline in these twenty years, with only Alexander and Camillus
among the new settlements in New York, and Illyria and the questionable swagger of Columbus in Ohio.

During these first two decades of the nineteenth century Ohio came
out of the condition of a sprawling territory into that of a great
state. From a population of about 50,000 at its admission, it expanded to one of 580,000 in 1820, becoming the fourth largest in
the union, larger than any of the states of New England from which
it took its aspect and tradition. The dominance of the Yankees did
not come from a preponderance of numbers. The northern third of
the state, being the old Western Reserve—jurisdiction over which
was ceded to the Territorial government in 1800—was very nearly
pure Yankee, the common farmhouse there being the Connecticut
"saltbox." The southern third, where the earliest Yankee settlements
had been made at and around Marietta, was overrun and conquered
by the Southerners. Between them the middle third was dominantly
of German derivation, some recently immigrated, the preponderance
from Pennsylvania and plentifully sprinkled with Scotch-Irish from
the Shenandoah Valley. As everywhere the Yankee and Rebel settlers
confronted each other with suspicion and contempt, the "enterprising Yankees fidgeting eternally for *improvements,* the long-sided
Kentuckians grumbling about elbow room."[28] The Frankfort (Ky.)
Commentator (March 2, 1800), reporting a murder committed by two

Yankee "adventurers," spoke for the whole South in transferring to Yankee parsimony its irritation at Yankee idealism:

> These two desperadoes are now somewhere in the western country, and will no doubt have the pleasure of shaking hands with many of their countrymen, whose hands like those at Botney Bay meet for the last time in their neighbors' pockets. Query—Would it not be proper for the people of the western states to instruct their representatives in Congress to pass some law to prevent the further importation or admission of Yankees, west of the Allegheny.[29]

The fidgety and pocketpicking New Englanders did, however, capture the state and define its policy, giving it a good educational system, always the mark of Yankee triumph over the Rebels. The Reverend Isaac Jennings, originally of Bennington, Vermont, devoted much of his life to setting up in Akron a primary and high school system which was widely copied throughout the state. Of wider influence was Caleb Atwater of North Adams, Massachusetts, who is commonly called the founder of Ohio's School System besides being, in his later life, a backer of the railroads against the canals, the first historian of Ohio, and probably the first advocate of the conservation of forests. He was "interested in almost everything except . . . making . . . money," and "lived and died a poor man."[30]

During these years between 1800 and 1820 Yankee characters and Yankee anecdotes passed into Ohio legend. Born about 1775 in Massachusetts—Boston and Springfield both claim him—John Chapman, better known as "Johnny Appleseed," tramped up and down the crude roads, planting apple trees with his hands, and with his voice roaring passages from Swedenborg. In the same first decade of the century a likewise well educated old gentleman from somewhere in Connecticut coveted a tract of 4,000 acres in Delaware County and combined Yankee humor and shrewdness in his way of getting it from the land sharks when it went up for auction. He appeared dressed as a tramp, and in the early part of the auction made himself conspicuous as an ignoramus, particularly in bidding against himself. When the tract he wanted came up, its value running well into thousands of dollars, the speculators agreed to let him hang himself. When, in the early bidding he raised his own bid to $1720, they stopped bidding and it was knocked down to him. To their astonishment he produced the money and refused to make a resale at a handsome profit.[31] Less noticeable was the coming of insignificant Owen Brown of Torrington, Connecticut. Yet in 1802 the Muse of History turned her head and looked when he moved to Hudson, Ohio, and set up a tannery, wherein his helper was his young son John.

This was the time of the organization of libraries in most of the towns in New England, and they sprang up accordingly in many of the towns of New York and Ohio. Most famous was the Coonskin Library of Marietta, established in 1804, the subscribers paying their subscriptions in coonskins which their agent, one Samuel Brown, carried to Boston and exchanged for the first fifty-one volumes.[32] One twelve-year-old subscriber, Thomas Ewing, "contributed ten Racoonskins—being all my hoarded wealth."[33]

In this period the leadership of the intellectual tradition was shifting from the pulpit to the bar, a change which was the more acceptable for being congenial also to the Southern Tradition. The lawyers were becoming a ruling class, its members commonly addressed as "Esquire" and putting on lugs accordingly. . . . "If a father had three sons," wrote Finley a little later, "and was able to give them an education, he selected the brightest for a lawyer, the next for a doctor, and the dullest . . . for a preacher."[34]

The shift of leadership from the clergy to the bar may or may not have been a sign of intellectual decline. There was no sign of it in Dr. Jones, a graduate of Brown, a lawyer, a doctor, and a man of personal charm who was showing, in 1805, a high contempt for the society of Marietta where he lived. ". . . He spent most of his time hunting and was quite intemperate. He often came in evenings when I was there, took off his moccasins, lay down with his feet to the fire and had me read to him—generally poetry of which he had several volumes."[35]

In 1820 the shadow of mediocrity was not yet visible. In the two decades then closing the Yankees had founded theological seminaries at Andover, Massachusetts (1805), and Bangor, Maine, (1816), besides Colgate College (1819) in New York, the University of Michigan (1817), and in Ohio, Ohio University (1804), Worthington College (1817), and the University of Cincinnati (1819). In the latter state they had conquered the Rebels and the Pennsylvanians culturally, and had imposed their stamp on them. A contemporary observer of the whole state says of all its people:

> They more naturally unite themselves in corporate unions . . . for public works and purposes. They have the same desire for keeping up schools, for cultivating psalmody, for settling ministers, and attending upon religious worship; and unfortunately the same disposition to dogmatize, to settle, not only their own faith, but that of their neighbour, and to stand resolutely, and dispute fiercely, for the slightest shade of difference of religious opinion. In short, in the tone of conversation, the ways of thinking and expressing thought upon all subjects, in the strong exercise of social inclination, expressing itself in habits of neighbourhood, to form villages, and live in them, in preference

to that sequestered and isolated condition, which a Kentuckian, under the name of 'range,' considers as desirable; in the thousand slight shades of manner, the details of which are too minute to be described, by most of these things, this is properly designated 'the Yankee state.'[36]

By 1820 Ohio was safe for Yankee idealism and Yankee crotchets. In the north, Michigan, under the territorial governorship, after 1813, of Lewis Cass of Exeter, New Hampshire, was yet sparsely settled, but was of almost pure New England blood. But Indiana, admitted in 1816 without a Yankee voice in its organization, seemed lost, and so did Illinois, admitted in 1818 with a Constitution merging those of Virginia and Kentucky, with the addition of the Prohibition of Slavery imposed by the Ordinance of 1787 under which the whole Northwest Territory was settled. Joshua Atwater of Westfield, Massachusetts, had settled in Madison County in 1809, and was teaching school there. Three Collins brothers were out from Collinsville, Connecticut, to anchor a Yankee salient at Collinsville, opposite St. Louis. Immediately they had set up a distillery, a sawmill, a cooper shop, a wagon shop, a blacksmith shop, a carpenter shop, a warehouse and a union meetinghouse which was used for both school and church. Soon after they had made this start, they came in some way under the baleful influence of Lyman Beecher's Temperance Campaign. Not only did they abandon the distillery but they chilled St. Louis by launching on the Mississippi a steamboat for the mutual trade and christening it with the frightening name of *Cold Water*. More congenial to the spirit of Southern Illinois in the early years was a letter written in 1820 by Gershom Flagg, late of Orwell, Vermont, now settled in Edwardsville, Illinois, to his kinsman Artemas Flagg back home:

> If you should wish to hear some large stories about the western Country read on. I raised about 5 or 6 waggon loads of watermellons this year many of which weighed 25 pounds each and I weighed one that weighed 29½ pounds. We had plenty of Melons of all kinds from the middle of July to the end of September. We feed our hogs great part of the time upon Melons, Squashes, & Pumpkins & cucumbers &c &c. The hogs now live upon Acorns which here grow as large as hens eggs almost.[37]

This kind of letter was congenial to the Rebel control of Illinois in 1820. But it was ominous also. For it fetched the Yankees.

Actually they were coming in increasing numbers after the end of the War in '15, and particularly after the cold year of 1816, called "Eighteen-hundred-and-froze-to-death," when New England had frost in every month. But it was the Erie Canal, opening in '25, that brought the idealistic and militant hordes who, though they rarely equalled the Rebels in numbers, yet gradually molded them, if not to their ways, then at least to their broader political policies. Between 1820 and 1840 Greater New England still sent relatively little fifth column into Indiana to undermine the Hoosiers from Kentucky, Tennessee and Carolina. But it captured Michigan and occupied the southern third of it, began competing effectively for the control of Illinois, bulged up into Wisconsin as far as Watertown and Madison, crossed the Great River to be a small minority among the dominant Rebels in Eastern Iowa, and in the persons of the leaders of the Mormons, sent a long and unquiet salient out across the Southern State of Missouri to Independence and the Territory northerly. In these two decades also, the Yankees began opening western flanks by establishing two new frontiers edging in from ships on the Pacific, a large and loosely held one sprinkled from San Francisco southward among the Spanish rancheros of California, and a single, missionary post at Walla Walla in what was going to be Washington Territory.

During these two decades, perhaps more than any others, we find the religious, political and intellectual idealism of New England high among the motives of pioneering. Lyman Beecher spoke for the age when he declared in 1835 ". . . the religious and political destiny of our nation is to be decided in the West." Population "is rushing in like the waters of the flood, demanding for its moral preservation the immediate and universal action of those institutions which discipline the mind and arm the conscience and the heart." And later in the same appeal he uttered that warning to Greater New England whose prophecy we now see partially fulfilled in our campaigns against education gathering out of Beecher's own Ohio, together with Wisconsin and strong elements in Indiana and Illinois:

> We must educate! We must educate! or we must perish in our own prosperity. . . . If, in our haste to be rich and mighty, we outrun our literary and religious institutions, they will never overtake us: or only come up after the battle of liberty is fought and lost, as spoils to grace the victory, and as resources of inexorable despotism for the perpetuity of our bondage. And let no man at the East quiet himself, and dream of liberty, whatever may become of the West. Our alliance of blood, and political institutions, and common interests, is such, that we cannot stand aloof in the hour of her calamity, should it ever come. Her destiny is our destiny, and the day that her gallant ship goes down, our little boat sinks in the vortex![38]

Typical of the Yankee method of migration was the Constitution drawn up by a congregation in East Poultney, Vermont, before the greater part of it with a few additions from other towns, altogether thirty shareholders in the Company, set out in 1836 under the leadership of their minister to found what became Vermontville, Michigan. ". . . A pious and devoted emigration," said the preamble, "is one of the most efficient means, in the hands of God, in removing the darkness which hangs over a great portion of the valley of the Mississippi." And a few sentences later they combined with their idealism the Yankee practical motive—"We believe that a removal to the west may be a means of promoting our temporal interest." The record of this group is in the pure pattern of Yankee migration and settlement. They sent a committee of three ahead with money to purchase land, lay out and clear the village around a square, each investor to have a ten-acre homelot located thereon "as well situated as those of any of his neighbors," besides a farm of 160 acres outside. Probably early in '37, the population arrived by Erie Canal, steamboat and wagon. By that autumn they were churched and all under cover, with a school flourishing. In '43 they founded their own Vermontville Academy whose tuition was $2.50 a quarter, board and lodging to be had in the town at between $1.00 and $1.25 a week.[39]

In this period Chicago—named for a "pungent onion" that used to grow in the swamp around the mouth of the River—was getting a start in that butchering which was to typify the future rather than the present. More characteristic of the '30's are two records left by pioneers who reached Log City, presently Galesburg, Illinois, in '37 and '36 respectively. The first is the diary of Jerusha Farnham, originally of Andover, Connecticut, subsequently a schoolmistress in New York State. At this time she is the wife of Eli Farnham who with four other families made up a covered wagon train that jolted out from Tully, New York, to help found Log City.

> Maternal meeting this afternoon. Here is an interesting society of females. . . . There are in this neighborhood two female prayer meetings, one the married and one for the unmarried ladies, a maternal association and sewing society. . . .

> . . . Received today four numbers of the Advocate [a publication devoted to the rescue of fallen women] from sister Martha. I've unfolded them all. . . . Well, we must have a moral Reform Society here in Galesburg.

> . . . My dear husband's birthday aged 34 years. How short the life of man upon the earth! How swiftly it passes away. Oh, that we may so number our days that we may apply our hearts to wisdom. This has been a very warm day, rainy and some thunder. Mrs. Buckingham has been here to-day assisting Eli about making brooms.[40]

The other memoir was by a settler at Log City in 1836 written in his great age. It contains a paragraph which, if we discount its rose glasses of antiquity, comes close to expressing the central spirit of New England culture in these '30's and '40's which were in Religion its last and in Humanitarianism probably its greatest flowering:

> I hope you will be able to get from what I have written a tolerable idea of Log City and its people. For myself I desire to say that I think there never was another company of people living together for one purpose who lived together so happily and worked with such mighty energy as the company of men and women who were the pioneers in the establishing of Galesburg and the great Knox College. They had marvelous faith and their works corresponded. . . .[41]

Incidentally, it is to be observed that Knox College, founded at this time (1837) by the Reverend George Gale of Adams, New York, who gave his name to the town, was a hotbed of the Anti-slavery movement, as was Illinois College, founded in '29 by the Yale Band—seven young graduates of Yale Theological Seminary.[42] Illinois by 1840 had three main lines of its Underground Railroad, and many branches. Illinois's first Anti-slavery Society was organized in '33, only two years after William Lloyd Garrison founded *The Liberator* and one year after the founding of the New England Anti-Slavery Society, and by '38 there were at least seven societies in northern Illinois.[43] Unquestionably the Yankees were moving in, and the fight was soon going to wax ugly.

In this period Wisconsin was in the ornamental throes of early settlement, the rumor of its riches being brought East by the 4,000 soldiers of the Black Hawk War in '32. The landoffices opened in '34. In '36 Caleb Blodgett of Vermont, New York, Ohio and Illinois arrived and, claiming 20,000 acres at a point south central in the Territory, hitched up his ox team and plowed a furrow around 100 acres in the virgin forest, an "improvement" sufficient to base his whole claim. Early the next year the New England Emigrating Company, organized in Colebrook, New Hampshire, paid Blodgett $2,500 for about a third of his claim. During the rest of the year the Company moved out and, while living in a boarding house, laid out the village with a prophetic "College Street," and put up buildings for the Church and the School which they at once called the Academy. The village became Beloit and the "College" Beloit College. The same process was substantially repeated in scores of other towns, the Yankees moving in shrewdly, establishing at once their school and church, and soon after their Academy, Lyceum, Magazine, Improvement Society, or some combination of these. In Wisconsin their chief rivals, who in many places outnumbered them, were not the Rebels, but the freshly immigrated Germans who generally stood with them against the Rebels, and whose offense was rarely more than making a merry holiday of the Sabbath. The Yankees had little trouble in getting early control of the Territory. By 1836 there were eleven private schools, not counting those in the larger towns of Milwaukee, Kenosha and Sheboygan.

Madison was being settled during the same years as Beloit, and its lore contains an example of libertarianism not rare on the frontier. Roseline Peck was the wife of Eben Peck of Shoreham, Vermont, and she had a "fiery, caustic wit." In 1837 she rode into Madison on an Indian pony, the first white woman there, and opened a tavern which became a political center. Whether before or after her establishment in Madison, her husband one day walked out and vanished without trace; and many years later he was living with a new wife and five children in Texas.

In Iowa the Yankees remained a negligible minority longer than they did in Illinois. In affirmation of the import of this minority one Allan from Maine challenged to combat one Points of Kentucky who was the champion of the region. The fight was "long and desperate," before a mostly Rebel audience who were guilty of no unfairness to Allan. Those being the days when fair fighting included gouging, biting and tearing, each man was "a mangled mass" when Allan admitted he was done. Both mangled masses were promptly arrested.[44]

The early Yankee frontier in California was not typical of the rest of the Great Migration, for most of its leaders married the daughters of rich Spaniards and went native. Exceptional was Jedediah Smith from somewhere in New York State, who went west to become a Mountain Man and in 1826 led out a group of traders, the first party to reach California by land. Exceptional also was Thomas Larkin of Charlestown, Massachusetts, who reached California in '32, was the secret agent of the U.S. government, publicly the enthusiastic correspondent of many Eastern periodicals, and so the first Booster of California.

Besides the energetic Planned Efficiency of settlements by groups or "companies," the early establishment of Churches, Schools and miscellaneous Improvement Societies, the easy practice of Desertion and Bigamy, the sharp and barely legal methods of acquiring Claims, the continuous war with the Rebels, pugilistic, economic and political, the issuance of lurid propaganda to bring out more settlers, besides all these another common incident of Yankee pioneering in the west was the establishment of usually evanescent missions to the Indians. Extreme among them was the Whitman Mission set up in Walla Walla in 1836, the first Yankee foothold in the Oregon Country. In 1847 the Indians murdered Marcus Whitman, his wife and twelve associates at the Mission, and the foothold was for the moment deleted.

Evidential always of the ascendance of Yankee culture was the sprouting of institutions of higher learning:

In Maine, Colby College (1813).

In Massachusetts, Wheaton College (1834), Mt. Holyoke (1837), Boston University (1839).

In Connecticut, Trinity College (1823) and Wesleyan University (1831).

In the still Rebel precinct of Indiana, the University of Indiana (1820), Hanover College (1827), Wabash College (1832), Franklin College (1834).

In Illinois, Shurtleff College (1827), Illinois College (1828), Lebanon Seminary (later McKendree College) (1828), Jacksonville Female Seminary (1835), Knox College (1837).

In Michigan, Kalamazoo College (1836).

In Iowa, Loras College (1832).

In New York, Hobart College (1822).

In Ohio, Kenyon College (1824), Western Reserve (1826), Dennison College (1831), Lane Theological Seminary (1832), and Oberlin (1833), first permanent coeducational college in the United States, first college in the United States to admit Negroes, more than Harvard or any other college of Greater New England the intellectual center and standard-bearer of the Evangelical and Reform Spirit of the age.

In the next duodecade, 1840-60, expansion accelerated under the urge of awakening nationalism or "Manifest Destiny" and every kind of leadership. "Fly," called Horace Greeley in the *New York Tribune*, "fly, scatter through the country, to the great west. It is your destination!" In Boston Edward Everett Hale preached a sermon on "The Christian Duty of Emigrants." The Yankee tide swelled out to include the rest of Wisconsin, the southern half of Minnesota, the rest of Iowa, eastern and southern Kansas, most of Colorado, and the Mormon salient up across Utah to the Great Salt Lake. California increased from 90,000 to 380,000, about equally from Yankee and Rebel immigration, accomplished its revolution against the Spanish in 1848 and was admitted as a state in plenty of time to stand with the North in the Civil War. On the Oregon frontier, Portland, Salem and half a dozen other towns were settled in Oregon proper, Seattle and Olympia in the new Washington Territory, while in the '50's the general expansion moved inland against the Indians, repopulating Walla Walla where the Whitmans had been murdered, and crossing the mountains to settle Wordensville, afterwards Missoula, Montana.

These were the years when the Second or Humanitarian Revival of Puritanism was at its height, while at the same time the forces of Greed and other forms of Individualism that were going to contract the Puritan Sky were becoming noticeable. Cheating by land speculators—often with the bribed connivance of Government agents—in the matter of the "improvements" necessary to make a claim of land valid became common practice. Houses, the chief "improvement" required, passed from pioneer to pioneer, sometimes for as little as $2. At first they were cabins that had to be taken down and rebuilt by each new "homesteader," but eventually they became shacks that roamed the navigable prairie on wheels.[45] Chicago had been boosted and boomed, had its Philip Armour and its Gustavus Swift, was already that gargantuan abattoir whose scent, though almost all of the founders were Yankees, was never, in Holbrook's phrase, "then or later," going "to remind any New Englander even faintly of home." The new Illinois Central Railroad—typical of many—had a grant of 2,300,000 acres in the state to dispose of, and its false and seductive brochures, complete with Victorian art and poetry, were the beginning of the great institution of American advertising. In all of this, together with Wage Slavery now appearing in a few industrial centers of New England, and which we shall notice later, we have intimations of the Big Business and the Robber Barons of the post-Civil War time.

The most lurid evidence of the decline of Puritanism was of course the '49 gold panic which was mostly in the '50's. There were 102 "Mining and Trading" Companies formed in Massachusetts alone. In '50 there were about 11,000 people in California censused as born in geographical New England. In '60 it was about 33,000. This does not take into account the western states of Greater New England, now much more populous than Old New England and sending out their sons in proportion. On shipboard the companies always showed that they were Yankees, having sermons, prayer meetings, lectures, bands of music, a complement of doctors and sufficient whiskey "for medical purposes." Boston's North Western Mining and Trading Company was composed of twenty-two Brahmins, including Charles Francis Adams, Jr., the historian, and all wore identical uniforms.

Very few of the Forty-niners got rich on gold, and the bulk of them lapsed into the unpredatory sanity and Equalitarianism of their culture. Some of them became distinguished men, including Adams and Hubert Howe Bancroft, historians, and Stephen J. Field, brother of Cyrus, appointed to the Supreme Court by Lincoln. But it cannot be denied that out of Greater New England somewhere between one and two hundred thousand Yankees panted westward seeking, not malleable soil or comfortable living, but riches. It could not have happened in the eighteenth century, let alone the seventeenth. Furthermore, another hundred thousand more or less did it again in the Pike's Peak gold rush of '59 when Colorado absorbed 20,000 Yankees, not counting those who went back home before the census takers of '60 could catch them.

Besides these direct and relatively healthy expressions of Individualism, we see it also appearing in this age in a subtler form that eventually was going to pervert its millions. The old Spiritual Equality of every man before God, including the secular extension of it which was one of the special Yankee traits, was tending, under the privations of the Frontier, to produce that superficial and conscious Equalitarianism which became the deadliest kind of Individualism whose aim is not to get my self ahead but to draw every other person down to my ignorant level. There is both a remnant of intellectual standards and an omen of mediocrity in the following record of life in a typical Ohio community in the 1850's:

> In a rural community, the necessity for cooperation and the desire for sociability, regardless of differences in capabilities, insured a relatively democratic society.
>
> There was no class founded on wealth, no one distinguished by either learning, ancestry, achievement, or pretentious estate, —we were all on the same level, wore the same home-made clothes, read or studied in dimly lighted rooms or by the light of wood fires, looked each other in the face when we met at each other's doors, all unconscious of that restless kingdom known as society, and in blessed, happy ignorance of what is now called refinement and culture.[46]

Here in a mind that still remembers distinction is the seed of that dead level of jealous ignorance that is ready to follow any ignorant leadership—the Know Nothing movement at the time of the record and the McCarthy movement today—that is eager to identify education with whatever may be the current social danger.

But stronger than the rapacity and the predatory jealousy, the old religious and intellectual motives were still dominant. A large share of the Yankee letters home from California evince more interest in the country, the people and the Spanish culture than in gold. There were probably more Yankees troubled by the Depravity of the gold-rustling life than there were practicing the Depravity.

Meanwhile, back east the culture was taking over the states where it had been weak. In Indiana James Whitcomb of Windsor, Vermont, and especially Caleb Mills of Andover, Massachusetts, put through a good educational system against the Southern majority. In Iowa the Yankee minority organized in 1844 the state Anti-Slavery Society,[47] and after the Kansas-Nebraska Bill in '54, the Southern majority, formerly six to one, was cut down by heavy immigration from the North. By '60 Iowa was a Republican state and the Rebels were leaving.[48] Meanwhile, in the curtain raiser of the Civil War in Bloody Kansas, the Yankee Fanatics had both physically and legally beaten the Rebel Ruffians, and in '58 Kansas came in with a free constitution.

Meanwhile the colleges and universities continued to be laid as the foundation stones of Yankee culture:

In New York, University of Buffalo (1846), University of Rochester (1850), St. Lawrence University (1856), Bard College (1860).

In Ohio, Ohio Wesleyan (1842), Baldwin-Wallace (1845), Otterbein (1847), Heidelberg (1850), Hiram (1850), Antioch (1853), Western College for Women (1853), Lake Erie (1856), Wilberforce (1856), University of Dayton (1858).

In Michigan, Michigan State (1855).

In Indiana, Evansville (1854).

In Illinois, Olivet (1844), Hillsdale (1844), Rockford (1847), Illinois Wesleyan (1850), Northwestern University (1851), Hope (1852), Monmouth (1853), Eweka (1855), Lake Forest (1857), Quincy (1860).

In Wisconsin, Carroll (1846), Beloit (1846), Lawrence (1847), University of Wisconsin (1848).

In Minnesota, University of Minnesota (1851).

In Iowa, Iowa Wesleyan (1842), Central (1843), Clarke (1843), Grinnell (1846), University of Iowa (1847), Coe (1851), University of Dubuque (1852).

In Kansas, Baker University (1858).

In California, University of Santa Clara (1851), University of San Francisco (1855).

In Oregon, Willamette (1842), Linfield (1857).

In Washington, Whitman (1859).

Beginning at the end of this period and running over into the '60's of the next, we have in comic opera form the solution of a problem that was universal on the Frontier, the need of Women. The problem was particularly grave in Washington Territory where in 1860 the ratio of women to men was as one to nine, all women above fourteen were married, and male fashions called for the hirsute and unwashed aspect of the Grizzly Bear. Asa Mercer, a native of Illinois, himself blessed with tolerable looks and charm, arrived in Seattle in '61 with an assignment to help clear a site for the forthcoming University of Washington. Immediately conscious of the Great Female Drought, he saw a vision, took ship for Boston, went to the mill town of Lowell which was in a state of depression and unemployment and, carefully concealing the fell purpose of matrimony but emphasizing the high wages to be had for school teaching, persuaded eleven undoubtedly virtuous maidens to take ship with him around the Horn, delivered them in Seattle on May 16, 1864 at midnight, received a powerful welcome in the lurid light of lamps, fires and torches, and in a short time ten of the girls were married.

Asa then returned to Boston for a further haul, this time with a contract signed by divers males, each of whom promised to pay him $300 for one wife to be delivered in full youth, comeliness and virtue. This time Mercer ranged up and down the east coast from New Hampshire to Maryland and collected a body of female "war orphans" variously estimated between 300 and 700. Complications, with much corruption and comedy, between the White House, Mercer and divers maritime tycoons, ensued in the matter of getting the whole ship needful to transport so large a complement. At last all was in readiness to sail from New York, when the *New York Herald* learned of the project and publicized it with the intimations that the war orphans were being shipped to populate the brothels of Puget Sound. Most of the maidens instantly resigned and all was to do again.

At last, in January, '66, the filthy troop steamship *Continental* pulled out of New York Harbor with what was probably about 400 A-1 wives for Washington Territory, and part of the epic is the miracle these Yankee girls instantly accomplished in putting the old hulk into civilized commission, themselves scrubbing the decks and the bulkheads, instituting the religious and intellectual routines that characterized all New England emigrating parties, and at least once taking over the galley and feeding themselves on gingerbread. An artist from *Harper's Magazine* went along to leave a fantastic record of the elevated charm of life on the old trooper, along with a text which entitled Mercer "The Moses of the Exodus from New England." After endless complications, the cargo finally shredded into Seattle in small, weary and undaunted groups during June and July, each maiden determined personally to shed the light of religion, virtue and truth among the tall forest shadows of the Northwest. In July Mercer himself married one of them, Miss Annie Stephens, and it is to this day a distinction in the environs of Seattle to be able to claim descent from one of the Mercer Girls.

Generally, between 1840 and 1860 the Yankees were rounding out Greater New England and consolidating the culture, as events presently proved, for the united front of the Civil War. Geographically it was 3,000 miles long by five hundred deep, with a population of about 14,000,000, almost half of the whole country—for the cities generally had not yet deserted the Culture for the industrial pseudo-culture—and within this 14,000,000, Old New England's population of about 3,000,000 was an archaic remnant. Almost everywhere the wilderness was subdued, the stumps gone, the hills rolling under the green carpet that man lays, tufted with his farm houses and his ornamental trees. Wealth was increasing faster than population, and besides the red, yellow or white frame houses, now generally of Classical or Greek Revival design, in almost every village four or five families were living pretentiously in one of the big new mid-Victorian brick cubes with the high front steps and the cupola on top.

But the people in the brick cubes were still the same as the people in the little farm houses. They all spoke the idiom of the soil, and they were all of the Puritan tradition that put the general good above the private advantage. In the cultural contest with the South in the states north of the Ohio, they had won in part because of this virtue. Holbrook sums up the contest:

> The pinchpenny habit in small matters was one of the many things about Yankees which tended to make them unpopular. The man from the South was likely, almost certain, to be hospitable and generous to individuals, either friends or strangers. He was lavish with his liquors, his food, his time; for even if he had little liquor or food, he simply had to live up to the code set by the wealthy planters. If he had nothing more than a mess of turnip greens, they were cooked and served with a flourish.
>
> On the other hand, "the Yankee"—so said Governor Thomas Ford of Illinois, who was no Yankee—"was the most liberal in contributing to whatever was for the public benefit. Is a school-house to be built, he wrote, a road to be built, a school teacher or a minister to be maintained, or taxes to be paid for the honor or support of government, the northern man is never found wanting."[49]

In the people of Illinois, as in those of New York, Ohio, Indiana, Michigan, Wisconsin, Minnesota, Iowa and Kansas, the culture was no longer pinched among the rocks of Connecticut and Vermont. On the old hilltops, the towns of the ancestors, the cellarholes, the highways and the walls, were already buried into creases under the leaves of fifty to a hundred years. The autumn silences were populous with the ghosts of the ancient culture. But the living souls of it had gone down into the valleys, and in a great army they had carried it westward to spread out over a new and fabulous land. In Old New

England where the Movement started, and all along its course, and in the branches and twigs of its destinations, as strong as the movement itself the force of a new and Third Puritanism, with its old flanking Heresies of Reason and Emotion, was playing out its drama.

In the post-war debauch at the end of the eighteenth century, the condition and prospects of Puritanism were probably dimmer than in the spree following King Philip's War a century earlier, and in terms of professed irreligion even darker than in that following the Civil War three-quarters of a century later. The nearest comparison would be with the orgy following the First World War a century and a quarter later, the sophomoric Materialism and naughty Paganism of the 1920's, the state called Infidelity in the vocabulary of the eighteenth century. Yale in the 1790's "was in a most ungodly state. . . . Most of the students were sceptical, and rowdies were plenty. Wine and liquors were kept in many rooms; intemperance, profanity, gambling, and licentiousness were common."[50] The individualism of the French Revolution was still fashionable with the young, in its foppish phase that aimed to "amuse, perplex and beguile," its sophomoric sophistication professing that "the end of creation is animal pleasure." The students formed enlightened societies in which they addressed each other as Voltaire, Rousseau, d'Alembert, even more daringly as Lucifer, Beelzebub, Belial. In 1799 not over five Yale undergraduates professed Christianity, and there was but one church member in the graduating class of 1800.[51]

At Harvard, paganism and licentiousness were also prevalent, though not so unanimously. There the greater menace, greater because it had infected the Faculty and the Trustees, was the Liberal Religion of Reason, Heresy alike to Puritans, Antinomians and Old Calvinists, spreading variously, as we have seen, from the Intellectual Arminianism of Mayhew to the Deism which denied any personal God at all. Where The River was Infidel, The Bay was Heretical. For many years Harvard avoided meeting the issue, though all the time it was pressing in from the periphery of the intellectual suburbs. As far back as the late 1740's Mayhew had denied the Trinity. In 1785 the Episcopalians of King's Chapel in Boston had accepted the Unitarianism of their minister James Freeman. In 1792 congregations in Portland and Saco proclaimed themselves Unitarian, and in 1800 the ancient First Church of Plymouth did the same. Still the great Liberals in Cambridge steered shy of the dread title.

In 1803 young William Ellery Channing, Harvard '98, moved in from his native Newport and was ordained in the Federal Street Church, Boston. He was known as a selfless and saintly Christian and a great systematic Liberal, though he also resisted classification because he wanted Christianity to remain free and catholic, not straightened towards bigotry within any sect. But the division between Liberals and both Puritans and Old Calvinists was already extreme beyond reconciliation, and authority at last must recognize it. In 1805 the Harvard Trustees courageously elected an avowed Unitarian, the Reverend Henry Ware, to the definitive Hollis Chair of Theology. Thus the University at the Bay aligned itself with awful doctrines which denied the Trinity, the Divinity of Christ, Original Sin, Free Grace, looked with doubt on Universal Depravity and Eternal Punishment, and espoused Free Will and a God of Mercy in human terms.

But already in 1805 a movement more inclusive than any at the Bay was well on its way. In the ordinary, historical cycle of things, the Revival of 1800, the Second Great Awakening, had been getting under way on schedule. Generally, our post-war debauches, with the exception of the sad little fiasco of still-born paganism in 1946, have lasted for not less than ten nor more than twenty years. Even while the bad little students at Yale were parading as Great and Infidel Encyclopedists, and the Enlightened Harvard Faculty was swinging into Heretical Reason, the forces of the new age were gathering among them all. Despite the wicked goings-on at the colleges, there was an increasing popular return to the churches during the 1790's, especially the Methodist Churches in response to the barnstorming of Jesse Lee, a tall Virginian, who started talking on the Boston Common in 1790, and in 1796 there were three thousand Yankees in the Wesleyan fold. In 1795 Timothy Dwight, grandson of Edwards and follower in a fashion of his New England Theology, was elected President of Yale; and in '96 he preached a short series of sermons in the College Chapel which shook Yale, and behind Yale New England. Soon thereafter he began his long Series of 173 sermons, *Theology; Explained and Defended,* which he recommenced every four years thereafter in order that no student should miss any of them. The tree began to drop its fruit in 1802 when a third of the students are said to have professed conversion.[52] Thereafter,

> Wherever students were found—in their rooms, in the chapel, in the hall, in the college yard, in their walks about the city— the reigning impression was, "Surely God is in this place!" The salvation of the soul was the great subject of thought, of conversation, of absorbing interest.[53]

Whatever similar tendency may have been stirring at Harvard was nipped by the appointment of Ware to the great Chair of Theology in 1805, for the Unitarians were against Revivals. But actually this intellectual resistance quickened the emotional swing of history. Jedediah Morse and other members of the faculty seceded to found, with Dwight's help, Andover Theological Seminary, which thereafter erupted Revivals about evenly with Yale, and together they comprised the parent religious volcanoes of the New Time.

During the next forty years, Yale had fifteen separate revivals,[54] and Dartmouth, Williams, Amherst, and the new Yankee colleges out through Greater New England were close behind. The procedure in all of these academic revivals was the same and was in distinction from the hullabaloo of Methodism and the Western Camp Meetings which often competed with them. Converted students conducted Prayer Meetings in every dormitory each evening, and the unregenerate who were concerned, if they were not duly "wounded" there, could usually go to more intellectual Inquiry Meetings held by the members of the Faculty, sometimes by the President. Oberlin, the collegiate leader of many of the chief trends of the day, had always a high record for Revivals. Knox seems to have stirred one up every winter as part of its regular curriculum!

In this new and evangelical age, the currents of Puritanism and its flanking Heresies, which we saw as two in the seventeenth century and expanded to three in the eighteenth, somtimes lose their sharp distinctions and blend into each other, while all alike are colored by a new influence which is the peculiar force of the age. This new force is Romanticism, representing the general trend of Western Culture, and to a degree of mankind. It is the experience of continuously arrested Mysticism, the Mystical impulse that never quite reaches full perception. It is Aspiration and Motion, always sensing distant truth but never grasping it. It believes in Perfectibility, in Perfection which may not be currently realized but is capable of realization, the past perfection of Old Forgotten Far Off Things, the future perfection that can be attained through Faith and Effort. Though the aims, the ultimate Truth and Perfection, of Romanticism are not immediately and sensuously present, they are none the less concrete. Romanticism does not address itself to the obvious surfaces but to the unique details of objects and persons, and especially the inner significances which the unique details imply to the Imagination. In addressing Society its interest is in all Individual Men, present or absent, not at all in Abstract Man. In society in the large it sees, not its surfaces but its possibilities, its contained intention that every individual can and will be raised from his wretchedness into a state of physical, moral and spiritual repose.

Romanticism is Perfectionist and Concrete; it is also Motile. And, as befits these qualities, it is Emotional. It is the emotion of travel and discovery, the exhilaration of possibility and expectation. It is also the emotion of perception, the emotion of detailed Imaginative Perception which is poetic. But while it remains Romanticism and is short of realized Mysticism, this perception is limited to particular things, and the full perception, the universal clairvoyance which is Great Art and Puritanism, is yet beyond it. Being frustrate of the full realization toward which it is moving, it is more emotional than is the wide and static aesthetic Perception of true Puritanism.

In moral expression Romanticism becomes Humanitarianism, a passionate concern for the Perfectibility and Salvation of every individual, and—the same in collectivized form—an equally passionate concern for the Utopian Perfectibility and Salvation of Society as a whole. Into this warm and concrete stream, Eighteenth-Century Liberalism, or Intellectual Arminianism, with its wide and cool Natural Reason dealing with a wide and cool Abstraction called Natural Man, disappears utterly, even in its mature form of Unitarianism which, along with every other trend in the new age, is going to substitute concrete Humanitarianism for abstract Humanism. The Social Objectivity of the Eighteenth Century, which directed itself upon Principles and overcame Religion during the Decline, is now going to direct itself upon actual Individuals and groups of actual Individuals. Old Calvinism with its Legal Arminianism is no longer going to rest smug in its own righteousness, but is going to set out to tear the beams out of its neighbors' eyes in the interest of this same Salvation of the Individual and Perfection of Society.

Antinomianism, the old Heresy or Error of Emotion, is going to get mixed up with Legal Arminianism in the pursuit of a new Ideal, not simply of the joyful Saving of myself but the moral perfecting of myself. The convert under Revivalism will no longer be overcome with repentance for his Self-centeredness, his Original Sin, his Alienation from God, but for his particular antisocial acts, his drunkenness, his adulteries, his lies. His determination for the future will be not only to love God but to behave himself respectably according to the book, partly, perhaps chiefly, to accomplish his own Salvation, but in part also to accomplish for its own sake an Ideal of his own Perfection, and at the same time to remove temptation from his Neighbor and to bring nearer that social Utopia in which all temptations, all sins and miseries will cease. Finally, and perhaps most significantly, the clairvoyant Perception at the center of proper Puritanism will be delicately colored by this feeling of human perfectibility. Over Third Puritanism there will lie a faint rosy light, something slightly anthropomorphic and suggestive of moral effort, something ever so mildly Arminian.

Much and conflicting authority tells us how the Romantic Movement reached America from Europe. It is said to have had something to do with the great Individualists of the French Revolution whose names we saw sported by the enlightened boys of Yale; yet, while it is true that in the '90's New England was beginning to hear of Jefferson, yet the French Revolution, its "French Infidelity" and its excesses were already discredited in America, even by the Democrats— then called Republicans. We are told that our Romanticism is imported from German Romanticism, and when the American Transcendentalists begin to occupy the stage, thirty years after the beginning of the play, that will be true as to them; but for the period around 1800, Coleridge is just beginning to import German Romanticism into England, the *Lyrical Ballads* are just published (1798), will not be published in America (Philadelphia) for another two years (1802), and it is a fairly safe guess that German Romanticism has absolutely nothing to do with Timothy Dwight, his evangelical sermons after '96, and with the sudden and astonishing effect they had on all of New England.

In literary terms, of course, we trace the English Romantic Movement along a line running from Thomson up through Collins, Gray, Shenstone and Chatterton, to positive expression in Blake, Cowper, Burns, Coleridge and Wordsworth, and so on this side into Bryant, Whittier and Longfellow. But English romantic poetry was in 1800 no more upon us than was German Romanticism. Timothy Dwight was a prominent Hartford Wit, and the Hartford Wits had heard of Shenstone. Yet so far as appears, he was all Pope to them, and neither Trumble, Humphries nor Barlow ever said a critical word that wasn't stolen from the good old Augustan cupboard. Timothy Dwight's father, to be sure—a giant of six feet four who could hold his doll wife, Edwards' daughter, straight out on the palm of his hand—Timothy Dwight, senior, like other Yankees of the Revolutionary time, was known for his "sensibility," and "sensibility" was one of the words by means of which the earlier romantics —notably Walpole and Shenstone—began to edge out of the Age of Reason back toward an age of honest emotion. But that is a pretty slim transition on which to found one of the two or three epic movements of this country.

American Romanticism was a force which had been gathering here subterraneously for a long time before 1800, as is proven by the explosive force with which it spread once it was released. A case might be made for the beginning of it in Franklin's curiosity about nature, or in Edwards' slightly earlier natural observations and his records of them. We might even go back to Edward Taylor's flowers and bees at Westfield. But the fact is that the Romantic Movement in America was only latterly related to either Nature or Literature. It was originally Humanitarian, and as such it was emergent out of the dominant abstract Humanism well back in the eighteenth century at about the time that English Literary Romanticism was also emergent. The ferment of it was working in the Universal Atonement of the New England Theology, and in the humanly utopian eschatology of Universalism, all well back in the 1750's. Certainly it was present in Hopkins' liberation of his specific slaves, and in the general movement of Emancipation. Humanitarianism was also stirring in England at the time, and either trend may have influenced the other. The simple truth is that it was a major World Movement and, like the "Birth" of *Homo Sapiens,* it occurred everywhere, and it seems petty to give it less than a planetary habitation and a name.

As in the early eighteenth century the First Great Awakening simmered for thirty years of random religious activity before Edwards integrated it in the Second Puritanism, so now the Second Great Awakening is going to boil along for a quarter of a century in a diffuse Humanitarianism and miscellaneous Religiosity before a new genius sends a creative light through it and forms it into a Third Puritanism. As already intimated, President Timothy Dwight of Yale must be given the credit of firing the first guns of the new Movement. He was a man of many small and facile talents, great stature, great snobbery, great conceit, great powers of self-propagation—"Particularly, I have coveted Reputation, and influence, to a degree which I am unable to justify"; altogether, in spite of his profession of his grandfather's Puritanism—Total Depravity, Predestined Election and all—altogether a man whom it is difficult to accredit with being a Christian at all.

And yet it was Dwight more than any other who took the tradition of the Eighteenth Century and gave it the turn and the new direction which became the Nineteenth. In 1798, while he was continuing the great series of sermons on theology that were going to set off the Revival in Yale, he took the lead in the formation of the Missionary Society of Connecticut, its purpose "to Christianize the heathen in North America, and to support and promote Christian knowledge in the new settlements within the United States." The Massachusetts Missionary Society was founded the next year, with the support of several local groups, including the "Boston Female Society for promoting the Diffusion of Christian Knowledge"; and thereafter similar organizations sprang up rapidly in Rhode Island, New Hampshire, Maine and Vermont. After 1800 all of these home societies had missionaries itinerating in the West, both among the Indians and in the new settlements. South of the Ohio the Rebel aspect of the Revival which was then roaring up to its peak in camp meetings such as the great Cane Ridge fracas in Kentucky in 1801 when 300[55] supposed ministers were exhorting 20,000 supposed people at once, the "slain" lay all about among the tree stumps, most of the living had "the jerks," and a diarist "saw at least five hundred swept down in a moment, as if a battery of a thousand guns had been opened upon them, and then immediately followed shrieks and shouts that rent the very heavens."[56] The Yankee missionaries of course had little to do with this gala Antinomianism, but pursued their more objective efforts to convert people in private or in small meetings. In 1809 the Connecticut Society had 23 missionaries itinerating about the West, riding vast circuits through the wilderness to preside over the little congregations they established. In 1814 there were 43 of them. In 1824 the Massachusetts Society had about 200. Meanwhile the Presbyterians, Baptists and Methodists were doing comparable work. In New York and Ohio appropriate Associations and Conferences were formed. By about 1820 the spade work for home missions was over, and the vast and slow ramification into every hovel and slum was beginning. The distribution of Bibles had kept pace. In 1812-13 and 1814-15 Samuel J. Mills, a Williams student from Kent, Connecticut, travelled 10,000 miles as a preaching missionary up and down the Ohio and Mississippi Valleys where he found shockingly few Bibles in the settlements. Through his efforts the American Bible Society was organized in 1816, and by 1821 had distributed 140,000 copies of Holy Scripture.

Meanwhile the Humanitarian urge of the Revival looked to larger fields than the domestic Reprobate. During the first decade of the nineteenth century, the same Samuel Mills just mentioned, along with a considerable group of other students at Williams, met at a haystack and formed a secret society, each member pledged to missionary service. Most of them went on to Andover Theological Seminary, where others joined them in the project. In 1810, through their urgency, the American Board of Commissioners for Foreign Missions was formed—Timothy Dwight being one of the Commissioners—and by the following year a fund of over $40,000 was raised. In 1812 five young men were ordained in Salem, and presently they set sail for India. On the way out two of them, Judson and Rice, though they were on different ships, turned Baptist separately from study of the Scriptures, and were duly received by the English Baptist congregation in Calcutta. The next year Rice returned to the United States, and through his efforts Baptist Missionary work, both domestic and foreign, was presently abreast of the earlier Congregational and Presbyterian leadership.

Like Missions, many of the other great Reforms of the century were intimated in the first two decades. At the end of the Revolution Noah Webster called attention to the low state of *Public Education,* publishing his *On the Education of American Youth,* a blast against the influence of Europe upon it and against the control of it by the Clergy. Between 1783 and '85 he issued the *American Reader,* the *American Grammar* and the *American Spelling Book,* the latter selling through the nineteenth century 100,000,000 copies, and the other two being close behind it. Webster also revised the ancient *New England Primer,* from which he deleted the old couplet for "A"—

> In Adam's fall
> We sinned all—

and substituted, "A was an Apple Pie made by the Cook." All of this was promising, but as late as 1820 Horace Mann was just entering Litchfield Law School, and Henry Barnard was only nine years old.

The *Prison* movement that was going to replace the old foul, pestilential, unheated, unsubdivided, crowded and whip-crazed "gaols," got under way in 1820 when Auburn Penitentiary, with solitary cells—too small—was built in New York; and Sing Sing was started soon after. New York also began the attack on the old barbarism of *Imprisonment for Debt,* passing a law in 1817 that limited the grounds for it to debts of $25 or more. And about 1820 New York City, followed in a few years by Boston, put in a Reformatory, recognizing that the common drunk and the tramp should be separated from the real criminal and put to work with the hope of reforming him.

The Education of Deaf-Mutes was inaugurated, and spectacular advances were made under the consecrated leadership of Thomas Hopkins Gallaudet, born in Philadelphia, graduate of Yale and Andover Theological Seminary. The Connecticut Asylum for the Education of Deaf and Dumb Persons was the first institution of the kind to be incorporated. When Congress gave it help, the name was changed to the American Asylum, and as such it opened in Hartford in 1817. Many states followed this lead promptly. Gallaudet himself married a deaf-mute, and his son continued the work in the great Columbian Institute, founded in Washington in 1857.

The first hospital for the care of the *Insane* was opened in Philadelphia in 1817. A year later the McLean Asylum was established in Massachusetts, followed in '24 by the Hartford Retreat in Connecticut, the latter taken thereafter as a model.

No attack was made in these years on *"The Woman Question"*

which was going to rock the '30's and '40's, Emma Hart Willard issuing premonitions in her *Plan for Improving Female Education*, 1819, and her establishment of the Troy Female Seminary two years later. The purpose of the older female academies had been chiefly to train women in the graces, at most to qualify them to be ministers' wives. The Troy Seminary—today the Emma Willard School—handed out healthy doses of Mathematics, History, Geography, Natural Philosophy (Physics), Political Philosophy (especially Locke) and Moral Philosophy (Paley), generally the subjects that young men were getting in their academies and the first two years of their colleges.

Of the two or three most spectacular crusades that were to follow, that for *Temperance* got a fair start before 1820. The consumption of spirits—generally rum in New England—was prodigious and increasing after the Revolution, estimated for the whole country at about seventy-five quarts a year per adult male in 1810, and a hundred and twenty-five in 1823.[57] In the middle of the second decade of the century Boston had a licensed saloon for every twenty-one males above sixteen.[58] The slogan of the initial movement was Temperance in the use of Spirits. There was little thought of Total Abstinence or of limitation on the consumption of wine and beer. The first attacks were in Pennsylvania by a few Quakers, also by the great scientific philanthropist Dr. Benjamin Rush, one of whose two chief assistants was the Rev. Jeremy Belknap, a predecessor of Channing's in the Federal Street Church, Boston. The first organizational attack was by the Methodists, whose General Conference in 1780 resolved disapproval of both the distilling and the drinking of hard liquors. Bishop Asbury, itinerating Greater New England, broadcast the phrase "Demon Rum," and in the West anyone who refused a drink was known as a "Methodist fanatic."

In Massachusetts the Reverend Ebenezer Sparhawk spoke of the physical ravages of rum with the naïveté of all laymen and most doctors in that age. Rum, in Sparhawk's opinion,

> puts the blood and juices into a most terrible ferment, and disturbs the whole animal economy. It vitiates the humor, relaxes the solids, spoils the constitution, fills the body with diseases, brings on meager looks, a ghastly countenance, and very bad tremblings, . . . introduces decay of nature, and hastens death faster than hard labour.[59]

In 1789 two hundred farmers of Litchfield, Conn., pledged not to use distilled waters that haying season (no restriction of course on cider which went to the fields with the men as a matter of course). Incidental to his Revival at Yale, President Dwight enjoined his students to sobriety. Generally, the Temperance Movement swelled with the Religious Revival. In 1811 the General Association of the

Presbyterian Churches in Philadelphia censured the "sin of drunkenness," and state associations in Massachusetts, Connecticut and Vermont, and the synods of New York and New Jersey took similar
action.

In 1812 the action of the Connecticut General Association of the
Congregational Churches, under the leadership of Lyman Beecher,
recently installed in Litchfield, was the most drastic on a large scale
up to that time. Mr. Beecher, attending an ordination in Plymouth,
Connecticut, the year before, had been appalled to find the ministers
of the Consociation tippling continuously, while in the house where
they stayed "the sideboard, with the spillings of water, and sugar, and
liquor, looked and smelled like the bar of a very active grog shop."[60]
After a preliminary battle, Beecher became head of a committee of
the General Association whose report, duly accepted, recommended
temperance sermons by all ministers, no drinking by the clergy at
meetings, abstinence by parents of the use of hard liquor in the
home, higher wages to workmen in place of the customary rum—and
even cider—rations, the circulation of temperance literature by the
churches, the fostering of lay organizations to work for temperance.
Beecher's adjuration to get the good work started was typical of
the religion of this always important figure in the General Reform
Movement that was to follow:

> Is it impossible for God to reform and save us? Has He made
> known His purpose to give us over to destruction? Has He been
> accustomed to withhold His blessing from humble efforts made
> to rescue men from the dominion of sin? . . . Immense evils,
> we are persuaded, afflict communities, not because they are in-
> curable, but because they are tolerated, and great good remains
> often unaccomplished merely because it is not attempted.[61]

Beecher's report is suggested by Tyler[62] as the true beginning of the
Temperance Movement in New England, which may be taken to
mean Greater New England. Many ministers were already in line, and
within two years they were joined by the Reverend Heman Humphrey, later President of Amherst, and Dr. Justin Edwards, later President of Andover Theological Seminary. In 1813, the Massachusetts
Society for the Suppression of Intemperance was formed. In view
of the honor the Methodists had earned as being the first organization in the field, a resolution of their General Conference in 1816
is a trifle anticlimactic: "Resolved, that no stationed or local
preacher shall retail spirituous or malt liquors without forfeiting his
ministerial character among us."

Most fateful of the Reform crusades, the Anti-Slavery movement
was slow in getting under way. In New England the early attackers
of it included Judge Samuel Sewall and James Otis, besides Samuel

Hopkins, and by 1800 all the Yankee states had given freedom to the children of their slaves. Slavery was forbidden in the Northwest Territory, the first increment of Greater New England, by the Ordinance of 1787, and by the Constitution the slave trade was supposed to end in 1808. In 1817 the American Colonization Society was formed under the highest auspices, including Roger Sherman and Daniel Webster, the object being to purchase the slaves of those who were willing to free them for compensation and to ship them to a Negro Utopia in Africa. The Society became active, built up two hundred local chapters, and in its peak year of '32 had an income of $43,000. Yet about a million dollars a year would have been necessary for its purpose gradually to eliminate slavery. Also, it never faced up to the fiery principle of human Equality, the method of deportation being an acknowledgment that the Negro Race was inferior.

The real Anti-Slavery Movement began with the appearance, after 1815, of out-and-out Abolition periodicals, courageous and fugitive, most of them, like the poetry magazines in the 1920's. The earliest started in Ohio in 1817, the *Philanthropist,* published by Charles Osborn. In the next three years, four sounded forth in the very South, two in Tennessee, one in Kentucky, one in North Carolina. The tempo of the epic increased imperceptibly in 1821 when Benjamin Lundy founded in Ohio the *Genius of Universal Emancipation.* For seven years later, the *Genius* having moved to Baltimore with its editor, he hired for Assistant Editor a twenty-three-year-old New Englander, William Lloyd Garrison, the most lurid figure in the Reform Movement, and high among the villains of American history.

Inconsistent with the Abolition Movement, and ironically so because most of the great Reformers belonged to both, was the Peace Movement. It first stirred in New York, but its birth was the issuance in 1814 of *The Solemn Review of the Custom of War, showing that War is the effect of a popular delusion, and Proposing a Remedy,* by the Rev. Noah Worcester, then of Brighton, Massachusetts. In 1815 the Massachusetts Peace Society was organized in the study of William Ellery Channing in Boston. Four years later there were sixteen more societies scattered over the country, the westernmost in Indiana. In a tribute to Worcester, who was secretary of the Massachusetts society until '28, Channing said:

> War rests on contempt of human nature; on the long, mournful
> habits of regarding the mass of human beings as machines, or as
> animals having no higher use than to be shot at and murdered
> for the glory of a chief. . . . Let the worth of a human being be
> felt; let the mass of the people be elevated; let it be understood
> that a man was made to . . . improve lofty powers, to secure
> a vast happiness. . . .[63]

Lyman Beecher's summons to battle against evil, quoted above, is typical of that great Reformer. So this celebration of the worth of every individual is typical of Channing, also a great Reformer but of a finer, a more truly Puritan quality and a larger historical significance.

Channing's ascendance and spokesmanship for New England may be dated from about 1820 and was generally synchronous with the acceleration of the random activities of the new and previously unintegrated Third Puritan culture. With the end of the War of 1812 in the peace of 1815, the whole Nation had burst into the spiritual, geographic, and economic expansion which was going to continue through the century. In 1817 New Hampshire, and in 1818 Connecticut, expressed the individualistic trend of the age by disestablishing the Congregational Church, Timothy Dwight and Lyman Beecher leading the defense in Connecticut. Thereafter it was only at The Bay, and there for only fifteen years more, that there survived that ghost of the Holy Commonwealth which even in the seventeenth century had never been fully embodied. In 1819, in his sermon at the Ordination of Jared Sparks in Baltimore, Channing said the key things that everyone had been thinking under their doctrinal differences, and so defined the Third Puritanism of Romantic Humanitarianism which was going to supply the central current of the new New England culture.

Some of the principles that Channing propounded at this time he had stated better earlier; some he stated better later; and a fair presentation of his significance in the Age calls for a combination of scattered pronouncements. But he implied them all here, and they struck with special impact at this time because it was an occasion of the first importance, the ordination of a respected Unitarian minister by another. The sermon was awaited and read eagerly because it was the first organized statement of Unitarian doctrine, but its ultimate importance was as a proclamation, not of Unitarianism nor of any doctrine at all, but of the Liberal, Romantic, Perfectionist, Humanitarian Vision of the age. And it was for that reason that it put Channing at once in a position of intellectual leadership in Old New England, and to a less degree in Greater New England, among many who opposed or ignored his Unitarianism.

In the Baltimore Sermon Channing announced six, and by a later addition they became seven, principles:

First, the New Puritanism is not going to be bound by any Old Puritan Orthodoxy:

We object . . . to that system, which arrogates to itself the name of Orthodoxy, and which . . . teaches, that God brings us into life wholly depraved, . . . that God selects from this corrupt mass a number to be saved, and plucks them, by a special influence, from the common ruin. . . .[64]

Second, the New Puritanism is based in the primary importance, and the primary responsibility, of every individual alone:

The ultimate reliance of a human being must be on his own mind . . . , in the power of forming his temper and life according to his conscience. . . .*

Third, to the New Puritanism the Central Meaning or God of the Cosmos is Moral, and the essence of Morality is human Benevolence:

We believe in the moral perfection of God. . . . God's justice . . . coincides with benevolence; for virtue and happiness, though not the same, are inseparably conjoined. . . .

* The first phrase of this quotation is from an earlier statement, "The Moral Argument against Calvinism," Channing, *Works* I, 225. Channing's best affirmation, perhaps the strongest affirmation for all time, of the old Puritan Equalitarianism, the Equality of all Individuals in the Eternal Scheme, was made in his Election Sermon, preached before the Massachusetts General Court, in 1830. His statement is a refreshing reminder that as late as a century and a quarter ago, when the nation was already under attack by the shallow Individualism of Competition and the Debased Equality of Mediocrity, America was still fulfilling her promise of a great and responsible democracy. The following excerpts are from *ibid*, IV, 70-3, 76 and 77:

"I . . . cannot better meet the demands of this occasion, than by leading you to prize, above all other rights and liberties, that inward freedom which Christ came to confer.

". . . The common . . . answer is, that it is freedom from sin . . . (But) it is not a negative state, nor the mere absence of sin; for such a freedom may be ascribed to inferior animals, or to children before becoming moral agents. Spiritual freedom is the attribute of a mind, in which reason and conscience have begun to act, and which is free through its agency, through fidelity to the truth.

"I call that mind free, which sets no bounds to its love, which is not imprisoned in itself or in a sect, which recognizes in all human beings the Image of God and the rights of his children, which delights in virtue and sympathizes with suffering wherever they are seen. . . . I call that mind free, which is jealous of its own freedom, which guards itself from being merged in others, which guards its empire over itself as nobler than the empire of the world. . . .

". . . The mind, after all, is our only possession, or, in other words, we possess all things through its energy and enlargement; and civil institutions are to be estimated by the free and pure minds to which they give birth.

". . . The human soul is greater, more sacred, than the state; and must never be sacrificed to it. The human soul is to outlive all earthly institutions. The distinction of nations is to pass away. Thrones, which have stood for ages, are to meet the doom pronounced upon all man's works. But the individual mind survives, and the obscurest subject, if true to God, will rise to a power never wielded by earthly potentates.

"A human being is not to be merged in the whole, as a drop in the ocean. . . . He is an ultimate being, made for his own perfection as the highest end, made to maintain an individual existence, and to serve others only as far as consists with his own virtue and progress."

Throughout his life Channing spent much time on this weak point in his position, the attribution of human virtue to God, thus rendering Him in part Anthropomorphic.

Fourth, since God is Moral, the New Puritan's worship is moral:

> Among the virtues, we give first place to the love of God . . . the true love of God is a moral sentiment, founded in a clear perception . . . of his moral perfection. . . . We esteem him only a pious man, . . . who shows his delight in God's benevolence, by loving and serving his neighbors. . . .

Fifth, God represents the perfection toward which the New Puritans, being Romantics, yearn:

> . . . We were made for union with our Creator . . . his infinite perfection is the only sufficient object and true resting-place for the insatiable desires and unlimited capabilities of the human mind. . . .[65]

Sixth, America may provide the Utopia, the social perfection, to which the New Puritan yearns:

> The United States, if true to itself, . . . will have the glory and the happiness of giving new impulses to the human mind.[66]

Seventh, the New Puritan is still a Puritan, for his religion is primarily a percept, an experience of the mind. Channing does not state this categorically, but it is assumed in most of the excerpts cited—"ultimate reliance" on the "mind"—"the true love of God . . . founded in a clear perception"—"the insatiable desires and unlimited capacities of the human mind"—and freedom of the mind to achieve its own percepts as expounded in the address to the General Court excerpted in the previous footnote. The undeniable Arminian quality in Channing is subserved to and swallowed up in true Puritanism. Moral conduct is not celebrated for its own sake but as perceived by the Conscience, a phase of the Imagination. As with Hooker and Edwards, Works are not primary but secondary. They depend upon and derive from a Psychological Experience which the Seventeenth- and Eighteenth-century Puritans called the Receipt of Grace, but which Channing, dispensing with Theological claptrap, described in his Romantic claptrap as a Perception of his "infinite perfection," which is also a "perception of" God's "moral perfection." It is all the same Imaginative experience fused of Reason and Emotion, only the Third Puritans conceived it in Romantic or Motile terms, where the First and Second Puritans had conceived it in more nearly final or Static terms.

There was of course nothing new in "Benevolence" with which, in Channing's view, "God's justice . . . coincides." It was a perfectly good eighteenth-century word of all schools, and both Dwight and Beecher had been giving it a new and specific flavor conformable to the new Humanitarianism, the new emphasis on the Particular Man. What Channing did that was new was to take it utterly out of its old Calvinistic frame—as not even the greatest Eighteenth-century Liberals had done—and identify it with the very fabric of Being, with God's Justice. Thus he attributed a moral quality to his Central Perception, and it is certain that both Hooker and Edwards would have rejected this anthropomorphic qualification on what to them was a Superhuman and Inscrutable God. Hooker recognized some value in certain Works as a possible Preparation for the recognition of Grace. But to him, as to Edwards, Grace itself was a clear and universal perception without any condition. It was the pure aesthetic experience, not a discovery of anything new, but a new and clearer way of seeing familiar things.

Channing professes a similar perception of "perfection," but he clothes it with a human condition, morality, benevolence. He places the love of God first "among the virtues," but he defines this love as "a moral sentiment," which is to say the love of Man. God is identified with the faculty of love between terrestrial Christian and Christian, between Neighbor and Neighbor. This is no longer the Christianity of the Seventeenth- and Eighteenth-century Puritans. That was *First-Commandment Christianity,* finding its instance in the Love of God. This is *Second-Commandment Christianity,* finding its instance in the Love of the Neighbor, a universal neighbor who is every individual on earth and who was "made for union with our Creator" and so "to improve lofty powers, to secure a vast happiness." The Christianity of Romantic Humanitarianism, with its emphasis on the individual, is Second-Commandment Christianity. But it is still Christianity, for it is founded in Love, not in a code of action. And it is still Puritan, for it is an aesthetic, an exercise of the "unlimited capacities of the human mind," a perception, in Hooker's standard phrase, of "things as they be."

With Channing we come down from the wide, thin-atmosphered eighteenth-century world of Abstract Man to the Concrete Reality of Individual Men. As eighteenth-century Man represented quantitatively a smaller concept, a smaller sky than that of the seventeenth-century Cosmos, so Channing's nineteenth-century sky whose stars are individual men is a still further contraction of Imaginative sweep. But qualitatively it is a real Sky again, its actuality being the actual sum of all the actualities of every individual person, his individual sufferings and joys, his hope of improvement, his romantic capacity to move toward "infinite perfection," to "improve lofty powers, to secure a vast happiness." The original Puritan's Idea or

Percept of God is continuing to shrink under the influence of Materialism and its Experimental Science which find reality in the concrete and the material. But the shrinkage is not yet all the way to the Material. The concretion, the Perception, of Third Puritanism, is still of the idealistic, the imaginative, the universal, the permanent, the timeless reality of every soul.

As was true of Hooker and the Seventeenth-century Puritans, and Edwards and the Eighteenth-century Puritans, Channing's objective perception of Truth, of his special Moral God and potentially Moral Individual Man, ran along the aesthetic line which we called the Holy Ratio, the line between too much Emotion, the Heresy of Antinomianism, and too much Reason, the Heresy of Arminianism. Channing is articulate enough in his fear of too much emotion, for all of the evangelists of this Second Great Awakening were well warned and desperately determined to avoid the excesses of James Davenport and the other Itinerants who in the 1740's had made a "shambles" of the First Awakening:

> Many have fallen into the error, that there can be no excess in feelings which have God for their object; and, distrusting as coldness that self-possession, without which virtue and devotion lose all their dignity, they have abandoned themselves to extravagances . . . Fanaticism, partial insanity . . ., ungovernable transports . . . [are not] piety.[67]
> . . . One surrender of desire to God's will, is worth a thousand transports.[68]
> Need I descend to particulars, to prove that the Scriptures demand the exercise of reason?[69]

And yet this Reason which Channing so urgently professes is a long way from the smooth and bright Natural Reason of Natural Man and his Natural Rights of the previous age. Channing deprecated brainless, emotional extravagances as Edwards did. But Channing was not for that cold. He was highly emotional in Romantic vein, with his "insatiable desires," his "infinite perfection," his "union with our Creator," his "lofty powers" and "vast happiness"; and the fact that he disciplined himself into a near-asceticism does not imply that the desires he suppressed were weak or that they were any weaker as sublimated into imaginative or spiritual experience. Channing doubtless started to think with a formal Natural Reason. But it had to grapple with plenty of emotion, and his final perceptions and their best expressions are the result of a nice fusion of the two, just as any artists are. His final Reason that he celebrates and whose results we see is what the old Puritans called Right Reason. It is the understanding that comes with Grace and Regeneration through a blend of Natural Reason and Natural Emotion in what

Ratio is as much a mystery today as it was in the days of Isaiah. Cautiously Channing does admit the necessity of emotion, and behind the disciplined admission, as behind all of his important statements, we feel the hot and distinguished soul at grips with its Benevolent God:

> We would not . . . be understood as wishing to exclude from religion warmth, and even transport. We honor, and highly value, true religious sensibility. We believe, that Christianity is intended to act powerfully on the whole nature, on the heart as well as the understanding and conscience. We conceive of heaven as a state where the love of God will be exalted into an unbounded fervor and joy; and we desire, in our pilgrimage here, to drink in the spirit of that better world.[70]

As to what fraction of the people in the first half of the nineteenth century enjoyed Channing's selfless, pure Perception, his Second-Commandment Christianity, his Third Puritanism, as distinguished from the strong Arminian and Antinomian forces that were also operative, it is as always impossible to say. Certainly Materialism, whether as doctrine or as avaricious practice, made but slight popular inroads upon Idealistic and Religious reality before the Civil War. Almost everyone still entertained at least a troublesome suspicion that the adventures and rewards of this sensate life were but incidents in a larger Plan. But how many of these were of a Puritanic rather than some other religious or quasi-religious disposition, it is specially difficult to determine because almost everybody spoke, and even thought, in the same Romantic idiom. Puritans, Arminians, Antinomians, Wild Sectarians and Atheists all talked the same language of Humanitarian Perfectionism, of a Social Passion which for universality, during about forty years after 1820, can hardly be equalled in the history of any nation. People wholly consecrated to selfless service would still adorn their activities with such tears, outcries and fallings to the knees as in either of the previous centuries we would have associated with the most absurd and self-indulgent Antinomianism. Even Channing within his restraint talks of "infinite perfection," of "union with the Creator," of the "insatiable desires of the mind."

In this World of Men we must take extravagant gestures as the universal manner of the times, and for classification we must look to subtler and deeper criteria. We must remember that true Antinomianism, exemplified by Mrs. Hutchinson, and again by Davenport and the Itinerants, actually defied The Law, whether Biblical, Ecclesiastical or Customary, and asserted as superior to it the direct communications of the Holy Ghost, in other words Personal Inspiration. In them there was a very clear assertion of the Self as the primary channel of Divine Authority. But among the Nineteenth-century Revivalists and Reformers, Romantic Ecstasy touching the Saving of a Soul or the Coming Perfection of Mankind, is typically the formal surface upon a wholly objective Perception and a Universal Love, such as Channing's, expressing itself substantially in selfless acts of service. In trying to distinguish Puritans here, we must shut our eyes and ears to performances that seem to us adolescent, and look for the quality of the Perception, the Light within, and of the Works without. Is the Perception a loving and objective one in which the self is lost in identification with the object, whether man or God? Or is it a mere garment upon the delight of private ecstasy? Are the Works done out of genuine shyness and concern for another's happiness alone? Or are they motivated mainly by the impulse to advance the self? These are more difficult criteria than we have used before. But it is necessary to use them here if we are to continue to trace the central thread of the Culture.

Among the leaders of the age, Charles Grandison Finney is one who, in spite of much extravagance in Revivalism, yet was surely impelled by an objective or loving Inner Perception into equally objective and loving outward Works. As Channing may be taken as the Intellectual Leader of the East and some of the West in this Age of Men, so Finney may be taken as the Emotional Leader of the West and some of the East. Yet neither was so extreme in his kind as to violate the Holy Ratio, and they shared without difference the same vision of Religious Humanitarianism, of Second-Commandment Christianity, which was the Third Puritanism. Channing the fastidious ascetic of Boston and Finney the weeping evangelist of the West were antipodal and incompatible in all things except this Central Thing, Universal Perception—Finney would call it the Sense of Grace—in terms of a God who was Loving in a comprehensible, human way, and who saw ultimate and Absolute Value in every individual human soul. Also it is to be observed of them both that, while they were close and favorable to most of the Reforms of the Age, each was chary of joining organizations, and always put Religion before any specific movement. Their effort was to convert the perpetrators of social evil rather than to crush them. To both of them Sin was essentially individual, not social; it was the separation of the individual from God which—Channing's repudiation to the contrary notwithstanding—was Original Sin.

There is much in Finney's account of his conversion which recalls that of Edwards. It occurred in October, 1821, when he was twenty-nine years old and had for several years been a practicing lawyer in

Adams in Upper Central New York. Finney was unique among preachers in combining a near void of Liberal Education with the special and minutely exacting mental discipline of the Law. In fact his serious, as distinguished from a mildly curious, interest in Christianity dates from his investigations of Mosaic Law as cited in his legal sources, and his discovery that the alleged Biblical foundations of the local Presbyterian minister's Calvinistic doctrine would never be acceptable as proofs in a court. Though revolted by Calvinism, he did move gradually into a state of religious anxiety, and out of that state came his conversion in the good old Edwardsean way of compulsive Grace. The visitation occurred after a restless night in which he fancied he was going to die and "sink down to hell":

> At an early hour I started for the office. But just before I arrived, . . . an inward voice said, 'What are you waiting for? . . . What are you trying to do? Are you trying to work out a righteousness of your own?'
> . . . I think I then saw . . . the reality and fulness of the atonement of Christ . . ., that instead of having, or needing, any righteousness of my own to recommend me to God, I had to submit myself to the righteousness of God through Christ. . . .
> North of the village, and over a hill, lay a piece of woods, . . . and . . . instead of going to the office, I turned and bent my course [thither]. . . .
> . . . Still my pride must show itself. As I went over the hill, it ocurred to me that someone might see me and suppose that I was going to pray. . . . I skulked along under the fence, till I got so far out of sight that no one from the village could see me. I . . . found a place where some large trees had fallen across each other, leaving an open place between. . . . I crept into this place and knelt down for prayer. . . .
> But . . . I found that my heart would not pray. . . . I would hear a rustling in the leaves, as I thought, and would stop and look up to see if somebody were not coming. . . .
> . . . I began to feel deeply that it was too late; that it must be that I was given up of God and was past hope. . . .
> Just at this moment . . . the revelation of my pride of heart, as the great difficulty that stood in the way, was distinctly shown to me. An overwhelming sense of my wickedness in being ashamed to have a human being see me on my knees before God, took such powerful possession of me, that I cried out at the top of my voice. . . . The sin appeared awful, infinite. It broke me down before the Lord.
> Just at that point this passage of Scripture seemed to drop into my mind with a flood of light: 'Then shall ye . . . seek me and find me, when ye shall search for me with all your heart.' . . .
> . . . I prayed till my mind became so full that, before I was

aware of it, I was on my feet and tripping up the ascent toward the road. The question of my being converted had not . . . arisen to my thought. . . .

I soon reached the road that led to the village, . . . and I found that my mind had become most wonderfully quiet and peaceful. I said to myself, 'What is this? . . . I have lost all my conviction. I have not a particle of concern about my soul.' . . .

I walked quietly toward the village; and so perfectly quiet was my mind that it seemed as if all nature listened. . . . I had gone into the woods immediately after an early breakfast; and when I returned to the village I found it was dinner time. Yet I had been wholly unconscious of the time. . . .

. . . The thought of God was sweet to my mind, and the most profound spiritual tranquility had taken full possession of me. . . .

I went to my dinner, and found I had no appetite to eat. . . .

. . . Just at dark Squire W—— . . . bade me goodnight and went to his home. . . . As I closed the door and turned around, my heart seemed to be liquid within me. All my feelings seemed to rise and flow out. . . . The rising of my soul was so great that I rushed into the room back of the front office to pray.

There was no fire, and no light, in the room; nevertheless it appeared to me as if it were perfect light. As I went in and shut the door after me, it seemed as if I met the Lord Jesus face to face. It did not occur to me then, nor did it for some time afterward, that it was wholly a mental state. . . . It seemed to me that I saw him as I would any other man. . . .

I returned to the front office, and found that the fire that I had made of large wood was nearly burned out. . . . As I turned and was about to take a seat by the fire, I received a mighty baptism of the Holy Ghost. Without any expectation of it, . . . without any recollection that I had ever heard the thing mentioned by any person in the world, the Holy Spirit descended upon me in a manner that seemed to go through me, body and soul . . ., like a wave of electricity. . . . It seemed to come in waves and waves of liquid love. . . . It seemed like the very breath of God. I can recollect distinctly that it seemed to fan me, like immense wings.

. . . I wept aloud with joy and love. . . . These waves came over me, and over me, and over me, one after another, until I recollect I cried out, 'I shall die if these waves continue to pass over me.' I said, 'Lord, I can not bear any more'; yet I had no fear of death.[71]

This conversion, it will be observed, has nothing of Channing's "Moral Sentiment" about it, and no immediate Humanitarian slant. It is the standard Puritan experience of Grace, signalized especially by Unexpectedness, Compulsion, the Hopeless Sense of Sin, the Loss of the Self and the Wide Calm, the Sense of Light, the Vision of Christ, the Excruciating Joy. It recalls the passages of ultimate Perception recounted by Edwards, the "new Sense of Things," the "calm, sweet Abstraction of Soul from all the Concerns of this World," the "Vision . . . of sweetly conversing with Christ," the sense of being "swallowed up in" God "for ever." The chief difference from Edwards' experience of Grace is that Finney seems to lack Edwards' sense of the Grandeur and Glory and Majesty of God. Instead he is inundated with waves of Love. This is perhaps the distinction between First and Second Puritanism together, both of them starting with the First Commandment, the love of the Omnipotent God, and Third Puritanism which is based in the Second Commandment, the Anthropomorphic Love of a Humane God, and of Neighbor for Neighbor.

Finney's first theology, that immediately ensuing upon his Conversion, was in many respects suggestive of Channing—the Denial of the Imputation of Adam's sin to all; the Denial of the Imputation of all Sin to Christ; the Denial of the Imputation of Christ's virtue to the Elect who must thereafter still go through the process of Repentance, seeming to make it all a system of Justice, not of Grace.[72] Affirmatively, Finney believed in Grace and Justification by Faith[73] in the old Puritan fashion, and his Faith probably required less of support by Works than Channing's did. Like Channing he saw Benevolence as the quality of the Converted and as "the whole character of God," and he defined it as "loving the happiness of others."[74] All this identifies him, not with the World of God, nor the World of Man, but with the World of Men.

Like all prominent Puritans, Finney has been so variously overvilified and over-praised by miscellaneous prejudices that it is hard to trust any record of him. It seems to be unanimous that he was a big man with a big voice, a big mop of hair, big eyebrows and big, deep-set eyes. As a basis of inference, it is well to remember the paradox of his training, that at the foundation he had no college, and very little other, education, but that professionally he was a lawyer with a lawyer's discipline in close reasoning and nice distinction. Between the Emotion of his basic ignorance and the Reason of his legal mind, we get his peculiar form of the Puritan Holy Ratio, the qualification for Objective, Universal, Gracious Perception for which most ministers are prepared through the means of College and Seminary.

Because of his lack of academic foundation, Finney took no delight in rhetoric or in large generalities. He talked very simply and specifically to the people, and in one sense he made himself the paragon of preachers in the Age of Individual Men. With the particularity of

Romantic Humanitarianism he made it a practice to address individuals, calling them by name if possible, seeking their cooperation in their own conversion. He was forever getting people to stand up in order to help them over the shame of professing religion in public —which, as we saw, had been one of Finney's own early blocks. His famous "Anxious Seat" down in the front of the congregation was not so entitled by him, and, by his account, it was not the scene of extravagant "exercises" as has sometimes been supposed. He says that it was during a revival in Rochester that he saw that some special treatment was necessary to overcome the pride of the Rich who often felt impelled to repentance and conversion but were ashamed to admit publicly that they had any such need. Finney provided them with this halfway step, where they might come publicly to occupy a seat that was for those who felt ready for conversion, but without the humiliation of standing and being personally addressed. He says that in this way he succeeded in making quite a dent in the upper crust of Rochester.[75]

There is no doubt that Finney was pretty far on the Emotional Left. Eventually he concluded frankly that most ministers were over-educated and over-intellectual,[76] though he did not go as far as some of the illiterate Methodists and Baptists who opposed an educated ministry altogether. After he became Professor of Theology at Oberlin in 1835, the Congregational and Presbyterian Churches generally looked askance at his graduates as candidates for pulpits. And Lyman Beecher, who stressed education as the center of the problem of developing the West, once presided at a convention in Cleveland from which the representatives of Oberlin were excluded. Finney, in his barnstorming from the Mississippi to the British Isles, in his prolific evangelism in the Free Broadway Tabernacle in New York that the Tappan Brothers built for him, was unconventionally far on the emotional side no doubt. Yet the gathering opinion[77] seems to be that he was nowhere near as wild as he has been painted, that, like the other Evangelists of the day—and Lyman Beecher himself ran second or third to Finney[78]—he had a fear of the methods of the roaring, eighteenth-century Lunatics who had brought on the New Light—Old Light controversy, and of the current methods of the Revivalists of Kentucky and Tennessee in whose Saturnalias Repentance, Liquor and Fornication were probably about equal ingredients. But, however extreme or moderate Finney's emotionalism may have been, it was in all cases objective emotion aroused by and identified with a concern for particular individuals before him at the moment. It was very far from the Antinomian emotion which is indulged as a pleasure, and carries with it the most vaunting implications of the importance of the self as a channel of God's will.

After all, Finney was for thirty-five years Professor of Theology and for fifteen years President of Oberlin, an institution that was notorious for Liberality but also had the full respect of all of Greater New England and much of Europe as a seat of higher learning. From the common accounts of Finney's weeping and kneeling and praying in public, it is interesting to turn to his mature *Systematic Theology*,[79] where a position of Modified Calvinism is far more fully and convincingly set forth than is Channing's Unitarianism in his elegant and unsystematic addresses.

Also, let it be remembered of Finney that, like Channing, he was distinguished from every complexion of Radical in his day in that he was Moderate in Reform, not condemning the perpetrator of Social Error, not attempting to punish him, but hoping simply and peacefully to bring him to the Christian Light under whose gentle revelation it would be impossible for him longer to Keep Slaves, or debauch Alcoholics, or abuse the Poor, the Insane or the Criminal, or Make War, or deprive Women of their Natural Rights, or take part in any of the scores of other time-honored social abuses against whose continuance so many Societies sprouted during Finney's life all over Greater New England. Finney's theory of Abolition was to convert the Slaveholders and leave the rest to them and God. The hundreds of his Oberlin graduates who went over the New West preaching Abolition both at the North and at the South, many of them under the immediate leadership of Theodore Weld, used Finney's peaceful method of persuasion, and it had an ultimately greater effect in history than did the violent and provocative vituperation of William Lloyd Garrison and his Radicals.[80] Garrison was a very real cause of the War. Finney and Weld did nothing to bring it on, but once it came they—Weld more than Finney—provided the Union with the united West which was one of the prerequisites of victory.

For a leader who followed his Second-Commandment Christianity into mortally dangerous action, and yet never did or said anything inconsistent with the basic, Objective, Loving Percept of Mankind, Theodore Dwight Weld is beginning to occupy the place of the most saintly Active Reformer in our history. Although for long periods subjected to violence, he never rose up, like John Brown, to meet evil with evil. Although hating Slavery with a passion that surely had an element of Arminian Moralism, he never, like Garrison, turned the hatred from the condition to individuals, and never, again like Garrison, used his passion to dictate, to oppose, and to seek to elevate himself into control of the Anti-slavery Movement.

Born in Connecticut in 1803, raised in the backwoods of Upstate New York, educated in Ohio, integrating the Abolition Movement in "Abolition House" in Washington in the years just before the War, living his last years and dying in 1895 in Hyde Park, near Boston, Weld's life spanned the culture of Third Puritanism in both space and time, and his importance is as the exemplar rather than the preacher of its Humanitarianism. While a student at Hamilton College he declared contempt for Finney and his revival methods, but presently became his follower and throughout his life did penance for his early error by the extremity of his devotion. Not long after their friendship began, Finney charged young Weld with pride: "If you don't take care I fear you will be spoiled by an idea of your own importance." He was referring to Weld's apparently ostentatious slovenliness in dress when he was lecturing, as he was already doing. Whether due to this or some other warning, Weld, though all of his life he was vague about dress, yet took from this early time a permanent lesson in humility.

The following anecdotes are selected from many more:

Though recognized everywhere as the greatest orator of the Abolition Movement, yet at the foundation of Lane Seminary in Cincinnati, 1832, he declined the chair of Sacred Rhetoric and Oratory "with his usual self-abasement," and enrolled as a student.[81]

While at Lane, he devoted all of his spare time to the free Negroes in Cincinnati: "If I slept in the city it was in their homes. If I attended parties, it was *theirs—weddings—Funerals—theirs—Religious meetings—theirs*—Sabbath schools—Bible classes—theirs. During the 18 months that I spent at Lane Seminary *I did not attend Dr. Beecher's Church once.*"[82] (Lyman Beecher was the President.)

Replying to an attack in a local paper on Weld's group who associated with Negroes to the public scandal, Weld very nearly stated the center of his own motivation: "Whom does it behoove to keep his heart in contact with the woes and guilt of a perishing world, if not the student who is preparing for the ministry?"

Wrote James Birney, the young Kentucky gentleman whom Weld brought into the Movement and who afterwards ran for President on its ticket, "I have seen in no man such a rare combination of great intellectual powers with Christian simplicity."[83]

In 1835, when Weld was asked to send for publication to the New York Headquarters of the American Anti-slavery Society a report of his capture for Abolition of the General Assembly of the Presbyterian Church, he sent a dramatic report but insisted that it be kept confidential, "for his fear of seeming vain or egotistical had become a haunting obsession."[84]

He consistently refused to speak at or even attend the annual meet-

ings in New York of the American Anti-slavery Society—"the state-
liness and Pomp and Circumstance of an Anniversary I loathe in my
inmost soul. . . . It seems so like ostentatious display, a mere make
believe and mouthing, a sham and show off. It is an element I was
never made to move in. . . . I am a Backwoodsman—can grub up
stumps and roll logs. . . ."[85]

Weld was a fanatic, but he overcame the common self-indulgences
of his kind, the refusal ever to be moderate, the joy in martyrdom.
When he was organizing the Ohio State Abolition Society against
organized and violent opposition he accepted the plea of the intended Colored Delegates that their presence would do more harm
than good. He saw nothing to be gained by "ostentatious display of
superiority to prejudice," and "blustering bravado defiance."[86] He
was mobbed hundreds of times—one of his scores of young disciples
said that when on lecture tour he came to expect a shower of eggs
and stones as "part of the introduction." Weld's method was to take
the mobbing at his first lecture, and usually at his second and third
and as long as the bullies—often set on by the gentry of a town—
chose to continue their attacks. Gradually they would decrease, and
their tactics would have strengthened Weld with the general population. Then he would stay on for five to ten more evenings, and
by the time he left he almost always left a local Abolition Society
behind him, together with contrition in the hearts of many of his
first persecutors. Though often injured, he never retreated but once,
from Troy, New York, where the mayor not only refused him protection but made the mob official and vitually unanimous by threatening to use the police to throw Weld out.

By his quiet, intrepid methods he captured Ohio and New York.
His disciples, fanning out from Oberlin where he went as a student
under Finney after leading the famous Abolitionist revolt at Lane,
captured most of Illinois, Michigan, Wisconsin and Iowa. They captured enough of the ruling opinion of New New England so that it was
the Moral Issues—the Utopia of the Union and the specific matter
of Slavery—that brought these states into the Civil War, against
their own economic interest which was with the South, and so provided the weight that was indispensable to the winning of it.

The number of Yankee leaders in the Age of Reform probably
runs into the thousands, great Puritans whose Grace was in a Perception of Utopia potential in the selfless instincts of men and in
the amelioration of their lot. There were the Tappan brothers,
Arthur and Lewis, born Yankees but migrants to New York City in

their manhood, richest philanthropists in the country, sustaining angels of Finney, Weld, Lane, Oberlin and the American Anti-slavery Society, contributing angels to the American Bible Society, the American Tract Society, Auburn Theological Seminary, Kenyon College, Oneida Institute, the American Education Society, the General Union for the Observance of the Christian Sabbath and numerous Missionary and temperance organizations, personal bene-factors of forgotten thousands of individuals, including more than a hundred divinity students at Yale. There was William Henry Channing, nephew of William Ellery, Christian Socialist, close to all reforms but hesitant about all, convinced that "Christ did not under-stand his own religion." Associated with Finney, there was George Washington Gale, whose Calvinism as minister at Adams, New York, so repelled Finney as to drive him to his own private throes and conversion. Gale was afterwards a disciple of Finney's, founder of Oneida Institute and of Knox College at Galesburg.

Associated with Weld, and more or less with Finney, there were Charles B. Storrs, President of Northwestern University; Elizur Wright, Professor of Mathematics at Western Reserve, one of the Founders of the American Anti-slavery Society, and its perpetual Secretary, editor of the *Emancipator* and numerous other Reform periodicals, including the *Chronotype* in which he attacked the Liquor Interests which duly had him indicted for libel, inventor, slave-rescuer, one of the founders of the Liberty Party that nomi-nated Birney for President, Insurance Authority and Massachusetts Commissioner of Insurance, authority on Forestry, author of books on all these topics, introducer of Whittier's first volume in 1844; Beriah Green, Professor of Sacred Literature at Western Reserve, President of the American Anti-slavery Society, active in the Temper-ance and Education movements; Asa Mahan, first President of Oberlin, afterwards President of Cleveland University and Adrian College; Henry B. Stanton, Abolitionist speaker and editor, and husband of Elizabeth Cady.

In Reform generally there were Amos Augustus Phelps, agent of the Massachusetts Anti-slavery Society, sometime editor of the *Emancipator,* at first the associate and afterwards the opponent of Garrison; Francis Jackson, wealthy Boston supporter of the Anti-slavery Movement who let the Female Anti-slavery Society meet in his house when violence was threatened; Oliver Johnson, occasional Assistant Editor of Garrison's *Liberator,* champion of Non-Resist-ance and Women's Rights—his wife was a Prison Reformer—Boston correspondent of the *New York Tribune* and afterwards Assistant Editor under Greeley; Henry C. Wright, eloquent lecturer on Im-mediate or Garrisonian Abolition, Non-Resistance, Spiritualism and Socialism; Charles B. Torrey who resigned as a minister to devote his life to the Slavery Conflict, was imprisoned in Baltimore in '44 for helping a slave escape, died in prison two years later from consumption brought on by neglect, and had a Boston funeral attended by thousands, where the sermon was preached by the brother of Elijah Lovejoy, followed by a mass meeting in Faneuil Hall where Channing, Whittier and Lowell were among many who performed; Samuel Joseph May, one-time assistant to Channing in the Federal Street Church, a man of infinite patience, humor and distinction, busy in Immediate Abolition—his house being a station in the Underground Railroad—Women's Rights, Public Education, serving at Mann's request as the first principal of the Nation's first Normal School at Lexington, called by many "the friend of mankind," but called by his brother-in-law Bronson Alcott "the Lord's chore boy"; John Pierpont, Abolition, Non-Resistance, Abolition of Militia, Abolition of Imprisonment for Debt, Phrenology, Spiritualism, Temperance; Charles Spear, founder of the Society for the Abolition of Capital Punishment and editor of the appealingly entitled magazine, *The Hangman;* Warren Burton, Pestalozzian educator, Phrenologist, author of *Helps to Education;* Dr. Henry Ingersoll Bowditch, Abolition, Public Health, Ambulances in the Civil War; Louis Dwight, Secretary of the Boston Prison Discipline Society, Agent of the American Education Society, Travelling Agent of the American Bible Society; E.M.P. Wells, founder of the reform school, the House of Refuge, in Boston; Josiah Quincy, mayor of Boston who reformed the Police, the Fire Department, the Schools, introduced a Reformatory for petty criminals, afterwards President of Havard; Samuel Gridley Howe, Surgeon in the Greek War of Independence, founder of Education for the Blind, and early in the care of the Insane, Abolitionist, husband of Julia Ward; Dorothea Dix, at first Governess in Channing's house, and afterwards lifelong and successful campaigner for humane treatment for the Insane; William Ladd, founder of the American Peace Society.

There were these and many more, including the hundreds of boys who went out from Yale and from Andover Seminary as missionaries: the "Illinois Band" of seven students who went out from Yale in 1828 and founded Illinois College; the "Iowa Band" of eleven from Andover who, with recruits from other sources, founded Iowa College, later Grinnell, and scattered through the state to found churches and schools; the Foreign Missionaries, male and female, who disappeared into Remotest Asia. There were all these, most of them now forgotten, who carried forward the Puritan Idealism in terms of Reform. And there are also the great names that survive, each in the lead of one or more of the separate Movements—Whittier, Lovejoy, Phillips, Parker, Alcott, Ripley, Mann, Barnard, Greeley, Harriet Beecher Stowe, Julia Ward Howe—including most of the leaders of the rising Feminist Movement: Lucy Stone, Catherine Beecher, Elizabeth Blackwell, Mary Lyon, Lydia Mary Child, Susan B. Anthony, Maria Weston Chapman. And along with these were the Ministers and the Reforming Politicians and Statesmen whose degree of Objective Idealism, as distinguished from Self-interest, can never be appraised.

All these and many more were leading the millions. But so were the apostles of the great traditional Heresies flowing on the Right and the Left of the current of Religion. Intellectual Arminianism or Liberalism had, as we have seen, disappeared for the time being into Romantic Humanitarianism. But Legal Arminianism or Moralism, while also dressed in Romantic Emotion, was no whit disguised by it, and was a great force from the very beginning of the century. Before taking it up, it may be well to distinguish it further from Third Puritanism which took some elements of it, like a faint coloring, into its Central Stream. We have seen that Channing attributed the moral quality of Benevolence to God. Still more Arminian seems his view that a man's actions, in application of Free Will, might earn him something like good Old Calvinist rewards and punishments.

Channing did gather from Scripture that a man's acts in this life will in large part determine his future status. He did not, however, as the Legal Arminians do, "presume . . . to be a prophet of the future,"[87] and he had no convinced concept of Hell. Furthermore, and most important in his doctrine, no "Sin" is possible until Conscience is active, and by Conscience he means the Sense of Duty that comes with the Perception of God's Moral Perfection. No act, in other words, is wrong in itself, as a violation of set Law, as with the Arminians. An act is wrong only as a violation of the Perception of God's Meaning or Truth—"to give the body a mastery over the mind, to sacrifice the intellect and the heart of the senses."[88] So much Moralism the First and Second Puritans entertained, presuming that once a man had enjoyed the self-losing or objectifying Perception of Grace he would be little disposed to the common self-indulgences.

In Channing no more than in Hooker and Edwards do we find the doctrine of Salvation by Works. Rather, with him as with them, Works are a *Sign* that the Perception of Holiness—call it Grace or not as you choose—has been attained. Correspondingly, Evil Works are a Sign either that the Perception has not been attained or that having been attained, it has been repudiated by that

Free Will that is part of the gift of Grace. The difference is in vocabulary and in emphasis. The self-loving, objective Perception of the
Meaning of the World remains the crux. And that is still Puritanism.

Finney is particularly eloquent in condemnation of the "Legalists,"
whom he places first among those who are "actuated" by "self-love"
in their religious observances:

> Their religious duties are performed as a task, and are not the
> result of the constraining love of God. . . . They . . . possess
> a legal spirit. . . . Their religion is . . . produced by the fear
> of disgrace or the fear of hell, . . . it is mostly of a negative
> character. They satisfy themselves, mostly, with doing nothing
> that is very bad. Having no spiritual views, they regard the law
> of God chiefly as a system of prohibitions, . . . and not as a
> system of benevolence fulfilled by love. . . . [They] are more
> or less strict in religious duties. . . .[89]

Finney is close to the tradition of Edwards, and is perhaps as
much a Second Puritan as a Third Puritan. Channing, on the other
hand, is nearer to the Mean of the Age. More widely across Greater
New England than the limits of his influence, there was a Nineteenth-Century Yankee type which suited his concept, one whose
Christianity was based in a genuine Imaginative Percept, and yet
a part of the Percept was an element of Moral Purity or Stainless-
ness which was consciously believed to be of the stuff of Religion.
It was a saintly type, and Weld and most of the leaders of Reform
doubtless belonged to it, probably more than belonged to Finney's
more robust Puritanism which put all emphasis on the Love or Perception of God and the Neighbor, and let conduct take care of
itself.[90] By definition Legal Arminians are sharply divided from
Puritans in lacking the latter's Mystical Perception. Yet the possession
or lack of this Perception may be in degree. Throughout the nineteenth century there was a wide intermediate strip of the people of
Greater New England who day in and day out were bound by the
Law. Yet they were gently bound, without suffering the Arminian
vices of Fear and Self-righteousness. Once or twice in their lives they
enjoyed the Clarity and the Light as Finney saw them. Good and
Benevolent conduct was part of the vision, in the manner of Channing. Yet it was the memory of the Light, though it might not recur,
it was the memory of the Light and not its moral ingredient, that
kept them throughout their days in the Puritan way, the Christian
way, the Second-Commandment Christian way.

It would be giving too much credit to Timothy Dwight or any
other individual to derive from him the strong Arminian or Old

Calvinist taint in the Revival of 1800. That had to come out of some generic trend, and Dwight became for a decade or two the religious leader of New England because he happened to integrate and express the course of history. I have not found a convincing account of this rise of Legal Arminianism, and do not presume to offer one. We can guess that a world long accustomed to live without Imaginative Percepts, to live in terms of the carnal images of War and the social concepts of Natural Reason, would prefer a religion that trafficked in the comprehensible Carnalities of pleasure and pain and presented itself under a Reasonable System in which certain procedures would lead to certain foreseeable results. Or perhaps it might be that as society tired of its post-war licentiousness it would ask a religion that branded as evil those courses of conduct which it was ready to renounce anyway.

For whatever cause, Timothy Dwight, starting in 1796 his famous series of sermons at Yale, gradually drew out a response which in half a dozen years was a social movement. Dwight professed to be a good Edwardsean, but he shied away from the modified Doctrine of Election that came down to him through Hopkins and Emmons, swung back toward the Old Calvinist insistence upon Works as a Means and Preparation for Grace, and said that an Unregenerate person became *less* of a Reprobate when he performed a good act than he would be if he did not perform it. What he preached as a practical matter was human Responsibility irrespective of Grace, Free Will *now*, and the need of immediate repentance; and he preached these things with warmth.[91] He did in fact throw in a little parenthetic Predestination and Election. But the boys in the College Chapel didn't bother about that; and the people in the churches where Dwight itinerated about New England, founding the *Connecticut Society for the Recreation of Morals,* didn't bother about it either.

At Yale, once the Revival was well under way, there was much genuine religious feeling—"Surely God is in this place!" But there was also a great deal of solemn conversation about the Salvation of the Soul. Jedediah Morse, quitting Harvard and its Unitarianism to found Andover Theological Seminary, spoke honestly for Old Calvinism—"Let us guard against the insidious encroachments of *innovation.*" What, in his view, was sound was Hell Fire. The hill where stood the Seminary and the equally revivalistic Andover Academy was known as Brimstone Hill. One day the Headmaster of the Academy dismissed the school with the announcement: "There will now be a prayer meeting; those who wish to lie down in everlasting burning may go, the rest will stay." Two went. An academy senior wrote in his diary that it was evident that some will be finally rejected from the Kingdom of Heaven and it is probable that it will be a part of their punishment to see . . . their former companions enjoying in that blessed state from which they are excluded by their own folly and sin. The . . . tortures of condemned spirits will be increasing to all eternity. How tremendous and overwhelming is the thought that the suffering of one soul will be greater than the united suffering of all in the universe for millions of ages.[92]

The Arminian element in the Revival of 1800 probably produced more Blue Laws than did any other period in Puritan history. The Sunday laws were especially fierce in Connecticut, where the Sabbath lasted from sundown Saturday to sundown Sunday. A law of 1814 forbade any travel on Sunday, except for necessity or mercy. A law of 1838 forbade work of every kind except under the same impulsion, and directed the appointment of tithing men to help the constables in the enforcement. The population supported both the letter and the spirit of the laws. Generally, children were forbidden to whistle or otherwise enjoy themselves on the Sabbath. A man living in a hollow near Hartford started on a journey after sundown on Sunday. When he reached the upland the sun was still up, and he sat down and waited for it to set. In 1803 betting on horse races was made criminal by law. In 1828 lotteries were outlawed, and thus a long-standing source of public revenue and private enjoyment was tabooed. In 1830 games of chance were banned, and in '39 the Circus was declared a public nuisance.[93] Ohio, the child of Connecticut, had its similar Blue Laws, forbidding work and pleasure on the Sabbath, and imposing fines on any who "profanely curse, damn or swear by the name of God," gamble, duel or "fight or box at fisticuffs."[94]

All across Greater New England, most of the common pleasures passed under the shadow of taboo. At Oberlin tobacco, tea and coffee were equally frowned on, and in 1837 a saint there was churched for drinking tea.[95] In '56, at the height of the Kansas War, Topeka had an effective "liquor spilling," recorded with unction by the biographer of the local minister who assisted actively: "The affair was participated in by a large number of our most prominent and respectable citizens . . . with the entire approval of the ladies, and resulted in the destruction of the entire liquor supply of the town."[96] The "City Fathers" of San Francisco passed ordinances in 1848 fining Sunday card-playing $10 to $50, and $25 to $50 if in a public place; and they seem to have enforced the ordinance more or less successfully through the Gold Rush.[97] For a vignette typical of the proceedings of Yankee communities all the way across the country,

we have the record of the doings of the First Congregational Church
of Beloit. The account starts with the report of a Temperance Revival in '42, and wanders:

> Continuous meetings were held several weeks. The total ab-
> stinence pledge, which had been adopted by the church, was
> adopted almost universally by the people, old and young. There
> had been but one place where liquor was sold and that was
> cleansed by the owner throwing the liquor into the street.
> . . . They disciplined and ex-communicated. . . . They over-
> did that perhaps. . . . They went as far as they could with the
> slavery resolution, and voted to open the meeting house, which
> some opposed, to anti-slavery lectures. . . . They disciplined
> under the Sabbath resolution, not sparing even the prominent
> members of the church for so slight a thing as terminating a
> journey on that day. And they disciplined under the amusement
> resolution, and in one case curiously and to us amusingly. They
> disciplined at a distance, away out nearly to the Mississippi
> River, through the aid of the local church there, a female mem-
> ber of this church for attending a ball there. And the discipline
> was effective, the woman confessing her fault. They withheld
> a letter of dismission and recommendations from a physician on
> the ground, for one thing, of complaints from his patients of his
> exorbitant charges.[98]

As here, with the flaring of Arminian righteousness and concern
for the mote in the brother's eye, we seem to get an increase in the
number of church trials. Two incidents in the ordeal of Brother
Clark in one of the New Haven churches will serve for illustration.
The record is the minister's:[99]

> At the pastor's study Saturday evening, 5 June [1840?]
> Present, the pastor, Dea. Whittlesey, Dea. Hinman, Br.
> Hotchkiss.
> Commenced the examination of witnesses in the case of Br.
> Clark.
> Miss Thursby—The evening when Mr. Knapp preached on
> the last judgt—house full when she arrived—Mr. Clark in Mr.
> Teasdale's pew—next the door—invited her to sit in the pew tho'
> crowded—afterwards he changed seats with his wife, & sat next to
> her as he said that he should lose his seat if he sat next the
> door. In the course of the exercises, she felt his hand in her
> muff, taking hold of hers—he sitting with his other elbow on
> the pew before him, & with his cloak so hanging from his arm
> as to hide what he was doing from the sight of Mrs. C. who sat
> at his right hand.
> Sometime after, she had been in an inquiry meeting in the
> basement of the Bap meeting house after the evening service.

Mr. Clark went home with her to Mr. Teasdale's—at the door, she opened the door and went in first, he followed and immediately put his face under her bonnet. She went in immediately and told Mr. Teasdale that she was sorry Mr. C. had come home with her. The next day she heard that Mr. C. had been seen to kiss her at the front door;—she supposes he was seen by some of the persons who were that eveg. surrounding the house.

Poor Mr. C. got off that time, but he seems to have been badly starved for he did it several times again, usually with married ladies, and finally for his incorrigible sinfulness was excommunicated.

In such records of Legal Arminianism—and there are hundreds of them available to the curious—rather than in the generally Consecrated and Selfless Seventeenth Century, the Puritan-burners can find some justification for their sweeping charges of "Puritanism" that are entirely false of the real Puritans in any age. How prevalent this prudery was before the Civil War, in contrast to genuine Puritanical Benevolence, how widespread the sympathy with the Blue Laws and how general their enforcement, there is as always no way of telling. We may presume, of course, that the small-time Arminians involved would be more aggressive than the Puritans, that they would tend to exult in the record concerning their high moral attainments, whereas the people of mature religiosity would be bored with it all and would not attend these baitings.

The truth probably is that most of the people of the Age of Reform were to some degree Moralistic or Arminian, yet were still sufficiently supported by belief in a God, a Meaning of the Human Dilemma and Drama, and a sense of Spiritual Equality, to save them from the need of stooping to persecute Brother Clark for drinking tea or good liquor or kissing Miss Thursby. Probably the most important general expression of Arminianism at this time was in its insistence on the Anti-Calvinistic "New Calvinism" of Free Will which suited and abetted the Romantic Individualism of the Age. Almost everybody was convinced that he was the Captain of his Soul. Yet he was not subjective in this conviction, because he was chiefly concerned, not so much that he should fetch his own vessel into port as that every other individual should also be the Captain of his soul and should steer it as he chose. As authoritative and unbiased a statement as I can find offers a panorama of the people of Greater New England at this time which shows them as devoted to their Central Idea of the Perfect Commonwealth, and as indifferent to Self, as had been their predecessors in the Seventeenth and Eighteenth centuries. Although the author uses the un-Yankee phrase "middle-class," although, like most historians of the Twentieth Century, he treats the essential Religious motive only tangentially, yet his presentation is superficially so true, and it so truly shows the emergence of Third Puritanism out of Second Puritanism in the background, and out of the Old Calvinism that immediately surrounded it, that I quote fully:

. . . Most significant of all American elements for their generation were the middle-class New Englanders. Like bees they lived in many communities. . . . Perhaps two thousand . . . villages, towns or small cities . . . dotted New England, western New York and northeastern Ohio—the "Western Reserve." To those formed to meet it, nothing could be more stimulating than the earnest conformity to community standards of plain living and high thinking, which characterized these places. . . .

The standards which they maintained represented one of the highest community achievements in history . . . faint shadows of English rustic dances remained. Muster day in May afforded some general merrymaking. Boys went to sea, men almost universally drank, occasionally heavily. The women gossiped, with each other and with the peddlers who brought news and wares from town to town. Occasionally bills flared on the sides of barns, a premonitory clown sported on the common, a bugler blew his trumpet, and the less pious gathered in the open air for a circus.

To such a people the new impulses of the period opened a world of light and happiness. More important than the economic opportunities which they were called to share was the change in spiritual outlook, . . . a growing, happy, moving conviction that all men were equal, not as they had thought of it, in sin, but in possibilities of good. This changed point of view rushed many off their feet into the excesses of religious revivals. Others, however, were too firmly grounded in the practice of a life based on reason to be overwhelmed. New England was like a well-made engine into which an electric current was newly turned, increasing its power of production.

Perhaps the most notable factor in this change, which escaped being a revolution, was the continuity of leadership . . . the New England ministerial families furnished a most unusual proportion of the leaders of her new activities. Hundreds of the radicals of the thirties and forties possessed the bone and sinew and the moral earnestness and mental habits of six or seven generations of ministers who would have regarded their aims and views as conceptions of the devil. With trained minds and steady habits, with economic resources adequate to its measured needs, with a high consciousness of its relative merits, and now thrilled by the enthusiasm of the hour into a belief that the great experiment of 1630 had finally succeeded and that its light should now shine penetratingly abroad for the regeneration of the world, the New England dominant, but not always ruling, middle class was prepared to do its duty.[100]

Throw around this panorama the inclusive frame of Religion, and you have the Third Puritanism that from here set out for Utopia and instead came up to Armageddon. It was the dominant thread of the Culture, but alongside it always was flowing that ominous Legal Arminianism which we must follow because it appeared at its worst in some of the leaders who put their mark on the age. When a person succumbs to Moralism so as to be preoccupied with Right and Wrong, he usually comes to be obsessed especially with Wrong, with Sin, not in the large sense of alienation from God but in the small sense of misconduct according to law or fashion. At first he is mostly concerned about his own sinfulness, but in due course it becomes more comfortable to attend to the sins of others. These others, these Neighbors, may be individuals, or classes in Society, or, in larger minds, all of Society, the sin appearing as an abuse, a cancer, in the Social Body. In the attack on the Sin, whether in Individual, in Class, or in Society, there is always danger that the Zeal of the Moralist will change from Christian Concern or Benevolence into Hatred, first of the Sin, and afterwards of the person infected with it. And in this hatred, this Judgment of another, the Reformer elevates himself to God's judicial prerogative, and so descends to the lowest depth of Original Sin. In a large mind with a true Social Vision, this Hatred becomes agreeable to Ambition, for in the condemnation of the Social Sin, the large Social Virtue of the condemner is modestly implied.

Among some of the finest minds of the Age of Reform, we find this Hatred for one or more Social Wrongs, variously swelling outward to include the perpetrators of the Wrongs. In Weld it was not so, for in him the hatred of sin was blocked by Christian Perception from personal hatred, even of his persecutors. In Theodore Parker, Universal Reformer, Transcendentalist, Socialist, we find the hatred of Social Evil still objective, still impersonal, but here less combined with Christian Love than derived from a fine Intellectual Arminian Social Vision which puts it in greater danger of slipping over into the self-glorification of personal hatred:

> . . . If there be a public sin in the land, if a lie invade the state, it is for the church to give the alarm; it is here that it may war on lies and sins; the more widely they are believed in and practiced, the more are they deadly, the more to be opposed. Here let no false idea or false action of the public go

without exposure or rebuke. But let no noble heroism of the
times, no noble man pass by without honor.[101]

In Lyman Beecher we go a long step beyond Parker, both in religious perception and in the perverted expression of it. In him we
see the tragic and paradoxical emergence of a hateful Arminianism
out of both an original Puritan perception and continuing Puritan
doctrine. His own conversion came unexpectedly and emotionally
in the usual Puritan fashion, when he was a young man home on va-
cation from Yale—though, prophetically enough, the immediate occasion of it was the perception of a drunkard passing the house and
his mother's comment of pity on him.[102] His doctrine was always of
Salvation by Faith, not by Works and the Law; he had a tender vision
of Christ, and he was not a preacher of Hell Fire. At the same time,
the center of his belief and preachment was Free Will. He made
much of the necessity of the Law and its Punishments to keep
earthly and Celestial Society in order. He made Moral Reformation
a condition of Grace.[103] With an eye on Channing, who denied the
whole cycle of Reprobation and Grace, he proclaimed his belief that
"the condemnation of those by whom offered mercy is rejected, will
be most fearfully aggravated."[104] And he emphasized that the Saint's
greatest concern should be lest, following Regeneration, he back-
slide into Sin. Beecher was personally a kindly, generous, courageous,
often humorous, lover of mankind. Yet there was in him from the
beginning a preoccupation with Sin and a delight to battle with it.
In comment on his first important sermon against a Social Evil—that
against duelling, preached in 1806 in reference to the Hamilton-Burr
affray, while he was an incumbent of his first pulpit at Easthampton,
Long Island—he said gaily, "Oh, I declare, if I did not switch 'em,
and scorch 'em, and stamp on 'em." Nineteen years later, in the six
great lectures in Litchfield that gave the first real impetus to the
Temperance Movement we have the indignation against Social Sin
mature and on the march:

> Intemperance is the sin of our land, and, with our boundless
> prosperity, is coming in upon us like a flood; and if anything
> shall defeat the hopes of the world, which hang upon our ex-
> periment of civil liberty, it is that river of fire which is rolling
> through the land, destroying the vital air, and extending around
> an atmosphere of death. . . .
> But it will be said, What can be done? and ten thousand voices
> will reply, "Nothing, oh, nothing; men always have drunk to
> excess, and they always will. . . ."
> Then farewell, a long farewell, to all our greatness! . . .[105]

And here he shows the tragic naïveté which most of the Reformers
suffered toward the Greatest Social Wrong of all:

. . . The abolition of the slave-trade, an event now almost accomplished[!], was once regarded as a chimera of benevolent dreaming. But the band of Christian heroes who consecrated their lives to the work, may some of them survive to see it achieved. This greatest of evils upon earth . . . is passing away before the unbending requisitions of enlightened public opinion.[106]

Beecher was at his worst in his bigoted denunciation of Catholicism which through increasing immigration was beginning to show strength in Greater New England. In 1834 he delivered on one evening three violent anti-Catholic sermons in Boston, following which —though no connection with his sermons is established—a mob in Charlestown burned down an Ursuline convent which had been doing a good job of educating some forty children of the rich in Boston.

And a step beyond Beecher, addressing the "greatest of evils upon earth," we find William Lloyd Garrison nominally announcing the appearance of the famous *Liberator* in 1831, but really announcing Himself and his subconscious determination to take over the direction of Mankind and to bring on Civil War:

. . . I *will be* as harsh as truth, and as uncompromising as justice. On this subject, I do not wish to think, to speak, or write, with moderation. . . . I am in earnest—I will not equivocate—I will not excuse—I will not retreat a single inch—AND I WILL BE HEARD.[107]

In the Peace Movement he went beyond the Organization's aim of international peace and anounced himself in a letter in similarly ostentatious terms:

. . . It is the duty of the followers of Christ to suffer themselves to be defrauded, calumniated and barbarously treated, without resorting either to their own physical energies, or to the force of human law, for restitution or punishment.[108]

Accordingly, when in '35 the Boston mob broke up a meeting of the Massachusetts Female Anti-Slavery Society, and dragged Garrison through the streets with a rope around his neck, tearing off his clothes, till the Mayor rescued him and jailed him for safekeeping, he exulted masochistically on his prison walls:

Reader, let this inscription remain till the last slave in this despotic land be loosed from his fetters. . . .
Confine me as a prisoner—but bind me not as a slave.
Punish me as a criminal—but hold me not as a chattel.
Torture me as a man—but drive me not like a beast.
Doubt my sanity—but acknowledge my immortality.[109]

And thereafter, with his unique genius for invective, he attacked, not Slavery but the Slaveholders and the South, in the hope of fetching on the violence which he subconsciously desired and professed to deplore:

> The men of wolf-like ferocity, who are multiplying the stripes upon the bodies of their victims, and making their yokes heavier and their chains more galling, and revelling in their blood, and basely withholding their wages, and excluding every ray of knowledge from their minds, and claiming a heaven-derived title to their bodies and souls. . . .[110]

Thus did Garrison, always in the name of Christianity, carry the Arminian hatred of Sin to the hatred of the Sinner, and beyond to heights where all sense of Sin and Sinner are lost in the Subjective Ecstasy of Rhetoric. What started as Legal Arminianism loses relation to Law and Morality, and merges into the ecstasy of Antinomianism, the identification of the private will with the will of God. Garrison was by talent a great poet of denunciation and satire. Much of his expression, both in prose and in verse, is worth preserving as literature for its own sake; but its relation to History, as well as Garrison's own delusions of leadership, might in charity be forgotten.

As Legal Arminianism, the Error of Reason, ran always dangerously along the Right Flank of the current of Third Puritanism in the first half of the Nineteenth Century, so Antinomianism, the Error of Emotion, ran as ominously along the Left Flank. Arminianism, occurring within the framework of the Law which is also the framework of Society, tended to lead, as we have seen, into Moral Snobbery, the Sense of Superiority or Inferiority by social canons, with appropriate competitive activities of Repression and Resentment. Antinomianism, on the other hand, was an exercise entirely between God and the Individual, giving the latter a lordly assurance quite above the necessity of comparing himself with less fortunate mortals. Wherefore, being innocent, honest and usually ridiculous, it was more appealing than Arminianism.

Not since Mrs. Hutchinson told the General Court at The Bay that God personally gave her instructions have we a purer case of it than that of the young perfectionist John Humphrey Noyes of Putney, Vermont, who, when catechized by his teachers at the Yale Divinity School, assured them that with his Conversion had come complete release from sin, "purity of heart and the answer of a good conscience before God."[111] Incidentally, in recalling Noyes's

youthful pomposity it is worth remembering also that his profession
may not have been far beyond his performance in the establishment
of the Oneida Community—New York—in 1848. In its Democratic
Communism, its unique control of Sex, its Progressive Education,
its system of Industrial Organization—from steel traps to silver
cutlery—, and withal its entire dependence on the Will of God as
revealed in the Bible, it was for thirty or forty years perhaps as close
an approximation of the Perfection which Noyes claimed as the
human record affords. Incidentally there was little that was Antinomian about it beyond Noyes's early extravagant claims, for its
people were always under close discipline. In terms of a community,
that at Oneida was perhaps the best application we have of Third
Puritanism, the Perception of Ultimate Truth in Moral Terms,
the Perception combining Reason and Emotion in the mysterious
proportion which is Grace.

The numerous Utopias which the Age of Reform produced were
usually touched with Antinomianism, especially on the part of the
leaders. Mother Ann Lee, the founder of the Shakers, learned
through numerous trances that as Christ had been the Male Principle of God on earth she was the Female Principle, wherefore, being the Second Incarnation of the Holy Spirit, she was in the 1770's
and '80's the "visible leader of the Church of God upon Earth."
Jemima Wilkinson, the "Universal Friend" who set up the New
Jerusalem on Seneca Lake in New York in 1788 and lived there in
some luxury, not only got her orders from God but probably was
herself God, since it was plain to her that in her youth she had
once died of a fever, and that when the spirit returned it was the
Spirit of Christ. The bulk of the Mormons were substantial, well-
disciplined Third Puritans. Yet without the fantastic communications of God, through strange Angels, Golden Plates, Mysterious
Language, and eventually forthright Revelation, to the ignorant,
credulous, handsome, naïvely conceited and lawless "Prophet" Joseph Smith, this great movement would neither have started nor
long continued.

Transcendentalism was after all a kind of systematic Antinomianism, and Bronson Alcott, in projecting his childish utopia at "Fruit-
lands" near Harvard, Massachusetts, was inspired to believe that
just there "the divine seed" was "to bruise the head of Evil and
restore Man to his rightful communion with God in the Paradise of
the Good." Brook Farm, involving much of the best brains of the
Age, chiefly under the direction of George Ripley, was distressingly
sane, and Emerson, who elsewhere declared, "We are all Antinomians now," regretted that he was not there "made nobly mad
by the kindlings before my eye of a new dawn of human piety."

Emerson also commented on the Age that it contained scarcely a literate man "but has a draft of a new community in his waistcoat pocket."[112] Adin Ballou, in founding his Hopedale Community, near Milford, Massachusetts, was also depressingly sane, being only a brilliant and brave Third Puritan, Unitarian preacher who sanely concluded that it was the duty of the disciples of Christ to work and pray for the practical establishment of His Kingdom on earth. Of the three Yankee Utopias which lasted longest, it is to be observed that the founders of Shakerism and Mormonism alike enjoyed extraordinary visitations and self-elevating revelations, while the founder of Oneida Community set about his work with the announcement that he was Perfect. There were during the period many other Utopias set up on Yankee territory besides those mentioned, but the most memorable of them, such as those at Zoar, Ohio, New Harmony, Indiana, and Amana, Iowa, were of foreign leadership and do not fit into the story of Yankee culture.[113]

Most of the Utopians were Millennarian in the sense that their Perfectionism, variously rationalized, told them that the Second Coming was due any day in the United States and that they would do well to be about preparing a proper reception for Christ. Indeed, something of the kind was in the mind of a large section of the citizenry who believed devoutly that the Union was God's own establishment in preparation for His Descent. But only William Miller, a consecrated, quiet, unsensational, uneloquent, meticulous and wholly sincere little Baptist minister in upper Vermont was able, by long calculations based upon literally taken statements by Daniel and other Prophets, to figure out just when the happy event was going to occur.

Mr. Miller found that it was to be in 1843; and probably nothing more would have come of his studies and his local preachings in Vermont and Eastern New York, had not Rev. Joshua V. Himes, minister of the Adventist Chardon Street Chapel in Boston, and probably the greatest publicity agent in America before Barnum, met the unobtrusive little man and seen the possibilities in his obsession. At once he started publishing *Signs of the Times* in Boston and *Midnight Cry* in New York, and within a year had Miller on the road, together with a circus tent, suitable bands and torches. This movement reversed the conditions of most of the Utopias, whereof the leaders were crazy and the rank and file mostly sane. Miller was the simplest, soundest little pseudo-Puritan imaginable—pseudo because his Puritanism was hopelessly compromised with the Arminianism of Respectability and Natural Reason, wherefore the Light he saw was only a bright idea and no Light. But he was far from Emotional and Antinomian in any way. Yet as Himes led him around the country, to which his was the very quintessence of good and expected News, first thousands, and presently hundreds of thousands, rose up to prepare themselves for The Day when they would meet their God. Before we reach The Day, however, it will be well to notice some of the other great movements that preceded it.

Characteristic of the Antinomian Individualism of the Age was the proliferation of Sects which began about as the Revival was getting under way in the last decades of the eighteenth century. We have seen the Congregational Church splitting off the Unitarians, the crack having appeared before the Revolution and being notice-able by the 1790's. Soon thereafter began a series of Schisms from the Presbyterian church, most of them starting in Virginia and spreading north across the Ohio: The New Light Schism (1803), presently organizing itself as the Christian Church; the Cumber-land Presbyterian Church (1810); the Disciples (1809); the Camp-bellites (the 1820's). There were the Republican Methodists, the Methodist Protestant Church and the Christian Connection Church. There were The United Brethren in Christ and the Evangelical Church, both of German origin and spreading north out of Pennsyl-vania. Later, as the slavery issue grew acute, every one of the old orthodoxies split into a Northern and a Southern section, and some split several ways.*

Besides these splits in orthodoxy there were numerous fly-by-night Antinomian sects, especially in New England, often distinguishing themselves by tonsorial or sartorial peculiarities for which they found sanction in the Bible. A spectacular one of these was the Pilgrims who assembled in Woodstock, Vermont, in 1817; their marks of saintliness were long beards, bearskin girdles, the prac-tice of fasting in sackcloth and ashes, foregoing the bath (their prophet did not change his clothes for seven years), free love and immediate divine inspiration for everybody. This sect held together long enough to trek out across New York, three hundred strong, and down the Ohio, to disband in Missouri.[114] In New England these numerous and transitory Antinomian sects were generally called Come-Outers, because their one positive performance was that they Came Out of the conservative godlessness of the Orthodox churches. In southern Illinois in 1835, one settlement of eighty fami-lies had fourteen sects most of which are today wholly forgotten.[115] During this period schism was so widespread within an almost universal profession of Christianity that it was said that every man's "hat is his church."

* The Episcopal Church did not split until secession.

Puritans, miscellaneous Arminians, and more miscellaneous Antinomians, all met together and quarrelled within the great and small organizations of Reform, of which we noticed some of the beginnings up to 1820. After that they all expanded rapidly until they blanketed Greater New England almost as fully as the Churches did. The chief among them can be divided into three groups. The Conservative group, typically Old Calvinist and well called the *"Benevolent Empire,"* was the far-flung Missionary and Charitable web of the Great Denominations efficiently united on an inter-denominational front for Conservative Religion, Conservative Charity and the Social and Economic Status Quo. Secondly, there was the *Radical Empire,* mostly religious in pretence also, and characterized by Antinomian passion or by Garrisonian passion of the Ultra-Arminian sort that is hardly distinguishable from Antinomian passion and fringing off into more or less socialistic doctrines. And thirdly, there was what we might call the *Moderate Empire,* typified by Rational and Liberal Social Consciousness not necessarily religious. The apportionment of the principal Movements and Manias among these three Groups might be as follows:

I. *The Benevolent Empire:* The orthodox Congregational, Presbyterian, Methodist, Baptist, and Episcopal Churches; based in these, the "Great Eight" among inter-denominational movements—namely, Religious Education, Foreign Missions, Home Missions, Bible Distribution, Tract Distribution, Sunday Schools, Preservation of the Sabbath, and Temperance; various less widespread charities, such as Colonization for Freed Slaves, Havens for Seamen, and Havens for Prostitutes.

II. *The Radical Empire:* Unitarians, and the various radical wings of the Presbyterian, Methodist and Baptist Churches; Quakers, Shakers, and Mormons; and all other kinds of Religious Utopians, Adventists—notably Millerites, Come-Outers, Deists, Free Thinkers, and Transcendentalists; Phrenologists and Spiritualists; "Immediate," Non-Political Abolitionists; Feminists, Non-Resisters, and No-Government Men; Radical or Pestalozzian educators; Absolute Prohibitionists or Teetotalers; Fourrierites, and all other brands of Socialists and Laborites.

III. *The Moderate Empire:* Gradual Emancipation, especially through political Third Party action; Prison Reform; Abolition of Capital Punishment; Abolition of Imprisonment for Debt; Care of the Insane; Public Health; Civic Sanitation; Prevention of Cruelty to Animals; Public Education; Manual Training.

Most active Reformers belonged to several Movements, often crossing the lines of this arbitrary grouping, but their temper was usually appropriate to one and only one of these "Empires." Beside the organizations appropriate to the movements named there were many others that came and went in a few months with their world-shaking periodicals, and there were many hundreds of local Improvement Societies that had no national affiliation. Almost every respectable town had something commonly called the Female Retrenchment Society whose purpose was to defend women against the hellish temptations of "tea, coffee, rich cake, pastry, preserves, snuff and tobacco, as well as wine and cordials."[116] Arthur and Lewis Tappan, leaders of large and interlocking segments of the Benevolent and Moderate Empires, were prominent in a group of rich men in New York who called themselves the New York Association of Gentlemen and pledged each other to devote their surpluses, not to accumulation, but to the Perfection, through philanthropy, of Mankind.[117]

Between 1820 and 1840, the greatest advance in Reform that proved permanent was in Public Education. In 1823 Rev. Samuel Read Hall of Concord, New Hampshire, established in his house the country's first Normal School, and a few years later was called to head a new school at Andover which also became a teachers' training school. There he worked for years with Horace Mann, lobbying to get Massachusetts to establish Normal Schools, a Superintendent of Education, and generally to improve the low state of public teaching. In '37 Mann became the first State Superintendent of Schools in the United States, and two years later the first State Normal School was established at Lexington, followed shortly by two others, while the state appropriation for Education was doubled and the teachers' salaries increased. Meanwhile New York, influenced by Hall's printed *Lectures,* provided special education for teachers through help to the Academies, and in 1838 Henry Barnard became Superintendent of Schools in Connecticut. Mann's classic Reports are the basis of American public education, or were until recent years when we have been defying his greatest warning by making our schools play-palaces to debauch the future voters to vote for more play-palaces. Said Mann:

> If we do not prepare children to become good citizens—if we do not develop their capacities, if we do not enrich their minds with knowledge, imbue their hearts with the love of truth and duty, and a reverence for all things sacred and holy, then our republic must go down to destruction, as others have gone before it; and mankind must sweep through another vast cycle of sin and suffering, before the dawn of a better era can arise upon the world. It is for our government, and for that public opinion which, in a republic, governs the government to choose between these alternatives of weal or woe.

During this period, namely in 1834 in the Masonic Temple on Tremont Street, Boston, Bronson Alcott set up a school based on the Pestalozzian teaching, which was virtually our Progressive or Dewey-esque method, becoming in practice the method of teaching the child nothing but drawing out the great mines of wisdom that are in his little brain and other ganglia. Alcott's school was popular until, with his passionate naïveté, he began to tell the children about sex, a realistic matter which Boston in the 1830's was already beginning to hide away in the Victorian closet.

Among moderate, and therefore not greatly celebrated Reforms, the Movement for Public Health and Sanitation made noticeable though unsure advances before 1840, having achieved the installation of quite unsanitary public water supplies and sewage systems in a few cities.

Of the great and spectacular Reforms, Temperance accomplished an advance and retreat. Lyman Beecher's big series of lectures, delivered in Litchfield in '25 and published and broadcast in '26, enlisted through succeeding years an imposing array of ministers, including Presidents Humphrey of Amherst, Nott of Union College, Appleton of Bowdoin, Lord of Dartmouth, Hopkins of Williams, Wayland of Brown and Day of Yale, not to mention the great and unpresidential Czars of Reform, Channing and Parker. In '26 the American Society for the Promotion of Temperance was organized in Boston, and revivalist lecturers, together with much professional propaganda, scattered forth to conquer. In '34 the Society claimed five thousand subsidiary societies and a membership of a million in the Nation. In '36 the American Temperance Union was organized at a Convention in Philadelphia in order better to integrate the old Society with its subsidiaries and especially with the numerous independent groups. There was conflict over the question whether the pledge to be urged on all citizens should be of total abstinence or of abstinence from ardent spirits only. The teetotalers, Lyman Beecher in command, won in the convention, but when the delegates tried to sell teetotalism to their constituencies the Union split into hundreds of angry factions. Between '36 and '39 the New York Association alone declined in membership from 229,000 to 131,000. By '40 the first campaign for Temperance was over. A reason for the decline of the Cause in the South was Garrison's espousal of it, for he was famous for integrating his Reforms and he was already wanted in several Southern states for Criminal Libel in his *Liberator*.

During these twenty years Garrison perfected his technique of Rule-or-Ruin with respect to the three movements where he most ardently exercised, namely the Abolition Movement, the Peace Movement and the Woman Movement, succeeding in setting back the first two and inadvertently begetting the third, though without bringing it to birth. He fancied himself the Head of all three, which delusion he took as justification for interpreting the general irritation with him as unfaithfulness to the Cause. Because he was for all three, he insisted that everybody must swallow them all or stand an inspired excoriating in the *Liberator*—not that that did anybody much harm, for the *Liberator* never had over 400 white subscribers, its real support coming from free Negroes.[118]

Garrison first garbled the Peace issue by drawing it down from the plane of War to that of individual Christian Non-Resistance, in the statement in 1835 which we noticed before. In '37 he got poor Angelina Grimke so confused in his three-way doctrine that, while lecturing first on Abolition, she found herself next combining this theme with that of Women's Rights, and then proceeded to break her engagement with Theodore Weld because he was not a "peace man." Garrison was behind all of this, as he was behind the little group of Radicals—including Adin Ballou, Henry Wright and Abby Kelly, female itinerater—who in '38 at a general Convention split every Peace Society in New England by insisting on Women's Voting Rights. This was already a known hobby of Garrison's, and at the mention of it the large Conservative minority at once withdrew. Garrison's residue then gaily formed a new outfit which he could control, the New England Non-Resistance Society, dedicated to the inviolability of life—thus solving the question of capital punishment —, together with Garrison's earlier principle of absolute, personal Pacifism. Thus he remained the boss of something, while the Movement as a whole was weakened.

Even before Garrison's effort to ruin Abolition by confusing it with the "Woman Question," he did a fairly successful job of demolition on account of the American Colonization Society which, as we saw, was the first real organization in the field, with Lyman Beecher the big gun, and to which most of the ministers of New England belonged. Beecher tried to unite the Colonization and the Immediate Abolition Movements, but Garrison would have no peaceful nonsense that might leave him in second place. In the *Liberator* he began to denounce the Massachusetts Association of Congregational clergymen for their "pro-slavery subservience," after which they showed a tendency to deny their pulpits to the paid and incendiary agents of Garrison's Massachusetts Anti-Slavery Society, until finally in a common announcement they denied them all to all kinds of Revivalists.

As they closed against him, Garrison bit by bit unbunged his best vitriol, till he was telling his readers that the Congregational ministers stood "at the head of the most implacable foes of God and man," toward whom "the most intense abhorrence should fill the breast of every disciple of Christ."[119] He reached the near peak of his genius when he discovered that the Methodist Church—which with the Baptist included two-thirds of the Abolitionists in New England—was "a cage of unclean birds and a synagogue of Satan." And after the middle '30's he habitually referred to all ministers as the "black-hearted clergy." Meanwhile, having been always orthodox, he proclaimed divers ostentatious heresies then current. Among other fresh insights he discovered that the Sabbath was a superstition, and that all ecclesiastical institutions confined the true Christian spirit. Also he renounced allegiance to all government and "nominated Jesus Christ to the Presidency of the United States and the World."[120]*

Garrison's best non-literary accomplishment, other than the Civil War, was the splitting of the American Anti-Slavery Society, centered in New York, whose leaders the Tappans, Elizur Wright, Presidential Candidate Birney, and other large-souled men, were really too much for the wiry, mirthlessly grinning, fearless little shrike from Boston. In '37 he planted trouble—later extirpated—by getting through the Annual Meeting a resolution to the effect that Abolitionists should neither organize a political party nor attach themselves to existing ones. But a little later, in June of the same year, he opened up the Woman Question in a way that was seriously going to rock the Movement. In that month the Grimke sisters, "Carolina's high-souled daughters," had heard the call of Anti-Slavery, and Angelina, as we have seen, was giving a series of lectures in Boston. At first the meetings were intended for women only, but after a "brother" or two had slipped in, the "door was wide open" and they found themselves addressing "promiscuous assemblies." Even the Abolitionists were shocked, excepting only Garrison and Francis Jackson, the philanthropic and courageous president of the Massachusetts Anti-Slavery Society. Garrison in a typically sudden and utter conversion saw the Rights of Women as identified with the general cause of Freedom, and took up for them with passion in the *Liberator*. Under

* Garrison was a greatly beloved and gentle husband and father, and was a clear, liberal mind where no question of his own power was involved. As an old man, in 1875, he presented to his son a Bible with the following inscription:

From his affectionate father, who presents it not as "the Word of God," as it is by many dogmatically assumed to be, (for that is from everlasting to everlasting,) but as a volume to be studied, criticised, and judged, without prejudice, credulity, superstition, or regard to any popular or prevailing interpretation thereof, and with the same freedom as any other book or compilation of ancient manuscripts; in which case, reason and conscience holding mastery over it, it will still be found deserving of the highest consideration for its incomparable truths, solemn warnings, and precious promises.

(Printed through the courtesy of Mrs. Faith Garrison Harwood who owns the Bible in question.)

his urgency Angelina shortly found herself giving a series of lectures, not against slavery, but in favor of Women's Rights.[121]

At this juncture the General Association of Massachusetts, representing "practically all" the ministers of the state, issued in July a Pastoral Letter to the churches, stating that the "perplexed and agitating subjects which are now common amongst us . . . should not be forced upon any church as matters of debate, at the hazard of alienation and division," and taking at the same time a fair whack at the heavy-jawed Grimke girls: "The power of woman is in her dependence. . . . When she assumes the place and tone of men as a public reformer, our care and protection of her seem unnecessary; we put ourselves in defence against her. . . ." In this dilemma Angelina plumped for protection and dependence. She at last agreed to marry the gentle Theodore Weld, who was for Women's Rights but never mixed his Reforms. Soon after the Pastoral Letter five ministers issued the famous "Appeal of Clerical Abolitionists on Anti-Slavery Measures," complaining of Garrison's excesses, particularly his assaults on moderate supporters which tended to drive them out of the movement. The signers of the "Appeal" claimed to represent nine-tenths of the Abolitionists. The day after its appearance, thirty-nine Abolitionists in Andover Theological Seminary issued a similar statement.

All of this gave Garrison great joy of combat, and the *Liberator* trembled with his weekly volleys. In the ecstasy of battle he wrote to the National Executive Committee in New York, demanding that they condemn the ministry of New England for the Pastoral Letter and Clerical Appeal. Lewis Tappan wrote him in the tone of a father reprimanding a bad boy for pulling his sister's hair. He regretted some of the things in the ministerial pronouncements, but he regretted also the behavior of the *Liberator*. Rather than censure the Appeal, Tappan would "censure those brethren who magnified the Appeal, and turned aside, at such a crisis, to wage battle with part of our own troops. . . ." Garrison thereafter behaved himself for several months as far as women were concerned. Then, at the annual meeting of the New England Anti-Slavery Society in '38, his lieutenant Oliver Johnson moved that women be admitted to full participation in the society. When the resolution was passed against opposition, Amos Augustus Phelps, wheel horse, and five other ministers and a layman asked to have their names expunged from the rolls of those present.

Garrison's next move was to inject the Woman Question into the National Organization, by which he did the Movement great and irreparable harm. He also set off a chain of events which culminated in the independent Women's Rights Movement, which thus became the child of Abolition by Garrison. Until 1839 the cells of what eventually would be the national women's organization had been local female auxiliaries of the American Anti-Slavery Society. In that year they determined to have a convention of their own in Philadelphia, at the same time that the American Anti-Slavery Society was having its annual affair in New York. Through manipulation by Garrison, or on his behalf, a lot of the "female" delegates on their way to Philadelphia stopped off in New York to see how the boys were doing. There being some doubt of their and other ladies' status on the floor, a resolution was introduced giving them full voting power, and—by the weight of the female vote before they had the vote—it was carried. A few days later, Phelps resigned as recording secretary of the Massachusetts Society, on the ground that it was no longer a simple anti-slavery society, but a "woman's-rights, no-government, anti-slavery society."

The chief problem of the American Anti-Slavery Society now was not slaves but women, and Garrison had them all in his pocket. The following year, the great year of '40, he determined to make good in his victory with a vengeance. For the annual meeting of the Society in New York in May, he chartered the steamboat *Massachusetts,* which lay in Lynn Harbor, offering a ride to New York at nominal cost to all who understood the purpose of their going. There were 500 delegates from Massachusetts.[122] The conservative or Tappan leadership had itself not been innocent of packing. The test came early, on the nomination by acting President Jackson of Abby Kelly to the business or steering committee. Garrison won by a vote of 560 to 450. Seeing that the jig was up, the old New York Executive Committee, including Lewis Tappan and Birney, withdrew with its full cohorts and reorganized as the American and Foreign Anti-Slavery Society.[123] The Garrison-controlled convention now elected three women to its National Executive Committee—namely, Lucretia Mott, Lydia Maria Child, and Maria W. Chapman, the last two Yankees. Furthermore, Garrison himself put through a resolution declaring that the American Church had given its "undisguised sanction and support to the system of American Slavery," and resolving, therefore, "that the church ought not to be regarded and treated as the Church of Christ, but as the foe of freedom, humanity and pure religion. . . ." Thus did Garrison exult over the authors of the Clerical Appeal. Thus did he ruthlessly widen national schism into a gulf. Thus did he gaily shrivel the hope of appeasing the church-going and partially Anti-Slavery South.

Meanwhile, the British and Foreign Anti-Slavery Society had sent invitations to a World Anti-Slavery Convention in London the forthcoming June.[124] The British invitation said that "gentlemen only were expected," but the American Radicals persuaded the girls to go all the same, the girls including Abby Kelly, Lucretia Mott, Elizabeth Cady Stanton, Ann Green Phillips, wife of Wendell, and other ladies of the best taste and courage.[125] After much embarrassment, they were excluded from the Convention and made to sit behind a curtain. In protest, Garrison, delegate from both the American and the Massachusetts societies, declined his seat and watched the proceedings from the Gallery. As Mrs. Mott and Mrs. Stanton, Quaker and Yankee respectively, sat in their modest seclusion, the Woman's Right Movement germinated in their minds, though it did not flower until eight years later.

Through 1840, the achievements of the Age of Reform, with its Third or Humanitarian Puritanism and Second-Commandment Christianity, had been impressive in but three important areas, namely the great Missionary Field of the Conservative Benevolent Empire with all of its subdivisions and corollaries, the Educational Field of the Moderate Empire, and the General Field of Religious Revival which included the Proliferation of Sects and was in some part of an Antinomian and Radical temper. In the lesser trends the last twenty years had continued to be mainly a period of the clashing of Experimental forces. The climax and parody of all these Random Trials, religious and otherwise, was the Chardon Street Convention, held in the Chardon Street Chapel in Boston on November 17, 18 and 19, 1840, with further and less impressive sessions in March and October of 1841.

The Minister of the Adventists who rented the Chapel from the adjoining Parkman family—it had been one of their stables, and Francis Parkman, Sr., spoke of it as "my mother's barn"—was Joshua V. Himes who just this year had discovered William Miller and his Prophetic Calculations about the great year of 1843, and was about to display them both luridly to America. The Convention was summoned by a self-constituted Committee who characteristically called themselves the "Friends of Universal Reform." Garrison was behind it, and among the signers the names we have already mentioned included Edmund Quincy, perennial Chairman of everything, Maria Chapman, perennial secretary of everything, Bronson Alcott, Henry Wright, William H. Channing, Theodore Parker and Oliver Johnson.

With the possible exception of the perhaps over-rational Parker, these seem to have been people whose religion was based in a genuine Objective, Universal Perception which qualifies them as Puritans; also, the great Puritans Channing and Emerson attended, though neither opened his mouth. There were Antinomians whom we shall notice especially, and besides these there were Legal Arminian Heretics of all shades except that of complacent and stupid morality for its own sake. Beecher did not show up, but there were numerous members of the Old Calvinist Clergy, with its Free-Will Calvinism. And there was Garrison the ecstatically self-righteous Hater of Social Sinners who discharged his broadsides in the face of the "Black-hearted Clergy" only less eloquently than in the print of the *Liberator*. The subject of the November session was the Sabbath—Was it or was it not of Divine Appointment? The subject of the March session —injected by Garrison—was The Ministry! No resolution was ever adopted on either topic, nor was anything accomplished beyond an Exhibition of wares of the Age of Reform, a Fair with several lively sideshows.

Nothing was concluded by the Chardon Street Convention. What was wonderful about it was its miscellaneity—"Madmen, madwomen, men with beards, Dunkers, Muggletonians, Come-outers, Groaners, Agrarians, Seventh-day-Baptists, Quakers, Abolitionists, Calvinists, Unitarians and Philosophers"—[126] not to mention a few Mormons, Spiritualists, Non-Resisters, No-Government Men, Millennarians, and Unidentified. What was wonderful about it was its Individualism, its free and Innocent Self-assertiveness and Anarchy, the fact that some of the finest minds of the century sat through the ordeal of its Pre-Organizational phase when the question was whether this Convention, or any Convention, or the World, or the Universe, would not do better without any organization other than that imposed by the Holy Ghost. The Chardon Street Convention is significant for an exceptionally pure display of Antinomianism, and its toleration by what was probably a majority of educated minds, both Puritan and Arminian.

The Convention of about 500 was assembled by nine in the morning on that November 17th in 1840,[127] and before the divers Anarchists knew what was happening, Edmund Quincy, presiding, had seen to the appointment of a Nominating Committee. But that was as far as he got with his dictatorial methods. When someone—doubtless planted—rose to move the nomination of a Steering Committee, the Antinomians scented the Enemy of Law and Order, and went into action. An unidentified man sprang up and gave off the view that no officers were needed, nor any committees either. He would not take his liberty of speech as the boon of a chairman or business committee, nor would he be constrained to address a chairman when he felt moved to address all his brethren. There was no need of a secretary, for reports would be made of course, and there was no point in resolutions for, after hearing the argument, everybody would know his own mind without being bound by a resolution. Without resolutions, there would be no need of a chairman to keep speakers to the point. He resented as the greatest of evils the existence of organizations to which the individual was subordinated.

Now a louder and surer voice rose in support. It was "Dr." Sylvanus Brown of Amesbury, Massachusetts, not registered as a delegate, formerly a Freewill Baptist, or Christian, or both, and a medical practitioner, now an ardent Antinomian Perfectionist.[128] "I am opposed to officers," he shouted. ". . . I came here to have a Holy Ghost meeting. Let us meet together as Christians, and wait upon the Lord, and speak as the Spirit gives utterance. And if anything is revealed to one that sitteth by, let him get up and speak, and not be called to order by a chairman. I want a free meeting. . . . I didn't come here expecting this meeting to be opened by man, or shut by man. I expected it would be opened and shut by God, who openeth and no man shutteth, and who shutteth and no man openeth. . . ."

Dr. Brown yielded to Thomas Davis, Cape Cod Come-Outer and signer of the Call. "We have met together on very important questions," said he, "quite as important as that which called the primitive Christians together, when they met to consult about circumcision and some other things; . . . But we don't read anything about their having a chairman. . . ."

"Amen!" shouted Dr. Brown.

"Nor about their having any president. . . ."

"Glory to God!" from Dr. Brown.

To the same effect, and amidst a gathering roar of approval, three or four others agreed that they wanted no officers, committee, bishops, popes or cardinals. Garrison was disturbed by the way his friends were behaving. "I fully agree," he said, "with these brethren about the importance of our meeting in the spirit of God; but I have frequently met them in anti-slavery meetings, and I never heard them complain before, that their liberty was infringed by the appointment of a chairman and secretary. I . . . marvel at this, and call on them to be consistent."

Then the Lord called on Dr. Brown to answer this challenge. After a little warming up, he cried out, "Those only are Christ's freemen who are out from under the yoke of committees, and chairmen, and ministers, and every such thing. The bondage in which men are to priests is a terrible one; . . . I can't be ridden by a committee or a chairman any more than I can by a priest. I hope the tide will rise here, . . . the Holy Ghost tide I want, and I hope it will rise so high as to wash out all the wood, and hay, and stubble, there is here. Glory to God! I want God to preside over this meeting. He that's joined to God is one spirit to God. . . . He that's joined to anything is one spirit with it. He that's joined to Van Buren is one spirit to Van Buren, and he that's joined to Harrison is one spirit to Harrison. . . . He that's joined to a chairman is one spirit to a chairman, and he that's joined to a committee is one spirit to a committee. . . . The Lord keep the meeting pure. If it would do any good, I would cry for thunder and lightning, if nothing else would do it. O for a Holy Ghost wind, to keep the meeting clear—such as they had on the day of Pentecost."

Apparently at this point Bronson Alcott provided an interlude which delighted the press. Launching upon one of his pet topics, vegetarianism, he gave off the opinion that meat-eaters gradually became all flesh, that they were converting their bodies into the bodies of brutes, that they were cattle, swine, sheep, geese and what not. At this he was interrupted by someone observing that, since his diet was confined to vegetables, it was fair to infer that he was in process of becoming a squash, a pumpkin, a stinkweed or any plant he chose.[129]

Now Dr. Brown again took over with a declaration that all organizations in nature revolve around some nucleus. "If there is any one here, who wants to be the nucleus of this meeting, let him stand forth. God is my nucleus. I didn't come here to put a stopper in any man's mouth; and I protest against one's being put into any brother's mouth, or any sister's mouth. I can't feel free in this meeting if any man is put over it. . . . Glory to God! I feel as if I was out from under every thing that is coming down, and as if I could cry out to everybody, Stand from under! stand from under! O my God, confound the yoke-makers!"

With this, Dr. Brown yielded to the Reverend Dr. Samuel Osgood, of Springfield, who said quietly, "I didn't come here to hear this rant; and if we are to be here without order, and like the town meeting of Ephesus, the better part not knowing whereof we are come together, I think we had better go home, and not stay here on expense, and to no purpose. . . ."

To which Brown shouted, "I'm here at the king's expense. Glory to God!" But as many people tried to interrupt at once, he restated his earlier doctrine, "If anything be revealed to another that sitteth by, let the first hold his peace."

At this, revelations began to come so fast to those "sitting by" that the meeting was entirely out of hand and Dr. Brown was compelled to "hold his peace." In the ensuing hubbub, he seems to have been suddenly impressed by the anarchy he had desired. Getting the floor again he put it to the meeting whether they would have a chairman or not, and the decision by acclamation was in favor of organization.

Thus the Chardon Street Convention passed out of its Antinomian or Individualistic phase into its Organizational Phase, and so out of its interesting into its uninteresting phase—in spite of the fact that Phelps, Parker, Dr. Osgood and others made able and pertinent addresses. Its little spree of Religious Anarchy at the beginning, though its equivalent doubtless has occurred frequently in Revivals, yet is perhaps the *purest*, the most Innocent, expression of Antinomianism actually on record. And yet we must remember that Antinomianism may also become complicated with self-aggrandizing, moralistic elements that are anything but Innocent. Mrs. Hutchinson mixed her doctrine and practice with strong Arminian poison, and James Davenport in the Eighteenth Century did the same, when they respectively passed judgment on the orthodox ministers and condemned them for Unregeneracy. Just as we saw, in the case of Garrison, Arminianism in its phase of hatred passing into a state of Personal Ecstasy which is hardly distinguishable from the Antinomian or exuberant kind of Self-indulgence, so Antinomianism may pass out of its phase of simple emotional joy—"Praise the Lord!"—into a phase of either Physical Violence or the Mental Violence of Censoriousness where its self-indulgent excesses are hardly distinguishable from those of Arminianism. Thus at the worst of each, the Egoisms of the two great Heresies may become virtually identical. So far, through the first two centuries of New English History, the wide central current of Puritanism, the Objective Perception of God, has kept them apart but for individual exceptions. In the Chardon Street Convention we have seen an Antinomianism of so exceptional and childish a Purity as to appeal for its very Innocence, its very Absurdity, and to lull us into the assurance that out of such Naïveté no dangerous self-assertiveness can grow. Yet out of this very exuberance, once it is well adulterated with Arminianism, we shall see developing the most deadly forces that have attacked the nation.

And what is true at this time of proper Antinomianism or Religious Individualism is true also of the Secular Individualism which, as we saw in the Eighteenth Century, may emerge out of it. In the nineteenth century the two kinds of Individualism do not come in sequence, but they tend to run parallel to each other under the same Romantic urge. As Innocent as was the anarchy at Chardon Street, so Innocent was the nation-wide Bumptiousness which bloomed after the Victory over England in 1815, and knew without doubt that America would soon exceed in Size—and, in those days, even in Quality—all that was Great and Good in the Old World. So Innocent was the Humanitarianism that knew that the United States would be the refuge for the Oppressed of the World, the Utopia of the Second Coming wherein even the Ungodly would any day now see very God with their very eyes. So Innocent was the Ambition that knew that every boy could become President if he would, and that held—as several State Constitutions stated literally—that every American was a King in his own country. So innocent was the Boastfulness—rather Rebel than Yankee—that identified itself with mythical Alligators and Bear and Tall Tales of Giants who could move Mountains, and was ready at a moment to lick anyone in naked and unregulated fight. So Innocent was the haste that washed down enormous meals with cold water, because one must be at Great Tasks, the Belief that there was no Labor on Earth, in Heaven or Hell that any American couldn't accomplish if he chose to give it his shoulder. So Innocent was the Jacksonian myth—rather Rebel than Yankee—that any ignoramus could run a great Government; the Yankees, being politically mature, knew better, but those of the West voted for Old Hickory in the hope of getting back the money that the Bank and the Eastern Manufacturers had stolen from them by way of the Panic of 1819.

So Innocent in this period—surely the most Inspiring the Republic has known, when Democracy was expansive but still maintained in its habits of mind the Aristocratic dream of Excellence—so Innocent was the determination that the current leveling should be a leveling Up rather than Down, that all should become Gentlemen rather than that the Gentleman as a word, a standard and an application of them should disappear.[130] So Innocent was the vast and Romantic exuberance of Manifest Destiny, an Empire to be "liberated" from the wicked Mexicans, another to be "liberated" from the wicked British in Oregon, a Continent being obviously prepared by God for our occupation and incorporation into this perfect Union that was designed by Him for his forthcoming Kingdom. So Innocent was Greeley and his cry, "Go West." And so Innocent was the faith that all this was being done right now before our eyes—Hurry!—Run!—Tomorrow is already late!

Finally, so Innocent was the Rhetoric of the Orators who put all this in phrases and spoke for the millions who heard and believed them. Here is A. A. Bennett, addressing his neighbors at Avon, New York, on the Fourth of July, 1827:

> . . . We may look forward to the period, when the spark, kindled in America, shall spread and spread, till the whole earth be illuminated by its light.[131]

And Chief Justice Robertson of Kentucky on the Fourth of July, 1843 (for, when it came to Rhetoric, the Rebels were never an inch behind the Yankees):

. . . The temperate zone of North America already exhibits many signs that it is the promised land of civil liberty, and institutions destined to liberate and exalt the human race. . . . Christianity, rational philosophy, and constitutional liberty, like an ocean of light, are rolling their united and restless tide over the earth. . . . Doubtless there may be partial revulsions. But the great movement will . . . be progressive, until the millennial sun shall rise in all the effulgence of Universal day.[132]

And Andrew Johnson, future Vice-President and tragic President:

I believe . . . man can become more and more endowed with divinity; and as he does he becomes more God-like in his character and capable of governing himself. Let us go on elevating our people, perfecting our institutions, until democracy shall reach such a point of perfection that we can acclaim with truth that the voice of the people is the voice of God.[133]

And in comment upon all this, less Innocent because more perceptive was Justice Story's warning near the beginning of the period:

. . . We stand the latest, and, if we fail, probably the last experiment of self-government by the people. . . .[134]

So Innocent in its harmless Individualism and Utopianism was Greater New England, and it should have been for the Great to see the Innocence in the frame of Irony and Tragedy which is Reality. Great in Understanding and Alarm over the danger of all this elation should have been the Transcendentalists of Massachusetts Bay—Ripley, Alcott, Bancroft, Thoreau, Margaret Fuller, Parker, Emerson— who did no whit undervalue their own importance, but did, in application of the Transcendental Individualism of their German Romantic Creed, signally fail to exercise the Responsibility which their Importance imposed on them. We must put the great weight of their failure on Emerson, for in some of his choices and in much of his too genial comment he showed that he foresaw the menace of raw Individualism; also, of the Transcendentalists, he was one of the two with the National audience and the national responsibility. Nor can we forgive Emerson in that he was himself perhaps the purest of all the Third Puritans on Record, his own life running almost perfectly the nice line between the Arminianism of Reason and Conduct and that Antinomianism of Emotional Indulgence which latter alone was what he recommended to America and the World. None was more sound than Emerson in perceiving the absurdities

of the more extreme and individualistic Reforms and Reformers
of his day. He believed in some of their Proposals, but would not
join their Organizations. When his friend Thoreau, in jail for refusing to pay taxes, said, "Waldo, why are you not here?," he did not
join Henry but paid his tax and persuaded him to return to the
wicked world. He went to Chardon Street, but opened not his mouth.
Referring, later, to this and similar gatherings he remarked that in

> these movements nothing was more remarkable than the dis-
> content they begot in the movers. The spirit of protest . . .
> drove the members of these Conventions to bear testimony
> against the Church, and immediately afterwards to declare their
> discontent with these Conventions, their independence of their
> colleagues, and their impatience of the methods whereby they
> were working. They defied each other, like a congress of kings,
> each of whom had a realm to rule. . . .
> . . . when a church censured and threatened to excommunicate
> one of its members on account of the somewhat hostile part to
> the church which his conscience led him to take in the anti-
> slavery business; the threatened individual immediately excom-
> municated the church, in a public and formal process.
> The criticism and attack on institutions, which we have wit-
> nessed, has made one thing plain, that society gains nothing
> whilst a man, not himself renovated, attempts to renovate
> things around him: . . . hypocrisy and vanity are often the
> disgusting result.
> Do you complain of the laws of Property? It is a pedantry to
> give such importance to them. Can we not play the game of
> life with these counters, as well as with those? . . . Let into it
> the new and renewing principle of love, and property will be
> universality. No one gives the impression of superiority to the
> institution, which he must give who will reform it. . . . Only
> Love, only an Idea, is against property as we hold it.[135]

And yet his solution for the faults of Individualism which he so
excellently points out is not to have less but more of it, not less
but more profound Self-assertion. In spite of the futility of these Fads
and Conventions, yet "in each of these movements emerged a good
result . . . an assertion of the sufficiency of the private man."
If Emerson, like Channing, had let the matter rest with External
Authority and Meaning, in the Over-Soul as an Objective Reality,
to which every individual must conform and in which every self
must be lost, he would have remained as an advocate what he was
as a person, the purest of the Late Puritans, the Purest because he
even rejected Channing's Moral and Arminian taint of "Goodness."
But to recommend to the Country what he was himself suited
neither his Puritan modesty nor his thrilling and un-Puritan theory

of Germanic Absolutism which went all over into Emotion and denied Reason and so the Holy Mean. He must preach always not less but more Individualism, more Romantic, Remote and Transcendental Individualism. In 1844 when he was making fun of the wild Antinomians, he already had many of the notes that were to become the stuff of his great *Essays* with their all too facile and memorable quotations:

> The power which resides in [each man] is new in nature, and none but he knows what that is which he can do, nor does he know until he has tried.
> I shun father and mother and wife and brother, when my genius calls me.
> A man is to carry himself in the presence of all opposition as if everything were ephemeral and titular but he.
> What I must do is all that concerns me, not what the people think.
> To be great is to be misunderstood.
> Trust thyself: every heart vibrates to that iron string.
> He who would gather immortal palms must not be hindered by the name of goodness.
> If I am the devil's child, I will live then from the devil.[137]

Dear, guileless Emerson thought that Evil, Self-Concern, was a passing affliction of adolescence. It was a phase, like the mumps, which you caught and got over, and thereafter the reality of every grown man was something good and true, as good and true as Emerson was himself. It had taken many generations of Puritan ministers to make him, and in consequence he was so utterly a Puritan, so utterly objectified and selfless in his vision, so absolute in his sense of Equality with all men, that he could indeed say to himself, "Be thyself," and become the better and the more selfless for the slogan. He could not know the people, the millions, to whom he was speaking, his readers and listeners who were most of America. In his Colossal Innocence, the expression and vindication of all the rest of the Romantic Innocence of the Nation, he could not know that most of these people were not born Regenerate and Guileless. He did not know or he forgot that the Universal Perception of God which was indeed potential in every man was deeply buried under a shallower Self that was weak and afraid and therefore aggressive and destructive, and that the True Perception, the Inner Light, the always Self-losingness, the Soul, must throw off the Outer Self before it could unite with the Over Soul, the Fact and Meaning of Being. He did not know or he forgot that it could do this only after the Outer Self was broken and blinded and drawn through the Darkness of the Valley, precisely as was said in the old Puritan books, precisely as was

said in most of the Christian books, precisely as was said in those
Hindu books which Emerson read and whose Truths on the Deeper
Planes were almost the same as the Truths of his own inherited
doctrine.

All this Emerson knew and forgot as he forgot the Air and the
Light, so that he must ignore it and go through it to something
more new and more exciting. What he thought he found was
that the very Outer Self, the Outer Shell of every man, was already
from birth undistinguished from the yet Unrealized Inner Reality,
that the Outer Self was not only qualified from childhood to perceive the God or the Over Soul but that it was already identified with
the Over Soul, and indeed was the Over Soul, not only could perceive the One but was itself One with the One. This was the extremity of Antinomian doctrine, which neither Mrs. Hutchinson,
James Davenport nor even the Hindu Sources would have endorsed.
The self which Emerson in his Sweet Innocence saw moving into
Samadhi and so into Nirvana was the Outer Self which the Hindu
must utterly overcome before approaching Samadhi and Nirvana, precisely as the Christian must overcome it and its Depravity before
qualifying for Grace. It was this Outer Self which had undertaken
to replace God at the Fall of Man and which, being resourceless and
timid, was always susceptible to the temptations to Self-Aggrandizement through the Aggressions of Arminianism or Antinomianism
or any kind of Individualism.

So Emerson the Great Saint became in fact Emerson the great
Advocate of Original Sin as the condition of Virtue, became in-
deed the "Devil's Child" without any experience or understanding
of what the Devil might in reality be. Wherefore one who was also
Great but no Saint, and who knew much about the Devil and His
Children, wrote a letter to Emerson and his Innocence and to the
Innocence of America:

Dear Mr. Emerson and Mr. America:—
Excuse me but I must tell you what you will get when you
tell every man to Be Himself, when you tell this Outer Self,
which to himself and to others is mostly what every man is, to be
Itself. You will induce this Self, which is in fact hopelessly
Dwarfed and Maimed and Dull and Empty of all feeling but
Fear, you will induce it to try to be Important and Strong. And
because it is not, and cannot be either, and knows itself Inferior and Afraid, it will have to create Something outside itself
which seems to be Important and Strong and yet can be Overcome, so that this insignificant self in overcoming it will be able
to persuade itself that it is Itself Important and Strong. Wherefore, from earliest awareness this Outer Self that you try to encourage will create a Chimera which will live and move in the

Deeps and which this Self, this Great Man, this transcendental Hero, will pursue from then on. And very early he will proclaim and will believe that it was the Chimera that dwarfed and maimed him, and from this he will have a Vaunting Motive for his Pursuit, a great swagger called Revenge. And from that time this Outer Self which is Little More than Nothing will pursue the Chimera which he has created out of nothing, until at last he closes with It and destroys It and in the same meeting is himself destroyed, not by the Chimera but by his own determination which attaches himself to the Chimera and so is drawn down into the same Deep, the Senseless Deep which is Animalistic Nothing and is not the valley in which the Self may be Overcome and out of which it may arise through Grace to Regeneration. This, Mr. Emerson and Mr. America, is what you will get out of this Self that you are asking your people to be. You will get Death without Rebirth, for the Inner Self which was real in Selflessness and True Identification with All Things and which you have never troubled to notice or nurture, will never be released from the womb of Almost Nothing that contains Him. Perhaps He will float off into Unconscious Being and some other trial, but this Trial that was to have been made here, in this particular Concentration of Mountains and Oceans and Plains, this Trial which the two of you might have made together, will not be made.

So Melville wrote to Emerson and America in 1851, but America did not read the letter at all, and Emerson smiled Benevolently at the rhetorical style, and put it aside and forgot it, and went back to his *Journals* and *Essays,* went on telling America to be Itself and Itself would be God.

Toward the end of this Age of "Ferment" and Experiment there were other intimations, some of future evil, some of future good, and there were some realized accomplishments. Important among the last were those of the Literary "Flowering" which were so miscellaneous that it is difficult to find in them a single significance. In the work of Bryant, Whittier, Emerson and Melville it was indeed a flowering of the Puritan tradition, its motivation that of the Cosmic Aesthetic, the perception of the whole meaning of the Scheme. Of the four, Whittier and Melville were deficient in the smaller Common Aesthetic of Art, so that one feels that their best expressions were matters of chance rather than of conscious craft. Bryant, on the other hand, and especially Emerson, besides having inclusive, Puritan perceptions, were conscious Artists. As such, Emerson was interested in the

original efforts of Whitman, and in Poe's excellent writing upon
trivial themes. An artist also was Longfellow, his pretentious material being thinner than Poe's and his talent weaker. In this group
Hawthorne was the finest and subtlest of them all. They were not so
much of their time as they were intimations of a remote second Puritan flowering when there would be little difference between the concept of Art, that of the common aesthetic, and the Sky of ultimately
shrunken Puritanism whose Meaning would be Self-expression, the
God of Self.

Besides the Puritan Poets and the Artists, a third group of the
writers of the Flowering were closer to the terminal trend of the age,
prophetic of the Great Decline that was going to come soon and suddenly like a new and complete Pseudo-Culture already secretly mature in the '60's. Rapidly after 1840 we see the Romantic Spirit, which
emotionalized and in a way ennobled most of the current trends, for-
saking the long and straight quest for actual goals and mounting the
merry-go-round of melodious subjective activity. The affectation of
Sensibility which we saw at the end of the Eighteenth Century
evolves on the one hand into the habit of indulgence of Emotion
for its own sake, which is Sentimentality, and on the other into a
code of wholly artificial Prudery whose application is the active expression of the sentimentality. About 1840, Emma Willard, the great
Rebel in Female Education, found herself shocked by the nudity of
the statues in the Tuilleries and wrote to her pupils:

> If your mothers were here I would leave you sitting on these
> shaded benches, and conduct them through the walks, and they
> would return, and bid you depart for our own America; where
> the eye of modesty is not publicly affronted; and where virgin
> delicacy can walk abroad without a blush.[138]

Of the Louvre she added:

> I am not ashamed to say I have not visited the statuary. . . . I
> should rather be ashamed to say that I had.

Fifteen years later a clerical friend of the "Sweet Singer," Mrs. Sigourney of Hartford, found the Elgin Marbles

> not altogether proper for the indiscriminate admission of visi-
> tors of both sexes. . . . Indeed, it was not difficult to perceive
> that the ladies here felt a little out of place.[139]

In keeping with this emergent Victorianism, sang Poet Marion Ward
in Griswold's *Female Poets*, 1848:

> 'I love to love,' said a darling pet,
> Whose soul looked out through her eyes of jet,

And she nestled down like a fondled dove,
And lisped, 'Dear Mama, how I love to *love!*'[140]

And in the same key were the sad sweet strains of Longfellow's original work, and much of Lowell, and some of Holmes.

More fully and ominously realized than the shams of Victorianism was the Degradation of Democracy which proceeded in step with the Individualism we have seen developing in Religious and Secular forms. As the masses of the Innocent and the Ignorant began to be mustered as the definitive political power, the same minds that saw the vision of their mustering perceived a way of using them when they were mustered. They saw how to encourage and turn to account derivatives of Fear—chiefly Vanity and the Sense of Inferiority—which are the Prerogatives of that Outer Man, that Hero, that Transcendental Self, which in these same years Emerson in his Innocence was also flattering. In the name of Democracy, irresponsible politicians, bent innocently on the destruction of the Republic for their advancement, replaced the Responsible Leaders, from among whom John Quincy Adams was the last President before Lincoln.

This great weed of Demagoguery, with its Promise of Dictatorship, had rooted as far back as the Itinerant Revivalists of the previous century, but it first blossomed rankly in the Jackson campaign when the old Colonial Aristocracy that had made the Nation was under justified attack, and the moderate democratic profession of half a century before began to enjoy extreme application. Jackson, while hastening to enrich himself and to revise himself—not without success—in the pattern of Southern Aristocracy, was in fact a bold and natively intelligent Hill Billy and he represented what the Southern Individualists of the Poor Farms, the Mountains and the Mississippi Valley wanted, together with the Northern Individualists of the accumulating Immigrations to whom America also meant opportunity for Advancement and Power. Jackson flattered all these by being of them, wherefore in 1828, with the help of the Yankees of the Northwest who discovered that they were producing too much and so passing under the control of the Eastern manufacturers and merchants, they elected him. It was a triumph, not for the Jeffersonian and Yankee Ideal of the Elevation of the Common Man, but for the Common Man himself just as he was, especially in Unelevated Innocence along the Frontier, half ignorant in the North, wholly ignorant in the South, persuaded that he could run the Government if he wanted to, just as he could whip any Englishman

or Spaniard or any other civilized swell who might question his
Greatness. Actually, the Yankees of the Northwest were still mostly
of the first and second generations out of Old New England, and the
evidence is not impressive that they were yet suffering from that
sense of Inferiority which is the death of Equality and the birth of
real self-assertive Individualism, the Individualism that substitutes
the impulse to level down for the old instinct to level up. The
Yankees who helped elect Jackson did so upon an Economic Motive. But the precedent of electing a Roughneck to the Presidency
was established, and leaders of the future saw that there was power
in the encouragement, imitation and profession of the qualities
which the ignorant admired.

The lesson was first well applied three campaigns later, the one
of '40 whose election just preceded the Chardon Street Convention.
Then it was the Whigs, not Jackson's Democrats, who did a good
job of debasing human decency in the interest of power. They devised the formula of presenting to the Electorate, not a man who
has ideas, ability and therefore enemies, but a handsome nonentity
who carries some bright badge, like a military record, to make him
shine, and whose soft spots are too little known to invite attack. Put
up an inoffensive candidate, and adorn him with inane slogans
which will offend nothing but good taste, will flatter the Plain
People, and may touch the humor of the rest, and you have a winner. In '40 the Whigs put up old General Harrison, the "Hero of
Tippecanoe," originally a Virginia and now an Ohio gentleman
living in a fine house, a worthy man of good education and small
brains. They portrayed him in hundreds of floats and thousands of
souvenirs and cartoons as living in a log cabin, drinking hard cider
and splitting rails. They composed euphonious slogans—Tippecanoe
and Tyler Too—and catchy songs, with singers who bawled them
along the highways across the Nation while rolling Gigantic Balls
from village to village, supposed to represent his snowballing majority. And poor VanBuren, the President and Harrison's opponent,
an able and experienced statesman who actually had risen from
humble origins in O(ld) K(inderhook), New York, they represented as
living off gold service in the White House, in the midst of fabulous
furniture minutely described, and drinking, not honest cider, but
expensive imported wines and cordials. The Whigs won, and a system was grafted on America which we see today in the operations of
Senators who struggle to draw the educated down to the level of
ignorance and jealousy. Yet, before the Civil War, while it elected
Presidents, this System of Mediocrity probably did not get far in its
larger objective of leveling the populace down. True Equalitarianism and suspicion of sham were yet a while stronger than ignorant

and jealous Individualism in the people of Greater New England.

Of the Infections that in a few decades were to prove fatal, the shams of Victorianism and of Farcical Politics were hardly in the blood stream before the Civil War. Even less evident were the greater corruptions, the two Materialisms, the practical Materialism of Greed and the Philosophical Materialism which eventually would release Intellectual Arminianism from both its Romantic and its Religious concealment.

Much was made by Southern Orators of Factory Slavery in New England, but the Industrial Revolution, while it was rising, was still far from qualifying the culture. Into the '50's the Walpole factories still paid their employees well by current standards, and worked them less than they would have worked on the farms. The famous girls in the Lowell Mills, chaperoned, educated, comforted, well housed, worked rarely over twelve hours a day, and paid better than anything agriculture could give them, were one of the Wonders of the Industrial World. Theodore Parker, in one of his most famous addresses, attacked the merchants of Boston for venality and hypocrisy. But he did not attack them for honest Atheism, let alone Frank Rapacity. As we shall see later, the pursuit of wealth as Power, rather than as evidence of having carried out God's injunctions to Diligence, was indeed beginning, and it would be a powerful reinforcement to both Antinomianism and Legal Arminianism. But it was hardly yet out of the Hypocritical Phase where it was practiced behind a façade of presumptive Religion. The acquisition of wealth was presumed to be the reward of good and deserving service of God, but it was not yet recognized as in itself a worthy and sufficient aim of life. The rich were not yet admired simply because they were rich, without scrutiny of the means of their attainment. "The capitalists . . . still, for the most part, sincerely believed in God."[141] Some of them had heard of Adam Smith, and most of them heard from their pulpits the Americanized version of his doctrine called Clerical Laissez-faire. But they were still a long way from the frank and unrestrained Ruthlessness which the rule would lead to when aggravated by the Civil War, Labor Trouble, enormous stakes, and the hypothesis of Natural Selection.

Before the Civil War the threat of Philosophical Materialism was even less than that of Applied Materialism. Natural Science had been a part of the expression of Natural Reason in the Eighteenth Century, but through the first half of the Nineteenth its fields of Experiment and Induction widened but slowly. Benjamin Silliman at Yale became the country's leading Chemist, and in '35 he delivered in Boston a series of lectures in Geology which raised the first doubts of the Six-Day Story of Creation. A little later Edward Hitchcock,

President of Amherst, discovered and described the famous Dinosaur
Tracks in the redstone of the Connecticut Valley. But Silliman and
Hitchcock were both good Congregationalists and at least Hitchcock
was a true Puritan; these were very faint presages of the barrage of
disillusionment that was to descend in twenty-five years. Joseph
Henry of Albany discovered magneto-electricity, and in '46 became
the first Director of the Smithsonian Institution in Washington, the
recent gift of an Englishman. In the same year Agassiz came to
Harvard from Switzerland to start his long career as one of the
leading biologists and zoologists in the world.

All of these men and their work were important, and all pointing
to a great Scientific Future, a triumph of Intellectual Arminianism.
But few knew it then, and a negligible number of the citizenry, if
any, were troubled in their Central Faith, their sense of kinship with
some central Power and Meaning of the Scheme. Like the Industrial
Revolution, the Scientific Revolution was in process, but the Anti-
ethical and Irreligious Revolutions which would be their ultimate
achievements were hardly yet indicated.

In 1840 and thereafter the forces of Decline were perceptible,
and eventually the ancient Heresies were going to appropriate
them to their uses; but before they could displace the Central Current of Religious Idealism, it was necessary that Religion itself
should thin away, letting the Heresies widen in to replace it in the
River. In the '40's the current of Third Puritanism was still flowing
wide and clear. The sky it reflected was contracted to the dimensions
of Second-Commandment Christianity, that of every Individual
human in the world; but for all that it was still an Objective Sky
with a Meaning or God. New England was still religious, and even
the few Skeptics and Atheists were troubled by the suspicion that
the external, unplumbed and mysterious Universe might yet actually Exist. The great Central Current fringed by its hardly yet
troublesome heresies, shining with Benevolence, flowed on toward
a romantically distant but visible Ocean of Human Perfection.
Only a few prophets—Story, De Tocqueville, Hawthorne, Melville—
feared the Ocean might be a mirage, and seemed to hear ahead a
Rumble as of a Great Falls, a great debacle, and a plunge into depths
unseen.

In the years just following Chardon Street there occurred two
events which may be taken as dramatically ominous. In '42 William
Ellery Channing died; Third Puritanism lost its prophet, its intellectual leader. Then came the Millennial Year of 1843 when the half-

million or so followers of William Miller believed with intense fanaticism that the Trump would sound and they would be caught up to Jesus in the air. Having put their affairs in order, many having given away all their goods, they repaired nightly to promontories suitable for the Leap. Under awful tension and sleeplessness the little huddles shivered on their hopeful hilltops while the Year came and passed and no saint rose. There were insanities and suicides. A small sect remained faithful to the sincere, confused and guilt-stricken Reverend Miller. But for most it was Final Disillusion. Their previously Innocent Antinomianism, in some part objective toward Christ, soured into readiness for sublimation into such self-expression of body or mind as the day might suggest.

Meanwhile, at least two of the three Great Reforms were expanding. In '40 the new-founded Liberty Party suffered an anticlimax when its James G. Birney got only 7,000 votes for President. But the next year Anti-Slavery moved into major action when Weld went down to Washington to operate "Abolition House," being a room in Mrs. Spriggs' Boarding Emporium. There he thenceforth coordinated Abolition with its Congressmen, notably ex-President John Quincy Adams, Joshua Giddings and Ben Wade of Ohio, Seth Gates and Gerrit Smith of New York, and William Slade of Vermont. The cohorts were of course much larger than this, but these are the ones we can be fairly sure of as proper Puritans, men who were pursuing a selfless Idea more faithfully than they were pursuing their interest or any emotion of hatred or destructiveness toward the slaveholders. All of them except old John Quincy Adams were subjected to miscellaneous assaults or challenges in and around Congress, and at least three adopted a technique not only of meeting these aggressively but, having in the case of challenges the choice of weapons, electing bowie knives, axes, raw-hide whips and other such coarse toys as gave the Southern Gentlemen pause. Giddings and Wade especially were men of great physical power and moral integrity whom the Rebels soon found it difficult to bully. Weld seems to have remained his old gentle self, thinking only of the freedom of the slaves, never vituperating the slaveholders, in fact often conferring with them. The Movement in New England benefited when Channing, just before his death, having all his life stayed clear of organized Reforms, yet made in Lenox a powerful address for Abolition.

In '40, the Temperance Crusade, which had been through a period of diffusion, started its strong march again with the Washingtonian Movement, won Boston for license under local option the next year, had the great reformed drunk John B. Gough barnstorming in '44, presented in '45 a new organization in the Sons of

Temperance, and soon turned a hundred towns dry. Meanwhile
Amelia Bloomer had introduced her comfortable costume; New
Hampshire, Vermont and Ohio had put in humane prisons on the
Auburn model; and Samuel Gridley Howe was teaching the deaf-
mutes to speak instead of relying on the sign language.

The year of '44 had at least four developments relevant to Reform.
Joseph Smith, prophet of the Mormons who was doing nicely in
his Independent City of Nauvoo, Illinois, had a revelation from
God authorizing Polygamy and undertook the same. Enflamed by
this and other irregularities, an Arminian mob from several neigh-
boring communities overcame the honest efforts of Governor Ford,
and so murdered the Prophet. The larger body of Mormons, about
6,000 strong, set out under Brigham Young to found their State of
Deseret on the Great Salt Lake, where in thirty years the numbers
increased, by various means, to 200,000.

In the election of '44 Birney did better than before, getting 60,000
votes. By a caption in the *Liberator* Garrison gave notice that the
Constitution was a "covenant with death, and an agreement with
hell." The same year Dorothea Dix, the heroic champion of the
Insane, having effected an expansion of the Worcester madhouse,
and the establishment of a good asylum in Providence, set out on a
ten-year Circuit that was going to take her 30,000 miles and set up
state asylums in Indiana, Illinois, Michigan and Wisconsin. A significant development, this year or the next, was the Conversion of
Theodore Parker from a moderate Anti-Slavery position to militant
Immediate Abolition and an increasingly vindictive and Garrisonian
attitude.

In '45 New York passed local option and five-sixths of its towns
voted dry. Antoinette Brown demanded to be accepted as a theological student at Oberlin, and was. The Transcendental Utopia at
Brook Farm, featuring most of the top intellectuals of New England,
decided to become a Phalanx of Fourierite Socialism. Theodore
Parker and Charles Sumner made pacifist speeches touching the
forthcoming Mexican War, while Horace Greeley in the *Tribune*
opposed it as aiming at the increase of the Slave Power. The American Peace Society and Garrison's Non-Resistance Society were both
going along nicely, being in liaison with the London Peace Society,
and the American Society being fortified by the membership of the
consecrated Elihu Burritt, the "Learned Blacksmith," of all the fair-
weather Pacifists the only one who was going to stay faithful in the
storm. In '46 John Humphrey Noyes, having just contracted a "complex marriage," left Putney discreetly and went to Oneida, New
York, where his disciples followed him two years later. In '46 also,
Maine went dry, and Henry Thoreau went to jail for nonpayment

of taxes, where when Waldo visited him, he issued his famous sarcasm to his friend. In '47 Brook Farm folded.

In '47 and '48 the Feminist Movement made strides. Lucy Stone, the first American woman to retain her own name in marriage, began itinerating for Women's Rights, was frequently mobbed and sometimes hurt. In '48 Elizabeth Cady Stanton and Lucretia Mott called in Seneca Falls, New York, the Convention they had projected eight years before when they were sitting behind the curtain of feminine chastity at the International Anti-Slavery Convention in London. Now they adopted a Declaration of Independence, in which the complaints of the colonists against King George were paralleled in both language and substance by equivalent complaints against the tyrannies of Man. The Delegation also incorporated a proposal of the Suffrage, but this went too far and cost them much otherwise possible support. Later the same year they had another Convention in Rochester, and in the next few years held them in Massachusetts, Ohio, Pennsylvania, Indiana, Wisconsin and Kansas. Organization in all these states followed shortly. In '48 New York passed the first law improving—though pathetically—the Property Rights of married women. Beginning in '50, regular, annual Conventions were held. Meanwhile, in '48 Elihu Burritt went to England and engineered an International Peace Conference. In the Presidential Election that year the Free Soil Party, which included the old Liberty Party, polled 300,000 votes.

The decade of the '50's was one of the fateful ones in American History, not only because with our hindsight we can see in it the slow alignment for the greatest Modern War to that time, but because we see also, as part of that preparation and parallel to it, the contraction and perversion of the tremendous forces of Puritanism that had made half the country. Through these years the dear old Reforms seemed to be running smoothly, and no one saw how grimly and inexorably the great and Objective Ideas of Religion were being squeezed out by Arminian Subjectivity and Hatred. Early in the decade Michigan, Iowa and Wisconsin put up modern prisons on the Auburn plan. In '50 the Sons of Temperance had 250,000 paying members. In '52 Vermont went dry and stayed so for fifty years; and soon thereafter Rhode Island, Minnesota, Connecticut, New Hampshire, Illinois, Indiana, Michigan, Iowa and Wisconsin all put in some kind of Liquor Control. In '52 also the New York Women's State Temperance Association was organized, and at its Rochester convention Mrs. Stanton tossed in her "bombshell" proposal that

Women refuse Intercourse to husbands who drank to excess—"Let no drunkard be the father of your children."

It was all very Earnest and Innocent, while the Forces of Destruction were gathering. In '54 Oneida Community moved successfully into the manufacture of traps, and presently into silk and so went strong for thirty years more. All of very great interest! In '56 Hopedale Community failed financially. Alas! In '57 the Columbian Institute for Deaf Mutes was founded in Washington, and in the same year the Blackwell Sisters—early Female Doctors—founded the New York Infirmary for Women and Children. A little more life, a little less suffering, while the Shapes of Cultural Death and National Agony were Deepening.

Also, the Benevolent Empire was upon its Benevolent business. The Y.M.C.A. was founded in '51, and by the end of the decade had 200 chapters. In the West in those days a thousand little churches were building annually, mostly for the Circuit Riders some of whom doubtless put their Antinomian Love of God and Man before the Evils of the latter, but many more of whom were presently howling Arminian destruction with the pack. Home Missions, Bibles, Tracts, all were getting around in bigger and more gratifying numbers. Church Membership was increasing, and so was the Proliferation of Sects.

But where was the Love that had been in the churches even up till '40? It was still in Finney, now President of Oberlin, perhaps in Weld, perhaps in Phelps and Wright and others of the little people we saw at Chardon Street. Channing was dead. Parker had contracted from what had been at worst a Transcendental Idea of Man to a Social Idea. Lyman Beecher had been persecuted at Lane, for the Humanitarian or Third Puritan features in his theology. He had won his fight, but had then resigned; his mind was weakening and he was presently going to live with his son Henry Ward who was making pleasant noises in Brooklyn. Garrison was throwing filth all over the nation with the *Liberator*, which nobody read but which all the newspapers, North and South, copied and passed out to their Readers, thus aligning them against each other in terms other than Innocence. Elihu Burritt engineered another Peace Conference in England in '52, but throughout the decade the Movement was decelerating and the membership of the two American Associations was falling off.

As we noticed the possibility of dating the two former Puritan Declines from the mid-century of each rather than from the follow-

ing decade, from 1650 and 1750 instead of 1660 and 1760, so now
we could date the downward turn of Puritanism from the passing of
the Compromise of 1850, with its Fugitive Slave Law. By this you
were made a Law-Breaker if you helped a fugitive on his way, or if
you hindered the U.S. Marshals in capturing and carrying off a piece
of human property who had no right to summon witnesses, let
alone to have a jury at his Hearing. Everybody in Greater New England had known since the Revolution that Slavery was evil, but it
was far away, and almost everybody gave thought to the economic
plight of the Southerners. Now they were required by law to compound the evil, something that was beginning to look like the
Greatest of Evils. Whittier had long been an anti-slavery propa-
gandist:

> What ho! our countrymen in chains!
> The whip on woman's shrinking flesh!
> Our soil yet reddening with the stains
> Caught from her scourging, warm and fresh.[142]

At the passage of the Fugitive Slave Law he wrote:

> For Pity now is crime; the chain
>   Which binds our States
> Is melted at her heart in twain,
> Is rusted by her tears' soft rain;
>   Close up her gates.[143]

When in '51 a Fugitive Negro William Simms was arrested and sent
back south under military escort, Whittier, speaking for Massachusetts, warned:

> That brave old blood, quick-flowing yet,
>   Shall know no check,
> Till a free people's foot is set
>   On Slavery's neck.[144]

Soon after the apprehension of Simms, Boston held a huge Mass
Meeting on the Common where Wendell Phillips and Parker spoke;
and on the Anniversary was held another Mass Meeting at which
Parker delivered one of his greatest and most deadly attacks on the
South. He entertained Fugitives in his home, and at least once wrote
his Sunday sermon with a pistol on his desk. Emerson had been wary
of Abolition, but it is reasonably clear that in the '50's he helped
runaway Negroes on their way. "I thought none," he said,[145]

> that was not ready to go on all fours, would back this law. And
> yet here are upright men . . . who can see nothing in this
> claim for bare humanity . . . but canting fanaticism, sedition
> and 'one idea.' . . . The whole wealth and power of Boston

. . . are thrown into the scale of crime: and the poor black boy . . . here finds all this force employed to catch him. The famous town of Boston is his master's hound. The learning of the universities, the culture of elegant society, the acumen of lawyers, the majesty of the Bench, the eloquence of the Christian pulpit . . . are all combined to kidnap him.

And Thoreau:[146]

I hear a good deal said about trampling this law under foot. . . . This law rises not to the level of the head or the reason; its natural habitat is in the dirt . . . and he who walks with freedom, and does not with Hindoo mercy avoid treading on every venomous reptile, will inevitably tread on it, and so trample it under foot.

There was not much selflessness left in these intellectuals, not much Puritan Perception and Objectivity. This was Arminianism, getting on toward its worst, judging people, condemning them, hating them.

And these views were not different from those of local leaders. A Vermont judge said he would not enforce the law without a "Bill of Sale from the Almighty." In Syracuse a Fugitive was rescued by a mob, and the Judge held the law Unconstitutional. In Oberlin a crowd of students protected a Fugitive and no legal action was attempted. The Supreme Court of Wisconsin held the law Unconstitutional, which nullified it for the whole state.

What the millions were feeling under this leadership we can only guess. Until now most had been apathetic. They had always been passionately Utopian about the Union, but until now they hadn't actually seen Utopia being violated. Now they not only saw wretches being dragged back into slavery, they were asked to wink at and even abet the process. They saw Utopia turned into a Coliseum for torturing human beings. They felt unclean, their Idea of America befouled. They were in a position comparable to that of the Southerners, who also knew slavery was Evil, but couldn't face it, couldn't even discuss it, couldn't do anything but get angry and fight about it. So now the Yankees saw, not all of Slavery, but enough of it to know its evil. They could fight about the corners of it they saw. They could and did increase the size and efficiency of the Underground Railroad. And they could and did rescue Fugitives from the Federal marshals.

But there was the whole Great Evil they glimpsed beyond the local incidents, and they could not fight about it because they didn't believe in destroying the South with Immediate Abolition and imperilling the Union that was to be Utopia. Also, it was true that they didn't like the Niggers much either, and this made them ashamed, like the Southerners. So they, like the Southerners, could only get angry and simmer. A resentment began to gather against a distant and unknown culture with its distant and unknown people. Increasingly it was assumed that the people and the culture were together Something Evil. The clean Idealism of Humanitarian Perfectionism and Benevolence began to run narrower in the River of Puritan History, to contract its Sky, and to edge over and make room for the widening current of Legal Arminianism which was that outer self that Emerson celebrated, mistaking it for the soul. And this current, boiling with self-righteousness, reflecting no outer sky, did what Melville had projected. It conjured far ahead a Shape. It formed out of its own sickly unquiet a Thing, a Thing of Evil to be judged and hated, and a Thing which the Self in its Weakness could follow and find and destroy. In Brooklyn the Yankee preacher Henry Ward Beecher began holding mock slave auctions in his Plymouth Church. Little newspapers and pulpits all across the North began to copy Garrison less and imitate him more, not in his demand for Immediate Abolition but in his excoriation of the Slaveholders.

And Garrison now need only copy from a Report of a Joint Special Committee of the Massachusetts Legislature:

> The slave holder profanes the soil of Massachusetts, seeking whom he may devour. His presence spreads terror among the colored people of our State. He is a hawk among doves—a wolf, a hyena, among lambs. . . . To our judgment, the *illegal* kidnapper on the coast of Africa, and the *legal* manhunter in Boston, belong to the same class of felons. They differ, however, *specifically,* and we think the native species far worse than the foreign felon, whom all Christian governments, and our own among the number, have denounced as a pirate.[147]

And the Fire-Eating press in the South, building pretexts for secession, continued to copy Garrison and to snarl, "This is the way all Yankees are." Some cool-headed Southerners sought a way of having him enjoined in Boston, in the interest of peace, but nothing was done.

In '52 Lyman Beecher's daughter Mrs. Stowe published *Uncle Tom's Cabin,* and in the North it did with Pathos what Garrison could not do with Billingsgate. There could hardly have been a more tender, a less vindictive author, and she wrote the book out of tenderness for the slaves. Eliza was actually Eliza Harris, a friend of Mrs. Stowe's in Cincinnati when she was there with her husband and father in Lane Seminary, and Eliza had in fact escaped from slavery by crossing the Ice of the Ohio as the author described it. It was the kind of tender book that drives men mad, especially in those Perfectionist days when it revealed the Thing, the terrible flaw in the Perfect Union. Five hundred thousand people bought the book in five years and probably four or five times as many read it. Almost all of the responsible North read it. That Evil Thing south of the Ohio began to take surer shape in the social fancy of the Nation. It began to swim in the psychic Deeps of every Yankee, and each of them alone and subconsciously began to scan the horizon, to hold himself tense to chase it and destroy it. The Yankee's notions of serving his neighbor, of perfecting his community, began to burn dim. Instead, his manhood, his Individuality that Jackson and Emerson had said was important, began to flare, and what its light saw was the Thing moving slowly and monstrously along the Deep somewhere down there below the Ohio. The Ocean toward which the Puritan River was flowing was no longer the Ocean of Romantic Perfection but a murky expanse where the Great Flaw swam and must be caught and destroyed. This was very far from the way any Puritan had ever felt before. It was even far beyond the way most Arminians had felt. Perhaps the Reformers of the 1680's and '90's had come near to it when the Evil Thing they were out to destroy was the Devil. But the Devil was a kind of person and the Natural Enemy of you and God. This was something Huge and amorphous and slow, something to do with a whole People who were supposed to be your Friends. The Devil was known to be wicked. It was his profession. There was nothing unhealthy about it for Him. These were your Brothers in Utopia who ought to be as Idealistic as you were. It was a family hatred and a sickly hatred, and it was worse for your own sense of guilt in submitting to it.

In '54 came the "Crime against Kansas," the Kansas-Nebraska Law repealing the Missouri Compromise which had made Kansas free soil, and leaving it to decide for itself whether it would come into the Union as a Free State or a Slave State. For eloquently opposing the Bill old Charles Sumner was beaten senseless in the Senate by a young bully from South Carolina. Garrison publicly burned the Constitution and said there could be "no union with slave states." Sarah Grimke, Weld's forceful sister-in-law, decided that the slavery question could be settled only in blood. The little Civil War began in "Bloody Kansas" and raged for five years. In New England divers Emigrant Aid Societies raised more money and sent out armed settlers faster than the South could. They sent in on the whole a very clean, well educated, militantly perfectionist lot who proceeded to establish learning and order in the Territory. The South had their usual resource of blustering alcoholics who were duly plied by the Gentlemen of Missouri and sent in to make trouble. They murdered a number of people and got into skirmishes with the Yankee Vigilantes. Their achievement was to set up a fake government, declare everything Yankee a Nuisance, and burn a good part of the promising "city" of Lawrence. The fanatic John Brown behaved worse than they did for he was intelligent and had some education. One night he and his boys took out the men of a slave-owning family and butchered them with edged tools. This was good Garrisonism, though a step nearer to psychosis. Garrison hailed the Bloody Mess in the *Liberator.*

Greater New England was partly ashamed and partly proud of Brown, but it was proud of everything else in Kansas. Psychologically, it was a Rehearsal. Every Yankee felt that he was involved. The Monster of Evil, the Chimera, seemed a little clearer in Fancy. It was as if people came back from the Sea and said they had sighted it, and told you its ways and its bigness. The Ocean ahead where it swam became again the Ocean of Romantic Perfection whose quality before had been perfect Love and was now perfect Hatred. After five years the Gentlemen of Missouri ran out of liquor and let Kansas have majority rule. She passed a Free Constitution in '59. The Yankees felt healthier than before, for there had been action. Emerson went, for him, very far in Arminian Condemnation:

Life has no parity of value in the free state and in the slave state. In one it is adorned with education, with skillful labor, with arts, with long prospective interests, with sacred family ties, with honor and justice. In the other, life is a fever; man is an animal, given to pleasure, frivolous, irritable, spending his days in hunting and practicing with deadly weapons to defend himself against his slaves and against his companions brought up in the same idle and dangerous way.[148]

In '56 the Republican Party was formed, comprising almost every Yankee we have named, and it made a showing in the election. A longer step than Bloody Kansas toward the Meeting with Evil was the Dred Scott Decision in '57 which not only held that a slave did not attain freedom by being brought into a Free State, but said in dictum that no Negro can ever become a citizen. The effect of this was not invigorating, like the news of tangible doings. It was sickly, filthy, perverse, contrary to humanity, like the Fugitive Slave Law. The same year occurred the serious Panic of '57. In the depths of it, in '58, there was a Revival, called a Great Awakening, much of it genuine and producing many thousand conversions. But it was a new kind, related to the pseudo-cultures of the now large cities, and having little relation to the earlier Yankee Great Awakenings. Its features were large daily union prayer meetings, decorously administered, with no Revivalistic fracas. The movement was nonsectarian. It had little if any effect in checking the current descent of Puritanism into Arminianism and rage.

The Churches and their great Associations of the Benevolent Em-

pire were already splitting, North and South, on the main issue of
Utopia against Bullying Economic Interest. The Western Unitarian
Conference adopted an Anti-Slavery Report, thereby driving out its
Missouri delegates. In '59 a Northwestern Christian Anti-Slavery
Convention was held. In '58 Lincoln debated with Douglas and
made the "House Divided" speech, and in the same year Seward
made his "Irrepressible Conflict" speech. In the North the phrase
"Slave Power" was as common as "Black Republican" in the
South, and it carried around it an awful aura of Perverse and
Psychopathic Malignancy. It was the Chimera, the Thing every
Yankee was creating to vent his Self on as his Idea of perfection
curdled. The tension all across the Continent was now very great. The
hunt for the great Diseased Whale was on, and the wonder was that
very few Yankees even yet believed it was going to be War. Something violent, something Heroic, something to swell the Arminian
Ego to indomitable size. But not Civil War. The Stream of Benevolence was still central in the Yankees and there was still Innocence
in the Antinomianism that flowed beside it. They did not yet know
that the little brain of the Diseased Whale was itself scheming to
lure them on, already preparing for War, delighting in Garrison's
ecstasies that the little brain could report to delude the Decent and
rouse the Half-Hearted to the job they must do.

Then the Heroic Symbol the Yankees sought to express their rage
was given them. On October 16, 1859, the bearded old lunatic John
Brown sprung his incredibly brave and foolish raid at Harper's
Ferry, Virginia, with some notion of arming local slaves and slavery-
hating whites, capturing Virginia, and thus leading the whole South
toward Emancipation. He was duly thwarted and properly hung
for murder and treason. And the Yankees, who were not commonly
given to condoning murder, saw their clarifying deed and rose as
one man and cheered. Through old Brown each of them had done
the Heroic and Self-Aggrandizing thing his Fury, his now inverted
and perverted Idealism, greatly desired to do. In the cruise of his
dream he heard the Look-Out of Consciousness cry out, "There she
blows!" And in the moment before he awoke he launched the boat
and threw the first harpoon at the Chimera's Heart. Then he
opened his eyes, and shouted with his like-minded neighbors and
lived a while in the vicarious glory. The depth of the Yankee
Psychosis appeared in the fact that Gerrit Smith, F. B. Sanborn, T. W.
Higginson and the great Theodore Parker himself were implicated
in John Brown's burlesque, and only Smith ever regretted it. On the
morning of his execution crepe hung on the churches and funeral
bells tolled all across the Continent. There were mass meetings
enough to let everyone speak. Here was Thoreau:

Is it not possible . . . that an individual may be right and a government wrong? Are laws to be enforced simply because they are made? or declared by any number of men to be good? . . . Is it the intention of law-makers that *good* men shall be hung ever? . . . Some eighteen hundred years ago Christ was crucified; this morning perhaps, Captain Brown was hung. These are the two ends of a chain which is not without its links. He is not Old Brown any longer; he is an angel of light.[149]

This is the "Higher Law" which all through this time the Yankees invoked against the Fugitive Slave Law, and asserted against the Dred Scott Decision. It was a part of Third Puritan Idealism, but it was now much crowded and blurred in every soul by the current of Hate and Destruction. Theodore Weld had at this time withdrawn from the management of Abolition House in Washington and was farming it in New Jersey. One of his neighbors succeeded in having the bodies of two of Brown's co-murderers shipped to their village where they buried them with honor. The following June the American Peace Society, for the first time in its thirty-two years of history, failed of a quorum, and it disappeared into the conflict, murmuring unctuous rationalizations. Elihu Burritt continued to work for the Pacifist Ideal, but now on an international and no more an internecine plane. Emerson voiced the dilemma of the Pacifist who is no longer a saint:

. . . I do not wish to abdicate so extreme a privilege as the use of the sword or the bullet. For the peace of the man who has forsworn the use of the bullet seems to me not quite peace.[150]

The North had now put its hand to the helm and there was no turning back. It was not a course toward Immediate Abolition. It was a course to block any inch of Extension of Slave Territory, and to do away with such diseased perversion as the Fugitive Slave Law and the Dred Scott Decision. It was a course, as it seemed, toward some kind of Clean Resolution, for every Yankee to meet the Great Chimera and sink his harpoon in it till it spouted black blood and rolled and returned to the Deep. In the face of convincing threats of Secession they elected Lincoln who, though born a Southern Individualist, now thought objectively as the Yankees usually did. He thought more objectively than most Yankees were doing now. In the face of the madness that followed his election, he remembered the Third Puritan dream of Benevolence and Perfection. Stopping in Philadelphia on February 22, 1861, on the way to take up his duties, South Carolina, Georgia, Florida, Alabama, Mississippi and

Louisiana already out and Texas going out tomorrow, he said what each Yankee believed, but he said it purely, unmixed with the widening current of Yankee hate:

> I have never had a feeling politically . . . that did not spring from the Declaration of Independence. . . . I have often inquired of myself what great principle it was that kept this confederacy so long together. It was . . . something in that declaration giving liberty, not alone to the people of this country, but hope for the world for all future time. It was that which gave promise that in due time the weights should be lifted from the shoulders of all men, and that all should have an equal chance. This is the sentiment embodied in the Declaration of Independence. . . . I would rather be assassinated on the spot than surrender it.[151]

And so there came Sumter, and out of the Yankee Love of Mankind Lincoln called for 75,000 Militia, and out of some Love and some Hate and some Buoyant Innocence the Yankees responded several times beyond need. The River of Puritan History quickened its flow toward the Distant Sea. The Sea was still the Idea of Human Perfection whose symbol was the Union, and it was the Ocean of perfect hatred where the Chimera of Evil swam. The Central Stream of the River was still the Puritan Stream of Benevolence, the Desire for Happiness of all Mankind, now specifically the Slaves. On the Left the Antinomian Stream was still Innocent and Exuberant and looked to lick the Rebels and be home for planting next week. But the Arminian Stream on the right was wide in its hatred, and could not remember that Objective Perception and Love had ever been. The world-old slogans of War came down from their classic shelves. Said Parker, "All the great charters of humanity have been *writ in blood,* and must continue to be. . . ."[152]

As always, the churches, or most of them, were the most bloodthirsty of the citizenry. The Northern cause was "sublime" and the cause of God. Said a Presbyterian Resolution on the State of the Country:

> This whole treason, rebellion, anarchy, fraud, and violence is utterly contrary to the dictates of natural reason and morality, and is plainly condemned by the revealed will of God.[153] [A very fine piece of Legal Arminianism at almost its worst.]

And the Ohio Baptist Convention in '62 promised to support the armies "in their endeavors to crush the wicked rebellion." The Methodists, the most numerous sect, gave the largest number of communicants and ministers to support the "cause of God" and suppress the "cruel and wicked rebellion," and, consistently with their general Arminianism, amended the church discipline by making slaveholding a sin.[154] Bishop Mathew Simpson, native of Ohio, was particularly effective in waving the Bloody Shirt all over the North while it was still indeed Bloody, raising audiences to utmost excitement with the simplest tricks of rhetoric accompanied by the display of some genuine Tattered Standard. Shortly after the war, the influential Baptist *Christian Watchman and Reflector*[155] made a definitive separation of the sheep from the goats:

> Any minister who during the rebellion did not develop the great Truth that Christianity demanded obedience to a beneficent government, and that rebellion and treason were odious, failed of fulfilling his whole duty.

Meanwhile, in July of '61, the Yankees had marched out to Bull Run to end the war in holiday spirit and dress. And they were routed by better leaders and angrier soldiers who had never known Benevolence or Innocence and whose Soil was Invaded. And so the Innocence faded also out of Yankee Individualism. And the Antinomian flow of the River quickened. And each man was the Agent and Power of God, and whoever opposed him must die. And the Arminian flow of the River quickened, and they told each other that Rebels were agents of Satan and less than human, and they all must die. Soon they were yelling and snarling and delving for blood with the best of the Rebels, most of whom had not known any culture but one of this kind.

In the War that ensued there was more Violence, more Self-indulgence in hatred and slaughter than in all wars that had gone before. There is nothing to approach it in the records of the French or the English wars where the enemy was foreign, or even in the Indian Wars where the enemy was sincerely believed to be the Devil's lieutenant. This was a war where the enemy was not only your Brother. The enemy was Yourself, a Flaw in your own Perfection, a sickly, subhuman flaw in that Union that God had designed for Utopia and had put in your care. After Bull Run they at last heard the thunder ahead and saw the rolling brink where the Perfection and the Flaw had led them. And the whole culture of fifteen million Yankees gathered and narrowed and, drawing its Heresies with it, plunged over the Falls.

And in the four years of descent into darkening Chaos the Arminian stream that was now the Blood-Hunt of Evil and the Antinomian stream that was now the Blood-Hunt for Glory spiraled and mingled and were a single Deluge of Violence on the right of the long Fall. This stream was the War of Destruction and Profiteers and Clerical Laissez-faire and the Churches. And soon in the Chaos below it would be Reconstruction and Corruption, and would flow away to the future in a separate river no longer the River of Puritan Culture but the Pseudo-culture of Violence and power.

And on the left of the Long Fall the old Central Stream of the River was pure in Lincoln with Malice toward none and the old Benevolent Idea that would free the Slaves and the old Utopian Idea that was the Union. And this too fell right down into Chaos, and it too would flow away in a Separate River that would have its Central Current and its new Heresies of Reason and Emotion. And this would be still the Ancient Puritan Culture, far in Decline but still the Ancient Puritan Culture.

In the Army of little boys who fought and died, perhaps a tenth were of the Stream of Self and Violence. And perhaps eight-tenths were sad little monkeys who were in it for wide-eyed adventure, or for the thirteen dollars a month, or under the pressure of hysterical public opinion, or in fear of the shame of being drafted. And perhaps a tenth were clear in the Puritan Stream. In the early declarations and later letters of these who gave the Army its meaning there is more of either the old Benevolence or the old Utopianism than there is of hate for the Rebels for trying to obstruct these Ideas of God.[157]

The commonest Idea was that of Utopia, frequently accompanied by an indifference or even a hostility to the Slaves. Wrote A. Davenport just after Antietam and the Emancipation Proclamation:

. . . I came out to fight for the restoration of the Union and to keep slavery as it is without going into the territories & not to free the niggers.

A doughboys' newspaper published in Williamsburg, Virginia, carried on its masthead, "The Union Forever and Freedom to all," but explained in its first issue that it meant freedom for "white folks" and not abolition. Wrote Samuel Storrow, enlisting from Harvard in '62:

. . . What is the worth of this man's life or that man's education if this great and glorious fabric of our Union . . . is to be shattered to pieces by traitorous hands . . . ? If our country and our nationality is to perish, better that we should all perish with it.

There were many such professions of idealistic patriotism, "fighting to maintain the best government on earth," and many of course got their patriotism hopelessly abstracted and rhetorically tangled with the Constitution, Free Speech, Free Government and the other stock phrases.

There was an impressive minority who were more concerned with Benevolence, with freeing the Slaves, than they were with the Utopianism of the Union. Here is Chauncey C. Cooke of Wisconsin:

> . . . I tell the boys right to their face I am in the war for the freedom of the slave. . . . I am for helping the slaves if the Union goes to smash.

Of the stuff of true Puritanism was Urich N. Parmalee who enlisted from Yale, "to free the slave," presently considered deserting because the North was not fighting for Emancipation, wrote without fanfare after the Proclamation, "I trust that no failure will dishearten me," fought through the whole war without asking for a furlough, was promoted for successive gallantries step by step from private to captain, and was killed at the head of his company a week before Appomattox.

Unlike that of Captain Parmalee, the visions of the boys of New England were liable to be blurred with the fury of Garrisonian Arminianism. Wrote Corporal Rufus Kinsley of Vermont:

> . . . Slavery must die, and if the South insists on being buried in the same grave I shall see in it nothing but the retributive hand of God.

John P. Sheahan of Maine took the wider view of God's wrath as including the whole nation:

> . . . We well deserve it, . . . god punished Phario for keeping the children of Israel in bondage and why should we go unpunished for we have committed a like sin.[158]

Probably the bulk of the boys who thought at all, like drops in the deluge of War, flew back and forth between the clear stream of Puritan Perception and the stream of its old Heresies, now one in Violence. They sang of Bloody Immolation and Boundless, Vicarious Power—

> Mine eyes have seen the glory of the coming of the Lord.
> He is trampling out the vintage where the grapes of
> wrath are stored;
> He has loosed the fateful lightning of His terrible
> swift sword.

And

> I have read a fiery gospel, writ in burnished
> rows of steel:
> "As ye deal with mine contemners, so with you
> my grace shall deal;
> Let the Hero, born of woman, crush the serpent
> with his heel."

And at the same time they sang the Eternity and the Affirmative Faith of the First Two Centuries of Puritanism, the song of the Soul's Preparation and the Soul's Receipt of Perception and Grace—

> He has sounded forth the trumpet that shall never
> call retreat;
> He is sifting out the hearts of men before His
> judgement-seat;
> Oh, be swift, my soul, to answer him! be jubilant,
> my feet!

Especially they sang of their own Third Puritanism and its Humanitarian Crusade which was the rhythm of their lives—

> In the beauty of the lilies Christ was born across
> the sea
> With a glory in his bosom that transfigures you
> and me.
> As he died to make men holy, let us die to make men
> free.

And, including all these, almost all the boys, whether they thought or not, sang instinctively the Idealism that was the Bedrock of Puritan-Yankee Culture, how John Brown's material body was rotting and his Idea was marching on.

Always while they lived they sang of John Brown and they sang the last stanza of the *Battle Hymn,* for these said what most of all they believed. As this war was unique in bitterness it was also unique in leaving in the soldiers who survived it no bitterness, no cynicism, no hint of Disillusion. Fifty and sixty and seventy years after their Hatred had caught the Chimera and plunged to Death with It, those cackling old Puritans and Yankees, in a world that was not their Utopia and which their Souls could not see, yet believed they had suffered and their friends had died in a cause that was the cause of History, the cause of the Cosmic Drama and God, and that in consequence of their victory His Truth was marching on.

2. THIRD DECLINE

As it was in the Seventeenth and Eighteenth Centuries, so in the Nineteenth, the forces that were going to curtail Faith and Imagination during the last four decades were developing during the preceding sixty years of Puritanism. In the Seventeenth Century the initial cause of Decline had been Economic, the complacency of the second generation resulting from the wealth accumulated through the struggles of the first—to which were added for good measure the postwar moral deterioration that followed King Philip's War, and the epidemic of Legal Arminianism that broke out to correct it. In the Eighteenth Century, the initial and chief cause of decline was Intellectual, the rise of Natural Reason, following Newton and Locke, resulting to a yet unimportant extent in Scientific Materialism, and to an important extent in the Liberalism or Intellectual Arminianism of much of the clergy—and to this again was added for good measure the postwar moral collapse following the Revolution. In the Nineteenth century the attack on Puritanism is going to come with great power from both intellectual and economic forces, besides being reinforced by the demoralization of war at the instance of the Decline. The intellectual force is the older and will ultimately be decisive, being the Rationality or Intellectual Arminianism of the eighteenth century revived and expressing itself now not only in Liberalism or Individualism, but equally in Experimental Science and Materialist Philosophy. This renewed Intellectual Arminianism is not going to be powerful until a critical time well along in the period. It is the economic force of Decline which, though little older than the beginning of the century, is to be the first to move effectively out of the War and Postwar chaos.

This economic force is to be Free Greed which, perverting the old Calvinist injunction to Diligence in one's Calling for the glory of God, is to become a respected motive irrespective of God and eventually even of Diligence. So profound will be this change that in those areas of Greater New England where the new Greed dominates the culture, we shall have to conclude that it is no longer Yankee, let alone Puritan, Culture but a Yankee Pseudo-culture, retaining some of the surface but none of the inner quality of the original current. There will remain, quite separate from the course of this pseudo-culture and running parallel to it, the original Puritan River, now more than ever narrowing between its Heresies in religion's greatest, and possibly final, Decline.

In the seventeenth century, in connection with John Hull the goldsmith and mintmaster, we discussed what I called the Grand Hypocrisy, the modernly incomprehensible attitude that undertakes diligence and frugality for profit because the Lord commands it and not for the enjoyment of the resulting hoard—

> . . . The Lord also hath made up my loss in outward estate. To him be all praise. . . . The Lord wean my heart more from these outward things, and fix it more upon himself!

From that time, through the apparent cupidity in the Decline at the end of that century, and through divers dubious doings respecting slaves and opium during the eighteenth,* the profession of doing God's work has remained primary. The Grand Hypocrisy of seeming cupidity in actual piety has often slipped over into the Common Hypocrisy of seeming piety in actual cupidity. But the profession of serving God and the genuine fear of His displeasure have continued with remarkable vigor. Even Franklin, who had no Faith and contracted his Sky from the dimensions of imaginative to those of sensuous perception, yet had his misgivings that the unknown God might yet be real, and thought it prudent to court His interest with a little prayer.

Even while the forces of honest Greed are gathering strongly in the first half of the nineteenth century, we find the ancient motive wonderfully troublesome to those whom God had greatly favored. Of the Boston merchant princes, William Appleton (1786-1862) was probably the wealthiest in his day. His diary[2] shows a lifelong fear of seeking money for its own sake:

> My mind is very much bent on making money, more than securing temporal friends or lasting peace. . . .

> I feel that I am quite eaten up with business; while in Church, my mind with all the exertion I endeavoured to make, was flying from City to City, from Ship to Ship and from Speculation to Speculation. . . .

> More than half a century have I lived: almost without parallel in the smiles of Fortune. . . . So much for me has been granted by kind Heaven, what have I done for my fellow beings? . . . My present intentions are to lessen my business, try to bring my mind to dwell on things of more importance, to associate more with religious persons. . . .

And at seventy-five, a year before his death, he confesses his essential sin of competitiveness, the desire to aggrandize himself above others:

> . . . I pray God to keep me from being avaricious, and proud of my success; but I cannot bear the shame of falling below my own powers and being left behind by those who are not my equals.

Scattered through the diary we find expressions about generosity which look like rationalizations of stinginess but, as we shall see, may well be honest reflections of ideas then fashionable among the Clergy:

* Journal of a Voyage by Gods permission from Providence . . . Rhode Island; toward Goree in Africa; on the Good Ship *Mary*. Captain Nathan Henry. May God grant success to the Ship and Crew. . . .
Monday 28th of December . . .

S.M. 4 Barrels of Cyder	Recd.
1 Tierce of Rice	6 Men Slaves
4 Do. Clarret	2 Women Slaves. . . .[1]

tianity than the sweetness of Home Missions, Bibles, Tracts and the
rest of the paraphernalia of the Benevolent Empire. This static wing
of clerical laissez-faire was unrelated to the future in so far as it
resisted the emergence of Individualism; but by deifying property
it did contribute to its eventual displacement of Religion in important quarters.

The other subdivision of Clerical Laissez-faire was ancestral
not only to the practical or Applied Materialism of the forthcoming Pseudo-culture, but also to the Philosophical Materialism which was going to support it. Although professed by otherwise
conservative ministers, it was not a pure conservative doctrine, for
it acknowledged the forces of change. To begin with, it carried out
the important rational manoeuver of identifying religion and science. Said the Reverend John McVickar of Columbia, no Yankee
but of great influence on Yankee preachers: "That science and religion eventually teach the same lesson, is a necessary consequence
of the unity of truth, but it is seldom that this union is so satis-
factorily displayed as in the researches of Political Economy."[9] This
identity being established, the laws of Nature, including the supposed laws of political economy, became "nothing less than laws of
God."[10] For "steadiness of action" the economic laws were taken to
be "on a footing well-nigh as safe as those of mechanical powers"—
this the expression John Bascom, President of Wisconsin and Professor of Political Science at Williams.[11]

Most relevant to the future was the content of these godly natural laws of political economy. As propounded by these pre-Dar-
winian divines, they were in fact early statements of "Social Darwinism," the social struggle for existence and the survival of the
fitter. Francis Wayland, President of Brown, was the most popular
author in the field in the pre-Civil War period. In his view the
basic laws are those of industry and idleness:

> If God have made labor necessary to our well being . . .; if
> he have set before us sufficient rewards to stimulate us to labor;
> and if he have attached to idleness corresponding punish-
> ments, it is manifest that the intention of this constitution
> will not be accomplished, unless both of these classes of mo-
> tives are allowed to operate upon man.[12]

That is, there must be no interference by government or any other
agency in the operation of these sacred laws, and charity, except for
the immediately afflicted, becomes a work of ungodliness. Said
Francis Bowen of Harvard:

> . . . The sight of the two extremes of opulence and poverty,
> —the hope of rising to the one and the fear of falling into

the other,—is the constant stimulus which keeps up the energy and activity of the human race. . . .[13]

President Bascom was for this same struggle for existence, but he added a corollary which showed a rudimentary Social Conscience. In his view, the operation of the law of acquisitiveness would eventually produce a higher type that would be above so base a motive. It is of interest that Bascom's book[14] appeared almost contemporaneously with the *Origin of Species* whose first American edition sold out in two weeks just before the Civil War. These business-minded clerics of the pre-War time had the stage all set for Individualism, religious and secular, to rush into a ruthless and quarterless battle royal. What prevented it yet awhile was the fact that this Individualism was in fact not yet Godless. Everybody still believed in God, and believed that He made these rules of competition and aggrandizement. Wherefore, in following these rules you were not excused from honoring His other rules, among them the rule of concern for the neighbor. As we see it today, God was accredited with promulgating the economic rules which must eventually displace His religious rules, His rules of Love and Grace. God was preparing the culture for the Economic Man, the Acquisitive Society, the Economic Interpretation of History, with its corollaries of Big Business and Marxism.

For a while yet, the fear of God and the awareness of the Second Commandment, which latter was directing the affirmative movements of the age, kept the merchants and industrialists from applying in full logic the rules of Social Pre-Darwinism which their ministers sanctioned on divine authority. Even as William Appleton was worried about his avaricious and competitive instincts, so the leaders of the concurrent Industrial Revolution, the employers in the new textile, shoe and miscellaneous factories had concern for their employees which we can not put down entirely to expediency. South of Boston, where child labor predominated, the evils of the British system were in part avoided by hiring family units. "Families Wanted" read an advertisement in the Providence *Manufacturers' and Farmers' Journal* for January 14, 1828: "—Ten or Twelve good respectable families consisting of four or five children each, from nine to sixteen years of age, are wanted to work in a cotton mill. . . ." Thus the children were given both the comfort and control of the parental presence. Some factories ran schools for the children evenings or on Sundays. In 1836 Massachusetts passed a law requiring all children under fifteen to go to school at least three months a year, and in 1840 Rhode Island passed a similar though weaker law.

Meanwhile the admired and fairly general system of employing women—mostly north of Boston—was the Waltham System which honestly aimed to combine education, decency and production. Care was taken in selecting the girls, usually enlisted from farms at ages close around twenty, and they were freely discharged for lying, laziness, profanity, and one factory let them out if they attended dancing school. The doors of the boarding houses—where the girls were required to live unless they had families in town— were locked against sinners who came home after ten o'clock, and the matrons were older women selected for their motherly intelligence. Likewise the overseers in the mills were men of virtue, free of the clutches of the demons alcohol and tobacco, usually married and commonly teachers in the Sunday Schools which most of the girls attended. At Lowell and elsewhere there were well attended Lyceums which imported the biggest names of the day, and there were societies for studying French and German. The Improvement Circle at Lowell published the literarily respectable *Lowell Offering*, and the "ladies of the loom" habitually tacked up on their machines bits of verse or prose which they memorized as they worked. For farm girls who could not go to an academy, their employment provided a kind of secondary education that was better than none, and after four or five years of it they would go home to marry or teach school.[15]

This industrial idyll lasted prettily till the dreadful panic of 1837 when wages fell thirty to fifty per cent, strikes were useless, years of great hardship followed, labor organization and class consciousness disintegrated, and employers generally abandoned the humanitarianism which had been one of their motives before. Labor, including the "ladies of the loom," petitioned for a legislative limitation of the working day to ten hours, and New Hampshire alone —in 1845—acceded. Presently the opening West and its Gold began to draw off the farm boys, and after them the girls for wives, teachers and missionaries. The tidal wave of European immigrants, especially of Irish—who would work for less than self-respecting Yankee girls—began. By the '50's the industrial parts of Old New England— eastern Massachusetts, northern Rhode Island, and central Connecticut—were approaching that state of tension between greedy wealth and desperate poverty which the clerics recommended with their Divine Laws of Laissez-faire, and which reversed the Puritan traditions of Idealism, Equality and Responsibility.

Meanwhile, less significant preparation for the Grand Debacle of the next age was to be seen in the 25,000, more or less, Yankee* boys who rushed to California after '48, and the 4,000, more or less, who rushed to Pike's Peak in '59. In these migrations there was probably less of designing cupidity than of the need for land and the common,

* This figure and the next are for Old New England only.

innocent exuberance of the age. It was yet a good way from tilting a pan of water watchfully on the slopes and foothills of the Sierra Nevada to selling gold bricks in the saloons of Chicago and Buffalo, watered railroad stock in the brokerages of Wall Street, and votes in the national and state legislatures.

Greater New England carried over the brink of the War these forces of Decline in varying degrees of development. On the left of the long Falls in the old Current of Puritan Faith, the Millennial Perception of God's Kingdom on Earth was contracted to the specific Union that must be saved; and the cosmic Benevolence of Second-Commandment Christian Perception was contracted to the specific vision of the Freed Slaves. On the right of the Falls the Legal Arminian current, now moralized into hatred of evildoers, specifically Rebels, and the Antinomian current, now brutalized into bloody self-advancement, were joined in the single Deluge of Violence. And the drops of this stream saw years below and ahead on the plain Visions of further Violence and Self-Advancement, greedy visions that rose naturally from the clerical doctrines they were accustomed to hear. They saw the vision of the still boundless West with its wealth to be won, its wars of Indian subjection continuing through the Great War, its dramatic Union Pacific Railroad beginning in '64 to creep in from both oceans. They saw the vision of the still fabulous Industrial World, with its cities and chimneys and ships and riches in profits and wages, continuing through the War its expansion under laissez-faire, gaining its intermediate objective of a high tariff. And, clarifying these visions, the drops in the Deluge of Violence heard around them the rustle of Great Ideas: the hardly disguised Materialist Philosophy of the Ministers who preached the identity of science and religion, especially the identity of the Laws of God and the Laws of Property; the deification by the same Ministers of the laws of unequal distribution of Wealth, the Laws of Poverty and Riches and the Virtuous Struggle between them.

These visions and these ideas the Deluge of Violence carried down the Falls of the War and into the whirlpool of chaos and Reconstruction. And thence it plunged on its separate way of Yankee Pseudo-culture out on the plain, full of rapids and shouting and tumult. And of all the self-aggrandizing voices along the River of Violence none was more loud than the boastful shouts of organized so-called religion. "The loyal churches of the North," bellowed George L. Prentiss in the *American Presbyterian and Theological Review*,[16]

> form a large army and wield a good deal of political influence —to say nothing now of their influence with the High and Mighty Ruler of the Universe.

Even more obscene were the Arminian screams of the churches for Sadistic Reconstruction, and their exultation over the prostrate South:

> How are the mighty fallen! Three fifths of their territory is wrested from them . . . Hallelujah! The Lord God Omnipotent reigneth! His right arm hath gotten him the victory![17]

And a consensus of the United Presbyterians, the Old School Presbyterian General Assembly and the Methodist General Conference proposed to secure the Republic against future subversion by passing a Constitutional Amendment declaring the sovereignty of God and the supremacy of Revelation.[18]

Thus the pulpit, long blinded to piety and empty of any affirmative imaginative theme, along with the political rostrum, settled on the nation both philosophic and predatory materialism, justifying them with negative Arminian thunder, the rhetorical art of implying the measure of one's own virtue by the magnitude of somebody else's venality. The formal leadership of the nation passed to the lachrymose preacher and the scowling politician, waving for fifty years the bloody shirt of unholy rebellion—and latterly the bloodless but dirtier shirt of communism. These were the leaders of the Pseudo-culture, the River of Violence as it plunged out of the postwar chaos into such spectacular expansion and prosperity as recalls that of Rome after she came back from destroying Carthage, gave over her earlier ideals, and overran the world. At the same time and over most of the same continental scene the original River of Puritan Culture also flowed out of the whirlpool of Reconstruction, and partook in decadence of the same spectacular Expansion.

Of the two aspects of the materialistic expansion of New England, the geographic and the industrial, the former was the one which as a movement of population was not necessarily inimical to the culture. Taking advantage of the Morrill Land Grant Act, the Homestead Act, and the luxuriantly advertised empire of 129,000,-000 acres—three times the size of Old New England—which the State and Federal governments gave to the Railroads, the endless wagon-trains trundled westward right through the War and for two and three generations afterwards. On May 10th, 1869, the western section of the Union Pacific—under the management of California's "Big Four"—Stanford, Huntington, Crocker and Hopkins—met the eastern section at Promontory Point fifty miles west of Ogden, Utah, where the great-funnelled engines faced each other and the nation listened while every telegraph instrument in the land reported the three strokes on the last spike—"One, two, three —done!"

By 1870 the line of settlement which in '60 had invaded Minnesota, Iowa, Kansas, Colorado, and had sent the Mormon salient out into Utah, had incorporated all of these states and territories into substantial settlement and was well out in the Dakotas and Nebraska. By '80 the settlers moving westward from the Mississippi and eastward from the Pacific had met in Montana for the North and in Nevada for the South, and the southern boundary of Greater New England was drawn to the Pacific. Within the area mopping up was well under way, with fifteen million bison butchered and three hundred thousand Indians butchered or herded into vassalage. In 1882 the Atcheson, Topeka & Santa Fe linked to the Pacific, in 1887 the Northern Pacific, and in 1882 the Southern Pacific. These great continental bands with their tributary lines were part of the general increase of railroads in the whole country from 35,000 miles in 1865 to 93,000 in '80, and, like the rest, their earnings averaged enough to pay the cost of their construction in about four years.

Out from the railroad lines the wheat began to ripple, and the cattle grazed and drove where the Indians and bison had roamed. In the cow country the pioneer civilization was partly Rebel and mostly "wild," where desperadoes and vice barons preyed on the brave and truculent cowboys in the little cow capitals with their false fronts, like Dodge City or Newton, Kansas. But in the main the settlers of greater New England were small-time Yankees, or their equivalent in German, Scandinavian, Bohemian or Polish immigrants, at first living or starving through a regime of dugouts or sod huts, buffalo chip fires and grubbed food, while they struggled hysterically to turn the plains into wheat and to buy the machinery that meant comfort. By the '70's the prairie was spinning with windmills, steam engines were drawing their gangs of plows, and the combined harvester-binder was releasing hundreds of thousands of hands to become owners. In four or five years prairie-dog towns were buried under great and bona fide cities like Lincoln and Wichita.

As always, the Yankees of the true culture set up their institutions as urgently as they established the means of existence. First, there were the churches and schools, and soon after them the Lyceums and the Improvement Societies. "The little sun-baked, blizzard-chilled hamlet that was talking of Indian raids one day might be talking of the *Atlantic Monthly*, the suffragist lecturer and Paris fashions the next."[19] Between 1860 and 1900, the founding of colleges accelerated, at least in physical terms, as did everything else in the period. In the four decades, 151 new institutions of higher learning were founded in Greater New England,[20] 17 of them in Old New England,[21] 55 in the Cis-Mississippi Old Northwest and Upstate New York,[22] and 79 in the new Trans-Mississippi West. These last included the University of Washington ('61), Kansas Agricultural ('63), and University of Kansas ('65), University of Denver ('64), Colorado School of Mines ('74) and University of Colorado ('77), Carleton ('66), (The University of Minnesota had been founded in '51), Lewis and Clark ('67) and the University of Oregon ('72), Iowa State ('68), (The University of Iowa had been founded in '47), University of California ('68), University of Southern California ('80), Stanford ('85) and Pomona ('87), Brigham Young University ('72), (The University of Utah had been founded in '50), University of South Dakota ('82), University of Wyoming ('87), University of Idaho ('89) and the Montana State University ('93).

Most of the new colleges, as distinguished from the great universities, were small and denominational, a fair proportion of them, both east and west, being Catholic, the student bodies of these recruited chiefly from the increasing tide of immigration. Greater New England, as well as Greater Pseudo-New England, was now continental and cosmopolitan, its culture absorbing with some success all but the most exclusive and stubborn islands of new arrivals. During the fifty years before 1900 the center of population had moved two hundred and forty-six miles westward from western West Virginia to central Indiana, since when it has moved only a hundred and twenty-seven miles more to the west. Meanwhile in 1890, the Census Bureau announced that there was no more frontier.

The pseudo-culture of Money and Factories and Great Cities concerns us here because it was the Outward Power of the age, and because it lured many Yankees away from the Inward Reality. So sudden and vast was the change in cities after the War, that to the new generation the civilization as it had been before 1860 was matter of ancient history. It was said that in New York City in 1866 there were more men whose incomes were $100,000 than in 1840 there had been men whose entire property was so much.[23] The established industries of textiles, shoes, mining, smelting, hardware, clocks and the earliest flights of gadgetry were already in boom when the war ended and, far from suffering from any postwar slump, continued to rise.

New Industries burst into solid, permanent and expanding mushrooms: Steel, when Alexander Holley of Salisbury, Connecticut, brought in the Bessemer process; western Meat, riding eastward through Chicago and Kansas City, at first in cattle cars and after

1875 in refrigerator cars; the milling of wheat, concentrated in
Minneapolis; Pennsylvania and Ohio Petroleum, beginning its consolidation in the Standard Oil Company of Ohio. Older industries
went into the phase of standardization and expansion of plant,
especially clothing, footwear and watches. The sewing-machine,
farm-implement, piano and organ factories improved their methods.
Milwaukee beer rose from 55,000 barrels in '65 to 260,000 in '73.
Between 1859 and '69 the number of manufacturies increased from
140,000 to 250,000. Banks increased geometrically to serve them.
British, Irish, Slavs, Germans and Bohemians poured in to operate
them, and industrial settlements swelled into cities over night. By
1875 seven and a half of the nation's forty million were foreign-born.

Due to the Panic of '73, immigration had slowed by '75 and, like
production itself, was not again in flood until '80. Between then and
'90, 3,000,000 came in.[24] The boom that brought them was largely
in terms of the consolidation of Trusts, the pyramiding of power
up to relatively few "Robber Barons." Between them they controlled
most of business and a fair part of government, and, of more permanent importance, they became the Pantheon of Gods of the
Pseudo-culture, the pagan part of the nation. Oil, Steel, Railroads,
Wheat, Distilling, Cordage, Sugar, Cottonseed Oil, Linseed Oil, and
many other basic industries concentrated into fewer hands, and
their trade names became the mottos of baronial escutcheons. Their
vassals included many million perverted Yankees and most of the
later immigrants who did not come to build America but to prey
on it and so to be preyed on.

Construction went on accelerating to the end of the century. In
the '80's alone 70,000 miles of railroad were built, more track
than any three countries of Europe had laid in fifty years. The
trackage that had been 75,000 miles at the end of the War was 193,-
000 miles at the end of the century. Steel profits between 1875 and
1900 were $133,000,000, of which $40,000,000 accrued in the latter
year alone, and of this $25,000,000 was Andrew Carnegie's personally.
It was estimated in '89 that a hundred men had incomes of $1,200,-
000 a year, and in 1902 that there were thirty-five hundred mil-
lionaires.[25] The total wealth of the nation had been about $16,000,-
000,000 in 1860, and in 1900 it was $126,700,000,000.

It is not specially significant that this golden period began just
after the War with four or five years of greater public corruption
than the country has known before or since, decisive numbers of
votes being purchased by lobbies in at least the New York, Illinois,
Iowa, Minnesota and Kansas legislatures, most big cities being run
by "Rings," and numerous Yankee Congressmen, including a future
president and a future candidate for president, being found in posses-

sion of the securities of railroads which enjoyed government patronage. Nor is it specially significant that at least three Yankees, namely Daniel Drew, Jay Gould and Jim Fisk, were involved—most notoriously in the "Erie War" in '68 and in the attempt to corner the gold market on "Black Friday" in '69—in what was for magnitude perhaps the most blackguardly commercial infamy in all of business history. The outright public and private corruption passed, as all postwar debauches have done. Against the contorted Drew, Gould and Fisk we could balance the upright and in the long run more powerful Cooke, Morgan and Hill. What was the significance of the human side of the expanding Circus of Violence was that all these Yankee leaders and many others like them, whether or not they retained a restraining responsibility, were all moving from the Culture into the psuedo-culture. Their entire affirmative motivation was the desire for self-advancement. From their angry and unctuous pulpits they learned nothing of Grace and God's business. So they turned to their own business.

If we take what are probably the two dozen greatest names in the nation-wide postwar pseudo-culture, either sixteen or seventeen of them are renegade Yankees. For railroads we have Huntington, Stanford, Crocker, Hopkins and Hill; for steel, Holley; for oil, Rockefeller and Rogers; for meat-packing, Armour and Swift; for flour-milling, Pillsbury and Washburn; for more or less constructive finance, Morgan and Cooke; for non-constructive speculation, Drew, Gould and Fisk. Hill was a borderline case, being born in Ontario of Methodist and Baptist background and living there till he was eighteen (1856) when he went to Minnesota and became, by its own official pronouncement,[26] its most distinguished citizen. All the rest were unequivocally Yankees.

In matters of origin and most matters of disposition they were miscellaneous. Of background approaching the sordid were Rockefeller, Drew, Gould, and Fisk, and in their dealings these four were probably the shiftiest and most furtive. Of poor but respectable rustic background and small education were Huntington, Crocker, and Swift, and of these only Huntington, the great lobbyist for the railroad interests of the Big Four—himself, Crocker, Hopkins and Stanford—was seriously charged with corruption. A cut higher in wealth, education or both were Stanford (wealthy farm family, Cazenovia Seminary, law studies and admitted to Bar in Albany), Hill (wide self-education after being disappointed of medical education by accidental loss of an eye), Holley (rich Connecticut iron family, Brown), Armour (Cazenovia

Seminary), Pillsbury (father in local railroading—Dartmouth), Washburn (Bowdoin and law studies) and Cooke (father a Congressman); and in widely varying degrees each of these showed a sense of public responsibility. Of a background of real wealth in Hartford and in England, and educated abroad, was Morgan, who did monumental things for art and letters, but was not interested in social reform nor much in private charity, and showed public responsibility chiefly in the example of integrity he set the country in directing a fair part of its business.

In all these men the Puritan desire for Objective Truth had inverted into the subjective desire for self-aggrandizement and power. Most of them were indifferent or hostile to learning. Although in '61 all of them were under thirty except Cooke and the California Big Four—who except for Hopkins were under forty—not one of them served in the Army, or otherwise showed any signs of Third or Benevolent and Utopian Puritanism. Although many of them supported and attended churches, and although we must discount their biographies which were generally written by Materialists who are shy of religion, yet it is significant that there appears no evidence that any of them was actively religious in the sense of Mysticism, the Puritan Perception of Grace. It is safe to infer from their most dastardly as from their most constructive deeds that each of them was natively equipped with Imagination of great and potentially Mystical scope; but in each it turned in the direction of expanding concepts of material power, leaving behind a piddling Arminian religiosity or none at all. Morgan's interests in art and in St. George's Episcopal Church in New York were genuine and drew large toll on his income; yet the field of his financial control was all the time expanding toward a billion. With the exception of Pillsbury, who went in for profit-sharing and helped at least the coopers' producer cooperative in Minneapolis, they all seem to have followed faithfully the discipline of Clerical Laissez-faire, especially its holding that neither they nor the state should concern themselves about the Individual Poor.

One thing they all—with the certain exception of the libertine Jim Fisk and the possible exception of Morgan—carried down from the Puritan Culture into the pseudo-culture was the Calvinist Economic Virtues of Diligence, Simplicity and Frugality. Only now wealth was no longer taken as a sign of Grace and an invitation to humility, as with John Hull and even as late as William Appleton. Nor was it any longer something hypocritically sought behind a façade of professed worldlessness. Now for the first time the frank cupidity of Franklin becomes the way of the gods. And a cupidity going farther than Franklin's, for he desired only enough wealth to release him to his real pursuits, while the Barons knew no satiety. Their diligence and frugality were not those of Calvinism, or even Franklinism, but of the Individualism of Jackson and Emerson as leading to tearing and gouging and maiming under the doctrine of clerical laissez-faire. Cried Rockefeller as a youngster when he had made one of his first killings, "I'm bound to be rich! *bound to be rich!*"[27] A little later, and thereafter until his death, he might have put it, "I'm bound to be richer!" In their commonly more reticent idiom, that was what his colleagues in Power murmured to themselves to the end of their lives. It was the diametric opposite of Puritanism or Yankeeism.

Such were the leaders of the great Materialist Debacle. And like them on their smaller stages were the thousands of local tycoons in the small industrial cities, who came into them from the farms, applied to the swapping of securities the same acumen that was a cultural trait in the swapping of cattle and other necessities, and, frequently to their confusion and to their wives' delight, woke up to find themselves rich. Such were the great leaders and the little leaders, and such were the millions who saw, envied, admired and imitated the latter. Within the precincts of the pseudo-culture, the "Epic of America" became the scramble for wealth which James Truslow Adams said it had always been.

The great River of Violence rushed on without Imagination, without Spirit, without Meaning, without any guidance but the alleged guidance of those Material laws of Competition and elimination which the ministers proclaimed as divine, which were said to embody the Natural Rights of the Declaration, and which were presently reinforced by the vogue of Darwin, Spencer and their American disciples. Thus sanctioned to pillage and despoil, the Barons, often restrained by the canons of common honesty, and usually serving the community in collateral ways, went on beating Labor's now Bloody Strikes and milking the people. In the election of McKinley in '96 the people declared for the pseudo-culture. They said they wanted to go on being milked, in the hope that they, and each of them, would be doing the milking tomorrow. Said the famous H. O. Havemeyer, President of the American Sugar Refining Company, at the end of the century when he was under government investigation:

> The consumer gets the advantage; every time it is the consumer . . . I think it fair to get out of the consumer all you can, consistent with a business proposition . . . I do not care two cents for your ethics. . . . Let the buyer beware. . . . You cannot wet nurse the people. . . . This wonderful individual you are talking about who must be supported . . . by a wet nurse called the government.[28]

C. W. Post, founder of the Postum Cereal Company and grand-father of General Foods, stated what all believed:

> Labor must be purchased as other items such as steel, wood, etc. . . . Labor is a commodity.[29]

At least in the early years of the pseudo-culture, and at least with respect to the small tycoons and the millions who followed them, the Yankee ministers, if they had experienced the Puritanism they professed, could have turned the River of Violence back in the Puritan Way. It was these thousands of little preachers who made gods of the Barons, and neither the Barons themselves nor the people who worshipped as they were ordered. It was they who out of all learning aggressively perverted the Imaginations of millions.

Still within hearing of the suffering of the Depression of 1873, the pious *Watchman and Reflector*[30] gave the green light to Ruthlessness:

> Labor is a commodity, and, like all other commodities, its condition is governed by the imperishable laws of demand and supply. It is all right to talk and declaim about the dignity of labor. . . . But when all has been said of it, what is labor but a matter of barter and sale?

And in '77, while the freight cars were still burning and the debris of artillery battle had not been cleared away, the nondenominational *Independent* discovered that the sacred Laws of Competition must be amended. When the employers fought with weapons of starvation they were public benefactors; but when the employees fought back with weapons of fire and lead they became rioters, "criminals in intent and criminals in fact . . . worse than wild beasts turned loose upon society."[31]

> If the club of the policeman, knocking out the brains of the rioter, . . . does not promptly meet the exigency, then bullets and bayonets, canister and grape—with no sham and pretense, in order to frighten men, but with fearful and destructive reality—constitute the one remedy and the only duty of the hour. . . . Napoleon was right when he said that the way to deal with a mob was to exterminate it.[32]

In May of '86, after Chicago policemen had shot a few strikers and, moving in to break up a peaceful meeting in the Haymarket, were bombed, and certain incendiary anarchists who had not thrown the bomb had been executed for conspiracy, the Christian press speedily went into action on the old line:

> When anarchy gathers its deluded disciples into a mob, as at Chicago, a Gatling gun or two, swiftly brought into position

and well served, offers, on the whole, the most merciful as
well as effectual remedy.[33]

And in the steel strike of '92, the highest religious authority was
still putting the maintenance of the divine laws of property above
all other interests:

> The battle of law and order must be fought to the end.
> . . . Despotism would settle this matter better than we can
> . . .[34]

Such were the voices of the priests of the industrial pseudo-culture,
most of whom were heirs of the Culture. By the '90's their message
of Moloch was weakening, but it had spread widely over the nation
and had itself become a tradition.

As the power of the River of Violence was Greed, its philosophy
Materialism, and its inspiration the Churches, so its surface was the
Victorian double code. We saw it appearing before as decadent
Romanticism. Now it reaches high development to serve the new Industrial Rich. Since the heart, the pseudo-reality, of the pseudo-culture was Greed, and since such a pseudo-reality can not express itself
otherwise than in the action of the Arena, all other forms of activity—
such as religion, art, recreation and manners—were frustrate. Wherefore, since all minds except the galvanized ones of the barons and
their cohorts felt the need of such activities, they had to build a system
separate from that of the underlying pseudo-reality, and even less
real than it was, a system which could be run without interfering
with the deeper course of the pseudo-reality. Thus we got the dichotomy which is Victorianism. It was chiefly a refuge for women who
dreadfully missed all Truth in their men, while themselves lacking both the independence and the education to envisage Truth of
their own.

Naturally the clergy of the pseudo-culture favored the dual system,
for it left the men to the Holy Battle Royal they loved. Wrote the
Reverend T. DeWitt Talmage, Presbyterian, wealthy by marriage,
and America's leading pulpit attraction, in the *Christian Herald*:

> Whether in professional, or commercial, or artistic, or me-
> chanical life, your husband from morning to night is in a
> Solferino, if not a Sedan. It is a wonder that your husband
> has any nerves or patience or suavity left. . . . If he come
> home and sit down preoccupied, you ought to excuse him.
> If he do not feel like going out that night . . ., remember he

has been out all day. . . . Remember, he is not overworking
so much for himself as . . . for you and the children.[35]

Thus you had Father's World, and Mother's World, and a tragi-
comedy between them called "Life with Father."

In this Half-Male, Half-Female culture in which the man spelled
"pray" with an *a* at home and with an *e* at the office, the perceptions of the female world were inhibited from looking all the way
into truth. Wherefore, emotion must not be that of Imaginative
Perception but something to be enjoyed for itself. It must be Sentimentality. The index of reality was not the cool omniscience of
Grace, but the delicious Extremity of Feeling, controlled, of course,
by good taste, but controlled that the telltale tears might rise to
flood level. The delicious Feeling was female Antinomianism. And
the Victorian Code itself, being identified with tender piety, was
female Arminianism.

For new-rich women who were too old to cultivate learning and
taste, the safest mark of Gentility was this Code which invited them
everywhere in the magazines and books of etiquette.[36] Founded in
the familiar moral Law, which Arminians had long presented as the
pattern of Grace and Salvation, the new law added numerous items
of manners, and the whole became a discipline equally of the church
and the drawing room. Here there was no split between Religion
and the World. A man might be either snubbed by society or criti-
cized from the pulpit for either adultery or waltzing, for theft or
for smoking in the presence of ladies. The formulae of religion and
"good breeding" were one formula. The common standard of excellence was tears hardly suppressed. They were the proclamations
alike of a divine vision, an evil thought, a *faux pas* or having
missed the party. The more absurd taboos, such as those about
drinking, smoking, card playing and like trivialities, had originally
been imposed in the belief, mistaken or not, that such indulgences
might divert the mind from the things of religion. Now they became the things of religion themselves, and sad and mighty were
the debates that wove around them.

Equally absurd with the life of the heart was the life of the mind
which the girls concocted to adorn their pseudo-culture. By and
large, education like religion was indistinguishable from Respectability. Its importance was to qualify you to appear in "Society."
Suitably elevated topics of conversation included "articles of virtue,
photographs of foreign subjects, paintings, or statuary to be admired, and the conversation may gradually center in the Egyptian
obelisk, or the Tower of London." Before going to a party it was
always a good idea "to outline your subjects and fortify yourself
by such study as you can make of them."[37]

Since the pseudo-culture ignored the Culture that had spawned it by Materialism, it became necessary to travel, to go to Europe to find "culture," and virtually anything out of the Eastern Hemisphere was at once beautiful and naughty. Art was thought to have "an ennobling and purifying influence"[38] which might protect an "elderly girl" of twenty-five or more in visiting an artist's studio without a chaperone. The common standard of literature, especially of criticism, was prudery. As the forms of sentiment replaced imagination in the liberal arts, fancy replaced it in the practical arts. Originality was identified with the bizarre, and brilliance with the diffuse. It was the time of minarets and flying buttresses, Gothic, Moorish, Chinese and simply Fantastic architecture, all acceptable if only it were lush in detail and unrelated to use. The interiors of the rich were museums of deeply carved mahogany, labyrinthine brass, fancily blown and embossed glass, deep carpets to the baseboards, lace and velvet by the ton, iron statues, onyx and marble slabs, stairs and fireplaces, peacock feathers or real peacocks, fountains, billiard tables and books by the yard. The interiors of the less rich were quainter museums of easels, bamboo tables, stuffed birds, gilded rams' horns, painted rolling pins, wax flowers under glass domes, china statues, Rogers groups, open fans on the wall, Japanese lanterns from the ceiling, cattails in a painted umbrella stand, and cosy corners hidden behind curtains of beads.

As false as was all this in that Woman's World, so false and paradoxical was the position of women themselves. On the one hand they were pampered and deferred to for their supposedly mysterious and noble "intuitions." On the other hand they were chaperoned, protected, deceived, misunderstood and frustrated as hardly in any other period of human history. In that time of the double standard, life in the demi-monde approached reality more nearly and more often than either the male or female life of the hermaphrodite pseudo-culture that made the show. Deprived of their husbands' masculinity in every sense, harangued upon their own innocence of emotion till some of them believed it, buried in clothes and compressed in corsets, the Victorian women of the rich and the near rich were unnaturally long-suffering, unnaturally tender, and unnaturally discontented. Out of the age came the real and successful impulse of the feminist movement.

The ultimate significance of the pseudo-culture was not in the Barons, the Baronesses and their imitators, but in their children. The first generation of the industrial rich was a kind of scherzo, a naïve overture from which a lapse into the old Culture would have been possible. But in the children there was announced a genuine New Theme that was neither Puritan nor even Yankee. From infancy their mothers surrounded them with proper servants, schools and travels to make them into the likeness of European ladies and gentlemen, and on the surface they often succeeded. The old folks had been brought up in Yankee Idealism and had perverted it. Being brought up in wealth, the young no longer suffered the insecurities of Greed and fresh Plutocracy. But no more had they reached the sureness of Aristocracy. In this America's first generation of great riches, the exciting smugness of being of the gay "upper crust," the "little four hundred," of any industrial town, the exciting power to buy every new thing with the fashion, all this pre-empted the Yankee Idealism, and all this for a time was sufficient. They knew the Victorian rules, but they snickered in church and made sacrilegious jokes, and they even began to make fun of the Holy Code and its pious pretences. This light generation, the froth of the River of Violence in the '80's and '90's, was the first ever in Greater New England that was brought up without religion and was not even teased by the God of the Puritans. His Sky was replaced by Society, His Idealism by the titillations of Vanity. In earlier periods of Decline, the Elect had sometimes been identified with the Elite. Now there was no meaning of Election. It was sufficient to be Elite and no more.

These charming First Fruits of the Pseudo-Culture had bright ideas, but they never knew Yankee Idealism. And they never knew Yankee Equality. Their strength was a sense of Class, but it was not a class of a strength that could yet afford to admit outsiders as Equal. Very few even stirred to *noblesse oblige* till the third generation. Likewise, the old Economic Virtues of Diligence and Frugality were forgotten as something foolish where wealth was assumed as part of the settled cosmic foundation. Finally, the Intellectual Tradition of New England was also discarded. The young, who enjoyed "the best education that money could buy," were ashamed of their fathers' ignorance but still they must admire them for providing what seemed the first proviso of "culture." Once the aristocracy had been of the Ministers, then of the Lawyers. Now it became the Businessmen, the "Men of Affairs," the men of the Banks and the Plants and the big gambling. Education went into second place and under suspicion. Intelligent men "didn't know the value of a dollar," and they must be kept out of office. When this generation was old it defeated Wilson's League of Nations, mostly because it was the work of a "snivelling college professor."

Idealism, God, the Christo-Puritan Theology, Equality, the Economic Virtues, the Intellectual Tradition—the removal of these from the Puritan House took away almost all of the frame and foundation. As far as the Industrial Pseudo-culture could remember, there had been no Old House, so long ago—a generation ago—it had been torn down and reconstructed. The second and third generation had chips of it, the Shrewd swapping, the Plain Style which became the Poker Face, the dry Humor. All the rest of the Pseudo-culture's house was replaced by the things that money could buy. Even the chimney of Selfless Grace was torn down and rebuilt of the glass bricks of Ambition. The Third Generation showed signs of responsible aristocracy. But by the maturity of the third generation the pseudo-puritan house was hurricane-stricken and the flood was rising. By then the River of Violence was churning its last Saturnalia as it ran to its leap into oblivion.

But the River of Violence was not the only stream that ran out of the Whirlpool of Reconstruction. Earlier we identified the pseudo-culture today with municipalities of more than 50,000 inhabitants. In 1950 these had a population of 23,000,000, out of a total population of Greater New England of 65,000,000. This leaves us today 42,000,000, about two-thirds of the total, who are still Yankees who live in the Puritan House and are reasonably pure of New England Culture. The population of Greater New England in 1890 was about 28,000,000, and a larger proportion of it, even in the great cities, perhaps 20,000,000 altogether, was still Yankee.

In the same years when the River of Violence plunged out of the chaos of reconstruction, the much wider and slower Puritan River ran out on the left of it, and they flowed along through the years near together and parallel. Before that, for the purposes of the War, the God of Third Puritanism had contracted into two limited Meanings, His Universal Benevolence into the Idea of Freed Slaves, His coming Kingdom, His Utopia, into the Union that must be saved. Each of these Ideas having been realized, they vanished from consciousness and the God with them. Accordingly, from this time Puritan Culture, the Puritan River, goes into its Third Decline. Henceforth, its Central Current of Imagination or Gracious Perception reflects only a small and contracted Sky, no longer a World with a single Meaning, but whatever perception each separate Yankee takes for his Central Idea. In place of the God who is lost it reflects, as we saw at the ends of the seventeenth and eighteenth centuries, flashes and flickers of Humor. The Puritan River in Decline tends, as always, to become the Yankee River.

The Yankee River in its central stream of Imaginative Perception is not all godless, for many Yankees are still in one way or another centered in religious ideas. Also, there is much profession of religion in the ancient Heresies that are wide and shifting bands of current running along the right and left flanks of the River, trying to preempt it. On the right the generally self-righteous Arminian Heresy of Reason and Free Will is nearest the River of Violence, and its own right-most element of Legal Arminianism was the one that first changed to a hateful current to wage the War and so cut off into the River of Violence. The distance between them is not great, and they sometimes toss spray—especially the spray of the Victorian Code and the preachments of its ministers—back and forth between them on the winds of fashion. Sometimes also they eat through the bank between them in little channels and exchange currents of people.

In the Central Current of the Yankee River there are commonly those who, whether they are religious or not, are content in their private Ideas, who are not Arminian, and who dislike Greed and wealth and all kinds of self-assertion; yet politically they side with the Great Ministers and the Great Barons and their right to exploit the public. The Idea is the Puritan one of Equalitarianism, which in this connection is commonly called Freedom. "This blustering pagan is a human being and as good as I am." He is entitled to do as he likes if only he doesn't preach Dangerous Error too loudly, and if his outward life conforms to common decency. Such Yankees were William Allen White in his youth, and Calvin Coolidge always. They are seeming atavisms in the industrial world, for in fact or psychology they are still part of the ancient Agrarian Culture. They are still naïve to the industrial world and the power of the Self and what evil can do to Good, what Individualism can do to their native Equalitarianism. It remains to be tried whether their Ideas, or some of them, are not absolute, whether, when the River of Violence is long forgotten, the New Industrialism will not adjust to them.

The typical drop in the Central Yankee Current in the Time of Decline between '60 and 1900 would be a countryman, one who got his fictional start before the war in Artemus Ward, Hosea Biglow and the other homespun philosophers. After the War he is pure to the point of caricature in country banker *David Harum* of Central New York who wasn't "much of a hand fer church-goin'," but looked "fer an honest man fer quite a number o' years" till he guessed he'd found him, who trimmed the hoss-tradin' "deackin" at his own game, threw out of his office a "wuthless pup" that came snivelling about a note due, but bought the poor widow's mortgage so he could forgive it on a pretext of repaying a kindness, and generally played fairy godfather to everybody in trouble.

On the urban and educated level we find the typical Yankee in the heterogeneous and passionate idealist named Hooker, Beecher, Hawley, Warner and Twichell who occupied Nook Farm on Asylum Hill on the then fringe of Hartford. Each fought his separate fight for his private substitute for discarded Calvinism and, with the possible exception of Harriet Beecher Stowe, found himself "without anchor in . . . a disorganized world."[39] Mark Twain, though only a Yankee by adoption, was of that society and loved it and fought a similar internal fight for the "benign determinism" with which he displaced his own discarded Calvinism, sank into "black despair" and became one of the casualties of the "great demoralization." In happier vein we find the godless but idealistic Yankee in Grover Cleveland who, when he was attacked during the presidential campaign for having an illegitimate child, said to his managers, "Tell them the truth." Of the examples cited, Cleveland is the one who is not much reputed for humor. The account of his private life, however, is that he was good company, a good story teller and mimic.

Perhaps the most convincing Yankee on record was William Allen White, the more convincing for having suffered early delusions in favor of the pseudo-culture and against humanly responsible government, and having emerged from them. Owner and editor after 1895 of the Emporia, Kansas, *Gazette,* his best expressions were uttered in the twentieth century, but he spoke for the end of the nineteenth. As Hooker, Edwards and Channing stood for three successive types of Puritanism, so White stood for Yankeeism. He called himself and the millions of his Middle West, Puritans. Yet his God was far more anthropomorphic even than Channing's, His village virtues so much more important than His Godhead that we hardly think of the latter at all. Channing with his concrete Benevolent God we can call Puritan. White with his Benevolent Local Mutual Spirit we must call Yankee. He distinguished the Middle Westerners from the people of Old New England partly in their freedom from Legal Arminian, Old Calvinist bonds, a distinction that was hardly real in his time. More convincingly he distinguished them for their quasi-mystical dream of Freedom as an Idea under their physically Big Sky. It was a dangerous idea, for that way lay the Equality of Mediocrity. But that was only faintly intimated in the nineteenth century.

White's idea of the Meaning, the God, of the Universe was of a Moral Force, a moral order whose violation brought retribution to the guilty individual or nation. This sounds like Legal Arminianism; yet in White's idea the moral order was not a code, it was not a Moral Law. It could not be reduced to rules. It was an idea or group of ideas that collectively are called Justice, "something fine in the heart of man which God put there when we got our manhood."[40] God administers human culture through this Justice—this Image of Him—that is stamped in every individual. Thus, as in original Puritanism, man is the implement of God's will, and a kind of Predestination survives. Society, especially the society of the small town where all know each other, rewards and punishes for God. Truth becomes the small town's composite idea of propriety.

> Was it God, moving in us, that punished Markley 'by the rod of His wrath,' that used our hearts as wireless stations for his displeasure to travel through or was it the chance prejudice of a simple people?[41]

This democratic God, like all gods, requires Faith to operate. Only in this case the requisite Faith is not really in the Mysterious God of the Universe, but in oneself and in one's fellow men. Early in the '20's White warned:

> The terror of a vast unbelief is gripping mankind in some sort of spiritual glacial epoch.[42]

He had not foreseen that this was inevitable where faith was actually no larger than social. Being himself so nearly a godly Puritan, he had not seen that Yankee culture alone, truncated of its head, its Puritanism, its God, could be only a declining culture, could not survive indefinitely with only its honest idealism and its honest humor.

Speaking at Harvard in 1939, four years before his death, White described his pioneer "Puritans" in terms of the essentials of Yankeeism. Here is the Central Idea, emotional as with the Puritans, and as with them disciplined in a rational frame:

> . . . The morals of the community grew out of a yearning for justice, the striving of men toward an ideal of human relations. . . . The aspiration in the hearts of the pioneers . . . represented . . . their relation to the forces outside themselves which they felt made for righteousness and which they called God. Their God was a spirit—an ideal—as unapproachable as justice, peace, love, liberty, mercy, judgement, or wisdom. Yet he was quite as real in their lives as these other aspirations.

Here is the Equalitarianism of the Puritans, as distinguished from the individualism of the Jacksonians and the laissez-fairists:

. . . (They took) a religion which contained an ethic and plan for human relations based essentially on a hazy vision of Liberty. Liberty is one thing you can't have unless you give it to others. A man does not establish free institutions unless he has faith in his fellow men.[43]

And here of most importance is the Objectivity of the Idealism, in Yankeeism as in Puritanism, as distinguished from the excesses of Emotion and Reason that beset them both:

The physical world is outside the religion of Jesus. . . . Alas, the religious creed of these little churches of many fields—the Methodist, the Campbellites, the Presbyterians, the Baptists, the Congregationalists, the Episcopalians—which the pioneers set up as they fought their way across the land, was channelled superficially on the one hand by the fear of hell and on the other hand by the hope of reward in heaven. But that surface channelling did not change the fact that the religion of the new West was essentially and in its deeper currents a religion of optimism and a profound faith that kindness pays in the deeper satisfactions of the human heart. . . . They built upon this ideal for the first time unrestrained by . . . the power or influence of any formal religion of authority.[44]

And yet this "ideal," this "hazy vision of Liberty," was not a God, and its perception was not the clairvoyance of Grace. Its content for White and for many others was a social concept seen perhaps in an objective and Christ-like spirit, but not itself having the objective reality of a God. And for many it was not even seen in an objective way.

David Harum, Harriet Beecher Stowe, Mark Twain and William Allen White were types of the central, idealistic current of Yankeeism. It had a humane warmth and limpidity, yet it was culturally a precarious current for the lack of any mutual percept of the One God, any inclusive theology to engage the Imaginations of all and hold them together. No more integrating were the various notions of God that survived in the flanking Heresies, the Antinomianism of Emotion and the Arminianism of Reason flowing along the left and the right of the central Yankee stream.

In these last forty years of the nineteenth century the extreme or camp-meeting form of Antinomianism was going out of fashion north of the Ohio, the Arkansas, and the rest of the southern boundary of Greater New England. At its strongest it was moving into the country of the pseudo-culture, trying to cope with the misery of slums which were the populous aspect of clerical and industrial laissez-faire. In numbers addressed and impressed, Dwight L. Moody of Northfield, founder of Northfield Seminary, bull-necked and bull-voiced, carrying two hundred and fifty pounds on his five-feet-eight of frame, was the greatest revivalist America ever had, surpassing both Whitefield and Finney. He had no high school education and no theology, preaching a simple biblical Fundamentalism, but he itinerated all over the English-speaking world and had the friendship of theologians, especially that of the Scotch evolutionist Henry Drummond. His audiences ran up to 10,000, and he adopted the qualitative standards of the pseudo-culture, measuring his successes and failures by the number of his conversions. A more obscure revivalist of the period, W. H. H. Murray, also working in the urban field, issued as stark a psychological definition of Antinomianism as we are likely to find:

> Separate yourself from all your kind, make of the world a solitude, depopulate the globe, and think of yourself as the only living soul upon which the attention of Heaven and Hell is fixed tonight. . . .
> Undue importance . . . is attached to the connection of Christians one with another. . . .[45]

Moody kept up the dignity of Revivalism through the century. After his death in '99 the mantle of Revivalist-in-Chief passed to the vulgarian Billy Sunday with his tents and trombones, his sawdust and his sliding into home plate shouting, "Safe for the Lord." And after Billy Sunday it was Amy Semple MacPherson with her sex appeal and scandals, her Angelus Temple with its Hollywood lighting and costuming, its female ushers and choir dressed as angels, its entrance of Sister Amy in a white robe, ermine cape with red lining, and a spray of red roses, its dramatic production of Bible stories in which Amy acted self-deprecatingly for Christ, its shameless raising of funds in the name of religion and their personal appropriation by Sister Amy.

Although old time Revivalism was on the wane toward the end of the Yankee nineteenth century, there was an indirect influence toward emotional religion in the tendency of the great sects to go respectable. As the second generation of the Middle West and its hiatus in book learning merged into the better educated third generation—William Allen White's generation—the Methodists, Baptists, Campbellites, Disciples and Christians, all of whom had had their phases of illiterate preaching and the roaring kind of conversion, lapsed into literacy, sweetness and sedate manners. The religious ignorant no longer had an easy place to go. The result was a bloom of inspirational sects and movements, appealing to all levels of religious naïveté, from the noisiest and least washed to the most ecstatic and effete.

Generally rustic in personnel and therefore closely identified with Yankee culture were the Russellites or Jehovah's Witnesses, founded by Charles Tass Russell of Pittsburgh in 1872. Concerning its growth in the nineteenth century, no statistics seem to be available, though the sect is thought to number around a third of a million today.[46] Its members are proudly the dispossessed, and the emotional appeal is in the Millennialism according to which the dispossessed will in due course inherit the earth. In intention there is an honesty and objective mysticism in this movement, together with high emotion and an Arminian Biblical Fundamentalism. There is a sinister element in some quarters where, in spite of the central tenet of pacifism, it is asserted that the dispossessed will one of these days accomplish their inheritance of the earth by bloody means.

The Salvation Army combines emotional religion with practical service, and is less identified with the Yankees than with the poor of the urban pseudo-culture. Marching in from England in 1879, it began to distribute in the cities great and small its simple comfort and its honest, brassy love. By 1900 it had about 700 corps with nearly 2,600 officers and employees, was conducting 45 workingmen's hotels, 5 women's hotels, 14 rescue homes for fallen women, 2 homes for artisans, 75 food and shelter depots, 107 industrial homes, 5 farm colonies, 20 employment bureaus, several salvage brigades, wood and coal yards, 2 children's homes, 1 day nursery and 21 slum settlements.[47]

Christian Science is scarcely a religion of emotional excess, for it combines a gracious and Puritan-like Perception, merging thought and emotion, with the most banal Materialism in the matter of wealth. Its beginning may be identified with either the publication of Mary Baker Eddy's *Science and Health* in 1875 or with her hegira from Lynn to Boston in the early '80's after which her cult began to grow rapidly. The great First Church was built in '95 and by the end of the century there were nearly five hundred groups with a membership of 35,000, mostly in the large cities of the Middle West.[48]

The last years of the century were rich in new sects—Theosophist, quasi-Hindu, Dowieite, and many others making their appearance at the World's Parliament of Religions at the Chicago World's Fair in 1893. But they were chiefly related to either the rich or the poor of the great cities and their pseudo-culture, and any Yankee connection was incidental.

Within Yankee culture proper the dominantly Emotional motif became sporadic or mixed with other impulses. In the evangelical churches periodic revivals were still held, but in small and orderly meetings no longer shaken by the thunder and lightning that used to mow down the thousands. In these almost anybody might be inconsequentially "wounded." Typical was Ralph Tower in Glenway Wescott's *The Grandmothers*,[49] he a pure Yankee farmer, motivated mostly by William Allen White's community conscience, without consistent religion so far as appears, certainly without theology. In a missionary meeting under a devout Christian, Tower suddenly stands up, declares in a shaking voice, "I know that my Redeemer Liveth," and sits down. It is something that might have occurred in a theater, or in watching a parade. There is no inference that his life was in any way altered by this quick, emotional orgasm.

Of more significance in the culture, because it was generally conceived at the end of the nineteenth century that these matters were for the women, was the religion of Ralph Tower's wife Marianne. It was subjective in experience and objective in application, none the less real for being a blend of Antinomianism and Legal Arminianism, the Antinomianism providing the touchstone and control. She had no mental concept of God at all. Giving herself to Him meant "merely being responsible for her life, her virtue, her usefulness to others and to the world as a whole. . . ."[50] She "knew no other god but God," and He was the God of "clean and respectable living, innocent thought, and industry."[51] All of this in her girlhood had been entirely subjective, a love affair with the great mystery which was not yet. And afterwards, in the person of her husband, the great mystery took form and lived in her house. ". . . She slept within reach of its strong, however tired arms. Mystery was in God the equivalent of passion. . . ."[52] By such women as Marianne Tower, rather than by their irreligious, tractable and socially responsible husbands, most of the churches of Greater New England were run.

Thus in the main Antinomianism, in its literal sense of Against-the-law-ism, was disappearing from Yankee culture, remaining rather as an emotional, a subjective, an individualistic impulse which might appear at any time or in any combination. Arminianism, on the other hand, remained strong in its traditional forms, as well as in divers new expressions. The most powerful Arminianism was that which was nearest to the River of Violence. It was so much of the Righteous Wrath that had fought the War as did not go over into Greed and the Pseudo-Culture but returned to the worship of God. Jehovah God of Battles had told men to die to make men free, and he now told them to be diligent and cultivate the earth.

There was Sherwood Anderson's Jesse Bentley,[53] big farmer in
Ohio, goaded by the same fury that drove John Brown and Drew
and Rockefeller, but there was in it with Bentley no hatred, no
rapacity, no greed. The self-assertive rage in him was fanatical in
the determination to do his duty as an ancient Hebrew patriarch
with his flocks and herds and retainers. He was under the Law, but
the strength of the Law was the will of God. He was not yet of the
time "when men would forget God and only pay attention to moral
standards."[54] Along with the Third Puritans who saw a God of
"Benevolent Sentiment," Bentley had been of the backbone of the
volunteer Union army. In his sad senility we see his like in Glenway
Westcott's Grandfather as a "bent old man" who

> . . . came down the path from the woodshed with a look of
> great exasperation fixed on nothing in particular. His beard
> was parted in the middle, and fell on each side of a large
> bone button in his collar; his rheumatic hands were clenched;
> and wherever he went, he seemed to be elbowing aside in-
> visible people in his way.[55]

These last four decades of the nineteenth century were the heyday
of that pinched Moralism so absurdly called "Puritanism." The
crop of Blue Laws probably exceeded that of the pre-Civil War
period, and surely that of any period in either the seventeenth or the
eighteenth century. It was the great season, gathering up to National
Prohibition in 1920, for efforts to revive decaying virtue by legislation. Most of the laws differed from those of the seventeenth century in being forced through timid legislatures by organized zealots
against the will of indolent majorities. It was a field day for Sab-
batarians, especially as there were now in the country many millions of wicked Germans and Italians who liked to combine their
rest with a little pleasure. Vermont passed a statute compelling
church attendance. Most of the states had statutes forbidding all
disturbing noise, and Connecticut in '88 fined anyone four dollars
for even attending a concert or a dance or "other public diversion"
on the Sabbath.[56] Throughout Greater New England the Victorian
Sabbath approached the sparsity of that of the Puritans, but there
was a very great difference in motive and in atmosphere. The ancient Sabbath was maintained by a pious people most of whom desired to spend it in listening to biblical exposition, in contemplation and in prayer. The Victorian straitjacket was imposed by a
few in order to exalt themselves in righteousness.

Women were now running many of the Reforms, and the drives
had a ruthless and shrill flavor when the evil attacked was

something that women recognized as a rival. The W.C.T.U. was formed and took over the Temperance Movement in 1879, and there followed the long war of unnatural restraint upon unnatural drinking, with Carrie Nation, late from an alcoholic husband, smashing saloons in the '90's as the fullest expression of virtue. Maine, New Hampshire, Vermont and Kansas went and stayed dry. The anti-gambling laws were universal and fierce. Iowa held by judicial decision that anybody who fled when a game was invaded was presumptively guilty of playing in it.[57] Indiana lumped under a maximum punishment of $100 the entering of either a house of ill fame or a gambling house.[58] Washington made it as criminal to let a minor play cards in your house—though not gambling—as to give him a drink.[59] Massachusetts had a salutary law against "profane swearing."[60]

Beside these atrocities, there was kindness in the Arminian world that was Victorianism and some of the little country churches like that of Masters' *Spoon River*. In that generally vindictive community little old maid Lydia Humphrey[61] found

> . . . brothers and sisters in the congregation,
> And children in the Church.

And there were mellow widows like David Harum's sister Polly Bixbee who professed the Victorian code, but chiefly enjoyed the touch of her sinful brother's humanity. There was Marianne Tower,[62] the Wisconsin farm mother we have seen, of an epic nobility, being "entirely concerned with works: with severities, kindnesses, abstinences, successes," her morality based in "a sense of responsibility to God before the nation."

Besides these there was the collective generosity that William Allen White assigned to the social judgments of small towns and which he called an expression of God's Will; he cited the ostracism of John Markley for cruelty to his kind wife in the forms of adultery and divorce. No doubt the male bar of the town gathered round the local paper was slow to condemn. And sometimes through the sacrament of a mutual event, like the death of one generally loved, or even a piece of genuine oratory,[63] the whole town was lifted into a common perception in which each was lost and which for the moment was pentecostal Grace.

But equally, on the testimony of other observers, that small town world could be one of repression and cruelty. Even Marianne Tower, generous in her personal relationships, yet "would have been willing to spread" her religion "by force, particularly in view of its importance to the nation as a whole, meanwhile coercing the doubtful with contempt and the lukewarm with enthusiasm."[64] The Reverend Joseph May, abolitionist, friend of Garrison's and known among liberals as "the saint," became the minister in Syracuse after the War where he gave all of his income above bare necessity to good causes; he forbade his wife to use more than one candle to read by, and so drove her blind. In Spoon River the Reverend Lemuel Wiley and Judge Somers persuaded a loveless couple not to get a divorce, which caused them to live out their own lives in fruitless desperation and to stunt their children.[65] Ivan Beede tells the story of how the bully of a Nebraska town took a frightened little homosexual out in the country and beat him.[66] In *The Grandmothers,* the grandfather ruined the life of one of his sons because "I didn't bring up my son to be a good-for-nothing singer." The same grandfather, having promised his grandson a penny for every five cabbage moths he caught, refused to pay for the males because the boy was old enough to know that only the females laid eggs. When he died it meant to the boy "that an old man who was too deaf to hear what was said to him would not complain of the noise they made anymore; it meant that they could go into the garden whenever they liked. . . ."[67]

But more terrible than individual brutality could be that ruthless pressure of the community[68] which White deifies but which others have compared to the "witch hunt" of 1692. Only the witch hunt of 1692 lasted six months, while the one of small-town Yankeedom lasted twenty-five or thirty years, and revives at this writing under the auspices of Senator McCarthy. It was the more cruel in that church trials were going out, so there was no confrontation of witnesses, and no chance for defense. We can admire without reservation William Allen White whose Yankee Idealism lifts him virtually into the Puritan tradition; but all the same we'd like to know what John Markley and his wife had to say about his adultery. We have not been shown that there was more fairness in his case than in that of Carl Hamblin whom the citizens of Spoon River tarred and feathered, and wrecked his press, for publishing a satire of the justice that hung the Chicago anarchists after the Haymarket Riot in May of '86. Extreme is the case of Mrs. Merritt[69] who sat

> Silent before the jury,
> Returning no word to the judge when he asked me
> If I had aught to say against the sentence,
> Only shaking my head.
> What could I say to people who thought
> That a woman of thirty-five was at fault
> When her lover of nineteen killed her husband?

So Mrs. Merritt, though she had struggled to prevent the murder, did her thirty years in prison and died there, while the community took the guilty boy back after fourteen years and accepted his penitence.

Most dreadful in Arminian communities because most universal are the indirect persecutions, where there is no action except in the "conscience," the communal sense, of the persecuted. Under this terror everyone is stunted, and the cases we see are only the extreme ones. Ethan Frome. Richard Cory. The boys who went off to the wars under the flags and the cheering and presently found they had been fooled—the youth in *The Red Badge of Courage*, Harry Williams who enlisted for the Spanish War from Spoon River.[70] And fundamental to them all, the lovelessness of this stark world of Works, the souls that are starved by neglect—

> I who loved you, Spoon River,
> And craved your love,
> Withered before your eyes, Spoon River—
> Thirsting, thirsting,
> Voiceless from chasteness of soul to ask you for love,
> You who knew and saw me perish before you,
> Like this geranium which someone has planted over me,
> And left to die.[71]

The most widespread form of this Terror of Social Conscience is the gas chambers of Mediocrity which levels whole communities. The Conscience here is provided by Individualism, Social Antinomianism. But the gas is Arminian, it is Social Judgement. Almost all the people in town, trying to swagger up out of their insecurity, don't get very far, so they collectivize at a low and easy common denominator. Instead of aspiring further upward or admitting defeat, they draw the few of distinction down to this fake and cadaverous equality that is no Equality but the most intense competition and jealousy. Being weak, they tear down the strong. Being poor, they tear down the rich. Being stupid, they tear down the intelligent. Being ignorant, they tear down the educated. All excellence is taboo, "swelled-headed." The new rich of the pseudo-culture make the collective suicide pact unanimous. Being Yankees, they are uneasy in their wealth which is not in their Tradition, and they know from their Intellectual Tradition that they do not deserve their power. They honestly long to be back with the boys at the corner and to let them know they don't feel superior. Also it's better policy to play equal than to accept the responsibility that power gives them, for responsibility might put conditions and limits to it. So they join the Terror against distinction, and they're all good and comfortable Americans together.

In that society of walking corpses there is "no sign of throughgoing candor; almost every speech is followed by a glance at someone, to see how it is being taken; each is playing up to the other."[72] Around the corner into the twentieth century Ivan Beede, the critic and fiction-writer, left his Nebraska small town in search of reality. Some years later he returned, accredited by a fine record as a foreign reporter, a collection of distinguished short stories, and a fund of exotic experience as one of the Paris Expatriates. His home-town newspaper welcomed him with editorial notice in which they paid him the supreme compliment that he had not changed, that he was still "the same old boy." It was their accolade. It was what they call democracy.

So on the right flank of the Puritan River in Decline, the Yankee River, we have an Arminian God of Judgement. And on the left flank we have an Antinomian God of Pleasant Emotion. In the middle the Yankee current is strong in Harum and White and 20,000,000 like them. But there's not much Puritan God in it. White's God is no god, and Harum and most of the other Yankees don't even profess any. Near the end of the century, 1091 California school children between six and twenty were asked to report their notions of God and his vicinity. In their composite view, He was "conceived as an old man with a long beard and flowing white garments, benevolent rather than stern of mien, but possessing power to 'have an earthquake at any time.' Heaven, suspended 'in the clouds,' had houses and streets of gold where angels flew about and strummed on harps. For Satan the conventional figure in *Faust* was the prototype, though two pupils derived their impressions more immediately from the labels on deviled-ham cans."[73]

But withal this Yankee River was no more narrowed than it was in the Hysteria of the 1690's or the Paganism of the 1790's, and each of them spread again into revival. Out of the vacuity of the 1890's it yet might have widened into a Fourth Puritanism to mature in its Fourth Century, but for another current that since the War had been spreading as Imagination contracted, replacing it gradually as if finally to cover it and prevent its reflecting a new and Meaningful Sky. As Third Puritanism shrank when the War had accomplished its Benevolent ends of Emancipation and the Union, it uncovered the old current of Eighteenth-century Humanism which its own Humanitarianism had embraced and had made specific. Now it emerged to run its separate and widening course along the inner border, the Intellectual fringe, of the Arminian current.

The dominant Rational Concept of this revived Intellectual Arminianism is now no longer the Abstract Natural Man of the Eighteenth Century. Now it is the generality called Society, and it is composed of Concrete Particulars, the same Individual Men who were the concern of Third Puritanism. It sees a sky like the Sky of Stars that Channing and Finney and Weld saw with Imagination; only this is an imitation of that, an artificial sky of Natural Reason and Science and Philosophical Materialism. It contains the Individual Stars, but they are seen only as parts of this general and fabricated sky, this Society. It is a sky of Social Virtue, but it is not an experienced sky, not a perceived sky. Its method of observation is not the method of religion. It is like Channing's sky, but with the difference that it sees no God who is greater than Men and Society and whose Meaning they must serve with the loss of Self. It is Second-Commandment Christianity with the Christianity deleted. In its maturity its work will be shared with kindly skeptics and atheists who aim simply at tangible Good without any interest in the relation the good may have to the reality of themselves or the objects of their benefaction. Its pulpits will preserve much of the vocabulary of Religion, but in the fashion of William Allen White it identifies God with Human Society, and the exercises of religion with the exercises of Society in its efforts to improve its own general Moral and Material Comfort. This rationalistic and kindly Quasi-religion will be called the Social Gospel.

We have seen the forces that will run together to make the great stream of this Quasi-religion. From the seventeenth century of Newton and Locke, the Natural Reason and its Natural Science that will surge again in this period to clarify the method and strengthen the work of the Social Gospel. From the eighteenth century, the Humanism, and from the early nineteenth the Humanitarianism that makes it specific. And from the nineteenth also the Romantic Optimism that knows that whatever man wills, that he can accomplish:

> It seemed to many of us . . . as if humanity were on the eve of the golden age. . . . The Kingdom of God appeared to be at hand . . . the reign of universal brotherhood.[74]

The Humanitarianism and the Optimism together will continue the great Reforms that started before the War—the Care of the Insane, Prisons, Temperance (now identified with the W.C.T.U.), Vice, Women's Rights, Peace; and to them other major movements will be added—the S.P.C.A., the Society for the Prevention of Cruelty to Children, the Red Cross, Indians, Negroes, Slum Clearance, Settlement Houses, Fresh Air, and finally competent administration of Charity through State Boards and Centralized City and County Organizations. All these movements continue with increasingly scientific and impressive results and increasing secularization.

In the line of descent of the humane Social Gospel also is that subhuman doctrine of Clerical Laissez-faire which we saw directing the River of Violence, the Pseudo-culture of Greed, in its sadistic excesses in the Labor Wars. Laissez-faire is eventually the enemy of the Social Gospel, yet in calling the attention of religion to the affairs of Society it is strong at the source of the trend that eventually overcame it. It is necessary again to pick up the thread of it after the War and to trace its changes, to see a force in the River of Violence sending influence like spray across to the Yankee River, and eventually the Ministers of Evil breaking through the barrier between the Rivers and flooding over to join the Ministers of Social Virtue.

After the War it is impossible to find the tenuous excuses we offered for the Clerical Laissez-fairists in the early days of the Industrial Revolution. The doctrine of Predestination and a man's Calling and Poverty as assigned by God no longer apply, for the Victorian ministers after the War no longer believed anything so precise and solid and inconvenient as Predestination. These fatuous ministers allowed the poor Free Will, and so blamed them for whatever made the ministers uncomfortable. The truth is, pontificated the rich and well accoutered Henry Ward Beecher, late of Litchfield and Cincinnati and now calling from Brooklyn, "The general truth is that no man in this land suffers from poverty unless it be more than his fault—unless it be his *sin.*"[75] Nor is there here any remnant of Aristocracy, of the genuine Class Feeling that concerns itself for its charges, the aristocracy of Williams and Edwards who loathed the Indians and served them, of Hooker who despised the ignorant and extended their political power, of Winthrop who in the great famine gave his last meal cake to a poor man who was nearer starvation than he was. Nor is there any longer for Beecher and his kind the excuse that the evils of the industrial system were not widespread, or of ignorance of the fact that old-fashioned Diligence and Frugality would not lift a family out of a slum where they were always below subsistence. Many other ministers, still in the Yankee River, discovered the truth of these things and changed their prejudices accordingly. In some of the strikes that anarchists influenced there may have been a scintilla of justification for a Conservative—but hardly a Christian—concern for the fabric of law and order.

It is evident that the concern—sometimes rising to panic—of the laissez-faire ministers and the laissez-faire clerical publications was not other than the normal concern of the owning classes for the sanctity of their ownership. The only intellectual excuse for the brutal line often followed was that they accepted the economics not only of Mill and Smith, but likewise of Malthus, Ricardo and Marx, and endorsed the Marxian dialectic of the economic interpretation of history and the class struggle. Unhappily we can not concede so much intellectual respectability to these ministers and their greedy parishioners, for few if any of them followed the professional economic thought of their time and would have been incredulous to find themselves identified with a materialistic and revolutionary dogma. Their vindication of Marx was in their blind support of the rich and material values, thus qualifying themselves as exhibits of that class of priests—universalized by Marx but relatively rare in American History—whose preachment is indeed the opiate of the people.

Increasing the early tendency of these ministers to meddle in economics was the trend, accelerated during the War, toward the identification of religion with every kind of secular activity. On the one hand this took the form of pulpit lectures on current secular issues. Said Beecher in '62:

> It is the duty of the minister of the Gospel to preach on every side of political life. I do not say that he *may;* I say that he *must.* That man is not a shepherd of his flock who fails to teach that flock how to apply moral truth to every phase of ordinary practical duty.[76]

On the other hand it identified profitable finance, that perpetual concern of the ministers of the pseudo-culture, with the Lord's business:

> Men who have tried it, have confidently declared that there is no sleeping partner in any business who can begin to compare with the Almighty.

> . . . God has need of rich Christians, and He makes them, and he assigns particular duties to them.[77]

All of this prepared the way for the Social Gospel by drawing attention from the God of the galaxies to the concerns of one of the smaller satellites of one of His smaller stars.

Essential, of course, to the whole trend of Intellectual Arminianism, the whole long campaign of Natural Reason against Imagination, was the growth of Experimental Science. Although it was enormously expansive and contributory to changing industry in the pre-War nineteenth century—complete steam, electric telegraph, factory and farm machinery, etc.—it was not yet of great importance in religious, social and intellectual life. There was Comte who, in spite of being branded infidel, sent important influence across the water. Although his own *a priori* method was old-fashioned, yet the positivist gravamen of his preachment was in the opposite direction, of the *a posteriori* method. Whether praised or damned, he accustomed many people to think in terms of actual, tangible observations. He prepared the way for *The Origin of Species,* published in America in 1860.

Although debated with passion in scientific and theological circles, Darwin never had a very wide direct popular influence. In the main he reached the lay public through Spencer whose more prolific and less severely scientific works began to be popular even in the '60's. Spencer's Darwinianism fitted the contemporary prejudices in economics; his morality was Victorian; he professed that his views were reconcilable with religion;[78] he had a busy publisher; John Fiske gave him weighty and energetic support in his lectures at Harvard, 1869-71; and in the '80's the prophet himself visited America.

Far more than Darwin, and somewhat more than Huxley, Spencer was the authority who assaulted the American churches with the same power theory in biological and social selection which many of them had been disseminating in economic selection. Incidentally, along with his theory of evolution there came the unavoidable inference that the biblical account of creation was not literally correct. Unhappily many intelligent and influential ministers, in this period which was perhaps the country's all-time low in theology, came out at first in defense of literal Biblicism or Fundamentalism. Thus they gave notice to the enlightened minds of a generation that was going to be mature in the '90's that Fundamentalism was of the stuff of Religion. So they turned them to Skepticism or still farther in the Materialistic direction.

Meanwhile, unintelligent ministers and congregations in great numbers withdrew defensively into extreme Fundamentalism or Biblicism. These were mostly the same Legal Arminians who concocted the Blue Laws, and generally proposed to stop the course of history by law.* All this helped the trend toward the Secularization of Religion, which was the trend of the Social Gospel.

* It was in the South rather than in Greater New England that official action was taken to scotch the impious rumor that Man was descended from a Monkey. In 1878 the distinguished geologist, Alexander Winchell, was ousted from Vanderbilt and the Tennessee Conference of the Southern Methodist Church resolved:

"The arrogant and impertinent claims of this 'science,' falsely so-called, have been so boisterous and persistent, that the unthinking mass have been sadly deluded; but our university alone has had the courage to lay its young but vigorous hand upon the mane of untamed Speculation and say: 'We will have no more of this.'"

The Southern Baptist brethren found similar courage the following year, and Crawford H. Toy was separated from their Seminary at Louisville, and four years later the Southern Presbyterians dismissed James Woodrow from their Seminary at Columbia, South Carolina. (Howard K. Beale, *A History of Freedom of teaching in American Schools* [New York, 1941] 202-07; Andrew D. White, *A History of the Warfare of Science and Theology.* . . . [New York, 1896] I, 313-16.)

Another effect of Darwin and Spencer was, of course, to strengthen
the theory of Laissez-faire, confirming it by identification with the
Struggle for Existence which was the way of Nature, the way of
Reality, the way of any god there might be. What before had been
Social Pre-Darwinism now became full dress Social Darwinism.
William Graham Sumner in his books and in his lectures at Yale
was perhaps the most consistent influential disciple of Spencer in
America. He went beyond his master in holding that the forces of
struggle and the survival of the fitter were resistless and not necessarily beneficent, and that any attempt to interfere with them
could be only absurd and mischievous. In his consistency Sumner
was not altogether comforting to the economic exploiters. For while
he opposed all kinds of relief for suffering, such as child labor laws,
he held artificial combinations like trusts and government coddling
like the tariff to be equally unscientific and presumptuous. He
said to leave the drunkard lying in the gutter, for that was just where
he belonged; but he also said to leave the rich man lying alone with
his investments and his risks. Sumner was too honest to be of much
help to the latter's raids on human and material resources. But his
ruthless materialism did help the increasing diversion of attention
from the things of Religion to the things of the Immediate Sensuous World.

Besides these negative and more or less brutalizing derivatives
from Darwin and Spencer, there was an optimistic school which
looked to the social struggle to cast up in the long run not only the
economically fit but the morally fit also. We saw earlier how President Bascom of Wisconsin espoused before Darwin a modified
Clerical Laissez-faire which held that once the able, industrious and
predatory had won their power, the continuing forces of competition would change rapacity into responsibility and Christian Love.
For the greater part of his life and influence Bascom was as con-
demnatory of strikes and social legislation as any, as prone to urge
the helpless poor to wait and pray. But if they waited and prayed
long enough, he told them that the forces that consumed them now
would produce a sweet society for their children's children's children—

> Interest, hidden as a seed by God in the dark, cold soil of
> society, initiates a growth it does not understand, pushes up
> into a higher region, and there finds and feels a heaven-de-
> scended warmth, which henceforth seizes upon it and draws it
> ever up, thirsting for that which is above.[79]

Here we are no longer in the field of biology, nor even in the
field of economics. Bascom and Sumner were pioneers in a new
science called Sociology through which the method and accumulated

doctrines of Science broke into Religion and soon preempted it. In 1865 the American Social Science Society was set up, with Bascom for one of its founders. The prominence and respectability of its personnel, which presently included President Grant and Charles Francis Adams, tended to dispel the suspicion of the Churches toward anything that called itself Science. Here the scientists, the gatherers and compilers of observed facts, worked at first shoulder to shoulder with the ministers in social inquiry. Gradually the ministers came to depend for their material less and less on God's Word or on Revelation in any form, and more and more on the data the scientists furnished to them. Thus the Scientists moved first even and then ahead of the Ministers as the leaders of opinion.

This was the same Intellectual Arminianism that had arisen in the mid-eighteenth century to undo the work of Edwards and accomplish great things politically. Now, working in terms of a better equipped and better disciplined Natural Reason, it arose to undo the work of Channing and to accomplish great things socially. The State of Grace and its perceptions of Right Reason retired into the vocabulary of rhetoric, along with other great concepts upon which the nation had been built. It seemed plain to all that Natural Reason, operating inductively upon carefully collected data, could diagnose all the ills of society and prescribe their cures. The administration of these cures in the name of Christian Charity, rarely paying more than lip service even to the Benevolent God of Third Puritanism, became the Social Gospel. It involved three great steps which often occurred together in the evolution of current thought, and of which we shall not often distinguish between the first two. First, there was the substitution, in the primary concern of organized religion, of the individual's Physical and Social life for his Imaginative or Spiritual life. Second, there was the substitution, in the same concern, of Society for the Individual. And third, the Method of Science was accepted as the Method of Religion.

The trends we have noticed supply a sort of developing stage setting against which we watch the last scene of what may be the last act in the three-century-long drama of the Decline of God. In the view taken in this book Puritanism was not destroyed by Economics under an axiom that men prefer Food and power to ideas. Nor yet by Science which threw doubt upon certain myths which a declining and frightened faith clung to in their prosaic literalness. Puritanism was not destroyed by either of these great forces, though they were both powerful temptations before the single and the collective minds that did make the choice of the Great Apostasy.

In the view taken in this book, every man is presumptively predestined at some time to hear the passing whisper, to see the flicker,
of Grace, of final Understanding, and while he can not initiate
the Perception, it is certain that he may refuse it. In the view taken
here, no man ever slipped into any Heresy, including the Heresy of
Intellectual Arminianism, or into Skepticism or Atheism, under a
compulsion to which his will did not at some time provide a definitive turn.

In this view the final quietus was not put on Puritanism during
the years between 1860 and 1900 by any force other than the
choices of leading minds in the Central Stream of the Yankee River,
exercising the Composite Choice of a determining number of the
people of Greater New England. We have the record of some of
those Intellectual Arminian choices, and it is ironic to aftersight
that they need not have been made. Good and Humane Works may
not fetch on Grace, but they do not forestall it. There is nothing
incompatible between Natural Reason and the larger vistas of
Imagination, Grace and Right Reason, for they contain Natural
Reason. But the men of the Great Apostasy, seeing Puritanism debased to Moralism and Ignorance by the Legal Arminians, and to
Brutality by the preachers of the River of Violence, seem to have
felt—though without admitting it to themselves—that the World of
Religion, the Sky of Imagination, was too far shrunken to be worth
Revival. In order to accomplish a program of simple kindness and
decency, such as the Conservative Churches were opposing, it seemed
necessary to proclaim in effect a Godless and Anthropocentric Universe such as would offer little of meaning for the after lives of those
whose Physical and Social conditions might be improved in it.

Horace Bushnell of Hartford, preaching all over the country in
the '60's and '70's, was the great transitional figure. On the one hand
he still talked a modified Laissez-faire, and on the other he still used
the traditional vocabulary of Theology. But his influence was away
from the first, and his theology moved so far in the Human direction that there was not much left of the Superhuman God with
humanly incomprehensible values. Though he forswore Unitarianism, he approximated Channing's denial of Original Sin and his
profession of man's goodness, and he saw the Atonement as an
Example rather than as a cosmic-psychic event. He denied eternal
punishment, and believed that God's Mercy dominated His Justice.
For practical purposes God expressed His will through human action, the supernatural through the natural:

> There is . . . a fixed relation between the temporal and
> the eternal, such that we shall best realize the eternal by
> rightly using the temporal.[80]

The ethic of the Universe was not different from the instinctive human ethic of fairness and Kindness. The quality of God to be taken seriously was no longer His transcendence but His immanence, His identification with human affairs. Henry Ward Beecher, going beyond Bushnell, made the criterion of right action a simple emotional one, "a state of the heart," and sometimes seemed to discard all theology in favor of an ethical Pragmatism:

> I gradually formed a theology by practice—by trying it on, and the things that really did God's work in the hearts of men I set down as good theology, and the things that did not, whether they were true or not, they were not true to me.[81]

Thus through Bushnell's revolutionary theology, and Beecher's escape from theology into a broth of emotion, American "humanistic optimism . . . flowed over at last into religion."[82] God was contracted to the size of Man and his Natural Science, and it was not impossible that He might shortly be let out of the picture entirely. Brotherhood was the controlling concept among the young men who followed Bushnell, Second-Commandment Christianity only with the religion extracted. The Imaginative Perception that is Grace was no longer the aim of life. Salvation would be connected with the service of Society. In the '70's, while Bushnell was thus trimming theology to human size, a less known minister, Jesse Jones, born in Canada of Yankee stock, was not only preaching the ancient Millennialism to the effect that the Kingdom of God would be on earth, but he was also specifying the nature of its Communistic society in sound Terrestrial Utopian terms.[83] The generally un-Yankee Episcopalians led in the development of the Social Gospel, with the generally Yankee Congregationalists, second. In spite of the reactionary expressions we heard in the thunder of the River of Violence, the Congregational press throughout the period was on the whole Liberal, which is to say Intellectually Arminian.

The first realistic profession of the Social Gospel, in terms of the central issue of Labor, was probably that of Washington Gladden, and he figures as the father of the movement. Raised on a farm in Owego, New York, confronted with Labor War in North Adams in the '60's, in Springfield, Massachusetts, in the '70's, and in the Hocking Valley in the '80's, he profited by his experience to proclaim the Error of Laissez-faire:

> . . . The wage-system when it rests on competition as its sole basis, is anti-social and anti-Christian.
>
> The doctrine which bases all the relations of employer and employed upon self-interest is a doctrine of the pit; it has

been bringing hell to earth in large instalments for a good many years.

The labor of the nation is the life of the nation; is that a commodity to be bought in the cheapest market and sold in the dearest?[84]

Thus Gladden stepped into the leadership in the beginning of the actual march toward a new world. But from the religious point of view, even more important than his actions was his early personal experience. As a boy he determined to be a minister, but encountered a block in his failure to enjoy an Experience of Grace. His solution was not to discard his plan, as he would have done even half a century before. His solution was to adopt the theology of Bushnell and Beecher, espousing a God Immanent in human affairs instead of one of cloudy transcendence with whom contact might or might not be of immediate importance to struggling humanity. If we were to place anywhere the turning of the page from Puritanism to the Social Gospel, it would be in the decision of Washington Gladden to pursue the profession of the ministry although—as Anne Hutchinson and the Itinerants of Edwards' time would have quickly discovered—he was not himself in Grace. But no one was concerned for that now. The Conservatives, clerical and lay, might quarrel with his Progressive Doctrine. But they, no more than Gladden, saw Religion any more as a primary consideration. In the same '80's when Gladden's influence was great, Newman Smith published *Christian Ethics* in which the ancient virtues were translated into social terms. Justice, he said, was "not fulfilled in the life of the man who, though himself just, has no will to get justice done in the world."[85]

Coming to the '90's, we find these materialistic and humanistic doctrines winning a status where they are hardly any more controversial. Josiah Strong, author of the great best seller, *Our Country*, a Yankee but involved less with Yankee culture than with the slums of the pseudo-culture, stated as axiomatic the theories of the Social Gospel and of the Economic interpretation of history—"the change in civilization, during the past century, from an individual to a social type," and "the progress of science which has revealed the interdependence of body and mind, and the influence of physical conditions on spiritual life."[86] Among the leaders of thought, Richard T. Ely the economist was one of the few who held out for moral values as superior to physical values in the form either of Socialism or of Social Darwinism.[87]

In the '90's the distinction between the work of the quasi-religious Social Gospelites and that of the Secular Reformers was disappear-

ing, especially in the cities, and they all worked together in centralized charitable organizations. One Philanthropic group frankly attached Christianity to its agenda for purposes of prestige only.
Among the Political Reformers, LaFollette in his youth was much
influenced by Bascom's proto-social doctrines,[88] and Roosevelt was
admiringly intimate with Gladden, W. S. Rainsford the great Episcopal Reformer, and Walter Rauschenbusch the Christian Socialist.[89]
Roosevelt announced the dogma of the Social Gospel:

> Under the tense activity of modern social and industrial
> conditions the church, if it is to give leadership, must grapple,
> zealously, fearlessly and cool-headedly with the problems of
> social and industrial justice. Unless it is the poor man's church
> it is not a Christian church at all in any real sense.[90]

And following Roosevelt we have William Allen White's "conversion" to the same godless view which made it easy for him thereafter
to identify God with the composite will of small town society:

> . . . Theodore Roosevelt and his attitude toward the powers
> that be, the status quo, the economic, social and political or-
> der certainly did begin to penetrate my heart.

> And when I came to the New Testament and saw Jesus, not
> as a figure in theology—the only begotten son who saved by
> his blood a sinful world—but as a statesman and philosopher
> who dramatized his creed by giving his life for it, then gradu-
> ally the underpinning of my Pharisaic philosophy was knocked
> out. Slowly . . . I saw the Great Light.[91]

During the last forty years of the nineteenth century, this substitution of Human Society for God and His Cosmos in progressive
minds was the widening drift of Intellectual Arminianism upon
which the wars of Labor for organization and living conditions and
the lesser wars of Temperance and the other Reforms were the
continuous surface storms. The old screams of Laissez-faire from
the pulpits of the pseudo-culture were silent forever—though they
continued to come from the ranks of employment. Most of the religious press had now moved back from the River of Violence to
the Intellectual Arminian stream of the Yankee River. They recognized the right of labor to organize and, under certain conditions
of unfairness and with taboo upon violence, to strike. By the depression of '94 the Liberals were all addicted to Bellamy's *Looking Backward* and George's *Progress and Poverty;* and most of them had been
in and out of one or more of the numerous socialistic panaceas which

all this time had been blossoming and fading in the flames of the industrial struggle. The war of Labor for human status was not won, it was only well started. But it had enjoyed an advantageous transfer of venue and was come into a new phase. It had come out of the twilight of obscurity and the darkness of radical intrigue and was spread in the open forum of the democratic process. It enjoyed the mature support of the Social Gospel, and with it a deep change in the public attitude generally.

By the '80's Reform was an issue in every industrial state. In '86 George got more votes than Theodore Roosevelt in the mayoralty election of New York. Tom Johnson of Cleveland, once a wealthy manufacturer, had undergone a spectacular conversion to the Social Gospel, and was about to be elected Reform Mayor. "Golden Rule" Jones who took Christ for his model in his humanitarian campaigns, was about to win the same office in Toledo. The recent indifference to general suffering upon the assumption that it was God's Will, and the older concern for the individual exclusive of his environment, which had been always a principle of all Protestantism, was gone very possibly forever. Henceforth, although the Church continued separate from the state, it might take any of the affairs of the state for its province.

The entrance of the churches into the rough and tumble world was in fact rarely happy. The clerical administration of the Social Gospel seems to have been on the whole ignorant, stupid and patronizing. Ministers preached about labor and housing conditions without knowing them, and when they talked to audiences of workers they were likely to remind them that they were "the masses" or "the ignorant classes," and to admonish them out of habit to the old virtues of frugality. Labor was almost solidly hostile to the Church because of its traditional stand against it. The ministers were accused of still harboring in fact the principle of Laissez-faire which they repudiated in theory:

> The fair field for individual merit to prove itself and win its due reward has been our pride so long that it is hard to believe it gone. But it is gone. . . .
> We are still blinding ourselves to the change, and insisting that the social system best suited to a condition when equality of opportunity for all men was the rule is best now that equality is no more.[92]

This was an age when, due perhaps to the abandonment of Religion to Sociology so that no official Puritanism remained to invite the imagination, the best young minds were turning away from the pulpit. We can fancy the unctuous little Victorians who in the '90's were going through the Seminaries, learning social theories but not how to apply them, learning nothing of actual humanity, and no living theology that could integrate their theories. Imagine Edwards standing lofty over his troubled audience, telling them that God's Love is holding them from dropping into the eternal fires of Self—that is First-Commandment Christianity. Imagine Weld on a rural platform, the windows breaking, rotten eggs dripping from his face, stones hitting his head till he is giddy, standing there evening after evening until ammunition and malice are exhausted and he can be heard—that is Second-Commandment Christianity. And imagine the thousands of others, women and men up the centuries who marched in the Central Stream and reflected the Sky of God. Then think of their successors, these comfortable ministers of the Social Gospel, in the rich churches of the '90's, boldly telling their employing congregations of the hardships of the lower classes, sometimes venturing to visit a Settlement House under safe chaperonage. Only a step beyond them is the twentieth-century Expert in Publicity, increasing the meaningless membership of his church, the fancy parish house with the gym, the games and the swimming pool, the glad hand, the clean fun, the good eats and the happy reputation—which I once heard a young minister confirm—for "not pulling too much of this Christ stuff."

There are plenty of relieving exceptions to the vacuous average of the clergy that began appearing from the seminaries in the '90's and has continued almost to date. There were the heroic slum workers, women and men, most of them free of church affiliation and the more genuine human beings for the freedom. There were some of the great surviving out of past—Bushnell, Josiah Strong, Jesse Jones—who were old in the '90's and had been raised in the Puritan tradition, and who remained in Grace whatever their doctrine. There were many of the more Radical Reformers who attacked with passion not particular abuses but the whole fabric of society—Charles M. Sheldon who spent nine weeks incognito among the poorest people in Topeka, and afterwards *In His Steps* sold 22,000,000; Hugh O. Pentcost, Christian anarchist, who denounced the execution of the Chicago anarchists and ran for mayor of Newark on the Labor ticket; Herbert N. Casson who identified the Labor Movement itself with Religion and set up the Labor Church in Lynn; George D. Herron, great Christian Socialist Evangelist through the Middle West who fell out of social grace when his wife divorced him.

But there were not enough of any of these to give the Social Gospel the semblance of Second-Commandment Christianity. Seriousness, the full life of the Imagination was lost, with God compressed into human clothing, his Transcendence gone along

with the metaphysical Atonement, the Grandeur of Sin condensed
into shallowly self-indulgent peccadillos.

In the Social Gospel nothing remained but a particularly shallow
Deism, a Deism without theology that was a shadow even of
Deism. Here are three statements that, spanning the period of the
Decline, spell out the evaporation of Religion. The first is by Adin
Ballou, one of the great pre-War Reformers, the founder of Hope-
dale, confessing his predicament after the War before the de-
Christianization of the movements of which he had been part:

> As to special reformers, they had mostly fallen away from
> the high ideals of Practical Christianity. The Non-resistants,
> with few exceptions, had failed in the hour of trial and
> yielded allegiance to the war-god. . . . Anti-slavery had be-
> come apotheosized by its war-power triumph and rested from
> its labors. All that could be done in its behalf was to carry
> words and deeds. The temperance cause called for involving
> myself in its reliance upon penal laws, arbitrary exactions, and
> final resort to violence. The same was true of the cause of
> women's rights. . . . Finally, the working people's movement
> flung its standard to the breeze and called for recruits to its
> heterogeneous ranks. I was interested in its objects and pro-
> fessed claims, as I had been in similar movements in America
> and England for many years, and I studied and watched it
> with sympathetic desire and hope. But I found in it little of
> the spirit of fraternity, of co-operation between the strong
> and the weak; little of the spirit of Christian brotherhood. It
> sought to level down but not up. Its trust was in legislation
> and governmental coercion. The sword was its dernier resort.
> It belonged to a moral and social sphere and to a field of re-
> form from which I had withdrawn forever.[93]

Here the *Nation,* attacking Gladden, Christian Socialism and the
Social Gospel in 1893, gives a good definition of Arminianism:

> . . . Every attempt to describe modes of action as essentially
> 'Christian' is an attempt to substitute a code of external ob-
> servances for a religion of the heart—the very evil against
> which Jesus uttered his most terrible denunciations—[94]

and we may add, Jesus and all of the Puritans from the beginning
of America. And here, in a quotation of R. E. Thompson, discussing the effects of science and economics on the Clergy, is the final
diminution of Intellectual Arminianism—that is, Christian Liberalism—into absurdity:

> . . . There is danger . . . of exaggeration. . . . We see it in
> the weaker brethren, who are carried most easily off their bal-
> ance by popular tendencies of any kind, and who talk some-

times as though men were to be regenerated by clean homes and fresh air, or as if the gospel had been superseded by political economy.[95]

And so New England Culture was given over to the Clerical Weaker Brethren and to the Liberals, both Clerical and Secular. And there was no more Puritanism. Increasingly after the War, the alternatives to "clean homes" and "fresh air" were dirty homes, no fresh air, and the mouthings of Beecher and the other rhetoricians of the pseudo-culture. No one, not even Bushnell had offered a more capacious Regeneration than that of Clean Homes, a Regeneration that would include the appropriate Uses of the things of the Earth, which in an age of gadgetry would be Clean Homes and Fresh Air, but would include also a Meaning for life in both temporal and eternal Homes, in both particular and universal Air. Now the Imagination that before had required the Cosmos and eternity to exercise in was diverted by much fashionable Busyness and the Ambition for ever cleaner and more snobbish little Homes.

At the turn of the twentieth century the Greedy River of Violence that had been slowed neither by the sprinkling of Reform blown across from the Social Gospel nor by the great splashings of Theodore Roosevelt's Big Stick, exulted in the Spanish War and Imperialism and thundered on to save or conquer the world for American Virtue.

Across the dividing bank the Yankee River flowed its wider and slower way. Between increasing Wealth and the Clean Homes and Fresh Air of the Social Gospel, the Antinomian Current was narrowing for the time being toward insignificance. But on the right the Legal Arminian Current of Righteousness was wide and strong, and it was this current that the Liberals and the Indifferent began now to identify with "religion." Also at this time the debunking of the Puritans was beginning; it became fashionable to identify the taboos of the Arminians with "Puritanism."[96] In the Central Current there was little true Puritanism left, but the small town people included enough like White and Harum and Coolidge to keep the Yankee culture strong without God.

Widening out from the Arminian side and appropriating increasing stretches of the Central Current, the stream of Intellectual Arminianism now spread over much of the Yankee River and itself was as strong and populous as the River of Violence. It was in all things the old stream of eighteenth century Intellectual Arminianism now emerged from the Romantic, Humanitarian, Second-Com-

mandment Christianity that for a while had absorbed it into
Religion. Like Chauncey and Mayhew and the Liberals of the eighteenth century, it now combined a Religious and Secular vocabulary. As the churches then identified themselves with the fight for the
political Rights of Man, so now the Social Gospel and Social Service
are one in providing the same healthy Fresh Air to the poor. As in the
eighteenth century the vista is wide and exciting and various, and
the sky of this Quasi-religion of Reasonable Humanism is bright although low. There is now the same irresistible Optimism that possesses the Fancy and almost persuades the Imagination. The
young ministers express it still in the language of Religion:

> It seemed to many of us who were . . . beginning our
> ministry in the eighties and nineties as if humanity were on
> the eve of the golden age. . . . The Kingdom of God ap-
> peared to be at hand. As the dawn of the twentieth century
> approached we felt sure that it meant the ushering in of the
> reign of universal brotherhood . . .[97]

But in this there was not, as there had been in 1690 or 1790, any
sign of Revival. The Ministers in the tradition of Bushnell and Gladden, along with the multitude of kind, socially conscious and skeptical Liberals, had small patience with any such metaphysical ob-
fuscation. They knew that Man was only beginning to use the full
powers of his reason to care for himself in the visible world. With
the imagination released from the shibboleths of priestcraft, the
flat vista grew long without limit. Except in its formal remnant in
the now religionless Puritan House of Yankee psychology, the experiment of 1630 was over. With the muttering ghosts of superstition silenced, America would soon move into a perfect world.

IV. The World of Me (1900-1960)

1. FOURTH PURITANISM (1900-1930)

THERE IS NOT MUCH doubt that the Frolic of the 1920's was a senile frolic instead of the May Day of a New Youth which it liked to call itself. It was the end, not the beginning, of something. Historically, we may take it as the end, the chute, of either of two trends, both of which we have seen running parallel to each other through the latter part of the nineteenth century.

One of the possible terminal significances of the 1920's was as the end of the complete life cycle of a Culture, a culture perhaps unique for short-livedness, having appeared, matured, flourished, decayed, borne fruit and fallen in about a hundred years. Generally, the great cultures have life cycles of between three and five centuries. This very special Yankee one, which we have heretofore called the Industrial Pseudo-culture, stirred perceptibly in the 1830's as the life and soul in the body of the Industrial Revolution, was born with the accession of the Profiteers in the Civil War, matured with the great financial Consolidations of the '70's and '80's, flourished until 1910, was in decay by 1912, rotted through the '20's, at the same time Bearing Fruit, and fell and vanished utterly in 1930.

If we accept this concept of the Industrial Pseudo-culture as an independent cycle of its own, then we must hold—as is entirely plausible—that Puritan Culture was fatally rotten in the pre-Civil War period when its final expression was in the Great Reforms, while incidentally it was bearing fruit in its Literary "Flowering." Under this hypothesis, it disappeared for good into the vortex of the War, and from that time the Pseudo-culture becomes the Second Culture of Greater New England. In discussing the nineteenth century we identified the pseudo-culture with what we called the River of Violence which was originally the force of Self-aggrandizement,

447

in the form of Arminian Self-righteousness, that was part of the
Yankee impulse in the Civil War. When peace returned the self-
righteousness combined with the equally extreme emotional Self-
indulgence of Antinomianism which the War fostered, and the
force of the River of Violence became that of the battle royal for
power that raged through the rest of the century. It was in this form
that the River poured into the twentieth century. The culture which
it carried and which we formerly called a pseudo-culture we may
here call the independent Gambling Culture. Its short life-cycle we
may conveniently attribute to modern acceleration.

As we have seen, the "philosophy" of the gambling culture was
Materialism, and the economic application of it was the doctrine of
Laissez-faire. The soul, the *zeitgeist,* of the culture was Greed or
rapacity, the necessity for self-ascendance in physical terms. In the
male world the self-ascendance was in the form of the power of
wealth in the Market. In the female world it took the form of the
power of wealth in Society. Besides the philosophy of materialism,
the economy of laissez-faire and the soul of greed, all the rest of the
gambling culture, including its religion, was contained in the Victorian Code whose purpose was to conceal the soul. The code did in
fact contain many noble precepts taken over from older cultures,
but its application of them was in the mere contemplation and
celebration of their affecting beauty, which was a tour not of action
but of sentimentality.

The tinsel nobility of the code and the administration of it by
rich women as the guerdon of gentility did conceal for some decades
the underlying greed and keep it within civilized restraint on the
social if not on the business plane. In the '90's, however, spores of
decay appeared in a few naughty youths of the rich who began to
make fun of the pruderies and the obvious hypocrisies of the code,
the concealment of humanity under tons of petticoats and other
thick conventions. As always, the concomitant of decay was artistic
production on the part of imaginations in revolt against the culture
that produced them. In the prose of Howells, Crane, the Adamses,
and Upton Sinclair, and in the poetry of William Vaughn Moody,
George Santayana (for literary purposes a Yankee), Robert Morss
Lovett, Norman Hapgood and many others, including the youngsters
Robert Frost and Edwin Arlington Robinson, the '90's began to
crack the armor of sweet Victorianism that was the façade on the
house of the gambling culture.

The social revolt continued into the new century—Jack London,
Hergesheimer, Dreiser. By the time of the Panic of 1907, corsets were
loosening and dresses were off the floor. During the next few years
there appeared a strange bloom of libidinous ball-room dances—the
grizzly bear, the bunny hug, the camel walk and the turkey trot—

where ugly and supposedly bestial intimacies of posture and sug-
gestiveness of movement were the measure of the unhealthy repression which healthy libidos had been suffering for fifty years. By
1910 Mr. and Mrs. Vernon Castle had got the terpsichorean anarchy
deanimalized and moderated into the One-Step, corsets were con-
tracting at both upper and lower edges, and sheath and hobble
skirts, while immobilizing women, were revealing the fact that they
were female, a matter that had been hidden from the men since 1860.
About 1912 the wicked French taught them to slit the skirt, and the
romantic limb became a shameless leg. Correspondingly it became customary for college boys to loosen their inhibitions with a
brace of "stingers" before going to dances, and some of the more
advanced girls would take a pull on both flask and cigarette in the
bushes. By 1915 dresses were loosening toward naturalness, the last
defensive armor was discarded, and women breathed as women, at
once bold, thrilled and vulnerable. Most of the girls smoked behind
their mothers' backs, and "petting" was elevated from a sacred ritual
in the garden to a parlor convention at which every self-respecting
young girl must be adept.

And so came the First War, and after it the last of the Victorian
conventions crumbled—formal dress, the chaperone, the calling card,
the social note, any interest in ideas or habits of people over twenty-
five, common courtesy to the same, common courtesy to anybody,
sobriety, common chastity, long hair, neckties, garters, belts, combs,
honor in all forms, the ancient virtues of diligence and frugality,
interest in any pleasures except nervous ones, any music but jazz, any
literature but sexy literature.

With the social taboos eliminated, and the surface of society
jiggling in anarchy, the insatiable Greed which before had suffered
some restraint drove out into the open and took control of the culture. It was like a big, shiny, luridly painted locomotive whose gilded
name was "Stock Market," and it began to accelerate with a clanking
and a ringing and a whistling, but without anybody in the cab and
without any brakes to apply if he had been there. Instead of the
River of Violence, the aspect of the Gambling Culture became that
of a track circling upward in a spiral where this locomotive like a
great, uncontrolled, mechanical toy, whirled always faster and higher
without any guidance but that of the mechanical law of its own geo-
metric acceleration.

The big toy locomotive whose name was Stock Market was the
reality of the gambling culture, for material reality was the only
reality. It drew after it a long train of cars filled with a gesticulating
and squealing population. In breaking free from Victorian restraint,
they also were escaping into a geometrically increasing physical
violence as limitless but less real than that of financial gambling. The

big toy locomotive was visible and audible. But the loaded cars it drew were ghost cars, only rarely perceptible in swift-passing moments of recollected humanity, and the voices of the jiggling millions at the windows were at an insect-high pitch which was inaudible and the squeals were provoked by microscopic events—"tremendous trifles" —on the train and in the outer landscape.

In the early '20's they had a Red Hunt that was almost as depraved as McCarthy's, and bore relation to the tragic execution for murder of two immigrants named Sacco and Vanzetti. The Ku Klux entertained itself with its ritual of persecuting the persecuted. But all this was too high-brow, like the good literature that was beginning to presage the final Decline. What the people on the train were really squealing at were things that had no humanity in them at all, not even evil humanity, the microscopic events which occupied the headlines that were their tiny newspapers—blindness and death from the Prohibition Law and Wood Alcohol—Bathing Beauties—"Yes, we have no bananas"—Bruce Barton's Christ as an Advertising Man—Imbeciles publicly canonized for murdering each other for Adultery (Hall-Mills, Gray-Snyder)—boys lost in caves—Peaches Browning—Dancing Marathons—Flagpole Sitting—Coué to cure everything—the Crime of Halitosis—Children of the Culture dissecting other children for fun—Florida as Paradise—Building Climbers and Cornice-sitters ("human flies")—Plays and Movies about "Life in the Raw"—Confused women celebrated for "It"—Pocketfuls of cards admitting to Speakeasies—Gangsters with bodyguards and Armored Cars—the Kindness of Al Capone—always and everywhere the jiggling of Jazz which was the motion of the train.[1]

While the locomotive and its cars were thus going faster and higher round their spiral of toy track, in the center of it New York and Chicago competed for which was the capital of the gambling culture, which had the most unnatural crimes, the least civilization and loudest squeals. Chicago won and deserved to win. The culture was a Yankee culture, and Chicago was more nearly Yankee in population than New York was. Also, Chicago wanted it more than New York did. It might be that the boys of Wall Street and the Big Board kept up more steam in the locomotive than the boys of the Loop did. But Chicago was purer in its devotion to Greed than New York was, more cleanly and unhypocritically consecrated to it. Once in Chicago a taxi driver turned and asked me in a kindly tone, "How rich are you, Bud?" There was in it no more insolence than as if he had been a different kind of devotee and had asked me if I loved God or if I knew that God loved me. Later on the same trip I was in a night club when the bass drum thumped for silence, the headwaiter announced that So-and-So the head of some little Company and worth So Much was coming to honor us and let's give him a hand, and so he went over and brought in the little fat man and we gave him a hand. This was the highest reality of the culture, an Idealism carried over from the Puritan time and attached to material power. New York might have been as powerful, but it wasn't as honestly idealistic.

So the big toy engine dragged its invisible train annually faster and bigger and better round the circular gambling culture that had no end but went spiralling each year above itself, each year steadily higher and higher, round and round and round. In 1929 it was invisibly high above the earth and everybody knew that poverty was abolished forever. The engine threw a wheel and careened, but it steadied and went on faster and faster and faster, and in 1930 it jumped the high track, dragging the train with it. Many people fell down from the sky and were hurt when they struck, but the engine and the train sailed into the empyrean and were not seen again. The gambling culture had piled up its pyramid and from the top had taken off into nothingness. It was as if the old River of Violence had for thirty years been running uphill, till it spilled over a height and fell into an abyss so profound that no noise of it ever came back. But many separate drops that were people sprayed out over the banks from the fall and were shattered and scattered and some of them reassembled into the river of the future.

This final, accelerating rise and fall of the century-old gambling culture is one explanation of the phenomenon of the '20's and it leads, as any explanation must do, to the end of the River of Violence, the obliteration of the industrial pseudo-culture of Greed which we saw flowing out of the Civil War and drawing much of Greater New England away from the Puritan tradition. The other explanation of the '20's, which is the one favored here, disregards the industrial pseudo-culture as always extraneous and lost, and emphasizes the Puritan tradition itself which, being then without any God, flowed into the twentieth century in the form of the Yankee River. Much of it, as we saw, was overflowed by the flanking current of Intellectual Arminianism whose religious pretense was that of the Social Gospel. The old central current was that of the pure Yankeeism represented by William Allen White who had no true God but whose objective idealism, and most of the rest of whose qualities, were those of the Puritans.

It was in this traditional Central Current that there gathered the essential stream of the '20's, reflecting what at least tried to be an actual Sky, a complete panorama of existence containing a central Meaning or God which all could worship. It was the smallest possible sky, being no larger than Myself, and it represented the final contraction of the Puritan world, from its seventeenth-century Cosmos, to its eighteenth-century Man, to its nineteenth-century Men, and now finally to its twentiety-century Me. Greater New England remained what it had been in external geography, but inwardly it contracted almost to the vanishing point. The Sky was Myself, and its God was Self-expression which for most meant Sex Expression. It was in this central current that the effective revolt against Victorianism was led, beginning with the intellectuals of the '90's, and it was its influence, blowing across like spray, that incidentally stimulated the collateral River of Violence into its gambling excesses.

Yet in the central stream of the Yankee River, the center of the revolt, for all the deification of Self and Sex, the ritual was not entirely subjective. It was a true deification. These Yankees, these ex-Puritans, were incapable of any pleasure, any "self-expression," except as it was the fulfillment of some Idea, the fusion of Reason and Emotion in some kind of Perception. Accordingly, the Self and the Sex involved here were actually objective Ideas, and no sensual delight was satisfactory except as it also satisfied these Ideas, this really one central Idea. Since this Idea was uniform for everyone, it was indeed a Meaning, a God, of their little objective Sky. And in the most intelligent of them this Sex-Self-God, following D. H. Lawrence, was not far from the Hindu concept of the Inmost Self which is one with inclusive Reality.

The central significance of the saturnalia of the '20's was as a kind of Epilogue, a superfluous Fifth Act—in this case a Fourth Act—on the long drama of Puritanism. It was a diminutive, a microcosmic revival, a sad and ridiculous kind of Fourth Puritanism taking a last turn in people who most earnestly professed their hatred of Puritanism, and who denied the existence of any God at all. One of its chief rituals was the debunking of all past principles, people and realities. And yet in all this there was a flaming Idealism. It was a pinched and restricted revival. It was a ghostly revival, like the spectral flowering that wine is said to enjoy in the wood the first and even the second spring after it is put down. But it was indeed a flowering, and if it was absurd it was also gallant, like the veteran of Napoleon's Guard and like Benedict Arnold who put on the old uniform to die.

Philosophically, the attitude of the Lost Generation is traceable from as far back as you choose to delve. Latterly it comes down from Transcendentalism through Pragmatism, Relativism and Pluralism into the famous Columbia Teachers College theory of Education—

usually accredited to Dewey—which knows no meaning, no reality, except that of the new-born child. This reality is asserted in the basic First Law of Malcolm Cowley's Standard Digest of the Laws of the Fourth Puritans:[2]

1. The idea of salvation by the child.—Each of us at birth has special potentialities which are slowly crushed and destroyed by a standardized society and mechanical methods of teaching. If a new educational system can be introduced, one by which children are encouraged to develop their own personalities, to blossom freely like flowers, then the world will be saved by this new, free generation.

2. The idea of self-expression.—Each man's, each woman's purpose in life is to express himself, to realize his full individuality through creative work and beautiful living in beautiful surroundings.

3. The idea of paganism.—The body is a temple in which there is nothing unclean, a shrine to be adorned for the ritual of love.

4. The idea of living for the moment.—It is stupid to pile up treasures that we can enjoy only in old age, when we have lost the capacity for enjoyment. Better to seize the moment as it comes, to dwell in it intensely, even at the cost of future suffering. . . .

5. The idea of liberty.—Every law, convention or rule of art that prevents self-expression or the full enjoyment of the moment should be shattered and abolished. Puritanism is the great enemy. [By "Puritanism" they meant Victorianism. Virtually no one in the period knew anything of Puritanism or of any other feature of American history.] . . .

6. The idea of female equality.—Women should be the economic and moral equals of men. They should have the same pay, the same working conditions, the same opportunity for drinking, smoking, taking or dismissing lovers.

7. The idea of psychological adjustment.—We are unhappy because we are maladjusted, and maladjusted because we are repressed. If our individual repressions can be removed . . . then we can adjust ourselves to any situation, and be happy in it. . . .

8. The idea of changing place.—"They do things better in Europe." England and Germany have the wisdom of old cultures; the Latin peoples have admirably preserved their pagan heritage. By expatriating himself, by living in Paris, Capri or the South of France, the artist can break the puritan shackles, drink, live freely and be wholly creative.

Life under this code, as embellished by bootleg liquor, was the life of the more nearly literate part of the bourgeois class of the United States which was in such earnest revolt against its own

bourgeoisness. It was necessary for men and women alike to be always
a little tight when socially assembled, though most women were
adroit at dumping their second impotable cocktail into a flower pot.
It was generally assumed that one's husband would get too drunk
to drive, and that somebody else's husband, being drunk, would
confide his unhappiness. Women were under a double motive sar-
torially. They must be liberated—which meant sexy—and they must
also be very masculine and casual. Short hair and the long cigarette-
holder were partial solutions. The rest was in the fashion of nudity
in ugliness, whereunder woman appeared very nearly bare except
for the essentially tender curves of breasts and hips which were concealed within repulsive and supposedly boyish meal sacks. Talk was
perpetually about or on the border of Sex. Liquor was used to drug
away the possibility of thought or conversation. Highbrow discussion wove around the honestly moronic novelists, especially Anderson and Hemingway. Cabell's somewhat more comprehensive
Jurgen was treated gravely. Ellis and Lawrence were also read, less
for their wisdom than for their sophisticated dirt.

Naturally, with the discarding of standards most children became
problems, and the sweet aura of sex could be evoked over any discussion of the tender young. Education must of course be Progressive
by the last bulletin from Teachers College, for the difficulties with
the young were due always to something repressed—something other,
of course, than the instinct of the child for Order and Knowledge
which *must* be repressed. Education for the purpose of inducing the
children to raise more hell was an admissible and profound topic
of talk. Also, there were in every town a few earnest and aggressive
highbrows who read the Reviews, discussed them and did, through
the Women's Club, fetch in sometimes good concerts and sometimes
even—Ah Beauty!—beautiful and dangerous poets or other presumably dirty writers.

On the whole, the natural monandry and fastidiousness of women
kept the adultery rate much lower than the men would have wished.
Most of the women suffered dreadful private anguish over their
chaste instincts and their cowardice. It was of the tissue of both
feminism and fashionable "philosophy" that they must Sin gaily,
must go about Sinning as casually as men did, must think nothing of
it either for themselves or for their husbands. Carnality was their
lofty Ideal, their desperate Challenge, their Pure Flame. It was
their Morality that they must be Immoral. Many worked at it with
some success, though the greater the success the greater was the
probability of an undesired divorce, of alcoholism or of both. Perhaps the happiest were those who slipped once or twice, got away
with it, felt they had fulfilled their religious duty and became normal

women again. But whatever fate did to the women, and to such of
the men as still pretended to think, they did remain consecrated
about all these things. For all their jazzing, charlestoning, strip-
pokering, and occasional open spouse-swapping, these Puritan girls
could not really tear off their clothes and scream for joy. In theory
they followed Pagan gods. In actuality they followed the God of
their fathers. In essence they were very silly little Puritans, but
withal Puritans, Fourth Puritans.

The center of Fourth Puritanism was Aesthetic, not in the Cosmic
sense of First, Second and Third Puritanism, but in the smaller
though still Imaginative and Gracious sense of creative Art. The
priests of Orthodox Religion were the Artists, especially the Writers,
who said the dear, wicked, beautiful, challenging things right out
in words. As Chicago was or ought to have been the capital of the
gambling culture, so it undoubtedly was the capital of Fourth Puritanism, and its "Renaissance" which marked the decay and coming
Death of one was also the fruition of the other. The sunrise of the
Renaissance is usually associated with the appearance of *Poetry*—
Harriet Monroe and Eunice Tietjens—in 1912, followed in 1914 by
Margaret Anderson's *Little Review*. The original Chicago crowd,
most of them coming in from the prairie, included Sandburg, Lind-
say, Masters, Sherwood Anderson, Van Vechten, Pound, Wescott,
Dell; and not far off in the Middle West were Dreiser, Cather, Lewis,
Carl Van Doren, Mark Van Doren, Hemingway, MacLeish, Eliot,
Fitzgerald, Crane, Thurber. Against this weighty battalion from
western Greater New England, the Middle and South East could
offer Mencken, W. R. Benet, S. V. Benet, Wylie, Dos Passos, Wolfe;
but Old New England could provide for the priesthood of Fourth
Puritanism only Amy Lowell, Millay, Cummings and H. D.—Frost
and Robinson were the purest Yankees of them all, but they were
not of the Fourth Puritanism. Amy Lowell issued thumping proclamations about the new movement in poetry being "less concerned
with dogma and more with truth," and how in 1917 it expressed
"the seething of new idealism" which was just then uniting America
in the First War. All this was good publicity for everybody, but it
had little to do with the Self-Sexual-Aesthetic God of the Lost
Generation.

Fourth Puritanism was a Middle Western contribution. As Old
New England had made its contribution in the first Flowering of a
century before, it was now the turn of Middle Western Greater New
England to lead a great outpouring of Imagination. It was very self-

conscious and local with the Middle Westerners who started it and
mostly led it. They were troubled with senses of inferiority about the
intellectual sparsity of their second- and third-generation pioneer
backgrounds. Accordingly, they had a lofty hatred of the Old New
England of their tradition, and found it convenient to accept and
cherish the current absurdities about "Puritanism," applying them to
Old New England exclusively. They could recognize the greatness of
Whitman because he was not immediately of New England, but in
dismissing Longfellow, Holmes and Lowell they must needs also
brush off the greatness of Emerson, Hawthorne, and of the best of
Bryant and Whittier. They could not give the Hartford wits their
little due as craftsmen. They could admire Franklin for his materialism, but must needs build cheap legends about Edwards. They
ignored the genius of Sewall, the high talent of Cotton Mather, the
greatness of Hooker and Winthrop, and they witheld the faint praise
to which Wigglesworth and Ann Bradstreet were entitled.

The Middle Western Fourth Puritans must keep themselves in all
things superior to their tradition. They determined to become, and
mostly did become, exquisitely cultivated beyond the possibility of
any condescension from Harvard and Yale. Since they knew very
well that all truth and beauty were not in Chicago, and since Old New
England was beneath recognition, they must needs, in their search
for post-graduate sophistication, vault all the way to the Left Bank
in Paris, recognizing cosmopolitan Greenwich Village as a halfway
station. Thus they set up a useful liaison with contemporary European art. On the other hand they performed the temporary disservice
of divorcing America from its past, identifying it with the Middle
West as "young," and so putting a hiatus in the normal growth of
the common Greater New England culture.

The doctrines of the priests of Fourth Puritanism submit to the
same divisions as those of all Puritanism into the Central Current
of Truth or Moderation, the Heresy of Emotion on the left, and the
Heresy of Reason on the right. They all present the basic current
"philosophy" to the effect that there are no external realities and the
aim of life is to express the Inner Self against the repressive and
therefore wicked laws and conventions of society. The books in the
Central Current would be those—I am not here noticing style or
offering criticism—whose story or preachment is of a moderate self-
expression or self-indulgence, avoiding extremity of either emotion
or self-righteous rationalism. Such would be Fitzgerald's *This Side
of Paradise* whose hero learns to know himself—the highest achievement of the age; Mr. Dos Passos' *Three Soldiers* and Mr. Cummings'
The Enormous Room, where inimical but untriumphant Reason is
represented by War and the Army; and Mr. Lewis' *Main Street,* Mr.

Masters' *Spoon River Anthology,* and Dreiser's *American Tragedy* where the enemy is in divers social repressions.

On the side of Antinomian or Emotional Excess, the classical example of Lost Generation Hedonism is of course the two-ended candle of the young Miss Millay in whom also "summer sang . . . a little while." *Roan Stallion* and much else of Mr. Jeffers would also be in this region of Carnal Immoderation, as would be Fitzgerald's *The Beautiful and Damned.* Many of Sherwood Anderson's characters wallow in sex with somewhat abnormal luxuriousness.

On the side of Arminianism, the preachment of the moral duty of expressing yourself carnally, the simple classic would be Anderson's *Dark Laughter* which at some length asserts that if you want your neighbor's wife take her and, conversely, if you have a very special desire for the hired man, go away with him—no very great originality in either preachment, but withal the profound Center of Fourth Puritan religion. Even more didactically moralistic is Mr. Hemingway who in his work of the '20's tells us straight that there is no real experience except in the violences of Sexual Coition, Hunting and Bull Fighting. By the last two he means Death, and thus he takes his manliness out of any suspicion of softness into a hard consistency. Physical violence is the thing, boys and girls, and death is part of it. It was of the quintessence of the '20's that so excellent a craftsman lacked the intelligence to look beyond the values of animal behavior and animal courage. In the '30's Mr. Hemingway advanced in age to high adolescence when he introduced a strictly human, moral value into his preachment, telling us in *For Whom the Bell Tolls* that violence, while it is still the ritual of Truth, may yet be true not simply for its own sake but as furthering a Cause. But that was in a later age when Fourth Puritanism was long lapsed into the Intellectual Arminianism of "Social Consciousness." A case of Intellectual Arminianism in the '20's—and here I speak in literary criticism rather than of any preachment involved—was Mr. Eliot's *Waste Land,* which was obviously concocted without emotion either of perception or of composition, and so does not stand among the honest creative expositions of the Hedonistic and Solipsistic doctrines of the period.

The clearest presentation of the Central Doctrine of Fourth Puritanism by one of its most distinguished priests is in Miss Cather's treatment of artists, an Artist as character within a Work of Art being about as far as you can go in the way of Self-expression. Miss Cather, of course, hardly rates as a Yankee and a Puritan, but in her preachment she out-Puritans any of the Fourth Puritans I know of, especially when she does it in pure aesthetic abstraction without any direct introduction of Sex. She catches the essential Holy Ratio of Perception as

Edwards understood it, translates it into the language of Self-expressionistic experience, and presents it to us in work that itself speaks with the clean moderation of the Holy Ratio. Her first announcement of the principle of the forthcoming Revival was in the short story "The Sculptor's Funeral," 1903. The sculptor, whose perceptions are "holy" and "precious," leaves his ugly Kansas town in the hope of self-fulfillment, duly fufills himself with success in the East, being so fulfilled dies young, and is brought home where an unfulfilled local lawyer issues a diatribe against small town life which is prophetic of *Main Street*. Here so early is our major theme of "the self as the measure of value,"[3] especially the self of the creative artist. The perceptions of this Self, like those of Grace in other forms, are absolute. The artist has "special insight not vouchsafed to the businessman, or the club woman, or the minister, or the lawyer, or the scientist, or the engineer, grosser beings all . . . The poet's criticism of life possesses finality, and his vision of society, simply because it is his, is ultimate." And yet any Club Woman might meet a poet! And surely she could Understand him!

In the *Song of the Lark* (1915) Miss Cather develops the cult of the Self-God, the Solipsist Universe, into some of its corollaries. Following Howard Mumford Jones's analysis,[4] we find that Thea Kronberg, great vocal artist, and all like her, are initiates in a mystery which can not be taught—"If you do not know in the beginning, you do not know in the end." This is Predestination. The truth, the work of art, the "life," rushes from within, not from without. This by itself is an Antinomian declaration, but it is presently qualified by the need of Discipline if the emotion is to attain to Grace or the Holy Ratio. The work must be passionate, emotional; it must also be Rational. As Thea Kronberg sees it, a mold like a bowl must be made to contain the secret, else it is nowhere—"In singing one made a vessel of one's throat and nostrils and held it on one's breath. . . ." This is the Reason, the Discipline. The resulting Holy Ratio or Perception is also dependent on the self being solitary—a dash of Protestantism—its central selfhood incommunicable. Finally, the truth which the idealistic, lonely, inward, passionate and disciplined self knows, has nothing to do with the truth of science, and it is beyond the grasp of the dull—which is to say it is a function not of Natural Reason but of Puritan Right Reason.

Although we miss here many of the qualities we are accustomed to associate with Puritanism—notably Equality, which Miss Cather may think too earthy a talent for an artist—yet, in terms of the larger members of the Puritan House, Thea Kronberg's creator qualifies her convincingly as Elect. It was the kind of Election which, in their secret chambers, the Fourth Puritan ladies most desired. In spite of their passionate efforts to conform to the fashionable Sexual Ideals, this was the kind of Election they could really understand and could share in warm and safe vicariousness. Thea Kronberg's kind of Grace was the quintessential Grace of the period, identifying it very closely with the older Puritanisms. The Sexual part of it, the Grace by Orgasm dispensed by most of the writers, was only a vulgarization of this deeper doctrine for the benefit of the Busy Mother and Businessman who were too harassed to think.

Fourth Puritanism, like the preceding Puritan Revivals, was intimated in the last stage of the previous Decline in the '90's of the previous century. It was integrated around 1912, and came into full maturity with the barrage of revolutionary and self-expressionistic books in and around 1920—*Spoon River* in '15, *Winesburg, Ohio* in '19, *This Side of Paradise* and *Main Street* in '20, *Three Soldiers* in '21, and *The Enormous Room* in '22. It flourished for four or five years only, and, unlike other Revivals and appropriately to its relative pettiness, it collapsed in '30 instead of lasting until '60. The coincidence of its collapse with that of the gambling culture was not due to any economic elements in Fourth Puritanism. A few newspaper and magazine writers lost their jobs, and, if they were abroad, had to come home. But very few of the young artists had produced under the support of boom finance, and if they had attained marketability by '30 they were better off thereafter than they had been before, depression or no depression. Fourth Puritanism collapsed of its own triviality. Its doctrines and intellectual poses were sound for a brief Artistic Renaissance, but there was nothing in them that could support a culture. As soon as their excitement of novelty wore off, normally intelligent minds had to look elsewhere for reality.

2. FOURTH DECLINE (1930-1960)

The decline of Fourth Puritanism was in process well before the Crash of '29, evinced among other things by the trickle of the expatriates back from Europe.[5] As a social movement it had been mainly negative, a revolt against Victorianism, spectacular chiefly in the way of demolition. Once the demolition was complete it had little more meaning for normally equipped human beings, except in its purely aesthetic aspect, and that was for the professional artists and their professional entourage. Even the artists wearied of the revolt, once

it was accomplished, especially as they began to lose the worshipful
coteries that had set them off in Greenwich Villiage and in the cafés
of the first migration. Their Self-expression as a positive way of life
had only a little more meaning than the gyrations of the Gambling
Culture which they abhorred. Also, the bourgeois culture they condemned was beginning to support some of them by the mid-decade,
and this dampened the ammunition of their revolt.

After '25 the glory of Revolution began to fade. Tourists were replacing sycophants in the dens of MacDougal Street, and the real
artists began to flee across Seventh Avenue. The Glory of the Deux
Magots in 1926 was not the fresh Glory that had been the Rotonde
in '20, the Dome in '22, or even the Selecte and the Viking in '23 and
'24. The first Expatriates had had the thrill of being Exotics—they
had been neither tourists nor Frenchmen but something—ah!—much
finer than either. They had been a shower of meteors. By '26 the
piling of saucers at the Deux Magots was become a Convention. The
Americans there were simply people who lived in Paris, and their
affinities were getting to be—remotely, to be sure!—with the substantial Frenchmen who also took their Vermouth there. With an exception or two, none of them wanted to become French. They had
no love for America, perhaps even less than when they came. And
yet, long before the tremor of '29, the collapse of '30, and the reports
of suffering in '31, they knew that they must either rejoin American
Culture with all its barbarisms or become Frenchmen, Englishmen,
Italians, or whatever else they knew they could never become. The
procession of repatriation was beginning by '27.

What the Crash did was to add a grateful Reality to what otherwise had been a grudging acquiescence in the common sense of
Return. They had thought of America's pseudo-culture of Greed as
hopelessly entrenched. Now it was shattered! Something might yet
be done! Now there were visible issues to be supported, not the old
"glittering generalities" and self-righteousness of "Puritanism" but
the concrete needs of actual, suffering people of flesh and blood. In
the '30's the former aesthetes and sexual rebels of the '20's enjoyed
yet another "Renaissance." This time the Light was of a kind of
Social Responsibility which, since most of these bad boys and girls
had not before thought of society except with abhorrence, they took
to be another new discovery of their unique genius. Grandly they
gave it a new name, they called it "Social Consciousness."

This social awakening of the highbrows of the '30's was an extension of that humanistic Intellectual Arminianism which, in the
form of the doctrine of Natural Rights, had led the Decline of
Puritanism after 1760, and in the forms of Science and the Social
Gospel, had done the same after 1860. Immediately it reinforced the

latter trend which throughout the irreligious spree of Fourth Puritanism had been flowing along through the churches and the public and private charities. There was, however, a difference between the Social Gospel of the '90's and the Social Consciousness of the '30's in that the former had been interested more in the theory of Service than in the particular individuals to be served, while the enthusiasts of the '20's, once they discovered society, were genuinely, passionately and immediately concerned with the sufferings of actual people. In this concern there was a very special kind of Joy. Self-expression after all had been still an Idea, it still had had something of the tabooed "Glittering Generality" about it. But in the social consciousness of the '30's there was no "unrealistic," inclusive Idea left, merely direct, personal and generous concern. In this Fourth Decline of Puritanism we find at last no glimmer at all of the original Puritan Sky, no Imagination at all, no remnant even of the Idea of Me.

This ultimate triumph of both Materialism and Individualism included the elimination of categories of experience that had bothered most of mankind through most of its history. One of these was of course Religion, and the now unqualified denial of it by the addicts of social Humanism divided them sharply, both from the ancient equally earnest Reformers of Third Puritanism, and from the Social Gospellites of the '90's, who had made at least a profession of Christian foundation. There was now plenty of the love of the neighbor about, but it was much contracted from the old Second-Commandment Christianity of the Third Puritanism of Channing who had still believed that such Love and Goodness were the way of the Cosmos and its God.

The denial of all idealism and all religion was loudest on the part of the highbrows, but it was implicit also in the new version of the Social Gospel in the '30's which went hand in hand with the social consciousness of the intellectuals. Most young ministers now gave up religion in the interest of filling their churches, striving to make them into clubs that could compete successfully with other social clubs and forms of entertainment, with the Y.M.C.A., the Elks, the Masons, the Women's Clubs, the Bridge Clubs, the Pool Rooms, the Bars, the miscellaneous Sporting Houses, the Movies and the Prurient Literature. The ministers of the '30's had two dominant motives. Their chief effort was the one that has characterized all Christian churches in all crises, namely to save their institutions, to get people into the pews by no matter what irrelevant or sacrilegious means. In this they were in competion with the highbrows who wanted to keep the people out of the churches. Secondly, the young ministers really wanted to make people physically and socially comfortable, to make life enjoyable here and now on this earth, irrespective of the "opiate" of religion. And in this they and the highbrows could work tolerantly together.

In the new Social Consciousness of intellectuals and divines alike they eliminated a second category of human experience with which previous ages had been preoccupied. Among the glittering generalities to be avoided, those of Politics were, after those of religion, the most glittering and empty. Wherefore it seemed desirable to these eager people to eschew broad social ideas, to concern themselves not at all with theories and principles of government and economics. All that was required was to be generous and kind, to help everybody who needed helping, and presently the malign and rhetorical State would wither away. So the political innocents joined any organization that turned up with a humanitarian profession, and proceeded to struggle to achieve its good ends against the predatory greed of the bourgeois world. The Communists were not slow to capitalize on this generosity and soon improvised the United Front to catch every naïve fly in the molasses of his own favorite charity. Many educated and kindly ignoramuses found themselves fronting organizations whose object was not to help anybody but to ease them and their admirers into the Party. Many of the little ministers who loved Peace were found preaching a Christian Socialism which prepared the equally innocent among their listeners for the Bloody Revolution. Many of both ministers and highbrows held offices in vicious organizations that one day would lead them into embarrassment vis à vis equally vicious and more ignorant inquisitors.

By the end of the '30's America had descended into a vacuum about as far as it is possible for a human society to do. It was empty not only of Idealism and objectivity but also of Individualism in self-concern, not only of Religion but also of the Greed which had supplanted religion. After the debacle of '30, competitive capitalism had left behind it a sour skepticism which might well last two or three generations, and everybody was willing to settle for three sure meals a day. The men of the '30's remembered also that the machine civilization had not saved them from selling apples in '31 and '32, and they had a simple conviction that as between materialistic phenomena, there was more reality in the stomach than in the gadget. The Last Puritanism of the '20's had left behind it nothing but a state of apologetic sentimentality on the part of its veterans, and during the depression the late feminists were busy discovering the slavery of the home, even that of the kitchen, with an amused and muddled relief.

By the end of the '30's even Social Consciousness was suffering its own disillusion in the discovery by many intellectuals that they had been the dupes of enemy agents, and the Moscow Trials had disgusted most of those who had been more or less consciously trading with the noble enemy. Roosevelt's liberal house-cleaning had enlisted the devotion of all the intelligent and humane, but by '40 the job was done, and curiously it left behind it no Political Idea, no immortal Slogan to follow. The task of sweeping away the rubbish of Individualistic Greed had been a needful one, but Roosevelt was not of the greatness which sees an affirmative vision and leaves it as a beacon for the future. He was a courageous gentleman who despised the new rich and wanted to take care of his people. But he never suggested any replacement for the brutal system he attacked. The New Deal was only the political expression of intellectual social consciousness, its business to cut out infection, to heal and soothe. Roosevelt's work was excision and suture. His followers awaited, and still await, some indication of either the imaginative heart or the politico-economic surface of the new world that is to replace Big Greed, some inspired prophecy such as the eighteenth-century Yankees heard about Natural Man from Wise, Mayhew, Otis and the Adamses.

By '39 there was no more Idealism and objectivity, and there was no more Individualism and subjectivity. There was not even any affirmative philosophy that was widely acceptable. Materialism, Pragmatism, Pluralism, Relativism, pseudo-Freudianism, all these had done well as part of the artillery of demolition, when there was a positive though decadent culture to demolish. Now they were simply themselves which was nothing, emptiness, negation with nothing more to negate, a vocabulary of flaccidity for girls and boys who hadn't heard of any point in life beyond Health, minimal Economic Security and feline Comfort. Finally the very continuum that held the social vacuum began to dissolve. The Great Priests of the long Theocracy of Science and Natural Reason started a recessional from their altar. They began murmuring confessions that their God and his Code of Reason may have been a false god and a shallow code. The Priests of Imagination might yet have to revive their rituals. But the Priests of Imagination were playing with the toys of the Social Gospel and "good fellowship," and they could not hear the Small Voice that now again became audible.

America in '39 was at nadir, was ready to move out along gray reaches in a gloaming that might be Hell, or Hel, or Purgatory, might be the twilight of evening or that of morning. Then a war came in sight and its promise of death stirred memories that there had been life. From '39 to '45 it provided a faint diversion for boys and girls who won it without enthusiasm or belief that they were fighting for anything. Then the grayness returned, and the arctic chill. A decade began on the bottom of existence, a decade populated by the colorless insects of caves, the blind fish of the abyss of the sea.

Any post-war age is a godless age, and it is usually one in which the godless ignorant release volcanos of vitality that the war pent up and raise miscellaneous, colorful hell. It is a time when the large minority of morons, whether they suffered from the war or not, must march about destroying things. Usually they do it with zest and strength. But after '45 there was not zest and strength enough to be healthily bad. The financial licentiousness which had followed the Civil War and the First World War was now impossible on several scores. The carnal licentiousness that had followed King Philip's War, the Revolution and the First World War did not invite a nation that was now sophisticated about sex, and took little pleasure in breaking taboos that were no longer there. Instead of pursuing any of these traditionally self-indulgent courses, the large ignorant minority plunged into an outlet which had not before been much used as a postwar safety valve. They discovered that this innocent and virtuous nation was under serious threat by the Russians, by its Allies, and especially by its own more intelligent leaders. So they threw out the leaders, empowered their own kind, and buzzed into a campaign of high terror. Instantly, like a great black spider feeling his web shaken by little wings, the Neanderthal Mind appeared from his dark cave and scowled terribly among the insects.

The McCarthy Phenomenon has occurred several times in our history. Its ingredients are always the same. There must be a strong but moronic Leadership which is incapable of self-criticism or ideation, is neurotically driven either to attain or to preserve power, and is equipped with animal courage and a rudimentary ethic which will admit rationalization of shrewdness, expediency and all kinds of malice and vice. Its Following must have three qualifications. First, it must be ignorant of all issues involved. Second, it must know itself inferior and so desire zealously to destroy what is superior and distinguished. Third, it must be able to identify something foreign about its proposed victim. Actually, these three qualifications are the same.

Perhaps the first appearance of the phenomenon of the Black Spider was in the 1650's, when the vicious John Endicott was able to bully a disapproving majority of the Massachusetts General Court into letting him persecute excessively a few aggravating Quakers and harmless Baptists. Somewhat similar was the much exaggerated little witch scare in Salem for six months in 1692, in so far as there is a possibility that some informed upon others for ulterior reasons. More nearly parallel was Connecticut's important New Light-Old Light controversy in the 1740's and 1750's when considerable numbers of inoffensive and godly people were identified by the Reactionaries with divers offensive, more or less "foreign" itinerant evangelists, and were seriously discriminated against in social, political and economic ways. Then there was the Nativist, Anti-Catholic movement of the 1840's and '50's which headed up into the American or Know-Nothing Party, committed much brutality, debauched justice, captured several states and appreciable influence in Congress. The anti-foreign planks in the platforms of this party were comparable to the Isolationism of the Black Spider movement today.

These movements are all alike marked by an ignorant mob (McCarthy's best mob is the American Legion) which is jealous about something, and has discovered a foreign scapegoat to lynch. But there is in the McCarthy movement besides a sinister element which has not appeared before. The quasi-tyrannies of Endicott, the Connecticut Reactionaries in the eighteenth century, and the Know-Nothings were all in fact native movements, with no foreign designs behind them. Perhaps the McCarthy movement was the same in the beginning. But we may be sure that by the time of the famous Hearing the Communists were in there pitching their very best and crying Havoc at the umpire. Probably no one but some of the F.B.I. knew how high their support reached, but we may be sure that it was as close to the top as they were able to wriggle their way. To this extent, the McCarthy Black Spider is probably more serious, more dangerously alien, than any before.

Surely the present shambles should not be viewed with indifference. Probably it will be in some such flat and gray period as this that some such filthy and sickly movement may move to an actual triumph of tyranny and an end of our long experiment in self-government. At the same time, it is hardly profitable to meet hysteria with hysteria, and it may be well to recall that in each of the preceding centuries there has been a movement comparable to the present one, of which those in both the eighteenth and nineteenth centuries mustered more strength than McCarthy has yet enlisted, and did more internal damage than he has yet done. It is well to know that this mob behavior under more or less psychopathic or Hitleresque leadership is necessarily an occasional phenomenon under democracy—like Jefferson's "bloodletting," and that it will probably vanish quickly at the first dawn of an idealism large enough to reassure the ignorant and the jealous. The greater work is not to oppose McCarthy directly, but to look for the dawn and try to integrate the Idealism in whose light he and his senatorial peers will disintegrate, and what little following has not escaped him will hang dead in the web.

This idealess twilight in which Spiders prowl and prey may be attributed to Man's rejection of God. It may also be attributed to a long psychological decline which has ended in a near stoppage of the flow of vitality not only of Man but of Woman also. To trace this devolution we must start with a Natural Man and Natural Woman as hypothetical and arbitrary as the Natural Man and his Natural Rights of the eighteenth century. Our Natural Man and Woman existed, of course, in a cave where they had a large family, a clan, and a good division of labor and responsibility between themselves.

Whether or not the polity of the cave was a matriarchy, it is certain that the Woman provided both the centripetal force and the continuum that held the sphere of the family together, their common place, their common pool in which they floated—for those who must still talk in such symbols, their common womb. This was not simply the physical continuity which the female line provides down the ages, but the spiritual continuity, the enclosing reality. This was Love, Female Love, that condition in which the Woman is always selfless, identified with those of her circle, her congregation, always in Grace, "Natural Grace" as Calvin called it. Masculine love is shallow and whimsical by comparison. Only exceptionally the male attains to the strength and inclusiveness of Female Love, though it is essential to his healthy being that he be contained within it. He is partnered to it. He shares it. Though it comes from the Woman it is as much his as hers. It is their mutual Being.

Conversely the Natural Man brings to the cave and the family what is his special proclivity, and this is as much the woman's as it is his. He provides the activity of the tribe in relation to the outside world. She provides its Being, and Loving, he its Doing and Seeing. He goes out into the environment and brings back the food. But more essential than that, he goes out into the environment and brings back the Truth. He goes up on the Mountain and comes down with the Tables of Stone. He spends hours on his knees in the hills and comes back and declares, "Thus saith the Lord." This activity of Imagination is as essential to the full life of the Woman as her Love is essential to the full life of the Man, not simply because she sees that it fulfills him but also because she needs to know the

Truth herself. She can live without it, but she cannot live fully without it, any more than the man can live fully without her Love. Without the man's word from God she cannot love utterly and completely. Without her love the man cannot utterly talk with God. So they are a circle which is a unit.

Besides these major qualities in which each in his field is unique, there are secondary sexual qualities in which the distinction is not so great. The woman is expert in observing and ministering to all the minutiae of the bodily activity, survival and comfort of the members of the family. And in derivation from this she is interested in all persons and the particulars respecting them. The man, on the other hand, is expert in building, fighting, killing and fetching. In these activities the man and woman can replace each other. Especially the man can, and often does, concern himself with the health and comfort of the clan, and even of people outside the clan.

The history of Western culture since the Renaissance, and specifically the history of Greater New England, has been a long Decline in Imagination, the major and unique prerogative of the Male, and a corresponding ascendance in man, not of the unique prerogative of the Female, which he cannot acquire, but of the Secondary Female Activities, those concerns with the Particulars of existence which the man can acquire and apply. The Middle Ages, embowering its women and concerning itself chiefly with Religion and other large and General Ideas, including the desiccated maleness of scholasticism, was probably weighted beyond the Natural Balance on the masculine side. But the Individualism of the Renaissance, the interest in the Particulars of life, notably the Material Particulars discovered and classified by Science, this was the beginning of a swing into female unbalance which only now may be ended. Perhaps the First Puritans were near the norm. But certainly as God began retiring from men's minds in the eighteenth century, their maleness began to shrivel toward the secondary femaleness of concern for Man, still abstract Man and so actually male, but trying to be female, trying to look like a specific, tangible man. By the time of the Revolution we have very many men, especially among the enlightened, who were far gone in Deism, indulging in the military swagger which is a sure sign of the loss of human maleness and the substitution for it of defensive animal maleness.

The great turn came in the middle of the nineteenth century when most people surrendered God for other activities, and Science began offering accounts of the world which dispensed with God entirely. Before the Civil War men were giving over their concern for the Meaning of life and were laboring in the interest of the poor and afflicted. We had the Age of Reform in which Christianity became

Female or Second-Commandment Christianity, the concern for the neighbor. After the War the last love of God evaporated through Transcendentalism which was in effect the love of the self, and progressively the battle for financial self-aggrandizement eclipsed other activities.

As men gave over their major function, the ego rose up in various animal ways to supply the want. The new doctrine of evolution suggested that the best men were the ones with the biggest muscles, and it was easy to infer from that that the best men were those with the biggest bank accounts. The more depraved men became in their imaginations, the more they swaggered their bodies. They discovered not only where woman's "place" was, but they discovered their "superiority" to her in general. Increasingly they sustained themselves by bullying her. By the end of the nineteenth century men's activities were divided between those of animal maleness or physical self-assertion, and those of secondary femaleness, namely, science, health, comfort and charity. The larger concerns which had been the masculine prerogative were survived by rhetoric, the Glittering Generalities against which the poets of the next century revolted.

Meanwhile, beginning in the end of the eighteenth century, as the Male was giving over his peculiar prerogative, the Female was losing hers too. Love was still the central meaning of her life, but one important channel of it was now blocked. You couldn't wholly love a man who was so little alive that he had to bully you to reassure himself. Your love for him became qualified with that mixture of contempt and compassion which is pity. Something entire that you had to give was no longer called for. It had no objective.

By the 1840's a good many women were discontented, and they set out, pretty ignorantly, to find for themselves what they weren't getting from the men. They rationalized that they were discriminated against in the man's world, that they didn't have "rights" enough. Being estopped from full female expression, they thought to find the answer in the secondary kinds of male expression, in matters of money and business and politics. They joined the men eagerly in the secondary female world of Reform. In fact, it was there that they found their largest expression. The heroic women of the settlement houses and the fresh air camps of the '90's were perhaps the healthiest phenomenon of the end of the century. In the service of the poor they found something like a substitute for the entire love which was no longer finding entire expression in their families. Thus Greater New England went into the twentieth century with the male mind shriveled to winning bread, gambling and taking a share in the female business of science, health and humanitarian concerns. The women were reduced to their part love at home and their charities, and it was their hope further to appease their discontent by winning the vote and the last citadels of what was thought to be masculine power.

In the intellectual world of the '20's, the world of Fourth Puritanism, the male secondary quality of bread-winning, with its corollary of gambling, was scorned as "Bourgeois" and "Babbitry." Therefore, in spite of women's sartorial and political sallies into maleness, the entire revival was in terms of the secondary female instincts, those for the healthy self-expression of myself, my babies, my friends and, as a social "philosophy," the healthy expression of everybody. There were of course cases of irrepressible major female love, but they were looked at as unnecessary, of doubtful taste, like "special love" in the Oneida community, a little old fashioned and unfortunate. As for men, the glittering generalities of ideas of any kind were taboo. They were entirely feminized except in their physical or tertiary sexual qualities.

In the '30's the female world continued in a different vocabulary. The God of Self-expression was deserted, and the last scintilla of male imagination that had been required to sustain the little idea of Him was gone. Everybody went in for deflating the pompous and feeding the hungry, and none of this required any God. Social consciousness and the New Deal were exclusively female exercises. Health and Comfort were acknowledged by all as the ultimate Good.

Thus by '39 there was not a living idea anywhere. We had reached bottom in the long Decline of Man, which, as it turned out, had been the long decline of Woman also. She had "won" most of the male secondary traits and powers, but she had noticeably failed to replace the male in the function of inquiring into the mysteries and meanings of life. It need not be concluded that only exceptional women are endowed with the power of the male imagination at its best. We merely observe that when the men were abysmally failing and the need of new Meanings was great, the women, but for a poet here and there, also failed abysmally to find any. They could do all the little masculine things. But, by and large, they didn't even approach essential malehood, true manliness.

By 1939 Man was utterly clipped of his maleness, and Woman, who had not acquired any, was shorn of her female power. There was nothing for him to do, so there was nothing for her to be. Their mutuality which once had been in mutual fulness where each shared the best of both was now in mutual emptiness where neither gave the other more than carnal titilation. By the beginning of the long twilight in '39 we had a leveling into sexual mediocrity even more terrible than the social leveling that was also going on. The war provided a postponement through its requirement of both male and female animality. But it was a trivial interlude, and in '45 the twilight returned more hopelessly than before. At least among the aging survivors of the Female Culture in its "triumph" and final reduction of Man, the wind along the dim reaches had the chill of trivial death.

The generation that was young in the '20's and '30's tries to carry their female world on through the '40's and '50's, but with the young glory of Miss Millay's candle long snuffed and the decent impulse of Social Consciousness perverted by disillusion and McCarthy. Aging men who idealized carnal matters in their youth find it hard not to continue to trust them, not to expect the secret in the next dear little loins; and they recall the sad poet who at 60 was arrested while bathing naked with a young girl in a public fountain, and so committed suicide. Aging men who did not fully develop the possibilities of the '20's and are unable to now, continue to preach the old law of the libido and to imagine themselves shocking and bold. Aging women who have forgotten that men ever walked with God, or that they ever desired to know such men, flatter the aging men for virilities they do not possess, and other aging women still ponder the romantic chance they once let pass and the road that perhaps might yet be taken. All alike have forgotten what Mankind and Womankind might be.

Among the Intellectuals the twilight world of Secondary Femaleness is the more dismal because it is here that Ideas are expected. Instead, it is here that the fashion of the tangible and the immediate very clearly shows itself as the Cult of Mediocrity. Here the Academicians know each other by their particulars in scholarship, their particulars in science, and not by their doctrines and their precepts. They live comfortably in their Relativism, their Tolerance and their kindly Good Fellowship. They are satisfied with the distinction of belonging to the right Faculty, and they avoid there what might alienate their peers. By lowering their brows, they adjust to the common Leveling of the age, the suspicion of Highbrows and Ideas. They do not try to lift the public to them but they vulgarize their style and they seek the truth in the records of the many, not the few. They issue digests and surveys of all knowledge, but none stands up and declares singular God. Whoever has a tendency to lead must conceal it, or he must walk alone, which is the farthest from leading. The students are taught many facts, but they are disillusioned of their first masculine hope that there might be Truth at the knees of the Enlightened, and that the informed might be also the wise.

The Mediocrity is most complete and most terrible among the

creative minds who are of the stuff of the prophets. Here the taboo
upon the life of the mind has become a thick armor, and those best
qualified to convey ideas are forbidden to have them. The best style
is the newspaper style which knows how to present the physical facts
in melodramatic or comical sequence, but makes no comment on the
facts and on life except such as a small child might make. The heirs of
great publishers forego responsibility and taste and become salesmen
of the newspaper styles or they delegate their choices to salesmen of
the newspaper style. All men of sensitive minds are deeply inhibited
against ideas, and women have so far forgotten that they once loved
them in men that they resent the ghosts of them as rivals. Who thinks
is proscribed. Men are no longer permitted to talk after dinner, and
since they can not address each other as men, they dare not reveal
their greatest strength and their greatest need and address women as
women. Their efforts at joint conversation are either banal factuality
or the infantile carnality they retain from their youth and which has
no relation to the maturities of sex.

Here Mediocrity goes beyond an adjustment to an affirmative
need. The dull must be raised to oracular status, ostensibly because
they are unhappy or are of a persecuted group, but their real qualification is that they are dull. When ideas are repressed the first sublimation is into vanity, and to elevate the worshipful mediocre becomes a service to the self. Also the irresponsible publishers know
that dullness sells best, and they forget that their ancestors struggled
to elevate the dullness. All distinctions, all standards of beauty and
truth, are taboo. Success is measured in praise, and is best assured by
membership in a clique that gives each a notorious prize. After vanity,
the next sublimation of thought is in alcohol, and the creative minds
lounge over their whiskey, and stare, and mumble, and soon reach the
vacuous desert where they most long to be. There they lounge—and
they drink—and they stare. And they curse the Black Spider, and curse
all but themselves—and they drink. Time carries them along the gray
reaches of futility—and they stare—and they mumble—and they drink.
In them the great curve does not rise from nadir, but goes out on its
level tangent into the dark. The last Man and the last Woman of
the Fourth Puritans sit in the darkness—and they drink—and they
search each other for lost truth—they stare—and they drink—and they
stare.

In the first section of this book the question was raised whether
we might be approaching, not a revival of exclusively New England
culture, but the emergence of a Third Culture of the United States
in which the psychological patterns of the two basic cultures of New
England and the Old South will fuse and supply the foundations of

what will be the first general culture of the Nation. It was suggested that the surviving pattern of Yankee Idealism might still be ready to supply a Religion, a Faith, and the Rebel Aristocratic tradition might still flower in a code of right and honorable behavior; also that Yankee Equalitarianism and Rebel Courtesy at their revived best might merge and find themselves the same thing.

It was also pointed out that the personal vigor and the economic strength of such a Third Culture would probably be in the newest new rich who inhabit the great pyramid based on the new Industrial South westward into Texas, and narrowing northward, mostly west of the Mississippi, up to Minnesota. This group, while typically ignorant, are frightening in their strange lack of the sense of inferiority which characterizes most new rich and argues a latent idealism. This crop, far from parading the ostentation that usually reveals an insecurity in its kind, is distinguished by its excellent manners, which come in on the Rebel side, and its indifference to anyone's opinion of it. This security *in vacuo* is disturbing as arguing a real loss in the genes, presaging no emergence of anything human but a further solidification of materialism, another step down from the heights of Athens to either the circus of Hitler or the ant hill of Russia.

But on the hopeful side, the smooth and shining smugness of these good people may turn out to be merely a function of the emptiness of the age. If any Idealism revives in the society around them, they may yet develop the insecurity of normal new rich, which means that their children will enjoy "the best education money can buy," and their grandchildren will be responsible citizens. Also, although the physical vigor of an emergent Third Culture may be found in this New Middle West, its guiding ideas may well develop elsewhere. There is a great deal of random intellectual activity up and down the Pacific Coast. At the other end of the Continent, much of the best brains of the country is buying up the walls and tenth-growth brush of New England in order to sit there and hear what Time has to say. While the industry and common metropolis of the new civilization will be in the Central Pyramid to which people will commute, the residential areas will be in these ocean-washed and mountain-broken suburban areas. And it may be that in these domestic regions the Ideas will be born and the new Culture will be matured.

Speaking only for Greater New England and the hope of its reviving and contributing the Idealism of a new Fifth Puritanism, we can comfort ourselves only so far as to hold that it is not impossible. In the '20's the Fourth Puritanism with its self-concerned sky did not ramify among the Yankee roots of rural and village life, and in the '30's, while the New Deal touched everyone, its emasculated genius of kindness without ideas did not spread much farther than Self-expression had done. Also, during the period of the rise and decline of Fourth Puritanism, the country's greatest prophets went their own ways and were not of the Faith. Mr. Sandburg had an Idea of size and eternity that was partly an Immigrant Idea, but it was more Yankee than it was Self-Expressionist, and its social application was epic, not particular and female. Mr. Frost is the purest type of Yankee, complete with humor replacing God. Robinson was very near to a First or Second Puritan, notably in the twin epics of *Merlin* and *Lancelot*, in the first of which the self-centered Rational solution of the human problem fails, and in the second the self-centered Emotional solution fails, and Grace comes when both are transcended.* However much or little they were read, Sandburg and Frost and Robinson spoke for more of the inarticulate Yankee millions than did Fitzgerald and Anderson and Hemingway. Their tradition is the Masculine one of the First and Second Puritans. They by-passed the Fourth Puritans and the world of the Immediate and Tangible, and it is in their current that a revival of Idealism will come, if it comes.

The young men and women who will live any Revival that comes were born in the '20's and '30's and matured in the void of the '40's and '50's. Before the war they supposed that life was a brief and faintly troublesome span without any meaning that might be worth effort. Then between '41 and '45 they learned about Horror and Death, and they began to listen with cautious curiosity for news of compensations as large as those negations. They heard no sound out of the '20's and '30's, and none out of the '80's and '90's, that spoke to their condition. They smiled with something between tolerance and contempt for the emptiness of their parents, and they waited for news in some new idiom they could understand. They saw

---

* Robinson's description of Grace, "the light of the Grail" as "a spiritual understanding of things and their significance" (*Selected Letters of Edwin Arlington Robinson* [New York, 1940], 113) is not different from Thomas Hooker's "brokenness of heart" that "brings a strange & sudden alteration into the world, varies the price and valew of things and persons . . .; makes things appear as they be" (*The Application of Redemption*, Miller and Johnson, 312). Frost is in the central Puritan-Yankee current in assuming a Holy Ratio, a medial line of Grace between Emotion and Reason. Most often with him the opposites became, as in the Bible, Mercy and Justice.

> You can't trust God to be unmerciful.
> There you have the beginning of all wisdom.
>
> ("A Masque of Mercy," *Complete Poems*, 619)

But again, there is a divine Order from which we probably cannot escape:

> The fear that you're afraid with is the fear
> Of God's decision lastly on your deeds.
> That is the Fear of God whereof 'tis written.
>
> (*Ibid.*, 641-2)

no harm in looking into the records of mankind's achievements. They discarded the Gambling Culture's cult of ignorance, and they became our first educated generation since the Civil War.

In these young men the Economic Individualism, the battling Greed which captured the country for Materialism in the nineteenth century, seems to have burned itself out without trace. In business today they seem to show a strange combination of apathy, docility and snobbery in accepting the company's dictation of what they should wear, what clubs they should join, what cars they should drive, whom they should entertain, and where they should send their children to school. Yet they take all this lightly, as part of the rules of the game, not because they are cutting each slant-eyed corner to get to the peaks of power, or that they want wealth beyond provision for average comfort among their financially average friends. In their new industrialism their job may be only a means of livelihood, or it may involve a public responsibility. But their personal values are not in the company and its mechanics. Their real values are in their families, their hobbies, their friends, in the books, the concerts and other mental nourishment that their leisure affords. Their talk is not the talk of their forebears of one, two or three generations. To match the recent college graduates of Greater New England for curiosity and mental equipment we must look back to the pre-industrial time before the Civil War when there weren't many college graduates, and we might have to look all the way back to the First Puritanism of the seventeenth century when there was a singular theological literacy and discipline among even the liberally illiterate.

The young men today are not apathetic. They have trained all their senses, and they are waiting and listening with increasing concentration. Everything that was celebrated in the last three generations seems to them to have withered and vanished. They have heard of something simple called Existence. In an earnest, responsible and detached fashion they are looking into it. And in their experiment on a clean slate these young men have an advantage which only a few of their happiest forebears enjoyed from the First right down through the Fourth Puritans. They have wives who are their intellectual equals, equipped with the same education, devoted to the same fresh experiment in Existence; yet they prefer to be women, to make their contributions of Being and Loving to the mutual experiment, and leave their husbands to make their contribution of Doing and Seeing.

For a long time while their elders were drinking in the twilight, the girls and boys waited and listened. First the girls saw a very long memory. They knew their mothers had failed to be men and had forgotten to be women, and so had been nobody. They remembered

about Female Love and how it takes all of you and gives reality to a
cave and a clan. And it was probably the girls also who first remembered about Male Imagination which their mothers had forgotten.
They were curious. They told the young men that they wanted to
be women. Together they suffered a Keatsian surmise. They did not
clothe the surmise with any high plans beyond those for a cave and
a small clan and an Existence that brought some of the outer world
into the cave. They thought carefully of these things, and they
waited. In their waiting all of the millenniums of womanhood returned into the girl and she was ready. And the millenniums of manhood began returning into the boy, and he stared out the window
and whispered, "Here am I. Take me."

These are all of our young men and women.[6] They are all starting
over from an equality and a mutuality such as men and women have
rarely enjoyed since the hypothetical cave of the Natural Man and
Woman. Then their equality was in brains that were filled only with
the things of the forests and hills and the seasons. Now their equality
is in brains that are filled with the learning and the hopes and failures
and glories of five thousand recorded years. But the tenderness and the
mutuality are as they were, and they will Exist together and advance
no more rapidly than is required. They will do all things together,
and for the clan, and no one will do anything alone.

They have heard from their elders of there being a God, and they
have heard from other elders of there being no God, and that religion is an evil thing, and there are Puritans who burn you when
they can. Of all this they know nothing, and presume to know nothing. They will wait, and exist, and perhaps one of these days they
will find that a God and a Cosmos are in fact part of Existence. Then
he will not hesitate to go up on the Mountain and fall on his knees
and watch the bush burning and hear the small voice. And her Love
will go with him, and God's words will come back to her when He
speaks. This fulness is today the fulness of all the young men and
women who walk hand in hand between the oceans. If a God does become part of their Existence, then what He tells them will be a new
Puritanism, a Fifth Puritanism, that will see as high and as deep as
the First, and as wide as the Science of Natural Reason has seen.

If the new Yankee boy and girl, and after them America, do again
awake and their Imaginations expand again toward a Meaning, it
will be in some ways a greater expansion even than that of the First
Puritans. It will not be a greater expansion of Imagination, for the
perception of Imagination is always absolute and cannot be ex-

panded. It will not be a larger Sky in any material sense, for the Cosmos is not a thing of material and temporal measurements. It will be a sky larger than that of the First and Second and Third Puritans in the number of material things it contains and which Science has discovered in its search for solutions in material terms. The Natural Reason which is a part of Imaginative or Gracious Perception will bring along with it a very great and inspiring baggage of galaxies and electrons and the means of controlling them, and all this will be included in the new Puritanism, the new balanced understanding which all will share. They will not be denied and excluded in the way of Fundamentalism, but they will be touched in the way of Puritanism with a Light, and Glorified and given a place within the One Meaning, the World of the God.

In another and more important material way, the new Puritanism, if it should arise, will expand beyond any of the older ones. It will expand in human and geographical ways beyond anything of people and lands that any Religion of Man has compassed before. For if Puritanism awakes again, it will not be as the activity of a small people called Yankees within a small country called Greater New England. In the movements of the future there will not be any more Yankees, or any more Rebels, or any more Greater New England, or any more Greater South, or any more United States, or any more this nation or that nation. There will be only the Land and the Peoples of Materialism and the Land and the Peoples of Religious Idealism. The question is going to be whether the former will absorb the latter by physical force, or whether the latter will absorb the former partly by physical force but mostly and necessarily by the force of Imagination, the Perception of the Meaning of Things.

And this question of who is to prevail between the Materialists and the Religious Idealists will depend on whether the two great families of Religions which between them contain the Affirmations of all the other great and small religions will be able to unite at the center and see God with a single Eye. Any revival of Puritanism in Greater New England and America will be as a minute and microcosmic element in this great union and Revival, like a detail in a painting which is at once a part and the whole, and it will occur in terms, not of any theology, but of the Inner Essence, the "Divine Ground," of Puritanism which will turn out to be identical with the Inner Essence or Ground of all Western Religion which is chiefly Christianity and all Eastern Religion which is chiefly Hindu, Buddhist, or some combination of them.

In the present tension of humanity, it is surely the first duty, as it is the deepest true impulse, of every person within all jurisdictions to struggle for a union of Christianity and that generic Oriental religion which we might call Hindu-Buddhism,[7] to merge apparent differences that are not real differences, to know what are the real differences, to devote all energy to their reconciliation, and to prophesy of any perceptions that may look in the direction of reconciliation. In this work the priests, the enlightened ones, will be the leaders, but it is the duty also of all communicants to prophesy, for the central perceptions of both of these universal religions are simple and profound and within the grasp of all persons.

Each of these two Families of Religions contains within it many sects that stand in theological difference and cleavage from each other. But the schisms within Christianity are the wider and deeper because most Christians believe their religion exclusive, while the central Being of Hindu-Buddhism, however entitled, contains all truth and recognizes all truth as true. Both great religions suffer a cleavage on the authoritarian-sacramental line, on the question whether the individual comes to Reconciliation with God by means or behaviors prescribed by the priests or whether he comes alone. This cleavage has accounted for much struggle and brutality and failure of Religion among Christians, and some among Asians. Yet all Mystics transcend it. Most Protestants yet acknowledge the need of priests, like those of the Puritans, whose learning is greater than that of the people and whose duty it is to expound and to assist the individual to his own Perception. Authoritarian Mystics assert no more than this, asking the communicant in the end to perpetuate his own Perception and perform his own Sacrament.

More grave between the religions is the difference we have seen in its extremity as that between Antinomianism and Arminianism, the coming to Union with God as an emotional experience imposed by God's will on the helpless soul, and the coming to it by the effort of Work and Free Will. Here the Hindus and Buddhists, though they may be indifferent to ritual, yet ask a long and voluntary discipline to master the self. Similar is the moral behavior prescribed by Authoritarian Christians, but different from both is the Protestant Christian belief that Grace is chiefly from God, that Free Will may open the door by works and by prayer but it cannot compel God to come. These are differences regarding the conduct of those who are not yet united to God. On the part of those who have attained Light there is no essential dispute in either the Temple or the Cathedral, at either the dissenting Chapel or the wayside Shrine, least of all in the Single Soul and the Light it has seen.

In the fundamentals of the House of Religion the similarity of Hindu-Buddhism and Christianity is virtual identity. Both rest upon the bedrock of Idealism; the final approach to Reality is through doorways in the Mind. Both assume the existence of an inclusive State of Being, from which the outer, active Self seems at the moment to be separated. In both, this state of Being is informed and motivated by an integrated Meaning or God. In both, the aim of life is Union or Reconciliation with this Meaning. In Hindu-Buddhism all individual souls will eventually achieve this Union, but the Christians are in sectarian dispute as to whether the Reconciliation is to be for all or only for some.

The differences in the first two of the four acts in the Cosmic drama are more apparent than real. According to Christianity every soul starts in a straitjacket of Original Sin or Self which he must break off and discard and become as a Child. According to Hinduism and Buddhism the universal Being in each person is surrounded with a clothing of Ignorance and Passions or Self-assertions; the first must be instructed away, and the second must be disciplined away and laid "at rest." The Christian sees God as helping the individual to master his Original Sin by assuming it Himself in human form and Overcoming or Atoning for it on a universal scale. Comparably, the Hindu-Buddhist Being, as in Krishna in the *Bhagavad-Gita,* is sometimes Incarnated to the end of helping men to universal Understanding; and one dogma has it that Buddha, while leading all aspects of Being through their degrees toward realization, yet holds himself short of it until every aspect and form is ready to move with Him into unification and peace.

Before passing on to the critical Third and Fourth Acts of the Cosmic Drama, which are fundamental to the respective Christian and Hindu-Buddhist Houses, let us look at some of the members in the superstructure which are derivative from the foundations and are nearly identical. In both systems there are offered learned disciplines of body and mind that are intended as Helps toward or at least as Preparation for Reconciliation with God. In both, Individualism is incompatible with Salvation, and indeed in Buddhism it is an illusion. Deep in both religions is the Fact of Equality, in Hindu-Buddhism the identity of all in their identity with Being, in Christianity the identity of all in their Perception of Being, their State of Grace. In both there is a good End, a Nirwana, a Heaven, wherein the shell or straitjacket of Self or Sin has been finally broken off and discarded. In both there is, as part of the discipline, a necessity of concrete mental Belief besides Faith or contact with God in Contemplation or Prayer. At the higher levels in Hindu-Buddhism and in both Authoritarian and Protestant Christianity, Belief is identical with Faith, being simply the perception of the meaning and purport of the symbolism of the Cosmic Drama. But many sects and doctrines within all religions encourage for the unregenerate a literal Belief in myths that are nonsense to both Reason and Imagination.

Between the two great families of religion the differences that seem real appear in the two last acts of the Drama. In the Third Act, the state which the Christians call Regeneration and the comparable penultimate state for the Hindu-Buddhists are alike in including complete illumination, complete Perception of all Being and all its Particulars, complete Light[8] And yet there is a significant difference in the manner in which they are attained. As a condition of Regeneration the Christian must lose his self utterly. He must become as Nothing, as Darkness, before he can be flooded with Light. He must lose his Soul before a new Soul and a new Will are given him. Furthermore, the new Soul is given him from without, as an unpredictable act of God's Grace, and he is helpless to compel it. Before this Gift he had in him only "ruined" remnants of the original soul of man and of the Free Will as they had been before he chose to elevate the Self at the "Fall." At best he can pursue a course of study and conduct which will help him to recognize God's Grace if and when it should appear.

For the Hindu and Buddhist the process seems to be reversed. All Reality was in the Inner Self from the beginning of time, and the problem is, not to lose or immolate this Self, but to peel off its covering and give It the fullest realization. The discipline of study and conduct can actually attain by force of Free Will the Mystical Union and Perception, as it could never attain Regeneration for the Christian without God's help. For the Oriental the means was single, a course of will and action of Man alone; in the case of the Occidental it was dual, a movement from God and its acceptance by Man. But in this penultimate state there remains a duality, even for the Oriental. The Inner Self, although it is itself all Being, is yet separate from Being and perceives it as the regenerate Christian perceives it. The difference between them, though it was real in the approach, is not yet finally real.

In the Fourth and final Act the difference seems vast and irreconcilable. In Salvation, at the end of the cycle of the Christian Soul, while it continues thereafter in Loving concourse with the central Consciousness or God, yet it retains its Separate Identity; and the condition is one of Action. In Nirwana, on the other hand, at the end of the cycle of the Hindu-Buddhist Soul, the Soul is utterly identified with and lost in the Consciousness of God which in fact it has been in microcosm throughout its pilgrimage; and the condition is one of Surcease. The Christian separate soul which had at first to be lost is replaced by another Soul which retains its particularity. The All of Being first contained in every Oriental individual and whose release was at first sought in separateness enjoys ultimately the loss of particularity. The Christian End of Love and the Oriental one of

Repose are both Real, and it would not seem that the initiate of either could afford to concede anything at this Heart of his Religion, this Center of his Cosmos, which is experiental and profound beyond theology. Here the East and the West would seem to stand at hopeless impasse.

The reconciliation of Hindu-Buddhism and Christianity would include as a matter of course the reconciliation with both and with each other of Mohammedanism, Judaism, Confucionism and every other Religion, Ethic or Code which presupposes a unified and Meaningful State of Being. The Reconciliation, the statement for all of what Aldous Huxley calls the "Perennial Philosophy," is a work for major Prophecy. While we await the Prophecy we can contemplate the differences, and question them, and prepare ourselves for understanding when the truth shall appear.

Is the ancient debate irreconcilable between the doctrine of Salvation by Works and that of Salvation by Compulsive Grace, both within Christianity and within the entire World of Religion?

In proceeding into ultimate mortal state, which the Christians call Regeneration, is there an essential and irreconcilable difference between the Hindu-Buddhist discipline of putting the passions at rest and the Christian discipline of losing the self? Is there an essential and irreconcilable difference between the Oriental's awakening into universal perception of outer Being through the stripping away of the passions from his eyes, and the Christian's similar awakening through the loss of the old self—the "old Adam"— and the receipt from without of a new and all-seeing Self?

In the final conditions of Repose in Nirwana and Love in Paradise, is there an irreconcilable difference between the monistic identification of the Hindu-Buddhist's individual consciousness with the all-seeing Consciousness of Being, and the Christian's equal but dualistic All-perception in Separateness through his concourse with God in Love? May it be that there is an essential parallel, differing only in scale, the inessential matters of time and place, between the Hindu-Buddhist Being's sending out perpetually new selves to travel their long cycle through inorganic, organic and human matter and so return, and the Christian God's establishment and maintenance of a cycle of Love perpetually with every separate soul? If we thus move out of temporal into metaphysical concepts, the differences would seem to diminish in importance, but not yet to lose their reality.

The disparity in understanding of the Cosmos is at the center of the outer differences between the East and the West, and it will require a perception equivalent to that of Christ or Buddha, an untrammelled Cosmic Perception, to reconcile the central difference and show as a matter of experience the Identity of Unity and Duality, of Repose and Love. Every artist perceives this Identity in detail, and the learning of both great theologies comprehends it. Yet no prophet has yet named it as the one indivisible fact of the One and the Many, the Each and the All.

If it is not the Will and Predetermination of this mutual God that this Reconciliation be accomplished, then it would seem to be His Will that both great religions shall fail. The Battles of Armageddon and of the Dharma will both be lost. The creature of imaginative uniqueness on this planet will recede instead of evolving higher. And the earth will be given back to the Materialists who desire to hurry Man into what for a little century will be well-fed brutality, before Animal Evolution has its obliterating way with the species as it did with the great Fish, the great Lizards and the Mastodons.

But it would seem more likely, from the indications, that the Will and Predetermination of the Cosmos is otherwise. As man's political units have steadily expanded by combination until soon there will be only two left which by some process, physical or spiritual, will before many centuries be unified, so Man's religious units have also accreted to a few large and inclusive ones, each having reconciled away differences with smaller sects which it has embraced. It would seem that as in geo-political things so in geo-spiritual things the Will of the God of the Cosmos impelling this planet is leading toward a unification and an elimination of the last errors in, and so the last differences between, the great religions. If the Unification occurs, then every cult and sect will pour into it out of its tradition whatever of the true and universal it always cherished in the midst of its theological confusion and partial blindness. One of these sects, along with other small sects of Asia and of the West, will be Puritanism. When they have all agreed, as they were probably Predestined to do from the beginning, the Puritans will at last be participating in a Kingdom of God which will include, quite incidentally, the one they projected for New England in 1630. Mankind will no longer be capable of destroying itself and will be, in the vocabulary of all prophecies at the heart of all religions, where in truth it has always been.

Bibliographical Comments

B ECAUSE LARGER BIBLIOGRAPHIES are available, it has seemed sufficient to group
the notes into periods, without appending an alphabetical list of sources. I
would like to mention specially the twenty-five or thirty books I have found
most useful, whether for stimulation or for factual reference. Of these, four have
influenced my attitude profoundly, so that without them the book, or considerable
parts of it, would have had a different flavor.

First, I must acknowledge the dependence of this book upon two of
Perry Miller's—while absolving Professor Miller from responsibility for the
elaborations I have spun out of some of his interpretations. To *The New England Mind—Seventeenth Century* I am indebted for originally fixing my attention
upon the Puritans, and for providing me with the foundation of such knowledge
of their theology as I have gained. Objection, unjust as it seems to me, is sometimes taken to Professor Miller's emphasis on the Federal Theology, and it would
be possible to question one or two of his other conclusions. But for scope and
thoroughness in examining one of the basic fields of American history it is unlikely that this work will soon be equalled. It stands alone as the classic exposition
of Puritan theology, and so of Puritan character, and so of Yankee character, and
so of much of American character.

In his *Jonathan Edwards* Professor Miller addresses the center rather than the
outer system of Puritanism, and relates it to history, metaphysics, science, aesthet-
ics and psychology. Before I read it I was approaching some such interpretation of Puritanism, including Yankeeism, as essentially a cult of poetic perception; but I doubt that I would have reached enough conviction on the point to
make it central if Professor Miller's book had not supplied me with the support
both of authority and of much documentation of which I was ignorant. One
reads and rereads this work with increasing admiration. In scope it does not
compare with the great Siamese volumes, Plato's Socrates, Coke's Littleton,
Boswell's Johnson. But for penetration to the center of human experience,
it belongs with these.

For an account of the decay of Puritanism into Liberalism in the eighteenth
century, the uncovering of the clerical channels through which the European
doctrines of Liberty reached New England, Alice Baldwin's *The New England
Clergy and the American Revolution* is, so far as I know, unique and standard.
It fills what is still a serious blank in the common textbooks and common
knowledge of American History, the lack of explanation of how the people of
New England, including the most remote and ignorant, were schooled in the
doctrines of Natural Rights, the Social Compact, and the Right of Revolution
for the Compact broken, long before the political leaders of the specific American

482

Revolution were anywhere articulate. Here is an indispensable link in the political evolution of one of the three sections of the nation. And it is generally ignored in the books.

Henry F. May's brilliant *Protestant Churches and Industrial America* is the story of the Puritan perversion and decline in the nineteenth century. In his account of "Clerical Laissez-faire," Professor May lays convincingly at the door of the churches the major responsibility for the epic swing of the nineteenth century into materialism and greed. Before I came on his book I was preparing to concede major motivation of the decline to the economic interpreters of history. But in May I found thorough documentation for what had before been no more than a groundless hope. I found that the great lapse was not a conquest of the righteous churches by the wicked scientists and the greedy business men, but that many of the churches, under the leadership of unctuous clerical apostates from the Puritan tradition, ran ahead of the scientists into the most sordid extensions of materialist doctrine. It is not necessary to grant even the great and glittering century to the cynical historians of the past fifty years! Professor May's book touches very nearly the line between scholarship and charm which many these days are aiming for, and it ought on every score to enjoy wide distribution.

The above four books sewed together comprise the central account of Puritan-Yankee adventure so far, and they provide the outline of my story: Miller's *Edwards* for the aesthetic crux of Puritanism; Miller's *New England Mind* for the spiritual-religious seventeenth century; Baldwin's *New England Clergy* for the intellectual-political eighteenth century; and May's *Protestant Churches* for the physical-economic nineteenth century. I have of course added other material and my own interpretations; and my conclusions sometimes bear small recognizable relation to the sources that instigated them. I think the interested reader would sometimes do well to compare my statements with those of these definitive secondary sources.

Besides the four books just mentioned and the standard primary sources of New England history, I have relied consistently on about twenty-five other volumes.

The Seventeenth Century:

Miller and Johnson's *The Puritans* is the standard source book for the seventeenth-century New England, including the eighteenth-century utterances of some of the contributors. I was first directed by it to many of the primary sources I have consulted for the period, and in cases where the primary sources are obscure I have cited Miller and Johnson without looking further. My one complaint against this work is not utilitarian but substantial, for its failure to include Thomas Hooker's famous political dicta in the section "The Theory of the State and of Society." To be sure, Hooker's political attitude is still matter of speculation, but until conclusive evidence is offered—as it may be shortly—it does seem that his well known expressions should be presented with such reservations as the editor may wish to make.

J. Hammond Trumbull's *Blue Laws True and False* is a useful handbook of the first codes of Massachusetts, Connecticut and New Haven, with often amusing selections from the records of the General Courts. The volume has unique value in its comparative presentation of some seventeenth-century penal laws and practices in New England, New York, Maryland, Virginia and England.

For general reference I have had constantly by me Charles M. Andrews' *The Colonial Period in American History,* and familiar matters for which no citation seemed necessary were generally verified in Andrews' first two volumes. For Massachusetts Bay specifically, and for proto-American Puritanism I have made the same general use of Samuel Eliot Morison's *Builders of the Bay Colony.* For the combination of scholarship, dramatic arrangement and narrative clarity, these two standard works can hardly be exceeded.

Except for one or two details taken from Hutchinson's *History*, I have cited nothing on the Hutchinson or Antinomian affair outside Charles Francis Adams' careful *Three Episodes* and *Antinomianism*. My only doubt concerning them would be in the author's seeming acquiescence in the common assumption that Winthrop wrote *A Short Story*, which was published in England in 1644, and to which Thomas Weld wrote the Introduction. It would seem that a reservation of judgment might be made here on grounds of style. In the offensive part of the account, the flavor, the personality, seems in contrast to the sometimes sarcastic but always dignified and gentle one of Winthrop in his authentic writing, and at least suggestive of that of the writer of the Introduction who had also been present at the trial. Since the whole history of *A Short Story* remains conjectural, it would seem prudent, pending further evidence, to withhold this unconfirmed and un-Winthrop-like shadow from Winthrop's character.

Undoubtedly the finest work on the end of the seventeenth century is Perry Miller's *The New England Mind—from Colony to Province*. Although I have used it as a mine of citations, I have depended on it for ideas and stimulation less than on *The Seventeenth Century* and the *Edwards*, for my book was already in first draft when it appeared.

The Eighteenth Century:

Ola Elizabeth Winslow's *Jonathan Edwards* creates a convincing picture of the character which I have adopted here, while trusting Miss Winslow also in factual matters respecting the leading Puritan of the eighteenth century.

For religious history, generally, and especially in the eighteenth century, I have drawn chiefly on M. Louise Greene's *The Development of Religious Liberty in Connecticut*. Although Dr. Greene's subject is geographically limited in her title, her exposition of the trends in Connecticut requires her to trace them elsewhere through New England. For the relation of religious trends in New England to those in the rest of the country, I have relied mostly on William Warren Sweet's compact *The Story of Religion in America*.

The finest store I know of Puritan-Yankee anecdotes on the sound rustic level is Ola Elizabeth Winslow's *Meetinghouse Hill*. It is mentioned here because I drew on it rather more in the eighteenth century than earlier or later.

George Allen Cook's *John Wise, Early American Democrat* is, so far as I know, the only collection of the material on this important but still somewhat hazy figure.

The Nineteenth Century:

As basic source for the great Western Migration, from the beginning of colonization but especially in the nineteenth century, I have used Lois Kimball Mathews' *The Expansion of New England*, which unfortunately carries only to 1860 and the Mississippi. Thereafter, while drawing statistics mostly from official sources, I have depended for anecdotes on numerous local histories, and above all on Stewart Holbrook's collection of them in *The Yankee Exodus*. Mr. Holbrook seldom fails to emphasize the humorous aspects of Yankee behavior, and sometimes over-emphasizes them; but so far as I know his facts, shorn of interpretation, are as sound as they are voluminous.

As a reference book for the great Reform Movement of the '30's, '40's and '50's I have used Alice Felt Tyler's *Freedom's Ferment*, along with certain work of my own and the sources there used. Miss Tyler's work is, I believe, the most comprehensive one on this aspect of the period.

After a somewhat unnecessarily melodramatic opening, Benjamin P. Thomas's

Theodore Weld, Crusader for Freedom becomes an excellent brief biography, giving a clear and well documented picture of this important character.

For the nineteenth rather than the earlier centuries, I have referred to the standard surveys of the *American Life Series,* especially Carl Russell Fish, *The Rise of the Common Man,* Allan Nevins, *The Emergence of Modern America,* and Arthur M. Schlesinger, *The Rise of the City.* Professor Schlesinger's *How to Behave* is a useful and entertaining compendium of Victorian manners.

For a presentation of the late nineteenth-century Yankee I have drawn, among other sources, on the more or less fictional picture galleries of William Allen White's *In Our Town* and *The Changing West,* Edgar Lee Masters's *Spoon River Anthology* and Glenway Wescott's *The Grandmothers.*

The Twentieth Century:
Of the several books on the 1920's, the one with the most comprehensive view, so far as I know, is Malcolm Cowley's *Exile's Return.*

Notes

KEY TO NOTES

For convenience in citation, repeated titles are often condensed into a short form, and those most frequently cited are listed in the following alphabetical key.

Adams, *Antinomianism.* Charles Francis Adams, ed., *Antinomianism in the Colony of Massachusetts Bay, 1636-1638.* Boston, 1894.

Adams, *Episodes.* Charles Francis Adams, *Three Episodes in Massachusetts History.* New York, 1892.

Andrews. Charles M. Andrews, *The Colonial Period of American History.* New Haven, 1934-38.

Commager. Henry Steele Commager, *Theodore Parker.* Boston, 1936.

Conn. Col. Rec. J. H. Trumbull and C. J. Hoadly, eds., *Public Records of the Colony of Connecticut.* Hartford, 1850-90.

Faust and Johnson. Clarence H. Faust and Thomas H. Johnson, *Jonathan Edwards, Representative Selections. . . . American Writers Series.* New York, 1935.

Greene. M. Louise Greene, *The Development of Religious Liberty in Connecticut.* Boston, 1905.

Greene and Harrington. Evarts B. Greene and Virginia D. Harrington, *American Population before the Federal Census of 1790.* New York, 1932.

Hammond. Chaptain Lawrence Hammond, "Diaries," *Proc. Mass. Hist. Soc.* 2nd ser., VII (1892), 144-72.

Hull. John Hull, "Diaries," *Trans. Am. Antiq. Soc.* III (1857).

Hutchinson. Thomas Hutchinson, *The History of the Colony and Province of Massachusetts Bay.* Lawrence S. Mayo, ed., Cambridge, 1936.

Mass. Col. Rec. N. B. Shurtleff, ed., *Records of the Governor and Company of the Massachusetts Bay in New England,* (1628-86). Boston, 1853-54.

Mathews. Lois Kimball Mathews, *The Expansion of New England.* Boston, 1909.

May. Henry F. May, *Protestant Churches and Industrial America.* New York, 1949.

Miller, *Colony.* Perry Miller, *The New England Mind: From Colony to Province.* Cambridge, 1953.

Miller, *Edwards.* Perry Miller, *Jonathan Edwards. American Men of Letters,* New York, 1949.

Miller, *New England Mind.* Perry Miller, *The New England Mind: The Seventeenth Century.* New York, 1939.

Miller and Johnson. Perry Miller and Thomas H. Johnson, eds., *The Puritans.* New York, 1938.

Morison. Samuel Eliot Morison, *Builders of the Bay Colony*. Boston, 1930.

Russell. Noahdiah Russell, "Diary," *New Eng. Hist. and Genealogical Register*, VII (1853), 53-59.

Schneider. William Herbert Schneider, *The Puritan Mind*. New York, 1930.

Sewall. Samuel Sewall, Diary, *Coll. Mass. Hist. Soc.* 5th ser. V-VII (1879-82).

Sweet, *Colonial*. William Warren Sweet, *Religion in Colonial America*, New York, 1942.

Sweet, *Story*. William Warren Sweet, *The Story of Religion in America*. New York, 1939.

Trumbull. J. Hammond Trumbull, *Blue Laws True and False*. Hartford, 1876.

Tyler. Alice Felt Tyler, *Freedom's Ferment*. Minneapolis, 1944.

Walker, *Creeds*. Williston Walker, *Creeds and Platforms of Congregationalism*. New York, 1893.

G. L. Walker. George L. Walker, *Thomas Hooker*, New York, 1891.

Winslow, *Edwards*. Ola E. Winslow, *Jonathan Edwards*. New York, 1941.

Winslow, *Meetinghouse*. Ola E. Winslow, *Meetinghouse Hill*. New York, 1952.

Winsor. Justin Winsor, ed., *The Memorial History of Boston. . . .* Boston, 1882-83.

Winthrop. John Winthrop, *Journal*. James Kendell Hosmer, ed. *Original Narrative Series*. New York, 1908.

NOTES

When a citation is given under an abbreviated title, its full title will be found either by looking back through the twenty notes preceding it or in the alphabetical key given above.

PART ONE—GREATER NEW ENGLAND

I. Geography

1. The bases of these figures are given later.
2. Brooks Adams, *The Emancipation of Massachusetts* (Boston, 1887).
3. Charles A. and Mary R. Beard, *The Rise of American Civilization* (Revised and enlarged one volume college edition, New York, 1934), 53.
4. Miller, *New England Mind*, 214.
5. *Abraham in Arms* (Boston, 1678), 15, quoted in Miller and Johnson, 393.
6. G. L. Walker, 51.
7. Morison, 184.
8. Winthrop, II, 18.
9. Morison, 101.
10. Trumbull, 10-11.
11. "Body of Liberties of 1641," Law number 45. In William H. Whitmore, ed., *The Colonial Laws of Massachusetts*, 1660-72. (Boston, 1889), 43.
12. Morison, 343.
13. Morison, 339-46. Winslow, *Meetinghouse*, 38-49. Schneider, 74-77. Andrews, I, 437.
14. New York, 1949, 13-14, and elsewhere.
15. New York, 1951, 32-38.
16. Compare Miller, *Colony*, "Prologue."
17. For guides to the literature on Turner, see: Ray Allen Billington, *Westward Expansion* (New York, 1949); also Robert E. Riegel, *America Moves West* (New York, 1930). For a symposium on the Turner theory, see *The University of Kansas City Review*, 18 (1951-52), 3-86.
18. Walter Prescott Webb, *The Great Frontier* (Boston, 1952).

19. Frederick Jackson Turner, *The Frontier in American History* (New York, 1920).

20. In 1860, at the end of the great wave of westward migration that began after the Revolution, there were about 6,000,000 people of Yankee descent in Ohio, Indiana, Michigan, Illinois, Wisconsin and Iowa, and 4,500,000 comparably pure Rebels in Western Georgia, Alabama, Mississippi, Tennessee, Kentucky and Missouri, each figure excluding immigrants from the other region and from foreign countries, which elements were more numerous in the Yankee Middle West—perhaps 3,500,000—than in the Rebel Middle West—perhaps 500,000. As we move back from 1860, the ratio of population changes in favor of the South. On the average, we can say that between 1790 and 1860 there were about equal numbers of Rebels and Yankees rubbing shoulders along the Ohio and contending, with increasing consciousness, for the control of the nation.

21. W. J. Cash, *The Mind of the South* (New York, 1941), 8.

22. Louis B. Wright, *The First Gentleman of Virginia* (San Marino, Calif., 1940), 56-57.

23. Cash, *Mind of the South*, 46.

24. All figures are adapted from the Census of 1950, as presented in the *World Almanac* of 1953.

25. Turner seems to be of this view, and he can probably be trusted not to err in favor of New England. See *Frontier in American History*, 227-28, 233-38.

II. Architecture

1. The quotations from Augustine and Hooker are both taken from Miller, *New England Mind*, 1.

2. Quoted without citation, *ibid.*, 10.

3. *Ibid.*, 11, with a quotation from Samuel Willard, *The Compleat Body of Divinity* (Boston, 1726).

4. Roger Williams, *Experiments of Spiritual Life and Health* (Philadelphia, 1951), 67-68.

5. Thomas Hooker, *The Application of Redemption*, (2nd ed., London, 1659), 55.

6. William Adams, *God's Eye on the Contrite. . . .* (Boston, 1685), 6-7.

7. *Puritans*, 60.

8. Hooker, *Application of Redemption. . . .*, 55.

9. G. L. Walker, 28-30.

10. Thomas Shepard, *The Autobiography of Thomas Shepard*, Allyn B. Forbes ed., *Publ. Col. Soc. Mass.*, XXVII (1932), 322.

11. *Personal Narrative*, Faust and Johnson, 69-70.

12. Cotton Mather, *Magnalia Christi Americana* (Hartford, 1820), 317.

13. *Personal Narrative*, Faust and Johnson, 57-58. 14. *Ibid.*, 58.

15. Winslow, *Edwards*, 172.

16. Sweet, *Story*, 189.

17. Cole's record is transcribed more fully in the account of the Great Awakening.

18. *Works*, John A. Albro ed., (Boston, 1853), II, 235, quoted in Miller and Johnson, 50.

19. *Personal Narrative*, Faust and Johnson, 66.

20. *Religious Affections, ibid.*, 236.

21. *Personal Narrative, ibid.*, 60-61.

22. *A Divine and Spiritual Light, ibid.*, 108. One wonders whether Edwards had been reading John Norton's similar passage which, for all its excellent rhetoric, yet uses light as a figure instead of as an experience as Edwards uses it: "Star-light cannot make it, otherwise than night. The light of nature

since the fall, hath not the proportion of Star-light, to the bright Sun-light at noon-day." (*The Heart of New England Rent,* [Cambridge, 1659] 12-13, in Miller and Johnson, 52.)

23. *Christ the Fountaine* (London, 1651), Miller and Johnson, 332.
24. *Experiments of Spiritual Life and Health,* 40.
25. *Winthrop Papers* (Mass. Hist. Soc., Boston, 1929-47) II, 90.
26. *Personal Narrative,* Faust and Johnson, 63-64.
27. *Ibid.,* 70-1.
28. *Ibid.,* 70.
29. *Ibid.,* 71.
30. *Magnalia Christi,* 303.
31. *Application of Redemption,* 54.
32. Edwards, *Religious Affections,* Faust and Johnson, 237.
33. Personal Narrative, *ibid.,* 63-64.
34. *Ibid.,* 60.
35. *The Soules Humiliation* (London, 1638), 77.
36. Winslow, *Meetinghouse,* 95-96.
37. *Application of Redemption,* 61-62.
38. Miller, *Edwards,* 160.
39. Confession of Faith, Article VII, adopted at Saybrook Synod, 1708. Walker, *Creeds,* 369. This is the Westminster Confession, the Savoy Confession, and is the Confession adopted by Massachusetts in 1680.
40. *Soules Humiliation,* 147-148.
41. *Heart of N. England Rent,* 12-13.
42. Miller and Johnson, 14.
43. *Ibid.,* 21.
44. *Application of Redemption,* 89-90.
45. Miller and Johnson, 11-12.
46. Cited in Ralph Barton Perry, *Puritanism and Democracy* (New York, 1944), 300.
47. *Institutes of the Christian Religion,* tr. by John Allen (6th Am. ed. Philadelphia n.d.) I, 649-650.
48. *Christian Directory: or a Body of Practical Divinity, and Cases of Conscience* (1673).
49. This is the opinion of Prof. Joseph F. Fletcher of the Episcopal Theological Seminary, Cambridge.
50. The quotations are as given in R. H. Tawney, *Religion and the Rise of Capitalism* (Mentor Book edition, New York, 1947) which offers many other examples of English Puritan encouragement to mercantilistic diligence.
51. See Mintmaster John Hull's *Diary.*
52. Published in *The Way of Life* (London, 1641), in Miller and Johnson, 319-324.
53. I Corinthians, 7, 31.
54. *Institutes,* I, 648. If the Pauline statement in Corinthians, *supra,* be read in connection with the passage preceding it, it seems to justify Calvin's interpretation as well as proposing moderation.
55. *Christ the Fountain of Life,* 119-120.
56. Miller, *New England Mind,* 42.
57. *Religion and the Rise of Capitalism,* 192.
58. In Miller, *New England Mind,* 25.
59. Preston, *Life Eternall* (London, 1634) pt ii, 6.
60. In Miller and Johnson, 482.
61. *Institutes,* 645, *et seq.*
62. Edmund S. Morgan, "The Puritans and Sex," *New England Quarterly,* XV (1942), 602.

63. *The Unbeleevers Preparation for Christ,* 69; *The Soules Implantation* (London, 1637), 47-48.
64. *Works,* John A. Albro, ed., I, 160-163.
65. *The Saints Guide* (London, 1645), 117.
66. *The Gospel-Covenant,* 51.
67. *Batteries upon the Kingdom of the Devil* (London, 1695), 108.
68. John Winthrop, *A Modell of Christian Charity,* in *Winthrop Papers,* II, 283.
69. *Ibid.,* 294.
70. *A practical Commentary . . . upon The First Epistle Generall of John* (London, 1656), 242.
71. *An Exposition of the Principles of Religion* (London, 1645), 46.
72. For a brief discussion of Ramian Logic, see the introduction of Miller and Johnson, 30-42.
73. *The First Principles,* 17, cited by Miller and Johnson, 35.
74. Miller, *New England Mind,* 433.
75. Edward Johnson, *Wonder-Working Providence of Sions Saviour,* in Miller and Johnson, 143.
76. Miller, *New England Mind,* 433.
77. Miller, *Edwards,* 239.
78. Quoted from *Religious Affections, ibid.*
79. Miller's paraphrase, *ibid.,* 241.
80. From *Religious Affections, ibid.,* 192.
81. True moral perception as combining both reason and emotion, though without suggestion of a ratio between them, is discussed as part of the experience of Grace or Conversion in Miller, *New England Mind,* Chap. X.
82. Quoted without citation, *ibid.,* 292.
83. *Ibid.,* 293.
84. *Christ the Fountain of Life,* 145.
85. *Religious Affections,* as quoted in Miller's *Edwards,* 179.
86. Miller, *Edwards,* 180.

PART TWO—YANKEES AND GOD

I. The World of the Cosmos (1630-1700)
1) First Puritanism (1630-1660)

1. There were 81 taxables in Plymouth Colony in 1634. (*New England Historical and Genealogical Register,* IV [1850], 253-54.) The taxables were generally the adult male residents, with a few widows, five on this particular list. They are commonly estimated at one-fourth of the total population, but the estimate is made complicated by the difficulty in knowing whether, in a particular place and year, the lower limit is put at 16 or 21. Greene and Harrington, p. xxiii.
2. In May, 1634, John Winthrop, reporting to the Earl of Warwick, estimated the population of the eight principal towns at "4000: soules & upwarde." (*Proc. Mass. Hist. Soc.* 1st ser., XX [1882], 43.) As that was a busy year of immigration, we could guess the population by the end of the year at nearly 5000.
3. In 1637 the Massachusetts General Court called for men from each town at the rate of approximately one per 38 inhabitants. (Greene and Harrington, 13.) Boston's levy was 35. (*Mass. Col. Rec.* I, 192.) Thus Boston in 1637 had a population of about 1330. The figure 750 is a guess, drawn from the later figures.
4. Unless otherwise indicated, the dispositions given here for 1634 are taken from the "Plan of Boston" for 1635, in *Series of Plans of Boston. . . .,* compiled by George Lamb (Boston, Municipal Printing Office, 1905) being a Sup-

Notes

plement to *Boston Town Records and Book of Possessions,* 2nd Report (1877). There seems to be a split of authority as to the location of Governor Winthrop's house at this time. Winsor, I, frontispiece, locates it at the head of the street where Lamb puts the Town House, while Lamb seems to locate it, in both 1630 and 1635, farther south, at the north corner of Milk Street, where Old South Church now stands. I am following Morison, 87, who, at the time of the May elections in 1634, has the Town House in existence on the site of the present Old State House, and has the Winthrop house where I have put it, down State Street on the south side, near the meetinghouse and on the site of the present Exchange Building, which carries a plaque claiming the distinction. Morison says that Winthrop moved "later" to the Old South location.

5. Winifred King Rugg, *Unafraid, A Life of Anne Hutchinson* (Boston, 1930), 73-74.
6. Adams, *Episodes,* 547; Winsor, I, 174, 360, 575 notes. Samuel Drake, *The Old Landmarks and Historic Personages of Boston* (Boston, 1873), 53-54.
7. See John Winthrop's account of the collapse of his farmhouse—Winthrop, I, 69, 70.
8. Anthony Garvan, *Architecture and Town Planning in Colonial Connecticut* (New Haven, 1951), 99.
9. Robert C. Winthrop, *Life and Letters of John Winthrop* (2nd ed., Boston, 1869) i, 43.
10. Hutchinson, I, 412.
11. The Fundamental Agreement of New Haven in Charles J. Hoadley, ed. *Records of the Colony and Plantation of New Haven. From 1638 to 1640* as quoted in Trumbull, 164.
12. *Mass. Col. Rec.* I, 79.
13. *Ibid.,* II, 38.
14. *Ibid.,* III, 109-10; II, 208; III, 264. See also Andrews, I, 459-61, and John F. Sly, *Town Government in Massachusetts,* 49.
15. Winthrop, I, 108.
16. Roger Williams, in *Publications of the Narragansett Club,* VI, 344.
17. Winthrop, I, 116-17.
18. Letter to Major Mason in 1670, in Miller and Johnson, 484.
19. Letter to the Town of Providence, 1655, *Publications of the Narragansett Club,* VI, 278-79.
20. Rugg, *Unafraid,* 73.
21. Winthrop, I, 299.
22. Testimony of Mr. Bartholomew at the examination of Mrs. Hutchinson. Adams, *Antinomianism,* 272.
23. For a somewhat imperfect condensation of Mrs. Hutchinson's Antinomian opinions, see Adams, *Antinomianism,* Introduction, 12-14, and Thomas Welde's Preface to *A Short Story, ibid.* 72-74. And for a more full examination of the "Errours" of her group see the findings of the Synod of 1637, *ibid.,* 95-124. It is customary to dismiss these eighty-two findings as absurd scholasticism, but that is due to religious indifference and accompanying theological illiteracy.
24. *Episodes,* 477. Adams invented the phrase on analogy to the modern legal shift of "constructive treason."
25. Winslow, *Meetinghouse,* 184.
26. Adams, *Episodes,* 551-58.
27. Joseph B. Felt, *Ecclesiastical History of New England* (Boston, 1862) II, 611, quoting Coddington.
28. Thomas Lechford, solicitor and diarist, reaching Boston in 1638 when the

feeling was still high, seems to despair of the democratic tendencies of the
Holy Commonwealth, because of "the errors and disorderlie proceedings we
run into and persist in dayly here, as sheep without a shepherd. . . . Christians
cannot live happily without Bishops, as in England; nor Englishmen without
a King. Popular elections indanger people with war and a multitude of
other inconveniences."—(Thomas Lechford, Esq., *Notebook* from June 27,
1638, to July 29, 1641, [Cambridge, 1885], 274.)

29. Adams, *Antinomianism*, 270, 275, 277.
30. Report of the Trial of Mrs. Anne Hutchinson before the Church in Boston,
    March 1638, Adams, *Antinomianism*, 285-336.
31. Adams, *Episodes*, 532.
32. Adams favors this view—*Episodes*, 538.
33. Adams, *Episodes*, 535.
34. *A Short Story* in Adams, *Antinomianism*, 168.
35. *Ibid.*, 286.
36. *A Short Story* and *The Examination* in Adams, *Antinomianism*.
37. *Ibid.*, 252.
38. *Ibid.*, 246.
39. So entitled in the appendix in which the report is printed, Hutchinson, II.
40. Shorter Oxford Dictionary.
41. *A Short Story*, in Adams, *Episodes*, 564.
42. *Ibid.* Despite good evidence pointing to Winthrop's authorship of *A Short
    Story*, the evidence is not conclusive. Against it is the fact that this ag-
    gressive and frequently vituperative work nowhere presents Winthrop's
    smooth and gentle style which is uniform in the considerable body of his
    known work and is unmistakable.
43. Adams, *Episodes*, 428-29.
44. John Cotton, *Controversie Concerning Libertie of Conscience in Matters of
    Religion* (London, 1646), 7.
45. Adams, *Episodes*, 568.
46. This is quoted in Miller and Johnson, 144-45. For the development and
    expression of the idea of the Holy Commonwealth, see Schneider, Chapter 1.
47. *Records of the Court of Assistants of the Colony of the Massachusetts Bay*
    (Boston, 1901-28) II, 16, 19, 35.
48. *Mass. Col. Rec.*, I, 177. See also below.
49. John Cotton, *Controversie Concerning Libertie of Conscience*, 8.
50. Cotton quoting Williams in *The Bloudy Tenent Washed and made white
    in the bloud of the Lambe. . . .* (London, 1647), 14.
51. *The Early Records of the Town of Portsmouth*, edited by the Librarian of
    the Rhode Island Historical Society (Providence, 1901), 66.
52. Greene and Harrington, 47, give the population of Hartford, Wethersfield
    and Windsor in 1637 as 800, citing Palfrey I, 455. As this neglects Spring-
    field, which was part of the same migration, and as it is also true that
    an unknown number came to Connecticut without going through Massachu-
    setts Bay, the figure would seem to be a conservative one.
53. Edward E. Atwater, *History of the Colony of New Haven* (2nd ed., revised,
    Meriden, Conn., 1902), 69.
54. Masson, *Life of Milton*, III, 108, 109, quoted in Adams, *Antinomianism*, 27.
55. Cotton, *Controversie Concerning Libertie and Conscience*, 7-8.
56. A letter entitled *New England's Lamentation for Old England's Errors*,
    quoted in Adams, *Episodes*, 564, n.
57. *A Reply to Mr. Williams his Examination; and Answer of the Letters sent
    to him by John Cotton*, 17-18, appended to *The Bloudy Tenent Washed*,
    etc. (London, 1647).

58. Miller and Johnson, 186.

59. For Massachusetts settlement see Albert B. Hart, ed., *Commonwealth History of Massachusetts* (New York, 1927-30) I, 525-532.

60. Andrews, II, 8.

61. Hooker complained of Cotton's too great insistence upon an account of an emotional experience of Grace as a qualification for admission to a church. On the other and political hand he complained that at the Bay the congregations did not sufficiently exercise their authority in excommunication.

62. There being no reliable figures, the populations given here are guesses compounded of the indications in three books, namely Greene and Harrington, Mathews, and Andrews.

63. *Conn. Col. Rec.*, I, 124, 127.

64. The Massachusetts *Laws and Liberties,* 1648 in Max Farrand, ed., *The Book of the General Lawes and Libertyes* (Cambridge, 1929), the Connecticut *Code* of 1650 in *Conn. Col. Rec.*, I, 509-563, the New Haven *Code* of 1656 in *New Haven Col. Rec.*, II, 559-616, all codifying laws most of which were long before published and enforced.

65. *Mass. Col. Rec.*, I, 126, 183, 274; III, 243. *Conn. Col. Rec.*, I, 64; II, 283.

66. Under "Heresie, Error" in *The Colonial Laws of Massachusetts. Reprinted from the edition of 1660.* . . . William H. Whitmore, ed. (Boston, 1889), 154.

67. New Haven *Code* of 1656, "Heresie."

68. Connecticut *Code* of 1650, "Ecclesiastical," and New Haven *Code* of 1656, "Ecclesiastical."

69. Lewis G. Janes, *Samuel Gorton, a Forgotten Founder of our Liberties.* . . . (Providence, 1896), 43-44.

70. Winthrop, II, 143-48. Also see *Mass. Col. Rec.*, II, 51.

71. Janes, *Gorton,* 63; J. R. Bartlett, ed., *Records of the Colony of Rhode Island.* . . . (Providence, 1856-65) I, 243.

72. Walker, *Creeds* 237.

73. *Ibid.,* 237.

74. *Ibid.,* 203-34.

75. Cotton Mather, *Magnalia Christi Americana,* (Hartford, 1820), 317.

76. Hutchinson, I, 129.

77. Hull, 144-45.

78. See "Extracts from the Letter Book of Samuel Hubbard," *Magazine of New England History* (1891) I, 173.

79. Connecticut *Code* of 1650, "Ecclesiastical," *Conn. Col. Rec.*, I, 523-25; New Haven *Code* of 1656, "Ecclesiastical," *New Haven Col. Rec.*, II, 587-89. George L. Clark, *A History of Connecticut* (New York & London, 1914), 137-39. Greene, 164-77. For an amusing account of Hartford's effort, somewhat later (1675), to disembarrass itself of some Quakers without harming them or invading their rights, see *Friends Library,* XI (1847), 148-49.

80. John Clark, *Ill News from New England* (London, 1652), in *Coll. Mass. Hist. Soc.,* 4th ser., II (1854), 1-113. The quotation is found on 47.

81. Adams, *Episodes,* 549.

82. Elbert Russell, the History of Quakerism (New York, 1942), 63-64. Roger Williams, *An Answer to a Letter Sent from Mr. Coddington.* . . . Boston, c. 1677. Society of Colonial Wars in Rhode Island and Providence Plantations, Publication no. 38, (Providence, 1946), 6-7.

83. Sewall, V, 43. George E. Ellis, in Winsor, I, 184.

84. Roger Williams, *George Fox Digg'd Out of his Burrows, Narragansett Club Publications,* V; also, *An Answer to a Letter Sent from Mr. Coddington,* etc.

85. Rhode Island Records, I, 376-78.

86. Sweet, Colonial, 147.

87. *Mass. Col. Rec.*, IV, pt. ii, 212.
88. *Friends Library*, XI (1847), 137-38.
89. *Mass. Col. Rec.*, III, 240.
90. The jailer eventually escaped a hearing. Joseph Besse, *The Sufferings of the People Called Quakers* (London, 1753) II, 185-187. See Brooks Adams, *The Emancipation of Massachusetts*, Chap. V (either edition), for other cases of aid or sympathy shown to the Quakers. For a slightly later example of popular sympathy see Zachariah Chafee, ed., *Records of the Suffolk County Court, Publ. Col. Soc. Mass.* XXIX, XXX, (1933), I, 519.
91. Clark, *Ill News from New England, loc. cit.*, 33-52.
92. Hubbard, "Letter Book," *loc. cit.*, 173.
93. Winsor, I, 185, n.
94. Winslow, *Meetinghouse*, 187-188. Citing manuscript Records of the Second Church.
95. Greene, 100 and note.
96. George L. Walker, *History of the First Church in Hartford* (Hartford, 1884), 159.
97. *Ibid.*, 214. See also a letter of Thomas Stoughton of Windsor to the General Court, May 17, 1658 (*mss.* Conn. Hist. Soc.) complaining that he is "persecuted" while dying, because the minister will not answer certain arguments of his. (The minister was John Warham, founding pastor of Windsor.)
98. Eugene M. Bushong, *Beginnings of the First Church in Wethersfield* (Cromwell, Conn., 1935), 12-17.
99. Michael Wigglesworth, *The Day of Doom*.
100. Greene, 101-04.
101. Walker, *Creeds*, 296.
102. Greene, 114.
103. Andrews, II, 116.
104. G. L. Walker, *First Church, Hartford*, 174.
105. Bushong, *First Church in Wethersfield*, 17.
106. Greene, 116-117.
107. For the state of opulence in Boston and elsewhere as early as 1640, see Andrews, I, 514.

I. The World of the Cosmos (1630-1700) (continued)
2) First Decline (1660-1700)

1. Solomon Stoddard, *An Answer to Some Cases of Conscience. . . ,* quoted in Miller and Johnson, 456-57.
2. Winslow, *Meetinghouse*, 92.
3. Quoted in George Allan Cook, *John Wise,* (New York, 1952), 12.
4. Hull, 152.
5. *Ibid.*, 157.
6. *Ibid.*, 161.
7. Precise figures of the losses in Philip's War seem not to exist. The estimates here combine elements from the "Harris Papers," a report on the war by William Harris in a letter to Sir Joseph Williamson (*Coll. of the R.I. Hist. Soc.*, X, No. 46), Mathews, 57-58, and Walker, *Creeds*, 411, who accepts Palfrey, *History of New England*, III, (Boston, 1865), 215.
8. Walker, *Creeds*, 412. Also Hutchinson, I, 295 n.; Winsor, I, 546.
9. Hammond, 145.
10. *Ibid.*, 155-57.
11. *Ibid.*, 162, 165.
12. *Christian History*, (Boston, 1743), I, 94.
13. These quotations and the longer one following are from Urian Oakes's

New England Pleaded With (1673), cited in Perry Miller's *Colony*, 34.

14. *Ibid.*

15. *History*, III, 41, note 3.

16. *Greene*, 128-29.

17. *Records of the Suffolk County Court, Publ. Col. Soc. Mass.*, XXIX, XXX, 1671-80, give 23 indictments (5 persons twice); 12 fined (including 6 for a second conviction and 2 Quakers); 9 admonished including William Chamberlain, Jr. who confessed not being to meeting for 4 or 5 years, and John Northy who confessed to an 18 month absence; 3 not proved.

18. Walker, *Creeds*, 427-32.

19. Miller, *Colony*, 36, citing the records of the General Court.

20. Samuel Nowell, *Abraham in Arms*, 15.

21. Russell.

22. *A Discourse Concerning the Danger of Apostasy*, (Boston, 1679, 2nd ed. 1685), 104.

23. Winslow, *Meetinghouse*, 185, quoting the First Church Records.

24. William B. Weeden, *Economic and Social History of New England*, 1620-1789, (Boston and New York, 1891), I, 180.

25. Winslow, *Meetinghouse*, 184 and 189.

26. *A Modell of Christian Charity*, in *Winthrop Papers*, II, 294.

27. Hull, 141 *et seq.* This and the quotations immediately following are from the "Private Diary."

28. Quoted in Morison, 171.

29. *Ibid.*, 181.

30. Miller, *Colony*, 36-37.

31. *Ibid.*, 50.

32. *A Farewell-Exhortation to the Church and People of Dorchester in New England*, (Cambridge, 1657), 16.

33. Miller, *Colony*, 37.

34. *Ibid.*, 50.

35. *Ibid.*, 51.

36. *Ibid.*, 37.

37. *Ibid.*, 46.

38. *John Dunton's Letters from New-England*, W. H. Whitmore, ed., (Boston, 1867), 73.

39. This development was alluded to in "Architecture," and is discussed by Perry Miller in "Preparation for Salvation in Seventeenth Century New England," *Journal of the History of Ideas*, IV (1943), 253-86.

40. Dunton, *Letters*, 71, referring to Massachusetts.

41. Walker, *Creeds*, 416.

42. Greene, 127.

43. Walker, *Creeds*, 427-32. The adoption by this Synod of 1679—as reconvened in 1680—of the English Savoy Confession of orthodox Puritanism, emphasizing Grace (Walker, 439, 367, 403) is a piece of remarkable inconsistency.

44. *Ibid.*, 419-20.

45. *Mass. Col. Rec.*, V, 240-41.

46. Greene, 128.

47. *Conn. Col. Rec.*, Acts of the General Court May, 1680, and May, 1681.

48. Captain Robert Keayne, *Notebook*, (Cambridge, 1889), entry for Sept. 13, 1640, 5-7.

49. *Proc. New Haven Colony Hist. Soc.*, V (1895), 138-48.

50. Charles Francis Adams, "Some Phases of Sexual Morality and Church Discipline in Colonial New England," *Proc. Mass. Hist. Soc.*, 2nd ser., VI, (1891), 477-516.

51. *Plymouth Church Records,* 1620-1859, *Publ. Col. Soc. Mass.,* **XXII-XXIII** (1920, 1923), I, 146-177.
52. *Some Important Truths about Conversion,* (London, 1674, Boston, 1721), 4-5.
53. *Soul-Saving Gospel Truths* (Boston, 1703, 2nd ed., 1712), 22-23. (There may or may not be a line of continuity in the circumstance that when Increase Mather was an undergraduate at Harvard in the '50's he lived mostly in Boston and tutored with John Norton, then teacher of the First Church and by all odds the most enlightened of the three Arminian triumvirs of the days of the Persecution.)
54. *Mercy Magnified on a Penitent Prodigal,* (Boston, 1684), 212.
55. *A Remedy against Despair,* (Boston, 1700), 42-43.
56. *A Dead Faith Anatomized,* (Boston, 1697), 87.
57. *The Principles of the Protestant Maintained,* (Boston, 1690), 110.
58. *Batteries upon the Kingdom of the Devil,* (London, 1695), 108.
59. *The Serious Christian,* (London, 1699), 21-24.
60. *The Plain Doctrine,* (Boston, 1659), 6th Sermon, 59.
61. Samuel Danforth's *The Cry of Sodom Enquired Into,* (Cambridge, 1674), 14-15.
62. Increase Mather's *The Greatest Sinners Exhorted and Encouraged to Come to Christ, and That Now Without Delaying,* (Boston, 1686), in William P. Trent and Benjamin Wells, eds., *Colonial Prose and Poetry, The Beginnings of Americanism, 1650-1710,* (New York, 1901), 221.
63. Samuel Moody, *The Doleful State of the Damned,* (Boston, 1710), 36-37.
64. Greene, 120-30. Also Sweet, *Colonial,* 107.
65. Walker, *Creeds,* 418-19.
66. Jonathan Pierpont, "Diary," *New England Historical and Genealogical Register,* XIII, (1859), 355-58.
67. Miller and Johnson, 734.
68. Dirk J. Struik, *Yankee Science in the Making,* (Boston, 1948), 23-24.
69. Miller and Johnson, 734.
70. Struik, *Yankee Science,* 23, quoting the preface to the fortieth volume of the *Transactions* of the Society.
71. Miller and Johnson, 732.
72. *The New England Historical and Genealogical Register,* VIII, (1854), 325-333.
73. Schneider, 43.
74. Russell, 54.
75. See Walker, 28-30, for Hooker's "Implanting into Christ."
76. "The Autobiography of Thomas Shepard," Allyn B. Forbes, ed., *Publ. Col. Soc. Mass.,* XXVII (1932), 361.
77. "The Diary of Michael Wigglesworth," Edmund S. Morgan, ed., *Publ. Col. Soc. Mass.,* XXXV, (1951), 414, 417.
78. Sewall, V, 419-20.
79. Marion L. Starkey, *The Devil in Massachusetts,* (New York, 1949), Chap. 1.
80. E. Cauldfield, "Pediatric Aspects of Salem Witchcraft Tragedy; Lesson in Medical Health," *American Journal of Diseases of Children,* LXV, (1943), 788-802.
81. Miller and Johnson, 735.
82. Starkey, *Devil in Massachusetts,* 155-56; Miller and Johnson, 736.
83. Miller and Johnson, 736.
84. A.L.S., Connecticut Historical Society.
85. Sweet, *Colonial,* 91. Trumbull, 19-23. Also Starkey, *Devil in Massachusetts,* 281.
86. T. J. Wertenbaker, *First Americans,* (New York, 1927), 145-48.
87. Starkey, *Devil in Massachusetts,* 272-75.
88. Trumbull, 21.

89. "An Account (taken from Mr. Harris) of New England, April 9, 1675"—*Harris Papers*, No. 39, R. I. Hist. Soc.
90. R. H. Tawney, *Religion and the Rise of Capitalism*.
91. The population was 13,000 in 1700. (Taken from Miller, *Edwards*, 3).
92. Miller, *Colony*, 113.
93. *New England's True Interest*, (Cambridge, 1670), 33, cited in Winslow, *Meetinghouse*, 105.
94. *Harris Papers*. A picture of the squalid side of Boston at this time is in the *Journal* of the Dutchman Jasper Danckaerts, 1679-80, quoted in Miller and Johnson, 404-11. In spite of his Anglophobia the picture is not convincing.
95. Elizabeth McClellan, *History of American Costume*, (New York, 1937), 92-93.
96. Sewall, V, 402.
97. *Winthrop Papers*, II, 89, 225.
98. Sewall, VII, 187, 190, 205, 255, 262, 274-75.
99. From Winthrop's letter to his wife, May 8, 1629, cited above.
100. Hull, 141, *et seq.*
101. This and the following quotations, from Sewall, V, 445, 446-47; VII, 165-66, 388-89.
102. *Ibid.*, 266-67.

II. The World of Man (1700-1800)
1) Second Puritanism (1700-1760)

1. Greene and Harrington, 9-10.
2. *Journal*, first published by Timothy Dwight in 1825. Available in Miller and Johnson, 425-47.
3. *Diary of Joshua Hempsted of New London, Coll. New London County Hist. Soc.*, I, (New London, 1901), 534.
4. 1693-97: First French and Indian War (King William's War).
   1701-13: Second French and Indian War (Queen Anne's War).
   1739-48: Third French and Indian War (War of the Austrian Succession).
   1754-63: Fourth French and Indian War or "Old French War" (Seven Years' War).
   1775-83: The Revolution.
   1786-87: Shays' Rebellion.
   1812-15: War of 1812 (Napoleonic Wars).
5. *The Heavenly City of the Eighteenth Century Philosophers* (New Haven, 1932), 29-32.
6. *Coll. Mass. Hist. Soc.*, 3rd ser., V, (1836), 177-243.
7. *Ibid.*, 229-30.
8. Sweet, *Colonial*, 289.
9. Greene, 169-70.
10. Miller and Johnson, 394 n., citing Percy A. Scholes, *The Puritans and Music in England and New England* (London, 1934), and 758, citing Sibley II, 496.
11. George Allan Cook, *John Wise*, 79-80.
12. Samuel Sewall drew the charter.
13. George L. Clark, *A History of Connecticut*, 229.
14. The quotations on this topic are taken from the late Ola Elizabeth Winslow's classic of New England culture, *Meetinghouse Hill*, Chap. X.
15. Cook, *Wise*, 20, citing *Publ. Col. Soc. Mass.*, XV, (1925), 156-68, and Samuel Eliot Morison, *Three Centuries of Harvard* (Cambridge, 1936), 31-32.
16. Clark, *Connecticut*, 229.
17. Joseph Easterbrooks, *Abraham the Passenger* (Boston, 1705), 3.
18. Greene, 224.

19. *Ibid.*, 223, citing Edwards.
20. *Ibid.*, 222.
21. *Ibid.*, 179-80.
22. Faust and Johnson, 56.
23. Quoted in *Sweet*, Story, 188-89.
24. Greene, 227.
25. *Religious Affection*, as quoted in Miller's *Edwards*, 192.
26. Timothy Dwight, *Travels in New England and New York*, quoted in Winslow, *Edwards*, 193.
27. *Personal Narrative*, in Faust and Johnson, 59, 60.
28. A.L.S., Connecticut Historical Society.
29. Winslow, *Edwards*, 192.
30. See Greene, Chapter X, for a full account of "The Great Schism" in Connecticut.
31. *Conn. Col. Rec.*, VIII, 452-57, 500-02.
32. Alvah Hovey, in *Life and Times of Isaac Backus*, (Boston, 1858).
33. Faust and Johnson, 189.
34. Quoted in Miller, *Edwards*, 321-22.
35. Winslow, *Edwards*, 284-85.

II. The World of Man (1700-1800) (continued)

2) Second Decline (1760-1800)

1. With a few alterations and additions the list is that of Carl Becker, already noticed, in *The Heavenly City of the Eighteenth Century Philosophers*, pp. 29-32.
2. Carl Becker, in the *Dictionary of American Biography*, VI, 585-598, esp. 597.
3. See Herbert W. Schneider, *A History of American Philosophy*, (New York, 1947), 41-42.
4. *Autobiography and Selected Writings*; Henry Steele Commager, ed., (New York, 1949), "The Way to Wealth," 210, 219, 220.
5. *Ibid.*, *Advice to a Young Tradesman*, 234.
6. Schneider, *American Philosophy*, 42.
7. Leon Howard, *The Connecticut Wits* (Chicago, 1943), 79.
8. John Davenport, *A Sermon Preach'd at The Election* . . . May 19th, 1669, in *Publ. Col. Soc. Mass.*, X (1904), 6.
9. *An Exposition upon the 13th Chapter of Revelation*, (London, 1656), 72.
10. Letter to John Winthrop, 1638, *Winthrop Papers*, IV, 82.
11. Sermon, probably before the General Court, May 31, 1638, *Coll. Conn. Hist. Soc.*, I (1860), 20.
12. *The Bloudy Tenent*, in Publications of the Narragansett Club, III.
13. *A Declaration of the Intent and Equitye of the Order Made at the last Court, Etc.*, 1637, from Thomas Huchinson, *A Collection of Papers Relating to the History of Massachusetts Bay*, (Boston, 1769), 69.
14. *Exposition*, 71.
15. *The Way of the Churches*, (1645), 4.
16. *A Discourse on Civil Government in a New Plantation*, (1663), 17.
17. *Nehemiah on the Wall in Troublesome Times*, (Cambridge, 1671), in Miller and Johnson, 238.
18. *A Sermon Preach'd at The Election* . . . *May 19 1669, loc. cit,* 6.
19. *Nehemiah*, in Miller and Johnson, 237.
20. Wise acknowledged Puffendorf as his teacher, and inconclusive internal evidence intimates that he had also seen Locke.
21. Quoted in George Allan Cook, *John Wise*, 48-49.

22. Except as otherwise indicated, the following quotations and references are taken from Alice Baldwin, *The New England Clergy and the American Revolution* (Durham, 1928).
23. *Ibid.*, 38, 39.
24. *Ibid.*, 40, 42.
25. *Ibid.*, 66.
26. *Ibid.*, 43-44, 69-70, 45, 87.
27. *Ibid.*, 56.
28. *Ibid.*, 60, 76, 78n.
29. *Ibid.*, 75-76.
30. *Ibid.*, 71-72.
31. *Ibid.*, 77-78.
32. MSS Conn. Hist. Soc.
33. Baldwin, *New England Clergy*, 97, 101.
34. *Ibid.*, 112, 116, 118.
35. *Diary of Elijah Backus, Jr., Connecticut Quarterly*, I, (1895), 355.
36. The original quotation is "What pity is it that we can die but once to serve our country."
37. From the separate reports of two Bristish officers who were present as set out in G. D. Seymour, *Documentary Life of Nathan Hale*, (New Haven, 1941), 292-310.
38. *Life and Works of John Adams*, C. F. Adams, ed. (Boston, 1850), II, 342.
39. Sidney Kaplan, "Rank and Status Among Massachusetts Continental Officers," *Am. Hist. Rev.*, LVI (1951), 318-26.
40. See John C. Miller, *The Triumph of Freedom*, (Boston, 1948), 186.
41. Charles Knowles Bolton, *The Private Soldier under Washington*, (New York, 1902), 242.
42. *Ibid.*, 41.
43. Rev. Ammi R. Robbins, *Journal*, (New Haven, 1850), 33.
44. *Ibid.*, 39.
45. Bolton, *Private Soldier*, 103.
46. *Ibid.*, 247-48, citing Elijah Fisher's *Journal*, 23-24.
47. Elisha Stevens, *Fragments of Memoranda . . .* (Meriden, 1922).
48. Evarts Boutell Greene, *The Revolutionary Generation*, (New York, 1943), 287.
49. J. Franklin Jameson, *The American Revolution Considered as a Social Movement*, (Princeton, 1926), 78-94.
50. Peter Thacher, *Observations upon the Present State of the Clergy of New England, etc.* (Boston, 1783), 4, 8, 13.
51. Rev. Francis Aspinwall, *Journal*, (1821), II, 102.

III. The World of Men (1800-1900)
1) Third Puritanism (1800-1860)

1. The Census of 1860 records 852,216 persons born in the New England states and emigrated to other states. Since this number would omit persons recorded as deceased, it seems reasonable to raise the total emigration in the period to approximately a million. But for a trickle into Missouri and Texas, this stream fanned out among the states and future states of Greater New England. (*Population of the United States in 1860*, compiled from the Original Returns of the Eighth Census, U. S. Census Office [Washington, 1864]).
2. The Census shows: for 1790, New England, 1,009,408; for 1860, New England, 3,135,283; the total of New York, Ohio, Indiana, Michigan, Illinois, Wisconsin, Minnesota, Iowa, Kansas, California, Oregon and the territories of Colorado, Utah and Washington, 12,275,364.
3. A computation from figures for the year 1850 (in Ray Billington, *Westward*

Expansion, 308). The secret in the basic statistics is in the preponderant number—2,331,000 out of a total of 4,501,000—of "Native" born. Presumably these were born of cultural backgrounds distributed about like those of the immigrants who came in during their lives. But already they are approaching or have achieved a similarity in culture which hardly reflects the four backgrounds in equal proportion. We can only infer from their record which of the four traditions has most nearly absorbed them.

4. *Puritans*, 12.
5. *We Were New England*, Barrows Mussey, ed., (New York, 1937), 115 ff.
6. The first citation is from Everett Dick, *Sod-House Frontier*, (New York, 1937), 233; the second from Harold E. Briggs, *Frontiers of the Northwest*, (New York, 1940), 353-54. The last three are from John Ise, "Pioneer Life in Western Kansas," in Norman E. Himes, ed., *Economics, Sociology, and the Modern World*, (Cambridge, 1935), 135, 133, which is based on personal interviews with pioneers.
7. The Rev. Nathan Perkins, *A Narrative of a Tour Through the State of Vermont from April 27 to June 12, 1789* (Woodstock, Vt. 1937).
8. Here quoted from *The Western Reserve, the Story of New Connecticut in Ohio*, Harlan Hatcher (Indianapolis, New York, 1949), 84-86.
9. Thadeus Mason Harris, "Journal of a Tourist into the Territory Northwest of the Allegheny Mountains; made in the Spring of the year 1803" (Boston, 1805), in Reuben Gold Thwaites, ed., *Early Western Travels* (Cleveland, 1904-07), III, 357-8.
10. Brown's *Cincinnati Almanac* (1816), quoted in Hatcher, *Western Reserve*, 192.
11. Boston Recorder (1867), quoted by Truman O. Douglass in *The Pilgrims of Iowa* (Boston, Chicago, c. 1911), 24.
12. Timothy Dwight, *Travels in New England and New York* (New Haven, 1821-22), II, 358-62.
13. Frederick Jackson Turner, *The Frontier in American History*, 37.
14. Carter Goodrich and Sol Davison, "The Wage Earners in the Westward Movement," *Political Science Quarterly*, LI (1936), 61-116.
15. Carl Russell Fish, *Rise of the Common Man* (New York, 1935), 63-68.
16. Rev. Henry Bushnell, *The History of Granville, Licking County, Ohio* (Columbus, 1889), 27.
17. Mathews, 180.
18. David Maldwyn Ellis, "The Yankee Invasion of New York, 1783-1850," *New York History*, XXXII (1951), 3-7; see also Mathews, 161.
19. S. P. Hildreth, *Biographical and Historical Memoirs of the Early Pioneer Settlers of Ohio* (Cincinnati, 1852), 450.
20. *Ibid.*, 448.
21. S. P. Hildreth, *Pioneer History: Being an Account of the First Examinations of the Ohio Valley, and the Early Settlement of the Northwest Territory* (Cincinnati, 1848), 278.
22. Stewart H. Holbrook, *Yankee Exodus*, (New York, 1950), 25-26.
23. Dwight, *Travels*, III, 266.
24. David Maldwyn Ellis, "The Yankee Invasion of New York, 1783-1850," *loc. cit.*, 7.
25. Lewis D. Stilwell, "Migrations from Vermont, 1776-1860," *Proceedings of the Vermont Historical Society*, new series, V (1937), 118.
26. Mathews, 178.
27. Dwight, *Travels*, III, 179.
28. Edmund Flagg, quoted in James M. Miller's *The Genesis of Western Culture: The Upper Ohio Valley, 1800-1825* (Columbus, 1938), 38.
29. *Ibid.*, 39.

30. Holbrook, *Yankee Exodus,* 38.

31. Rev. Henry Bushnell, *The History of Granville, Licking County,* 81.

32. Miller, *Genesis of Western Culture:* 152.

33. "The Autobiography of Thomas Ewing," ed. Element L. Martzolff, *Ohio Archaeological and Historical Quarterly,* XXII (1913), 150-51. Ewing was not a born Yankee, his father being from New Jersey and himself born in Virginia in 1789. Being brought to Marietta in 1792, he became the first graduate of the college there.

34. James B. Finley, *Sketches of Western Methodism* (Cincinnati, 1855), 180.

35. Ewing, "Autobiography," *loc. cit.,* 151.

36. Timothy Flint, *Recollections of the Last Ten Years* (Boston, 1826), 44-5.

37. Solon J. Buck, ed., "Pioneer Letters of Gershom Flagg," *Pub. No. 15 of the Illinois State Historical Library, Transactions of the Illinois State Historical Society for the year 1910* (1912), 166.

38. *Plea for the West* (Cincinnati, 1835), 11, 30-31.

39. Holbrook, *Yankee Exodus,* 79-80.

40. *Log City Days: Two Narratives on the Settlement of Galesburg, Illinois. The Diary of Jerusha Loomis Farnham; Sketch of Log City, by Samuel Holyoke* (Galesburg, 1937), 42-3.

41. *Ibid.,* 76-7.

42. Theodore Calvin Pease, *The Frontier State, 1818-1848.* (Chicago, 1922), 420, 437, 439.

43. *Ibid.,* 369-70; R. Carlyle Buley, *The Old Northwest: Pioneer Period, 1815-1840* (Indianapolis, 1950) II, 622.

44. Irving Berdine Richman, *Ioway to Iowa: the Genesis of a Corn and Bible Commonwealth* (Iowa City, 1931), 292-3.

45. Seth K. Humphrey, *Following the Prairie Schooner* (Minnesota, c. 1931), 17-18. Also, Everett Dick, *Sod House Frontier,* 32-6.

46. Francis P. Weisenburger, *The Passing of the Frontier,* 1825-50 (Columbus, 1941), 131, quoting Morris Schaft, *Etna and Kirkersville* (Boston, 1905).

47. William Salter, "My Ministry in Iowa 1845-56," *Annals of Iowa,* XX (1935), 41.

48. Truman O. Douglas, *The Pilgrims of Iowa,* (Boston, Chicago, c. 1911), 292.

49. Holbrook, *Yankee Exodus,* 64.

50. Lyman Beecher, *Autobiography, Correspondence,* &c, Charles Beecher, ed. (London, 1863-65) I, 30.

51. Tyler, 29.

52. Sweet, *Story,* 326.

53. Noah Porter, as quoted by Robert Baird in *Religion in America* (New York, 1844), 201.

54. Tyler, 30.

55. P. G. Mode, ed., *Source Book for American Church History* (Menasha, Wisc., 1921), 331-42.

56. *Autobiography of the Rev. James B. Finley,* W. P. Strickland, ed. (1856), 166-7.

57. Tyler, 312, gives for these two dates four and a half and seven and a half gallons respectively for the entire population, of which the adult males may be taken approximately as a quarter.

58. *Ibid.,* 321.

59. *Ibid.,* 313, citing John Allen Krout, *The Origins of Prohibition,* 67.

60. *Autobiography,* I, 214.

61. *Ibid.,* 217.

62. Tyler, 320.

63. William Ellery Channing, *Works,* 8th ed., (Boston, 1848), IV, 401.

64. *Ibid.*, III, 85-86.
65. *Ibid.*, III, 85, 82-84, 94-95, 94.
66. *Works*, 1903 ed., 104.
67. *Works* (1848), III, 95.
68. *Ibid.*, III, 96.
69. *Ibid.*, 63.
70. *Ibid.*, III, 96.
71. *Memoirs of Rev. Charles G. Finney, Written by Himself* (New York, 1876), 13-21. The excerpt of the account of the conversion given here omits several incidents and presents little of the dramatic suspense of the entire passage.
72. *Ibid.*, 57-58.
73. *Ibid.*, 23.
74. Rev. Charles G. Finney, *Lectures to Professing Christians* (Oberlain, 1879), 212.
75. *Memoirs*, 288-89.
76. Finney, *Lectures to Professing Christians*, 88-9.
77. This is the opinion of Professor Roland Bainton of Yale Divinity School, and I do not know whether it has been published.
78. Other great revivalists of the day, varying in degree between the fairly clear Puritanism of Finney and the Arminian tendency we shall notice in Beecher, include Nathaniel W. Taylor, first Professor of Theology at Yale Divinity School, and Asahel Nettleton, one of the founders of Hartford Theological Seminary.
79. Rev. J. H. Fairchild, ed. (New York, 1878).
80. William Warren Sweet, *Revivalism in America* (New York, 1944), 158.
81. Benjamin P. Thomas, *Theodore Weld, Crusader for Freedom* (New Brunswick, N. J., 1950), 43.
82. *Ibid.*, 73.
83. *Ibid.*, 83.
84. *Ibid.*, 96.
85. *Ibid.*, 113.
86. *Ibid.*, 94.
87. "The Evil of Sin," *Works*, IV, 151.
88. *Ibid.*
89. "Legal Religion," in Finney, *Lectures to Professing Christians*, 90-3.
90. See "Christian Perfection," *ibid.*, 339-53 *passim*.
91. For a condensation of Dwight's theology see Williston Walker, *A History of the Congregational Church in the United States* (1894), 288-306.
92. The above paragraph is taken, much of it directly, from Tyler, 30-1. The long quotation Tyler takes from Lyman, *John Marsh Pioneer*, 30.
93. George L. Clark, *History of Connecticut*, 371-3.
94. Beverley W. Bond, Jr., *The Foundations of Ohio* (Columbus, 1941), 245.
95. Francis P. Weisenburger, *Passing of the Frontier*, 1825-50, 162.
96. Russell K. Hickman, "Lewis Bodwell, Frontier Preacher; the Early Years," *Kansas Historical Quarterly*, XII (1943), 296-7.
97. "The Moral Aspect of California, a Thanksgiving Sermon of 1850," by Rev. Charles A. Farley of the First Unitarian Church of San Francisco, Clifford Merrill Drury, ed., *California Historical Society Quarterly*, XIX (1940), 299.
98. *Services at the Fiftieth Anniversary of the First Congregational Church, Beloit, Wisc. . . .* (n.p., n.d.), 40, 44.
99. Photostat provided through the courtesy of Thu Wright Jr., and now in Yale Library.
100. Carl Russell Fish, *Rise of the Common Man*, 21-3.
101. *The True Idea of the Christian Church*, as quoted in Commager, 166.

102. *Autobiography*, Charles Beecher, ed., (London, 1863-65) I, 32.
103. *The Gospel According to Paul—A Sermon* . . . (Boston, 1829), 10.
104. *Ibid.*, 15.
105. Lyman Beecher, *Works* (Boston, 1852-53) I, 349.
106. *Ibid.*, 407-10 *passim*.
107. *The Liberator*, Vol. I, No. 1, January 1, 1831.
108. F. J. and W. P. Garrison, *William Lloyd Garrison* (New York, 1885-89) II, 52.
109. *Ibid.*, II, 28.
110. *The Liberator*, January 2, 1836.
111. Allan Estlake, *The Oneida Community* (London, 1900), 21.
112. Tyler, chap. vi.
113. Letter to Carlyle, Oct. 30, 1840, quoted in W. P. and F. J. Garrison, *Garrison*, III, 25.
114. Lewis D. Stilwell, "Migrations from Vermont (1776-1860)," *Proceedings of the Vermont Historical Society, new series*, V (1937), 148.
115. Carrie Kofoid, "Puritan Influences in the Formative Years of Illinois History," *Pub. No. 10 of the Illinois State Historical Society, Trans. of the Illinois State Historical Society, for the Year 1905* (Springfield, 1906), 326.
116. Bertha-Monica Stearns, "Reform Periodicals and Female Reformers, 1830-60," *American Historical Review*, XXXVII (1931-32), 678-99.
117. Benjamin P. Thomas, *Theodore Weld*, 28.
118. Gilbert H. Barnes, *The Antislavery Impulse, 1830-44* (New York, 1933), 50.
119. *Ibid.*, 93.
120. *National Enquirer*, III, 23.
121. Barnes, *Antislavery*, 155-60.
122. *Ibid.*, 169-70. Garrison's official biographers have the good ship *Massachusetts* sailing from Providence, and they point out that special trains were provided to deliver the Boston contingent to the pier. Doubtless both accounts are correct. The *Massachusetts* collected what she could from the strong Garrison town of Lynn, then proceeded to Providence.
123. *Ibid.*, 175.
124. *Ibid.*, 171.
125. Tyler, 453.
126. Emerson, "The Chardon Street Convention," in *Complete Works* (Riverside Ed., Cambridge, 1883), X, 352.
127. For an account of this meeting, see Amos Augustus Phelps, *A Sketch of the Proceedings of the Convention*, etc. (Boston, 1841).
128. A search of the *Vital Records of Salisbury, Mass. to the End of the Year 1849* (Salisbury containing Amesbury), and of three local histories reveals plenty of Browns but no Sylvanus. A Sylvanus Brown died in Pawtucket in 1824 (*National Cyclopedia of American Biography*).
129. *Dedham Democrat*, quoted in *The Liberator*, December 4, 1840.
130. Carl Russell Fish, *Rise of the Common Man*, 8.
131. A. A. Bennett, *Oration*, quoted in Ralph Henry Gabriel, *The Course of American Democratic Thought* (New York, 1940), 23.
132. George Robertson, *Oration*, quoted *ibid.*
133. Andrew Johnson, *Speeches*, Frank Moore, ed. (Boston, 1865), 56; quoted in Fish, *Common Man*, 10-11.
134. Joseph Story, *Miscellaneous Writings* (1825), 86, quoted in Gabriel, 23.
135. Emerson, "New England Reformers" in *Works*, III, 239-40, 242, 248, 249.
136. *Ibid.*, 241, 242.
137. "Self-Reliance" in *Works*, II, 48, 53, 52, 55, 59, 49, 52, 52.
138. Gordon S. Haight, *Mrs. Sigourney, the Sweet Singer of Hartford* (New Haven, 1930), 54.

139. *Ibid.*, 53.
140. Clifton Joseph Furness, *The Genteel Female*, an Anthology (New York, 1931), XXXIV.
141. Gabriel, *Course of American Democratic Thought* 9-10.
142. "Exposulation."
143. "In the Evil Days."
144. "Moloch in State Street."
145. Ralph Waldo Emerson, *Complete Works* (Boston, 1903-04) XI, 185.
146. Henry David Thoreau, *The Writings of.* . . . (Boston, 1884-93) X, 179.
147. Quoted in *The Liberator*, April 18, 1851.
148. *Works*, XI, 247.
149. *Works*, X, 53.
150. *Journals of Ralph Waldo Emerson.* . . . E. W. Emerson and W. E. Forbes, eds., (Boston, 1909-14) IX, 362.
151. Nicolay and Hay, *Complete Works of Abraham Lincoln*, (VI, 156-8) quoted in Gabriel, *American Democratic Thought*, 24.
152. Commager, 193.
153. Sweet, 450.
154. Sweet, *The Methodist Church and the Civil War* (Cincinnati, 1912), 39-40.
155. September 20, 1866, p. 2, quoted in May, 40.
156. Benjamin P. Thomas, *Theodore Weld*, 244.
157. The following quotations are from Bell Irvin Wiley's *The Life of Billy Yank* (Indianapolis and New York, 1952), 338-44, *passim*.
158. For more extreme statements of hatred of the Rebels, see *ibid.*, 346-50.

III. The World of Men (1800-1900) (continued)
2) Third Decline (1860-1900)

1. "Journal of the Ship *Mary*, 1795-1796," in Elizabeth Donnan, *Documents Illustrative of the* . . . *Slave Trade* (Washington, 1930-35) III, 360-61.
2. The quotations are from Susan M. Loring's *Selections from the Diaries of William Appleton*, as quoted in Cleveland Amory's *The Proper Bostonians*, (New York, 1947), 81-6, *passim*.
3. Taken from a long excerpt in Commager, 182.
4. May, 7-25, *passim*.
5. *Inequality of Individual Wealth the Ordinance of Providence* (Boston, 1935), cited in May, 21.
6. *Political Economy* (New York, 1840), 282, cited in May, 15.
7. May, 21. Also, Stephen Colwell, quoted in May, 19.
8. *Ibid.*, 22-3.
9. *Outlines of Political Economy* (New York, 1825), 69, quoted in May, 14.
10. Potter, as cited in May, 15.
11. *Political Economy* (Andover, 1859), 11, quoted in May, 20.
12. *The Elements of Political Economy* (4th ed., Boston, 1852), 118, quoted in May, 15.
13. *The Principles of Political Economy* (Boston, 1856), 499, quoted in May, 17.
14. *Political Economy*, 136, quoted in May, 20.
15. Edward C. Kirkland, *A History of Economic Life*, (Revised ed. New York, 1946), 332-41.
16. IV (1866), 330, quoted in May, 43. For more morsels of this type, see May, 39-44, *passim*.
17. Gilbert Haven, "The Great Election," *Methodist Quarterly Review*, XLVII (1865), 263, quoted in May, 41.
18. May, 43.
19. Allan Nevins, *The Emergence of Modern America* (New York, 1927), 123.

20. *World Almanac,* 1953.
21. Among these were Bard ('60), Bates ('64), Wellesley ('70), Smith ('71), Radcliffe ('79), American International ('85), Clark ('87).
22. Among these were Vassar ('61), Marquette ('64), University of Illinois ('68), Cornell ('68), Purdue ('69), Syracuse ('60), Ohio State ('70), University of Detroit ('77), University of Chicago ('90).
23. D. A. Wells, *Recent Economic Changes* (1889), 65, quoted in Nevins, 31. Generally, the events between the War and '79 are taken from Nevins. *Scientific American,* Sept. 15, 1866, quoted in Arthur M. Schlesinger, *Learning How to Behave* (New York, 1946), 27, gives the figures for the incomes.
24. Generally events between '80 and 1900 are taken from Ida M. Tarbell, *The Nationalizing of Business* (New York, 1936).
25. Schlesinger, *How to Behave,* 28.
26. At the Pan-American Exposition in San Francisco in 1915 each state named its first citizen.
27. Matthew Josephson, *The Robber Barons* (New York, 1934), 49.
28. Report of the Industrial Commission (Government Printing Office 1899) 114, 118.
29. *Proceedings of the Eighth Annual Convention of the National Association of Manufacturers,* 1903, 123.
30. June 4, 1874, 6, as quoted in May, 55.
31. *Independent,* July 26, 1877, 16, quoted in May, 92.
32. *Ibid.,* August 2, 1877, p. 16.
33. *Congregationalist,* May 13, 1886, 16-17, quoted in May, 101.
34. *Christian Advocate,* July 28, 1892, p. 507, quoted in May, 105.
35. Reprinted in *The Wedding Ring* (New York, 1896), 80-3, and quoted in Arthur M. Schlesinger, *The Rise of the City* (New York, 1938), 126.
36. "Thank God, now my wife can be a lady!" said the Irish prospector as he struck gold in Colorado—Schlesinger, *How to Behave,* 29. For an accurate and excruciating delineation of Victorian manners, see this volume, Chapters II and III.
37. Schlesinger, *How to Behave,* 36, citing several sources.
38. Sherwood, *Manners and Social Usages* (New York, 1884), 163-4, quoted in Schlesinger, *Rise of the City,* 123.
39. Kenneth R. Andrews, *Nook Farm* (Cambridge, 1950), 76. The three short quotations that follow are successively from pp. 69, 74, and 76 of this book.
40. Editorial in the Emporia *Gazette,* July 27, 1922, as quoted in Walter Johnson's Introduction to *Selected Letters of William Allen White* (New York, 1947), 22.
41. *In Our Town* (New York, 1906), 119. This theme is fully developed in *A Certain Rich Man* (1909).
42. *Collier's,* 1921, as quoted in Johnson, 19.
43. *The Changing West* (New York, 1939), 9, 10.
44. *Ibid.,* 12-13.
45. *Music-Hall Sermons* (Boston, 1870), pp. 102 and 106, quoted in May, 73-4.
46. Frank S. Mead, *Handbook of Denominations in the United States* (Nashville, 1951), 102.
47. 1900 World Almanac; 399; Commander Booth Tucker, *The Social Relief Work of the Salvation Army in the United States.* Vol. XX in Herbert B. Adams, ed., *Monographs on American Social Economy* (Albany, 1900).
48. Schlesinger, *Rise of the City,* 337-38.
49. Glenway Wescott, *The Grandmothers* (New York, 1927), 259.
50. *Ibid.,* 238.
51. *Ibid.,* 239.

52. *Ibid.*, 250.
53. *Winesburg, Ohio* (New York, 1919), "Godliness."
54. *Ibid.*, 80.
55. *The Grandmothers*, 34.
56. *Connecticut Revised Statutes*, 1888, p. 384.
57. McClain's *Annotated Code of Iowa, Statutes Supplement* (1888-92), 303.
58. *Rev. Stats.* 1883-89 (William F. Elliott), 96, 97.
59. *Annotated General Statutes* (William L. Hill) (1891), 690, 135.
60. *Sup. to Pub. Stats. of Massachusetts* (C. A. Merrill) 1893, p. 903.
61. Edgar Lee Masters, *Spoon River Anthology* (New York, 1915), 223. When the citation from this work can be found in the Table of Contents, no reference will be given.
62. Wescott's *The Grandmothers*, 238-9, 241, 244.
63. See Aaron Hatfield, *Spoon River Anthology*, 230.
64. *The Grandmothers*, 237-8.
65. *Spoon River*, 80, 82.
66. *Prairie Women* (New York, 1930).
67. *The Grandmothers*, 173. 35, 55.
68. See Stewart G. Cole, History of *Fundamentalism*, (New York, 1931), 12-15.
69. *Spoon River*, 172.
70. *Ibid.*
71. *Ibid.*, 197.
72. *Goodbye, Wisconsin*, 20-21.
73. Arthur M. Schlesinger, *Rise of the City*, 321.
74. John W. Buckham, *Progressive Religious Thought*, 316-17, quoted in May, 232-3.
75. *Plymouth Pulpit*, New Series III (New York 1874-5), quoted in May, 9.
76. "Speaking Evil of Dignities" in *Freedom and War. . . .* (Boston, 1863). 394-5, quoted in May, 40.
77. *Congregationalist*, June 21, 1876, 196; July 14, 1869, 12, quoted in May, 50, 51.
78. May, 47.
79. "The Natural Theology of Social Science," *Bibliotheca Sacra*, XCV (1868), 315, quoted in May, 49.
80. *Sermons on Living Subjects*, 270, quoted in May, 84.
81. *Statement before the Congregational Association of* New York and Brooklyn, etc. (New York, 1882), 13, quoted in May, 86.
82. May, 84-5. Most of the material on the Social Gospel is paraphrased from May, as the quotations are taken from him.
83. May, 75-6.
84. *Applied Christianity*, 33, 135-6, 52, as quoted in May, 173.
85. *Christian Ethics*, (New York, 1914), 378, quoted in May, 196.
86. *Religious Movements for Social Betterment* (Monographs on American Social Economy), XIV (New York, 1900), 4-6.
87. May, 140-1.
88. *Ibid.*, 228.
89. *Ibid.*
90. *The Foes*, 224-5, as quoted in May, 228.
91. *Autobiography* (New York, 1946), 325.
92. Charles Worcester Clark, "Applied Christianity; Who Shall Apply it First," *Andover Review*, XLX (1893), 18-33, as quoted in May, 224.
93. *Autobiography*, 462-3.
94. *Nation*, LVI (1893), 381-82, quoted in May, 215.
95. *De Civitate Dei. . . .* (Philadelphia, 1891), 1. quoted *Ibid.*

96. Brooks Adams, *The Emancipation of Massachusetts* (Boston, 1887).
97. John Buckham, *Progressive Religious Thought* 316-17, as quoted in May, 232-3.

IV. The World of Me (1900-1960)
1) Fourth Puritanism (1900-1930)

1. Most of the highlights of the '20's are taken from either Frederick Lewis Allen's *Only Yesterday* (New York, 1931) or Frank Sullivan's *In Our Times* (New York, 1937).
2. Malcolm Cowley, *Exile's Return* (New York, 1951), 60-1.
3. Generally, the comment on Willa Cather is from Howard Mumford Jones's *The Bright Medusa* (Urbana, 1952). This and the following quotation are from pp. 13-14.
4. *Ibid.,* 24-9, *passim.*

2) Fourth Decline (1930-1960)

5. For a more extended analysis of the movement of repatriation, see Cowley, *Exile's Return,* 284-92.
6. I dare venture this tentative generality, having known many of the youth in several universities, and not having found any exceptions. I refer also to a survey of the wives of the Yale Class of 1937 ("Mrs. 1937," *Yale Alumni Weekly,* November, 1952) in which all of 266 who filled out the questionnaire, coming from 36 states, eschewed careers for themselves and said their first duty was to their husbands.
7. In the cursory comparisons that follow, I have relied somewhat on my own general knowledge of Hindu-Buddhist and Christian classics, and immediately I have referred to five secondary sources: Aldous Huxley's Introduction to the translation of the Bhagavad-Gita by Swami Prabhavananda and Christopher Isherwood (Hollywood, 1944); Mr. Isherwood's exposition of the Cosmology of the Gita, in the same; Mr. Isherwood's Introduction to *Vedanta for the Western World* (Hollywood, 1945); Swami Prabhavananda's essay "on Divine Grace" in the same; corrections of my manuscript and suggestions by Professor Norvin Hein of Yale Divinity School. Since there are some convenient inconsistencies in my text, and no pretense of definition, discretion suggests that I acknowledge these sources generally, without specific citations. The purpose is merely to set up for the layman some of the similarities and contrasts between the two greatest religions on earth. I have not mentioned Mohammedanism because, in the points touched upon, its doctrines seem to coincide nearly with either those of Hindu-Buddhism or those of Christianity.
8. Here especially, it would seem the most advanced folly for the Occidental who is but shallowly versed in Oriental theology to propose a state of identity between Christian Regeneration and any particular station on the Oriental, Mystic Way. Suffice it that Evelyn Underhill recognizes five steps common to the progress of all mystics, Christian or otherwise, though without attaching theological names to any of them. The last step, which is involved here, is simply that into *Union* with the God, though it is still a dualistic "union" and not final to the monistic necessity of both Hindus and Buddhists. I dare call it "Regeneration" for the Christian, but dare not claim for it any of the subtle states of both Hinduism and Buddhism, though there are several which invite. In this connection the work of A. J. Appasamy, the Indian who became a Christian bishop, is as valuable as any I know. He does not hesitate to use Hindu vocabulary to describe Christian experiences. See especially, *An Indian Interpretation of Christianity* (Christian Literature Society for India, 1924).

Index

Adams, Brooks, 7, 445
Adams, James T., 9-10, 38, 413
Adams, John Quincy, 379, 383
Alcott, Bronson, 357, 362, 367, 370
Allen, Ethan, 185, 268
American Culture: charge of youthfulness examined, 17-30; extent of contemporary cultural centers in, 44; possibility of composite materialistic culture, 44-45; possibility of composite immaterialistic culture, 45-46, 471-73; possibility of 5th Puritanism, 473-75; a vacuum at end of 1930's, 462-64; See also Puritan Culture; Puritan-Yankee Culture; Puritanism, 1st, 2nd, 3rd, 4th; Yankee Culture.
American Revolution: John Wise and, 236; social and political rationalization of, 1725, 275; Religion, 275; ministry prepares for, 278-80, 284-85; during, 285; political idealism in, 283-84, 285-86, 287-88; mobs, 285-86; Yankee officers in, 286; soldiers, 287-88; licentiousness and religious indifference after, 288-90
American Tragedy, 456-57
Anderson, Sherwood, 454, 455, 459; Jesse Bentley of *Winesburg*, 426; Antinomianism of characters, 457; *Dark Laughter*, 457
Andover Theological Seminary, 321, 348, 365
Andros, Edmund, 231, 236, 277
Anglican Church and Anglicans: aristocratic assumptions of, 25, 86; and inner Independence, 82-83; on Predestination, 53; on interpretation of the Bible, 85-86; why the Puritans excluded, 123; rise in early 18th Century, 241-43; raid Connecticut, 232, 242; send SPG scouts into Connecticut, 232-242; victories in Connecticut, 242; "Great Apostasy" at Yale, 242; protest Connecticut's intolerance, 232; toleration of in Massachusetts, 231;—and ecclesiastical taxes, 231; toleration of in Connecticut, 232-33;—and ecclesiastical taxes, 233; flourish in Boston by 1720, 231; limited importance of, 243; not within New England Culture, 243
Anti-Slavery Movement: first Abolition law, 171; in Rhode Island, 265; after the Revolution, 288; in Illinois, 311; in Iowa, 315; American Colonization Society, 329; Abolition periodicals appear, 1815, 329; L. Beecher on, 355, Weld's actions in, 342-43; members of, 343-45; attack on Massachusetts Female Anti-Slavery Society, 355; ministry in, 363-64, 365; Garrison's disruptive efforts, 366-67; Women's Rights mixed with, 364-67; "Abolition

House" and abolition Congressmen, 383; Liberty Party, 383, 384; develops Psychosis, 1850-1860, 387-96; Romanticism of, 324; in Radical and Moderate Reform Empires, 360
Antinomianism, Heresy of: source, 116-17; relation to Pure Calvinism, 58; psychological definition of, 424; widens application of inner Independence, 83; Puritans associate with libertinism, fear, 58; Covenant of Grace as answer to, 116-17; and Anne Hutchinson (*see*); Edwards leans towards, 251; Great Awakening, an outbreak of, 117 (*see* also Great Awakening); —attacks Edwards' Holy Ratio, 259;— leaders of, 259; moves out of the River, 265; under Romanticism, mixed with Legal Arminianism, 322; in Humanitarian Perfectionism, 335-36; in Utopian Communities, 357-58; Sects, 359; of Garrison, 355-56; of Noyes, 356; of Transcendentalism, 357; Emerson, on extent of, 357;—desires to be, 357;—advocates, 373-77; its Radical Empire of sects and Reform, 360; pure, at Chardon Street Convention, 368-70; Violent Phase, 37; merges with Arminianism, 395;—remains united in River of Violence, 396; female, of Victorianism, 416; declines in Revivalism, 423-24; literal, disappears, 426; becomes Emotional Religion (*see*); Social, and Social Conscience, 430; weak in 1890's, 445; of 4th Puritanism, 457;—in Willa Cather's artists, 458
Aristocracy, in New England, 25; different in the Bay, the River, the Island, 26, 87; Puritan's was intellectual, 87-88; accepted in Church Covenant, 106, 107; code followed, 143, 433; in Winthrop's politics, 167; and sumptuary laws, 170; in Boston (*see*); Divinely and Socially Elect, confused, 93, 98; unity of—assumed, 196, 214, 215;—and genealogy, 214-15; lawyers become leaders of, 88, 307; Businessmen become the, 418;—developed responsibility of, 417-18; none in Clerical laissez-faire, 433; of F. D. Roosevelt, 463
Arminianism, The Heresy of, 19, 29; demands Justice of God, 116; destroys Predestination, 59; Grace and Atonement, 69, 70; Reason, 59, 203; Covenant of Grace as answer, 116, 117; Hell-fire, 80-81; Individualism, 202; preached, 1679-99, 104; strong minority of ministers hold, 117; stronger after 1679, 201-02; heresy laws, 170; Violent Phase, *close to extreme Antinomianism*, 371; Garrison as example of, 355-56;—mob murders Joseph Smith, 384;

508

248; eschews Covenant of Grace, 117; Education and Grace, 250; Equalitarianism, 250; on standards for church admissions, 240, 261; his doctrines distorted during the Great Awakening, 83-84

Elect, The: and the Saints, 100; Puritans attempt to discover that they were among, 55; plutocracy seen as in Boston, 98; Elite become, 214; and genealogy, 214-15; Willa Cather puts Thea Kronberg among, 458

Election: in pure Calvinism, 57-58; in middle view of Predestination (Hooker), 60; Free Grace, 60; preparation, 60; Regeneracy, 57, 60, 70; loses meaning for children of Industrial Rich, 418; 4th Puritan ladies' views of, 458-59; Sexual, mere vulgarization, 459

Eliot, John, 137, 143, 208

Eliot, T. S., 21, 455, 457

Emerson, Ralph Waldo: purest of 3rd Puritans, 373, 375; Channing compared with, 374; German Absolutism, 374-75; desires to be Antinomian, 357; fails to warn of danger of Individualism, 373-77; as Puritan artist, 377-78; describes equalitarianism, 110; at Chardon Street Convention, 367; Thoreau and taxes, 374; Arminianism develops on Slavery issue, 387-93

Enormous Room, The, 456, 459

Emotion: Heresy of, *see* Antinomianism; in Romanticism, 322; in Victorianism, 416; discipline of by Willa Cather's artists, 458; *See also* Holy Ratio

Emotional Religion: residue of Antinomianism, 426; considered a woman's matter, 426; revivals and, 426

Emotional Sects: increasing respectability of great sects, results in bloom of, 424-25; various, discussed, 425

Endicott, John: intolerance of, 13; and Winthrop, 134-35; cuts royal standard, 138; one of bloody triumvirate, 173-74; death, 177; leads Black Spider Phenomenon, 464-65

Enlightenment: role in America, 1760-1800, 267; doctrines of, 267; pseudo religion of, 267; education in, 272; science in, (*see* Franklin) Rational Aesthetic of, 270-71; Political Liberalism, the essential quality of, 272-73; 1760-1780, age of pure reason in New England, 283-84

"Epic of America," (James T. Adams), 38

Episcopalians, 360, 439

Equalitarianism: explained, 25; examined, 105-11; in small town America today, 110; historic sources of, 25, 105, 109-10, 110-11; religious assumption in, 25, 106, 109-10; in Edwards, 250; conflict with aristocratic tradition refined, 25-26; assumes an aristocracy, 106; corollaries of, 26-27; materialistic historians' explanation of, 110-11; expansion of beyond the churches, 108-09; secularization of, in politics in the River, 167-69, 280-82; social, 225, 280; in Puritan educational theory, 85, 88-90; a source of Yankee humor, 112; and competition, 109; materialism destroys the roots, 110; contrasted with individualism, 37, 109; check on

Individualism, in 18th century, 109; mixed with individualism, 1704, 224; basis for democracy, 37, 109; not democracy, 109; of Yankee Revolutionary officers, 286; Channing on, 331, 331n; Yankee '49ers lapse into, 314; tends on frontier to individualism, 315; sense of Inferiority the death of, 380; class tensions reverse, 405; forgotten by children of the New Rich, 418; called Freedom, is Idea of 3rd Decline, 420; Wm. A. White on, 422-23; not in Willa Cather's 4th Puritanism, 458

Expatriates, 453, 456, 459-60

Faith: is relation to Truth, 99; realized as part of Grace, 99; and relation to God, 99; confusion of with belief, 100; Wm. A. White on, 422

Faith, Salvation by: doctrine of examined, 99-105, *pass.*; Finney on, 329; *See also* Grace; Works

Faithful Narrative of the Surprizing Work of God, A, 246

Federal Theology: 115, 482; Covenant of Grace, 115-17; protection against Antinomianism, 116-17; protection against Arminianism, 117

Female Love: woman's primary prerogative, 466; is "Natural Grace," 466; and man, 466-67

Feminism: part of Radical Reform Empire, 360; to the kitchen, 462; *See also* Women's Rights

Finney, Charles Grandison, 336; quality of his religion, 336; as a 3rd Puritan, 336, 339, 347; Emotionalism, 340; Perception as Grace, 336, 338, 339; Concept of God, 336, 338, 339; Sin, 336, 339; Atonement, 337, 339; Justification, 339; Faith, 339; Benevolence, 339; his *Systematic Theology*, 341; his education, 337; view of educated ministry, 340; his conversion, 336-39; his technique, 340; condemns Legalists, 347; emotional leader of Greater New England, 336; mistrust of, 340; and Reform, 336; Method of, reform the individual, 341; and Clerical Laissez-faire, 402

Fish, Carl Russell, on Yankee Culture, 352-53

Fiske, John, 435

Fitzgerald, F. Scott: 455, 459; *This Side of Paradise*, 456; *Beautiful and the Damned*, 457

Forgiveness of Sin: Christian remedy for sense of guilt, 66

Franchise: and Equalitarianism, 108-09; in the Bay, 108; in the River, 109

Franklin, Benjamin, 267; a River Yankee, 268-69; first true Yankee, 270; place in Puritan decadence, 269; passion for science, 268-69, 270; utilitarian, 269; debasement of Economic Virtues, 269-70; humor, 270; literary theory, 270-71; satire of C. Mather, 268; and Whitefield, 255

Free Enterprise: beginnings, 1650's-1670's, 195; and Massachusetts government of 1684, 196; *See also* Capitalism; Industrialism

104, 201-02; as sign of Election, 61, 98,
100, 103-04; Yankees on, 104-05; and
Hell-fire, 202; Edwards, 332; Dwight,
348; Channing, 332, 346
World of Cosmos: 17th century Puritan sky,
127; contracted, 214, 227; in 18th century, "superstitious" imagination, 227
World of Man: (Abstract Man) part II,
chap. ii; 18th century Yankee sky, 127,
227, 269; "superstitious" Imagination retained, 227; described, 226-27, 273, 283-
84; affirmative Religious forces of, 227-30;
Franklin contracts, 269; force for Romanticism, 322-24; See also Enlightenment; Humanism
World of Me: part II, Chap. iv; 20th Century Yankee sky, 127; its sky, 451-52; its
God, 452; deification of self and sex, 452
World of Men: part II, Chap. iii; 19th century Yankee sky, 127; and Romanticism,
321-24

Yale: founding as conservative school, 237;
level of education and library of, 1700,
240; "Great Apostasy" of 1722, 242;
Bishop Berkley donates books, 242; opposes Great Awakening, 258-59; opposes
Edwards' Holy Ratio, 359; depravity and
infidelity at, 1790's, 290, 319; Revivals,
1802-1840, 320-21, 348
Yale Band, The, 311, 345
Yankee: the word, 3
Yankee Culture: 3-4, 6; original nucleus of,
45, 125; now a psychological system, 125;
transmission of to non-Yankees, 43; boring of materialism into, 41, 98; about
1700, 214-23; location and extent in
1890, in 1950, 419; present status of, 45-
46, 125, 127; Thought of: Idealism of,
45-46, 49-50, 51, 221-22, 292, 305-06;
Idealism has shrunk, 50, 97, 214; accepts Puritan's underlying assumptions,
50-62; belief in external reality, 50-51;
belief in Meaning in Cosmos, 51; Will of
God, 51-52; predestination, 62; Original
Sin, 66-67; Atonement, 70; on Grace, 80;
Belief substituted for Faith, by religionless, 100; on Belief, 117-18; on Heaven
and Hell, 80, 82; on Economic Virtues,
98-99; Grand Hypocrisy of, 193; reversal
into Petty, 98-99; imports perverted English doctrine of calling, 214; Franklin,
269-70; present view of wealth, 98-99;
Code of Decorum, 214; Equalitarianism,
105, 109-11; changing bases for, 109-10;
today, 110; secular, 225; Individualism
in during Great Awakening, 84; Inner
(Religious) Independence, 83-84; restraints, 85; desire and respect for learning, 39, 41, 85, 92; Moderation, 121,
124-25; Optimism, 115, 292; believes in
invincibility of reason, 90; and common
sense thinking, 113-14; revivalism in, 84;
doctrine of works, 99, 104-05; See also
Franklin; Greater New England; Sewall
Yankee Culture, 19th century: Expansive
Phase (1800-1860), 291; dominance in
Greater New England, 292; qualities of,
292; values maintained, 291-93, 352-53,
397-98; Channing proclaims Vision of,
330; 3rd Puritanism the dominant thread,

353; Three Empires of Churches and Reforms, 360; Petty Hypocrisy in, 381;
Greed in, 314-15, 381, 404; Idealism in
352-53, 398; individualism, 330, 351;
checked by belief in God, 404; intellectual standards, 317, 352; quality of religion of, 318, 335-36, 347, 351-53, 382;
Legal Arminianism in, 349-51, 353-56;
Humanitarian and Religious movements in
early 19th century, 324-30; Humanitarian
Perfectionism as universal language 1820-
1840, 335; Antinomianism in, 335-36;
Imaginative Perception of, 336, 347; Reform and Reformers, 341-46 (see also
Reform); Antinomianism in, 356-59; to
Violent, Legal Arminianism in slavery controversy, 387-96; See also Humanitarianism; Perfectionism; Romanticism; 3rd Puritanism; Union Yankee Soldiers
Yankee Culture, of 3rd Decline: 314, 382;
location of, 419; God, Benevolence, Utopia vanish, 419; Humor replaces God,
419, 421; each finds own Meaning, 419,
421; Arminianism in, 420; Equalitarianism, the Idea of, 420; naive to Industrial
World, 420; David Harum, typical of
rural, 421; Nook Farm, typical of urban
educated, 421; William A. White, most
convincing Yankee, 421-23; danger of,
423; strong without God in small towns,
445; Religion in, 420; emotional sects,
424-25; revivals, 425; emotional religion,
425; women's business, 425; literal Antinomianism disappears, 425; Arminian
Righteous Wrath into worship of diligence
for God, 426-27
Yankee Humor: 4, 17; origins, 111-12; in
Equalitarianism, 112; in aging of Puritanism, 221-22, 270; early example of, 212;
Franklin and, 270; of children of New
Rich, 419; increased in 3rd Decline, 419-
21
Yankee Pioneers: idealism of, 34, 38, 41-42,
299-300; methods, 39; See also under
Greater New England, Settlement of
Yankee Pseudo-culture: 6; changing, 45; location and extent of today, 419; origins
in Arminian-Antinomian Violence, 395-
96; where Greed dominates, 399; life
cycle of, 447-48; on work and wealth,
98-99; Greed, the pseudo-reality of, frus-
trates other activity, 415; splits culture,
415-16; reverses Puritan idealism, 418-19;
churches voice self-aggrandizement and
Arminian sadism of Reconstruction, 406-
07; and Post-war Expansion, 406-07; materialism of, preachers justify, 406-07;
into Industrialism by desire for self-advancement, 411; Industrial leaders of
Yankee background examined, 411-13;
Laws of Competition, 413; on labor, 414-
15; ministers permit, 414; Victorianism,
the surface of, 415-17; children of Industrial Rich, the froth of, 418; no contact with Yankee culture, 418-19; host
to extreme revivalism, 423-24; and new
emotional sects, 425; Gambling Culture
of 1920's the end, 447-51; See also River
of Violence
Yankees: different from Puritans, 17, 48, 54,
221-23, 270